# The Canadian prairies: A history

GERALD FRIESEN

# THE CANADIAN PRAIRIES

## A HISTORY

UNIVERSITY OF NEBRASKA PRESS

Lincoln and London

Published in the United States by
the University of Nebraska Press
ISBN 0-8032-1972-5

Publication of this work has been assisted by the
Canada Council and the Ontario Arts Council under their
block grant programs.

TO MY PARENTS

AND

TO JEAN

# Contents

# Maps

The maps appear in a section between pages 90 and 91.

# Illustrations

The photographs appear in a section between pages 338 and 339.

Greek Catholic church (PAC: Frank Royal)
Ranch pond (PAC: Frank Royal)
Old store (PAC: Frank Royal)
Dust storm (GA)
Continental Oil Company wells (PAA: H. Pollard)

Two cartoons appear in the text: 'Separating the farmer from his profits' (MA: Russenholt, *Grain Growers' Guide*, 28 December 1921, page 6) on page 187, and 'Clout' (Roy Peterson, *Vancouver Sun*, 25 April 1980) on page 450.

# Preface

The prairie west is rich in historical literature, but it has never been the subject of a scholarly synthesis that tells its story from the days of Indian-European contact to the present. No single volume establishes a framework within which readers can place their reflections on the region's past. *The Canadian Prairies: A History* was written in response to that need. It is intended for the general reader and the student. It is based on the most recent scholarly research. It is as comprehensive in theme and detail as space would permit. And it attempts to entertain as well as to inform.

Having lived most of my life in the prairie west, I am too close to my subject to be entirely objective. I like to travel the grid roads, to chat over coffee in highway cafés, and to participate in the heated debates that are the glory of prairie politics. As the late W.L. Morton once observed, these communities are distinguished by a superficial friendliness that makes daily contact between people of very different backgrounds not only possible but likely. I confess to a bias in favour of this democratic, egalitarian spirit.

Prairie society, like any other, attracts and repels for a variety of reasons, but among its positive qualities, in my view, are the accessibility of those who hold power and the democratic veneer of daily life. There is an apparent openness in public affairs that puts premiers on a first-name basis with their voters and requires oil and grain barons to participate in the local community. At the heart of prairie culture is a most democratic sport, curling, and the most common prairie social occasion is also the most inclusive – that is, the community-wide celebration that takes the form of a dance, fowl supper, school concert, or 'social.' Two crucial sectors of the prairie economy, agriculture and government, are controlled by 'the people.' Such an open polity can experience problems, particularly when majorities wish to assert their wishes against minorities or when social criticism is mistaken for subversion; but it also has strengths. Perhaps the most attractive aspect of the prairie community is that it has offered a relatively peaceful and comfortable home to immigrants from around the world and has given its children a hopeful future. The process of adaptation was never easy, but suspicion and recalcitrance have usually given way to grudging respect and, eventually, acceptance. That is a considerable accomplishment.

The single most important challenge to this optimistic assessment is the status of prairie native people. In a small way, this book attempts to address that issue, too.

Volumes of synthesis such as this one are speculative undertakings because they do not have the rigorous foundation of primary sources that is the hallmark of the scholarly monograph. The support of a publisher is essential to their completion. This book owes its existence to Virgil Duff of the University of Toronto Press. He initiated the project, convinced a hesitant author of its potential, sustained it for five long years, and defended a handsome product in a time of publishing austerity. I wish to thank him for his kind encouragement.

As Mr Duff recognized when he first cast about for an author, prairie historical research has been something of a collective enterprise for over fifteen years. The atmosphere of co-operation and debate has made the scholarship stronger and has made a synthesis possible. This study is built on the social history of Indians, fur trade families, cities, working people, and ethnic groups that the recent generation of scholars has revealed. And it owes much to the generosity and work of dozens of specialists.

A number of these colleagues sacrificed their time in order to explain issues with which I was unfamiliar, to give me advance copies of new work, and to criticize the manuscript. Among the critics, I would like to give special thanks to five University of

Alberta scholars, Rod Macleod, Doug Owram, John Foster, David Hall, and Mike Percy; to several colleagues at the University of Manitoba, especially Ed Rea, Morris Mott, and Hal Guest; to John Thompson of McGill, who offered much useful advice; and to my friend Bob Young, a French historian with prairie roots, who tackled the passages that were impenetrable to the non-specialist. I would also like to thank two friends, Ian MacPherson and Del Muise, who heard more than they wished about this enterprise. It was a pleasure to work with Mrs Alice Grover, who typed the manuscript, and the staff at St Paul's College and the University of Manitoba. Mrs Maria Weise made the work possible. Mrs Georgeen Klassen at the Glenbow-Alberta Institute provided guidance in the selection of illustrations, and Caroline Trottier of Winnipeg drew the maps. John Parry was a thorough and kind editor. Richard Ens helped with statistical material and footnote verification. Alexander Usher calculated electoral results. Joe Friesen was always available for consultation. I committed the errors by myself and would be happy to hear about them.

I wish, above all, to thank my wife, Jean, for her support during this very long process. Not only did she endure the writing with patience and humour but she also did her best to explain ethnohistory to an innocent. For reasons that do not require words, the book is dedicated to her and to my parents.

# The Canadian prairies: A history

# 1

# Introduction

Three landscapes confront the visitor to the western interior of Canada: the prairies, which roll seemingly without end west and north from the Red River toward the Rockies and the Arctic; the parkland, where a profusion of birds and lakes, gentle hills and valleys, and fertile soil suggest a crescent-shaped oasis at the northern edge of the prairies; and the boreal forest, with rock outcroppings, cold lakes, and miles of spruce and pine as little travelled today as they were 400 years ago. These three landscapes have been bound by economy and history into a single region for most of the past three centuries. Their unity provides the rationale for the story that follows.

Inhabitants of the western interior have long recognized generalizations about the region's three landscapes: prairies, parkland, and forest. Popular images reinforce their perceptions: the prairies are flat, the parklands rolling, the forest vast and impenetrable. The prairies are the home of the meadow lark, whose distinctive song suggests images of shimmering heat waves above parched soil and grasses; the parklands are the home of the red-winged blackbird, whose crimson and gold shoulder tabs flash as he swoops to harass a lumbering crow; the boreal forest is made sinister by the raven, a raucous ebony intruder, and lightened by whisky-jack, the grey-clad thief and clown of the deep woods.

The seasons seem to provide complementary images for each landscape; autumn is a delight in the parkland, for there the gold of poplar, the scarlet of sumac, and the brown of maple and oak mark the turn of another year; the deep cold of winter is best endured where the boreal forest meets the parkland – in those protected valleys where trees and game provide sustenance, shelter, and fuel in the most difficult months of the calendar. The western interior is not simply W.O. Mitchell's 'basic requirements of land and sky,' the kettle lakes and bluffs of Gabrielle Roy's water-hen country, or the remote forests and mountains of Ralph Connor's Mounted Police – it is all three and more.

The unity that binds three landscapes into a region originates in the prairie economy. Native exploitation of resources customarily relied upon seasonal movement between at least two if not three habitats. The European fur trade was established upon these native cycles and itself came to depend upon exploitation of each of the three zones. Adaptation to international capitalism disrupted native life in the three zones when region-wide policies – Indian reserves, the square survey, the railway – imposed a new order upon the land. But the single dominant feature of the new agricultural economy was, again, a region-wide phenomenon – the so-called National Policy of the federal government. And each of the modern prairie provinces, Alberta, Saskatchewan, and Manitoba, has established an economy that marries the agricultural productivity of the prairie and parkland to the mineral, timber, and hydro-electric resources of the northern forests.

The cultural history of the western interior reinforces this economic unity. The unusual circumstances of the western fur trade, in which native and European co-operated peacefully for two centuries, between 1640 and 1840, underlie the first modern era of regional experience. In the second era, from the 1840s to the 1890s, the market economy and industrial capitalism re-created the entire region even as it had transformed England a century before. The third era of regional history encompassed the first four decades of the twentieth century; an agricultural economy was set in place and the political arrangements of a democratic capitalist state were challenged and confirmed. In the fourth era, from the 1940s to the 1980s, regional distinctiveness was simultaneously destroyed and affirmed; paradoxically, by becoming a neighbourhood in a multinational economy and culture, the prairie provinces and the prairie region remained vital and distinctive elements in human history.

The story itself is sufficient justification for the choice of boundaries. In these pages we will follow a single human society through more than three hundred years of dramatic change. The physical size of the region (750,000 square miles) makes its story intrinsically interesting. Its range of experience, from native hunting parties to petrochemical technology, spans the history of mankind. At the centre of the narrative lies the crucial experience of modern times – the industrial revolution. And the limited size of the region's population – perhaps 40,000 in 1800 and about 4 million today – makes it an ideal community to study. A history of the prairie west is sweeping but manageable; it is diverse and yet not exceptionally complex; it is an ideal introduction to the history of recent times.

Modern commentators would describe the pre-1840 prairie west as part of another age, a separate era in the history of the world. What was it like to travel in a pristine environment? Several scientific expeditions have left exhaustive commentaries on the experience.

As James Hector concluded in the late 1850s, the western interior lay on three great planes, rather like three steps on a stair. These 'prairie levels' were separated by gentle scarps that appeared as long low chains of hills. Thus, the hills of the Manitoba Escarpment, when seen from the west, have a gentle elevation of about 200 feet, but when approached from the east rise 500 to 800 feet above the surrounding country.[1] Hector described the levels as the three 'prairie steppes,' an adaptation of a term usually reserved for the type of vegetation found in Russia, but the usage has stuck and we still think in terms of mounting steps – and steppes – as we travel west across the prairies. The first prairie level averages 800 feet in altitude and corresponds to the bottom of glacial Lake Aggasiz, which dried up about 6,000 to 7,000 years ago. The second level, with an average altitude of 1,600 feet, lies between the Manitoba Hills (Pembina, Tiger, Riding, Duck, Porcupine, and Pasquia) and the Missouri Coteau, which rises along a line from Weyburn to Moose Jaw before turning north along the Saskatchewan-Alberta border. The third level, with altitude varying from 2,200 to 4,000 feet, slopes from the foothills of the Rockies in a northeasterly direction toward the Athabasca country.[2]

If these were its only hills, the region would unquestionably deserve the dismissal of today's weary travellers who, having motored
across its southern edge from Winnipeg to Medicine Hat, argue that
the interior is flat and boring. But this is not the case. Even a century
of cultivation cannot conceal the fact that the region is dotted with
tree-clad hills and valleys. They interrupt the miles of rolling plains,
sometimes as low blue ranges on the horizon, sometimes as winding slashes cut deep into the surface of the land. The hills and
valleys were created about 5,000 to 10,000 years ago when vast ice
sheets began to melt and to slide northeast toward Hudson Bay.
These glaciers left behind a discontinuous cover of stony till and
stratified drift as much as 1,000 feet in depth and deposited thick
accumulations of end moraine 'capped by forest and studded with
myriad kettle lakes.'[3] The sequence of birch and poplar forests, hills,
and sky-blue lakes in central Saskatchewan, extending from the
Birch Hills south to Wakaw Lake, is an example of this type of
landscape. And the melt water from the ice also cut flat-bottomed,
steep-banked spillways across the plains which we now associate
with the marvellous valleys of the Qu'Appelle, Assiniboine, Saskatchewan, and Souris rivers and which can be as much as four
miles wide and 300 feet deep. Where they now provide aesthetic
relief, the hills and valleys once were crucial islands of food and
shelter, hunting grounds as well as places of refuge.

The escarpments and the other ranges of hills were important to
the Indians, especially in the southern interior, but were less prominent except as landmarks or post sites in the mind of the fur trader.
To him, as to the Indians who became intermediaries in the trade,
the single most important geographical feature of the region was the
river system. From the trader's perspective, the interior was divided
into territories based upon the major rivers: the Red River Country,
the Saskatchewan Country, and the Athabasca Country (the latter
based upon the drainage basin of the Mackenzie), as well as several
smaller 'countries' along the rivers south and west of Hudson and
James bays. As Eric Ross's imaginary guidebook of 1811 concluded,
the interior possesses 'a remarkable system of rivers and lakes
which are distributed with an evenness and closeness that make it
possible to travel by light canoe from any one point in the Northwest to almost any other with a minimum of interruption. It is these
waterways, more than anything else, which has made possible the
rapid exploration of the Northwest, and it is also they which have

made practical the fur trade which, in turn, has greatly stimulated exploration.'[4] The rivers flowed north and northeast, of course, from a cold to an arctic winter climate and were prone to flooding in spring when early melt water rushed northward toward lands that were still frozen solid. This was especially significant along the Red, where miles of rich lands were regularly threatened by floods. The river system determined also the direction of trade flows and, as a result, affected the conduct of native diplomacy. Perhaps most important, river valleys were also rich in food resources. And where food was plentiful, there Indians would congregate and traders find a market.

European visitors often remarked upon the 'natural' character of the landscape. By this, they meant that the environment bore little evidence of human occupancy; instead, animals and plants dominated the earth. Their characteristics – the sounds they made, the smells they left behind, and the markings that they inscribed upon the surface of the land – were the dominant features of the region. Perhaps the most profound of all the changes that occurred in the western interior in the last half of the nineteenth century was that thereafter the landscape would be dominated and moulded by humans rather than by forces of nature, except in those rare moments – a flood, a blizzard, a forest, or prairie fire – when nature reasserted its power.

Some types of nineteenth-century landscape were recorded by explorers, and others have been reconstructed by modern-day scientists. The consensus is clear. In the southern plains, on the less fertile brown soils of Palliser's Triangle where precipitation in the growing season (May to September) is lowest, short grasses of six inches to one foot in height provided up to 80 per cent of the vegetation cover although sage and common cactus were also present. Surrounding this district was an arc of 'mixed-grass prairie' (short grass as well as mid-grasses which were two to four feet high), where the dark brown soils were more fertile and the precipitation was a little more certain. On the eastern fringe of this arc, on the plains of Manitoba's Lake Agassiz between the Red River and the Escarpment, lay the lush grass cover, over five feet high in places, of the 'true prairie.' The moistest area of the interior, the Red River Valley always possessed rich resources. Between the prairie and the boreal forest lay the parkland transition zone, a belt of prairie dotted with bluffs of aspen or aspen and oak. Here the soils were a

rich black, high in organic content and possessing perhaps the best
agricultural potential in the country when moisture was adequate.
The boreal forest of the interior was vast, of course, since it was part
of the system that stretched from Newfoundland to Alaska, and
shared with the rest of the mid-north the characteristic spruce, fir,
and jack pine. Still farther north lay the tundra, which was marked
by dwarf shrubs, permafrost, and the absence of tall trees.

The natural landscape in the southern prairies was dominated by
buffalo (or bison) rather than by man. These animal giants travelled
in herds numbered in the thousands and tens of thousands in the
summer time and simply swallowed up the land in their path. Isaac
Cowie's party met buffalo near the Qu'Appelle valley: its 'route took
us into the midst of the herd, which opened in front and closed
behind the train of carts like water round a ship ... the earth trem-
bled day and night ... as they moved ... over the inclinations of the
plains. Every drop of water on our way was foul and yellow with
their wallowings and excretions.'[5] The sound of the bisons' roaring
could be heard for miles and the path upon which the animals
travelled resembled a war zone, marked as it was by wallows that
might measure 40 by 15 feet, each a foot or more deep, created when
they rolled to escape insect attacks. Bison dung was sufficient to fuel
camp-fires for generations, and bison bones sustained a small fertilizer industry in the modern pioneer era. Bison trails criss-crossed
the plains like highways. Where the herds encountered bluffs, the
trees would become rubbing posts, and the barks of stronger specimens would be torn off to a height of six feet; the smaller brush
would simply be beaten to death by the cyclonic force of the bisons'
passage. The buffalo landscape had a character all its own.

The same might be said for some of the smaller-scale landscapes
of the natural world. Beaver, for example, built dams and marshes
that spread over large areas in valleys and along creek beds and
thereby created an ideal habitat for waterfowl and moose and for
swamp vegetation. Villages of prairie dogs were common on the
short-grass prairie and, if the estimate of the Lewis and Clark expedition is typical, could riddle the land with burrows for several
miles. Grasshoppers, or locusts, were so numerous on occasion
that, to cite the example of the Hind expedition, they could be
mistaken for a great grey cloud hanging low in the sky and could
devastate herbage for miles.

The overriding feature of every vista and every event in the western interior was that they were all created by the unaided forces of nature. Here was the world, William Butler commented in 1872, as it had taken shape in the hands of the Creator. Here too was vastness. The area of the three prairie provinces is about 750,000 square miles, or 480 million acres, an area that would encompass most of western Europe. The distance from the eastern edge of the plains near the Red River to the foothills of the Rockies is over 800 miles, roughly the distance from Paris to Warsaw. And of this vastness only about 9,000 acres – fourteen square miles – was being cultivated when Palliser reached the western interior in 1857. Not that plants were not grown and harvested by the natives – they were – but European-style agriculture, which eventually held sway over the entire region, scarcely existed there after two centuries of European presence.

# 2

# Native history:
# An introduction

The history of the western interior has long suffered from ignorance about the lives of its first inhabitants, the native people. When Bishop Taché wrote about the Indians of the west for a European and European-Canadian audience in 1868, he found it necessary to start with the assertion that natives were as much members of the human race as were his readers: 'The native is a man, for he is born amid weeping, he grows up amongst tears or dreams ...' He was trying to break down the prejudices of his time, to force his contemporaries to step beyond the perception of natives as exotic remnants of another world and instead to see them as humans with a range of problems and institutions not entirely different from those of their European counterparts. Yet when W.L. Morton in the 1950s wrote his classic history of Manitoba, he was unable to say anything of consequence about the era of native dominance in the region. Research had not yet established the richness and variety of these native societies.

We still do not know when different types of humankind emerged. It seems certain, however, that the Indians of the Americas descended from Asian peoples and that they migrated across the Bering Straits between twelve and seventy thousand years ago. This was not a long journey; a gap of only sixty miles, half of it studded with islands, separates the two continents today, and, in an age when the sea was much lower, there was a land bridge. It takes only a small leap of the imagination to watch a number of hunters and their families following their prey – mammoths, bison, bears, and moose – across this spit of land into the vast hunting territories of North America. In the centuries that followed, the children of their children would have continued to hunt, perhaps moving into the interior of the Yukon, south along the eastern slope of the Rocky Mountains, and eventually onto the great plains of the continent. About 11,000 to 11,500 years ago (or 9500–9000 BC), these big-game hunters were pursuing the mammoths that then abounded on the plains, attacking them in bogs or at water-holes. The spears they used had distinctive leaf-shaped stone points that constitute crucial evidence of Palaeo-Indian activity on the continental plains. Changes in climate and over-hunting seem to have caused the extinction of the mammoth (in the next thousand years) and the development of more specialized hunt-based cultures, as the discovery of variations on the stone projectile points suggests. Thus, as the centuries passed, native technological and cultural change responded to ecological change.[1]

Great ice sheets, thousands of feet thick, covered much of North America when the first Indians entered the continent. The centres of glaciation, one in British Columbia and the other around Hudson Bay, gradually pulled apart to create two gigantic sheets and an ice-free corridor along the Rockies. As the climate continued to warm and the glaciers receded (around 6000 BC) new cultures developed to take advantage of the wild food resources that replaced the extinct mammoth. One such culture continued to hunt a giant version of the bison on the plains; a second, based in the eastern woodlands, developed grinding implements – milling stones and mortars and pestles – in order to harvest such foods as seeds, nuts, roots, and berries which supplemented the hunt. The people of a third culture, whose residences included the southwestern desert but extended from Oregon to Mexico, used fully the scarce food resources of these arid lands, including fish, game, and plants. It was they who made the technological breakthrough that underlay the foundation of the justly celebrated civilizations of Central and South America.

Agriculture, in America as in the Old World, was crucial to the development of more complex societies. Recent archaeological dis-

coveries of primitive varieties of corn in the highlands of Mexico
demonstrate that these breakthroughs had occurred at the latest by
5000 BC in the Americas. By 3400 BC, cultivation of maize, pump-
kins, kidney beans, cotton, avocados and peppers, the fabrication of
pottery utensils, and the development of small villages marked this
central American culture as especially rich. In the era when Egyp-
tians were constructing the pyramids and the empires of Greece and
Rome bestrode the Mediterranean, these people were achieving
comparable feats. Thus, the chief ceremonial centre of the Teotihua-
can civilization, which reached its greatest heights between 300 and
600 AD, occupied a site of seven square miles in the region northeast
of the present Mexico City; there, the people built spectacular palaces, pyramids, and ceremonial mounds that still seize the visitor's
imagination. This civilization fell, perhaps to northern barbarians,
only to be succeeded by the Toltecs and eventually the Aztecs.
When the Spaniards under Cortez marched into central Mexico in
the early sixteenth century, they were awed by the magnificence of
the civilization that confronted them, by the canals that drained the
marshes, and especially by the great walled fortress of Tenochtitlan
with its lighthouses and twenty-five temples rising from the lake.
The forthright soldier Bernal Diaz recorded in his reminiscence:

> We were amazed and said that it was like the enchantments they tell
> of in the legend of Amadis, on account of the great towers and tem-
> ples and buildings rising from the water, and all built of masonry.
> And some of our soldiers even asked whether the things that we saw
> were not a dream ... I say again that I stood looking at it and thought
> that never in the world would there be discovered other lands such
> as these ... We did not know what to say, or whether what appeared
> before us was real, for on one side on the land, there were great
> cities, and in the lake ever so many more, and the lake itself was
> crowded with canoes, and in the Causeway were many bridges at
> intervals, and in front of us stood the great City of Mexico, and
> we – we did not even number four hundred soldiers.[2]

These great civilizations of Mesoamerica influenced the peoples to
the north during several thousand years, and if the nature of the
contact and its results are not yet certain the outline is fairly clear.
Corn cultivation and the use of ceramics spread northward, and,
between 500 and 1000 AD, items as diverse as decorative traditions,

ball courts, and copper bells were diffused along the Mississippi and Missouri River valleys. Farther afield, in eastern North America, the so-called Woodland tradition, which developed around 1000 BC, had borrowed such aspects of Mesoamerican civilization as corn, pottery, mortuary mounds, and ceramic figurines. To the north again, in the two millennia from about 1000 BC to about 700–1000 AD, these Woodland peoples developed several distinctive cultural traditions, including the hunting-gathering life of the Atlantic seaboard, the agricultural and hunting life of the area around the lower Great Lakes, and the various combinations of fishing, hunting, and gathering that distinguished the bands of the upper Great Lakes and Hudson Bay regions.

The next great era in the native pre-history of the western interior began around 700–800 AD and ended with contact between natives and Europeans in the seventeenth century. Archaeological and ethnohistorical research is not yet sufficiently detailed to explain the rhythms or even the exact identity of these pre-contact cultures. But, as a result of study during the last quarter-century, we have significant clues where before we knew nothing. During almost a millennium, according to archaeological evidence, members of these Woodland cultures established a constantly evolving relationship with their natural environment and their neighbours. Travel, trade, war, and the quest for food marked their existence. The native peoples of this region manufactured and decorated jewellery and pottery vessels. They possessed dentalium shell that could have originated only on the Pacific coast, and they worked with stone materials that could have come only from the foothills of the Rockies or the northeastern fringe of the plains.

In the area that particularly concerns us, the western interior of Canada, four native cultural traditions were evolving in the millennium after 700 AD: Plains Village, Plains Woodland, Plains Hunter, and Sub-Arctic. Those of the Plains Village tradition eventually established a more sedentary culture rooted equally in the hunt and the field: thus, in addition to their harvests at buffalo surrounds and jumps where arrow and spearheads have been found, these natives cultivated corn, beans, and squash along the fertile river bottoms, using digging sticks and hoes made from bison scapula. The Plains Woodland tradition retained connections with the boreal forest while using plain and parkland as well; it seems to have relied upon fish, fowl, big game, and plants for a considerable proportion of its food supply but to have embarked upon bison hunts in the milder seasons of the year. The Plains Hunters relied more heavily on the plains bison hunt; but their skin tepees and constant movement across great distances resulted in a meagre legacy of material remains. The Sub-Arctic tradition, based in the northern reaches of the Shield and the low Arctic, would have relied more on the caribou as a fundamental food source and might be seen as the precursor of modern Athapaskan or Dene peoples. (Another tradition, located in the high Arctic and on the very shores of Hudson Bay and the Arctic Ocean, was the foundation of Inuit culture. These latter people were biologically distinct from Indians and probably originated in a common culture in northeast Asia that had taken form before 4000 BC.) And, despite the 200 language groups in North America (and nearly 2,000 in Central and South America), the western interior of present-day Canada contained only three language families, Algonkian, Siouan, and Dene or Athapaskan.[3]

Scholars are still uncertain about many aspects of this Late Woodland millennium. In the past, they were too quick to classify distinct cultural groups on the basis of their material remains (such as projectile points and ceramics) and on the assumption that different cultures occupied or possessed separate parcels of real estate. It is now suggested, however, that food resources, military calculations, and even personal whim might have determined whether and where a particular band would hunt, fish, or travel in a given season. Moreover, it is now recognized that a number of bands might have occupied the same territory at different seasons; thus, one group might use a parkland site for a winter bison hunt, a second for springtime exploitation of wildfowl and tender giant reeds, a third for summertime berry picking, and a fourth for autumn fishing and wildfowl hunts. Such overlap becomes even more likely as scholars increasingly emphasize the role of plant resources in native diets: wild rice and maple sugar, cattails and greens, seeds and berries, rosehips and acorns, hazelnuts and breadroots were probably part of annual food cycles.[4]

These cultures were not poor by today's standards. Indeed, the wealthiest example of the Plains Village tradition, the city of Cahokia in the Mississippi Valley near present-day St Louis, contained in 1000 AD more citizens than London (30,000, compared to 20,000) and had been using corn as a dietary staple for several centuries. The Plains Hunter tradition, which some might dismiss as less 'advanced' because it had not intensified its agricultural activity, relied upon a bison population of 50–60 million (at 1,000 pounds of meat per animal) and thus was founded on an ample resource base.[5]

How many people lived on the continent? This has been a subject of much scholarly debate and has yet to be established with certainty. Following the cautious estimates, we may conclude that between 6 and 10 million people lived north of Mexico at any time between 1000 and 1500 AD. The greatest population density occurred where intensive agriculture was practised, and the lowest would be on the plains and in the northern sub-arctic, where food resources were more limited. Thus, in the northwestern interior, which stretches from Lake Superior to the Rockies, and from the Missouri to the Arctic, there may have been as few as 15,000 and as many as 50,000 people at any time in the pre-contact era.

The quest for food has been a central concern for all human groups at all times but for Indians in early North America it was a concern that touched every individual. Natives were careful to adapt to nature's dictates. The efficiency and economy of, for example Chipewyan-made caribou-skin clothing and moccasins, their skin tents, their snowshoes and toboggans are impressive by any cultural or technological measuring stick. These were societies built on stone, bone, skin, wood, and snow. Nature was teacher and master and companion to the native peoples of the Americas; they derived important insights and benefits from the relationship.

Indian religious beliefs emphasized the importance of reconciliation with the supernatural and usually found their expression in metaphors drawn from the natural environment. As the Saskatchewan Plains Cree warrior Fineday told anthropologist David Mandelbaum, 'Everything has got the spirit of Manitou in it, even a blade of grass, or else grass couldn't grow.'[6] The native's relationship with the supernatural was often sought through a withdrawal experience or vision quest, usually at the time of puberty. Often, young men and women would fast or subject themselves to various ordeals (Fineday looked toward the sun for four days), until they made contact with the supernatural force and obtained some message about their unique gifts, songs that they would sing to call upon their guardians for help, and talismans or tokens that would serve as their guardian spirit. Thus, some would learn that they would be hunters, others would be leaders of ceremonies, others warriors, and, most prized of all, others would cure the sick. When he experienced this contact with the supernatural in a dream, Crowfoot, later one of the most famous chiefs of the Alberta Blackfoot, was told by a buffalo spirit to make a pair of leggings from the skin of a buffalo calf; these would be his holy charm when he became the 'father of his people.' Later, he was given an owl's head, which he wore in the famous top-knot in his hair throughout his life and which was said to be both his protection and his guide to greatness as leader.[7] The holy songs, the talismans, and the contact with a representative of the supernatural were the group's and individual's support in an unpredictable world.

Whatever the particular religious beliefs of his culture – and the range of beliefs was vast – the North American Indian 'almost invariably was a believer in some force outside himself. Yet, at the same time, he often recognized, through dreams, the unconscious forces within himself which seemed to link him to the larger forces of the universe. His ability to empathize with other humans and with nonhuman living creatures who seemed to share the same life force provided the Indian with a coherent and meaningful world view.'[8]

Warfare was a powerful factor in the life of every individual and group in the western interior of the continent. Proof of bravery, of skill, of supernatural support all could be attested by a daring raid against 'the enemy.' But in addition to such acts of prestige, and equally common acts of revenge, economic motives also precipitated warfare and affected the determination of one's friends and opponents. War was so much a part of plains Indian life that, by the nineteenth century, according to David Mandelbaum, the plains Crees lived a 'metaphor of battle':

This meant that whenever a man had to do something special or unusual, he announced that he was able to do it because of some similar act he had performed against the enemy. For example, in preparing for the Sun Dance ceremony, several tepee covers were needed to make the big Sun Dance lodge. A man who had been victorious in battle would go around with a little stick, would strike a standing tepee with it and say, 'Just as I struck a tepee of the enemy and slashed it so do I take this tepee cover for our Sun Dance.' Or if a man had to perform one of the police functions of a warrior society, which might include destroying the possessions of another man, he would say, 'Just as I destroyed the possessions of the enemy on such and such an occasion so do I now destroy these possessions.'[9]

For males in these cultures, participation in warlike activities was mandatory if they were to be fully accepted as members of the group, let alone candidates for leadership or for positions of high honour.

Generalizations about broad patterns of behaviour among diverse cultures can be misleading, but a number of additional points should be made to clarify aspects of native social organization. It is sometimes assumed that Indian groups were led by powerful authoritarian chiefs whose word was law or, conversely, that organization within the bands was so loose as to be meaningless. Neither assertion is valid as a description of the plains and woodlands bands of the western interior. Political and diplomatic decisions were normally taken after discussion in councils composed of most male adults, but bands had leaders, as do most human groups. These men – and they were customarily men – exercised the usual leadership functions, were chosen generally by ability as well as by heredity, and exerted their authority by persuasion and example rather than decree or force. This governmental system may be informal by today's standards, but it met the needs of native society. Police functions were regularly carried out during the summer gatherings of the plains band by a warrior society, particularly during the all-important buffalo hunts when discipline was essential to success. Humour and public ridicule were extremely effective weapons in a number of woodland cultures and apparently served as well as today's jails in regulating behaviour.[10]

Indians were traders long before the arrival of Europeans. They exchanged goods with members of their own band or with other bands of their culture and dealt with bands from other cultures, even if they had to undertake great journeys in order to do so. Thus, the Assiniboines of the southern prairies might make a month-long trip at the end of summer to the Missouri River valley to visit the Mandans, with whom they could exchange their hides and crafts for corn and other goods. These exchanges were more than simply an anonymous economic transfer, of the type that occurs in a modern supermarket; the negotiation that preceded the native trade, the ceremony that accompanied it, and the games and dances that surrounded it have no parallel in modern commercial relations. A better comparison in today's world would be an international treaty-signing ceremony that is sealed by an economic agreement and formalized at a conference that includes social events.

However, the native event would normally occur annually and would certainly involve each member of the band as well as its leaders; in this sense, the native's journey provided a break in routine, offered new challenges to the male hunters, enabled the adolescents to see the way others lived, and permitted the family to stock up on prize items such as Mandan corn or Cree beadwork that were not readily available at home. Trade was not merely an economic event, therefore, but a gift-exchange ceremony and a time of celebration. Underlying the social characteristics, too, was a significant political dimension: the regular renewal of contact, as between the Mandans and Assiniboines, served to consolidate a diplomatic alliance, to say that they were friends who exchanged gifts; the implication, as with modern pacts of 'mutual assistance,' was that the two cultures had a common enemy with whom they were sometimes at war, who would be a regular target for raiding parties and against whom they might fight as one. Trade ties were political and diplomatic statements; and trade exchanges were very much a part of pre-contact native culture.

A common assumption today is that Europeans could, according to their own beliefs and laws, 'discover' the continent and 'claim' it for their respective sovereigns without acknowledging native rights to the land. In fact, in the sixteenth and seventeenth centuries, when contact was made, Europeans were quite prepared to recognize both the legal existence and the military power of the native peoples, to accept native possession of the land, and to negotiate with them for privileges of use and occupancy by the customary tools of diplomacy, including, of course, war. It was only later, when time and acquaintance had worked their way, that European nations began to distinguish between their own 'dominion' over North American territory and the native 'possessory rights' to certain portions thereof. This occurred in the western interior only after several centuries of contact. Thus, a long era of peaceful relations, during which natives and Europeans were equal, preceded this later phase of European dominance. As is customary in international relations, the diplomatic relationship was founded on the natives' power to assert their will on the battlefield as well as in a court of law or at the council table.[11]

The pattern of native personal and domestic life is so diverse that it defies generalization. None the less, recent works of synthesis do emphasize several themes. Native child-rearing was notably patient, gentle, affectionate, and even permissive, it seems, and emphasized co-operation while discouraging competition. Though corporal punishment was rare, children would be shamed or ridiculed into the proper behaviour. To pledge one's word was to make an unalterable bond, and, even at the risk of betraying oneself or one's people, one was supposed to maintain such a pledge. The keenest edge of legal custom was that of retributive justice: a wronged family was permitted, indeed required, to take vengeance for injury by inflicting similar pain on the transgressor. But Indian generosity was also justly famous because the concept of sharing one's riches was actually an operative principle. This was a survival mechanism in an uncertain world, of course, because one never knew when one's own needs would be great. But it was also a mark of status to be able to share wealth. As a result, co-operation, like retribution, was very much ingrained in Indian life.

Children spent their early years close to their mother and their camp, where girls learned to carry out such tasks as making clothing and boys began to shoot with toy bows and arrows. Adolescence marked the time of transition from childhood to adulthood. For boys, this included withdrawal from camp and vision quests. They would also accompany their elders more frequently on hunting and trapping expeditions and there learn the arts of survival. The first hunting prize of an adolescent male, like the first successful hunt of the season, was an occasion for celebration in which all the hunters would share the bounty and congratulate the hunter. For girls, adolescence was also a turning-point. At first menstruation, Cree girls were removed a small distance from camp for a time of fasting and seclusion. On their return, they were expected to remain aloof and respectful for some time but then to be prepared to embark on the life of an adult. Marriage was arranged by the parents and was not usually accompanied by special rites but rather was made formal by public proclamation. Divorce was effected in similar fashion. Polygamy was acceptable but, naturally, depended especially upon the wealth and ability of the male provider. Childbirth was the mother's responsibility but, in most cultures, midwives assisted at the event. Abortions were induced by special potions. Death was accompanied by public expressions of grief, including wailing and self-mutilation, and by formal burial ceremonies in which the body would be dressed in fine clothes and either placed in the ground, under logs, or on a scaffold accompanied by the weapons, ornaments, and utensils of the deceased.[12]

Native economies in the Americas were not poorer, more precarious, or more miserable than their contemporary European counterparts. Indeed, recent studies of hunting and gathering societies suggest that the natives of the western interior may have lived a life of relative comfort and plenty. Skeletal analysis of palaeolithic remains in Europe and Africa, for example, indicates that the hunter-gatherers of the stone age were taller, stronger, and healthier than were people in the intervening millennia. The hunter-gatherer did not labour endlessly in quest of food. Indeed, it is apparent that when societies give up a hunt-based economy in favour of agriculture, they actually increase the per capita work-load. The argument that native societies were 'poor' depends, of course, upon our evaluation of material accumulation; if we agree that our human needs are finite – perhaps consisting of health, food, shelter, a sense of belonging to the universe – then these societies were as wealthy as they wished. Moreover, because they chose the easier life of hunting, they necessarily accepted the need of mobility and the impossibility of property accumulation. But, responds the sceptic, what about the times of famine, the improvidence that fails to set aside for the morrow? Trust in one's hunting ability, one's fortune, and nature's generosity may partially account for the hunter's attitude, but we should recall that food storage implies stasis, which in turn exhausts local resources and thus enforces mobility on the hunting band. The hunting and gathering societies of the western interior achieved economic, political, and religious arrangements as satisfactory and as conducive to human happiness, for most members of the community, as those of any other society.[13]

Not all Europeans dwelt in Versailles or debated with Plato. The great mass of people in ancient Greece were either very small farmers or slaves; agriculture was the basic economic activity. Agriculture was the principal occupation and source of income in the Roman Empire, too, and was conducted either by slaves or by peasants who farmed just enough land to feed themselves and their families and, perhaps, to trade for a hoe and a knife and other small implements. Eileen Power's classic account of the ninth-century French peasant Bodo, his wife Ermentrude, and their three children suggested a daily round of constant toil for everyone in the household. Christian in name, Bodo remained as 'superstitious' as his Frankish ancestors, saying charms over the sick – his children and his cattle alike – and incantations over the crops and the bees and the aches in his joints. The jolliest of his few holidays was an annual fair which must have resembled the Cree trading expedition to the Mandans. The whole family attended the fair, perhaps for several days, roaming among the stalls of cheeses and wines and feathers and salt and almonds and monkeys and cloth, listening to strange tongues, sniffing the spices, and exchanging a few pennies for exotic morsels of food and a minstrel's song and, of necessity, salt for the winter's meat. Only in Bodo's era did sufficient iron become available for the production of a new and better type of felling axe and a new heavier plough that permitted the expansion of agriculture into the richer alluvial lowlands of northern Europe.

Daily life for the peasant in the seventeenth century would have altered little from the pattern established three or even five hundred years before: illiteracy; physical tiredness; quarrels over incursions into crops by a neighbour's animals or a traveller's retinue; inadequate diet, precarious health, and taxing labour; isolation from the so-called main currents of political and intellectual life of the age; small houses, often shared with animals, in which privacy was almost impossible; superstition, especially concerning illness and other calamities; and physical endurance combined with physical hardship. This was the lot of most Europeans – perhaps 70 to 90 per cent – until the Industrial Revolution.[14]

The cultures of the western interior of Canada were successful adaptations to the environment. Like their European peasant counterparts, the first peoples of this region were attuned to the rhythms of nature, dependent on the myth and magic of traditions then thousands of years old, and not significantly affected by the technological changes that were to shake the globe in the following centuries. The natives were travellers, traders, hunters, soldiers, and family members, and, though it might not have seemed evident to any single generation, they were evolving with changes in local ecology, regional diplomacy, and continental technology.

# 3

# The natives' fur trade
# 1640–1840

The pattern of native diplomacy and the rhythm of native movements continued to change – indeed, began to change more rapidly – during the two centuries after 1640. But the natives' seasonal
round of existence, methods of child-rearing, transition to adulthood, hunting and trading expeditions, and material culture – the
houses, food preparation, and clothing that lay at the foundation of
life – remained little altered by contact with Europeans. The images
of European culture as 'pattern-maker' and of native culture as 'clay'
were never accurate descriptions of fur-trade relationships. Such
European goods as blankets, cloth, hatchets, and awls did not de-
base native culture. They were technologically superior means of
carrying out functions already required by the natives and were
readily adopted for that reason. However, guns and horses and
European diseases did represent significant new factors in native
life and should be recognized as European contributions of a different order. The advent of Europeans and European trade goods
marked the beginning of a new era – an era two hundred years
long – distinguished by adaptation, peace, and co-operation.

To examine prairie history from the native point of view requires
several revisions in the conventional wisdom. Chief among these is
our perspective on the fur trade. The customary discussion of the
trade focuses on the competition between business enterprises

based in Montreal and Hudson Bay and finds watersheds in the Conquest of 1759–60 and the coalition of fur companies in 1821. Native history has a different rhythm. Following the American historian Wilcomb Washburn, we can discern four eras in the post-contact native experience: the first was marked by native equality with Europeans; the second began when native equality was challenged and ended when it was destroyed; in the third, which extended almost to the present, the native 'existed on a plane of inequality, his destiny largely shaped by whites.'[1] The fourth commenced in recent decades and represents a native cultural and political resurgence. In the western interior, the era of equality endured from the 1640s to the 1840s. It was challenged and destroyed in the following half-century. The third era began in the 1890s and ended only in the last generation, about the 1940s. The final era extends from the Second World War to the present.

At the time of the first European contact with natives of the western interior, during the seventeenth century, five prominent cultural groups existed in the region. The Saulteaux, or Ojibwas, dwelt along the north shore of Lake Huron and Lake Superior and may have established a village-based society. The Crees lived north and west of these bands, between Hudson Bay and the Manitoba lakes and travelled more than their Ojibwa cousins whose language was a version of their own Algonkian tongue. The Assiniboines, who probably lived south of the Crees, and west of the Ojibwas, in the region of the Rainy River corridor from Lake Superior to Lake Winnipeg, were a Siouan-language group and an offshoot of the Sioux nation; they had established peaceful relations with their Algonkian neighbours and adopted an economy comparable in its essentials to these woodland hunter-gatherer cultures. The Blackfoot probably lived west and north of the Assiniboines and relied more on the buffalo hunt for their subsistence. The Chipewyans lived yet further north, along the Churchill watershed, where caribou provided one firm foundation for their food cycle. Each of these five peoples experienced significant change during the first two centuries of contact with the European fur trade.

The Ojibwas are one of the important groups in today's native politics. They are divided into four communities. The southeastern group lives in the lower Michigan peninsula and southern Ontario; the southwestern Chippewas occupy Wisconsin and Minnesota; the plains Ojibwas (Bungi) moved into western Manitoba and Saskatchewan at the beginning of the nineteenth century and have there remained; and the northern Ojibwas inhabit the forest lands that stretch eastward from the Manitoba Interlake to Hudson and James bays and Lake Superior. This remarkable growth and dispersal of population was the product of a relatively small group, perhaps 5,000 in 1640, that occupied a thin strip along the neck of water connecting Lake Superior to Georgian Bay.

The Ojibwas' territory was rich in fish, plant life, and game – it is said they harvested 2,400 moose in the winter of 1670–1 on Manitoulin Island – and the bands found little reason to move very far from their villages of 100–300 people except in the depths of winter when they dispersed into the forests to hunt large game. By mid-seventeenth century, great numbers of Ojibwas (1,500 and more), were gathering annually at Sault Ste Marie to trade with the Europeans from the St Lawrence and to enjoy a more intense social life, but their annual calendar was otherwise little altered by trade in the early years of contact. They had begun to act as middlemen for the French, carrying European goods to the Crees and Assiniboines and returning with rich harvests of furs that they exchanged at great advantage to themselves. After the Hudson's Bay Company set up posts on the Bay in the 1670s and 1680s, some Ojibwas seem to have travelled there – a distance of 1,000 miles – to obtain an alternate source of goods. Many Ojibwas moved west into the country north of Lake Superior in the following generation (1690–1730), perhaps in company with the expansion of the French fur-trade network. Thus, the Ojibwas were not true sub-arctic peoples when they encountered Europeans, but, during the next century, they became greater travellers and traders as they participated more determinedly in the European-native trade network. Aside from the migration northeastward and the increased emphasis upon travel, they remained a separate cultural group. Language, kinship, art, and ceremonial life – from the Feast of the Dead to lacrosse – distinguished them from their Algonkian-speaking cousins, the Crees.[2]

Modern-day Crees recognize three major components of their people. The land stretching from east of Lake Winnipeg to northern Quebec is inhabited by the 'swamp people,' the forests of northern Saskatchewan and Alberta and northwestern Manitoba by the 'woods people,' the plains and parklands of Saskatchewan by the 'prairie people.' Their empire, like that of the Ojibwas, is testimony to the changes of the last three centuries.

When the Crees first met European traders and Ojibwa middlemen in the seventeenth century, they were hunters in the Shield
country between Lake Superior and Hudson Bay and travelled as far
west, perhaps, as the Saskatchewan River at The Pas. During late
spring and early summer, they gathered in large bands – as many
as 1,000 or more – to renew friendships and to enjoy the festive
atmosphere. During the rest of the year, they dispersed in smaller
bands to hunt and fish in widely separated lands. Everyone in the
smaller group was a relative – brother, father-in-law, aunt – and
thus the family hunting band was a close and supportive unit.

The Crees were travellers, especially in the summer, when their
birch-bark canoes carried them along the river systems of the interior, but also in winter when showshoes and sleds were their means
of conveyance. Their travel, like their social structure, was based on
the ecology of the Shield and parkland. The hunting bands carried
their houses with them in the form of moose or caribou skins which
were thrown over a conical skeleton of small poles collected from
the woods around the campsite. These houses have been described
as clean and warm; indeed memories of a floor of fresh pine boughs
and beaver skins and the wood fire in the centre have kindled many
fond reminiscences in literature of the fur trade. Fish, fowl, and
game constituted the main elements of the Cree diet; food was
dried, roasted, or boiled. Utensils were of bone, flint, and wood.
Nature provided fresh plants and meat or ready refrigeration for
most of the year, and so preparation of food was rarely a problem.
Clothing was made from animal skins and furs, decorated by
coloured quill work and, at times, by painted designs. The Crees
captured animals with the aid of snares and deadfalls in winter and,
in all seasons, by shooting with bows and arrows and later with
guns. Moose and woodland caribou were particularly important in
their diet. They caught fish in nets and perhaps in weirs. The now-
rare sturgeon was commonly speared, and this method was probably used for other species too. The resource base could not be
described as exceptionally good but it was adequate, given the careful planning and movement of the hunting bands, to sustain the
4,000–5,000 Cree who occupied the vast region in the 1640s.

The establishment of regular European trade at both Hudson Bay
and Lake Superior encouraged the Crees to move west with the
French traders in the decades around the opening of the eighteenth
century and, with their new-found allies, the Assiniboines, to become middlemen in turn to the natives who lived yet farther west.

This profitable alliance of Crees and Assiniboines was to endure for a century and to cause great changes in the western interior.[3]

The Assiniboines were members of the Siouan language group and thus were not readily understood by the Algonkian-speaking Ojibwas and Crees. Before European contact, they probably lived west of the Ojibwas along Lake Superior and the so-called boundary-waters corridor stretching toward Lake of the Woods. Within a few years of European contact, probably by the 1640s, they became customers of the Ojibwa middlemen. But the Assiniboines, like the Crees, benefited from the arrival of traders on Hudson Bay and, by the 1680s, were making the long trek northward to secure European goods and thus became middlemen in their turn. During these expeditions, they formed closer diplomatic relationships with the Crees and thereby initiated a new alliance among the western interior peoples.[4]

The Blackfoot are now recognized as the natives of southern Alberta and Montana. Their confederacy comprised the Piegan, Blood, and Siksika (Blackfoot proper) tribes and, from the early nineteenth century, was allied with the Athapaskan-speaking Sarcees. The Blackfoot retain the image of plains warriors in popular mythology, an appropriate depiction given that they were probably buffalo hunters – pedestrian and later horse-mounted – for centuries. Before Europeans arrived on the continent, they would have followed the herds from parkland to plains, using the jump and the pound to kill sufficient animals not only to supply their basic dietary needs but also to provide materials for clothing, shelter, tools, and fuel. The Blackfoot ancestral home, for perhaps ten thousand years, was a portion of the northern plains, perhaps west of the south branch of the Saskatchewan River. Unlike their forest-based neighbours, they never depended on fish or built canoes; rather, their distinctive material culture was based on buffalo-skin tepees, straw basketry, and clay pottery. The men did the hunting, butchering, and war-making; women processed the skins, gathered plants, and supervised the children. Winter bands might consist of a dozen tepees, while the annual summer camp might bring hundreds of households together for a great buffalo hunt and festival. The Blackfoot became customers of the Crees and Assiniboines in the early eighteenth century and, as they traded skins for European goods, were integrated into the growing diplomatic alliance system that the Cree and Assiniboine bands were creating.[5]

The Chipewyans lived north and west of the Crees along the Churchill River system and in the low Arctic. With their Athapaskan-speaking neighbours, the Beavers and Slaves (who are also part of what is often called the Dene nation), they are the inhabitants of the northern reaches of the three prairie provinces and the southern parts of the Northwest Territories. Like the Crees, the Chipewyans were travellers, but their language was Athapaskan and thus quite different from the Algonkian tongue of their southern neighbours. Their small bands might range over several thousand miles in a year as they followed the food and seasonal cycles of their vast homeland. The centre of their existence was the caribou, but moose, bear, beaver, and fish were also basic items in their diet. During the annual migrations of the caribou herds, the Chipewyans would set up converging rows of sticks to guide the animals into enclosures made of branches where snares would make easy the task of hunters equipped with bows and arrows. The Inuit to the north and the Crees to the south were, at the time of European contact, traditional enemies of the Chipewyans, but, until the spread of European weapons in the eighteenth century, warfare was not a deadly occupation. In the 1780s and 1790s, as the North West and Hudson's Bay companies extended their operations into the Lake Athabasca region, guns sharpened enmities and changed, to some degree, the course of Chipewyan history.[6]

Despite this emphasis on native contact with European technology, the single most important theme in native history in the seventeenth and early eighteenth centuries was continuity – both in the retention of most aspects of native material and domestic culture and in the maintenance of the accustomed seasonal movement associated with the food cycle. European trade was fitted between annual migrations that had, for generations, followed the changes in animal location and plant resources. Native history in this era was also distinguished by the emergence of native middlemen. Native traders rapidly became indispensable to the operation and expansion of the European fur trade. Acting as traders, transporters, and advertising agents, the native middlemen used the trade to increase their own status, to improve their hunting and domestic tools, and to reinforce their military power. Whether the natives controlled the trade or were increasingly dominated by it, however, has been a subject of debate among scholars.

The existence of numbers of native middlemen has been attested by the records of fur traders and priests. Extant writings suggest the development of two different native migration patterns during the first century of the fur trade. One cycle of movement can be illustrated by the experience of two Hudson's Bay Company employees, Joseph Smith and Joseph Waggoner, who joined a Cree party as it left the Bay for the interior in 1756. The traders soon discovered that the natives were not planning to spend the winter trapping for the English but rather would devote their energies to their own survival. They paddled into the interior for two months, from 23 August to 18 October, and then, having navigated Nelson River, the northern tip of Lake Winnipeg, and Cedar Lake, they abandoned their canoes and set out on foot across country. For two months they walked west and south, along the Manitoba Escarpment in the forest region south of Lake Winnipegosis, hunting moose and fishing for jack (northern pike) and eventually coming upon a small herd of buffalo. Once this boon was discovered, camp was made and the band remained there for two more months, killing buffalo and subsisting thus during the cold snowy weather. The group moved on in early February, hunting moose as it walked northeast toward the Swan River valley. Here, again, camp was made, and, for another two months, while the band lived on dried meat and fat, trees were cut, bark was gathered, and canoes were constructed for the return trip to York Factory, which began in mid-May.

Similar activity and movement cycles were recorded by other European travellers with Indian bands in this era. The Indians wintered in the parklands, where food was relatively more abundant, and trapped or traded for furs in late autumn or early spring in the adjacent forests. In spring they would set up their fishing camps along a lake or river, and, perhaps in June, part of the band would canoe to York Factory on Hudson Bay, returning in the autumn to recommence the cycle.[7]

The pattern witnessed by Smith and Waggoner, which can be described as a forest-parkland cycle, had its counterpart in a second pattern, the plains-parkland cycle encountered by Jesuit missionaries and by the French fur trade expeditions of the La Vérendryes in the mid-eighteenth century. Crees and Assiniboines would leave the parklands around the southern shore of Lake Winnipeg in the early spring to trap in the Riding Mountain district or to fish along the rivers and lakes of the parklands margin. Once their families were established at the fishing camps, too, the young men might head south to Sioux territory to participate in war raids on their enemies. In middle and late summer, the natives moved out onto the high plains to hunt the herds of bison that had been fattening on rich plains fodder and to hold the summer festivals where hundreds would worship, celebrate, and exchange trade goods. These summer migrations often included a visit to the Mandan villages along the Missouri River where used European goods could be traded for beans and corn and Mandan crafts. Then, as the leaves turned and the nights grew colder, they would head toward the parklands to prepare for winter. Thus, the summer migration of some Assiniboine bands differed from the woodland Crees in direction but had as its object trade and visits with other groups as well as food gathering, just as the northern expeditions did.[8]

The Cree and Assiniboine experience is illustrative of the effect of middleman status upon native history. Individuals in these two cultures had quickly seen the advantages of European technology and, by the mid-seventeenth century, were important suppliers of furs to the French on the St Lawrence via Ojibwa, Ottawa, and Huron middlemen. When the Hudson's Bay Company moved into posts along Hudson and James bays in the 1670s and 1680s, the Crees and Assiniboines started to patronize these establishments. With the aid of English guns, the most powerful military weapon in the native arsenal, they consolidated their hold on the Nelson River district, through which their enemies had to travel to reach York Factory. A measure of the importance of their control was that, as early as 1684, 300 canoes containing over 700 people visited York Factory, the Hudson's Bay Company post at the Hayes estuary on the Bay. Another measure is the careful estimate that 70 per cent of the pre-1760 York Factory trade was conducted not by those who trapped the animals but by native middlemen.[9] Thus, the Crees and Assiniboines became middlemen in the trade, imposing tolls on those who came from upriver or trading at high profits with the more distant bands and conveying the furs thus gained to Hudson Bay.

The terms of trade were, for political purposes, very hard. If a Cree paid 14 prime beaver pelts to Hudson's Bay for a musket, he might resell it to the Blackfoot for 50 beaver. Similarly, the price of a hatchet rose from 1 to 6 beaver, of an axe from 1/3 to 4 beaver; the pattern seemed to be that tools of war cost three to six times more than the York Factory price when the Crees resold them to their inland allies. Even a kettle would rise from 8 to 20 beaver in price, however, so the cost of doing business with a middleman – and we should recall that the goods he sold were often well-used – was never small.[10] And the enemies of the Cree-Assiniboine-Ojibwa alliance, among whom the Dakota Sioux were most important, would simply be excluded from this trade. As A.J. Ray concluded, the crucial aspect of the trade system was the power of these middlemen: 'They were able to dictate the terms of the trade to Europeans and other Indians alike. Further, because of the nature of the system that evolved, they largely regulated the rate of material culture change, and to a considerable extent they also influenced its directions.'[11]

The Crees, Assiniboines, and Ojibwas used their domination of European trade to dictate diplomatic arrangements in the western interior of the continent. By the end of the first century of trade, the three groups with their Blackfoot allies, controlled the entire region from the Bay to the Rockies and from the South Saskatchewan River to the Churchill River. Their power was a product of their strategic location and was proof of their negotiating skill as well as good fortune. It was also an almost-accidental by-product of a way of life that had evolved in preceding generations, in particular of food-gathering and trade patterns. Because of their geographical location and their seasonal migrations, the Crees and Assiniboines continued their pre-contact way of life in all its essentials and yet were able to acquire valuable tools and much greater political power. In the generations after contact, European trade enriched rather than demoralized the Cree and Assiniboine peoples.

The actual trade event was a remarkable combination of native theatre or ritual and European bargaining. Whether the Europeans controlled the process, as is sometimes alleged, is dubious. Rather, both sides retained considerable autonomy in the first century of the fur trade.

The traders at York Factory, the largest Hudson's Bay Company post, have left fascinating descriptions of the transactions. Their narratives take up the story from the time the Indian canoes near the trading post. The native trading captain would halt the brigade briefly in order to levy a small tax of one or two pelts on each of his followers and to marshal them in formal fashion, perhaps in ranks of ten canoes abreast with a gap of several hundred yards between each rank. The trading captain might carry a flag in his canoe and would signal the fort by firing his gun in the air as he neared the landing place. The British would reply by discharging their cannon and raising the Union Jack. The captain and his lieutenants disembarked and entered the governor's room for formal introductions while the native women set up camp some distance from the walls of the fort. The men exchanged greetings and speeches on the state of the country, the governor received the gift of pelts from the captain, and the native leader was given a fine suit of clothing – red or blue cloth coat with regimental trim and lace, a white shirt, stockings with garters, English shoes, and a hat with feathers – and a range of other items, including tobacco, prunes, and brandy. A procession then formed; to the fore went drummers and soldiers and company servants, bearing the gifts; trading captain and governor followed, deep in conversation. This formal parade stopped at the native camp, where the gifts were distributed and more speeches were made. When the company servants left, a party ensued that might last for two or three days. Trade then commenced.[12]

To start the exchange, the natives and traders once again gathered in the fort, this time to smoke the grand calumet (pipe of truth and friendship) and to establish the ground rules. The natives pointed the pipe in each direction and twirled it in the air to symbolize the bond between the two parties and then passed it round for each participant to smoke in turn. The trading captain and the governor then spoke again. The former emphasized his loyalty and, of course, implied that there were other traders with whom he could deal. He explained his desire to have good-quality items, including 'thick' kettles and blankets, 'lightweight' guns with 'locks that will not freeze in the winter,' and 'moist hard-twisted' tobacco and mentioned his concern that the measures be fair, even ample. 'Tell your servants to fill the measure,' he would say, 'and not to put their thumbs within the brim ... Give us good measure of cloth; let us see the old measure; do you mind me?' Trade commenced with the roll of a drum each day at 5 a.m. and ceased with another drum roll at 8 p.m. It was conducted out of a window in the trading room and might involve much debate about the quality and worth of individual pelts and the measures of particular trade goods. When the bargaining was over, the trading captain received another substantial collection of gifts, the fort's cannon was fired, and the canoes set off for the winter hunting territories.[13]

Was either the European or the native duped in the exchange? We have no standard by which to judge. Native peoples traded surplus skins obtained during food-based seasonal migrations for implements of great utility and for entertainment costs during a period of intense socializing. In the exchange, they also consolidated military power and personal or group status – achievements of real if immeasurable worth. Europeans acquired food that was essential to their survival and traded goods of smaller monetary value for furs of greater monetary value – as evaluated by European markets. Whose culture will provide the measure of gains and losses?[14] The trading parties depended on each other. Insofar as the natives were influenced by the process, they were the subject of non-directed culture change, a much more benign process than was to occur when white Canadian church and government officials assumed responsibility for their guidance in the late nineteenth century.

Native consumers demanded a predictable range of trade goods. Most important on this list were weapons, including guns and the shot, powder, and fire steels to operate them. Next were materials for clothing – broadcloth and blankets – and household metal goods such as flints, kettles, hatchets, knives, awls, ice chisels, needles, and files. Finally, there were the 'luxury' items – tobacco, beads, and brandy. The natives were aggressive consumers: their complaints about the design and quality of goods drove local officials of the Hudson's Bay Company to despair but did encourage constant efforts by the company to improve its products. The natives were also careful: in the early generations of the trade, they would ensure that their fundamental needs were met before splurging on luxury goods.

In their reaction to price changes, they did not adhere to European market predictions about supply and demand: higher prices for furs at the post (higher demand) did not encourage the natives to bring in more furs (increased supply). On the contrary: because the natives' needs were relatively inelastic and their cargo-carrying capacity limited, they would respond to higher prices by bringing in fewer furs. However, in periods of intense competition between the French and the English, when traders were willing to expend greater effort in order to meet Indians near their own hunting territories, natives did accept an increase in the cost of trade goods. That is, natives would supply more pelts to obtain European goods at a convenient outlet and, in that sense, would respond as European market theories predicted.[15]

It is sometimes said that natives did not receive adequate recompense for their pelts and, especially, that the luxury trade in liquor, beads, and tobacco was exploitive. It is true that 100–200 pounds of beads were traded annually at York Factory between 1720 and 1774. In the same period, an average of 2,000–3,000 pounds of tobacco and 300 to 400 gallons of brandy and rum were traded annually. But what do we make of such a trade when we note that the natives utilized 70 MB (Made Beaver) to satisfy their basic needs, according to trader Andrew Graham, and another 30 MB to 'squander' on luxuries? We should recall that liquor was consumed in a few brief parties at a time customarily reserved for native celebrations – before the canoes departed for the hunting territories and a renewal of the annual cycle. Even if the middlemen alone used the beads and consumed the liquor and tobacco – which was probably not the case – they and their families must have been several hundred in number. In the first century of the trade and, indeed, until the 1770s and 1780s, brandy, beads, and tobacco were an outlet for excess purchasing power and a means employed by Europeans to win native custom; these items were luxury goods in the native world.[16] This is not to ignore the fact that liquor became destructive to the trade.

Histories of the fur trade at one time emphasized that European material culture revolutionized native life in very short order. Indeed, historians once suggested that native adoption of European technology was irrevocable. Thus, it was supposed that the gun replaced bows and other hunting techniques, that cloth replaced skins, and that eventually European produce replaced the products of the hunt: 'European supplies were necessities, not luxuries, for the Indians who traded to the Bay, and to many times that number of Indians living inland. Within a decade of their becoming acquainted with European goods, tribe after tribe became utterly dependent on regular European supplies. The bow and arrow went out of use, and the Indian starved if he did not own a serviceable gun, powder and shot.'[17] As recent studies have demonstrated, such generalizations are misleading, if not nonsense. Guns were not crucial hunting weapons in the eighteenth century; traditional

modes of trapping such as snares and deadfalls were still used in the
twentieth century. Moreover, cloth was especially used by natives
who chose to remain – probably for the first time in history – on the
barren grounds near the Bay rather than to return inland where
bigger game would supply their clothing needs. The food balance at
Eastmain post between the late seventeenth and late nineteenth
centuries, to cite one instance, was overwhelmingly on the side of
native contributions to the Europeans rather than the reverse. But
these are random examples. They suggest that the trade relationship between native and Europeans varied with the season, the
native culture, the pressures of native and European power politics,
and a dozen other factors. But they demonstrate, too, that native
dependence was not a central theme in the first century of trade and
that use of particular goods did not necessarily entail the loss of
earlier skills.[18]

In recent revisionist studies of the fur trade, some scholars have
argued that the trade relationship was not only founded on native
ritual but was also subordinated to native diplomatic priorities.[19] In
this view, the fur trade should not be seen as a market relationship,
conforming to European conventions. Scholars such as Abraham
Rotstein have suggested instead that the trade relationship was an
outgrowth of 'treaty trade': it was a collective rather than an individual undertaking and was founded on native cultural requirements.
Crucial to this case is the contention that trade was built around a
ceremony in which military alliances were confirmed, friendly celebrations staged, and kinship obligations remembered.[20] Other scholars, such as A.J. Ray and Donald Freeman, have disagreed with
Rotstein's thesis. They have argued that the use of native ritual in
the trade ceremony concealed the Europeans' manipulation of trade
institutions to serve their own ends. In their view, the gift-giving
and the speeches were designed to encourage loyalty in the face of
competition from other European traders; 'credit' was provided
with the same intent; extra kindnesses were shown the trading captain in order to enhance his status and thus his ability to persuade
others to return to the post next year. In this latter perspective, the
trade relationship was said to have taken its character from the
'market' and, thus, was quickly restructured by the European
approach to economic activities.[21]

Whose culture determined the nature of the trade relationship?
Whose culture determined price, selected customers, chose sites,
and dictated the slope of supply-demand curves? These are compli-

cated questions. Though several books have addressed these very issues in the Canadian fur trade, no satisfactory synthesis is available to explain the eighteenth-century trade in the western interior. Scholars agree that both natives and Europeans bargained intensely to secure better terms. This was not a purely treaty trade wherein prices and alliances were fixed and unvarying, in other words, but rather was a market, where natives pitted the French against the English and where the traders sought customers from every culture and varied their measure – shorter yardsticks, thinner cloth, diluted brandy – to secure profits; natives and Europeans tried to best each other on matters of price, quality, and supply. However, the natives who controlled the English trade (the Crees, Assiniboines, and Ojibwas) would deal only with their allies (Blackfoot and Mandans) and tried to ensure that such enemies as the Dakota Sioux and Gros Ventres did not secure access to European goods. In this sense, natives were engaged in treaty trade in their own political environment. As long as the Europeans did not try to break this native monopoly, the treaty relationship remained intact. Moreover, the natives' perception of the relationship was probably founded on their assumptions about reciprocity: as in many traditional societies, the natives of the western interior expected to share the product of their hunts (the pelts) with their allies, the Europeans, and to receive European goods on a similarly generous basis.[22] How this perception changed over time and how it varied within and among native cultures has yet to be determined. Nevertheless, we can conclude that the very attitudes with which native and European commenced the exchange – reciprocity and treaty trade on the one hand, market trade and profit on the other – make it likely that their differences in cultural perspective remained to some degree throughout the eighteenth century.

Continuity and autonomy were central aspects of the native experience in the early fur trade, but so too was adaptation. It can be argued that the diplomatic and technological context of native life changed rapidly after the advent of Europeans even though native seasonal migrations seemed little altered. Two items of European origin, the gun and the horse, had a particularly important impact upon native history on the prairies. The gun entered the continent from the northeast, the horse from the southwest. They met on the central plains in the mid-eighteenth century and, by their marriage, created a dramatic new native culture. The image of mounted armed plains warriors has since become the epitome of 'Indians' – the origin of North America's 'cowboy-Indian' version of western history – but it represents merely a brief moment, a century of flamboyance, in a story that is at least ten thousand years old. Nevertheless, the plains warriors' single century of prominence – from the 1730s to the 1850s – brought pivotal changes to the natives of Canada's western interior.

General descriptions of native seasonal cycles and migration patterns might seem to suggest that individual bands and even entire cultural groups lived in the same areas for centuries, hunted in the same valleys, and fished in the same lakes. This is not the case. In fact, we now know that the native peoples of the western interior made dramatic changes in home territory during the two centuries after European contact and, indeed, probably experienced comparable movements before that time. As A.J. Ray has pointed out, the Assiniboines in the 1680s occupied a corridor extending from near Lake Superior to the Manitoba lakes. By 1760 they had moved west and north through the parklands. By 1820, they had moved south, onto the plains between the Saskatchewan and Missouri rivers. It is not surprising that each of these shifts in location entailed an important change in economic activity and in material culture. Similar observations can be made about the Ojibwas, who moved northwest from the shores of Lake Superior to the Manitoba Interlake in the same period. The pattern of Cree migration was more complicated because the Cree bands moved west from Hudson Bay to control a vast territory extending from the Saskatchewan to the Churchill River system by 1760. In the succeeding half-century, the Crees split into two groups, a plains and a woodland type, the latter remaining north of the North Saskatchewan system while the former moved to the parkland fringe of the plains from the Qu'Appelle valley to the North Saskatchewan. The Blackfoot, too, moved west and south in the eighteenth century. And the Chipewyans moved west and north. These migrations were the product of new factors in native life, especially the gun and the horse, and brought about crucial changes in native history.[23]

The Crees, Assiniboines and Ojibwas moved westward in order to maintain control over the English and French trade. They were able to do so because of the military advantages provided by European guns – without such powerful weapons they could never have dictated the patterns of trade within the native world. However awkward the process of loading powder and shot, however difficult the operation of firesteels, however unreliable the lock, and however prone to explosion the barrel itself, the gun was pivotal in warfare and, thus, in native diplomacy. The remarkable narrative of the Cree leader Saukamappee, as recorded by the explorer David Thompson, suggests how the history of the region was altered by these European weapons. In the late 1720s, as a youth of about sixteen, Saukamappee accompanied a party of twenty Crees led by his father to aid the Piegans (a Blackfoot group) against the Shoshones. They carried metal and stone-tipped lances, bows and arrows (also with metal or stone points), knives and axes, and thick leather shields. After feasting and dancing and the selection of a war chief, the Cree-Piegan force of 350 went in search of the Shoshones and eventually discovered an enemy camp of at least their number:

> After some singing and dancing, they [the Shoshone] sat down on the ground, and placed their large shields before them, which covered them: We did the same, but our shields were not so many, and some of our shields had to shelter two men. Theirs were all placed touching each other; their Bows were not so long as ours, but of better wood, and the back covered with the sinews of the Bisons which made them very elastic, and their arrows went a long way and whizzed about us as balls do from guns. They were all headed with a sharp smooth black stone [flint] which broke when it struck anything. Our iron headed arrows did not go through their shields, but stuck in them; On both sides several were wounded, but none lay on the ground; and night put an end to the battle without a scalp being taken on either side, and in those days such was the result, unless one party was more numerous than the other.

Thus, in pre-gun warfare, shields were adequate to defend against arrows, offensive tactics were static rather than dynamic, and the result was not carnage but rather a few honourable wounds.

Saukamappee's tale resumed with an account of a battle with another enemy, the Snakes, that occurred about ten or fifteen years later when his Assiniboine-Cree-Blackfoot force could muster ten guns as well as the usual arrows:

> Those of us who had guns stood in the front line, and each of us [had] two balls in his mouth, and a load of powder in his left hand to reload ... The War Chief was close to us, anxious to see the effect of our guns. The lines were too far asunder for us to make a sure shot,

and we requested him to close the lines to about sixty yards, which was gradually done, and lying flat on the ground behind the shields, we watched our opportunity when they drew their bows to shoot at us, their bodies were then exposed and each of us, as opportunity offered, fired with deadly aim, and either killed, or severely wounded, every one we aimed at.

The War Chief was highly pleased, and the Snake Indians finding so many killed and wounded kept themselves behind their shields; the War Chief then desired we would spread ourselves by two's throughout the line, which we did, and our shots caused consternation and dismay along their whole line. The battle had begun about Noon, and the Sun was not yet half down, when we perceived that some of them had crawled away from their shields ... The greater part of the enemy took to flight, but some fought bravely and we lost more than ten killed and many wounded; Part of us pursued, and killed a few, but the chase had soon to be given over, for at the body of every Snake Indian killed, there were five or six of us trying to get his scalp, or part of his clothing, his weapons, or something as a trophy of the battle.[24]

The gun flowed into the western interior from the north and east, giving the natives nearest British and French posts the advantage in warfare. Diplomatic and territorial upheavals followed.

As the Cree and Assiniboine traders moved westward in the late seventeenth and early eighteenth centuries, they cemented their alliances with the Ojibwas, the Mandans, and the Blackfoot. Naturally, these alliances also confirmed their common hostility to other native bands, among whom the Dakota Sioux were most prominent. Thus, by the 1730s, a diplomatic map of the western interior would have placed the Assiniboines and Crees at the centre of an alliance system that stretched from Hudson Bay to the Rockies. At its southeastern margin, the Sioux were pre-eminent as enemies, but the Snakes, Gros Ventres, Nez Percés, Shoshones, and Kutenais were also hostile neighbours on the southern and western frontiers. This pattern had been stabilized, and Cree-Assiniboine security confirmed, by the gun. Then, in the decades from the mid-1730s, the arrival of horses began to reorganize the diplomatic map.

The mustang of the plains was a larger, coarser version of the Arabian. Introduced to Mexico by the Spaniards during the sixteenth and seventeenth centuries, this small, well-muscled, and fast animal was notable for its strength and endurance. It could carry 200 pounds and haul 300 pounds whereas dogs, the previous beasts of burden, could carry about 50 pounds and haul no more than 75 pounds on a travois. Best of all, the mustang brought the millions of buffalo within hunting range at almost any season. During the eighteenth century, as the number of horses on the continent increased and as the trading and raiding of horses became a central aspect of native life in the southwestern plains, the horse culture became a force in native politics. Group after group in the central plains converted from a pedestrian and agricultural to a horse-based buffalo-hunting economy and to mounted warfare. They did so not because Europeans required such a transition but because the military and economic advantage of a horse-based culture seemed evident.[25]

The Crees and Assiniboines discovered a new economic role at this time. After the fall of Quebec in 1760, the fur trade in eastern Canada had been reorganized by entrepreneurs who, under the title of the North West Company, pushed their canoe-based trading system from Montreal to the Pacific and Arctic oceans by the early 1790s. The Hudson's Bay Company matched them in the construction of inland trading posts and, in the process, helped to eliminate the role of the native middleman. Henceforth, the trading post moved with the Indian trappers; access to it could no longer be controlled by native traders. Simultaneously, the demand for food at the inland posts – over 1,000 labourers were now employed in the interior and hundreds more in the canoe brigades – provided an alternative occupation for the Crees and Assiniboines. As the resources of the forest and parkland dwindled and the fur company labour force grew, the companies turned to the buffalo for food. Pemmican, that greasy mixture of buffalo flesh, fat, and berries delivered in ninety-pound hide bags, became the fuel of the trade machine. It was supplemented by fresh meat (canoemen consumed eight pounds of fresh meat or one to one and a half pounds of pemmican per day) and, where available, fish and fowl. Buffalo products were collected from native hunters at a chain of posts scattered along the fringe of the parkland and stored in warehouses located at important transportation nodes such as Cumberland House (the junction for Athabasca trade), Norway House (between the Bay and the Saskatchewan interior), and Bas de la Rivière (or Fort Alexander, between the Assiniboine and Lake Winnipeg routes to the interior, on the one hand, and the main avenue to Lake Superior and eastern Canada, on the other). Thus, 'a new economic link was welded between the parkland-grassland region and the forest country.'[26] The crucial aspect of this link was that many Crees and Assiniboines who had lost their role as middlemen in the collection and carrying of furs now gained a new function as provisioner for European traders and their canoemen.

The Assiniboines adapted to the role of provisioner very quickly and, from being an important supplier of furs to the Hudson's Bay Company in 1768, they had become suppliers of pemmican by 1780, when they first burned the prairies around Hudson House on the North Saskatchewan to ensure that buffalo did not venture near the fort and fall prey to the European traders. By 1790, their former interest in trapping and freighting was replaced by an overriding quest for buffalo. They acquired new power in the process, of course, because European traders had become dependent upon them for food; the Assiniboines had only to threaten to boycott a post to bring the trader to an appreciation of their interests, be it better prices or rejection of trade from enemy bands. Thus, in the era of competition and rapid change, from the 1770s to the 1840s, the Indians of the southern interior – Crees and Assiniboines for the most part – lost the fur resources upon which they had depended and were bypassed as middlemen traders by the advance of trading posts inland, but they acquired a crucial new role as provisioners to the fur trade. Their new occupation increased the pressure on the food resources of the plains and parkland but also ensured the natives' continuing autonomy in the economic system of the trade.

To emphasize the native functions in the fur trade could be misleading. In fact, the trader remained at the rim of the native universe, a supplier of arms and luxuries and a few technologically advanced items rather than a director of operations. The native agenda continued to centre around the quest for food, the seasonal cycle of movement, the usual process of birth, maturing, and aging of every individual and family, and the negotiations with adjacent cultures that distinguished enemies from allies. These latter relations, which can be termed native diplomacy, underwent considerable change between the 1770s and 1840s.

The stability of native political relations in the eighteenth century was founded on the Cree, Assiniboine, and Ojibwa domination of the European trade. Because these three groups controlled access to European technology, particularly guns, they were most attractive trading partners – and thus allies – to the Mandans and Blackfoot. The arrival of trade competition, the extension of trading posts across the northwestern interior, and the advent of American traders (Lewis and Clark travelled the length of the Missouri 1804–6) upset the Cree-Assiniboine-Ojibwa trade monopoly. Even more important from the native point of view was the emergence of the horse trade as a pivotal factor in native diplomacy and warfare. Competition for control of the horse trade from the south and anger over horse-stealing were central to the collapse of the Cree-Blackfoot and Cree-Mandan alliances between the 1790s and 1820s. That the stealing was no small event was attested by the officers at Fort Edmonton, who reported the loss of 650 horses in their area alone in 1810. In these new conditions the Crees and Assiniboines, in particular, were caught without a source of supply for horses and without a unique item of trade. The Mandans, through their vast trade network to the south, could acquire horses from the Minnetarees, Cheyennes, and Crows, their new allies in the early nineteenth century. The Blackfoot, too, had a source of horses in the Gros Ventres (or Atsinas). Moreover, with the arrival of American traders and the extension of Hudson's Bay and Nor'West trade operations, neither Mandans nor Blackfoot relied on the Crees for guns. In this period of instability, concludes John Milloy, we see 'the conscious and rational attempts by the Cree and other plains tribes to construct new military and trade patterns to replace those which, because of changed circumstances, had failed ... War remained a communal undertaking based on strategy which encompassed more than merely a quest for individual status.'[27]

As late as 1823, the Crees and Assiniboines of the plains remained confident of their ability to handle all that fortune might decree. In that year, the governor of the Hudson's Bay Company, George Simpson, complained: 'The Plain Tribes ... continue as insolent and independent if not more so than ever; they conceive that we are dependent on them for the means of subsistence and consequently assume a high tone, but the most effectual way of bringing them to their senses would be to withdraw the Establishments/particularly those of the Saskatchewan/for two or three years which ... would enable us to deal with them on fair and reasonable terms ... This however cannot be affected until Red River settlement has the means of furnishing us with a considerable stock of Provisions for our Transport business.'[28] The circumstances awaited by Simpson were soon realized. The union of the two fur trade competitors in 1821, the increasing numbers of metis, and the subsequent growth of the Red River settlement created an alternate supplier of plains provisions and a labour force. The emergence of the metis 'new nation' will be discussed later, but its importance in the realignment of political power in the mid-nineteenth century, especially in undermining the role of the native plains hunters, must be emphasized.

If the rise of the metis had been the only new factor in native history in the early decades of the nineteenth century, the Indians might have adjusted easily. But the metis were only one of a number of factors that affected the native cultures of the western interior. The American buffalo robe trade, the devastating smallpox epidemic of 1837-8, the exhaustion of game resources in the eastern fringes of the forests, and the resurgence of the Chipewyans were the most important factors in this equation.

Pressure on the plains buffalo population increased dramatically in the nineteenth century, and, contrary to popular myth, it was not only the American hunter who was responsible for the slaughter. In 1805, the largest company in the western interior, the North West Company, traded for 1,135 buffalo robes; between 1830 and 1843, the American Fur Company and the Hudson's Bay Company, then the two largest operations, traded 70,000 and 10,000 buffalo robes respectively, each year.[29] The growth was attributable to an increase in European and eastern North American markets, to the new strategy of the Blackfoot, who were determined to maintain a secure supply of guns and ammunition in a time of dissolving native alliances, and to increased hunting by Red River metis and American plains hunters. The result was a sharp reduction in buffalo population.

One consequence of the new situation was a significant change in Blackfoot culture, which flourished and expanded with the growth of the robe trade. Prosperity stimulated 'expansion,' as Oscar Lewis has explained, and tepees grew larger, buffalo corrals bigger, the number of wives per hunter higher, and the individual hunter's string of horses longer. The consequent dependence on European trade – on clothing and utensils that had supplanted native dress and pottery, for example – increased Blackfoot reliance on the buffalo. Thus, the seeds of Blackfoot despair were sown in the first half of the nineteenth century, the era in which they seemed the most independent, prosperous, and flamboyant people on the plains.[30]

The Ojibwa experience was much different. In the eighteenth century, an era of relative abundance of game both large and small, the Ojibwas travelled in large groups (twenty to thirty-five people) and exploited large hunting territories communally. But by early to mid-nineteenth century, this social structure had been drastically changed. Small family bands became the rule, as did the use of relatively private family hunting territories – well-demarcated tracts of land to which the family habitually returned, in which it enjoyed more or less exclusive rights to resources, and which might be passed on to the eldest son. The evidence for this development is strong, especially in the trading-post journals which would note, for example, that one Indian planned to winter 'on his own lands' and that another would be changing the post which held his account because the first was 'too far from his father's land.' What had happened? It may have been a long-term cycle of the ecozone. Perhaps intensive trapping and hunting, a product of the flourishing fur trade during the years of North West Company competition with the Hudson's Bay Company, may have simply exhausted the large game resources of the forest, especially caribou, moose, and beaver. Whatever the explanation, food and clothing shortages led to Ojibwa dependence on small animals, especially rabbits, and on the trading posts. Mobility was thus reduced and the bands became smaller, and by the 1830s and 1840s intensive exploitation of small private hunting territories became the rule. Like the Blackfoot, the Ojibwas were becoming increasingly tied to the European trading system and losing their room to manoeuvre as autonomous individuals. But if their way of life changed in the first half of the nineteenth century, it did not end. The Ojibwas were still the hunters, fishermen, and wild rice gatherers of the eastern forest margin, and some had even joined the plains buffalo hunt culture by the end of the 1830s.[31]

The experience of the Chipewyans, the Assiniboines, and the Blackfoot illustrated one other crucial aspect of native history in the fur trade era. If the advent of European technology resulted in diplomatic change and greater economic potential for the native peoples, it also stimulated population change. Though the evidence is too scattered to be conclusive, the native population probably increased dramatically in the eighteenth century. The consequent pressure on food resources and the introduction of European diseases to which the native had little resistance then permitted the spread of such scourges as whooping cough and smallpox, which must have been calamitous in their effects. Thus, when the fur trade pushed into the Lake Athabasca–Great Slave district in the 1770s and 1780s, it provided the Chipewyans with the guns that would enable them to hold off the Crees, but it also introduced smallpox. Samuel Hearne, who traded in the district, thought that perhaps 90 per cent of the Chipewyan population was wiped out in the 1780s, and, though his estimate seems high, it is none the less an indication of the scale of the disaster that swept the western interior in that decade. Whooping cough and measles hit the plains bands 1818–20 and may have killed half the Assiniboines (or three thousand of six thousand) and one-third of the plains Crees. But the best-documented case was the smallpox epidemic of 1837–8 which struck the plains bands a devastating blow and practically eliminated the Mandans and Assiniboines as factors in prairie diplomacy.[32]

The fur trade era brought significant change to the natives of the western interior. By the 1830s, they inhabited territories and employed technologies that were far distant from anything their ancestors of the 1630s had known. They remained confident of their power, however, and believed they were as autonomous as their ancestors. They were increasingly dependent on the trade and technology of Europeans, but one need not read into this dependence a moral about native folly or European duplicity. The people of the globe were becoming interdependent during this same era. There was nothing in the native-European relationship to suggest that either was unfairly exploited by the other. After nearly two centuries, natives and Europeans lived side by side in relative peace. If there was cause for concern, it lay in the specialization of the region's economy. A few items – animal food products, furs, and robes – sustained both home consumption and the export market as they had for centuries. An abrupt change in 'production capacity' or 'market potential' or a sudden depletion of resources would have devastating consequences.

# 4

# The Europeans' fur trade
# 1640–1805

There were two fur trades, one controlled by the natives and the other shared by Indians and European entrepreneurs. There were, similarly, two perspectives on the early history of the western interior. To walk from the Indian encampment to the palisades at York Factory was to move from one way of life and one set of assumptions to another that was radically different. For an earlier generation of Canadian scholars, business and the arrival of European 'civilization' were the sum and substance of pre-1840 prairie history. Companies, profits, competitive strategy, and personnel rather than contact between natives and Europeans constituted their approach to the history of this era.[1] It is fair to say that from the mid-seventeenth century to the first decade of the nineteenth century, the northwest was remote from the struggles of imperial armies, the missions of religious orders, and the quest for riches that marked the history of European overseas expansion.

European interest in the western interior was, for 150 years, limited almost exclusively to the fur trade. Throughout these many years, two trading empires were established in the region. One was associated with the investment community of the City of London and, from 1670, was conducted by the Hudson's Bay Company. The other was created by the merchants of New France and sustained by the labour of French-Canadian engagés or tripmen; after the Conquest of 1760, the French system was reorganized by a new group of Montreal merchants and, eventually, as the North West Company, came to dominate the western trade in the closing decades of the eighteenth century. The two avenues of entry into the northern half of the continent, Hudson Bay and the St Lawrence–Great Lakes basin, provided the foundation and help to explain the existence of two competing trading networks. The waxing and waning of the fortunes of the trade provided the one matter of interest to European observers of the region.

The relative lack of other types of European activity in the northwest for two centuries can be explained by the unimportance of the territory's exploitable resources. When compared to the fabled wealth of the Incas, the varied riches of China, or even the fertile lands of Virginia, the rock sheets and icy rivers of the Pre-Cambrian Shield, which offered only furs as an item for international shopping lists, were a poor bet for imperial investment in the seventeenth century. Despite the consistent profits of the trading companies, the development of fur auctions and a fur processing industry, and the regular native market for furs, leather, and blankets, the fur trade was a minor chapter in European economic history.

There were two types of fur market in Europe. The first, the luxury fur market, served then as now to place fine pelts, whether marten, fox, bear, or seal, on the backs of well-heeled buyers through such intermediaries as fine tailors and furriers. The second was not for fur at all but for 'felt,' a strong and durable manufactured fabric that used the hair and discarded the skin of an animal pelt and for which the bottom layer of hair on a beaver pelt, about one inch long and equipped with numerous barbs, was ideally suited. When the hair was mixed with a paste or compost, the resultant flexible material could be used for armour and protective fabric of various types. It was particularly suited to the production of men's felt hats and for over 200 years, through the changing fashions of the European upper class, found a steady market in that rather specialized outlet. In an age when every European gentleman wore a hat and perhaps owned several, this was an industry of some importance.

The quest for furs and felting material in North America began accidentally in the sixteenth century. Fishermen and explorers who visited the continent had begun the exchange, and Jacques Cartier's first voyage to Canada in 1534 not only defined a portion of the coastline but also resulted in an informal fur trade session. The Indians, who obviously knew their business, were eager to exchange furs, including the skins they wore, for European goods; the sailors were equally happy to discover an additional source of revenue. The quest for fishing grounds and the search for a short sea route to Japan opened the fur trade of the northern continent. But fur coats, the felting process, and felt hats alone converted this desultory trade into a thriving business.

The geographical pattern of the continental trade was determined in part by the river systems and in part by the beaver themselves. When European traders arrived, the beaver habitat extended from the Atlantic and St Lawrence drainage basins west and north as far as the Rocky Mountains and the sub-arctic and produced especially fine specimens in the cold waters and winters of the Pre-Cambrian Shield. The fur trade put great pressure on the beaver population and, as a result, increasingly pushed west and north in search of new supplies of beaver pelts; inevitably, trade followed the rivers. As Harold Innis, the economic historian who first perceived the pattern in the Canadian staple trade, concluded: 'The problem of the fur trade became one of organizing the transport of supplies and furs over increasingly greater distances. In this movement the waterways of the beaver area were of primary importance and occupied a vital position in the economic development of northern North America.'[2]

From the time Samuel de Champlain first established his habitation at Quebec in 1608 to Louis xiv's institution of royal government in 1663, the history of New France was intimately bound up with exploration, religious missions to the Indians, and, underlying and supporting all other activity, the trade between Indians and Europeans. Like their neighbours, the Dutch and the English, the French discovered that the Indians were quite prepared to participate regularly in the trade and, indeed, to use the Europeans to further their own ends. Within a few years of his first contacts with the Indians, Champlain had been forced to choose among native allies and, by accepting the Hurons, the Algonquins, and the Ottawas, to make the Iroquois confederacy his enemy. It was a fateful choice, because it tied the French to the Indians of the Ottawa valley–Georgian Bay region and thus to the Great Lakes route into the interior of the continent. Despite the tragedy of 1648–50, when the Iroquois confederacy destroyed the Hurons and created martyrs of several Jesuit missionaries, including Brébeuf, the French remained tied to the St Lawrence–Great Lakes route to the west. Down the great river travelled Radisson and Groseilliers in their path-breaking expedition to Lake Superior in 1659–60, Jolliet and Marquette in their investigation of Lake Michigan and the Mississippi (1669 and 1673), La Salle in his voyage to the Gulf of Mexico (1682), and La Vérendrye in his bid to open the western interior to the French trade (1731–43). The French also maintained their early alliance with the Algonkian-speaking peoples who ranged along this route, in particular the Ottawas, the Ojibwas, and the Crees. Thus, the water route and the diplomatic patterns fitted together. 'It was significant,' as Innis noted, 'that La Vérendrye had laid down the boundary of Canada in the search for the better beaver of the northern areas.'³

The French empire reached the western interior because of the ability of individual entrepreneurs. These men, the leading merchants of New France, regularly put together a pool of investment capital, a fleet of canoes, a complement of voyageurs, and a stock of trade goods. They then hired a trader to guide this expedition through difficult wilderness to a point some one or even two thousand miles from Montreal and there establish a suitably agreeable relationship with the leaders of hunting and trading bands of natives. Finally, when the expedition was once again safe in Montreal, canoes low in the water with the rich skins of the northern forests, a merchant would find an outlet for the pelts in European markets.

If individualism was the hallmark of the trading enterprise, the overall direction of the colony was marked by the considerable centralization required by the French imperial system. New France soon left behind the mercantilist ideas of Colbert, developed in the 1660s, which argued that the colony should become a self-sufficient community confined to a limited territory. Instead, following the ambitions of an early governor, Louis Buade, comte de Frontenac, the colony established a far-flung fur trade system upon the narrow base of agriculture and fishing and a few small industries in the most heavily settled territory along the banks of the St Lawrence. Its loosely linked outposts stretched south to the Gulf of Mexico, west to the Rockies, and north to James Bay. But this system was not created in defiance of Versailles. Rather, like the imperial ports on the coast of Africa, it had strategic as well as economic functions: European empires, especially the French and British, had interests around the globe in the seventeenth and eighteenth centuries, and, where they came into conflict, as in America, it was natural for one to wish to confine, harass, and otherwise preoccupy the other. The North American fur trade became an instrument of international power politics in the hands of the French government, and, whatever the eventual fate of individual entrepreneurs, it served its purpose if it forced the British to divert military forces or extra expenditures to these 'few acres of snow' (Voltaire's phrase) from more important theatres elsewhere.[4]

English interest in North America did not follow the French pattern, in part because of accidents of geography and also because of cultural differences. The English claimed the more fertile regions of the central and southern seaboard of the continent and thus found richer agricultural lands than did the French. Because their fur trade was always secondary to agriculture, the English never seriously challenged the French hegemony in the interior. But the English acquired a second foothold on the continent, unexpectedly, when the defection of two French traders with innovative ideas about the fur trade offered control of another great avenue to the interior, Hudson Bay. Unlike the other two entrances to the northern half of the continent, the Hudson River from New York and the St Lawrence from Quebec and Montreal, the Bay offered ready sea access to the vast fur-rich territories of the northwestern interior. Though the voyage was difficult and the shipping season short, the economies of this route were so great as to be irresistible. Here, a trading operation that seemed opposed in every respect to that of the French, a monopoly company with centralized organization and a few fixed trading posts, contested the French for domination of the northern trade for almost a century.

Pierre Radisson and Médard Chouart, sieur des Groseilliers, traders from New France, were responsible for the English trading enterprise. Adventurous, impatient, and remarkably single-minded, these brothers-in-law had journeyed west from the St Lawrence to Lake Superior in the late 1650s and returned to Quebec with not only a fine cargo of furs but also a plan that would revolutionize the fur business in North America. Having seen that the finest pelts came from the northern forests, having by-passed the native middlemen in the southern Great Lakes, and having learned that these rich resources were easily reached by a 'Bay of the North Sea,' the two traders proposed that the long canoe journeys to the west be abandoned for the much shorter sea trip down Hudson Bay. As

Glyndwr Williams has concluded: 'In their proposals lay the origin of the maritime bias of the fur trade and of the English Hudson's Bay Company.'[5] But the reaction of officials in New France, far from the enthusiasm that Radisson expected, was to fine the two adventurers for unauthorized trade (and perhaps to imprison them, though this is uncertain) and thus to drive them into the arms of the English. After a failed expedition from New England to the Bay, Radisson and Groseilliers travelled to England in 1665 to seek stronger patronage. In the court of Charles II, where interest in colonial trade and an overseas empire was considerable, their much-exaggerated tales of the riches and the wonders of the 'North Sea' found a growing circle of wealthy gentlemen prepared to invest a little money. Thus in 1668, Mr Radish and Mr Gooseberry (thus did the English translate their names) boarded the *Eaglet* and the *Nonsuch*, each with a cargo of trade goods, and headed for Hudson Bay. The *Eaglet* was forced to turn back, but the *Nonsuch* carried on alone, reaching the mouth of the Rupert River on James Bay in the fall of 1668; Groseilliers set up a small log house and wintered without incident. In the spring, three hundred Indians came down to trade. The *Nonsuch* investors found a ready market for the high-quality furs in England. As Radisson and Groseilliers had predicted, a new and profitable fur trade organization could be established on the basis of this sea route to the interior of North America.

Investors were now prepared to back the scheme on a more permanent basis. On 2 May 1670, with the support of Prince Rupert (the king's first cousin) and 'some of the most important men in Restoration England,' the definitive royal charter of the Governor and Company of Adventurers of England Trading into Hudson's Bay was issued. The company was granted 'sole Trade and Commerce' of the Hudson Bay drainage system and declared 'true and absolute Lordes and Proprietors' of this vast region, but it is easy to exaggerate the importance of this royal assertion of monopoly. Because competition with the French and, later, Montreal and American traders was inevitable, the company's own strength as a trading organization, not the royal charter, would determine its fate. However, in the difficult years of warfare during the company's first half-century, 'the official recognition which the Royal Charter bestowed gave the Hudson's Bay Company a vital international and diplomatic status' that was to be an influential factor on several occasions.[6]

With the extension of French fur trade activity into the upper Great Lakes and the arrival of the English at Hudson Bay, competition for the furs of the western interior was joined. For the next generation, until the Treaty of Utrecht ended the War of the Spanish Succession in 1713, traders of the two nations fought for, conquered, and lost the posts on Hudson and James Bay at what seemed to be regular intervals. The English company had established its trading operations on a reasonable footing in the 1670s by outfitting posts on James Bay at the mouths of the Moose, Albany, and Rupert rivers. These posts were visited annually by ships from England, and, though losses still marked its ledgers, fur sales in London and on the continent were promising. The French debated whether to oppose this northern competitor by sea or overland and eventually, at the urging of the indefatigable Radisson and Groseilliers, who had rejoined their motherland, conquered the English posts in 1682–3 by means of a seaborne expedition. Ironically, the French government, wishing to avoid diplomatic embarrassment, connived to return both the trading posts and Radisson to the English in the following year. But this was just the beginning of what could well be portrayed as *opera bouffe*.

In 1686, the chevalier de Troyes journeyed overland from the St Lawrence to James Bay with a hundred men to seize two posts, Moose Fort and Charles Fort, where the defenders were caught in their nightshirts, and then turned on the largest, Albany Fort, using cannon taken from a company ship. Caught at dinner, the English officers suffered untold horrors as one shot passed beneath the arm of a servant pouring wine and a second whizzed past the governor's wife, who fainted. When asked by his men 'if Wee should fire or Contrive some means to oppose the French,' the harried governor, with wife and wine at risk, allegedly replied 'doe what you please.' The fort's complement then retreated to a cellar where they roared in unison for mercy. This the famished French were only too pleased to grant in exchange for a little food and drink. In the many skirmishes that followed this unpromising episode, the shifting fortunes of war raised Pierre LeMoyne, sieur d'Iberville, to heroic stature and diminished the fighting reputations – if ever they enjoyed such distinction – of the hapless traders and labourers in the company employ. But the French also suffered reverses. Between 1686 and 1697, 'of ten attacks made on Bay posts by French and English forces, only two had failed.'[7]

The problems of the fur market were even more burdensome than the military adventures. The English company had paid its first dividends in the 1680s and continued to function well in the diminished market of wartime Europe. But the French, with furs pouring into their ports from vast North American operations and with export markets cut off by the military conflict, saw great warehouses of pelts reduced to putrifying masses of waste by rodents and vermin. Thus, at the peace negotiations, the French were cool to the idea of retaining their Hudson Bay operations and eventually agreed to return the entire Bay region to the Hudson's Bay Company by the Treaty of Utrecht in 1713.[8]

With the return of York Fort (1714) and the establishment of a new post at Churchill (1717), in addition to the James Bay posts of Albany and Moose and three small satellites at Eastmain, Rupert River, and Severn, the Hudson's Bay Company resumed its conservative routine. For the next half-century, three or four ships sailed into the Bay annually, bringing trade goods and supplies as well as replacements for some of the 150 men (the total complement in Rupert's Land) who had had their fill of this remote country. Though the total value of fur exports from the Bay was far smaller than that of Canada, the shareholders were satisfied with the steady if unspectacular annual dividends which were issued after 1721 (only once in this era did the dividend exceed 10 per cent) and the average annual profit of about 30 per cent.

The quiet prosperity of the Hudson's Bay Company was a matter for congratulation rather than complaint within the exclusive and unpublicized ranks of the shareholders. So private was the company in this era that the 'last quotation of company stock was in 1700, and transfers of shares in the eighteenth century were arranged privately'; no correspondence on the affairs of the company was to be undertaken by its servants; and even 'letters brought home on the ships were to be delivered to the Committee for scrutiny.'[9] Secrecy is a crucial weapon in any commercial operation and especially so in a monopoly, which must face both foreign and domestic rivals, but it was even more important to the company because of the campaign against chartered operations that rocked British commerce in the early eighteenth century. In an era when chartered trading companies were under attack, when the infamous South Sea Company burst like a bubble (1720), when the Royal African Company was dissolved (1750) and the Levant Company Charter 'altered,' even survival was an achievement. The company was not immune and despite its low profile sustained a fierce attack in the 1740s, including dozens of pamphlets, broadsides, and petitions, an investigation by a parliamentary committee, and a full debate in the House of Commons. Despite the best efforts of Arthur Dobbs, MP, an aspiring explorer-capitalist, the argument that the company had failed both to develop its hinterland and to enlarge British naval capacity fell before the gloomy company descriptions of the difficulties of trade in the northern wilderness.[10] The company was left to its own devices because no one had a better idea of what to do with this forest vastness.

The traders of New France were more enterprising than the English critics of the Hudson's Bay Company and than the company itself. While the company servants 'for eighty years slept at the edge of a frozen sea ... [failing] to penetrate farther themselves, and have exerted all their art and power to crush that spirit in others,' to quote company critic Joseph Robson, the French pushed beyond the bottom of James Bay under the able and courageous leadership of Pierre Gaultier de Varennes, sieur de La Vérendrye, who used the fur trade between 1727 and the 1740s to search for the fabled Mer de l'ouest. The innovation of La Vérendrye that distinguished his work from that of the individualist coureurs de bois who preceded him was a series of carefully chosen fur trade posts that became the basis for the rational advance of the French into the distant interior. He even selected the staging post for a two-phase transportation system, Kaministikwia at Grand Portage (near Thunder Bay on Lake Superior), which was about two months' journey from Montreal and another five hundred difficult miles from Lake Winnipeg. He then went on to found Fort St Charles on Lake of the Woods (1732), Fort Maurepas on the southern edge of Lake Winnipeg (1734), Fort Rouge near present-day Winnipeg (1737), Fort La Reine on the Assiniboine near present-day Portage la Prairie (1737), and Fort Dauphin on Lake Winnipegosis (1739); his family and other French traders, following where he led, continued this policy after his retirement from the west in 1742, founding Fort Bourbon on present-day Cedar Lake, where the Saskatchewan River flows in from the west (1748), and Fort la Corne near the forks of the Saskatchewan River (1753). This chain of posts was designed not only to control the highways of the fur trade and to protect the most effective route to the Rockies and the western sea, but also to cut directly across the flow of furs to the English on the shores of Hudson Bay. Thus, the competition between French and English intensified once again. As was the case at the close of the preceding century, the French won the lion's share of the trade.[11]

Made sensitive to the need for activity by their London critics, as well as by declining revenues at their Bayside posts, the Hudson's Bay Company finally accepted the oft-raised suggestion of its servants in the field and decided to dispatch an emissary to the Indian hunting bands to encourage them to trade at the Bay rather than with the French. The result was the famous expedition of Anthony Henday. But, as the company had pointed out during the parliamentary investigation of 1749, there had been an earlier voyage into the interior under its sponsorship, and, though the record is not entirely clear, its leader, Henry Kelsey, earned the honour of being the first European to visit the inland Indians. The problem with Kelsey's claim was that the authenticity of the record of his travels in 1690–1 was questioned by company critics. When the papers of one of these critics, Joseph Dobbs, were presented to an archives in 1926, it was found that they contained both a complete manuscript journal inscribed 'Henry Kelsey his Book,' which described his famous expedition, but also a curious rhyming prologue which has since attained considerable fame as explorer poetry:

> In sixteen hundred and ninety'th year
> I set forth as plainly may appear
> Through Gods assistance for to understand
> The natives language and to see their land ...
> The Inland Country of Good report hath been
> By Indians but by English yet not seen ...

And then, as Kelsey warmed to his tale, he described the environment through which he travelled:

> This wood is poplo ridges with small ponds of water
> Here is beavour in abundance but no Otter ...[12]

Whatever one makes of his literary skills, Kelsey was an able and resourceful young man. He travelled with little assistance and few trade goods, encountered a large number of natives, and showed no trace of fear in his narrative, though he came close to starvation on several occasions. The direction of his journeys remains the subject of debate but it seems certain that he accompanied an Indian band from the Bay to the region of present-day The Pas on the Saskatchewan River in 1690 and thence, in 1691, toward the vast plains that had probably never before been visited by Europeans; here he passed through the endless herds of buffalo and subsisted on the rich resources of the parkland, where deer and fish and fowl were plentiful; by comparison with the shores of the Bay, it must have seemed rich to his eyes, and the number of Indians must have far surpassed his expectations. He succeeded in this remarkable adventure because of his ability to speak Cree and to live easily with his Indian hosts, but he failed to make an impact on company trade practices or, because of the company policy of secrecy, on the public, and thus his feats remained almost unknown for over two centuries. Despite two trips to the northwest among the Chipewyans, by William Stewart (1715–16) and Richard Norton (1717–18), the company abandoned the tactic of the commercial traveller until British critics and French competitors shook its complacency in the early 1750s.

An obscure labourer, Anthony Henday, volunteered to travel inland when the company again responded to French competition. He was to have an important, if delayed, impact upon trade policy and thus upon the history of the western interior. Henday left York in June 1754 in the company of a Cree trading party. At Fort Basquia (The Pas), when this party encountered French traders, he feared that he would be arrested, but his Indian hosts laughed at his anxiety, saying the French dared not stop him. The party travelled up the Saskatchewan into its south branch, crossed overland to the north branch, and at the end of July finally encountered a band of Assiniboines, who told Henday bluntly that they preferred to trade with the French. Further cross-country travels led him, in September, to his first sighting of a great buffalo herd, so numerous that his guides had to 'make them sheer out of our way,' and so easily hunted that the party took only the tongues and other delicacies.

In mid-October, near the Red Deer River, Henday met a band of Blackfoot, with 200 tents allegedly pitched in two rows. He asked that some young men be dispatched to York to exchange furs for guns, to which the Blackfoot leader replied that 'it was far off, and they could not live without buffaloes flesh, and that they never would leave their horses, and many other obstacles which I [Henday] think very just, the chief of which was, they never wanted provisions.' Like his successors, Henday urged his Cree guides to trap furs, much to their amusement and derision; his Indian companion set him straight: 'My bedfellow informs me that ... they would get more wolves and beaver etc. from the Archithinnes [Blackfoot] and Aseenepoets [Assiniboines] than they could carry ... She said that the Indians that traded at York Fort were supplyed by them, and that we should see them in the spring.' Of course, this was the case. He was travelling not with trappers but with middlemen. Henday himself acquired thirty wolf skins in the spring rendezvous. But when his party commenced the long journey toward York, their sixty newly built canoes heavy with the furs they had gained in trade, they did not breeze past the French posts as Henday had hoped but rather stopped at each one for a little relaxation. At Fort la Corne, for example, 'the master gave the natives ten gallons of adulterated brandy and has traded from them above one thousand of the finest skins.' The story was repeated at Fort Basquia, and when the flotilla reached Hudson Bay in late June, many of the best and lightest furs had been left behind with the French, and only the heavier, less valuable pelts remained to be traded to the English.

Henday's tour was an important lesson in the operations of the fur trade system. He had discovered the middleman role of the Crees, had observed the workings of the Cree-Blackfoot-Assiniboine alliance, and had been a helpless bystander when the French scooped off the best of the native fur harvest. But little of this was communicated to the London committee of the Hudson's Bay Company. Because of internal politics in the company, the committee saw instead only an expurgated version of Henday's full journal, and his information was not acted on for another two decades.[13]

The war in Europe and North America, known as the Seven Year's War in North America, handicapped French trade operations in the mid-1750s and, by the end of the decade, cut them off entirely. Left alone in the field by 1759–60, the English assumed control of the entire trade of the western interior for the first time in a century. But their monopoly was to be brief. In the wake of the British victories at Quebec and Montreal, the St Lawrence fur trade was immediately reorganized, the veteran voyageurs and traders were rehired, and the expeditions again departed from the island of Montreal, this time under the sponsorship of Anglo-American and

British as well as French merchants. The leaders of these partnerships and coalitions were soon fighting an equal battle at the bottom
of the Bay. By the end of the 1760s, they had established their
pre-eminence in the crucial Lake Winnipeg–Saskatchewan River territory. Founded upon the enormous skill and capacity of the Canadian engagés supplemented now by the credit and the high-quality
trade goods of London, the Montreal-based trade was simply too
effective for the unreformed Hudson's Bay Company. As Andrew
Graham, a valued Hudson's Bay Company trader, discovered: 'The
Indians resort to them in the winter for ammunition, and the whole
body of the natives build their canoes not far distant from the residence of the traders, and finding they can procure tobacco and other
necessaries so near, and being in liquor, every inducement to visit
the Company's Factories is forgot, and the prime furs are picked out
and traded. The refuse is tied up and brought down to us.'[14] The
arrival of the horse in the western interior around mid-century had
hastened the Crees' and Assiniboines' abandonment of a middleman role in the trade, but so, too, the arrival of Canadian pedlars in
the heart of the Winnipeg–Saskatchewan middleman district reduced the need for native intermediaries in the trade. Moreover, the
Canadians, building on a century of French experience with native
marriages as a tool of trade and diplomacy, delighted in establishing
close personal liaisons with their native customers. Thus Wapenes-
sew, a faithful ally of the company for at least two decades, was
seen on Lake Winnipeg in 1771 or 1772 in a contingent that included
the shrewd Canadian trader Thomas Corry and no fewer than seven
large canoes laden with furs; the Indian trade captain passed on a
message through Corry to his former Hudson's Bay Company ally,
Andrew Graham: 'He hopes you will knot Be angre with him as he
has Drank So much Brandy this winter he canot Com';[15] it was
apparent that the Canadian and the Indian lived in the same house
and ate at the same table. Such relationships could not be countered
by the company as long as it remained on the shores of the Bay. The
British system of coastal trade from fortified factories was simply not
integrated into native society to the degree of the French-Nor'-
Wester system.

The Montrealers revolutionized the western fur trade between the
mid-1770s and mid-1780s. New and stronger groupings of traders
began to appear from 1776, and, by the winter of 1783–4, the famous
sixteen-share partnership known as the North West Company had

been established on a firm footing. It was dominated by Simon
McTavish and the Frobisher brothers, but at various times in the
next two decades encompassed almost all the great names of the
Canadian trade, including such explorers as Peter Pond and Alexander Mackenzie, such surveyors as David Thompson, and such
merchants as Edward Ellice. Its first accomplishment was the creation of a transportation system that conquered a vast area of
wilderness with an efficiency that would do credit to modern shipping firms. The heart of the system was a series of ships (on Lake
Superior) and schooners (on the lower Great Lakes) and a giant
warehouse as transfer-point at Grand Portage, later moved to Fort
William, on the west shore of Lake Superior. The Montreal–Fort
William run was accomplished with amazing efficiency by the man-
geurs du lard whose canots du maitre carried trade goods and supplies westward in the spring and great cargoes of furs on the home-
ward journey in high summer. The hivernants, or winterers, in
turn, made their annual trip from the interior in lighter birch-bark
canots du nord, fuelling their endeavours with fresh meat, fish, and
especially the pemmican purchased from the new plains dwellers,
the plains Crees and Assiniboines. The system was smooth but
violent and flamboyant. Nothing could compare with the June rendezvous of wintering partners, Montreal traders, and canoemen at
Fort William. It was a party so wild as to satisfy the rough-and-ready
for a full year – brandy and rum by the gallon, roast meat by the
quarter, women, fighting, tests of strength, the thrill of gambling for
large sums, the laughter of old friends – and it made the isolation
and the struggle worthwhile. Moreover, the rendezvous brought
the policy-makers and the field-men – the wintering partners –
together in an atmosphere that ensured frank exchanges and hard-
headed planning. The Nor'Wester system of profit-sharing and
regular consultation, in which the wintering partners could contri-
bute to crucial decisions and profit from their implementation, was
the ideal structure for the expanding fur trade. It is little wonder that
the great Hudson's Bay Company surveyor Philip Turnor could mix
envy with malice in his description of his opponents: 'They give
Men which never saw an Indian One Hundred Pounds Pr. Annum,
his Feather Bed carried in the Canoe, his Tent which is exceeding
good, pitched for him, his Bed made and he and his girl carried in
and out of the Canoe and when in the Canoe [he] never touches a
Paddle unless for his own pleasure.'[16] The North West Company

introduced not only murder and assault and mean exploitation but also energetic business management to the western fur trade.

One great strength of the Montreal traders was their ability to expand their trade network into new and ever richer areas of fur-bearing animals. They concentrated upon the most valuable pelts – mink, fisher, marten, and prime beaver – which were less bulky and left the heavier, less valuable wolf, bear, and moose hides to their English competitors. Their first breakthrough was achieved by the cut-throat Peter Pond, who became the agent for a loose coalition of pedlars in the Saskatchewan–Lac la Ronge country. Having been given a pool of trade goods at the end of the winter of 1777–8, Pond was able to move north from the mid-Saskatchewan in early summer rather than having to make the long spring voyage to Lake Superior. He paddled through the spruce and pine forests north of Île à la Crosse until he reached the Methy portage, where a sandy trail crossed the height of land between the Churchill and Athabasca rivers, and thus he pushed five large canoes of goods – an adequate supply for a year's trade – into the land of Lake Athabasca, the Eldorado of the trade as it came to be known. He was now beyond the reach of the monopoly of the Hudson's Bay Company. This foul-mouthed New Englander was not an entirely honourable hero – he was twice suspected of murdering competitors in 'scuffles' – but he did make possible the next great explorations of the northern reaches of the continent.

Bitter conflicts within the ranks of the pedlars, of which Pond's excesses were only an example, forced the leaders of the North West Company to reorganize their partnership in 1787 and, by including Gregory, McLeod, and company, to establish a virtual monopoly over all the northern fur trade operations out of Montreal. The new unity also enabled them to make better use of their personnel in the expansion of their trading territory. The career of Alexander Mackenzie illustrated their technique. Mackenzie had worked in the office of a Montreal trader and had served briefly at a small post in the northwest when he was dispatched to Athabasca to work with none other than Peter Pond, who still believed that the Arctic and Pacific oceans were just a little beyond the reach of his canoes and who, in the mean time, was taking 20,000 MB in fine skins a year out of his Eldorado. Pond left the fur country in 1788, a year after Mackenzie's arrival, but he had had ample time to implant his convictions about fur trade geography in his young colleague's mind. In

June 1789, continuing his mentor's search for the western sea, Mackenzie took a small party northward down the Slave River to Great Slave Lake and thence, after being tied up by ice and the search for an outlet, into the great river that was to bear his name; however, after 900 miles they were carried not into the Pacific but into the Arctic Ocean, a sea 'eternally covered with ice'; in his dismay, Mackenzie called his highway the River Disappointment.

Though Mackenzie had proven to be a fine general, he was conscious of his shortcomings as an explorer. When he met the skilful Hudson's Bay Company surveyor Philip Turnor shortly after this epic voyage, he was mocked: the company man said Mackenzie could not make observations and could not describe precisely where he had been. Having been slighted again at the 1790 meeting of the Nor'West partners at Grand Portage, Mackenzie went to England to learn the surveying techniques that would complement his undeniable brilliance as a traveller. (This latter may seem of little importance in our day, but the term comprehends the ability to plan a route, provision canoemen, negotiate with fearful crew members, overcome the military alliances of the native diplomatic system, and muster the energy necessary to drive an expedition and oneself, day after day, in extremely difficult physical conditions, to an unknown or ill-defined destination.) Mackenzie returned to Fort Chipewyan on Lake Athabasca and immediately began preparations for a second journey in search of an overland route to the Pacific. With seven Canadians and two Indians he left an advance post in May 1793 to pass through the Peace River Canyon and connecting streams to the great Fraser River. Threats from Indians and the danger of the river itself finally forced him to strike overland; having then found the Bella Coola River and aid from the friendly Bella Coola Indians, he pushed his exhausted crew the remaining miles to salt water. On the shore of the Pacific, he triumphantly scrawled his classic message on a rock: 'Alexander Mackenzie, from Canada, by land, the twenty-second of July, one thousand seven hundred and ninety-three.' The journey that had consumed two months on the way out took little more than one month on the return, and Mackenzie, then thirty years old, could call his remarkable days of exploration finished. He had proven not only his great personal qualities but also the strength of the commercial company that had supported him. His Nor'Westers stood astride the continent, brilliant technicians in market and travel organization and successful, if at times brutal, managers of the trade itself.[17]

The Hudson's Bay Company had not disappeared under the on-slaught of the North West Company, but it had assumed a distinctly inferior status in the fur trade of the western interior between the late 1760s and 1810. It tried to compete on equal terms but simply lacked the leadership and organizational flexibility to capitalize upon its chief natural advantage, the short economical sea route into the heart of the continent. As a result, it was always a step behind its competitors, never willing to give up the struggle but never incisive enough to strike first into new territory or to seize quickly upon new strategies. The pattern became clear in the late 1760s, when the returns at the most lucrative company post, York Factory, began to decline. York had traded 25,000–40,000 MB annually be-tween 1720 and the late 1760s, but in 1768 the total declined to 18,000 and remained at that level for the next four years, despite 'a new trade standard which gave the Indians better terms for prime marten, bears, and foxes.' By 1773 the returns had dropped to 'the derisory figure of 8,000 Made Beaver,' and the company was clearly losing its influence in the Lake Winnipeg–Saskatchewan River dis-trict.[18] Even before news of this last harvest had reached London, however, the managing directors of the firm, the committee, had finally decided to establish inland posts as some of its employees had been advocating since Henday's return almost twenty years before. In so doing, of course, the company was reversing the prac-tice of a century; the wonder may be not that the decision was late but that it was taken at all. So ill-prepared were the company's servants that Samuel Hearne's expedition of trade goods, supplies, and a dozen men, undertaken in the spring of 1774, had to be transported in small, two-man canoes with Indians who were re-turning to their wintering lands; because of the haphazard depar-ture arrangements, half of Hearne's crew never did join him. And when his canoes reached the district of The Pas, he discovered that the 'Pedlars' (Nor'Westers) were in full command of the territory, and so he pushed on sixty miles to Pine Island Lake, just off the Saskatchewan River, and there built Cumberland House, the first permanent company post in the interior. But this proved to be merely a way-station. As the explorations of Pond and Mackenzie rapidly pushed the trading frontier far to the north and west, the company responded slowly and methodically by mapping the waterways and extending its network of posts across the Saskatchewan. Only in 1791 did its servants even reach the Athabasca, and its first post on that lake was not built until 1802, over twenty years after Pond first crossed the divide. Even a series of trading posts could not rescue company fortunes completely, however, and its dividends declined from 8 per cent in the closing years of the century to 4 per cent between 1801 and 1808 and, in the five years from 1809, to zero. It was a time of crisis indeed.

The company was simply unable to match the skill and ruthlessness of the Canadians. Its share of the trade was approximately £30,000 in the 1780s, compared to the Nor'Westers' exports of £165,000 to £242,000, and it did not much exceed that proportion in the following two decades. In 1800, for example, the Hudson's Bay Company sent £38,000 in furs to London, the Nor'Westers £144,000. The vaunted company efficiency also declined. Scurvy broke out at York Factory, rotten meat was sent inland, tobacco was too damp to be burnt despite attempts to mix it with oil and molasses, and sour cheese and butter had to be abandoned at the Bayside. Even when one makes allowances for the usual problems of the trade, the company record in this period was poor. The great David Thompson, a product of Grey Coat School in London and an extremely talented explorer-surveyor, was sent to investigate a new route from the Bay to Lake Athabasca in 1795–6, with the aid of two Chipewyan guides but almost no equipment or food. He and his companions had not only to build their own canoe but also to rely upon a fishing net for their daily sustenance. When he finally did reach Athabasca, Thompson lost the canoe and its contents in a waterfall and had resigned himself to death when a chance encounter with an Indian family saved him. Shortly afterward, Thompson defected to the Pedlars' ranks. It was no surprise.

In 1795–6, the Hudson's Bay Company sent 132 men inland from York whereas the Canadians employed 1,120 canoemen and 35 guides alone in their admittedly much more demanding transportation system between Montreal and the far northwest. Despite some bright spots, including the extension of the post network to the Rockies (Edmonton House was founded in 1795 and Acton House, at the edge of the mountains, in 1799) and the development of an extremely efficient transportation system with the introduction of the capacious shallow-draught York boats on the Saskatchewan in

1797, the company was in dire straits by the end of the first decade of the nineteenth century. As European fur markets collapsed during the Napoleonic wars, and as directors were asked to provide cash for current operations in the face of a £50,000 overdraft at the bank, the company faced the greatest crisis of its existence.[19]

If only the Pedlars could have maintained peace in the northwest and ensured the unity of their uncertain partnership, they might have captured the Bay route and perhaps even the charter privileges of the Hudson's Bay Company on their own terms. But peace and harmony were never strengths of the Montreal people. Instead of consolidating their monopoly, they merely intensified the competition between 1790 and 1810. At the heart of North West Company politics were two sets of conflicting interests: within the Montreal community, the dominance of the powerful marquis of the North West Company, Simon McTavish, was challenged by a number of strong independent firms, including McGill-Todd, Forsyth-Richardson, and Grant-Campion; and, within the Nor'Westers' own ranks, the interests of the Montreal and London agents were often seen to be in conflict with those of the wintering partners. Thus discord within the Montreal merchant community and disagreements within the ranks of the Nor'Westers themselves complicated the intense struggle for profits.

The competition among the merchants was especially serious in the fifteen years after 1790. Simon McTavish had clearly asserted his hold over the North West Company by this time, and his competitors, many of whom traded southwest of the Great Lakes, were increasingly dissatisfied with their share of the upper Great Lakes operations. These problems intensified in 1794 when, with the signing of Jay's Treaty by Britain and the United States, Canadian access to posts south of the border, including Detroit, Chicago, and the northwest shore of Lake Michigan, was 'interrupted.' That is, despite the apparent liberality of the treaty in its support of trade by British subjects and American citizens on either side of the frontier, the Montrealers were in fact forced to choose between the Canadian (northwestern) trade and the American. Several firms switched their attention north of the Great Lakes, and soon these important operations, including Forsyth-Richardson, Grant-Campion, Parker-Gerrard-Ogilvy, Phynn-Inglis, and Leith-Jameson, all of Montreal, as well as John Mure of Quebec, were disputing the North West–Hudson's Bay dominance of the western interior. By 1798, Forsyth-

Richardson and Leith-Jameson had created a partnership to pursue the trade with greater vigor, and in that year they were even able to carry their challenge into the Athabasca district. In 1800, when Alexander Mackenzie joined their firm, this New North-West Company, also variously described as the XY Company (after the marking on their bales of goods which distinguished them from the Nor'Westers') and as Sir Alexander Mackenzie and Company, had become a significant factor in the west. And when the battle between the Nor'Westers and XY was joined, the Hudson's Bay Company was forgotten: the Canadians assumed, in their flamboyant way, that the English plum would be picked by the victor.

If this competition between Montreal companies was serious, it was made particularly significant by the disagreements between the wintering partners and the Montreal agents within the North West Company. Whoever controlled the largest number of shares in the company naturally exercised the greatest power in policy and personnel decisions. And the choice of postings could be very important at a time when profit-sharing, which was just another form of commission trading, was the rule. Moreover, the big shareholders obviously took down a healthy profit when the final accounting of the year's trade was made. In the shifting affairs of the Nor'Westers, where new agreements were constantly being negotiated (in 1779, 1780, 1783–4, 1787, 1790, 1792, 1795, and 1802–3), the winterers believed that they were losing money to the agents. When the winterers found a champion in Alexander Mackenzie in the 1795 renegotiations, they created a crucial split in Nor'Wester unity. And when Mackenzie's contract with the North West Company expired in 1799, it was natural that he should look to the XY Company for a better deal and that a number of dissatisfied winterers should accompany him on his switch into the new concern. Thus was the struggle between XY and the Nor'Westers intensified.

Mackenzie was by now a man of great stature in England as well as Canada, and the publication of his *Voyages* in 1801 earned him a knighthood and a hearing for his visionary scheme to reorganize the trading structure of the empire. He would, he said, create a great new British trading concern, the Fur and Fishery Company, which would subsume the privileges of the Hudson's Bay Company, the East India Company, and the South Sea Company. Using the sea route to the Bay, and linking the China trade to fur posts on the Pacific, a united Canadian fur trading structure could form the heart of an international trade system. But Mackenzie's grand idea fell before the resistance of Simon McTavish and the North West Company. It was left to an American, John Jacob Astor, to pick up the elements of the scheme some years later.

The competition between Nor'Westers and the XY Company may have undercut Mackenzie's world trade scheme, but it could not be sustained indefinitely because it was simply too damaging to all parties. West Indian rum, the 'Fiery Double distilled Rum,' was now being shipped into the western interior in immense quantities to fuel the competition between traders. In 1800 alone, over 10,000 gallons of the liquor arrived in the interior, and, as the Montreal competition increased, this figure reached over 21,000 by 1803, 16,000 imported by the Nor'Westers and 5,000 by the XY Company: 'The Indians were not only spoiled and debauched,' E.E. Rich concluded, 'they were bullied and abused as well.' For reasons of profit if not of humanity such practices could not be allowed to continue, and when, in 1804, the death of Simon McTavish removed a key source of personal animosity between the two concerns, a coalition was quickly negotiated. Henceforth, an even more powerful Montreal-based company would control the fur trade of the western interior. Negotiations to take over the Hudson's Bay Company – or at least to use the prized route from York Fort to Athabasca – were commenced in the expectation that the English would inevitably give way to the superior Canadian company.[20]

The political fate of the northern part of the continent – a British nation and an American nation – had been largely determined by the close of the eighteenth century. As a result of French, Hudson's Bay, and North West fur trade activity, the western interior remained under the British crown at the close of this period. And, though competition between the English and Montreal companies continued and even intensified as the nineteenth century began, the creation of a monopoly enterprise was now within reach. What was the place of the natives in the calculations of the entrepreneurs? They were part of the environment, presumably, to be used by the victorious European company. So far distant were the worlds of native and European as the nineteenth century began.

# 5

# Maintaining the old order 1805–44: The metis, the fur trade, and the Red River settlement

Several new factors were introduced into western Canadian history in the first half of the nineteenth century. One was the 'new nation,' composed of the children of the fur trade marriages between Europeans and natives. Another was Lord Selkirk's colonization experiment, the Red River settlement, which was the harbinger of British and European industrial capitalist conventions. The fur trade itself underwent important changes. Between 1800 and 1820, an unprecedented degree of violence marked the struggle between the Montreal and London fur companies. After a new monopoly enterprise was created in 1821, Governor George Simpson and the company's London committee created a leaner, more aggressive trading operation and, against their will, a civil administration in the growing settlement at the forks of the Red and Assiniboine. None the less, despite extraordinary upheavals in native and fur company society, the trade and the hunt continued apace, on the surface little affected by these deeper currents of change.

James Isham provided one perspective on the new forces at work in fur trade society when, in his *Observations and Notes*, written between 1743 and 1749, he declared that Cree girls were 'very frisky when Young ... well shap'd ... their Eyes Large and Grey yet Lively and Sparkling very Bewitchen.'[1] He might have added, as was attested in a dozen other fur trade journals, that Indian women also made moccasins and showshoes, preserved food, harvested fish and berries and wild rice, dressed furs, and sewed canoe seams. Moreover, they acted as interpreters and intermediaries in trade negotiations: marriage between the daughter of a prominent Indian and a European fur company man might cement a trade relationship and outflank the opposition in a way that was otherwise impossible.

The interest of European males in native companions was reciprocated by some Indian women. Physical attraction may or may not have been important to the women – there is no evidence comparable to the European traders' expressions of enthusiasm – but the domestic and diplomatic gains secured by such family ties were very useful to the Indians. The marriage of one of their band to a trader could provide them with credit and help in tough times; it could give them an advantage in trade negotiations; it might mean that enemy bands did not secure European weapons. For the individual woman, such a relationship ensured access to wealth in the form of labour-saving domestic tools, a lighter work load, a more secure food supply, and, in the case of officers' wives, such marks of status as being lifted into and out of canoes and having one's tent and bed prepared by others. There were drawbacks, too, including a higher fertility rate and separation from one's native family, but these problems emerged only as the custom of marriage became firmly entrenched in fur trade society. Sexual liaisons, marriages, and children were, in short, a fundamental aspect of fur trade history.

The stability of fur trade marriages depended on the circumstances of the European and native societies from which the individuals were drawn. When the Indian bands were moving regularly with the changes in season and food supply, and when European traders had only brief contact with the bands, relationships would probably have been brief. But as the trader established more permanent bases and as some Indians became attached to these supply centres, lasting liaisons became possible. The institution of marriage 'according to the custom of the country' (à la façon du pays) was established on Indian rules in the eighteenth century. It usually required parental consent and payment of a bride price to the woman's parents. It might be formalized by a calumet ceremony similar to that employed in trade talks, by a ritual washing of the bride, and by the exchange of native garments for European. Marriage was not necessarily a lifetime contract in the eyes of either partner, and, in the eighteenth century at least, the women could return easily to their own bands with their children.[2]

Two patterns of family formation, one associated with the Montreal and one with the Hudson's Bay operations, developed in the early fur trade. French entrepreneurs had set down permanent roots in Indian country by the late 1690s, and, during the next century, their offspring established a distinctive culture based on a combination of European and native customs. They settled along the rivers and lakes of the Chicago–Green Bay region and populated as many as fifty villages and towns. They erected their log cabins on the waterfront, cultivated peas and potatoes in gardens that stretched behind, created a distinctive costume that combined native moccasins and leggings with European ruffled shirts and waistcoats, and established control over the middle rungs of the fur trade economy. They were frontier traders, brokers between eastern companies and western natives; they were guides, interpreters, ferrymen, oarsmen, and mail carriers, but, most of all, they were buffers between natives and Europeans. Neither one nor the other, they became the metis.[3]

The Hudson's Bay Company families were located near the company forts on the shores of the Bay. Though company journals are reticent on the subject, it appears that fur trade marriages were at first the prerogative of senior officers and that alliances between junior officers or servants and native women were less formal and rarely resulted in the establishment of families within the walls of the posts. None the less, British men and native women did make liaisons and a new community – the Home Guard Indians – eventually developed. Many of these hunters and jacks-of-all trade were related to or the offspring of native wives, but they did not acquire, as did the French Metis, a separate social status. If they lived with the natives and travelled in their hunting bands, they were native. On the rare occasions when fathers participated in their upbringing, encouraged their education, and perhaps aided in securing company positions for them, they became English. A middle racial category did not develop in the eighteenth-century British fur trade.[4]

The children of mixed European and native parentage exercised greater influence in the half-century from 1770 to 1820. In these two generations of increasingly intense trade competition, the number of servants, posts, families, and, of course, children increased markedly. Alexander Henry's rough census of 1805 enumerated 1,090

The Metis (Labor)

Fur Trade —

" " page

69

Fraser, Herald

WAYNE UDE                    513 MARSHALL        MANKATO MN                      56001
PHONE-                       BIRTH-03/10/72      LOCKER-1547
HOMEROOM NUMBER - 0100                           RUN DATE 09/04/84

| CRS | SEC | SEM | PER | DAYS | PER | DAYS | COURSE TITLE | ROOM | TEACHER |
|-----|-----|-----|-----|------|-----|------|--------------|------|---------|
| F100 | 06 | 3 | 1 | ALL | | | ENGLISH 7 | 0203 | WILIGEN |
| F013 | 01 | 3 | 2 | ALL | | | RESOURCE 7 | 0100 | MEYER |
| A700 | 05 | 1 | 3 | ALL | | | HOME EC 7 | 0115 | POTZLER |
| B720 | 06 | 1 | 3 | ALL | | | IND ARTS 7 | 1201 | MILLER |
| F920 | 01 | 3 | 4 | MW | | | ORCHESTRA 7 | 0127 | DUNN |
| F808 | 02 | 3 | 4 | TR | | | PHY ED 7 | GYM | HESSE |
| F050 | 01 | 3 | 5 | ALL | | | LUNCH | | STAFF |
| F300 | 03 | 3 | 6 | ALL | | | GEOGRAPHY 7 | 0109 | RUSS |
| F200 | 08 | 3 | 8 | ALL | | | MATH 7 | 0107 | LUNDBERG |
| S100 | 06 | 3 | 1 | ALL | | | ENGLISH 7 | 0203 | WILIGEN |
| S013 | 01 | 3 | 2 | ALL | | | RESOURCE 7 | 0100 | MEYER |
| S500 | 05 | 2 | 3 | ALL | | | ART 7 | 0227 | ADAMS |
| S808 | 02 | 3 | 4 | TR | | | PHY ED 7 | GYM | HESSE |
| S920 | 01 | 3 | 4 | MW | | | ORCHESTRA 7 | 0127 | DUNN |
| S050 | 01 | 3 | 5 | ALL | | | LUNCH | | STAFF |
| S300 | 03 | 3 | 6 | ALL | | | GEOGRAPHY 7 | 0109 | RUSS |
| S200 | 08 | 3 | 8 | ALL | | | MATH 7 | 0107 | LUNDBERG |

Nor'Westers in the interior but also 368 women and 569 children. His more careful count at his own post revealed 36 men, 27 women, and 67 children.[5] The phenomenon of unchecked population increase was so obvious that in 1806 the North West Company forbade its servants to marry Indian women; henceforth, only metis wives would be acceptable. The labour demands of these far-flung trade empires also ensured that a growing number of 'country-born' (Canadian-born) would find company jobs rather than return to their mothers' bands. They learned English or French, picked up the elements of reading and writing, cultivated kinship ties, and, in dress and outlook, became more European and less Indian than the preceding generation. Some of them – as many as 30 Nor'West boys between 1790 and 1810 – were educated in Canadian or British schools and returned to the northwest as 'gentlemen.' By reason of their number, their cultural differences, and their education, these children of mixed parentage began to think of themselves as a distinct group with distinct interests.

The children of the Montreal trade, offspring mainly of French and Ojibwa parents, were the most numerous and settled of the new native-born population. Their heritage was a century old. Their homeland, which stretched from the southern tip of Lake Michigan to Red River, was vast, and their economic support lay both in agriculture and in the powerful Montreal fur trade. But pressures exerted by the westward expansion of the new nation, the United States of America, began to disrupt their world between 1800 and 1820. In this crisis, many metis simply were absorbed into the American population. Others moved westward. Jean-Baptiste Nolin, for example, sold his fur trade operation at Sault Ste Marie in 1818–19 and re-established his large metis family at Red River. And when Cuthbert Grant returned from his years at school in the 'outside world,' he too established himself in the Red-Assiniboine country. Thus, as Nor'West competition with the Hudson's Bay Company intensified after 1810, the Montreal fur barons found natural allies in their company's offspring, the metis of the northwest.[6]

If the metis can be viewed as a new factor in fur trade operations, they were not the only addition to the competitive situation in the northwest. In this same period, the Hudson's Bay Company was changed so drastically that it became almost a new organization. Its dramatic rescue included the adoption of trade incentives in the field, severe economies in the head office, and, most famous of all, the foundation of a British outpost in the region, the Red River colony. The consequence was an extension of the trade war and an intensification of violence.

Lord Selkirk is often placed at the centre of these events. He did not single-handedly alter the entire course of western Canadian history, as is sometimes said, but he did exert an important influence upon it. Thomas Douglas was born in 1771, the seventh son of the fourth Earl of Selkirk, and because of his place in the family was permitted to pursue a leisurely education at Edinburgh University and then to take a grand tour of the Continent. A bright student, he was frequently included in a brilliant circle of young Scotsmen that numbered a future essayist (Francis Jeffrey) and a novelist (Walter Scott) among its number. His brothers died in rapid succession, and, in 1799, when he was twenty-eight years old, Thomas assumed leadership of his clan and the earldom.[7]

The new earl was deeply touched by the economic plight of his people, and, as he travelled his estates and saw the conditions of the farmers and crofters who were ostensibly dependent on his good offices, he decided that he must act to improve their lot in life. An obvious solution was emigration, and for the next decade Selkirk devoted himself to that idea. He considered setting up a colony in Louisiana and purchased some lands in New York state, but he preferred to retain these people under the British crown and, therefore, gave more serious consideration to Canadian sites. His first endeavour, the Baldoon Farm near Lake St Clair in Upper Canada, was plagued with problems. The second, on Prince Edward Island, enjoyed reasonable success. While establishing these settlements in 1803–4, Selkirk visited Montreal, was entertained by the Nor'Westers at the Beaver Club, and began to develop his scheme for yet another colony, in the western interior. At a time when North West control of the entire trade was conceivable, Selkirk's plans did not seem to conflict with those of the Nor'Westers. His relationship with Alexander Mackenzie and their joint plan to purchase Hudson's Bay Company shares probably grew out of these early contacts. But Selkirk had a shrewd sense of business politics and, rather than tie his fortunes to those of the Canadians, he brought two allies into his confidence, his wife's brother, Andrew Wedderburn Colvile, and his wife's sister's husband, John Halkett. The trio took control of the Hudson's Bay Company at the nadir of its economic fortunes, in

1809, and instituted the reorganization that was to stand the fur trade on its head in the next decade.[8]

Of the three, Colvile, a senior partner in a firm of sugar brokers, was a substantial businessman and an important addition to the leadership of the Hudson's Bay Company. To commence the rescue of the company, Colvile devised a Retrenching System that leaned heavily on Nor'Wester experience and his own concern for careful accountancy and shrewd buying and selling in the London market. His most striking innovation was the adoption of the Nor'Wester system of profit-sharing for payment of traders in the field – that is, payment by results or commission rather than by regular wage – but retrenchment involved also the creation of a more efficient administrative structure for the North American operations and, though we are less sure about this, of a more flexible standard of trade in dealings with the Indians. The mixture of economies and incentives worked wonders, and by 1812 the company could report a small profit. Its revival spelled real problems for the fur trade, however, because it coincided with Lord Selkirk's next emigration scheme and because it made a North West Company takeover bid much more difficult.

Why Selkirk chose the forks of the Red and Assiniboine rivers for the focus of his new emigration plan is something of a mystery, but perhaps the popularity of the site in the previous century and company officers' praise for the fertility of its land influenced him. Equally important, no doubt, was the exhaustion of the fur resources of this district, the proximity of the buffalo plains (which stretched west of the Red River between the valleys of the Assiniboine and the Missouri), and easy access to the company transportation route from York Factory. The choice of site was at once the great strength of the colony and a source of much grief: strength, because the plains did indeed feed the settlement and the trade; grief, because the colony was placed astride the critical provisioning routes of the North West Company and thus appeared to threaten the very existence of the Canadian company's operations.[9]

But if the site at the forks created problems for the fur company, it was well chosen as the first agricultural experiment in the western interior. Here, for the first time, as the London committee and its critics, including Arthur Dobbs, had dreamed, serious experiments could be undertaken in the production of field crops, slaughter animals, and dairy herds. The dreamers would discover whether this distant wilderness could supply its own food requirements and thus end the reliance on 'plains provisions' and the importation of food-stuffs. Moreover, a settlement in the interior would resolve another growing problem by providing a home for retired servants and their Indian or metis wives, many of whom had no desire to live in the British Isles or the Canadian provinces. If these servants could retire to a stable and comfortable settlement in the interior, the directors of the company believed, a whole new generation of young traders might be created, thereby laying to rest the company's problems in labour recruitment. So the Selkirk experiment coincided with the needs of the Hudson's Bay Company and jeopardized the operations of its competitor.

Selkirk took his plan to the London committee in 1810, but, because of the opposition of Alexander Mackenzie, who remained a large shareholder, the scheme was delayed until a General Court of the whole company – a public shareholders' meeting – could consider the plan. And there, in early 1811, despite the hasty plans of the Nor'Westers to defeat the proposal by buying sufficient shares to dominate the meeting, Selkirk was triumphant. He was granted for the nominal sum of ten shillings a tract of 116,000 square miles, known as Assiniboia, or the Red River Colony. In return for this huge tract of land, five times the size of Scotland, Selkirk was to provide the company with two hundred servants a year, to permit the company to set up trading posts within the colony, to forbid settlers to participate in the fur trade, and to provide land for retired servants. The company, in addition to granting the land, agreed to provide free transportation and equipment for the colonists, to give the colony's governor a commission (thus adding the authority of the company's charter to his rulings), and to enrol the colonists as company servants to ensure further the maintenance of discipline.[10] Was it any wonder that the Nor'Westers saw the fur trade company and the colony as two arms of the same corporate body or that the Nor'Westers should wage war on the one as they did on the other? At a time of unstable European markets, rising costs of competition in the interior, and growing demands for plains provisions from the vast North West post system, the threat posed by the colony to the vital food supply system of the North West Company had to be confronted. The story of the following decade was the battle between the Canadian Goliath and the English David. Red River, as it proved, was a crucial factor in the combat.

The struggle began in Scotland, where Selkirk's choice as governor, retired army officer Miles Macdonnell, was recruiting settlers. Agents of the North West Company dogged his heels, rousing fears of the distant wilderness and of company support: 'Even if [the emigrants] escape the scalping knife, they will be subject to constant alarm and terror. Their habitations, their crops, their cattle will be destroyed, and they will find it impossible to exist in the country,' wrote the Highlander (the pen-name of Simon McGillivray of the North West Company) in the *Inverness Journal*.[11] The expedition of 105, including mainly labourers but also some families and company employees bound for trading posts, departed the wind-swept dock at Stornoway in the Hebrides late in the season of 1811, leaving goods behind them in their haste to escape the dire prophesies of the North West agents. But the words of the Nor'Westers were as nothing compared to the tribulations of the Selkirk settlers in the following fifteen years.

The suffering of the Red River settlement has been enshrined in the history of the west. Indeed, from the late nineteenth century, through the writing of R.G. MacBeth and George Bryce, among others, the colony has been seen as the epitome of the spirit that conquered the wilderness. While recent decades have required less uniformly British, more multicultural heroes, of whom Louis Riel is paramount, no cultural changes can erase the pain and the hardship faced by these ill-prepared contingents of men, women, and children. It was not that survival was impossible – generations of Indians and traders put the lie to such exaggerations – but that the immediate adaptation required of these farmers was immense, the ignorance of local conditions displayed by successive leaders was criminal, and the uncaring fur company combat into which they were thrust put their very lives in jeopardy.

The first party of labourers arrived on the shore of Hudson Bay in late September 1811, much too late to attempt the voyage to Red River before freeze-up, and there remained; the makeshift huts, miserable weather, sparse game resources, and frustrated talk would stand out in their memories forever after. The trip to Red River in four large crude boats occupied the best part of the summer of 1812, and thus, when the sites of the new farms were set out in September, the colonists again faced a long and hungry western winter. The men moved south to a metis settlement, there to learn the skills of the buffalo hunt from the natives of the country in order to stave off starvation. At least they had begun to establish a stable base, however, for a second party of colonists, Irish and Highland Scots, about eighty in all, had set out from Ireland in June 1812, reached York Factory in August, and pressed straight on to Red River, arriving there at the end of October to tax the already slim resources of the group that had preceded them by little more than two months. The hunt, in large measure the work of the metis huntsmen rather than of the colonists, sustained the community during the winter of 1812–13, despite the burden imposed on the fur company's provisions, and in the spring of 1813 the immigrants began to build in earnest. Along the west bank of the Red River, about a mile north of the Assiniboine junction, they built log houses and sowed their small crops on long narrow river lots. Though the harvest was disappointing, it at least supplemented the buffalo hunt in the winter of 1813–14.

A third contingent of settlers had been expected, ninety Scots from Kildonan including many sturdy young men, but a series of disasters intervened: fever killed five en route, the landing was made at Fort Churchill rather than York Factory, their ship ran aground, and the absence of preparation in this more northerly post was made worse by the threat of starvation, scurvy, and typhus, all of which forced the party to remain at the Bayside in makeshift shacks. It was an arduous beginning, but the Kildonan families proved their mettle by walking overland from Fort Churchill to York Factory in the late winter (behind the skirling of a Gunn's bagpipes, as novelist Margaret Laurence's creation in *The Diviners* would have it), in order to be ready to depart as soon as the Nelson River broke up. They reached Red River in early July 1814, to find turbulence and uncertainty in every household. But their very arrival inspired confidence, crops were planted, and the colonists once again prepared to face the winter.

The winter of 1814–15 was no easier than the two preceding, however, because food shortages and the fear of Indians, metis, and Nor'Westers played on the settlers' nerves. When the spring of 1815 finally brought warmer weather, 140 settlers accepted the North West Company's invitation to embark in company canoes for Canada; they had had enough of hardship and uncertainty. The 60 settlers who remained expected to be left in peace. But the metis rode through their crops, burned their houses, and finally drove them into their boats. At the top of Lake Winnipeg, they were met by Colin Robertson, the quick-witted, quick-tongued agent of the Hudson's Bay Company. Robertson talked them into turning their boats around and sailing back down this vast lake to their abandoned settlement. With the promise of his support they did so, and, once again, this time under his cheerful direction, they made preparations for winter. Robertson's noble plans were doomed, however, by the hostility of the Nor'Westers.

The North West Company, including both the partners in Montreal and the winterers in the interior, had been suspicious of the link between the colony and the Hudson's Bay Company from the beginning. Events in Red River only increased their fears. Not only had the settlers relied on the metis huntsmen's plains provisions – fuel of the North West canoe brigades – but also in January 1814, when food was short, the colony's governor, Miles Macdonnell, in his famous Pemmican Proclamation, had prohibited the export of provisions from the district. He later forbade the running of buffalo (hunting from horseback, metis-style, stampeded the herds out of range of the colonists) and also seized some North West Company pemmican stored at Fort La Souris. These were direct blows at the North West supply system and were made worse by Macdonnell's insistence, as his proclamation made plain, that the Selkirk colony owned the land on which the North West posts sat and the fruit thereof.

The response of the Nor'Westers was immediate and blunt; they pressed the young metis men of the district to harass the colony or, as it was put, 'to commence open hostilities against the enemy in Red River.'[12] Since many of these men hunted buffalo for the North West Company and were affected by Macdonnell's presumptuous ruling, they were happy to oblige. The metis negotiated at gun point to secure North West food supplies in 1814, and they conducted a campaign of terror in 1815, including the destruction of crops, the theft of animals and implements, and the burning of some houses, but they did not resort to attacks on the settlers themselves. In August 1815, when Robertson arrived at the forks with the 60 settlers who had been driven our several months before, the metis did not oppose their re-establishment, and when a new governor, the distinguished American Loyalist Robert Semple, and his contingent of 80 Sutherland settlers arrived in November 1815, affairs were so peaceful and the harvest so bountiful (the crops had survived the worst efforts of the horsemen) that metis threats seemed irrelevant. Semple blithely assumed that the crisis was over, to the dismay of Colin Robertson, who eventually left for Hudson Bay in frustration. Robertson's fears were justified by the events of 19 June 1816.

To understand the occurrence in the shady grove of trees known locally as Seven Oaks, we must recall not only the commitment of the metis to the North West Company cause but also the violence of fur company competition and plains warfare. Narratives of western life – by such diverse characters as Samuel Hearne, John Tanner, Peter Pond, and Saukamappee – suggest that local incidents of violence and death were simply an expected part of the seasonal round of existence. Thus the tragedy of June 1816 was not an unexpected aberration but a predictable flare-up in an intense conflict between a fur trade empire under challenge and its lightly regarded opponent.[13] Similarly, the metis were not ruthless, thoughtless renegades who fought from some primordial bloodlust, as later Red River apologists tried to demonstrate, but soldiers in what they perceived to be a just cause. Their young articulate leader, Cuthbert Grant, had returned to the west in 1812 from an extended period of schooling (whether in Scotland or Canada is not certain) and employment as a clerk in Montreal. He had become a well-dressed young gentleman during his eleven-year absence, but, despite his frock coat, breeches, beaver hat, and boots, he was welcomed as a native of the country. He married a local girl, Elizabeth McKay of Brandon House, 'according to the custom of the country' and took up his duties as a trader in the Qu'Appelle district, where he demonstrated that he was 'proficient in the way of life of the plains, as horseman, hunter, and warrior.' He was emphatically neither a villian nor a brutal cut-throat but a loyal son of the fur trade and of the North West Company, in whose service his father died and in whose ranks he had been raised and educated. According to his biographers, 'Grant's readiness to follow the plans of his superiors and to use his growing influence with the metis to rally them to the cause of the North-West Company and of their own rights in the soil was to be the principal factor in the Nor'Westers' harrying of Selkirk's colony.'[14]

Cuthbert Grant, together with three other young metis, had been selected as captains of the metis by the North West Company agents when the campaign against the colony began in earnest in 1814 and had marshalled his forces both in that first confrontation and again in the summer of 1815. He was, quite clearly, the leader of an organized movement to drive the colonists out of the country. In the winter of 1815–16, while Colin Robertson and Robert Semple regrouped, Grant and his colleagues continued their preparations for the third season of conflict: 'Give my best wishes to all the Young Fellows of the *bois-brulés* that you see,' Grant wrote Seraphim Lamar in December; 'you must impress on them that they keep up their courage and take good care what they do for come spring we shall see the *bois-brulés* from Fort des Prairies [Edmonton] and from all sides.' The winter passed quietly; Colin Robertson attempted to win the metis from their alliance with the Nor'Westers and Semple toured the district. But the quiet was deceptive. As Cuthbert Grant demonstrated in an oft-quoted letter of 13 March 1816 to J.D. Cameron of Sault Ste Marie, the third campaign would be the harshest yet:

> I am as yet safe and sound thank God, for I believe its more than [Colin] Robertson or any of his suit dare to offer the least insult to any one of the Bois Brûlés; altho' Robertson made use of some expressions, which I hope he shall swallow in the Spring ... The Half Breeds of Fort Dauphin, de Pra[i]ries & English [Churchill] river are all to be here in the spring, it is hoped we shall come off with flying colors and never see any of them again in the Colonizing way in Red River, in fact the Traders shall pack off with themselves also, for having disregarded our orders last spring; according to our arrangements, we are to remain at The Forks & pass the Summer for fear they should play us the same trick as last Summer of coming back, but they shall receive a warm reception.

It is clear, therefore, that Grant planned an attack on the settlement that would, once and for all, remove it from the western interior. His position was confirmed when the Nor'Westers named him 'Captain-General of all the Half Breeds' (the title as reported by a Hudson's Bay Company trader) in the spring.[15]

There existed a rough balance between the forces of the North West Company and the settlement as the snows melted in 1816: Colin Robertson and his forces controlled the Forks and the Nor'-Westers' provision supply route from Qu'Appelle to the Winnipeg River; Cuthbert Grant and the metis could seize the Hudson's Bay Company pemmican supply at a moment's notice. The metis acted in May, first capturing the Hudson's Bay Company pemmican boats as they manoeuvred single-file through the Grand Rapids of the Qu'Appelle River, and then riding pell-mell into the yard of Brandon House, the Hudson's Bay Company post, to capture and plunder that bastion. They then moved east again, about thirty to forty horsemen in each of two parties on either side of the Assiniboine River, Cuthbert Grant in command, constantly on the watch for some retaliatory force from the colony and carefully shepherding the huge shipment of pemmican that lay in the flotilla of boats on the river between them. They reached the portage (Portage la Prairie), fifty miles west of the forks, without incident, and there made plans to get their cargo to the North West canoe brigades on Lake Winnipeg, another fifty miles north of the forks. Since the river would be blockaded by the colonists, their plan was to carry pemmican overland by cart on a route which, as in the hypotenuse of a right-angled triangle, would avoid the settlement. Then, in the longer term, they could simply starve the colonists into submission.

Accidents can alter the course of events, however, and in this case they were pivotal. When Grant's expedition tried to leave the Assiniboine for the overland trek, the banks were so wet and marshy that the horsemen travelled much closer to the forks than they intended. Thus, rather than a ten-mile margin, their exit at Catfish (Omand's) Creek left them only three miles. Worse, the overland route to the Red was wet and marshy, Grant's horses were soon belly deep in the swampy fields, and the party veered even closer to the fort – perhaps a mile and a half from its palisades. Semple, who had been warned by sympathetic Indians and metis of Grant's approach, foolishly decided to go out with a small party to inquire about the metis mission and to assert his authority over the district. Having seen only the small advance party of about fifteen in contrast to the larger group with the carts and pemmican that numbered almost fifty, Semple took only twenty-odd men with him. When warned of the larger group by several farmers whom he met en route, Semple did order that a three-pound field piece be brought up, but he was too impatient to await its arrival and instead plunged on to confront the interlopers. They met at Seven Oaks.

The Grant and Semple parties spread out cautiously along a wide front, eyeing each other, clearly uncertain about the situation but quite prepared for trouble. Thus, though entirely unplanned, a tense and volatile confrontation had been created by a series of accidents and, it must be admitted, Semple's thoughtlessness. The sun was sinking lower and the air was growing cooler as the two lines faced each other, silent but for the stamp and snuffle of their horses, until after several minutes Grant ordered an aide, François Boucher, to ride forward with a request that Semple's men either surrender or be fired on. Boucher and Semple spoke; each irritated the other; Semple grabbed at the horseman's reins and gun; Boucher slid from his horse and ran for safety; shots were fired, the metis took cover behind their horses and began a heavy volley that was answered by scattered musket shots; their volley finished, the metis threw themselves to the ground to reload, French-Canadian style; the remaining men in Semple's force cheered, thinking they had finished off the enemy, but the metis rebounded, firing and charging on foot. Some of Semple's men fought savagely, others broke and ran for cover, but most were shot or speared within minutes. Six escaped and a seventh was spared after tearful pleas. Twenty-one of Semple's party died, one of Grant's. The accidental confrontation had become a bloody battle – but it is not properly called, as is too often heard, a massacre. The significance of the event lay in its impact on the metis and the fur trade, not in the ultimate fate of the colony itself. The colonists would eventually accept that the events of Seven Oaks were the result of an accident; in this understanding lay the later reconciliation of metis and colonists, of Grant and the Scotsmen, and thus the peaceful coexistence of these communities in the following half-century.

But the battle did affect the metis, who had clearly been moulded into a community by the events of 1814–16. Before these struggles they had simply been traders and hunters and employees, family members and relatives, but now they were a collective force, an association larger than a family and with more important bonds than a company; they were, as they described it, a new nation, the bois-brûlés. Seven Oaks sealed their unity; before the night of 19 June was over the events of the conflict had been immortalized in song by Pierre Falcon, Grant's brother-in-law:

Ah, would you had seen those Englishmen,
And the Bois-brûlés a-chasing them!
One by one we did them destroy
While our Bois-brûlés uttered shouts of joy!

Their political interests would henceforth be defined as the right to run buffalo and to live freely according to the custom of the country. They insisted that they could claim the benefits of their maternal heritage. They even negotiated a treaty in which 'whatever presents may be given annually to the Indians, ... the Half breeds shall have an equal share with them.' As this protracted struggle had made clear, they had an identity separate from both the Europeans and the Indians: they were part of both cultures. The importance of the campaign to the French-speaking metis of Nor'Wester origin cannot be overestimated. Seven Oaks was their ordeal by fire. It gave them a sense of nationhood that was to be reinforced by Riel and Dumont later in the century.[16]

On the morrow of the clash, the settlers, broken by the loss of family and friends and by the sight of the mutilated bodies, hastened to collect their belongings and depart. Cuthbert Grant, once more a clerk rather than a war captain, took an inventory of the goods left behind, signed the lists of thousands of items for hours on end, and, then, after two days of these last details, he watched the colonists sail northward, leaving his metis once more in command of the forks.

The crushing blow did not destroy the Selkirk settlement. Reinforcements were even then making their way to the west, this time under the command of Lord Selkirk himself and with the protection of about ninety mercenaries from the Swiss and German de Meuron regiment that had fought in Canada during the war of 1812–14. Selkirk captured Fort William, the North West headquarters, and arrested several company officers. He also discovered evidence that linked the Canadian company to the deaths at Seven Oaks. Having weakened his opponents, Selkirk proceeded to Red River in 1817. He soon placed the colony upon a sounder foundation, signed a treaty with representatives of the local Crees, Assiniboines, and Ojibwas to extinguish aboriginal title to the land, and a stable prosperous existence was once again a possibility. What was more, the Nor'Westers were now on the defensive, harassed by the Hudson's Bay Company in the trading districts and by Selkirk in the courts. They retaliated on both fronts, of course, but the strains upon the loose federation of North West partnerships were beginning to weaken its entire fabric.

One source of discomfort for the Nor'Westers, perhaps the most serious because it jeopardized their profits, was the escalation of fur trade competition between 1815 and 1819. Athabasca was still the Eldorado of the trade, and any Hudson's Bay Company activity in this district was cause for concern. The end of the Napoleonic wars in Europe had stimulated the revival of fur markets and Colvile's economies had worked wonders in London. The London committee was now emboldened to tweak the Canadian giant's nose, however expensive the adventure might be in the short run, in the hope that the Bay company might multiply its share of the trade in the longer term.

The Hudson's Bay Company's Athabasca campaign was specifically designed to carry the battle into the enemy stronghold. When Colin Robertson was forced to remain in Red River to supervise the rebuilding of the shaken settlement in 1815, responsibility for the enterprise was placed in the hands of John Clarke, a determined but less able trader. He took his party north to Lake Athabasca and there founded Fort Wedderburn. Unfortunately, Clarke had contemptuously refused to 'drag grease' (pemmican) into Athabasca.[17] His men set up other posts in the Athabasca region in the summer and fall of 1815, but then, recognizing that they were dangerously short of food, they attempted to return to the Peace River country. In a case of extraordinary cruelty, however, North West Company officers prevented the contact between Indians and Bay men that might have meant an exchange of goods for food; in the end, 16 Bay employees suffered a horrible death by starvation, 13 of them during a desperate attempt to reach Lake Athabasca. Clarke barely survived the winter by collecting frozen berries, according to his own report, but he lived to lead another badly planned expedition the following summer, though this time no deaths resulted from his failures. The Hudson's Bay Company did not give up on Athabasca or the competition easily, however, and in 1818 it sent a huge force under Colin Robertson, including 26 officers and 160 men, into the fray. With the advantage of an early start and 'mischances' that he left along the Nor'Westers' portages, Robertson cut into North West trading territory in decisive fashion. Not only did the Montreal company suffer trading losses in 1818–19 but it suffered also the indignity of having seven North West wintering partners and a number of servants arrested as their canoes filed through the Grand Rapids of the Saskatchewan; their captor, Hudson's Bay trader William Williams, had arranged a small cannon on a barge and another cannon and two swivel guns below the rapids. Confronted with this remarkable arsenal as they emerged from the portage through the

woods, the Nor'Westers could only surrender. The arrests constituted a crippling blow to the North West Company trade operations
and to the company's prestige as the dominant force in the district.

The so-called Athabasca War was expensive and dangerous to
both parties, but it was only one of a number of problems that
plagued the fur companies in the years after 1816. The issues were
especially serious for the North West Company because the customary tension between the Montreal agents and the winterers
(which harkened back to the flare-up in 1795–1804) was exacerbated
by the extremely competitive and therefore costly trade wars, by
kidnapping and assault, and, perhaps worst of all, by the excesses
that had led to the death of innocent traders, labourers, and settlers
both in the trade districts and at Red River. The arrest of the seven
wintering partners on the Saskatchewan in 1819 also hurt morale.
Looming behind all these matters was the need to establish a new
partnership agreement for the Company before the season of 1822.
The Nor'Westers were in trouble because their financial structure,
which called for the annual distribution of profits, did not permit
the establishment of a reserve fund and thus worked against the
wintering partners in years when the company experienced losses.
Though the 1820 gathering between winterers and Montreal agents
at Fort William was uneventful on the surface, since it arranged as
usual for the dispatch of the Athabasca brigades, it was significant
for one great omission, the failure to reach a decision on the renewal
of the partnership. This time, the heated arguments between winterers and agents inspired the former to appoint a special delegation, consisting of John McLoughlin and Angus Bethune, to travel
to London to negotiate a new deal with either or both of the North
West agents and the Hudson's Bay Company in 1820–1.

If the wintering partners were losing their stomach for rough
tactics and financial setbacks, the British Colonial Office was equally
dismayed by the continual outbreaks of violence and the welter of
legal disputes that Selkirk and the two companies had inspired.
Slowly but surely, despite an initial bias in favour of the politically
powerful Nor'Westers, the government came to recognize that fault
lay on both sides. The report of William Coltman, a commissioner
sent from Canada to investigate the Seven Oaks tragedy, was a
perceptive analysis of the situation: the colony, and the entire western interior, had experienced not criminal acts by individuals but
violent incidents in a 'private war' between two trading empires,
Coltman concluded, and therefore 'common sense required not so

much the prosecution of individuals as the restoration of order and the pacification of the parties.'[18] But before this view could prevail, a confusing series of court cases had begun in Quebec, in Montreal, and in Toronto, the whole marked by 'connivance, laxity, ignorance and prejudice,' as the historian E.E. Rich has commented.[19] The publication of a parliamentary Blue Book 'Relating to the Red River settlement 1815–1819' further emphasized the need for new solutions. Thus, the financial and personnel problems of the North West Company, the inadequacy of Canadian law and administration, the violence within the western interior, and the injury to the interests of both investors and Indians precipitated British government support for a compromise agreement.

The death of Lord Selkirk smoothed the way. He had worked tirelessly for the interests of his colonists in 1817 and had returned to the Canadian provinces to answer charges arising from the confused legal situation. But after the first series of cases had been heard in Quebec and Montreal in 1818, the whole business had been shifted to Upper Canada and recommenced from the beginning. Selkirk was bothered by ill-health and, rather than sit through the entire proceedings again, retired in despair to England and thence, his health deteriorating, journeyed south through France; at a villa in the graceful gentleman's retreat of Pau, within sight of the mist-shrouded Pyrenees, he died in April 1820. He was buried in a modest grave in the nearby village of Orthez, far from the hills of Scotland and the plains of the western interior the destiny of which he had so much affected. And the legal cases that had tried his patience and absorbed his capital lingered on and then collapsed, one by one, in obscure or irrelevant conclusions.

With Selkirk gone and balance sheets and government officials demanding attention, negotiations for a compromise proceeded apace in London during the winter of 1820–1. McLoughlin and Bethune represented eighteen wintering partners; Edward Ellice and William McGillivray acted for the London and Montreal agents; Colvile, Deputy Governor John Henry Pelly, and others acted for the Hudson's Bay Company. Where so many previous talks had foundered, these had the advantage of urgency and also of a sense of generosity, especially on the part of Colvile and Pelly. A new Hudson's Bay Company was the result.

The conclusion could not have been surpassed in its wisdom and tact. The 'coalition' managed to marry the administrative and financial stability of the chartered company to the field experience and flexibility of the Nor'Westers. The annual profits 'were to be divided into one hundred shares: twenty to the Hudson's Bay Company proprietors, twenty to the North West Company proprietors, forty to the traders in the field, and the remaining twenty split between Selkirk's heirs, Simon McGillivray and Edward Ellice (to compensate for the loss of their London agency), and a reserve fund.'[20] Though a compromise board was originally supposed to govern the company, this plan was dropped within three years and the old London committee, to which only Edward Ellice of the North West agents was appointed, resumed its position as the chief governing body of the corporation. The London organization of the Hudson's Bay Company and its charter rights to the soil of Rupert's Land remained inviolate and to these were added, by royal licence, a monopoly of the fur trade in the rest of British North America (excluding Upper and Lower Canada and Rupert's Land) for twenty-one years. Fifty-three traders were selected to become partners in the company (25 senior men as chief factors and 28 junior officers to be known as chief traders) and to share 40 per cent of the profits; 32 of these partners were chosen from the ranks of the North West Company, an appropriate but not extraordinary recognition of the greater size and experience of the Montreal operation. And, as in the old Montreal company, the chief factors were to meet once a year to determine policy, promotions, and other matters of interest to the trade. The new operation also abandoned Fort William as the depot of the trade, and thus, as William McGillivray wrote, 'the fur trade is forever lost to Canada.' But the decision in favour of the Hudson Bay route was obvious, and the 'snug business' of the agents who brought in supplies through Montreal was consequently forfeited.[21]

The powers of the London committee of the Hudson's Bay Company and the interests of the wintering partners of the North West Company were preserved. The Montreal agents won handsome financial rewards, but their power was eroded beyond rescue. And, with the ascendancy of a new North American administrator of the Hudson's Bay Company, George Simpson, which was consolidated with amazing speed between 1820 and 1826, the London committee found that its authority over the western interior was virtually unimpaired for the next twenty-odd years.

The problems faced by the new Hudson's Bay Company may have seemed less serious than the hurdles that had just been cleared, but they were none the less daunting to the administrators and traders who began to pick up the pieces after a generation of bitter competition. There were still opponents of the company to be faced on the periphery of its territory: American and Canadian traders in the eastern forests of the continent; the American Fur Company south of the forty-ninth parallel in the western interior; and Americans and Russians along the Pacific coast. A huge surplus of trading personnel would have to be handled with tact once the duplicated effort was eliminated. The Indians, who had grown accustomed to high prices and plentiful gifts, would have to adjust to the new situation. Even the ecology of fur-bearing animals would have to be considered carefully because over-trapping had exhausted the fur and food resources of some areas. And, of course, fierce enemies, men who had harassed and fought and even killed for their company's advantage, would now have to learn to live and work together as colleagues in a common cause. But if the tasks were considerable, they were mastered with remarkable ease.

To understand the fur trade of the western interior in the half-century after 1821, one must start with the 'Little Emperor' of the Hudson's Bay Company domain. More than anyone else, George Simpson dominated the history of the epoch. As E.E. Rich concluded, Simpson was 'shrewd, purposeful, and little troubled by scruples'; according to Glyndwr Williams, he 'brought to his task a combination of energy, administrative ability and capacity for reasoned judgement rare in the fur trade.' He had a prodigious memory for business detail, an extraordinary ability to see beyond the ledger books and inventories to the vital broader patterns that affected policy and required decisions, a cold and even ruthless standard by which he measured his subordinates, a passionate devotion to the affairs of the company that can be seen as admirable but also as repellent, a prodigious enthusiasm for work and travel, and a smiling geniality that could charm a business acquaintance or an important politician in the wink of an eye.[22]

Simpson took the trade operations in hand with remarkable speed, considering that in all his thirty-five years he had never been more than an able clerk and accountant in Colvile's sugar-importing firm and had probably never before visited North America. Within a year of his arrival in 1820, he had been named governor of the vast Northern Department (its boundaries were Hudson Bay, the Arctic and Pacific oceans, and the Missouri Valley) and had commenced the task of reconciliation and reorganization. His first formal joint banquet of the great traders, held at York Factory in October 1821 (coinciding with the birth of a daughter to his metis companion, Margaret Taylor), was a showcase for his powers of diplomacy. At the formal dinner in the great hall, two long narrow tables were set for the seventy-three guests. Alexander McDougall was to sit across from Alexander Kennedy; they had not been close, to put it mildly, since 1813, when they had fought a duel at Swan River. McDougall 'was just sufficiently master of himself to spit, not on the table but on the floor,' as a witness recalled, and 'it was "dollars to dough-nuts" ... whether the entertainment would be a "feed" or "fight."' But there were peacemakers, among whom Simpson was supreme: 'The two sections of the guests, at summons of the bell, entered the great hall in silence, and kept wholly apart until the new governor moving in the throng with bows, smiles and introduction, brought about some conversation or handshaking between individuals.'[23]

Poise was partnered with firmness. Simpson pressed older officers to retire, fired recent recruits and traders who were judged incompetent, and slashed wages with such vigour that even the London committee winced. There was method in his fierce decisions. The lower wage scale permitted a reduction in price levels, which had been pushed up during the years of competition, and thus partially soothed the irritation of the employees who could buy goods only at the company store; and the new scale also encouraged an enthusiasm for economy that was Simpson's trademark. He reduced the flow of alcohol to the Indians, and, to compensate for the loss of this important gift and trade item, he instituted a 'more generous regular standard of trade.'[24] He experimented, largely without advantage, in the use of new transportation routes and wherever possible replaced canoes with boats, which were larger and thus more economical and reliable. Always, it seemed, he was racing to the next post, in a beautiful light canoe manned by a picked crew of at least a dozen voyageurs whose powerful paddling and rhythmic singing left an impression on so many observers; and in the middle of the canoe, ornate snuff box nearby, an amanuensis often at his side, ready to devour the account books and quiz the trader, sat the emperor himself.

No one man could run the trade single-handedly, and behind Simpson the council of chief factors and the London committee continued to operate as a kind of company government. The former became a weak institution, useful chiefly as a forum for discussion and for assessment of personnel, but the British directors always kept a firm hand on administrative matters. Thus, though Simpson embodied the company to North American observers, having assumed control of all the company operations on this continent in 1826, he was still subject to the oversight of the great capitalists of the City. The principles by which they operated were fixed and sure: in the areas safe from competition, trapping was to be carefully controlled, the Indians were to be treated fairly, even with paternal care, and profits must certainly be high; in the areas where competition was intense, opponents must be beaten off whatever the cost.

It would be wrong to treat the company trade success as simply the product of the monopoly granted by royal charter in 1670 and by royal licence in 1821. The company secured control of trade in its territory and beat off incursions by reliance 'on its business efficiency rather than on its charter rights.' Had it been unable to compete, as was demonstrated by the expansion of the French between 1680 and 1760 and by the dominance of the Montrealers between 1770 and 1821, it would have suffered commensurately. Its victories after 1821 testified to the business acumen of its leaders, its officers, and its men.[25]

One crucial area that concerned the company in the decades after coalition was the district west of the Rocky Mountains: Columbia (which extended from the valley of the Columbia River to the Pacific, including Vancouver Island) and New Caledonia (from the Russian territory north of Sitka south through the Queen Charlotte Islands to the upper reaches of the Fraser River). This had been a North West Company preserve during the first decades of the century when Simon Fraser had descended the river now bearing his name and when David Thompson had carefully explored the northern reaches of the Columbia River. Control of the southern trade had been contested by John Jacob Astor's American Fur Company, which founded Fort Astoria at the mouth of the Columbia in 1811, but the Nor'Westers took over the post two years later and again assumed dominance in the area. To the north, in the district below Alaska, the Russian American Fur Company was active, and though it remained close to the coast it attracted the trade of Indians well into the interior. In their attempts to compete effectively, the Nor'Westers had shipped goods from Montreal, an expensive and time-consuming business, but their solutions to the problems of transportation and to the uneasy state of Indian diplomacy in the area had never been entirely satisfactory. Thus, the new company inherited significant difficulties in the district west of the mountains, both in the southern territory around the Columbia and in the northern coast and interior, where a reorganized Russian opposition provided serious competition.

In the south, where the British-American boundary convention of 1818 (renewed in 1827) gave free access to citizens of both countries for a ten-year period, the company concluded that profits would never be large and that the country should be 'trapped out' – the fur resources totally exhausted – in order to create a cordon sanitaire and thus to discourage incursions by American traders into the more valuable territories further north. This was the object of the successful Snake River expeditions by Peter Skene Ogden and John Work (1824–32). Under their cover, the company withdrew north of the Columbia and awaited the results of the boundary negotiations, which they assumed would leave much if not all of the Columbia department in American hands.

New Caledonia was more important to the company, but the means of successfully operating in the wilds of the interior and of competing against the Russian and American free traders on the coast were not easily settled. Chief Factor Dr John McLoughlin, a great bear of a man and the most powerful figure west of the Rockies, wanted to establish posts at a number of strategic locations; Simpson preferred to use ships. McLoughlin liked to buy out American competitors or use them as agents in the trade; Simpson preferred to undersell them until they were driven from the scene in ruin. These disagreements remained beneath the surface of their friendly or at least polite relations in the 1820s and 1830s, when the company enjoyed trading rights as far north as 54°40′ by virtue of an agreement with the Russians, and appeared on the road to peaceful solution when in 1839 the company won the further concession of a ten-year lease on trade in the Russian portion of the Alaska panhandle. Unfortunately, just when a company monopoly on coastal trade from the Columbia to Alaska seemed to have ironed out their differences, Simpson and McLoughlin had a falling out over other questions of policy and over the tragic murder of McLoughlin's son in 1841. Though too much can be made of the personal feud, it coincided with and complicated the difficult conditions that the company faced in the crucial decade of the 1840s.

Of the new complications, the most important was the arrival of increasing numbers of American settlers in the so-called Oregon Territory, particularly in the rich Willamette Valley south of the Columbia. In this era of American western expansion – this was the decade of decision for Texas and California too – Oregon fever became a factor in American politics. It produced demands in Washington for annexation of the northwest (the slogan '54°40' or fight' fuelled James Polk's successful presidential campaign in 1844) and eventually placed great pressure on the Hudson's Bay Company. So heated was British-American discussion in 1844–5 that war over the Oregon boundary seemed entirely possible. President Polk was confronted with equally pressing problems in Texas and California, however, and preferred to settle the northern boundary issue peacefully in order to be free to 'thrash' his southern neighbour, Mexico. The result was the Oregon Boundary Treaty of 1846, in which the British lost and the Americans gained ground by the decision to extend the prairie boundary line of the forty-ninth parallel to the Pacific.[26] As E.E. Rich concluded, the agreement 'conformed in its essentials to the purpose which the fur-traders had followed from the beginning. They had meant to sacrifice the Columbia Department and to retain and develop New Caledonia. In 1846 the names were changed, but little else. The United States secured Oregon Territory; the British retained British Columbia.'[27]

British North America acquired a Pacific coast line as a result of Nor'Wester and Hudson's Bay Company activity. The significance of the contribution of Thompson, Ogden, McLoughlin, and their colleagues to the development of the region and of Canada cannot be exaggerated. Without access to the Pacific, the history of the northern half of the continent would have taken a very different course.

Red River, too, became a stable flourishing community in the 1820s and 1830s. The coalition permitted the settlers to live in peace, encouraged superfluous servants to retire with their families to a life of farming and hunting in the populated centre, and provided a role for the metis buffalo hunters as provisioners of both Red River and the northern fur trade. In 1821 the population of Red River was about 400, half Scots, one-third Canadians (French), and a few German and Swiss. The latter left within five years but the population of the district multiplied as many of the metis who had been living at Pembina accompanied Cuthbert Grant to St Francois Xavier, twenty miles west of the Forks, there to establish a large settlement that was to be a force in the northwest for the next sixty years.

The European and Canadian population of Red River grew very slowly in the next two decades and reached a total of about 1,000 by the mid-1840s. The Scottish nucleus had been supplemented chiefly by a contingent of English farmers (thirteen families in 1836) and retired English troops with their families (Chelsea pensioners increased the population by 200 in 1848). But the metis population increased so dramatically that by the early 1840s the French-speaking and the English-speaking metis scattered along the banks of the Red and Assiniboine rivers numbered about 6,000, split more or less equally between the two language groups. It was an unusual community because it had so little economic reason to exist, but it survived to become a significant factor in Hudson's Bay Company calculations and in the history of the west. Selkirk's child was healthier than ever he could have expected, though very different from his original vision.

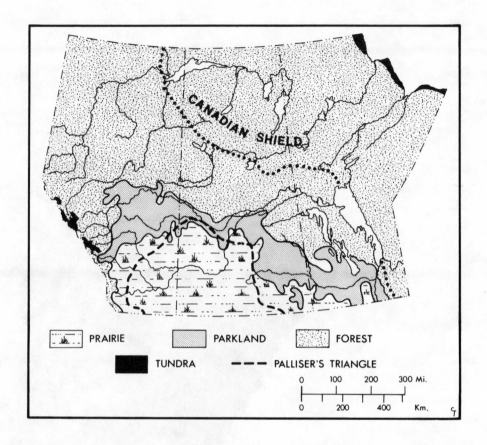

PRAIRIE    PARKLAND    FOREST

TUNDRA    — — — PALLISER'S TRIANGLE

Vegetation of the western interior

Physical features of the prairie west

God's
Lake

BASIN

DRAINAGE

Reindeer
Lake

Lac
la Ronde

Nelson

River

River

River

Cross
Lake

Hayes

500

500

1000

1000

1000

1000

2000

2000

2000

2000

2000

2000

1000

1000

1000

Saskatchewan

River

Cedar
Lake

Lake
Winnipeg

Lake
Winnipegosis

Lake
Manitoba

Assiniboine

River

River

Red

Lake

allaston
Lake

**Elevation**

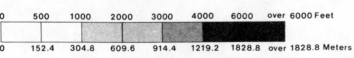

| 0 | 500 | 1000 | 2000 | 3000 | 4000 | 6000 | over 6000 Feet |

| 0 | 152.4 | 304.8 | 609.6 | 914.4 | 1219.2 | 1828.8 | over 1828.8 Meters |

Major drainage divides

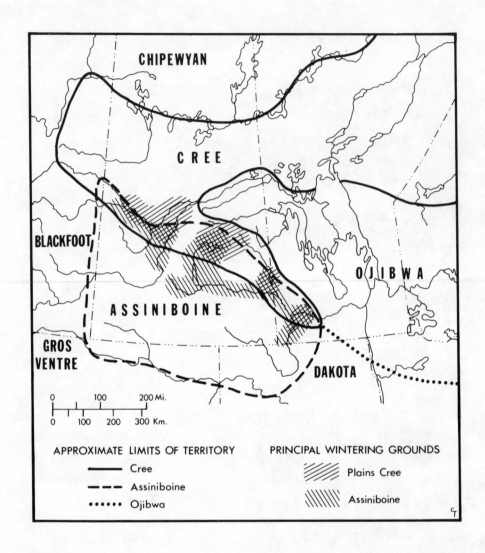

CHIPEWYAN

C R E E

BLACKFOOT

OJIBWA

A S S I N I B O I N E

GROS
VENTRE

DAKOTA

0      100      200 Mi.

0    100    200    300 Km.

APPROXIMATE LIMITS OF TERRITORY

——— Cree

‒ ‒ ‒ Assiniboine

•••••• Ojibwa

PRINCIPAL WINTERING GROUNDS

Plains Cree

Assiniboine

Indian territories of the prairie west ca 1820

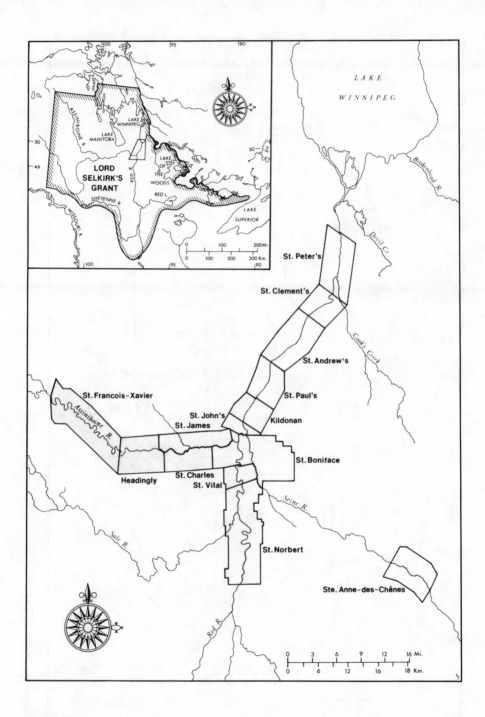

The Red River settlement

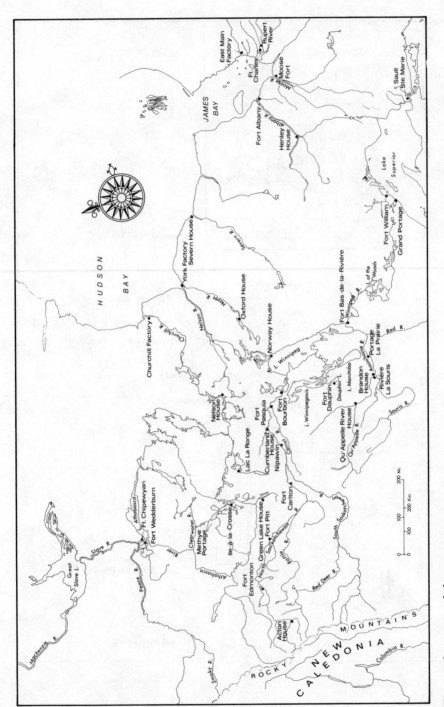

Fur trade posts of the west

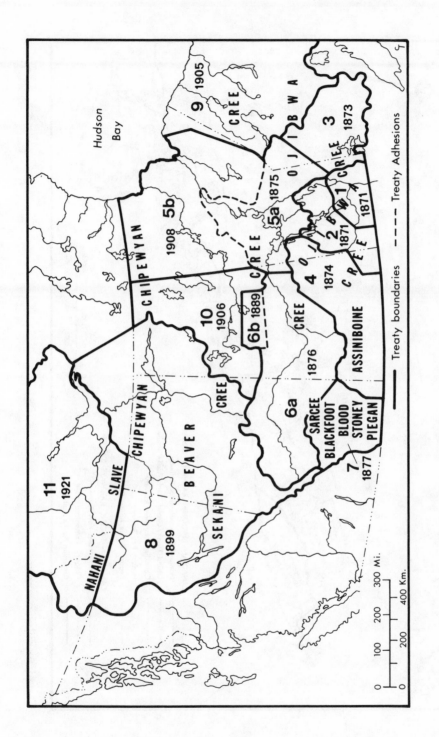

The numbered treaties of western Canada

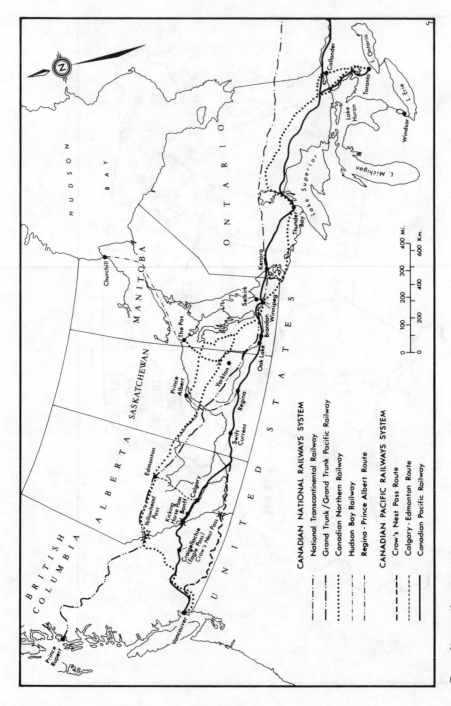

CANADIAN NATIONAL RAILWAYS SYSTEM

.—.—.— National Transcontinental Railway

———— Grand Trunk / Grand Trunk Pacific Railway

············ Canadian Northern Railway

.··.··.·· Hudson Bay Railway

.·.·.·.· Regina - Prince Albert Route

CANADIAN PACIFIC RAILWAYS SYSTEM

– – – – Crow's Nest Pass Route

————— Calgary - Edmonton Route

————— Canadian Pacific Railway

Canadian railway routes

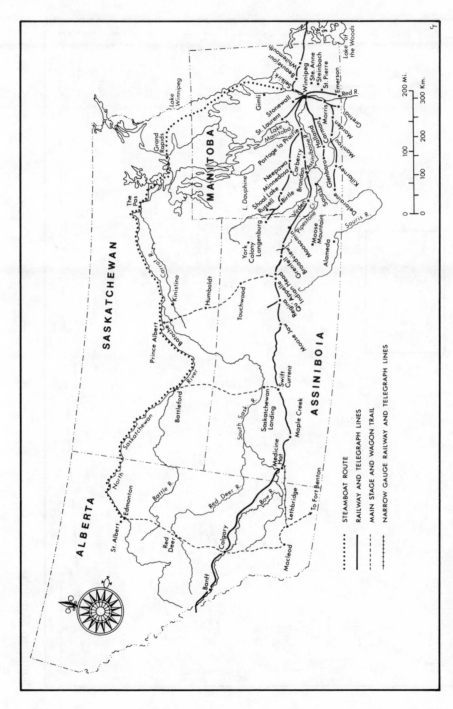

Western Canadian settlement in 1886

........... STEAMBOAT ROUTE

——— RAILWAY AND TELEGRAPH LINES

– – – MAIN STAGE AND WAGON TRAIL

+++++ NARROW GAUGE RAILWAY AND TELEGRAPH LINES

ALBERTA

SASKATCHEWAN

ASSINIBOIA

MANITOBA

Edmonton
St. Albert
Red Deer
Calgary
Banff
Macleod
Lethbridge
To Fort Benton
Medicine Hat
Maple Creek
Swift Current
Saskatchewan Landing
Battleford
Prince Albert
The Pas
Humboldt
Touchwood
Kinistino
York Colony
Langenburg
Qu'Appelle
Indian Head
Grenfell
Moosomin
Broadview
Moose Mountain
Alameda
Virden
Pipestone
Deloraine
Glenboro
Souris
Brandon
Carberry
Holland
Carman
Morris
Stonewall
St. Laurent
Portage la Prairie
Neepawa
Minnedosa
Shoal Lake
Russell
Birtle
Killarney
Manitou
Morden
Gretna
Emerson
St. Pierre
Steinbach
Ste. Anne
Winnipeg
Selkirk
Beausejour
Whitemouth
Gimli
Grand Rapids
Red R.
Lake of the Woods
Lake Winnipeg
Lake Manitoba
L. Dauphine
North Saskatchewan
South Sask. R.
Battle R.
Red Deer R.
Bow R.
Carrot R.
Battle R.
Souris R.
Moose Jaw
Moose Jaw

200 Mi.
300 Km.
100
200
100
0
0

5

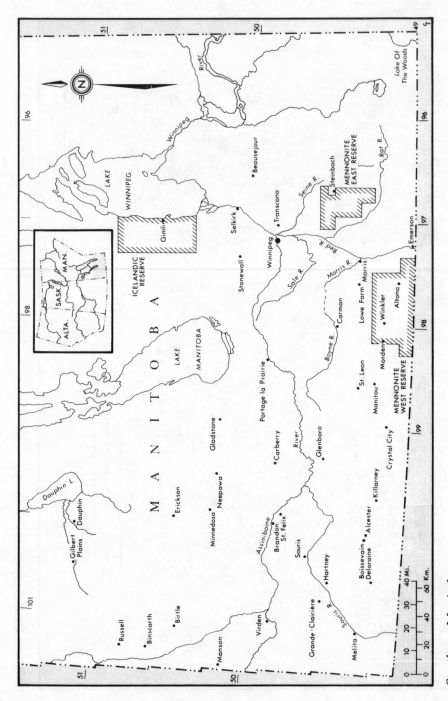

Southern Manitoba

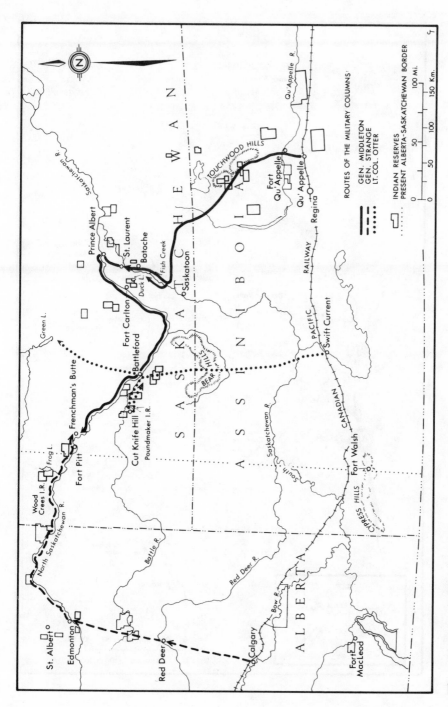

The 1885 North-West uprising

ROUTES OF THE MILITARY COLUMNS:
GEN. MIDDLETON
GEN. STRANGE
LT. COL. OTTER

INDIAN RESERVES
PRESENT ALBERTA-SASKATCHEWAN BORDER

Alberta

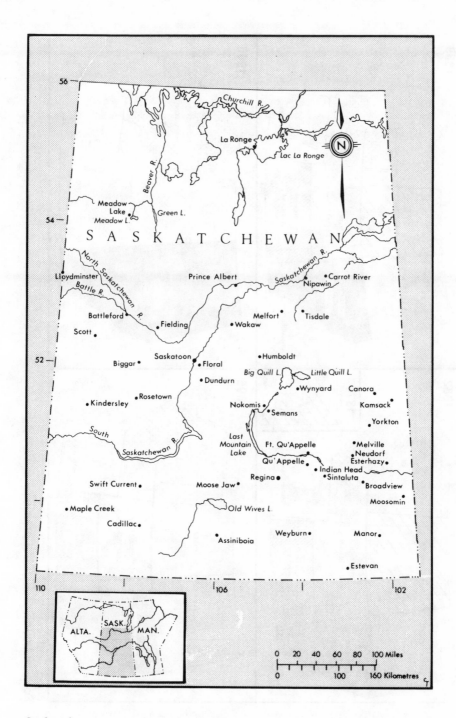

Saskatchewan

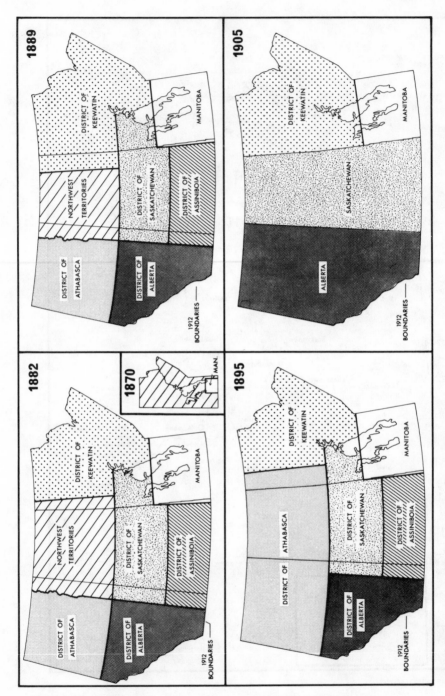

Political boundaries of the prairie west 1870–1912

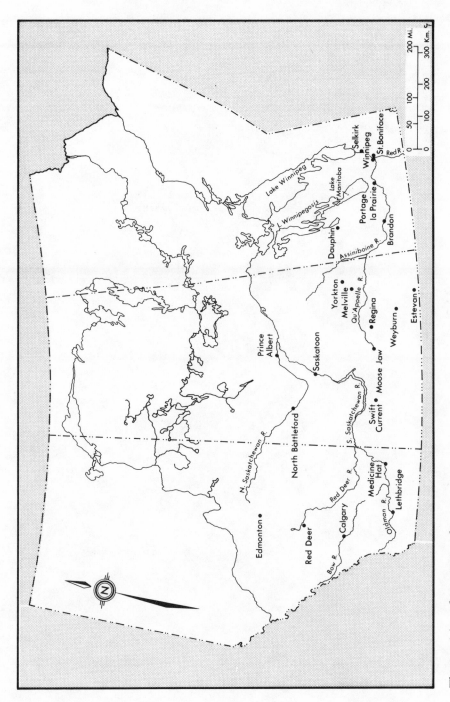

The prairie urban network

# 6

# The metis and the
# Red River settlement
# 1844–70

The prairie west changed dramatically in the last half of the nineteenth century. The 1840s can stand as a dividing line between one era and another. The metis, in particular, were seeking new outlets for their ambitions and energies in that decade. All around them the institutions of European industrial capitalist society were taking root. New ideas such as race, respectability, and progress were becoming current. Attitudes associated with church marriages, illegitimate children, the servant class, and the 'proper' lady were hardening into social conventions. In this changed environment, the children of liaisons between natives and Europeans found themselves at a disadvantage. Nevertheless, they responded to this adversity with the pride and independence of a self-reliant people. In their resistance to the social prejudices of the new order, they were never victorious but they were able at least to win acceptance. In their struggle for a livelihood, they challenged the economic hegemony of the Hudson's Bay Company and won their freedom. As the pressures from outside forces increased, however, they learned that the expansion of European settlement in North America was irresistible. Thus, when a political crisis finally was precipitated in Red River in 1869, they seized Upper Fort Garry and attempted to direct the Canadian annexation of the region.

Measurement of the change in prairie society can take many forms. Perhaps the simplest index to the new order was the health of the buffalo hunt. In the 1830s, the Crees and Assiniboines and Blackfoot were still in command of the northern hunt, harvesting as much as they wished and selling great quantities of hides and pemmican to the fur companies. In the 1840s and 1850s, the Red River metis challenged Indian hegemony and probably became the most important processors of pemmican for the Hudson's Bay Company trade. By the 1860s, both Indians and metis were travelling farther and farther west in search of buffalo herds and were coming into conflict over this once seemingly infinite resource. By the end of the 1870s, the herds had disappeared forever. The Indians were on reserves, the metis in disarray, the whites in control.

Another measure of the transition was the mode of employment in the region. At the start of this era, most Indians hunted and travelled according to the rhythms of the seasons and the demands of the resource cycle, pausing to fit in the hunting, trapping, or trading that would supply the necessary ammunition and a few luxuries at the European posts. Some Indians and many more metis participated to a limited degree in the wage labour system of the Hudson's Bay Company. They divided their time between the hunt and the company, hiring on for specific periods – a boat run or a cart brigade or for spring packing – as contract labour. In these circumstances, they were paid a credit in the company's account books that would be spent on trade goods during the following months. This labour system might be described as typical of a non-industrial society and, in its informal work discipline and rough measures of time, not far removed from that of the casual farm labourer or cottage artisan in seventeenth-century England. If this system was common in the 1840s, it was in retreat in the 1880s. By then, Winnipeg newspapers were listing daily and weekly variations in wage rates for such narrowly defined skills as machinists, boilermakers, and pipefitters. Private employment agencies had sprung up along the main streets of the city to provide a meeting place for jobseeker and employer. The labourer now was responsible for his keep, whether on or off the job. His overhead, including food, clothing, and shelter for himself and his family, was solely his responsibility. No longer would the community – the trading post, the parish, and the hunting group – accept collective responsibility for his survival. And he discovered that, due to the migration of workers and the rise and fall of work projects, he would henceforth ride the economic roller-coaster of boom and bust. As the economist H. Clare Pentland would have put it, the labourer had been present at the creation of the capitalistic labour market in western Canada.[1]

A striking transition comparable to that of the hunt and the labour market also occurred in the prairie attitude to property. In native cultures, property was moveable and, to a considerable degree, held in common. But, as the experience of the Ojibwas demonstrated, the increasing pressure on game resources forced the hunting bands east of Red River to recognize 'private' family hunting territories in the second quarter of the nineteenth century. The development of conflict between metis and Crees over access to buffalo hunting grounds near Qu'Appelle in the 1850s and 1860s could be seen, too, as a dispute over resource control. The economist Irene Spry has suggested that this phase of dispute over resources marked the transition from a 'common' to an 'open access' property system – from a perception that resources belonged to all and should be shared to one with the governing principle 'first come, first served.' No sooner was this new idea introduced than it was obsolete. The arrival of increasing numbers of settlers and the necessity of government treaties with the Indians made inevitable the introduction of a third approach to land and resources – that of private property. Henceforth, one could possess the land and the water, the animals and the plants; one could require that others not 'trespass' or 'steal'; if even land was to be in short supply, one could make rules to ensure that the first in the race – the shrewd and the competitive – would be rewarded.[2] As the victors would have explained, those who lost did so because they lacked moral fibre or, more simply, because they arrived too late.

These fundamental changes in labour and property relations were irresistible because they were aspects of a technological and economic revolution that encompassed the globe. They were accompanied by equally profound changes in the way humans regarded each other. The consequences of this aspect of the great transformation are still, a century later, poisoning social relations in the prairie west. One recalls how easily men from Europe and women from native communities established families in the eighteenth century and set up new institutions – marriage arrangements, economic roles, and distinctive artistic expressions such as architecture and costume – that accommodated an intermingling of peoples.

As late as 1840, when Letitia Hargrave arrived at York Factory to be the wife of that post's leading officer, she could exclaim at the sympathy and the support she found among the metis women with whom she associated. Changes in race and class perceptions were already evident among the fur traders, however, and Letitia soon saw things differently. What pure-bred gentlewoman from bourgeois England would willingly consort with people who were born out of wedlock or had had several spouses or were only steps removed from the life of Indians? By 1848, Letitia was writing that her friend Isobel Finlayson, the English-born sister-in-law of Nicol Finlayson, would be 'in agony' because Nicol, having had 'two distinct families' in his first twenty-five years in the fur trade, was about to marry a metis girl and presumably start a third. Five years later, while in Sault Ste Marie, Letitia told a correspondent that she herself was in agony: 'We expect Wemyss Simpson and his wife here on Monday. I hate the very thought of a half breed visitor.' Letitia had learned about 'racial differences' in the intervening years and had been lectured to about respectability and the sanctity of the family. Now she had relegated her former friends to an inferior status.[3]

Letitia's change of heart originated in changing conceptions of race and class and, to an equal degree, in the missionary activity sponsored by the British churches. Race, class, and religion were as powerful as guns and trade in shaping the British Empire. The new racial perspective was a product of nineteenth-century scholarship, an offshoot of Darwin's work on the origins of life and of the new discipline of anthropology. But it was also a product of the political crises of the era, including the debates over slavery and concerns about 'miscegenation.' At the foundation of the new racial stereotypes was the eclipse of the Enlightenment's ideal of the 'noble savage' and the widespread acceptance of another eighteenth-century notion concerning 'stages of civilization.' The assumption that humankind had developed progressively through a sequence of cultural stages from 'savagery' and 'barbarism' to the highest rank – Victorian England – might be viewed as optimistic. At the least, this outlook, known as monogenesis, suggested that all members of the human family had a common origin and that the alleged 'childlike' character of some groups was due to isolation rather than to biological inferiority.

Though it denied the competing claims of polygenesis, which posited the biological inferiority of some 'races,' the monogenesis argument reinforced popular perceptions of 'savagery' and 'civili-zation' and contributed to uneasiness among Red River citizens. Theories of 'racial miscegenation,' which suggested that marriage between 'races' damaged the blood stock of the superior race, must have circulated from time to time, and so too would such innova-tions as phrenology or cranium measurement, which was presumed by some to be an index to brain capacity and to vary among the 'races.' Where there was talk of division within the human family based on 'blood' or 'race,' there would inevitably have been gossip about individual and family attributes. In the string of little villages that was the northwest, such talk could divide the community. Was it any wonder that James Ross, the bright young Red River boy who had been sent to the University of Toronto for advanced studies, should react like a wounded child to this gossip? As he wrote to his sister: 'What if mama is an Indian! ... Remember the personal quali-ties that ought to endear mama to us. Who more tender-hearted? Who more attached to her children ...? What avail those accom-plishments in etiquette and fussy nonsense of which she happens to be destitute?' 'Race,' as Ross's outburst suggested and his failure to write to his mother may have indicated, was an explosive notion.[4]

The second aspect of Letitia Hargrave's change of heart concerned her prejudices about social class. She had been raised in a protected environment in the 1820s and 1830s when Britain was itself dis-covering new perspectives on society. Amid the shifting fortunes of the rising industrial and commercial bourgeoisie, the struggling landed gentry, and the impoverished slum dwellers and farm labourers, she and her prosperous contemporaries learned that suc-cess – money and advancement – went to the strong. Conversely, weakness – sloth, irresolution, inability to control one's passions – brought poverty and misery in its wake. In the perspective of Letitia's family, the best human qualities included aggression, com-petitiveness, and a willingness to work; their reward was the badge of respectability. What could one make of these tenets in the declin-ing fur trade world of the western interior? Surely the officers of the trade must fight to maintain their rank and their wealth. Surely their wives must assist them by establishing solid respectable households and by inculcating tried and true British values in their children. Just as metis and Indians were said to be inferior to British officers be-cause of their race, so labourers and canoemen were alleged to be inferior because of their status. Neither Indian nor labourer possessed the necessary qualities to succeed in the Victorian world. The Hargraves did. By emphasizing competition and survival of the fittest, these intensely moral and self-critical individuals created an intolerant and even violent empire. Not only the 'lesser races' but also the 'lesser classes' bore the brunt of the bourgeois crusade to improve humanity and of the bourgeois commitment to self-preservation.[5]

The Bible was said to be the secret of England's greatness in the Victorian era. If Red River was representative, there was truth behind the slogan. British missionaries helped to develop new rules of comportment in many colonial outposts, and despite the variable fortunes of business and war their influence over colonial social structure was considerable. One could argue that British versions of Christian doctrine provided the crucial vehicle by which divisive notions about race and class were introduced throughout the empire.

In Red River, the Hudson's Bay Company was as important as the church in introducing the new mores. George Simpson, the company's governor, who confined the metis to unskilled labour, had no qualms about accepting race-based assessments of the local population. And, as one who believed in the superiority of European males, he apparently treated native women with contempt and hypocrisy, casually exploiting them as mistresses while describing them as 'bits of brown,' 'fluff,' or 'my commodity.' His marriage to his delicate and beautiful English cousin, Frances, and her subsequent brief stay in Red River, where she was isolated from native society for fear that she might encounter evidence of George's earlier life, introduced racial considerations into the marriage decisions of fur trade officers. But even Simpson's influence would have been fleeting had it not been for the constant labour of the missionaries, especially those of the Anglican Church Missionary Society, to reform and to Christianize the northwest. Their watchwords were 'permanent' settlement, as opposed to Indian movement through the seasonal resource cycle and metis travel on the hunt, and 'Christian' families, as opposed to either native marriages or the unchurched liaisons – however stable – of the fur trade. The missionaries were consistent in their teachings, relentless in the establishment of new schools and churches, and disputatious when issues that affected marriage, baptisms, and the hunt threatened their ideals. Though it was not their goal to create race and class divisions, this was the result of their work.[6]

Perceptions of race, class, and religion sustained numerous social divisions in Red River. Alexander Ross, the literate and moral patriarch of a mixed-blood fur trade clan, argued that his group, the English-speaking metis and the Scots settlers, were part of a 'European or agricultural party' and thus closer to 'civilization.' In contrast, he said, the French-speaking metis, who continued to travel far afield on the hunt or on trading expeditions, were veering toward 'the native or aboriginal party.' French metis informants might have distinguished between their group and the Ojibwas by reference to their own literacy and their adherence to the Roman Catholic church. The Anglican parson's wife, Mrs Cockran, might have claimed that her race placed her in a separate category from the Anglican metis and that her religion placed her on a higher plane from the French Roman Catholics. High-ranking fur trade officers such as George Simpson might slight Mrs Cockran, in turn, because she was a 'dolly-mop' who excelled only in conversation about 'the scouring of pots and pans' – in other words, she did not share their bourgeois sense of refinement. Roman Catholics knew in their hearts that they alone belonged to the true church. Most fundamental, no doubt, were the social divisions based upon differences of language, occupation, and place of residence. The unique French-Ojibwa or French-Cree dialect of the metis, the sharp contrast between a full-time farmer and a hunter-trader, and the undoubted distance between a Catholic parish such as Ste Anne and a Protestant parish such as Kildonan all separated the citizens of the settlement. And yet, if the extended village of Red River seemed divided against itself, why had it not experienced riots and petty assaults? Perhaps the stability of the community had yet to be tested.

The state of the economy would have had a bearing on the public peace. For the metis, who had become the single largest group in Red River, the strict regulations of the Hudson's Bay Company did present obstacles to their economic well-being in the 1830s and 1840s. An obvious economic activity for the metis was employment in the company, and dozens of young men entered the company's service after 1821. Few of these appointments, however, were to the officer category. Rather, the metis were placed in the ranks of the labourers and were expected to man boats, build posts, hunt provisions, tend horses, chop wood, cut hay, and perform the countless other tasks associated with jacks-of-all-trades in any non-industrial society. Between 100 and 200 metis would have been employed, whether on seasonal contracts or on two- to three-year engagements, in 1830, accounting for about one-fourth of the servant-level employees, and this proportion rose to about one-half of the larger employee total in the 1850s. In addition to these 'unskilled' employees, about eighty metis were hired as apprentices in the skilled trades (including carpenters, blacksmiths, tinsmiths, boatbuilders) between 1830 and 1866, an average of about two per year. These boys, who were required to be at least fourteen years of age, signed a seven-year contract as they would have done in the British apprenticeship system and were paid £8 per annum to start and about £15 per annum at the end of their term. As is obvious, the unskilled and skilled positions did not promote the metis into the officer ranks of the company. Company policy was to regard the metis community as a labour pool for the lower ranks. According to Governor Simpson, 'If brought into the Service at a sufficiently early period of life they will become useful steady Men and taking all things into consideration I think they will be found the cheapest and best servants we can get.'[7]

Though the company provided satisfactory employment opportunities for many male children of former servants, especially for young men without families, it did not offer an outlet for the ambitious – or for the children of the ambitious. In earlier decades, many metis had risen into the officer ranks; these retired gentlemen, who possessed large estates in Red River and, in several cases, considerable wealth, wanted their children to have equal opportunities. Similarly, Europeans who had married natives of the country, whether Indians or metis, expected that their offspring would rise to positions of power. And yet, as the Scot James Sutherland (himself a former chief factor) discovered, his racially mixed children were doomed to inferior status: 'I am very much at a loss how to settle my Sons. I have now four Sons at the house with me the two Oldest are now men fit for any duty but in this part of the World there is no opportunity for young People to push themselves forward in any way, better than Labourers, either as farmers or Boat men, in the Co's Service, and either way they can barely make a living – my two youngest sons has now a better Education than I had when I came to this Country yet it will be of no use to them as they cannot employ it beneficially.'[8]

The company, and Simpson in particular, did not bend in this matter. Despite the protests of disappointed fathers, the company's only concession was to create a new position for the metis, apprentice postmaster, at the bottom of the administrative hierarchy and below the level of apprentice clerk, the usual starting point for Europeans, at £20 per annum. Twenty of the 21 young men who were hired at this rank were metis, 19 were the children of officers; two-thirds of the group (14) eventually reached the level of clerk (£40 to £50 per annum) and 3, all children of Chief Factor Richard Hardisty, eventually became officers and won a regular share of the company profits which would amount to £250–£500 per year for a chief trader in the 1850s. Aside from this route, which began at the race-based position of apprentice postmaster, only a handful of metis moved into the officer rank. When we recall that the population of the northwest was overwhelmingly native – there were almost no 'European' children in the territory – and that almost all the officers were imported from outside, the frustration of the metis takes on some importance.[9]

The best alternative for able young men was to embark on a trading career outside the monopoly company, a path that was followed by several in the 1820s and 1830s. To Governor Simpson's dismay, this private trade got out of hand. Andrew McDermot and James Sinclair were primarily responsible for the crisis, but, had they not been in Red River, another ambitious trader would have precipitated a fight. McDermot and Sinclair conducted retail operations in Red River, exported tallow to Britain, and traded in the territory's staple, furs, with the Hudson's Bay Company.[10] To their chagrin, they became entangled in American competition with the company. In the summer of 1844, Norman Kittson, an American businessman, set up a trading post at Pembina, just inside American territory on the Red River, not more than seventy miles from the Upper Fort, and began to deal in furs. Though the economics of the competing shipping routes through Hudson Bay and the American eastern seaboard probably still favoured the chartered company, the very existence of an alternate market and source of supply naturally attracted some of the metis.[11] Simpson's fierce reaction, which threatened to destroy the McDermot and Sinclair business operations in the tallow and freighting trade as well as the American operations in furs, pushed the many Canadian free traders into Kittson's arms.

What had begun as a minor conflict, in which fledgling entrepreneurs flexed their muscles, became a full-blown confrontation between the company and the Red River settlers. And when the colonists enlisted Alexander Isbister, the mixed-blood Rupert's Lander who had become a distinguished figure in London, to present their case to the British government, the quarrel over trade was translated into the language of early Victorian Britain, wherein innocent native confronted guileful merchant, free trade struggled against chartered monopoly, and self-government was resisted by grasping imperialists. The foundation of the company's case thereupon shifted, as E.E. Rich has suggested, 'from the fact of economic subordination to the theory of legal subordination,' and would henceforth depend upon the company's ability to enforce the law. In a world where metis hunters constituted the single most powerful military force, the company's hegemony had become a hollow shell.[12]

A metis trader, Pierre-Guillaume Sayer, provided the symbolic occasion for the test of Hudson's Bay Company power. Between 1846 and 1848, the company had maintained its position with the aid of 300 British regular troops, obtained by Simpson on the pretence that the Oregon boundary crisis threatened to become a general British-American war in western North America. But when the troops and their money departed, to be replaced by pensioned soldiers and their families who were neither awesome nor affluent, the trade dispute arose again. Chief Factor Ballenden, the company administrator, decided to face the issue in the spring of 1849 by arresting four metis, including Sayer, on a charge of illegal trafficking in furs. With the pensioners as his bulwark and the charter of 1670 as his reference, Ballenden went to the General Quarterly Court of Assiniboia to vindicate the Hudson's Bay Company monopoly.

The Sayer trial of 17 May 1849 was an important event in the history of the western fur trade. The metis, whose numbers had not yet been reduced by the departure of the spring hunt and the boat brigades, had organized an informal self-defence committee and were present in large numbers, armed to the teeth, at the Ascension Day mass that coincided with the opening of the court. When, after a number of minor cases involving bootlegging and assault, the defendant Sayer was first called, there was no answer in the subdued court room because the metis were assembled on the opposite bank of the Red River, around the steps of St Boniface Cathedral, listening to Louis Riel sr's call for free trade. But 200 to 300 metis converged on the courthouse after lunch, waving their rifles, shouting defiance, and even threatening to shoot or ride down the court officials. Perhaps because he saw the necessity to keep order, the English-speaking metis James Sinclair became the free traders' spokesman. A jury acceptable to both sides was empanelled – powder horns and shot pouches still at their belts – and Sinclair was appointed as Sayer's counsel. The trial was conducted smoothly and without incident. The evidence clearly demonstrated that Sayer had traded liquor for furs. After a brief recess, the jury found him guilty as charged, though it also recommended mercy on the ground that Sayer had believed the activity was legal. The company's representative, Chief Factor Ballenden, declared his satisfaction with the verdict, accepted the recommendation of mercy, and dropped the charges against Sayer's three companions. On the face of it, Ballenden and the company had won a satisfactory verdict in a fair trial before a representative jury. But, as in any state, law must be supported by force; in Red River, the company's sole basis of support, the pensioners, had not even been called out of their barracks for fear they would be slaughtered by the hunters. Thus, when Sayer emerged from the court to announce that he had been released without punishment, the assembled metis recognized that trade in furs was free: guns were fired in delight rather than anger, and the metis shout became a declaration of the era: 'Vive la liberté! La commerce est libre!'[13]

Alvin Gluek attributes the collapse of the Hudson's Bay Company monopoly to the work of Kittson; Irene Spry, following Governor George Simpson, emphasizes the role of McDermot, Sinclair, and 'the mobility, the restless energy, and the resourcefulness of the native free men of the plains.' It is a small point of difference. The monopoly was broken, and the settlement was no longer subordinated to the company's larger fur trade strategy; Red River had acquired an economic life of its own.[14]

During the following quarter-century, the free traders were active across the entire western interior. Not even Governor Simpson's wooing of Andrew McDermot and James Sinclair (who moved to the Columbia and was shortly thereafter killed in the so-called Indian wars) could halt the growing assault upon the company's position. Fur sales in St Paul rose from $5,000 in 1845 to $40,000 in 1855 and an average of over $150,000 annually in the following seven years. These were the fruits of the free traders. From Fort Alexander on the Winnipeg River to the Qu'Appelle lakes, Fort Edmonton, and even Athabasca, company officers reported the activities of the merchants. And, of course, with the traders came whisky and further disruption of Indian life. By the 1860s, competition for the diminishing buffalo herds was increasing, and metis settlements, at first wintering stations but soon permanent communities, were forming nearer the western buffalo grounds in the Cypress Hills, in the upper Saskatchewan River territory (near St Albert and Victoria), and on the South Saskatchewan River (at Batoche and St Laurent). With the gradual development of this fur economy, the metis acquired new occupations, becoming freighters, horse traders, guides, interpreters, and government servants, but the trade in furs, robes, and plains provisions continued to be their favourite and most consistently rewarding enterprise. As with the Indians, so too with the metis, the buffalo and other fur-bearing animals were the underpinnings of their freedom. When James Hector of the Palliser expedition met some of these men in December 1857, they gathered round the fire and spent the long cold evening 'laughing, joking, and playing on the violin'; at this point, the metis seemed to be in control of their destiny.[15]

Once again the metis had won an economic niche for themselves as their forefathers had done in the Great Lakes region a century before. They were the intermediaries, the traders and translators and guides; they were a buffer between European and native. And, as in that earlier incarnation, their viability depended on the continued paramountcy of the fur trade and the hunt. Many metis were travellers and traders, not farmers alone. This relationship between their economic existence and their personal and collective autonomy was crucial. It was also a frail reed in the changing circumstances of mid-century.

While enduring a transformation in economic institutions and social perspectives in the decades around mid-century, the northwest was also undergoing a physical re-examination. We must keep in mind, in surveying this remarkable development, that our perception of the environment is selective. It is influenced, as a geographer has noted, 'not so much by the quality of our vision, as by the visions we have in mind.'[16] So it was in the prairie west. Some saw fertility, others saw deserts. Some revelled in the freedom, others worried about the need for constraints. But, by the 1850s, a consensus was taking shape. The west was perceived increasingly as a land of opportunity and even as a potential agricultural frontier.

The earliest visions of the northwest in the English-speaking world were prepared by Arthur Dobbs in the 1740s and 1750s and by their very optimism created an image of a fertile utopia. Dobbs, a publicist and entrepreneur, was a leader in a campaign to extend British overseas commerce and, more particularly, to abolish the Hudson's Bay Company trade monopoly. Noting that the latitude of the western interior was the same as that of southern Poland or Holland and that, according to contemporary science, latitude determined climate, he claimed that the northwest interior required only 'convenient Houses with stoves' to create habitable settlements similar in nature to those of north-central Europe. From scattered fragments of testimony by fur traders and travellers, Dobbs argued that the interior was well wooded. And, because wooded soils were deemed to be obviously fertile, Dobbs concluded that the region held considerable agricultural potential.[17]

Two contemporaneous situations provide an ironic commentary on Dobbs's estimate of northwest fertility. The first was the extraordinary fact that Dobbs never released to the public his own copy of Henry Kelsey's manuscript journal which described the western interior as an area that contained 'Nothing but short Round sticky grass.' Such a territory could never have been seen as fertile by an Englishman, and thus the Kelsey journals would have defeated Dobbs's campaign. The second testimony was the Hudson's Bay Company explanation of its failure in several agricultural experiments on the icy shores of the Bay: the company attributed its losses not to poor soil or poor climate but rather, because it believed the land had 'layne fallow it may be from Creation,' to the very richness of the land. The soil was so fertile, in other words, that it overwhelmed the seeds and plants![18]

Despite the obvious shortcomings of these long-distance estimates of western agricultural potential, an image of the northwest had been created by Dobbs and his contemporaries: the land stretching from Hudson Bay into the western interior was vast and fertile; it consisted of woodland punctuated by meadows extending for hundreds of miles into the continent and was as suited to agriculture as the plains of northern Europe. The image was not unlike the vision of America conjured up by Crevecoeur a few years later and, like that vision of plenty and opportunity, was to be just the opening phase of a love affair between a land and its propagandists.

The image of fertility and of a hospitable climate was accepted by a number of British writers in the first half of the nineteenth century. Thus, when the Earl of Selkirk described the Red River valley to prospective settlers, he said it contained millions of acres equal in soil and climate to any other such district in British America. And when the railway became a practical means of transportation in the following generation, armchair empire-builders concluded that the western interior would permit the construction of a rapid rail-sea link between Britain and Asia as an underpinning for the global empire. An economic boom was simply assumed by these British propagandists, none of whom had ever visited the land, and the clichés thus flowed from their pens unimpeded: 'pictures of certain prosperity and grandeur and enterprise crowd upon the mind,' according to a tract written in 1850 by F.A. Wilson and A.B. Richards, 'with the prospect of a wilderness peopled – a remote ocean converted to an immediate and familiar high-road.'[19] The actual conditions of soil and climate did not concern these men, whose minds were occupied with higher matters, and so their conclusion, like that of Arthur Dobbs a century before, was a stirring call to duty: for the sake of empire, the northwest must be developed.

If the optimistic picture of the northwest had relied only on such shallow propaganda, it would never have taken a grip on the British public and would have been erased by harsher judgments. But the perception of fertility had much stronger foundations than these empty predictions. One of the most enduring lay in the tradition of imperial adventure fiction which was established in the mid-nineteenth century and reached its apex at the end of Victoria's reign with the writings of Kipling and Henty and Winnipeg's own Ralph Connor. An early practitioner of this genre in Britain was Robert M. Ballantyne, who had served as a junior clerk at York Factory and undoubtedly had been affected by the American wilderness tales of James Fenimore Cooper. Cooper's stories, including *The Pioneers* and *The Last of the Mohicans*, portrayed the noble savage and idyllic wilderness as sympathetically as was possible. Here was the freedom of a life close to nature. Here a man's strength and virtue determined his fate. And here, best of all, was escape from the constraints of polite society and the pressures of an increasingly urban, rapidly industrializing Old World. Ballantyne adapted this genre to the cricumstances of the British Empire and the fur trade of the Hudson's Bay Company. Because he had actually worked in the northwest, unlike many such authors, Ballantyne wrote of the fur trade with authority. He described an 'almost untrodden wilderness' where individuals could leave behind their past mistakes and make a new start. Conditions for the pursuit of excellence, he claimed, were greater there than anywhere else: '"Roughing it" I certainly have been [says Ballantyne's fur trader], inasmuch as I have been living on rough fare, associating with rough men, and sleeping on rough beds under the starry sky; but I assure you, that all this is not half so rough upon the constitution as what they call leading an *easy life*; which is simply a life that makes a poor fellow stagnate, body and spirit, till the one comes to be unable to digest its food, and the other incompetent to jump at so much as half an idea.'[20] This was the stuff that would sustain a western myth in another generation.

Gentlemen travellers reinforced the image created by the writers of fiction and by western painters. Looking for adventure in lands that had not yet succumbed to the machine age, men such as the Earl of Southesk, Viscount Milton, and W.B. Cheadle, and the most exciting prose stylist of them all, Capt William Butler, wrote glowing accounts of the vastness of the territory, the wealth of natural life, and the apparent fertility of the land.[21] Their stirring renditions of life on the margin of empire, as they often put it, emphasized the silence and the loneliness and the beauty of this frontier. For drama, they introduced 'natural' phenomena: the prairie fire, for example, was likened to 'a volcano in full activity,' but it could not be properly described or imitated 'because it is impossible to obtain those gigantic elements from which it derives its awesome splendour.'[22] Above all, they emphasized that the isolation of the region was temporary: by their very presence in the land, as well as by their visions of manor houses on the lip of the Qu'Appelle valley or of farmers on the Portage plains, the gentlemen travellers were saying that this frontier was ready for development. In recording their love of prairie sunsets and mountain shadows, they added another strand to the western tapestry: this was a land of awe-inspiring beauty where one could live life close to the natural order as it had taken shape at the creation. And it was a land whose development by international forces was imminent.

If wilderness could be beautiful, it could also be dangerous. And where Rousseau's conviction that man in nature was good and pure promised a greater society in the new land, the heirs of a conservative and Christian world-view worried rather about the dangers when people escaped the bonds of tradition, ignored the teachings of the church, and lived without such civilizing forces as class, school, and family. Thus the image of natural harmony and grace in the western interior was juxtaposed with a much darker picture of this land. British leaders had yet to hear of the horrors of the Belgian Congo or to read the lessons of Joseph Conrad's *Heart of Darkness*, but they knew very well that for every planned utopia in the wilderness there could result a kingdom of evil.

'What kind of moral nurse is mother nature, a Christian has no need to ask,' wrote Bishop Mountain in his account of a tour through the western interior. The missionaries who were sent by the Hudson's Bay Company to Red River, including the Reverend John West, believed they were responsible for the maintenance of a 'civilized' existence in the face of nature's temptations. What is more, they had before them the example of Indians who 'endured all the miseries and privations inseparable from a state of barbarism.' Thus the church had the self-imposed responsibility of 'rescuing' the natives from their present state and saving Europeans in this moral wasteland.[23]

In the palmy days of evangelical religion, the days of Shaftesbury and the crusade against slavery and child labour, the church's concern for Indians received widespread public attention. One campaign, in particular, brought the northwest to the attention of the British public and established a new strand of thought concerning this frontier. A.K. Isbister, the child of a fur trader and an Indian woman, was born at Cumberland House in 1822 and educated at school and university in Scotland. He returned to Canada to enter the fur trade but eventually left the northwest for a more settled life in London, England. There he took up the cause of the natives of the Hudson's Bay Company territory, arguing that the chartered company was concerned solely with the pursuit of profit and that it maintained the Indians 'in a state of utter dependence ... to pass their lives in the darkest heathenism.' When associated with economic questions about the company's monopoly of trade and intermittent diplomatic difficulties with the United States, Isbister's attack upon the alleged negligence of the company helped to create an image of the northwest as a moral and political wilderness. The image sat poorly with the simultaneous perception of beautiful vastness but it did encourage one identical conclusion: civilization must be extended into the new frontier.[24]

Knowledge of the northwest was supplied by scientists and explorers as well as by romantic travellers and moral crusaders, but, for a variety of reasons, this rather prosaic information accumulated very slowly and did not result in a convincing synthesis on the western environment in the first half of the nineteenth century. David Thompson, the great explorer, whose perceptions of the continent were remarkable for their breadth and inclusiveness, was one of the first to perceive that the Saskatchewan country was part of the continental plain that stretched south to the Gulf of Mexico, but his ideas did not receive general circulation in the nineteenth century. A number of other fur traders reported that the western interior contained two very different landscapes, thus distinguishing between the woods of the northern country and the grasslands that stretched south of the Saskatchewan River. Aside from these elaborations on the reports of Anthony Henday, it was not until the 1850s, a full century after Henday's travels, that the character of the interior was more clearly defined.

American exploration made several important contributions to this process. From the days of Lewis and Clark, the district along the Missouri River and south toward the Arkansas River was regarded as sterile, and slowly but surely a concept of a Great American Desert became fixed in American literature. The concept was not immediately applied to the Hudson's Bay Company domain north of the Missouri, because there, as the fur traders had reported, the great herds of buffalo created a truly rich environment rather than a desert wasteland. Changing purposes can change perceptions, and, as travellers began to think of the western interior in terms of agricultural capability rather than the fur trade, soil and climate – the conditions for crop production – rather than buffalo herds created a new definition of its character. It may have been accidental, but, as this new definition took shape, the concept of the American Desert was extended to include part of the western interior in British territory.[25]

Pressures in the United Kingdom, the United States, and Canada to learn more about the western interior resulted in the dispatch of two important exploring expeditions in the period 1857–60. The

British party was led by Capt John Palliser and included such very able members as geologist James Hector, botanist Eugène Bourgeau, and magnetical observer Thomas Blakiston. The Canadian group was led by S.J. Dawson, a civil engineer, and H.Y. Hind, a geologist. Though they never met or even corresponded, each expedition built upon the reports of the other to add vast amounts to the knowledge of the southern reaches of the western interior and, as geographer John Warkentin concluded, to lay 'the basic conceptual framework for our present interpretation of the physical geography of Western Interior Canada.'[26] The most important of their ideas was the concept of two vast sub-districts in the western interior, one rich and Edenic, the other sterile and forbidding. The first, stretching in an arc from the Red River settlement northwest to the Saskatchewan River valley and the Rockies, contained magnificent soil and was called the Fertile Belt; the second, a triangular-shaped region that extended into the prairies from the United States, was designated the Arid Plains, the Great American Desert, or, in popular parlance, Palliser's Triangle. Though the generalizations were the products merely of extrapolation from American scientific literature and of a cursory survey of actual conditions in the western interior, they were not easily removed. And despite the inaccuracy of their 'desert' label, the expeditions did suggest that fertile soil was present in abundance in the western interior. The Palliser and Hind-Dawson reports can be taken as the point of transition from fur trade to agriculture in the thinking of outside observers. As Warkentin concluded: 'Prior to Palliser's and Hind's expeditions to the interior, there had been a generally passive, largely uninformed, yet on the whole positive, appreciation of the nature of the land. After the expeditions a myth of good land in the North Saskatchewan country was reinforced ... and a myth of bad land in the southern interior was started ... Their work marked the beginning of a direct, not just a speculative, concern with the resources of the region, and the problems of devising strategies for administering the area, building transportation links, and colonizing the land.'[27]

One of the great issues that bothered would-be developers of the west was its climate. It took only a reasonably observant person to note that prairie winters were rather cold, that the first frosts arrived early, and that spring was often late. The variability of rainfall was also obvious. However, with the publication in 1857 of a remarkable scientific work by the American climatologist Lorin Blodget, the great agricultural potential of the interior was finally made apparent. Climate was not a function of latitude alone, said Blodget, but of ocean currents, the continental land mass, and winds. Using the relatively new concept of isothermal lines (which link places with the same mean seasonal or annual temperatures), Blodget argued that the northwest was as warm as Poland, just as Arthur Dobbs had asserted a century before: 'We find the isothermal of 60°[F] for the summer rising on the interior American plains to the 61st parallel, or fully as high as its average position for Europe.' He concluded that the 'commercial and industrial capacity' of the region was 'gigantic, and but for the pernicious views entailed by the fur traffic as to the necessity of preserving it as a wilderness, it would long since have been opened to colonization.' Blodget had silenced the prairie west's critics with one grand stroke. His work became widely known in Canada and Minnesota and served as an important tool in the hands of the propagandists who were now embarking upon the next great imperial adventure on the North American continent.[28]

The 1850s marked a crucial change in the perception of the western interior. The land came to be seen not as a wilderness but as a potential home for a great civilization. Descriptions of the rough contours of the wilds were softened, and in many writings the land took on the appearance of English or eastern Canadian countryside. Thus, the Qu'Appelle valley, once perceived as a rough slash in the face of the southern prairie, became a rounded secluded refuge. When a member of the Hind expedition, James Dickinson, found himself 'looking down upon the glittering lake 300 feet below, and across the boundless plains, no living thing in view, no sound of life anywhere,' he foresaw the day 'when will be seen passing swiftly along the distant horizon the white cloud of the locomotive on its way from Atlantic to Pacific, and when the valley will resound from the merry voices of those who have come from the busy city on the banks of the Red River to see the beautiful lakes of the Qu'Appelle.'[29] It is sobering to reflect that his vision came true within thirty years.

The British government was the central factor in determining the fate of the northwest. Its image of the territory in the 1850s and 1860s was influenced by its responsibility for the administration of a North American empire within a world-wide empire. Faced with insistent problems in the Pacific and in the Crimea, not to mention uncertainties in Africa and Asia, it would have been content to leave the western interior to the Hudson's Bay Company as had been done for two centuries. But the licence of the company, which had been extended in 1838 for another twenty-one years, was due to expire and thus would have to be reviewed. Moreover, the pressure from the opposition benches, especially from Little Englanders such as John Bright and anti-colonialists such as William Ewart Gladstone, was matched by a propaganda campaign from aboriginal protection societies about the failures of the chartered company and the virtues of native evangelization. The cost of administrative alternatives such as crown colony status was prohibitive, in the government's view, and so room for manoeuvre was minimal. The Palliser expedition and the 1857 parliamentary inquiry into the Hudson's Bay Company demonstrated British official recognition of the need for change in the northwest but resulted in the depressing acknowledgment that Her Majesty's Government could offer little help in the process. Committed to free trade, colonial self government, and protection of native peoples, the British administration pursued a policy that seemed to contradict its principles in every respect. It attempted to postpone decisions in these mid-century decades, placing its confidence instead in the Hudson's Bay Company and in the hope that Canada would eventually take the problem off its hands.[30]

If the official British attitude toward the western interior was cool, the American government seemed little more enthusiastic about acquisition of the territory in the 1850s. Preoccupied by the slavery issue, and in no mood to add new 'free soil' matters to the north-south debate, successive presidents were none the less pressed by Minnesota advocates of 'Manifest Destiny' to consider the future of the northwest. The ambitions of St Paul merchants were short-lived. Despite the amazing northwestward advance of settlement in Minnesota – the population of the area rose from 6,000 in 1850 to 172,000 in 1860 – and several grand designs for a transcontinental railway across the northern plains, the depression of 1857 destroyed Minnesota dreams of a northern empire by cutting off credit for expansionist projects. And before the dreams could again be translated into business enterprises, the outbreak of the Civil War and of the hysteria-laden Sioux Wars of 1862–4 undermined Minnesota's aspirations. The hiatus of nearly a decade ensured that the province of Canada would be able to claim the western interior as its own.[31]

The Canadian movement to annex the west had acquired strength and influence in 1856–7, just as British and Minnesota interests turned to serious consideration of the territory. It was led by a handful of men, perhaps twelve to fifteen in number, but their positions were so important and their commitment so genuine that they determined the fate of the western interior and, consequently, of the northern half of North America.[32] In a century of national organization, the vast federation they created was one of the globe's grandest designs; the western interior, as the propagandists so often said, was the keystone in the arch of the Canadian empire.

The reason for the outburst of annexationist enthusiasm in Canada West (now Southern Ontario) lay in the changing economic circumstances of the 1850s. Farmland, formerly available in the rich peninsula of the lower Great Lakes, became increasingly scarce as the decade progressed, and though farms could still be purchased the prices were higher than in the competing regions of the adjacent American states. Moreover, the explosion in railway construction in the Canadas, as in the United States and western Europe, prompted visions of commercial wealth that could be fulfilled only in the west. Such ambitions inspired businessmen in the two areas most affected by the need for fresh hinterlands, the Ottawa valley and the city of Toronto, to press for the Dawson-Hind expedition and for Canadian government intervention in the hearings of the British Parliament's select committee. Eventually, Canada renewed its claims to the western interior by right of French exploration in the eighteenth century. The Canadian goal was the creation of a larger trade network, whether based on fur companies in the western interior, on Pacific merchants, or, when at its most expansive, on China and the South Pacific. As the powerful Toronto Reform party leader George Brown wrote in his paper, the *Globe*: 'Let the merchants of Toronto consider that if their city is ever to be made really great – if it is ever to rise above the rank of a fifth rate American town – it must be by the development of the great British territory lying to the north and west.'[33] The western interior was, in this view, the foundation of an empire. It was a source of trading activity, not an area with ambitions or interests of its own, and it would make Canada a world leader: 'With two powerful colonies on the Pacific, with another or more in the region between Canada and the Rocky Mountains, with a railway and a telegraph linking the Atlantic with the Pacific and absorbing the newly-opened and fast-developing trade with China and Japan ... who can doubt of the reality and accuracy of the vision which rises distinctly and clearly before us, as the Great Britannic Empire of the North stands out in all its grandeur.'[34]

While these storm clouds were building up around the Red River settlement in the 1850s, the residents became tense and factious. Or, at least, that has been the picture drawn by a number of historians in the intervening century. Indeed, several students have suggested that Red River was on the verge of collapse in this era, whether from forces exerted by the annexationists or from internal disputes that set the colonists against each other. Neither perspective is entirely satisfactory. Rather, if one regards Red River as a metis community in transition, the few pieces of evidence we possess do not suggest irreconcilable divisions within the settlement or that intolerable pressures were being exerted by Canada, the United States, and Great Britain. The people of Red River were managing very well in the 1850s and 1860s despite growing concerns about their food supply and control over property.

The view that Red River was in crisis was best expressed by the historian George Stanley. In *The Birth of Western Canada* (1936) Stanley depicted the colony in the 1850s as a quiet backwater about to be assailed by 'an army of white immigrants and settlers.' The metis, he suggested, did not want to adapt: 'Their racial origin was different from that of the Canadians, their historical life was distinct from that of Canada, and all intercourse, social or economic, between the two peoples had been prevented by natural obstacles ... With the advent of the Canadians in Red River the day of the buffalo hunter and the small freighter was at an end. A primitive people, the half-breeds were bound to give way before the march of a more progressive people.'[35]

Another explanation of the Red River crisis was presented by Frits Pannekoek. It relied in part on two sex scandals, but its strength was greater than that provided merely by the settlement's dirty linen. Pannekoek emphasized the impact of European women and the Church Missionary Society on local mores, especially on marriage patterns and racial stereotypes. The growing gulf between metis and Europeans was illustrated by an extraordinary court case in 1850. Gossip in the settlement that year suggested that Mrs John Ballenden, an English-speaking metis and wife of the highest company officer in the district, was permitting a dashing young officer in the Chelsea pensioners, Capt Christopher Foss, to 'park his boots under her bed.' To clear their names, Mrs Ballenden and Capt Foss brought charges of defamatory conspiracy against four of the gossips. The trial alienated the English-speaking metis, defenders of Mrs Ballenden, from the Europeans, who tended to believe the whispers and to support the four scandal-mongers.[36] A second scandal, according to Pannekoek, further separated the English-speaking metis from the Europeans. It involved the Reverend Griffiths Owen Corbett, an Anglican clergyman who had been leading a campaign against Hudson's Bay Company rule in Red River and in favour of crown colony status. In 1863, after six years in the settlement, Corbett was arrested by the company on a charge of having tried to induce an abortion in an English-speaking metis woman whom he had allegedly made pregnant. Corbett was convicted and eventually sent out of the colony, but not before a popular movement on his behalf had resulted in two jail-breaks and much unrest. In Pannekoek's view, the Corbett case also illustrated the alienation of the English-speaking metis community from the Hudson's Bay Company. By the mid-1860s, Pannekoek claimed, the English metis turned to the newly arrived Canadian annexationists for leadership. The English metis would not only accept a British-Canadian Protestant view of the world, according to this perspective, but they would also distrust the French metis and eventually oppose Riel's protest movement in 1869–70: 'The Riel resistance of 1869–70 was in part caused and certainly exacerbated, not by the racial and religious antagonisms that were introduced by the Canadians, but rather by a sectarian and racial conflict that had roots deep in Red River's past.' The resistance was, in short, a 'civil war.'[37]

Both Pannekoek and Stanley have depicted the settlement as divided and unstable. Such a view exaggerates the weaknesses of the community and underestimates the abilities of its residents. A truer picture would give greater attention to the regular performance of daily duties and the development of political interest groups in these years. Red River was becoming integrated into the wider world in the late 1850s and the 1860s. Travellers, trade goods, and even settlers were arriving in numbers. The death in 1860 of the strongest defender of company interests, Sir George Simpson, symbolized the passing of the trade era. The metis adjusted quickly to the new economic opportunities, and the far-sighted among them soon began to assume the characteristics of an entrepreneurial class. Extended families grew up around the most prosperous individuals, men such as Narcisse Marion, Jean-Baptiste Lagimodière, and Salomon Hamelin. The sons of these leaders found employment driving the carts or working the fields of the patriarchs. These leading men were joined by French Canadians from Quebec to form an educated, politically aware French-speaking elite in the settlement.[38] Though less is known about the English-speaking metis community, it is probable that a similar development was occurring there; certainly, the presence of men such as James Ross and James McKay suggested the existence of such a group. These individuals were community leaders because of their relative prosperity or education and occupied prominent positions when crisis beset the settlement in the 1860s.

The growing traffic in goods and ideas increased international interest in the fate of the Hudson's Bay Company territories. To the observers of the day, there seemed to be three alternatives. The United States was preoccupied by Civil War between 1861 and 1865, but Minnesota leaders remained determined that their manifest destiny would be realized. Canadian politicians were divided by partisan and cultural loyalties, especially the strong opposition of French Canada to western expansion, but some, particularly Reform party leader George Brown of Canada West, assumed that Rupert's Land should be theirs. Finally, if the Hudson's Bay Company rule on behalf of the crown had ceased to be effective, the British government might, with reluctance, adopt the strategy it had employed for British Columbia and Vancouver Island: that is, it might create a crown colony in the northwest. None of these alternatives was to become a reality in the decade after 1857 for the simple reason that Canada and the United States were unable to act and Great Britain was unwilling to do so. The Hudson's Bay Company's exclusive right to trade in the northwest and on the Pacific, a right granted by the 1821 royal licence, which was itself a supplement to the 1670 charter, was allowed to lapse in 1859, and thus 'Government in the Northwest hung on a legal thread, the sovereignty of the British Crown and the charter of 1670.' The Royal Canadian Rifles had provided some order as well as social interest in the settlement after their arrival in 1857, but the departure of their boats down the Red toward Lake Winnipeg in the spring of 1861, a moving sight as recorded in a settler's diary, marked the end of effective company authority and a return to the uncertain legal situation of the days of Guillaume Sayer. The eruption of popular protest in the Corbett jail-breaks several years later made evident what everyone knew:

because the company had no power to enforce its decrees, a political and legal vacuum existed in the territory.[39]

Land thus became a topic of great concern. What was clear title? What was meant by aboriginal and squatters' rights? These were now matters of private anxiety and public debate. The Hudson's Bay Company had inherited Lord Selkirk's treaty with Chief Peguis and had created a system of 'clear titles,' in British law at least, along the Red and part of the Assiniboine River valleys, but elsewhere there was no land law. Rather, as Irene Spry has suggested, the native concept of common property resources had given way to a system of open access and now to property ownership. Where government was unstable and land rights were uncertain, political troubles were likely to follow.[40]

Dissatisfied settlers in the English-speaking part of the community tended to focus this criticism on the Hudson's Bay Company. The company had resisted agricultural development in order to protect the fur trade, they said, and had opposed such positive solutions as crown colony status for its own advantage. Furthermore, it had persecuted the Reverend Mr Corbett, dominated local commerce for too long, and was run by a distant, unknown, and, no doubt, uncaring committee. Led by the small group that from 1859 published the *Nor'Wester*, though not composed exclusively of these people, the opponents of the company became increasingly shrill during the 1860s. Tradition and simplification have given the title 'Canadian party' to these critics. The work of W.L. Morton has tended to sharpen the focus even more by suggesting that the group 'was in fact John Schultz and such Canadians as were under his influence at any given time.' The picture was completed by Roderick Campbell's aphorism that, in Schultz, 'Fate had manufactured a scoundrel out of material meant by Nature for a gentleman.' Upon this perspective Pannekoek constructed his view of the English-speaking community in Red River: bereft of leadership, the English metis turned to Schultz and thus became Canadian annexationists and anti-French zealots.

Such a view is too simple. In fact, as life in any village will reveal, the Red River settlement was not alone in being united and divided by neighbourhood loyalties, kinship networks, and other social obligations. It can be agreed that many English-speaking metis were, for a variety of reasons, alienated from both the Hudson's Bay Company and the French-speaking community. It is evident, too, that residents of the district were worried by political events in the 1860s and anxious to establish their own place in the rapidly approaching new order. But the influence of one leader, even so persuasive a man as Schultz, was never so overwhelming that it encompassed more than a fraction of the total. Merchants such as Bannatyne and McDermot, clergymen such as Black, home-grown literates such as James Ross and John Norquay, and Upper Canadian imperialists such as Charles Mair and Walter Bown could not be classified as a group despite their common tongue and their residence in Red River. And when their shifting loyalties are traced through the troubles of the late 1860s, the argument that they constituted one of two factions in a civil war seems weak.

Red River was beset by anxieties in the 1860s, that is certain. Drought and grasshoppers destroyed the crops in 1862–5 and again in 1868; in the latter year, even small game, the plains hunt, and the lake fisheries failed. Public appeals for relief were sent to Minnesota and Ontario, a relief committee was set up, and food and seed wheat were distributed in the winter of 1868–9. And still, in the midst of this destitution, settlers were arriving from Ontario and staking out squatter's claims that challenged metis, Indian, and company assumptions. It appeared that a land rush was about to be unleashed in a territory where neither a government nor a system of justice would ensure customary rights.

The British and Canadian governments moved slowly to remedy the situation. The crucial step toward resolution of northwest problems was taken in 1864 when Canadian politicians finally buried their differences and agreed to work toward a British North American federation. The process was long and complicated but successful, and on 1 July 1867 four of the British colonies in North America became the new Dominion of Canada. As a federal union, the new nation ended the French-English deadlock and thus opened the way to Canadian annexation of the northwest, a prospect that had been crucial in the achievement of Confederation. But the arrangement for the transfer of the northwest from British to Canadian sovereignty had never been the subject of serious negotiation and certainly had never included consideration of the residents of that land. As W.L. Morton emphasized, no guarantees of native rights, of land titles, or of participation in government were made: 'These things might have been done, but they were not attempted, and the consequences were to be serious. The responsibility for the failure is perhaps to be ascribed to the Imperial rather than to the Canadian government. One of the greatest transfers of territory and sovereignty in history was conducted as a mere transaction in real estate.'[41]

The English-speaking metis were probably disposed to rely on the goodwill of the incoming Canadian administration, but some of the French metis were not. They recognized, perhaps, that French and English were often at loggerheads in the government of the united Canadas before 1867 and that French and Catholic rights would not necessarily be protected as a matter of course; they certainly were aware of the bold claims of the English-speaking arrivals from Ontario who threatened to ride roughshod over their lands and, presumably, their church and language.

The summer and autumn of 1869 were marked by British and Canadian discussions with the leading Hudson's Bay Company officers in London about extinguishing the company's charter rights and, in Red River, by public meetings and much informal talk concerning the fate of the settlement. The only solid evidence about the changing status of Red River was the arrival of a Canadian government survey party in August, apparently to prepare the way for the long-predicted land rush. That the chief of the party, J.S. Dennis, accepted the hospitality of Dr Schultz merely confirmed the fears of the French metis.

The central reason for the turbulent events of 1869–70, as W.L. Morton has concluded, was the French fear of English-Canadian rule in Red River and, more precisely, fear of the elevation of Dr Schultz and men like him, land-hungry Protestant fanatics, to positions of authority. There are two sides to this story. Behind their suspicion of the boastful Canadian expansionists, the French-speaking metis were groping for a sharper definition of their own aspirations. This was not the retention of the hunt alone, but a defence of their rights as full citizens in the new order: to own the land they now farmed, to sit in government, to hold jobs in the civil service and in the businesses that would spring up. Such demands would have been guaranteed without question by the Canadian authorities, but Ottawa was never to hear such requests in the calm atmosphere that was necessary. In addition to these demands for recognition of individual rights that were part of the British heritage and modern industrial capitalism, the metis were expressing vaguer and more difficult concerns. These included language, faith, kinship networks, and schools – all reinforced by parish and neighbourhood patterns – and have been described as corporate rights, the rights of the metis 'new nation' as a community within the community. This concern for their collectivity, for their culture in the broadest sense, not for 'frontier' and not for language and religion alone, underlay the metis struggles of 1869–70.

Popular movements of protest require leaders as well as grievances. Three groups in Red River, in addition to the metis themselves, might have supplied this direction. The Roman Catholic clergy, the American trader-merchants, and the Hudson's Bay Company officers all had reason to distrust the Canadians and to seek an alternative to Canadian annexation. But each of these groups was small in number, and none, despite the fulminations of their critics, was critical in the direction of events. Rather, the dominant figure in the uprising was the young and persuasive Louis Riel.

So great is the accretion of popular imagery around Riel that we now find it difficult to perceive him as a human being. He was very young to be prominent in these events, but at twenty-five he displayed a remarkable maturity of judgment. From the little that is known of his early years, we must believe that he was without experience in leadership of a group and yet he commanded a large and turbulent force through extremely troubled times. For one with so little knowledge of public affairs, he possessed extraordinary daring, courage, and determination. As Oscar Malmros, American consul at Red River, described him, he was 'ambitious, quick of perception, though not profound, of indomitable energy, daring, excessively suspicious of others and of a pleasing and rather dignified address.' As a speaker, he was fluent and forceful; as a strategist he was quick and innovative; as a public personality, he was intense and utterly dedicated to his cause. His fate was the metis fate; he became the embodiment, not just the leader, of his people.

Riel was born in the Red River settlement in 1844, the eldest of eleven children in a deeply religious and politically prominent French-Canadian family. Though his father's mother was probably French Chipewyan from Île-à-la-Crosse, Louis's early life was spent almost exclusively within the bounds of the settlement where he acquired a reputation as an able and pious student. Perhaps in part because of the educational background and economic ambitions of the Riel and Lagimodière families, Louis was one of three students selected by Bishop Taché to receive further schooling in the Sulpician College of Montreal in 1858. He remained in the east for ten years, acquiring a solid training in the humanities and the classics, a smattering of law, and a good deal of experience in the politics of French Canada. He also sustained some significant reverses. The death of his father in 1864 moved him very deeply and, as his letters home suggest, left him in a profound depression. In the following year, the handsome young man of twenty-one fell in love, dropped out of school, tried a number of occupations, and was prevented from marrying by his fiancée's parents. In despair, he threw up his excellent prospects as an articling law student and wandered from Chicago to Minneapolis, whence he returned to Red River in July 1868. He may have been prey to uncertainties – perhaps a mixture of insecurity, guilt, and ambition – when he returned to help his mother and her large family, but he was also a competent and talented young man. Only the pressures of the next eight years prevented him from maturing into a secure personality and a prominent public servant.[42]

The metis resistance led by Riel was a movement not of the entire French-speaking community, let alone of all Red River. As in any political event, the resistance won and lost adherents throughout its life of ten months. The alignment of factions is thus uncertain. Riel was opposed by the Canadian annexationists associated with John Christian Schultz and by the recent Ontario settlers west of Winnipeg on the Assiniboine River. He was opposed also by the Indians of the 'Lower Settlement' where Schultz and British patriotism were strong. Riel was supported with varying degrees of enthusiasm by the Roman Catholic clergy, the Americans, and many of the French-speaking metis. And some of the French and many of the English-speaking settlers – metis, Scot, Orkney, Canadian – were in the middle, ready to move from side to side depending on the issue and the circumstance. The heart of the resistance lay with the men mobilized by Riel – the cartmen and boatmen who wintered in the settlement and were quite prepared to serve as an army in a good cause.

The resistance took shape slowly and deliberately between June and October 1869. Several public meetings and numerous gatherings at church doors on Sundays addressed the issue of the transfer, but, despite rumours of Canadian annexation and uncertainty about the consequences, no decision was reached on a course of action. Then, on 11 October, as the Canadian survey party reached the metis river lots near St Vital, Louis Riel and a few followers rode up from the river to join the owner of the farm, André Nault, in challenging the right of the Canadian government to cross their lands or, more important, to conduct any survey in the northwest. It was a considered political act, symbolic of the metis determination to stand up for their rights. As the survey party withdrew to safer tasks in accordance with their instructions, the metis began to organize in earnest. Within two weeks they had created a National Committee, administered oaths of loyalty to their members, erected a barrier across the main trail to the United States – the site has been called La Barrière ever since – and begun to police the highway and the plains stretching to the west in order to control access to the settlement. They now had to prevent William McDougall, member of the federal cabinet, noted Canadian annexationist, and the man nominated to be first lieutenant-governor of the North-West Territories, from taking up his commission. McDougall ignored the first message requiring him to remain in American territory, but the armed party of metis horsemen that confronted him on 2 November was more convincing. He retired across the border to Pembina, never to return and never to fulfil his task. As in the challenge to the survey, so in the opposition to McDougall's entry, the metis had made it apparent that they would not only assert their concerns but also prevent annexation to Canada until they had won recognition of their rights.

These opening skirmishes were doubtless illegal, but they were not violent and did not involve property. However Riel could not stop at symbolic acts. He lived in a land where guns and violence were well-known and where an Indian rising or a Canadian-metis skirmish was quite possible. Again he showed the decisiveness that was his mark. On 2 November, he sent several hundred metis to the tree-covered south banks of the Assiniboine from where, in groups of three and four, they crossed to Upper Fort Garry. Without a shot being fired, the metis soldiers seized the strongest bastion in the settlement, including cannon, small arms, and considerable stores of pemmican (sufficient to feed an army for the winter) and thereby established the military dominance that would sustain them for the duration of the resistance. An illegal violation of company property rights but a brilliant stroke of tactics, the seizure of the fort was the single most important act in the metis campaign. Winter was fast approaching, and with it protection from outside intervention for at least six months. Henceforth, Riel negotiated from a position of military strength.

His great task was to create common cause with all groups in the settlement in order to present a united front to the Canadian government. To that end, he called a convention of twelve English- and twelve French-speaking parish representatives for 16 November. Riel proposed to that convention that they form a provisional government to replace the moribund Hudson's Bay Company administration. While this and other possibilities were being debated and the leaders of the settlement's various factions were jockeying for power, William McDougall made his last appearance on the western stage.

McDougall had been languishing at Pembina for a month, observing the construction of a log cabin – his own – and awaiting advice from Ottawa on his next step. He had been told to do nothing until he heard that the transfer had actually occurred, but because the mails required two weeks for delivery he was not abreast of events and therefore assumed that the original date for the transfer, 1 December, remained unchanged. Moreover, he assumed, wrongly as it happened, that the government of the Hudson's Bay Company expired at the transfer and that he must be in a position to inaugurate Canadian authority. Having received no new instructions, he crossed the border on the night of 30 November and read a proclamation to the wind and the stars announcing the transfer and the commencement of his rule. He was wrong. Prime Minister John A. Macdonald, having learned of the metis resistance and of McDougall's forced sojourn at Pembina, had wired London in late November to postpone the transfer on the grounds that Canada was entitled to peaceable possession. Thus, the rule of the Hudson's Bay Company remained intact and McDougall's proclamation was void.

Riel was still regarded as a law-breaker by many in Red River because he had seized the fort. However, he had refused to challenge the sovereignty of the crown, and so most residents did not view him as a rebel. Then came the news of McDougall's proclamation and the circulation of McDougall's commission to John S. Dennis to put down those in arms against constituted authority. At this point, the community moved to the brink of armed conflict. The Canadian loyalists moved to the area of Lower Fort Garry, twenty miles north of Riel's base and in a site equally defensible as a military redoubt. Armed deadlock would have resulted had there not been a Canadian government shipment of pork in Schultz's house in the village of Winnipeg within gunshot of Riel's troops. Though guarded by Schultz and fifty men, and fully sufficient to sustain the

Canadian loyalist army throughout the winter, the pork had not been removed to the safer ground of the Lower Fort. Riel seized the initiative once again and on 7 December compelled the surrender of the house, pork, and garrison. This was a significant blow to his opponents.

Even more important as a factor in defusing opposition among the English-speaking settlers was the relative moderation of Riel's political program. The convention of twenty-four had received McDougall's proclamation on 1 December and, of course, believed it to be valid. It had also heard a list of rights prepared in haste by the French members which seemed a reasonable declaration. But the delegates had been unable to agree on their next move. The English wished to permit the queen's representative (as he was thought to be), McDougall, to enter the territory; Riel was adamant that he should not, for fear that he would rally the Canadian loyalists and destroy his plans for a united negotiating stance. The convention then dissolved, and Riel went forward with his French metis supporters alone.

On 8 December, the day after his raid on Schultz's house, Riel proclaimed the establishment of a provisional government. In the accompanying declaration, often described as the Declaration of Metis Independence because of its obvious similarity to the American document of 1776, he and his adviser, Father Dugas, argued that the Hudson's Bay Company had ceased to provide effective government and that its transfer of the northwest to another authority without the consent of northwest inhabitants violated the 'rights of man'; therefore 'the law of nations' supported the metis right to proclaim a provisional government. This new government was prepared, however, to treat with Canada on terms of union. The document, W.L. Morton concluded, 'is no more than an assertion of the right of the metis to negotiate the terms on which Canadian authority would be established in the North-West.'[43] Riel thereby won the silent sympathy, if not the political support, of the English-speaking settlers. That sympathy, coupled with the military blow to the Canadian forces in the battle over government pork and the intervention of several Protestant ministers who dispersed the loyalist military force, was sufficient to maintain Riel's control over Red River. In the mean time, McDougall had been defeated. In mid-December, he collected his belongings and headed across the plains for St Paul and, eventually, Canada.

Riel was now in command of Red River and it had become the turn of Prime Minister Macdonald to find a means of commencing negotiations. His first tactic, six months late in conception, was to dispatch two commissioners to explain that Canadian intentions were honourable. His second was to prepare for a military expedition in the summer of 1870. His third was to re-establish Hudson's Bay Company rule through Donald A. Smith, chief factor in charge of company affairs in North America, who was made a special commissioner and asked to buy off the insurgents or otherwise break Riel's hold over the colony. The two innocent commissioners, Thibault and de Salaberry, were powerless. The armed force was to come into play only later. But Smith initiated a new phase in the resistance.

Shrewd, cool, and decisive, Donald A. Smith was a match for Riel. He had the power of the Hudson's Bay Company at his disposal at a time when the tripmen usually required credit to get through the winter, and he had Macdonald's commission in reserve. His goal was to negotiate the transfer with the people of Red River, whereas Riel wished that Canada deal only with his provisional government. Smith forced Riel to convoke an extraordinary general meeting of the entire settlement at Upper Fort Garry on 19 and 20 January 1870. There, with settlement notables standing on the gallery of the mess hall, and over a thousand people below them in the courtyard, and despite the −20° (Fahrenheit) cold, Smith assured the settlers of liberal treatment by the Canadian government. For reasons that have never been explained, he did not press his advantage by reading his proclamation and thereby making continuation of the provisional government a rebellious act; instead, perhaps because the compromise had been arranged in advance, he acquiesced in Riel's call for a new representative convention, the so-called convention of forty, to consider his proposals.

Once more Riel was in command, and Smith, whatever his hopes for the new assembly, had lost. The result was a second convention, a second list of rights, and an agreement to send delegates to Ottawa to negotiate terms of entry into Confederation. Riel did not secure the convention's repudiation of the Canadian bargain with the Hudson's Bay Company or its approval of provincial as opposed to territorial status. But he did win its approval for the establishment of an interim provisional government, representative of the entire settlement, with himself as president. It was the culmination of the campaign he had begun the previous October to create a united settlement. By 10 February, when the convention ended, Riel seemed to have won his way.

The crisis of the following week set in train the events that led to Riel's downfall. Canadian loyalists, including members of the Canadian survey party and men who had escaped or been released from Fort Garry after the capture of Schultz's house in December, apparently decided to attempt to release the remaining prisoners in the fort. They met with Schultz and others in the lower settlement and then, probably because Riel was fulfilling a promise to the convention by releasing the prisoners, decided to disband. Unfortunately, Riel had already decided to meet them in combat. His armed horsemen surrounded their opponents in deep snow just as they passed the village of Winnipeg on their return home and imprisoned them in the fort. Capt C.A. Boulton, leader of the group, was sentenced to be shot as an example to the rest and perhaps, too, as an example to the Canadian government. But this threat passed; Boulton's sentence was commuted, the new provisional government was elected, and the settlement seemed still to be awaiting peaceful annexation to Canada.

Two individuals who had been involved in this latest military fiasco were now brought to the fore and, almost alone, destroyed the settlement's unity. John Christian Schultz had escaped arrest in the loyalist 'march' and had set out for Duluth, Minnesota, across country, smouldering with resentment. He was headed for Ontario where he planned to launch a crusade to save the northwest from the French Catholic metis. Thomas Scott, a twenty-eight-year-old labourer from Ontario, had been captured for the second time in two months and soon managed to make himself the most hated man in the barracks. His dysentery and his contempt for the metis irritated his captors beyond endurance. When the guards almost shot him on the spot, the metis leaders, perhaps including Riel but certainly Ambroise Lepine, ordered that Scott be given a military courtmartial. He was sentenced to death. In the early morning of 4 March, a still incredulous Scott was led into the sunshine behind the fort and cut down by a firing squad. Riel may have believed that the execution was necessary to pacify the metis guard. He may have wished to hasten the completion of the transfer by impressing his opponents with the depth of his resolve. But the 'murder' of Scott was a fatal error because it created a political martyr. John Christian

Schultz arrived in Ontario to discover that the bullets that had executed Thomas Scott provided ample ammunition to ensure the conquest of Riel and the metis.

The resistance had run its course by April 1870. Only two inter-related issues had to be settled. The first was the negotiation between the Red River delegates and the Canadian government of the terms of entry into Confederation, including, of course, the question of an amnesty for those who had participated in the event. The second was the means by which authority over the territory would be transferred from President Riel and his still-unrecognized provisional government to the new lieutenant-governor and the Canadian state. Failure to reach appropriate agreement on these matters was to render futile all Riel's efforts in the preceding year.

The Red River delegates left for Ottawa at the end of March with a third list of rights as a basis for negotiation. This list owed much to the work of the convention of forty but was not identical to its so-called second list of rights. The important changes, inserted secretly at the insistence of Riel, it would appear, called for the admission of the northwest as a province rather than a territory, for a bilingual lieutenant-governor, and for a general amnesty covering all acts and all participants in the resistance. This third 'secret' list was supplemented by yet another, or fourth list, probably at the instigation of Bishop Taché, who had returned to Red River just before the delegates departed. In this final list, the delegates were instructed to seek the establishment of denominational schools and the creation of an upper house, or senate, as well as an assembly, following the Quebec model. These were significant departures from the will of the community as expressed in the convention of forty and caused much disagreement – were never approved, in fact – when presented to the legislative council of the provisional government in early May. But the lack of Red River support for these lists was not known in Ottawa, where the delegates arrived in April. There, the three Red River men discovered that the agitation over the death of Thomas Scott was still growing. Only after two of the three had passed an unpleasant sojourn in jail were they permitted to carry out their assignment by meeting representatives of the federal cabinet and negotiating the terms of transfer.

The new province of Manitoba was created by the Manitoba Act, which received royal assent on 12 May and came into effect when proclaimed on 15 July 1870. It embodied most of the rights de-

manded by the metis, including responsible government and provincial status, bilingual institutions, denominational schools, and
guarantees of land titles and of federal respect for Indian title. But in
several crucial matters the negotiators failed. The related issues of
provincial status, control of lands, and metis land rights were handled skilfully by Macdonald. He created not a province of the Northwest, but a tiny self-governing province of Manitoba – approximately one hundred miles square – and a vast unit called the North-
West Territories, administered from Ottawa. In both jurisdictions,
the federal government retained control of public land and natural
resources, the only area in the country where this was to be the
case. As W.L. Morton commented, 'Thus was Riel's demand for
provincehood at once granted and made almost a mockery.'[44] To the
English- and French-speaking metis, Macdonald granted security of
tenure within accustomed plots of land, for whatever that was
worth, and he reserved 1.4 million acres to be allotted to their unmarried children. But he had not granted great blocks of land intact,
as the metis and Bishop Taché probably desired, and thus had not
created a buffer and a preserve for the maintenance of metis culture.
And, despite the pointed demands of one of the negotiators, Father
Ritchot, an amnesty had not been granted in writing. Despite these
considerable failures, the demands of the colony had been heard
and an agreement quite unlike the federal government's original
intentions had been won. Even with the considerable omissions,
and assuming that the amnesty issue would be resolved satisfactorily, it was an acceptable deal. The results were greeted with relief in
Red River and accepted without dissent by the provisional government.

The question of what would happen to the provisional government still remained. In December, when casting about for a means
of handling the resistance, Macdonald had set plans under way for a
military expedition to Red River. The reason for such a military
adventure had long since ceased to exist, but Col Garnet Wolseley
had set off in the spring none the less, with the 60th Rifles, symbol
of British concern for the farthest marches of the empire, and volunteers, chiefly from the Ontario militia, to reinforce Canadian authority. The expedition was a product of political necessity – a challenge
to American annexationists and a sop to Ontario nationalists for the
death of Scott. As might have been predicted, it was a punitive
expedition, despite Wolseley's declaration that his was 'a mission of

peace.' Wolseley himself explained privately to his wife: 'Hope Riel will have bolted, for although I should like to hang him to the highest tree in the place, I have such a horror of rebels and vermin of his kidney, that my treatment of him might not be approved by the civil powers.'[45] Riel, uncertain about the nature of Wolseley's commission, could rely only on the word of his advisers, Father Ritchot and Bishop Taché. They, in turn, could only trust their most powerful acquaintance in the federal cabinet, George-Étienne Cartier. In telling Riel that an amnesty was certain, Ritchot and Taché were transmitting the assurances they had received in Ottawa. But Macdonald would not sustain Cartier's promise. Given the political storm over Scott's death, the Canadian government refused to grant such an amnesty, and the imperial government, to which Ottawa handed the matter, was not yet prepared to act. Riel had no way of knowing these problems. He had considered resistance to the Manitoba Act because of the absence of an amnesty and had continued to drill metis troops in May and early June, but when the pressures of the season – the annual employment on the hunt and the cart and boat brigades – forced a decision, he had accepted the word of his advisers and permitted the dispersal of his men. For the rest of the summer he was isolated, a president of a rudimentary government with, as of 15 July, no authority and little apparent support.

Bishop Taché perceived the difficulty of the metis, particularly of Riel, and rushed to Ottawa in July in a vain attempt to hasten the departure of the newly appointed lieutenant-governor, Adams Archibald, in order that the civil authority might be securely installed before Wolseley and the military arrived. Taché failed, and the Wolseley expedition reached the settlement a week in advance of the governor. The timing was important if only as symbol because, instead of a peaceful transfer of power from Riel to Archibald and an implicit reconciliation of contending forces, the settlement was suddenly turned into an armed camp. The imperial troops moved upstream through the lower settlement in purposeful fashion, landed in a rainstorm on Point Douglas, where they immediately assumed battle formation, and advanced toward the Upper Fort as if expecting an armed encounter. Riel was warned of their impending arrival and fled across the river to St Boniface leaving, it was said, his breakfast unfinished on the table. He travelled south to the metis settlement of St Joseph, (now Valhalla) in American territory, to begin an exile that never really ended until his death fifteen years later. English-speaking troops invested the settlement, asserting the authority of Canada. More important, they asserted the determination of Ontario to remake the west in its own image.

The events of 1869–70 had great significance for the new Canadian state. They culminated in the transfer of the northwest to Canada rather than to Minnesota and thus ensured that a continent-wide nation would be established. They also reinforced the principle at the heart of Confederation by extending an essential part of the 1867 compromise – 'a dual culture in political union' – to the first new province of the dominion. Because it contributed to the creation of a tiny Manitoba and to federal control of public lands, the resistance helped to establish the western 'bias' – the theme of western regional dissatisfaction and grievance – that has been an important aspect of Confederation from that day to the present.[46] But one must always return to the French- and English-speaking metis, for Red River was overwhelmingly their settlement. Riel had given the metis a voice and a program, it is certain, but he had not solved their political problems. He had won a temporary victory on land tenure and, in the 1.4-million-acre grant, a potential buffer against Canadian encroachment. He had created a political and institutional framework in which the metis could assert their rights, especially in the regulations concerning the assembly, language, and schools. But Riel himself had been driven into exile. And his victories could easily be overturned. The metis had made their presence felt by means of the resistance and had defended their right to an equal start in the incoming order, but they could neither hold back the tide of newcomers nor guarantee the integrity of their community. Their ability to command political and economic power would determine how they fared in the new order.

# 7

# Prairie Indians
# 1840–1900:
# The end of autonomy

In the crucial decades of the 1850s and 1860s, Red River was an important factor in continental affairs. As a result, it has long been the focus of historical attention. That is proper, because events in the settlement helped to determine the shape of Confederation and, to a degree, the place of the prairie provinces in the Canadian nation. But concentration on Red River obscures the role of the Indians in the era of transition to Canadian rule. By choosing to make special arrangements for Manitoba, and by setting aside a land grant for metis children in Manitoba, the Canadian government had acknowledged a distinctive status for the metis in the new nation. In the 1870s, it acknowledged yet another category of citizenship for Indians. Neither metis nor European Canadians, Indians would be treated as wards of the state – put bluntly, they would be treated as children – until some date in the distant future when they had met a number of unusual requirements. Confined to reserves in the wooded areas of the plains, parklands, and forests of the western interior, Indians embarked upon a very different course from that of the larger society. They entered the twentieth century by a different door and at a different time than their European Canadian neighbours.

The last half of the nineteenth century constituted a revolution for most of the native societies of the western interior, particularly those of the plains and parkland. None of the changes in the native way of life in the preceding two centuries could be compared to the extraordinary upheaval of this period, and, what is even more striking, nothing could compare with the speed of the change. A typical Cree youth might have been hunting buffalo and raiding for horses in the 1860s just as his grandfather had done sixty years before; in the 1870s, he might have succumbed to the whisky trade or been struck by an epidemic; almost certainly he would have been removed to a reserve and perhaps even taught the rudiments of agriculture. In the 1880s, some of his children might have been attending school, and he, having faced starvation for three or four years in succession, might have participated in the violence associated with the 1885 uprising. But nothing within his power could alter the circumstances of his life: the buffalo had disappeared, trains and fences and towns now dominated the plains, and the old ways had disappeared beyond recovery.

The Ojibwas, especially those living in the woodlands on the eastern prairie fringe, were the first to taste the new way of life. In the 1820s and 1830s, they had adapted to the disappearance of moose and caribou by hunting small game on family hunting territories. By the 1860s, some were taking part-time employment as canoe men, cart drivers, and labourers in the fur trade or had hired out to Red River farmers. Others continued to hunt and trap, but, because the buffalo herds had moved far to the south and west, they could no longer combine early- and late-winter fur gathering with the mid-winter buffalo hunt.

An illustration of the new order was the Riding Mountain district where, in order to retain the services of Ojibwas as fur gatherers, the Hudson's Bay Company imported pemmican from its western posts and there exchanged these 'plains provisions' for the pelts of mink, marten, and fisher. Henceforth, the Ojibwas were dependent on the trading company for food. As time went on, pemmican was supplemented by flour and biscuits, and, eventually, the old native diet gave way to a European diet. The hunters had virtually become company employees: 'They trapped for the company and were provided with nearly all of their requirements at the company store on credit.' By a sleight-of-hand, it must have seemed, these Ojibwas had exchanged the autonomy of a hunting-gathering band for employee status and food.[1]

The condition of the plains bands was considerably more insecure. Sporadic warfare between Blackfoot and Cree-Assiniboine forces, usually with control of the horse trade as object, continued to mid-century. As the American buffalo robe trade prospered, the pressure on the buffalo population – still the crucial factor in plains Indian culture – increased. As a consequence, the annual metis-controlled hunts from Red River became an issue in the 1850s, and both Dakota (Sioux) and plains Crees resisted metis incursions into the best hunting grounds. A Cree council at Qu'Appelle in 1857 criticized the metis and Hudson's Bay Company for their presence on the open plains, blamed European goods for the hard times now faced by the Indians, and resolved not only to forbid metis and European hunting in their territory but also to forbid all travel through it except that associated with the conduct of trade. When the redoubtable English gentlemen Milton and Cheadle reached the Cree camps in 1862–3, they received a lecture along similar lines. The once-secure Crees, who had seen themselves as the centre of the universe and had scoffed at the European greenhorns, were beginning to recognize that their single crucial resource, the buffalo, was disappearing.[2]

Because the decade of the 1860s was a time of scarcity on the plains, the Crees despaired of the hunts and the horse supply in their own territory (Fort Edmonton to the South Saskatchewan elbow to the Yellowstone-Missouri river forks) and began to move west into the neutral zone that separated them from the Blackfoot. Raids and truces were the rule until 1865, when the Crees moved into the 'last refuge' on the western plains, the game-rich forests and deep sheltered valleys of the Cypress Hills, about 150 miles west of the traditional Cree-Blackfoot border. Isaac Cowie, the fur trader, visited a Cree encampment in the hills in 1869 and found that it consisted of 'three hundred and fifty large leather lodges, containing a mixed population of probably two thousand five hundred or three thousand people, of whom about five hundred were men and lads capable of waging war.'[3] These people had ventured into enemy territory not because they sought to expand their empire but rather because their very survival depended on more successful hunts. Violence between Crees and Blackfoot was the increasingly likely result of this migration.

The single most significant step on the descent toward war occurred in the spring of 1869 when the famous Cree diplomat and peace-maker Maskepetoon was invited to resume his quest for a Cree-Blackfoot understanding. Earlier in the decade, Maskepetoon had won a reputation as a diplomat because of several truces he had negotiated, but this time he was given no chance. His fate was reported by the Methodist missionary, Reverend John McDougall:

> The Cree and Blackfeet were in proximity, having been forced there by the movements of the buffalo, and the Blackfeet made proposals of peace, which Maskepetoon answered favourably, and himself and his son with a small party set out to arrange and ratify the compact. As he approached the camp of the Blackfeet, the latter came out to meet him with loud acclaim, and seemed very friendly, and the whole crowd of both sides sat down to quietly converse, and, as far as Maskepetoon was concerned, to smoke the pipe of peace. But while this function was going on, at a signal given by one of the Blackfeet, the massacre of the old chief and his people began, and very soon all were killed by this consummate treachery.[4]

Revenge was necessary, of course, and by 1870 a state of war existed along the Cree-Blackfoot frontier from the Missouri to Fort Edmonton.

This plains warfare has been eclipsed by the publicity given the Red River uprising of 1869–70, but it was an important watershed for the participants. Isaac Cowie, a young fur trader, claimed that he heard of as many as 700 violent deaths in this era of bloodshed. And the battles were only a part of the tragedy of the plains Indians in the deadly decade 1865–75. Two devastating epidemics swept through the Cree and Blackfoot camps in those years; estimates of the death toll ranged upward from several thousand to half the plains population. Another deadly enemy, the whisky traders from the Missouri River posts, particularly Fort Benton, moved north into the Cypress Hills–Oldman River district in the late 1860s and began to dispense their powerful violence-breeding concoction.[5] Murderous quarrels, the threat of starvation, and the dissolution of families and bands followed in their wake. But if the sorrow and hardship were great, they caused only a brief hiatus in the plains war. At a Cree war council in the autumn of 1870, one chief declared: 'Advance and capture the Blackfoot nation ... The small pox killed most of their fighters so we won't be opposed by any great number.' A great war party of Assiniboines and Crees, including the chiefs Big Bear, Piapot, Little Mountain, and Little Pine and their 600 to 800 warriors, moved west with horses, tents, and a variety of weapons ranging from Hudson's Bay Company muskets to bows and arrows.

They met a large force of Bloods and Piegans (Blackfoot) near the junction of Oldman and St Mary's rivers, not far from the whisky post Fort Whoop-up, and launched a full-scale attack. If surprise was on their side, fire power favoured the Blackfoot, who were equipped with modern repeating rifles, needle guns, and revolvers. As Jerry Potts, later a guide and interpreter for the North-West Mounted Police but then a member of the Blackfoot force, reported: 'You could fire with your eyes shut and would be sure to kill a Cree.' The surprise attack was quickly repulsed and the Blackfoot then counterattacked, driving the Crees across the river and into a bluff of trees. Bodies littered the bank of the river, the water's edge was red with blood, and the fast current carried many more bodies downstream. It is certain that 200 to 300 Crees and perhaps 40 Blackfeet died that day at the Oldman River.

The battle of Oldman River ended the last plains war. The Crees sent tobacco to the Blackfoot in the spring of 1871, and a formal peace was concluded at a meeting of chiefs at the Red Deer River in the autumn. Both sides had been exhausted by the conflicts, the epidemics, and the whisky trade. They now hunted across the plains without regard for territorial limits, pursuing the remnants of the buffalo herds, while the spectre of a white Canadian invasion was slowly translated into reality.[6]

The so-called Cypress Hills massacre was a brutal reminder of the violence of the frontier and an example of the treatment Indians might expect in an uncontrolled confrontation with whites. The Cypress Hills rise out of the wide dry plains of the southwest prairie like the foothills of the Rocky Mountains, from which they are several hundred miles distant, and constitute a remarkable oasis between the valleys of the Missouri and the South Saskatchewan. To climb into the hills, a trip of a few miles, is to discover a world of forests and valleys, streams and glades, birds and insects, quite unlike the plains that stretch away for miles in every direction. A kind of animal sanctuary when they were a no-man's land between Blackfoot and Cree-Assiniboine territory, the Hills became a busy crossroads for both hunters and traders in the late 1860s. Besides the Indians, the most common residents of the hills were independent traders, usually associated with the American supply companies at Fort Benton on the Missouri, whose cart trains creaked north in the autumn and returned in late spring with profitable cargoes of furs and robes. Though liquor was an illegal trade good in both American and British territory, only the Americans had troops in place to enforce the law, and so the traders usually carried whisky – often mixed with the most appalling dilutants – when they worked north of the border. The traders' posts were rude affairs, consisting of rough log palisades, about ten feet in height, enclosing two or three log shacks – roofs of sod, floors of mud – and might house a handful or several dozen people, but they were centres of attention, especially in the long winters.

In the winter of 1872–3 two such posts, those of Moses Soloman and Abel Farwell, sat on opposite banks of a quiet bush-covered stream, perhaps 200 yards apart, deep in a valley within the Cypress Hills. Nearby, in a coulee, a succession of Cree and Assiniboine bands had camped, as they brought in their furs and traded for supplies before moving off again. In late May 1873, an Assiniboine band of about 30 lodges led by Little Soldier (Manitupotis) and a number of smaller groups including 13 lodges under Little Chief (then known as Inihan-Kinyen) were in the coulee, their horses tethered, camp-fires smoking, dogs barking, while they enjoyed the comforts of plentiful wood and water as well as the provisions of the nearby posts. The atmosphere was slightly troubled: whisky was still readily available, horse stealing remained an irritant in Indian-white relations, and quarrels were numerous, but fights did not unduly worry Soloman and Farwell, who between them employed or housed about twenty people and were accustomed to confrontation. Testimony to their sang-froid was the fact that, though one of their traders had been murdered by Indians in April, the event caused little more than a ripple in the trading season calendar.

The arrival of a gang of wolf hunters disturbed the calm at Battle Creek. These quarrelsome characters, about a dozen in number, hunted wolves with strychnine for the bounty payments and probably stole horses on the side. They were lamenting the loss of about forty horses to Cree raiders and enjoying the remaining whisky at Farwell's post when one of the post employees, himself drunk, burst onto the scene complaining that his horse had been stolen. What happened next is far from certain, but the wolfers and several traders seem to have collected their guns – mostly recent models of Winchester and Henry repeating rifles – and approached the Assiniboine camp in the belief that the stolen horse was there. The Indians had been drinking that day and may have been incapacitated by this time. Moreover, they were no longer on good terms with one of the traders, Soloman, and thus might have been expected to greet the oncoming delegation with hostility, even belligerence, despite their unpreparedness for battle. Warned by a metis from the post of the wolfers' attitude, the Indian women and children scattered, but a number of the Indian men waved their guns in the air and offered to fight. Attempts to negotiate delivery of another horse as compensation for the alleged theft quickly collapsed, shots were fired, and the wolfers then riddled the camp with a deadly hail of bullets. Not a white was injured in this attack. One died later while hunting down native survivors. About twenty Indians were killed, most by rifle fire though one was clubbed to death; his severed head was later to be erected on a lodge pole near the post. Five Indian women were captured and raped in the ensuing drunken debacle. The traders and wolfers moved out the next day, leaving the posts in flames in order to deprive the Indians of a last revenge. The remaining Indians, including a boy of twelve whose reminiscence provides a sad commentary on the events, fled the smoking ruins of their tepees in the valley and eventually joined other bands in the area.[7]

The story of the Cypress Hills massacre has often been told. But what is its moral? It is true that some of the perpetrators of the crime were eventually tried, five in an extradition hearing in Montana in 1875 and three in a murder trial in Winnipeg in 1876, but conflicting testimony and vagueness in details permitted the acquittal of all those arrested. Neither the speed nor the justice of this example of law enforcement would have impressed the Assiniboines. It is also true that the grisly details hastened the dispatch of the Mounted Police to the west in the autumn of 1873, but whether events in the Cypress Hills did more than speed up a process already in hand is doubtful. The real significance of the massacre lay in its uniqueness. It was not part of a pattern of overt racial violence, and, despite many problems in the following decades, such unbridled barbarity, unleashed in a land then beyond reach of law, was never permitted to occur again.

The violence of the decade after 1865 only made plain what everyone already knew, that the inhabitants of the western interior required new political and judicial arrangements to replace the now irrelevant authority of the Hudson's Bay Company. One of the most pressing issues was the Indian claim to sovereignty. This had not concerned the fur trade companies, but had been of sufficient concern to Lord Selkirk that he had negotiated a treaty with five Cree and Ojibwa chiefs in July 1817. By this agreement, the Indians ceded to the crown strips of land two miles wide on either side of the Red and Assiniboine rivers from Lake Winnipeg to near Grand Forks and the Muskrat River respectively. In exchange, the Indians were to receive 200 pounds of tobacco annually. But this example of Selkirk's scrupulous concern for propriety was the only well-documented case wherein native rights to soil in the northwest had been extinguished. With the transfer of the entire region to Canadian control in 1870, this issue immediately pressed on the federal administration and its agents in the small province of Manitoba, because 'Indians, and land reserved for Indians' were matters of federal responsibility under the British North America Act.

The Canadian authorities did not lack for guidance in their deliberations. The basis of Canadian Indian policy had been set out over a century earlier in the British proclamation of 1763, which provided the rules for the administration of the former territories of New France, and in the administrative practices of Sir William Johnson, superintendent of Indian affairs. By this policy, the British acknowledged Indian aboriginal rights to the soil while asserting crown title as well. Thus the crown accepted that it must formally extinguish Indian rights before settlement or other distribution of the land could occur. Only the crown could undertake such negotiations with the Indians, and thus private parties could not legally arrange for their own claims to Indian land; negotiation was to occur at an open assembly before all the people rather than in closed sessions among a few representatives. Treaties of this sort, often with a military alliance in view, were negotiated in the eighteenth century, and, though the object became one of paternalist concern, others were negotiated in the Maritime colonies and Lower Canada in the first half of the nineteenth century. A significant departure in this system occurred in 1850 when the so-called Robinson treaties were negotiated with the Indians of the Lake Huron and Lake Superior territories. Here, rather than a small acreage required for immediate settlement, as had been the case in the past, the treaties covered huge districts far removed from settled areas. As an example of a carefully organized move by imperial authorities to clear the way for future development, the Robinson treaties set the pattern for the treaties in the western interior in the 1870s.

A treaty was a much more formal and explicit conclusion to an agreement between Indians and Europeans than was the exchange of gifts, medals, or trade goods, but like those earlier and (to Europeans) less binding ceremonies it was a means of cementing a relationship between peoples and setting out the rules by which that relationship would be governed. Though often scorned today as an empty form imposed by a conqueror on the conquered, the treaties of the 1870s should not be dismissed so quickly. The Indians had much less autonomy in the negotiations than would have been the case twenty-five years earlier, but they still negotiated as firmly as they could, won concessions where possible, and produced a settlement that had positive as well as negative features for their group. The Europeans entered the negotiations with limited financial resources to pay for concessions, little military power to enforce their will, and a great deal of nervousness as to what the Indians would accept. Thus the necessity of a treaty was more than a mere formality in the view of the Canadian government. The Indians were a sufficiently powerful military force in the early 1870s to evoke fears in official circles and, if nothing more, to threaten immigration prospects for a generation. The fact that there 25–35,000 Indians in the western interior in 1870, and another 10,000 metis, and fewer than 2,000 Europeans or Canadians reinforced the government's concern.

The treaties were also sufficiently important to both sides to create a liturgy of their own. The negotiations were accompanied by great pageantry. They featured long and rhetorical statements, often laden with exaggerated metaphors (wherein, for example, the crown and Queen Victoria became the 'Great Mother'), and had their own symbols, such as uniforms and peace pipes. They were marked by intense debate, both within the camp of the Europeans and in the deadly serious, often faction-ridden councils of the natives. To our ears, the pompous rhetoric of the mid-Victorian politician rings hollow, whereas the simple nature-based images of the Indians seem to sing of honesty and innocence. However, as in any set of negotiations, one should beware of judging either side simply on the basis of appearances.

The topic of treaties was first raised in the Fort Frances–Rainy River corridor when the Canadian government sought to conciliate the Ojibwas in order to assure the safe passage of the Wolseley expedition to Red River. The response of the Ojibwas was most instructive: they would permit the passage of troops, as well as steamers and even railways, in exchange for appropriate payment (one report said they wanted ten dollars per Indian to relinquish control over the right of passage by immigrants), but they would not permit settlers on their lands. In other words, the treaty concept was not questioned by the Ojibwas, but the proposed terms of the treaty were apparently going to be stiff. As it happened, Wolseley did distribute gifts to the Indians but, probably because of the range of Ojibwa claims, did not conclude a treaty in 1869–70. The Indians around Fort Garry also were prepared to negotiate a treaty as soon as the lieutenant-governor arrived, and presented their case with considerable persistence during Lieutenant-Governor Archibald's first year in Manitoba. At the same time, federal government commissioners opened negotiations with the Ojibwa Indians in the Fort Frances district. The Fort Frances team made no progress in 1870–1. In fact, it was told by one of the Ojibwa leaders: 'We want … much that the white man has to give and the white man, on his part wants roads and land. When we meet next summer you must be prepared to tell us where your roads are to pass and what lands you require.' The Indians would retain sovereignty, in this view, and the government would acquire corridors running through it. But this was not acceptable to the federal government, which wanted instead to extinguish Indian claims to the territory once and forever. When the commissioner, Wemyss Simpson, member of Parliament for Algoma, presented this proposal to the Ojibwas in 1871, he was unable to win agreement and may even have been insulted by the Indians. Simpson retreated to Winnipeg where, with Lieutenant-Governor Archibald, he began another set of negotiations. Because they were the first to result in a treaty, these latter talks were crucial to the settlement of Indian claims in the west.[8]

Archibald and Simpson convened an assembly of about 1,000 Indians at Lower Fort Garry on 27 July 1871. Government provisions were made available, and liquor was banned. Uniformed troops were present as symbols of the power of the crown. Chiefs and headmen were formally selected by the Indians – in order that the authority of the treaty signatories could not be questioned – and opening statements were then made. Archibald and Simpson argued that reserves were to be set aside but that these would not be as large as some Indians seemed to assume. The concern of the government was the peace and welfare of its people, Archibald explained:

Your Great Mother wishes the good of all races under her sway. She wishes her red children to be happy and contented. She wishes them to live in comfort. She would like them to adopt the habits of the whites, to till land and raise food, and store it up against a time of want ... Your Great Mother, therefore, will lay aside for you 'lots' of land to be used by you and your children forever. She will not allow the white men to intrude upon these lots. She will make rules to keep them for you, so that as long as the sun shall shine, there shall be no Indian who has not a place that he can call his home, where he can go and pitch his camp, or if he chooses, build his house and till his land.[9]

These were memorable words, particularly when seen from the perspective of the land surrenders that occurred in the following half-century, but they were accompanied by an ultimatum that left the Indians little room for manoeuvre. Archibald was offering a treaty in exchange for the cession of all native rights and the grant of land reserves; but, whether the Indians accepted the treaty or not, he was saying, settlement was bound to occur. Given the circumstances, one wonders whether either party had much choice.

The Red River Indians responded with demands that sounded remarkably similar to those of the Fort Frances group. Their fundamental assumption seemed to be that they would retain the bulk of the land – over two-thirds of Manitoba, as Archibald commented later – while relinquishing small portions to the government. This was unacceptable, Archibald replied: 'If they thought it better to have no treaty at all, they might do without one, but they must make up their minds; if there was to be a Treaty, it must be on a basis like that offered.' The Indians withdrew to reconsider their position and, presumably, to discuss the relative merits of no treaty as against reserves of 160 acres per family of five. Three days later, negotiations resumed, this time not on the contentious issue of reserves but rather on limited matters such as government assistance in education, the provision of farm animals, and the supply of farm implements. After three more days of negotiations – and there was give and take at the sessions – an agreement was reached that satisfied both the Indians (except for Yellow Quill) and the government representatives. The Indians agreed to surrender title to all their territory, to keep the peace, and not to molest the property or persons of Her Majesty's other subjects. In return, they were to receive an immediate gratuity of three dollars each, an annuity of fifteen dollars in cash or goods per family of five, reserves in the amount of 160 acres per family of five, a school on each reserve, and protection from intoxicating liquor. A number of additional items – clothing for the headmen, farm animals, and implements – were not contained in the written text but rather were assented to informally; they were none the less binding. Later, when the government failed to carry out these clauses of the oral agreement, the Indians complained bitterly. After four years of argument, the Ottawa authorities finally acknowledged that these so-called outside promises were indeed part of the treaty. In early August 1871, the negotiations were complete. Pipes were smoked, drums rumbled, shots rang out, and the Lower Fort treaty, treaty 1 as it came to be known, was completed.[10]

The remaining prairie treaties differed in substance as well as detail. Treaty 2, covering the Lake Manitoba area, was signed within a month of the first, and because the results of the earlier negotiations were well known, apparently roused little debate. As earlier experience suggested, the Fort Frances–Lake of the Woods agreement, treaty 3, was more difficult. Wemyss Simpson failed to make headway in 1872, perhaps because rumours of silver discoveries had prompted the Indians to hold out for a higher price. The government offered higher gratuities and annuities, however, partly to counteract the influence of higher settlements across the boundary in the United States, and added an additional sum for chiefs and headmen, but still encountered difficulties. The Ojibwas were divided over whether the terms were adequate; what the federal negotiator, newly arrived Lieutenant-Governor Alexander Morris, termed 'divisions and jealousies' among the Indians stemmed from disagreements over whether to grant absolute sovereignty to the crown. As one Ojibwa said: 'The sound of the rustling of gold is under my feet where I stand; we have a rich country; it is the Great Spirit who gave us this; where we stand upon is the Indians' property, and belongs to them.' The Indians went so far as to place guards around Morris's own camp to ensure that no native broke rank. But Morris, too, had brought troops in order that Indians sympathetic to his case would be secure enough to state their views.

Morris refused to accept the notions of Indian sovereignty and of limited transfers to the crown. His offer of a larger annuity – five dollars per capita – was greeted by an Indian counter-proposal of ten dollars per capita as annuity and requests for numerous other 'gifts,' including farm animals, implements, clothing, buggies, seed, tools, twine for fishing nets, and additional supplies for chiefs. Moreover, this Indian proposal specifically postponed the issue of land reserves for discussion at a later date. The Ojibwas had learned much from the American and Red River negotiations. Morris took the only tack he could: he refused to back down and tried to find a crack in the chiefs' united front: 'I told them if so [if this was the Ojibwas' final offer] the conference was over, that I would return and report that they had refused to make a reasonable treaty, that hereafter I would treat with those bands who were willing to treat, but that I would advise them to return to the council and reconsider their determination before next morning, when, if not, I should certainly leave.'[11] A Lac Seul chief then deserted his brothers and, although 'the others tried to prevent him' as Morris reported, asked for a treaty including farm instruction and a school, in order that his children might gain 'the knowledge of the white man.' Indian unity broke down in the next twenty-four hours, and a treaty was concluded along the lines that Morris had desired. The Indians lost on the crucial issue of sovereignty, but they won much better terms than had been provided in the first two treaties, including a land grant of 640 acres, rather than the 160 acres of treaties 1 and 2. Treaty 3 also provided for a $12 gratuity (as opposed to $3 in 1871), a $5 annuity ($3), an extra salary for chiefs and headmen of $25 and $15 per annum respectively, a suit of clothing every three years (not given in 1871), $1,500 per annum for twine and ammunition (not given in 1871), as well as farm tools and implements, carpenter tools, seed, and cattle to be given one time only (a much larger list than that in the 1871 treaties). This was very close to the Ojibwas' demands of 1869, except that the provision of tools and supplies was not to be renewed at eight-year intervals as had been requested in the earlier proposal, nor was there a huge cash settlement as the Indians had demanded.[12]

Treaty 4, covering the Ojibwas, Crees, and Assiniboines in the southern prairies between Fort Ellice and the Cypress Hills, produced yet another significant bargaining ploy on the Indians' part. Having set the meeting place at the Hudson's Bay Company post situated in the winding valley of Qu'Appelle, Lieutenant-Governor Morris arrived only to face an Indian request that the conference tent be moved away from the company reserve because that plot was itself at issue. The Indians said they would not even commence negotiations until the issue of company land had been settled. As

The Gambler, an Indian leader, argued, the Indians were still in control of the territory, and, because they had not given up any land, the company should not be able to claim the Qu'Appelle post site as a reserve. Indeed, the £300,000 paid to extinguish company claims in the northwest should have been paid to the Indians, Pasqua, another spokesman, argued. As in every other treaty negotiation, the real issue in the session was where ultimate sovereignty lay. The Gambler said: 'The Company have stolen our land. The Queen's messengers never came here, and now I see the soldiers and the settlers and the policemen. I know it is not the Queen's work, only the Company has come, and they are the head, they are the foremost.'[13] When asked what the company had stolen, Gambler replied: 'The earth, trees, grass, stones, all that I see with my eyes.' Again, Morris hoped to divide the militant Indians from the passive. As he reported: 'The Crees were from the first ready to treat, as were the Saulteaux [Ojibwas] from Fort Pelly, but the Saulteaux of the Qu'Appelle District were not disposed to do so and attempted to coerce the other Indians. They kept the chiefs "Loud Voice" and "Coté" under close surveillance, they being either confined to their tents or else watched by "soldiers," and threatened if they should make any overtures to us.' But eventually the Crees' desire for a treaty broke the Indian ranks, and the Ojibwas went along with the rest. Treaty 4 was in most respects similar to treaty 3.[14]

If one prairie treaty stands out from the others it is probably treaty 5. Though future economic development was in part the government's motivation for the treaty, the urgent need of the Indians themselves was also a precipitating factor in its completion. In the territory of Lake Winnipeg and The Pas, employment with the Hudson's Bay Company had dropped with the introduction of steamboats and the use of the American as opposed to the Bay route from England, and the Indians were pressing for the allotment of reserves and supplies in order that they might begin to farm. This Indian concern, coupled with Canadian interest in the timber, mineral, and transportation prospects of the Saskatchewan River–Lake Winnipeg territory, led to the treaty discussions. The negotiations were very rapid; at each of three sites in September 1875, the talks opened and concluded within a single day. Whether these Indians, more distant from the main travelled routes of the plains, understood the implications of the agreement was uncertain. They wanted reserves immediately, and, despite the usual administrative problems, that was achieved. But whether they wanted to bargain away their sovereignty over the territory is unknown. In 1876, when a negotiator returned to secure further adhesions to the treaty among bands who had not been present the year before, he encountered Indians at Grand Rapids who claimed that the 1875 talks were merely preparatory to the signing of a treaty. Whatever the sincerity of this misapprehension, it produced little further debate at the time.[15]

The great plains Cree community had been quarrelling with the government and with its Indian enemies since the mid-1860s, and though the war at Oldman River in 1871 had cooled the temper of the warriors the disappearance of the buffalo ensured that they would remain edgy and combative. The dispatch of waves of government observers and of the North-West Mounted Police provided a stream of information on their restlessness, but, for a variety of reasons, the long-promised Saskatchewan treaty negotiations were postponed from season to season to the point where both Lieutenant-Governor Morris and the plains Cree chiefs were angry. In the summer of 1875, the Crees interrupted both the geological survey and the construction of the telegraph line from Winnipeg to Edmonton on the grounds that they would not permit such trespassing until a treaty was completed. These actions were little different in nature or implication from that of the Red River metis who in 1869 stopped a government survey party and thus precipitated the resistance. After four years of sparring, Morris finally received Ottawa's permission to negotiate a treaty at Fort Carlton on the North Saskatchewan River in the summer of 1876:

On my arrival I found that the ground had been most judiciously chosen, being elevated, with abundance of trees, hay marshes and small lakes. The spot which the Indians had left for my council tent overlooked the whole.

The view was very beautiful: the hills and the trees in the distance, and in the foreground, the meadow land being dotted with clumps of wood, with the Indian tents clustered here and there to the number of two hundred.

On my arrival, the Union Jack was hoisted, and the Indians at once began to assemble, beating drums, discharging firearms, singing and dancing. In about half an hour they were ready to advance and meet me. This they did in a semicircle, having men on horseback galloping in circles, shouting, singing and discharging firearms.

They then performed the dance of the 'pipe-stem,' the stem was elevated to the north, south, west, and east, a ceremonial dance was then performed by the Chiefs and headmen, the Indian men and women shouting the while.

They then slowly advanced, the horsemen again preceding them on their approach to my tent. I advanced to meet them accompanied by Messrs. Christie and McKay, when the pipe was presented to us and stroked by our hands.

After the stroking had been completed, the Indians sat down in front of the council tent, satisfied that in accordance with their custom we had accepted the friendship of the Cree nation.

Morris emphasized in his opening statement that he was sent by the queen not to trade for short-term goods or palliatives but to help in the creation of an agreement that would endure 'as long as that sun shines and yonder river flows.' After the Indians adjourned to nominate their 'recognized leading chiefs,' Morris explained the terms of the proposed treaty, noting that 'we did not wish to inter-fere with their present mode of living, but would assign them reserves and assist them as was being done elsewhere, in commenc-ing to farm.'[16]

Once again, the crucial issue in the negotiations was retention of sovereignty. Upon hearing the terms, Poundmaker, then an impor-tant man but not yet a great chief, objected to the size of the pro-posed reserves: '"The government mentions how much land is to be given us. He says 640 acres one mile square for each band. He will give us, he says," ... and in a loud voice, he [Poundmaker] shouted "This is our land, it isn't a piece of pemmican to be cut off and given in little pieces back to us. It is ours and we will take what we want."' A wave of approval greeted this protest, and a number of Indians stood up, waving their hands and shouting yes in Cree. Morris was shaken by the incident but took his usual line: because settlement was inevitable, the Indians would be crowded out unless they had reserves. He did not discuss the implied issues of relative size of reserves or of development policy itself. The talks then adjourned. The Indians spent a day in informal discussion and another day in a formal council separate from the Canadians. According to a metis observer, Peter Erasmus, the resistance of Poundmaker and those of his persuasion was overwhelmed by the weighty speeches of two senior chiefs, Star Blanket (Ahtahkakoop) and Big Child (Mistawasis). In the face of rapidly declining food resources, these elders feared that death by starvation was the only alternative to the treaty. As Star Blanket said: 'For my part, I think that the Queen Mother has offered us a new way and I have faith in the things my brother Mistawasis has told you ... Surely we Indians can learn the ways of living that made the White man strong.'[17]

When the Indians returned to the bargaining tent with Lieutenant-Governor Morris on the following day, they devoted their entire attention to the food supply question. 'They were not exacting,' Morris reported, 'but they were very apprehensive of their future, and thankful, as one of them put it, "a new life was dawning upon them."' The next day was spent on a list of more precise demands, ranging from farm animals to aid for the blind and lame. This list included a free supply of medicines and, in case of war, exclusion from liability to serve in the military. Morris did agree to provide a medicine chest (a clause that was to return to the courts in modern times), to provide additional aid in the first three years of farming, and to add to the treaty a famine clause indicative of the concerns of the Saskatchewan bands: that is, if famine or pestilence ever struck, the queen would grant assistance 'to relieve the Indians from the calamity that shall have befallen them.' When Morris had approved the revised terms, Star Blanket called on the people for assent, which they provided by shouting and holding up their hands. But again Poundmaker intervened, saying that he could not see how their children would be clothed and fed on what was promised and that he did not know how to build a house or cultivate the ground. His warnings fell on deaf ears. Mistawasis called Peter Erasmus aside and asked him to ensure that all the promises were actually written into the treaty, but, aside from that precaution, the negotiations were concluded on a basis similar to the others. Some plains Indians, notably Big Bear, refused to sign the treaty, but it was assumed that they, too, would soon come to terms.

The Blackfeet of the Rocky Mountains foothills, whose territory extended from the Missouri to the North Saskatchewan, had had less regular contact with Europeans during the two centuries of fur trade, but they too had been drawn into the orbit of development in the 1860s. They might have settled on either side of the forty-ninth parallel, depending on the movements of the buffalo and the political situation, had the North-West Mounted Police not arrived in 1874. By suppressing the excesses of the whisky trade and providing a rough but effective judicial system, the Mounted Police acted as a buffer in the times of great trial in 1875–7 when the buffalo hunt failed and thousands of Sioux refugees fled across the border before the American cavalry. The result was that in September 1877 the last of the prairie treaties, number 7, was negotiated at Blackfoot Crossing, with representatives of the units of the Blackfoot confederacy, the Piegans, Bloods, Siksikas (or Blackfoot proper), and Sarcees, as well as a few mountain Assiniboines (Stoney). Hundreds of tepees, ten thousand horses, feathered headdresses, and the inevitable dogs created an exciting scene. The usual ceremonies were conducted, the newly appointed commissioner, David Laird, made the usual opening speech, the chiefs were recognized, and then an adjournment was called in order that the Indians might consider their position. The Blackfoot were as divided as their compatriots in the earlier treaty sessions had been. It appears that the two crucial individuals in the deliberations were Red Crow, a senior Blood chief, and Crowfoot of the Siksikas. The latter, who had been impressed by the activities of the Mounted Police and by Commissioner Macleod, feared the day when settlement overwhelmed his people: 'That would be the time they would need to rely on the white man for help.' Crowfoot swung the balance in favour of the treaty.[18]

The signing of treaty 7 marked the conclusion of an eight-year debate on Indian-white relations. In the years that followed, a small number of additional bands signed the prairie treaties and separate treaties were negotiated in northern Alberta (treaty 8, 1899) and in northern Saskatchewan and Alberta (treaty 10, 1906–7).[19] The translation of the western interior from aboriginal possession to clear crown land and to private ownership had been accomplished with extraordinary dispatch. The government had achieved title to the soil, according to its view of the law, and the Indians had achieved recognition of their needs and some measure of protection against the seemingly inevitable influx of Canadian settlers. In return for relinquishing sovereignty, the Indians had won a permanent direct relationship with the crown which, they believed, would serve them in case of disputes with local administrators.

To weigh the relative gains and losses of a treaty is a difficult matter. These were not simply imposed settlements as is sometimes suggested. The Indians won more in the negotiations than the government had planned to give, but they lost on the crucial issue of ultimate sovereignty over the land. One might well ask, however, given the time of the discussions and the assumption of rapid development that both parties accepted, whether a better result was possible for either side. Some Indians, perhaps a considerable proportion of the total, particularly among the Ojibwas but also including recognized militants such as Big Bear, wanted to reject the terms. None the less the negotiators were always able to win over the 'doves,' who could be induced to accept the agreement because of their fears for the future or because they wished help in the process of adjustment. Once some adherents had been obtained, the government negotiators enjoyed the luxury – from the standpoint of a bargaining session – of threatening to settle the deal with those receptive to a compromise while omitting the advocates of a hard line; that is, the government would have been able to extinguish native title and leave the recalcitrants out of the financial arrangements. Indian solidarity was never sufficient to resist this threat because, when forced to make a decision, the greater proportion of Indians – leaders and followers – was persuaded by the case for compromise.

Whether the Indians appreciated that they had agreed in principle to a sweeping change in property relations has been debated ever since. Did the Indians understand the implications of the transfer of sovereignty and, in particular, of the white Canadian perception of private property? Irene Spry has suggested that the Indian notion of property encompassed common property, wherein members of a defined group used an area according to certain rules, and open access, in which the resources were used by everyone as they saw fit. But, she contends, the Indian view did not encompass private property, the actual possession and trade of real estate, and thus the Indians were not capable of appreciating the treaty. They thought they were admitting whites into the territory to share the resources given by the Manitou to all his people, Spry argues; they assumed that in certain parts of this territory – the reserves – resources would belong exclusively to the Indian people and that elsewhere open access would be the rule.[20]

Spry's interpretation corresponds to the Indian perception of property as recorded by Edwin Denig in the mid-nineteenth century:

None of these ... tribes claim a special right to any circumscribed or
limited territory ... All the ... territory in the West [known to them]
and now occupied by all the Indians was created by Wakonda [Assini-
boine Creator] for their sole use and habitation ... Now each nation
finds themselves in possession of a portion of these lands, necessary
for their preservation. They are therefore determined to keep them
from aggression by every means in their power. Should the game fail,
they have a right to hunt it in any of their enemies' country, in which
they are able to protect themselves ... It is not land or territory they
seek in this but the means of subsistence, which every Indian deems
himself entitled to even should he be compelled to destroy his
enemies or risk his own life to obtain it.[21]

This argument also supports the view reiterated by Indian elders during this century: Indians gave whites the use of the land for farming
purposes, but did not relinquish the water, timber, fish, birds, mountains, or minerals. Such debates must be entered with caution. Not
only is there much at stake in the contemporary review of aboriginal
rights but also each treaty differs in crucial ways from every other. In
treaty 5, of course, the explanations were brief and perhaps incom-
plete. In treaty 3, the implications of the settlement seem to have been
recognized. Jean Friesen argues that the Ojibwas in the latter treaty
negotiations knowingly exchanged their property for guarantees of
continuing economic and political assistance from the state. In this
view, Mawedopenais, a leader of the treaty 3 people, understood
very well what the bargain implied: 'And now in concluding this
treaty I take off my glove and give you my hand and with it my
birthright and my land – and in taking your hand I hold fast all the
promises you have made as long as the sun rises and the water flows
as you have said.'[22] There is no short answer to the issue of Indian
perception of property relations and sovereignty in the treaties.

There will never be agreement on what the original parties did, let
alone what they thought they had done. Nevertheless, it seems
clear that a fundamental divergence in Indian and government
views of the treaty has marred Indian-white relations from the 1870s
to the present. For the crown, the treaty was a single transaction. A
price was arrived at, aboriginal title was extinguished, and the two
parties had no further claims on each other except as specified in the
clauses of the treaty. For the Indians, in contrast, the treaty, like the
fur trade exchange, was an alliance. It was subject to renewal each

year and implied a continuing relationship between two peoples. The Indian people assumed they had given up their land or birth-right, however they understood this concept, and in exchange acquired political protection, economic security, and education not just during the troubled era of transition but forever. As the custom of annual treaty payments recognized, this was not a one-shot event, in their eyes, but a relationship that would be reviewed in order that the spirit of the contract, as well as the letter, was main-tained.[23]

In the mid-1870s, while the last prairie treaties were being negoti-ated, while the prairie bands were beginning the process of reserve selection, and while the first white settlers were moving onto the open grasslands to experiment with cereal crops, native apprehen-sion about the new order was slowly growing. Some experienced observers of the region, native and white, assumed that fifty years, a century, perhaps an eternity would pass before the fur trade and the hunt ended. But others feared that hard times were ahead. No one, it can be said with confidence, anticipated just how difficult the next decade would be. Who among the residents of the prairie west imagined a transition that, for most of the sub-districts within the region, was completed within ten years of its start? Adams Archi-bald, addressing the Indians at the Stone Fort in the negotiation of treaty 1, said that the queen thought it good that the Indians adopt 'civilized ways' but would not compel them to do so. They would have to cease hunting over the land as it was settled, but 'there will still be plenty of land that is neither tilled nor occupied where you can go and roam and hunt as you have always done, and, if you wish to farm, you will go to your own reserve where you will find a place ready for you to live on and cultivate.'[24] And yet by 1870 there had been no buffalo near Red River for some time; by 1876 there were only a few in the region of Qu'Appelle; and by 1879 even the herds of the Cypress Hills region had melted away. The transition was over, for all intents and purposes, by 1885. This turbulent decade, 1875–85, ended in violence and, it must be said, betrayal of the Indian people.

The heart of the problem was the virtual extinction of the Cana-dian buffalo herd between 1874 and 1879. No satisfactory explana-tion, aside from an incredible slaughter by native and white hunters who were supplying the American robe trade, has ever been offered for this sudden destruction of the prairie food supply. A variety of half-hearted conservation measures was considered by the Canadian federal and territorial governments, but no effective limits were adopted in time. Heavy hunting in the mid-1870s depleted the breeding stock, and by 1878 most of the Canadian herd had been driven into Montana. Similar pressure in 1879, allegedly planned by the American authorities to ensure that Sitting Bull and his Sioux soldiers would starve in their Canadian refuges whence they had fled after the Little Big Horn, drove the animals south of the border again just as they were about to make their annual migration into the Saskatchewan country. By the end of 1879, the buffalo had disappeared forever from the Canadian prairies. Though some Indian bands travelled south to the Missouri for another three summers, even those herds were soon destroyed. The plains equestrian way of life, rich and fulfilling as it had been for over a century, had come to an end.[25]

The results were disastrous, especially for the hunters of the western prairies who had relied so completely on the buffalo. The Blackfoot, it was reported, were 'selling their Horses for a mere song, eating gophers, mice, and for the first time have hunted the Antelope and nearly killed them all off ... Strong young men were now so weak that some of them could hardly walk. Others who last winter were fat and hearty are mere skin and bone.'[26] Reports of hardship and of death by starvation were legion during the 1880s. If the government had been slow to react to the destruction of the buffalo, it did move quickly to feed the Indians. Emergency rations, including flour and cattle, were distributed by the federal authorities on numerous occasions.

What is striking, in retrospect, is the government's apparent use of food rations as a means of coercing reluctant Indians into the treaties and, later, as a tool for controlling Indian diplomatic activity. The problem lay with those plains Crees who had not been satisfied by the treaties of 1874 and 1876. Led by Big Bear, Piapot, and Little Pine, these bands had sought vainly to restrict the buffalo hunt to Indians only and then had demanded more generous gifts of food and capital equipment from the government. Though Piapot acceded to treaty 4 in 1875, the other two leaders stayed out of treaty 6 until the food supply crises. Under pressure from his followers, Little Pine gave up in 1879, but Big Bear, who was sustained by the most militant hunters, continued to resist until 1882, when starvation drove him to take the treaty in exchange for food rations. Even after they signed, however, these three leaders struggled to improve on the treaty settlement. Their goal was the creation of contiguous reserves where, as in the Indian territory established by the American reservation system, populous and extensive Indian communities might retain considerable autonomy. This the government could not accept. Indeed, Indian Affairs Commissioner Edgar Dewdney used food rations as a weapon to push Piapot into the Indian Head region and to send the Little Pine and Big Bear bands to Battleford and Fort Pitt respectively. But he could not prevent them from talking. Though separated by 300 miles of prairie, the Indian leaders continued to agitate for revision of the treaties.[27]

Big Bear was a key actor in subsequent events. One of the most independent and influential plains leaders of his generation, he had been consulting native leaders across the region for a decade. He had met Riel during a visit to the Missouri valley, had spoken with Sitting Bull after the defeat of General Custer, and had maintained constant contact with militants such as Piapot and moderates such as Crowfoot. W.B. Cameron, who knew him, reported many years later that Big Bear possessed 'great natural gifts: courage, a keen intellect, a fine sense of humour, quick perception, splendid native powers of expression and great strength of purpose.'[28] In 1884, Big Bear sent runners to all the plains Indians, even the Blackfoot, calling on them to attend a sun dance near Battleford, on the adjoining reserves of Poundmaker and Little Pine, undoubtedly in the expectation that a chiefs' council would follow the religious ceremony. When the great assembly began in June 1884 – probably the greatest assembly of plains chiefs in history – a violent confrontation between a starving Indian and a stubborn Canadian farm instructor led to Mounted Police intervention, a near-riot, and, apparently, the temporary discrediting of men such as Little Pine and Big Bear who prevented a slaughter. But Big Bear proceeded to another large assembly at Duck Lake, where, incidentally, Louis Riel spoke to the Indians and where it was agreed that an even bigger council would be held in the summer of 1885. The Indian protest was supported by the Duck Lake people, who drafted a petition detailing government violations of their treaty and accusing the federal commissioners of misleading them in the treaty negotiations. Big Bear's work was nearly complete. With Little Pine and Piapot, he had united the plains Crees and even interested the

Blackfoot in the proposed 1885 council where demands for an enlarged 'Indian territory' and greater Indian autonomy would be
approved and forwarded to Ottawa. A Cree revolt – a political
rather than a military uprising – was brewing.

The Canadian authorities were abreast of these developments.
Commissioner Dewdney relied on a number of informants, among
them the distinguished Cree chief Poundmaker, to follow the course
of the Cree diplomatic campaign and to determine his own policy.
In the face of this campaign and violent Cree opposition to his
threats of ration cuts, Dewdney abandoned his 'submit or starve'
policy in the summer of 1884. Instead, he would single out the
troublemakers and imprison them. 'Sheer compulsion,' he told
Prime Minister Macdonald, was 'the only effective course' when
handling most Indian bands. In the summer of 1884, as Indian solidarity grew, Dewdney won Macdonald's support for an increase in
the size of the Mounted Police force and for an amendment to the
Indian Act that would permit the arrest of any Indian who was on
another reserve without the approval of Indian Affairs officials. He
suggested also that Macdonald contact the stipendiary magistrates
in the region to ensure that jail sentences be used wherever possible
to remove troublemakers. Dewdney was ready for trouble by the
end of 1884, but he did not expect violence.

If government officials had known more about Little Poplar, they
might have been less sanguine. This war chief, a member of Big
Bear's own band, rejected his leader's long and slow diplomatic
campaign for Indian solidarity. Little Poplar advocated violence –
execution of Indian agents and government representatives – as a
means of restoring Cree independence. He found a sympathetic
response among the unruly youths in the Fort Pitt–Frog Lake area.
Because of Little Poplar's agitation, Big Bear, whose successes had
been achieved at the expense of much time away from his people,
was no longer the unchallenged leader of his band. Power among
his 500 followers passed to the warrior society – the Rattlers – and
to the war chiefs, Little Poplar and Wandering Spirit, and to Big
Bear's son Imasees. The militants were spoiling for trouble, and
news of a fight between metis and Mounted Police at Duck Lake,
over 200 miles east of their camp, pushed them into open warfare.
They vented their anger against whites, anger that had been building for a decade, by seizing the Hudson's Bay Company store at
Frog Lake on 2 April and killing nine white men in a few brief

minutes of rifle fire. Only the company agent and two white women were spared. With news of the 'Frog Lake massacre' came the chilling realization in households across the territories that Indians as well as metis were ready to die for the native cause. Among British Canadians, who knew of General Gordon at Khartoum and General Custer at the Little Big Horn, the Frog Lake incident created an atmosphere of terror. As if to make the threat immediate, stores at Fort Pitt, Lac La Biche, Cold Lake, Green Lake, and even the town of Battleford were pillaged by native soldiers. The protest movement had apparently become a general native uprising of the type familiar to every citizen of the empire.[29]

The terror among white settlers and the coincidence of the metis skirmish at Duck Lake with the Cree action at Frog Lake have combined to influence historical interpretations. Inevitably, the '1885 rebellion' is described as a metis and Indian uprising. Inevitably, too, these interpretations have suggested that Big Bear and even Poundmaker were associated with a Cree military movement planned to reinforce the metis under Riel and Dumont. These suggestions are wrong. As John Tobias has argued, the so-called Indian uprising was really the outburst of a few young warriors in each of the Cree and Assiniboine bands in central Saskatchewan. It was not approved by the chiefs and, indeed, did not attract widespread support. But it did offer the government an ideal opportunity to smash the Cree diplomatic campaign for native unity and revision of the treaties. The political goals of Dewdney, the panic of white settlers, and the assumptions of historians have created a concerted Indian-metis war where, in fact, sporadic raids for food and violent acts by a few young Indian rebels happened to coincide with the metis uprising.[30]

Insofar as it was possible, the leading chiefs remained aloof from the battles of 1885. After Frog Lake, Big Bear restored his authority over his band, convinced them to permit the peaceful withdrawal of the police detachment at Fort Pitt, and then headed into the bush country north of the North Saskatchewan where his followers would be far from the action. Beardy, another chief, and his followers refused Riel's invitation to join the metis. Piapot, whose reserve received a special contingent of troops, was never involved. The Blackfoot, likewise, resisted the temptation to strike back at the whites in this time of starvation and of government vulnerability. In their case, perhaps, Dewdney had acted wisely by inviting four chiefs of the Blackfoot confederacy, including Crowfoot, to travel by rail to Regina and Winnipeg in 1884 to view the numbers and achievements of the whites. The tour impressed the chiefs with the futility of defiance. Thus, when their young followers argued that the Blackfoot should join the metis in rebellion, the old chiefs temporized. Two of them, the Blood chief Red Crow, a long-time enemy of the Crees, and Eagle Tail, a Piegan, were adamant in their refusal to join the revolt. Crowfoot was uncertain. In the end, he followed the lead of Red Crow and sought to use his peaceful stance as a bargaining tool to acquire greater concessions from the federal government. Nevertheless, despite his refusal to ally against the whites, Crowfoot provided shelter for all Cree refugees who reached his camp and despised the Canadian military presence. His decision not to take up arms was a measure of his assessment of the military situation, not a statement of loyalty to the federal government.[31]

Poundmaker, whose soldiers were accused of participating in the metis rising, was also responsible for rescuing a portion of the Canadian military force from certain slaughter. In devising a strategy to deal with the vast territory and the confused situation, Canadian authorities had sent three columns of troops north from the newly constructed Canadian Pacific mainline, from Qu'Appelle, Swift Current, and Calgary. The Swift Current group, under Lt-Col William Otter, reached Battleford without difficulty only to discover that the so-called siege was actually a Cree foray in search of food that had escalated into pillage and vandalism. Otter had had the temerity to pursue Poundmaker into his own country, the wooded and hilly land to the west of the village. There, at Cutknife Hill, famous for a Cree victory over the Sarcees not many years before, Otter's 325 men surprised the Indians early in the morning of 2 May. The Cree soldiers immediately scattered through the bush and coulees surrounding the hill and began to fire at the exposed troops on the bald summit above them. As the morning passed, the troops' position deteriorated, the number of casualties increased, and the Indians almost completely surrounded the hill. Fearing disaster, Otter retreated and, to his surprise, was able to escape without further bloodshed. Little did he know that his men had been saved by Indian kindness. Poundmaker, who had never approved of this war, had ordered his own men to leave the Canadian soldiers in peace. Though he had not participated in the uprising to that date, the battle of Cutknife Hill drove Poundmaker to consider uniting his force with that of Riel. However, the fall of Batoche occurred as Poundmaker was leading his men toward the metis bastion, and, within a week, he too sought terms of peace.[32]

Big Bear's men had remained in their own territory around Fort Pitt, between Edmonton and Battleford, throughout April and had begun to move east toward Poundmaker's camp only in early May and then had stopped to hold a thirst dance in order to restore harmony and confidence among their disparate group of wood and plains Crees. However, when the third military column, Maj-Gen Strange's force from Calgary, reached the Cree camp at French-man's Butte, near Fort Pitt, Big Bear's soldiers installed themselves in deep rifle pits above the surrounding plain. A brief Canadian attack was enough to convince Strange that the Indians held a supe-rior position, and so he withdrew to Fort Pitt while the Cree, dis-turbed by the cannon fire, retreated in the opposite direction. The subsequent pursuit of Big Bear in the bush land west of Battleford was ponderous and extremely taxing – one soldier died of exhaus-tion after three weeks' march – but the Cree camp was tracked until it broke apart under the weight of internal dissension. Big Bear, ever the plains warrior, turned in his tracks and evaded the troops in a solitary trek to the territory of his birth around Fort Carlton, where he surrendered on 2 July. With the arrest of the leader of the plains Cree diplomatic campaign, the government had achieved its objec-tive. It was the turn of the courts and the law to ensure that Indians acquiesced to Canadian rule.

As in the discussion of the military events of 1885, so in the analysis of the legal proceedings, one must distinguish the whites and metis from the Indians. In the trials, Commissioner Dewdney had an ideal opportunity to break the independence of the Crees. He ensured that over 100 prisoners were processed during the sum-mer of 1885, including 2 whites, 46 metis, and 81 Indians. Most of the trials were for treason-felony, and only a fraction resulted in convictions. The judicial result included the imprisonment of 44 Indians and 7 metis. The bias of the system against the Indians could not be more evident. One experienced legal observer said Poundmaker was 'convicted on evidence that, in any ordinary trial, would have ensured his acquittal without the jury leaving the box.'[33] Big Bear, Poundmaker, and the other Indians found guilty of serious crimes were transported to the Stony Mountain federal peni-tentiary, north of Winnipeg, to serve three-year sentences within the stone walls of the fortress. The two chiefs had their long hair cropped, were required to do menial jobs, and, it is clear, were unable to adjust to prison life. Both converted to Roman Catholicism but their perception of this action is not known. Poundmaker was released in the spring of 1886, Big Bear in 1887, both, it is said, broken in heart and spirit. Neither lived out the year of his release. And the Cree diplomatic movement to create a single large reserve and better treaty terms was decisively defeated.

The events surrounding the treaties and the violence of 1885 have been the chief subjects of historical discussion of prairie Indians in the modern era. The attention is warranted, of course, but it should not obscure the fact that thousands of Indians continued to live in the prairie west after the death of Big Bear and Poundmaker and continued to struggle with government policy, agricultural assistance, and a new educational system. And, despite the undeniable hardships, they retained their sense of themselves as a different people. Piapot, whose quick tongue had inspired them so often in the past, could still provoke laughter at the whites and, in the process, suggest that Indians retained a degree of autonomy. One day shortly after the arrival of a new Indian agent who happened to have had a leg amputated, Piapot told a few members of his band that he had never trusted the white man's treaty and now he had proof that it was worthless; the whites had promised to maintain the treaty as long as the rivers flowed, the grass grew and men walked on two legs. Now they had sent him an agent who had only one leg.

The period from the mid-1870s to the mid-1880s had been terribly difficult for the prairie Indians because of the widespread food shortages, but there were other burdens placed on them in this era that were to remain with them for generations to come. The signing of treaties and the establishment of reserves marked the commencement of the process that scholars describe as 'directed social change.' One social group, in this classic model of social analysis, dominates another, guiding and forcing the latter's adaptation to its culture. In this view, white Canadian expectations and policies would slowly replace the ideas and plans of the Indian people; the social changes in the Indian community would conform increasingly to the rhythms of change in the larger society. Eventually, according to some theorists, there would cease to be a distinguishable native identity. But such enormous changes take time, as students of older societies can attest. School and reserve and administrative fiat would not transform Indians into European Canadians overnight.[34]

The political status of the prairie Indians was actually determined before they negotiated their treaties but was never explained to them or made a subject of negotiation. Instead, unilateral governmental decisions reduced them to the position of minors or wards. The government's Indian policy was a product of its dissatisfaction with native communities as they had evolved in the century after 1760. The Indian settlements, especially those in Upper Canada, had functioned well enough as economic and political units, but the Indians themselves, in the official view, remained distressingly separate from the larger community. To 'civilize' them, British authorities concluded, the principles of private property and the franchise would have to be inculcated more effectively. This was the purpose of the Gradual Civilizing Act of 1857. When Indian leaders refused to permit the whittling away of their reserves by the creation of fifty-acre private holdings, and when only a handful of Indians applied for enfranchisement, the new Canadian government, which inherited the British policy and outlook, imposed legal sanctions to control native self-government. By 1876, when the Indian Act was passed, the federal government and its agents had established a system of 'wardship, colonization and tutelage' that limited native self-government and even native economic development. Into this situation stepped the native people of the prairie west. They were assumed to possess aboriginal rights when they signed the treaties, to be sure, but they were not informed of the Indian Act's limits on their actions. Rather, only in the years after the treaty did they learn of these restrictions.[35]

The Indian Act, which has governed Canada's Indians since it first consolidated various pieces of legislation in 1876 and, in a more thorough revision, in 1880, requires the government to supervise the economy, politics, education, land, and even many personal decisions of the Indian people. As a former superintendent of Indian affairs once said, 'Probably there is no other legislation which deals with so many and varied subjects in a single Act. It may be said to deal with the whole life of a people.' The Indian Act is at once protective and coercive. It aims to protect and nurture the Indian people but also to assimilate them into Canadian society. It shows little respect for Indian society and expects few contributions by Indians – as Indians – to the larger community. However, it evinces a respect and concern for Indians as individuals worthy of integration into the Canadian mainstream. The Indian Act, in brief, is an example of the Victorian mind at work in a 'missionary' field.

An Indian, according to the act, is someone designated as an Indian. This includes individuals who are members of recognized bands as well as the wives, children, or widows of registered Indians. A white woman who marries an Indian becomes an Indian, as do her children; an Indian woman who marries a white thereupon loses her Indian status, as do her children. Traditional Indian government was superseded in the act by band chiefs and councils whose elections, terms, and powers were carefully set out. Despite the apparent latitude of local band administration, all Indian decisions were reviewed by administrators – usually whites – at the level of the band and then at regional and national supervisory offices. The bureaucracy was and remains a remarkable case of state direction of a community, as the example of Indian reserve land will illustrate. The purpose of reserves was to permit the Indians to learn European Canadian ways at their own pace; that is, the reserve isolated them from whites in order to integrate them more effectively at some later date. Reserves, by uniting the Indians in close-knit political and social arrangements, actually worked against this end. One important reason for the existence of reserves was officials' fear that if Indians were given individual title to plots of land they might fall prey to white swindlers. To combine the protection of the reserve with the educational virtues of private property, the administrators created 'location tickets' or certificates of ownership. By this system, plots of land would remain in the possession of individuals at the pleasure of the band council and the minister of Indian affairs and could not be sold except to the crown. It was an unusual and creative solution but, despite the advantages of this private-public tenure, state power over Indian land, including the power to expropriate, has caused problems. The ultimate goal of the Indian Act was to transform Indians into whites by means of the franchise, which implied not just the right to vote but also the right to hold and produce private property, to use liquor, and to pay full taxes. Enfranchisement, in short, meant that the Indian turned his back on his heritage, left his reserve, and became a non-Indian in the 'mainstream' of white society. Few chose this option in the first century of the act.[36]

Another source of friction between government and prairie bands lay in the agricultural policy for the reserves. Because food was the fundamental need of the natives and because training in agriculture seemed an obvious means to 'civilize' them, the government placed great hope in its farm policy in the 1880s and 1890s. By hiring white instructors, establishing 'model' farms, and employing increasing numbers of agents, the government planned to solve the problem of food supply within just a few years. In order to ensure that Indians did not evade the demands of farm labour, the 'pass system' was used to permit only those who had obtained an agent-approved ticket to leave the reserve. Then, when some bands commenced large-scale export agriculture and contracted debts to farm implement companies, the government introduced a 'permit system' that cut off produce sales beyond the reserve except with the approval of the agent. As this unusual imposition made plain, the Indians were expected to learn individualistic peasant agriculture and to cultivate with hoe and scythe, not to become cash-crop farmers who shared the work and rewards on a collective basis. The spread of the agricultural economy on the reserves was slow, and the returns were poor. By the early twentieth century, the government's native agricultural policy was acknowledged by some officials, particularly by Frank Oliver, minister of the interior 1905–11, to be a failure.[37]

The arrival of hundreds of thousands of immigrants offered an obvious alternative: pressure from settlers, railways, and town site promoters on the 'empty' reserve lands could be translated into capital for new Indian development projects. During the next generation, as much as one-half of the reserve land was sold off. In southern Saskatchewan's treaty 4 area alone, 270,000 of 520,000 acres were sold by 1928. There were benefits in such a policy because pools of capital were created for individual bands, but there were great shortcomings, too, as succeeding generations were to discover. An example of relative success was the Blackfoot reserve east of Calgary, where the surrender of 125,000 acres, nearly half the reserve, produced a trust fund of over $1 million by 1920. Henceforth, the reserve could provide its own social security system – weekly food rations, medical care, housing, and some farm equipment. Not all reserves were so fortunate. And, even in this case, the provision of basic material needs did not ensure the satisfaction of the reserve Blackfoot or the avoidance of social problems. As Hugh

Dempsey concluded: 'Those reserves which surrendered lands showed no noticeable advancement or long-term benefits over those which did not ... Rations which should have been used as an inducement to work, had just the opposite effect. The use of firearms was restricted. Travel was limited, and anyone leaving his reserve required a pass. The marketing of grain and hay was strictly regulated, and everywhere an Indian turned, he was greeted by restrictions on his freedom. In the end, it was easier for many to continue the welfare pattern established during the early starvation years than it was to break out of the mold to make a viable living on the reserve.'[38]

The great hope of administrator and missionary alike was that education would break the hold of tradition and create a properly 'Canadianized' Indian. As a result of the campaign to 'civilize' and 'Christianize' Indian children, schools became an issue in native-white relations as early as the 1880s, and native educational institutions, such as the various ceremonies encompassed in the term 'sun dance,' remained a source of conflict even thirty years later. The goal of white education policy was, of course, to protect Indians from the worst features of white society, to prepare them for the labour market, and to 'save' them for the sake of their souls. Church and government co-operated in the provision of three types of institution, the day school on the reserve, the boarding school, and, most elaborate of all, the industrial school. At the latter, children were required to live apart from their families for extended periods in the expectation that Indian attitudes and customs would be forgotten. At the Qu'Appelle Industrial School, for example, the children were expected to learn not only a European language but also European Canadian concepts of time, work discipline, and public order. They spent half their day in trades workshops or in the kitchen, laundry, or dairy and the other half in the classroom. Their recreations were such Canadian pastimes as cricket, football, checkers, and, of course, the brass band. The industrial schools were phased out in the first decades of the twentieth century, partly because they were costly but also because they were failures.[39] The boarding schools continued for another two generations, always under white supervision. Their record has yet to be established by scholarly investigation, but, aside from the predictable academic successes and failures, such schools have been the target of Indian criticism ever since because of their harsh insistence on conformity to Canadian cultural practices.

One reason for the failure of the industrial schools and, by extension, of the government's assimilationist policy was the conscious resistance of the Indians themselves. Too often, students of Canadian history have been told that Indian society 'collapsed' before a 'more advanced' civilization. In fact, prairie Indians did not acquiesce to the pressures for assimilation. Instead, they fought back as best they could, employing passive resistance when their children were recruited into boarding schools and, later, organizing political associations to oppose the excesses of the Indian Act. One of their most important expressions of resistance was the annual summer gathering of the plains communities. This sun or thirsting dance had been the occasion for games, courtship, and visiting as well as for worship in pre-treaty days, and it remained a crucial event in plains Indian life even after the turn of the twentieth century. Despite regular government attempts to proscribe the dancing, it was only when charges were laid that the activity was curtailed. And, even then, the dances remained on the fringes of summer fairs and sports days, illegal and yet all the more powerful for the fact that they were conducted in secret.[40]

Much had occurred in prairie native history during the last half of the nineteenth century. Members of hitherto autonomous hunting bands were confined to reserves in several dozen districts across the west. The Canadian government set the policy for off-reserve travel, for the sale of agricultural goods, for the provision of education, and even for religious worship. It was beyond the power of native leaders to influence the legislation that governed Indian life, the so-called Indian Act. This unhappy circumstance was to remain virtually unchanged for another half-century. Only in the 1940s and 1950s would the two sides begin to address the extraordinary problems that beset this relationship, and only in the 1970s and 1980s would solutions begin to emerge.

# 8

# Canada's empire 1870–1900: The region and the National Policy

The millions of acres of western real estate were expected to serve the interests of 'old Canada,' in the view of those who lived east of Lake Superior. After all, the 3.5 million citizens of the four eastern provinces (in 1871) had paid for the land and had accepted the transfer of the imperial burden to their shoulders. Because previous economic booms had accompanied the expansion of agricultural settlement, they planned to establish a new 'investment frontier' that would open the west and enrich the east in one fell swoop. Their hopes lay with the pioneer farmer who, far from being the self-sufficient recluse of folk-tales, would initiate an economic take-off by buying lumber, groceries, and agricultural implements, on the one hand, and shipping grain and livestock, on the other. To encourage western settlement, a railway must be constructed. Until then, Canadian sovereignty would be asserted in the face of American competition by the dispatching of a police force. But the ultimate goal was the arrival of settlers; mile after mile of farmsteads would demonstrate to American annexationists the sincerity of Canadian intentions and provide a hinterland for the manufacturing plants of central and Maritime Canada. These plants, in turn, were defended by yet another facet of the so-called National Policy, the protective tariff. Police, railway, settlement, and tariff were central elements in the national design imposed on the western interior.

Some scholars have argued that Confederation itself was a plank in the entrepreneurs' National Policy. Businessmen needed economic growth if they were to prosper. In the face of the abolition of imperial preferences by the British government in the 1840s and the termination of the reciprocity agreement by the United States in 1866, Canadian leaders were left with the northwest as a field for investment. As the economist V.C. Fowke argued: 'The decision to create and develop an integrated economy on a national basis was adopted because of the disappearance of not one but two more highly regarded alternative possibilities – those of imperial and of continental economic integration.'[1] The transfer of the northwest from the Hudson's Bay Company to Canadian control in 1870 was only part of the design. In the next year, Prime Minister Macdonald took advantage of favourable circumstances to negotiate the entry of British Columbia into Confederation and thus to complete the physical integration of a continent-wide 'new nation.' But it was one thing to achieve sovereignty over this vast empire, quite another to consolidate a national economy and to establish Canadian institutions throughout.

The series of Indian treaties between 1871 and 1877 completed the bulk of the negotiations concerning the recognition and extinguishment of aboriginal title in the western interior. As the tragedy of the Cypress Hills massacre made plain, however, treaties could not ensure that natives and newcomers respected each other's rights. Into this troubled situation, according to legend, rode the 300: coats of red, helmets of white, rifles slung beside their saddles, these were the Mounted Police. Younger sons of Europe's great and titled families, gentle iron-willed servants of justice, they were said to be representatives of all that was best in Canada. But, as with other national symbols, it is difficult to know where truth fades and myth takes over.

The North-West Mounted Police force was formed in 1873, added the prefix Royal to its title by grant of Edward VII in 1904, and, when its exclusively western mandate ended in 1920, became the Royal Canadian Mounted Police. The force is central to an understanding of western Canada and, by extension, of Canada as a whole.

The importance of the force in Canadian history can be demonstrated by reference to the 150 tales of adventure and romance that have placed the Mounties in a prominent role. Such adventure stories conform to a formula and could be dismissed as merely escapist, of course, but they can also be seen as the expression of basic cultural values. In the years between the 1880s and the 1920s, the Mounties attracted considerable attention both at home and abroad. They became a symbol for the aspirations of the nation. Their presence in formula adventure stories reflected this prominence.[2] The hero in these stories, as in American dime novels and British imperial adventures, had a tough exterior and a heart of gold. He was usually British, intelligent, handsome, and kind. He preferred the company of his horses and his comrades – until the 'loving girl-wife' arrived on the scene. The challenge presented to this hero was similarly out of a formula: the forces of evil, represented by Sioux 'renegades,' whisky runners, or armed robbers, threatened the forces of good. Victory always went to the forces of good, predictably, but the manner in which the Mountie triumphed was significant. Again and again, the novelists noted that a handful of men patrolled an area larger than western Europe. Their life was lonely and austere; they were driven by their sense of duty and sustained by powers of endurance and iron discipline.[3] When the crisis came, the lone rider faced danger with unflinching courage:

'Put it down there, my man. Do you hear?' The voice was still smooth, but through the silky tones there ran a fibre of steel. Still the desperado stood gazing at him. 'Quick, do you hear?' There was a sudden sharp ring of imperious, of overwhelming authority, and, to the amazement of the crowd of men who stood breathless and silent about, there followed one of those phenomena which experts in psychology delight to explain, but which no man can understand. Without a word the gambler slowly laid upon the table his gun, upon whose handle were many notches, the tally of human lives it had accounted for in the hands of this same desperado.

...

'Now listen!' gravely continued the youngster. 'I give you twenty-four hours to leave this post, and if after twenty-four hours you are found here it will be bad for you. Get out!'

The man, still silent, slunk out of the room. Irresistible authority seemed to go with the word that sent him forth, and rightly so, for behind that word lay the full weight of Great Britain's mighty empire. It was Cameron's first experience of the North West Mounted Police, that famous corps of frontier riders who for more than a quarter of a

century have ridden the marches of Great Britain's territories in the
far northwest land, keeping intact the Pax Britannica amid the wild
turmoil of pioneer days. To the North West Mounted Police and to the
pioneer missionary it is due that Canada has never had within her
borders what is known as a 'wild and wicked West.'[4]

As Dick Harrison has suggested, this passage from a novel by
Ralph Connor epitomizes the myth of the Mountie. In the classic
show-down, a slim young fellow, unarmed and alone, faced down a
deadly desperado. He won not because of a faster draw or some
other outstanding personal quality – here is no American individualist at work – but because he represented an irresistible force.
Behind the stripling Mountie, whether riding into an Indian war
dance or a den of thieves, was a thousand years of British law,
parliament, and church. His strength was not an individual accomplishment but the gift of an invincible culture. As a bad man in one
novel wisely perceived of his Mountie captor: 'He knows that the
hull damn Force is back of 'im, an' back of that the British Empire,
Army an' Navy combined. Touch 'im and ye touch the hull con-
sarn.'[5]

The real-life Mountie was closer to his romantic adventure counterpart than we might expect, if not in his handsome bearing at least
in his reputation and influence. For the most remarkable fact about
the North-West Mounted Police in this first generation of its existence was that it was loved and respected. The comment of an
American train robber, captured in British Columbia after a flight
across the border and a sizzling gun-fight, may serve as the expression of public opinion: 'You may think it funny coming from me, but
I certainly admire the way you boys do your work.'[6] The Mounties
were an outstanding success. As the most recent study of the force
concluded: 'A few hundred men decisively influenced the development of the prairie West.'[7]

The North-West Mounted Police was an essential part of the
National Policy because it ensured that peace would prevail in an
area that could have been extremely violent. Particularly in dealings
with Indians, but also on the unstable frontier of European settlement, it constituted the most important institution in the territory.
Where the Americans spent $20 million annually fighting plains
Indians in the 1870s, the Canadian government, whose total annual
budget was $19 million, spent less than $400,000 per year on the

Mounted Police. The result was that the government could afford to participate in crucial development projects such as the railway, the survey, and experimental farms. Prime Minister Macdonald had advanced an unusual idea and taken a considerable gamble when he launched the force, but time proved him right in his belief that frontier violence could be anticipated and prevented by a small unit that combined features of the military, the police, and minor judiciary.

The idea that a police force might express Canadian sovereignty and act as a vehicle for maintaining good relations with the Indians was first suggested by Sir John in late 1869 just before the metis resistance spoiled his plans to take over Red River: 'I have no doubt, come what will, there must be a military body, or at all events a body with military discipline at Fort Garry. It seems to me that the best Force would be *Mounted Riflemen*, trained partly as Cavalry, but also instructed in rifle exercise. They should also be instructed as certain of the Line are, in the use of artillery. This body should not be expressly military but should be styled *Police*, and have the military bearing of the Irish Constabulary.'[8] The idea collapsed in the face of the resistance, to be replaced by Wolseley's military expedition, but was revived in the early 1870s as a means a handling the still-insistent needs of the vast North-West Territories. The turmoil in Manitoba demonstrated the evils that must be avoided; the first two lieutenant-governors, Archibald and Morris, emphasized to the point of shrillness their concerns about Indian unrest. And Col Robertson-Ross, head of Canada's militia, who had been sent west in 1872 to assess the military situation, had reported that American whisky traders in the Fort Benton–Cypress Hills region posed a serious threat to peace. Legislation to enable the government to establish judicial institutions and a police force in the territories was passed by the House of Commons in the spring of 1873, but the order-in-council to implement the bill was delayed while Macdonald struggled through Liberal charges of corruption over the creation of his next project, the Canadian Pacific Railway. Then, late in the summer of 1873, news of the Cypress Hills massacre began to filter eastward. Lieutenant-Governor Morris called for police help once again, and this time Macdonald decided to speed up his timetable. Instead of waiting until the summer of 1874 to dispatch the force, he authorized the immediate departure of a rapidly assembled contingent. The survival of the Mounted Police was a narrow thing; the troop left Ottawa on 1 October, and in November Macdonald's Conservative government fell.[9] Its successor, the economizing administration of Alexander Mackenzie, might well have refused to authorize its establishment.

The Mounties commenced their duties in the Northwest with the famous Long March of 1874 which brought them as close to extinction as they ever came. They travelled along the southern route parallel to the international boundary rather than north along the well-travelled Saskatchewan or Carleton Trail and were soon lost in a mapless stretch of sunburned plains with inadequate water and grass for their horses and oxen. They were fortunate to reach the foothills. Their famous confrontation with the lawless elements of the west at Fort Whoop-up, former capital of the 'whisky-traders' empire, was no crisis at all; the troops found only a single anxious hunter in residence; had there been an army of roustabouts, the police might well have collapsed at their feet from sheer exhaustion.

The frontier military role of the force never did materialize. Instead, as Macdonald had hoped, the Mounties soon became the most important arm of the central government in its administration of the Northwest. They helped to supervise local Indian affairs, delivered mail, took the census, collected customs duties, provided medical services, established meteorological records and crop reports, issued relief supplies, and, perhaps most important, acted as justices of the peace and thus 'tried the great majority of the suspects they apprehended.' The force was not at all an outgrowth of the English (and hence American and Canadian) common law and police tradition, wherein the local government supervised the police and the constables, as officials solely of the magistrate's court, were confined to upholding the criminal law. Instead, it was closer to the European tradition where the police were agents of the central government, supervising not only criminal law but also aspects of civil law as well as other administrative arrangements. As a result of their broad responsibilities and, especially after the appointment of L.W. Herchmer as commissioner in 1886, their concern for the collection of information, constables became experts in every aspect of life in their districts. In the late 1880s and 1890s, they systematically patrolled the entire Northwest, regularly visiting 'almost every farm and ranch,' covering an annual average of one and a half million miles on horseback. They settled rumours of Indian uprisings, noted the arrival of unusual visitors, and provided a thorough report on the state of the region upon which the government and police headquarters could act to control potentially troublesome situations. The information included such things as reports of new settlements that required police attention, deficiencies in the Criminal Code that left offences unpunishable or made enforcement unnecessarily difficult, and unusual increases in the incidence of particular types of crime. This useful intimacy with every aspect of life in the west ensured the police would be trusted and respected. And it was this extraordinary popularity, coupled with a series of accidents, that alone ensured the survival of the North-West Mounted Police beyond the era of early settlement.[10]

The Liberal government that assumed office in 1896 distrusted a Tory-created organization staffed presumably by loyal Tories. Prime Minister Laurier was planning to disband the force when two events, the gold strike in the Yukon and the Boer War, reinforced the reputation of the Mounted Police. The outbreak of the war disrupted plans to replace the military functions of the force with a prairie militia on the eastern Canadian model; the Yukon required an infusion of trained officers that could come only from the current prairie system; and, of course, the people of the west insisted in message after message to their political representatives that they wanted the Mounted Police to stay. Laurier relented, and, when Saskatchewan and Alberta were created in 1905, the constitutional requirement that the provinces assume responsibility for the administration of justice was negated by two simple devices: the provincial attorney-general replaced the federal minister of justice as the source of legal authority and advice for the Mounted Police, and the provinces agreed to pay a portion of the cost of the force in return for its services. This system operated until 1917 and thus ensured the continuance of the Mounted Police into the modern era and its eventual translation from a territorial troop into a national police force.

The explanation of the Mounties' success lies as much in the society of the western interior as in the police force itself, for each nurtured the other. The officers were crucial in the process: 'As a group the officers of the Mounted Police were elitist, sure of their position in society and, as such men tend to be, secure in their strongly held opinions and attitudes. They came to the North-West determined to mould it according to their image of what Canadian society should be. For these men the frontier environment was not an active force in the shaping of the social order, but a passive framework within which social roles could be worked out.'[11] The western frontier in Canada was not, as the American frontier was reputed to be, a classless egalitarian world. Rather, from the time of the arrival of Ontario immigrants in the 1870s, the west was assumed to have, as did the rest of Canada, a 'better class' and 'lower elements.' Within this general grouping, the Mounted Police officers were the cream of the crop. When a doctor in Fort Macleod wrote to apply for admission into the force as surgeon in 1887, he added that if enlistment as an officer were impossible, he would accept an appointment to the Canadian Senate. Perhaps this anecdote stretches one's imagination, but it does indicate the power and the status of the officers.

These men were not, as fiction would have it, younger sons of British gentry. They were, rather, members of the élite of the eastern provinces, Anglican or Roman Catholic in religion, and experienced in military affairs. They were well-educated (many were graduates of Royal Military College), increasingly were promoted from the ranks, and, as in other cases where federal political priorities had to be respected, they represented the regional, ethnic, and religious balance of the national population. Inspectors were entitled to one servant – a constable – and superintendents two, ample indication if more were needed of the social outlook of the officer class. The officers' living quarters in the late nineteenth century were furnished with *Punch*, the *Illustrated London News*, and *The Times* of London as well as the *Canadian Illustrated News*. Their social events, particularly the formal evening ball, were highlights of the season. From that day to this, the Mounties fulfilled ceremonial duties, such as aides-de-camp and guards of honour, which would in other societies be the prerogative of the military, and they appeared at the important community rituals, from Dominion (Canada) Day to the annual fair, as symbolic representatives of the power of the state. The officers numbered only 25 to 50 at any given time, but their social power was immense: the very embodiment of the gentleman class, they ensured that the 'better element' would set the tone of western Canadian society.

This social pretension was the outgrowth of the traditional British and European assumption that officers were gentlemen and other ranks were recruited from the lower orders. The same assumption influenced perceptions of crime. The Mounted Police had to determine, as do all police, which crimes were significant and which were merely a nuisance. In the northwest, it placed first priority upon the maintenance of order and thus emphasized crimes of violence, especially those involving guns, and was concerned least with moral offences such as gambling and prostitution. Here, again, assumptions about social class influenced their activity. Members of the middle class, including the officers themselves, possessed the crucial civic virtue, respectability, and their behaviour set the standard by which all others were judged. They lived in a stable environment, often in a family setting, they were sober in public, and they never engaged in violent activities. Members of the 'lower element' might be respectable – indeed, it was worth remark when they were – but if they engaged in violence, were drunk on the streets, or frequented bawdy houses, they were only fulfilling the expectations of their social betters. As a result, vagrancy was a serious crime in the northwest because it involved young unemployed males who might become violent. Prostitution was a nuisance but not a threat to social stability. And rustling, which involved relations between neighbouring, presumably 'respectable' ranchers, was not a 'crime' but a thorny 'problem.'

Stability was the ideal of middle-class society, and the Mounted Police, who shared this ideal, ensured that it would be maintained. Violence there was aplenty in the Northwest as there was in the United States: 'The thing that shocked Canadian observers of life in the American West was not violence per se, but the fact that it sometimes occurred among social and economic groups which in Canada would have fallen into the category of the respectable middle class. What conditioned the Canadian view of the United States was not so much hypocrisy, although there was undoubtedly an element of that, as a different view of the relationship between crime and class.' In Canada, by definition, the middle class was law-abiding; and in Canada, by definition, law-breakers belonged to the lower elements in society. The members of the Mounted Police, 'left largely to themselves, did what they thought was necessary to build a just and orderly society' and thus to reinforce the ideal of respectability. Their powers were very wide and yet, because the force exercised its authority with discretion and commonsense – terms that themselves embodied the values of the dominant class – they were not accused of being despotic or tyrannical. 'This state of affairs can only be explained by abandoning all Turnerian assumptions about the influence of the frontier. Canadians in the West, exposed to the same environmental influences as American frontiersmen, demonstrably possessed very different ideas about politics and society. The political culture of the Canadian North-West was derived almost entirely from eastern Canada and in fact was partly the creation of the police themselves.'[12]

The Canadian Pacific Railway, as much an element of Macdonald's National Policy as any other plank, has also assumed mythic proportions in the story of nation-building. Popular songs such as Gordon Lightfoot's *Canadian Railway Trilogy* and television spectaculars such as the CBC's presentation of Pierre Berton's *National Dream* merely reflect the conventional wisdom that the railway built the nation or at least ensured its survival. An epic narrative poem by E.J. Pratt, too, translated the Canadian Shield into a dragon and the railway into the knight that vanquished it. Such a view has historical support. Indeed, one of the greatest Canadian historians, Donald Creighton, was as much as anyone responsible for placing the Canadian Pacific Railway in the national pantheon. But, as with the North-West Mounted Police, so with the CPR, it is important to separate fact and reputation. What is a national dream to some may be a terrible nightmare to others. The story is often told in western Canada of the farmer who watched the finest wheat crop in the history of his district dashed to pieces by hail and, as his dreams of prosperity disappeared, turned to roar at the sky, 'Damn the CPR.'

The basis for the celebration of the railway lies in two assertions. First, the actual construction of the line was, in Creighton's words, an 'astounding success,' the product of 'brilliant individual enterprise'; the achievement, Creighton wrote, justified the elevation of CPR president George Stephen to the status of 'perhaps the greatest creative genius in the whole history of Canadian finance.' Second, the completion of the railway was central to the development of the fledgling dominion. As Creighton has said, the railway was 'a project only less formidable than that of the Dominion of Canada itself. The Dominion and the railway would both encounter the same acute difficulties for they shared a common ultimate objective. The prime purpose of Canada was to achieve a separate political existence on the North American continent. The prime function of the Canadian Pacific Railway was to assist in this effort – to help in the building of the national economy and national society which alone would make this ambition possible of achievement.'[13] Thus, in Creighton's powerful interpretation of Canadian history, Macdonald, Confederation, and the Canadian Pacific Railway were the sustaining roots of a single tree, the Dominion of Canada. This view, expounded so persuasively in the 1940s and 1950s, was adopted by Pierre Berton in his popularization of CPR history in the 1970s. But, just because it was popular in the last generation, the national dream should not be viewed as a fanciful revision of the past concocted to fit the needs of an embattled Canada in the present. Rather, this interpretation was evident even as the last spike was driven home in 1885. Alexander Morris, who had come to know the Northwest firsthand in the 1870s, wrote Prime Minister Macdonald on the completion of the railway to congratulate him on 'the second crowning triumph of your more recent life, second only to that of Confederation. You have now created the link to bind the provinces indissolubly together, and to give us a future and a British nationality.'[14] Those who criticize the CPR must first come to terms with its achievements.

A Canadian railway was believed to be important in the era of Confederation because it would demonstrate the capacity of the nation to stand at the forefront of technological achievement – rather like space platforms and communications satellites in the late twentieth century – and because it would assert Canada's claim to the Northwest against American competitors. Thus, national pride, economic interest, and territorial integrity all were bound up with the drive for a national rail link. The concern about American competition, which Macdonald felt very keenly, may have been justified in the early 1870s. The revival in 1869–70 of plans for a Northern Pacific railway by which the financier Jay Cooke hoped to link the Great Lakes to Minneapolis–St Paul and the Pacific Ocean, threatened to tap the Canadian Northwest from just below the border and, of course, raised the spectre of eventual annexation. Though Cooke's plans collapsed in the international depression of 1873, the scheme was revived by James J. Hill in the early 1880s and seemed to pose a serious challenge to the Canadian transcontinental for the following two decades. It was this American presence that moved Macdonald, who always found the American way of life distasteful, to defend the Canadian line with such determination.

The answer to the American threat was not easy to formulate. The appropriate Canadian repository of capital and experience was the

Grand Trunk Railway, which linked Montreal to Toronto and Sarnia, in the west, and to Portland, Maine, on the Atlantic coast. But, aside from its uncertain career as a financial undertaking, the Grand Trunk clung to the dream of a commercial empire in the American Midwest and thus insisted on building south of the Great Lakes and through Chicago, a determination that was not to change until Laurier's great railway barbecue at the turn of the century. So the Grand Trunk was as unacceptable to Macdonald as the Northern Pacific. But if the right railway entrepreneurs were difficult to find, Macdonald did not despair of finding them. In the negotiations for British Columbia's entry into Confederation, his government guaranteed that it would commence the construction of a railway to the Pacific within two years of the date of union and complete it within ten; this bold promise, which became one of the terms of the eventual agreement of 1871, indicated the importance of the rail line to the prime minister and his government. And, though his first effort ended in disaster, Macdonald never wavered in his determination.

That first attempt to secure a suitable railway consortium resulted in a struggle between two groups. Sir Hugh Allan, steamship king and perhaps the wealthiest man in Canada, carried the hopes of the Montreal business community but was handicapped by his reliance upon American money and technical support. Senator D.L. Macpherson was the leader of a Toronto-based group of capitalists – one sees here the growing sense of competition between the original Canadian metropolis and its rising Ontario rival – that would have made an ideal complement to the Montreal team. But Allan was determined to go it alone, to run the company as president, and to choose its course, including its relationship with his American backers. And, in order to have his way, he created a political machine in Quebec that undermined the power of Macdonald's closest ally and most important partner, Sir George-Étienne Cartier. Allan then attempted to buy the contract for the Canadian Pacific Railway, which would include millions of dollars in grants and millions of acres of land, by donating heavily to the Macdonald-Cartier party in the 1872 federal election. He was successful, but only briefly. Macdonald created his own Canadian Pacific Railway Company in February 1873 with Allan as president and with representatives of the business communities of Toronto, Montreal, and the other provinces as directors. This first CPR was short-lived. Allan's American allies, who did not like being treated as dupes, leaked news of his political scheming to the Liberal opposition in the House of Commons. The Liberals found further information in the files of Allan's lawyer – a fine piece of skulduggery in itself – and then, in the spring of 1873, confronted Macdonald with the evidence of his heavy reliance in the election on the financial contributions of Sir Hugh Allan, who now was president of the government-created railway company. The Pacific Scandal brought down the government and the first CPR in November 1873. Ironically, Canada's railway dreams were left intact because Jay Cooke and the Northern Pacific had collapsed two months earlier. Once again, Canadian and American entrepreneurs would have to start as equals in the struggle for economic empire in the northwest.

The Liberal government of Alexander Mackenzie, despite its poor image in history books, carried out a reasonably successful railway policy from 1873 to 1878. It completed the Intercolonial Railway from Levis (across the St Lawrence from Quebec City) to Halifax in 1876, the eastern end of an eventual transcontinental link, and it prosecuted the essential surveys for the Pacific line with vigour. Because of the crippling effects of the depression, Mackenzie could do little on the 2,000-mile link to the Pacific except to prepare the way and await the formation of a consortium of capitalists; that was the accustomed procedure in the nineteenth-century Atlantic world.

The consortium did not come together until 1879–80. By then, the depression and Sir John's remarkable politicking, particularly his memorable picnics in the summers of 1877 and 1878 and his stirring advocacy of the so-called National Policy, had swept Mackenzie from office in the federal election of 1878. And then into Macdonald's lap fell the offer that he, like Mackenzie before him, had awaited. A Canadian syndicate, with strong financial support at home and in the international investment community, was prepared to build the Pacific railway.

The 'Syndicate,' as it was known at the time, came together in the late 1870s to rescue a railway in Minnesota and, of course, to make the windfall profits that such an endeavour could produce. Its members included Norman Kittson, the American fur trader who had opened the Pembina post in the 1840s and who had had an interest in Red River steamboat transportation since the 1860s; James J. Hill, a former Canadian who had merged his transportation holdings with those of Kittson in the 1870s to form the Red River Transportation Company and who was already showing signs of the interest in railways that would make him one of the greatest figures in North American railway history; Donald A. Smith, the chief North American officer of the Hudson's Bay Company, who had established himself in Manitoba in the 1870s and, through the Hill-Kittson group, had linked the Hudson's Bay Company to the Red River Transportation Company; and, finally, George Stephen, president of the Bank of Montreal, textile manufacturer, industrialist, and – the decisive factor – cousin of Donald Smith. Kittson, Hill, and Smith were wealthy, they understood the west, and they recognized a business opportunity when it was presented to them; Stephen too was wealthy, and, more important, he had the connections in the international investment community that could mean the difference between success and bankruptcy in the dangerous world of railway finance.

The four were brought together by Hill's interest in the St Paul and Pacific, a railway destined to run from Minneapolis to Winnipeg, which had been launched in 1871 and had collapsed with its parent, Cooke's Northern Pacific, in 1873. It retained valuable assets, including four million acres in land grants, if it fulfilled its promises, and thus seemed to represent a property worth $20 million, excluding its considerable potential simply as a profit-making railway. Hill calculated that the company could be purchased and rehabilitated for about $6 million but he acknowledged that the risk, in legal complications and financial troubles, was considerable. He provided the management in Minnesota while Stephen conducted complex financial negotiations in Europe and North America that held the package together. Crucial in this latter respect was Stephen's relationship to John S. Kennedy, a New York financier, who supplied money and introductions. The fledgling syndicate was very successful. The resulting railway company, the St Paul, Minneapolis and Manitoba, opened its line to Winnipeg in December 1878, had net earnings of between $1 and $2 million in each of its first two full years of operation, and came to be seen as one of the great investment coups of the era. The four principals, and Kennedy, the fifth, must have made an instant paper profit of several million dollars each, excluding annual dividends on their substantial shareholdings, because bonds with a face value of $17.2 million dollars had been purchased for $3.7 million dollars. A very profitable operation had been set in place and so it is little wonder that the syndicate was ready for a bigger challenge.

An upswing in the international economy encouraged a number
of companies to investigate the Canadian transcontinental project in
1879–80 and thus provided Macdonald's government with a rough
idea of the subsidy required to stimulate serious bids. But after a
round of discussions in London in the summer of 1880, George
Stephen's syndicate alone remained in the running. A deal was
struck in the autumn, and after an interminable debate in the House
of Commons the CPR bill was passed. On 16 February 1881 the
company was incorporated. The syndicate was built on the foundations laid by the Minnesota venture: Stephen, Smith, and Hill each
put up $500,000; so too did Stephen's associate in the Bank of Mont-
real and successor as president, R.B. Angus; a new ally, Duncan
McIntyre, who controlled the Canada Central Railway, an essential
link between the Ottawa–Montreal area and the proposed Pacific
railway terminus near Lake Nipissing (itself near Georgian Bay),
subscribed a like sum. A larger amount, about $740,000, was put up
by Morton, Bliss and Company of New York, and another $500,000
was subscribed by John S. Kennedy of New York. Finally, a Paris
firm, Kohn Reinach and Company, also joined the syndicate. It was
an international consortium that had its roots in the Red River association of Hill and Smith and the Scottish family tie of Smith and
Stephen. It was Canadian by virtue of the roots of its dominant
partners and nationalist in inspiration, but it was founded on the
ideals of western entrepreneurs – American and Canadian westerners – and the potential of western investment. It was also a multinational enterprise: only about one-sixth of the stock was held in
Canada during the next half-century, while majority ownership
slowly shifted from American to British hands.[15]

When discussing such great development projects, one must
keep in the forefront the purposes they are to serve. The CPR was in
part a political undertaking, intended by the Canadian government
to knit the nation together. But it was also an adventure in capitalist
investment, intended to return a profit to its supporters. An illustration from another continent will place the project in perspective. At
about the same time the CPR was being launched, British and American capitalists wished to open Africa to 'modern' economic and
social influences. In part the inspiration was profit; in part, it was
'civilization': the railway would put a stop to 'that most fearful of all
crimes – the trading in human souls,' as American railway entrepreneur Samuel Huntington explained. In a classic statement on the

relationship between profit and mission, Huntington informed a colleague that unless the African railway 'is a financial success it can hardly be one in respect to the higher objects it has in view – of substituting civilization for barbarism, of extending commerce, with all of its blessings, over the vast country that has lain for so long neglected by the Christian people of the more favored parts of the world.' In his fondest dreams, Huntington told the British traveller H.M. Stanley, he foresaw a day when 'all that vast country that you have explored will be occupied by civilized man, and I dare to hope that that man will be an *African*.' But, he insisted, he could organize American investment assistance only if the project promised to be a '*financial success*.'[16]

Railways had a dual purpose in the nineteenth century: as a vehicle of 'civilization' and a fertile source of investment profits. It had, as a result, two masters: private entrepreneurs who undertook the usual responsibilities and accepted risks in order to make the usual gains; and government, in the name of the people, which would regulate them in order to ensure that national purposes were served. As Sir John commented to George Stephen in 1881: 'With five years ahead and a favourable Government at the head, the CPR can go on its own way for its own interests, and in the long run its interests and those of the Dominion are identical.' The CPR would be a joint achievement of government and private enterprise. Nevertheless, Van Horne's later statement to an American Senate committee – 'The Canadian Pacific was built for the purpose of making money for the share-holders and for no other purpose under the sun' – cannot be ignored. The CPR was both a privately held, profit-oriented corporation and a state enterprise; that was its strength and its weakness, and when its board of directors, or the Canadian people, ignore the inconvenient half of the dualism, they merely open themselves to greater irritation.

The contract was in most respects a reflection of the ideas that had been discussed for a decade. The railway company agreed to build and operate a rail line from Callander, near Georgian Bay, to the Pacific on Canadian territory. By agreeing to operate the completed enterprise, the company was guaranteeing that it would not be a one-shot outfit that skimmed the profits and fled for safety. The through line was to be in operation within ten years and was to meet specified construction standards. In exchange, the company was to receive direct grants of $25 million and 25 million acres of land (land 'fairly fit for settlement,' as the company prudently specified). It would also receive tax exemption in perpetuity for company property in the North-West Territories, duty-free importation of construction materials, including rails and spikes, exemption of land grant property from taxation for twenty years after selection or until sold, a gift of several hundred miles of completed railway, and, most contentious of all, a 'monopoly clause,' whereby for twenty years no rail line was to be constructed south of the CPR main line unless it acted as a feeder to that main line, nor could such a line approach nearer than fifteen miles to the American border. These last were useful advantages to the company, of course, but they were to cause much political grief and to foster ill-will toward the CPR that has never entirely dissipated.

The CPR construction work consisted of three distinct phases: 650 miles of difficult Shield country from Georgian Bay to Thunder Bay; 850 miles of relatively easy prairie land; and 400 miles of terrain in the Rockies and Selkirks that was as difficult as any in the world. The route had been selected and surveyed in the 1870s but now was revised by the syndicate. The significance of the change was to move the transcontinental from the northern park-belt (Lake Manitoba and the North Saskatchewan River) to the southern plains stretching from the Assiniboine River to the region south of the South Saskatchewan River and thence northwestward via the Bow River valley to the Rockies. Thus, the main line would now cross the Red River at Winnipeg rather than twenty miles farther north at the ambitious village of Selkirk; it ignored the hopes of the already established citizens of Prince Albert, Battleford, and Edmonton and instead created wholly new urban centres at Brandon, Regina, and Calgary. And it crossed the mountains into British Columbia via the Kicking Horse rather than the Yellowhead Pass.

No more profound alteration could have been implemented; that we understand it so imperfectly is testimony to the secrecy and power of the syndicate. The reasons advanced for the change of plans are plausible but not obviously decisive. They include the two arguments presented in Parliament and that are given most credence by the latest study of the CPR: that the southern route was quicker and cheaper to build (there are only two large bridges in the 832 miles from Winnipeg to Calgary), and that, because it was closer to the American border, the new route would enable the company to compete with potential American rivals. Additional explanations include concern over the northern growing season, which was said to be too short for the maturation of the grain strains then available; the already recognized potential for coal development on the southern route, which would provide valuable traffic as soon as the line was completed; the reduction of interference with the fur trade, a reflection of Donald Smith's position in the Hudson's Bay Company; the prospect of profits on the town sites, which had already been pre-empted by speculators on the northern route but not, of course, in the south; and the testimony of John Macoun, propagandist and botanist, who claimed as a result of his travels that the so-called Palliser's Triangle was not as arid as previously depicted and, indeed, was 'well suited for agriculture.' Though any of these explanations might have been pivotal, we cannot say that any one was, and thus there seems little reason to contest W.K. Lamb's conclusion. Railway men were swayed by railway arguments: Van Horne and Hill, using Macoun to bolster their preference, chose the line that would be constructed fastest and would return freight revenue most quickly.[17]

The construction of the rail line was accomplished with astonishing speed. William Van Horne, then thirty-eight years old and the general manager of an American railway, assumed control of operations at the start of 1882 and was soon joined by two other Americans, Thomas Shaughnessy and John Egan. An American firm, Langdon and Shepard of St Paul, Minnesota, accepted the construction contract that had been fumbled in 1881 by two other American appointees, and, when they in turn were found wanting in 1882, the CPR set up an American subsidiary to carry on the construction work in the following season. The eventual result was the creation of indigenous expertise. Canadians such as James Ross, Herbert Holt, William Mackenzie, and Donald Mann learned construction and entrepreneurial techniques on the job for the CPR. Though it is customary to dwell upon the role of Van Horne in the completion of the line, the rise of these secondary figures to positions of prominence in the world of management should be emphasized.[18]

By the end of 1881 the prairie line had reached Oak Lake, near Brandon; by the end of 1882, it was past Swift Current, over 575 miles west of Winnipeg, and trains were covering the Winnipeg–Regina run regularly; by the end of 1883, the end of track had passed Calgary and was near the summit of the Kicking Horse Pass, 962 miles from Winnipeg. The more difficult section north of Lake Superior required greater resources and was not completed until the spring of 1885. And, in the far west, the greatest task of all, the road through the Rockies and the Selkirks, proceeded with immense difficulty and with the aid of 6,500 Chinese as well as 2,000 Canadians at the height of activity. Van Horne had decided that the meeting place of the east and west lines in Eagle Pass should be called Craigellachie, a Highland gathering place for the Scots warriors of the clan Grant; both Smith and Stephen were related to the clan and had used the word as their rallying cry at the darkest moments of the struggle to build the line. The last spike was driven by Donald Smith in the presence of Van Horne, Sandford Fleming, Major Rogers, and others, leaders and labourers, who had built the line. The event on 7 November 1885 was a simple ceremony, but a moving one; the photograph of the event is probably 'the most famous of all Canadian historical photographs,' and Van Horne's five-second speech – 'All I can say is that the work has been well done in every way' – is one of the most famous utterances in national rhetoric. And then, according to Fleming, there was silence: 'It seemed as if the act now performed had worked a spell on all present. Each one appeared absorbed in his own reflections.' Then there were cheers, the leading men boarded their rail cars, and the labourers held their own last-spike ceremony.[19]

The Canadian Pacific was far from a finished transcontinental rail line – much construction and improvement remained to be done – but it could begin regular operations from Montreal to Vancouver in 1886. Stephen and Van Horne had yet to negotiate the purchase of railways in Ontario and Quebec by which they would extend their traffic from Georgian Bay to Montreal and the lower Great Lakes, but their program was soon successful. With the completion of the rail links, the west had been tied to the rest of the dominion by the closest possible bonds of that era. The railway was a vehicle for export and import, a medium for rapid communication, a means of travel, that brought the west and east within hours rather than weeks of each other. The CPR transcontinental line was not the only vehicle that could have accomplished this feat – indeed, its subsidiary, the St Paul, Minneapolis and Manitoba, had done the same thing – but it was the first regular national link to do so. By absorbing the Minnesota connection, the CPR controlled the west's access to the world. That was its great accomplishment and its great burden. The CPR represented the long-awaited liberation of the

Canadian west; but such promises could never be entirely fulfilled, as Stephen, Van Horne, and Macdonald were soon to discover. When all was said and done, the CPR was still a privately owned corporation as well as a national dream. Its profits benefited a few, not the nation as a whole. And this contradiction between railway as public service and as private profit-making company has plagued relations between the west and the CPR and between west and east, as well as historical interpretations, ever since.

The Mounted Police and the CPR would be irrelevant without a western farming community. Indeed, without large-scale agricultural development, Macdonald would have to admit that his National Policy was significantly flawed. Thus, in the same period that the rail link and the police force were first considered by the federal cabinet, immigration and land policies were set in place. Though revised in detail from time to time, these policies established the basic structure of settlement and remained significant determinants of western history throughout the period 1870–1930 during which the federal government retained responsibility for prairie land and natural resources.

At first glance, the decision to retain federal control over prairie lands during the settlement era might seem an anomaly. Certainly, no other province within Confederation, whether part of the original 1867 agreement or added after 1870, was required to relinquish control of its lands. In British constitutional practice, as Chester Martin has demonstrated, the administration of public lands 'uniformly devolved upon British provinces with the achievement of responsible government,'[20] and so the departure from this principle in 1870 (for Manitoba) and 1905 (Saskatchewan and Alberta) was significant. Control of the lands became an issue in party politics and eventually resulted in federal compensation payments to the prairie administrations; it should be no surprise, therefore, that later assertions of provincial control over natural resources, whether oil or land, were vehement: local governments had chafed at this very restriction for two generations.

Despite the agitation of prairie politicians, the federal government did have the constitutional authority to control prairie lands 'for the purposes of the Dominion,' and prairie citizens probably were 'not without pride in having been able to lend, so to speak, to the Dominion the resources without which these great national enterprises could ever have been effected.'[21] When all the partisan rhetoric about 'provincial rights' had been exhausted, the fact remained that the federal government had retained control of the lands for overriding national purposes: to build a transcontinental railway, to attract settlers to the western interior, and thus to establish a secure national entity on the northern half of North America. There was little doubt that as early as 1870 the Canadian government planned to encourage railway construction by means of land grants. It recognized that, if Canada were to compete with the United States, it would have to offer free homesteads to immigrants. As Prime Minister Macdonald argued, 'It would be injudicious to have a large province which would have control over lands and might interfere with the general policy of the Government in opening up communications to the Pacific, besides the land regulations of the Province might be obstructive to immigration. All that vast territory should be for purposes of settlement under one control, and that the Dominion legislature.'[22]

By the BNA Act, Ottawa and the provinces were to hold concurrent jurisdiction over agriculture and immigration, but Macdonald's determination to retain control over prairie lands meant that Ottawa set policy in these crucial fields. The first step was the survey. The delay of two years occasioned by the Red River resistance altered the system that was employed. From April 1871, when the cabinet passed an order-in-council on the subject, the west was to be subdivided into square-mile units nearly identical to those then in use in the United States. With the historic exception of long narrow river lots that were retained along the Red, the Assiniboine, and several other rivers where settlement preceded the surveyors, the entire west was surveyed according to a single system. The baselines, the Fort Garry meridian and the forty-ninth parallel, served as the axes for the entire west. The basic unit of landholding was the section – one mile square or 640 acres – which was divided into quarter-sections of 160 acres – one-half mile square. Thirty-six sections, six miles square, would compose a township. The townships were numbered northward from the American boundary; the ranges were numbered west or east from the 'first' meridian and, as settlement moved west, from second and third and fifth meridians. Thus, by this one sweeping decision, all rural addresses in western Canada were established according to a single principle. A farm at Se 6, 2–4, w1 (the southeast quarter of section 6, township 2, range 4, west of the first meridian) was thus twenty-three miles west of the prime meridian and six miles north of the forty-ninth parallel. The system was uniform, easily understood, and, because founded on astronomical observations rather than a magnetic or solar compass, remarkably accurate. An iron stake driven into the ground by the surveyors to mark each unit as they staked off the surface of the plains became the reference point for every pioneer, the solution to almost every dispute about boundaries.

While the surveyors moved west, marking out the plots of land even before settlers arrived, the federal government was establishing the regulations by which the land could be occupied. From the passage of the Homestead Act of 1862 in the United States, whereby a settler could obtain a 160-acre farm for a nominal fee of ten dollars, the fame of the 'free homestead' had spread around the world and ensured that any nation competing for immigrants must appear to be equally generous. Canada could offer no less. By orders-in-council in the spring of 1871, entries were to be accepted on 'homesteads' for 160 acres (a quarter-section) in exchange for a fee of ten dollars. A residence requirement of five years was to be fulfilled, after which clear title would be granted to the applicant. The landmark legislation that introduced the principle of the free homestead in Canada, a Dominion Lands Act of 1872, reduced the residence requirement to three years. In this offhand manner, Canada matched the American offer of free homesteads.

Dominion lands were intended to pay for railway construction as well as to attract settlers. In the land policy of 1871–2, cabinet and Parliament excluded from the homestead provisions a forty-mile belt of land, twenty miles on each side of the Pacific railway, which would be reserved for sale by the railway or the government; this plan collapsed with the Macdonald administration in 1873 and was revived only in part by the next Macdonald administration. By the regulations of 1882, all even-numbered sections would be available for homestead. Nevertheless, the dual – and to some degree conflicting – purposes of federal land policy remained until 1894, when the railway land grant system was ended, and even until 1908, when the last railway land grants were actually selected. In this way, 25 million acres were set aside for the CPR and another 7 million acres were reserved to aid in the construction of other rail lines.

These restrictions upon the selection of homestead land might not seem extraordinary, since they amounted to only 32 million acres, but one must recall that there were additional claims upon the available free land. Of these, the most important were the requirements of the Hudson's Bay Company and of school lands. The former, part of the transfer of 1870, reserved to the company up to 50,000 acres around its posts and one-twentieth of the Fertile Belt (usually section 8 and three-quarters of section 26, or about 6.6 million acres) as part of the compensation for relinquishing its exclusive right to trade. The so-called school lands were two sections (usually numbers 11 and 29) in every township that were to be auctioned at the best available price and the proceeds 'set apart as an endowment for purposes of education.'[23] Almost 5 million of the 9 million acres had been sold by 1930. Two smaller programs, the University of Manitoba grant and a Manitoba government swamp-drainage project, placed an additional 1 million acres on sale. The federal government itself, through direct sales and special grants to former soldiers and former mounted policemen in particular, removed another 5 million acres. Thus, despite the Canadian advertising program that emphasized 'free lands,' about 60 million acres of the prairies were available through purchase, not through the free homestead system. When we recall that only 56 million acres were permanently taken up by the free homesteads, the dual purpose of western lands becomes even more apparent. The fertile lands of the western interior were intended to attract immigrants, it is true, but they were also used to pay for railways, schools, swamp drainage, military service, and the extinguishing of Indian title and the Hudson's Bay Company charter. These various purposes were not wholly harmonized, as V.C. Fowke has commented, but they did produce remarkably satisfactory results.[24]

One reason for the eventual prairie satisfaction with the dualism inherent in federal policy was that free and sale lands were often available in adjacent packages. If a settler homesteaded an even-numbered section, he would often find an odd-numbered section for sale next door when he wished to expand his operation. From 1872 to 1894, and again after 1908, the land regulations actually encouraged a settler to think in terms of a larger farm by permitting a 'pre-emption' to be filed. That is, after filing on his homestead, the farmer could make an interim claim upon an adjoining quarter-section – if available – and later purchase it from the government when he had secured the patent on his homestead. Thus, the systems of pre-emption and sale reinforced the trend to larger farms by making these sale lands readily available to homesteaders.

The land policy, like the railway policy, was intended to create conditions in the western interior that would attract immigrants, but the government was still obliged to advertise the virtues of the prairies if Canada was to win the attention of prospective settlers, both at home and abroad. The chief function of the federal Department of Agriculture from 1867 until 1892, when the responsibility was transferred to the Department of the Interior, was the promotion of immigration. It was an uphill struggle. Of Europe's 2-1/2 million emigrants between 1853 and 1870, 61 per cent had gone to the United States, 18 per cent to the Australian colonies, others to Brazil and Argentina, and only a very few to Canada. What is more, emigration from Canada to the United States was alarming. The federal Immigration Branch did what it could with a limited budget. Starting from a faith in the importance of free land, the branch spent large sums on maps, pamphlets, prospectuses, and other printed advertising material in a wide range of languages – probably at least a million pieces per year after 1870. This literature was distributed in various ways but, in particular, through a second important part of the branch program, the immigration agencies that were established in Canada, Britain, and continental Europe. The government also offered commissions – per capita rewards, in effect – to agents for the recruitment of immigrants and created a system of passenger warrants that provided reduced steamship fares for certain classes of newcomers. Starting in the late 1870s, as the trade in Canadian live cattle to Britain grew in importance, the government took advantage of the advertising potential of the trade by inviting delegations of British tenant farmers on expense-paid tours of Canada, and it later extended this program to other groups in Britain and Europe. The results of these various efforts were not impressive: in the thirty-two years from 1867 to 1899, only 1.5 million immigrants entered Canada; by comparison, 5.5 million entered the United States in the 1880s alone and 2.5 million entered Australia between 1879 and 1890.[25] Admittedly, those countries, too, suffered high rates of emigration. But Canada had made a start, and, as experience was to demonstrate, the start was of critical importance: much of the later immigration to Canada has been described as 'chain migration,' that is, linked to the citizens already in their new homes; attracting the first newcomer from a village or neighbourhood was crucial.

The most important immigration activity in the first generation after Confederation was the encouragement given to groups or colonies to settle as discrete homogeneous units in the prairies. As early as 1872, the government had approved the reservation of three blocs of land for group settlements of Swiss, Germans, and Scots, and, though little came of those early proposals, the principle was well received and well used in following years. The first significant colonies to settle in the west were Mennonites from Russia (1874 and after), French Canadians from New England (1874 and following), and Icelanders (1875–81). In the wake of these important experiments, the government also licensed a number of company colonization attempts in the 1880s, but of the nearly thirty sub-contracts little was accomplished beyond the enrichment of a few company directors. More effective by far were the so-called nominal reserves, which did not bar outsiders from homesteading but encouraged specific groups to congregate. In the 1880s and 1890s, significant groups of settlers of no fewer than fourteen cultures, from English and Scottish to Romanians, Finns, Swedes, and Jews, took up land under this informal system.[26] Immigration to western Canada was an established fact, if not an overwhelming success, by the end of the nineteenth century; firm foundations had been established for the flood that was about to commence.

The National Policy encompassed railways and settlement, according to V.C. Fowke, but also tariffs, freight rate agreements, Indian treaties, and the North West Mounted Police. The policies were not just the creation of Sir John A. Macdonald but, rather, were established in the generation before and the first two generations after Confederation. They may have worked together to make the nation strong, but they may also have penalized the outlying regions to the benefit of central Canada. Did the national policies discriminate against the west? The accusation is built on a number of charges: that the freight rates levied in western Canada under transcontinental transportation policies were too high, that Canadian consumers paid too much for manufactured goods and that the surplus found its way into the pockets of central Canadians, that the western failure to achieve economic diversification through manufacturing was a result of the tariff policy, and, finally, that the west 'paid' a disproportionately high share of the cost of nation-building through its contribution of the revenue from land and resources alienation – a provincial endowment in the rest of the country – to such projects as the CPR. These considerations led the dean of Canadian econo-

'Separating the farmer from his profits' (Russenholt, *Grain Growers'*
*Guide*, 28 December 1921)

mics to comment: 'Western Canada has paid for the development of Canadian nationality, and it would appear that it must continue to pay. The acquisitiveness of eastern Canada shows little sign of abatement.'[27]

At the heart of the debate in both popular and scholarly forums was the protective tariff. No other federal program was so universally disliked in the settlement era. The tariff, which was a customs duty or tax levied on imported goods, generated about 60 per cent of Ottawa's revenue in the 1870s. In this era, almost a half-century before personal income tax, direct levies on personal wealth were unthinkable, and so alteration of customs duties was an issue of great sensitivity. The tariff arrived at after Confederation, a compromise between the higher rates in central Canada and the lower rates in the Maritimes, was a tax of 15 per cent ad valorem, that is, added to the value of each imported item. This rate remained relatively unchanged through Macdonald's first government and was raised slightly in 1874 by the Mackenzie administration to compensate for the slump in imports and consequent drop in government revenue. Pressure from manufacturers for protection from American competitors and their alleged dumping practices resulted in a proposal for another tariff increase in 1876, but, under pressure from Maritime representatives and doctrinaire low-tariff men in the cabinet, Mackenzie and his finance minister, Richard Cartwright, decided to hold the line. They were adhering to a rigid policy when the times seemed to require flexibility; the Conservatives immediately attacked the decision as cruelly neglectful of the manufacturer and, in subsequent months, advocated a tariff not just for revenue but for 'incidental protection' – that is, a tariff not just for government needs but for the manufacturers. Within a year of their 1878 election victory, the Conservatives had implemented a complex new tariff schedule that was clearly protectionist. Though the manufacturers had not won on every issue, they recognized that the new tariff schedule constituted a manufacturers' budget.[28]

The 1879 tariff has been described as a crucial element in the National Policy because it was so closely tied to the completion of a transcontinental railway and the establishment of an integrated 'national' economy: 'Construction of a Pacific railway would make possible the economic development of the West. Protective tariffs would foster interprovincial trade in place of international trade. Canadian manufacturers would be assured as fully as possible of exclusive rights to the total Canadian market. Together, railways and tariffs would integrate the expanding area of economic activity. Tariffs would ease the burden of improvements in transportation by providing railway traffic and a more diversified economy as a source of tax revenues.'[29]

The assertion that the tariff was the linchpin of the National Policy originated with the economist Harold Adams Innis in the 1920s and was supported by the influential work of Donald Creighton in the 1940s and 1950s. Today, scholars are not prepared to acknowledge that Macdonald and his colleagues had in mind a grand design to integrate the national economy. What is more, they do not even agree that the policy was a success. One of the critics of the National Policy, John H. Dales, has argued that the 1879 tariff produced economic growth that was too fast, too large, and unacceptably inefficient. Another, V.C. Fowke, has suggested that it discriminated against the prairie region and against the wage labourer. The controversy is far from over.[30]

The most interesting recent contribution to the tariff debate was made by the economist Kenneth Norrie. He suggested that the tariffs did not inhibit the industrialization of the prairies, as many westerners, including especially the Alberta nationalists, have contended. We may agree that Ontario and Quebec industrialization was artificial, he wrote, but this development was at the expense of the United States rather than of western Canada. Norrie also noted the argument made by some economists and used by the western provinces in their debates with Ottawa in the 1970s that the tariff redistributed income among regions by giving only central Canada the benefits of job creation. Again, he was not convinced. Because almost all prairie development occurred after the tariff barrier was erected, prairie economic decisions must have taken the tariff into account, he argued, and the costs of adjustment were consequently minimal. Norrie used the example of land values to illustrate his point. In the absence of tariffs, the farmer would have earned greater returns, but this higher income would have pushed up the sale price of land by an equal amount; thus the real losers in a low-tariff community would have been the big land-sellers – the federal government, the CPR, and the Hudson's Bay Company. Norrie admits that the settler on a free homestead lost economic rents but argues that, because these immigrants arrived after the tariff was in place, they went into farming with their eyes open, already aware of the costs of doing business. Or, as the bloodless language of the economists' discipline would have it: 'Factors moved into the region anyway, with the decision to do so based on observed price ratios rather than on some kind of free trade shadow prices.'[31] Norrie's argument is reasonable, but it is not the last word. For every immigrant who arrived on a prairie farm with a clear idea of the costs of production, there must have been ten who did not. For every immigrant who was prepared to accept the economic insecurity of a prairie farm because it was infinitely better than the alternative in his homeland, there must have been ten who concluded that the predetermined price ratios were unjust and that they had a political right to redistribute national income. The tariff debate has not ended, in other words, but it has moved to new ground.

A second source of debate about the National Policy was the eternal Canadian issue of freight rates. Incredible though it might seem, the cost of shipping a ton of steel west or a carload of wheat east does interest many citizens of the prairies – indeed, there have been few quicker ways to start an argument among groups of western business and agricultural leaders than to air one's opinions on transportation economics. Prairie residents claim that they have paid higher transportation costs than other Canadians because of 'a discriminatory rate structure which has been built into all Canadian transcontinental transportation policies.' The injustice originated with the publication of the first CPR freight rate schedule in 1883, they say, and has abated not a whit in the intervening century. Thus, in the admittedly extreme case of the 1883 schedule, wheat would travel 200 miles for over twenty cents per bushel on the prairies and well below ten cents per bushel in central Canada. The practice was eventually described and approved by federal regulatory agencies as 'fair discrimination.'[32]

Railway presidents and federal politicians have defended themselves by pointing to the elementary evidence of Canadian geography. The CPR faced stiff competition from other rail lines and from much cheaper water transport in eastern Canada while having to bear the cost of 'unproductive' stretches of rail north of Lake Superior and through the Rocky Mountains. Who was to make the entire system economic? The West. And why not? The railway was built and the rates established before large-scale agricultural settlement took place and therefore must have been part of the economic calculation of the potential homesteader. The very purpose of the railway was to open the region for development, and so why should the beneficiaries object to a levy on hitherto unrealizable profits? Moreover, the next best alternative, American railway competitors, charged just as much as the Canadian lines. And, finally, freight rates have actually dropped steadily since 1897; if one assumes that the price of farm acreage reflects the capitalized value of the farmer's expected return (net income after expenses), the established homesteader reaped a capital gain in the value of his land with every decline in freight rates.

The prairie response yielded to none of these arguments. The railway benefited east as well as west and, therefore, its cost should be paid by both. If the American Midwest suffered from the same injustice, then a corrective should be applied there, too; the American case proved only that railways were a natural monopoly and had to be regulated or nationalized. The economic rents (or unexpected gains) accruing from increases in land values and decreases in relative freight rate levels did not reach the prairie farmer but rather were 'stolen' by the owners of the grain-handling companies or were dissipated by the inefficiency of eastern manufacturers.[33] Thus, the prairie case remained, then and now, unwavering: the fundamental principle of Canadian transportation policy should not be regional discrimination but rather should be national equalization of railway rates.

Western opposition arose as soon as the 1883 schedule appeared. Within five years, the railway and freight rate issues had ended the political career of John Norquay and given Thomas Greenway's Liberals an unassailable majority in the Manitoba legislature. Still the issue refused to go away. Then, in 1897, the lure of rich mineral deposits in the Kootenays produced an unusual bargain that was a fixture in Canadian life until 1983. This was Holy Crow – the Crow's Nest Pass freight rate agreement. To defeat American competition in the remote valleys of southeastern British Columbia, the CPR would have to build a spur from its main line at Lethbridge, Alberta, to Nelson via the Crow's Nest Pass. Such an expensive undertaking would necessitate a federal grant, eventually set at $11,000 per mile for the 330-mile line, to cover about two-thirds of the construction costs. But a grant would be politically palatable in western Canada only if the CPR made concessions on freight rates. Thus, in exchange for access to a mineral empire – the great mining corporation Consolidated Mining and Smelting Company (Cominco) became one of the first CPR industrial subsidiaries – the CPR agreed to reduce its freight rates, including the rate for grain eastbound from Winnipeg to Thunder Bay and the rates on westbound settlers' effects such as binder twine and tarpaper, by approximately 20 per cent. The Crow rates went into effect in 1898 and 1899.

The exciting atmosphere of the economic boom at the turn of the twentieth century turned heads in Canadian boardrooms and cabi-net chambers. At the Winnipeg headquarters of a burgeoning prairie railway, the Canadian Northern, William Mackenzie and Donald Mann overestimated their income once too often as they tried to extend their branch line network toward Thunder Bay and Edmonton. In order to stay afloat, they were forced to rely upon Manitoba government bond guarantees. In return, they promised to haul prairie grain to the Lakehead at a rate even lower than that stipulated in the Crow's Nest Pass agreement. The 1901 deal, which was soon matched by the CPR, was denounced by some eastern Canadians as an unacceptable attempt by western regional interests to shift the burden of the CPR to eastern shoulders but, in the face of unanimous western support for the arrangement, Prime Minister Laurier did not intervene. The Manitoba government's unilateral action had pushed Canada toward nation-wide equalization of freight rates.[34]

The unbounded optimism of these years soon undid the prairie victory. In 1903, the Laurier government decided to build a second transcontinental on the foundation of eastern Canada's Grand Trunk Railway. Because this new system threatened to curtail the Canadian Northern links to the Grand Trunk, which were crucial to Mackenzie and Mann's battle with the CPR, the westerners chose to build their own – Canada's third – transcontinental. If one line north of Lake Superior was an economic risk, what could justify three? The answer came quickly. The end of the boom in 1913 and the unpredictable economic circumstances of the First World War forced the federal government to take over the two ruined lines under the newly created Canadian National Railway. During the war, too, the 1901 Manitoba-Canadian Northern freight rates – and even the Crow rate – were set aside. As the war ended, prairie citizens once again organized to campaign for national equalization of freight rates. The prairie protest of the early 1920s produced paradoxical results. Farmers secured as much as they could have expected when, in July 1922, the Crow rate on outbound grain and flour was restored. In July 1925, this deal was enshrined in a federal statute. There the rates remained, untouched and sacred, for over half a century. As W.L. Morton once commented, the Crow rates were a kind of 'offset' which made 'the burden of the tariff tolerable on the prairies.'[35] But the special rates on settlers' effects were not restored, and the relative burden of freight rates in the various regions was not re-examined. As a result, the discrimination that had been built into the Canadian rate system in the early years was perpetuated and made worse for every sector of the prairie economy except for producers of cereal grains. Was it any wonder that western industrialization seemed difficult? Or that prairie manufacturers and processors fumed about freight rates for the next two generations?[36]

In contrast to the debates over the regional justice of tariffs and freight rates, which remain lively, little has been added to the discussion of western land policy in recent decades. One aspect of the prairie case has never been convincing. Western lands did indeed 'pay' for national projects such as the CPR, and Ottawa did retain control of these lands until 1930, but federal transfer payments to the provinces were sufficiently generous that prairie citizens had little reason to complain. A second charge carries more weight. It contends that Ottawa's administration of the lands was poor and that the settlement of arid areas, for example, resulted in unnecessary social expenditures in later years. With the benefit of hindsight, we can see that the southeastern parts of Alberta should never have been open to settlement, of course, and we may believe that local administration would have been wiser. But these are moot points. On the whole, federal land administration, despite some serious flaws, was sensible and successful.

Kenneth Norrie concluded his 1978 article with the assertion that 'the claims of prairie economic discrimination currently so casually thrown about are not supported by the evidence.' In his view, the few feasible alternatives to the federal railway, tariff, and land policies would have weighed just as heavily on the residents of the prairie west. In general, he is right. But his arguments are based on 'counterfactual' propositions, that is, on what would have happened in the west if the next most likely policy alternative had been adopted. This logic would not have satisfied prairie pioneers. The arguments of the prairie west were built upon local perceptions of political and economic 'justice' – that is, not what was likely but what was desirable and even 'fair.' Prairie protesters demanded nation-wide calculations of income and, as we shall see, nation-wide redistribution of wealth. The prairie arguments were important because increasingly, as the decades passed, the prairie region was gaining influence in the Canadian family of regions. Though the National Policy was designed to integrate the west into the nation, it eventually became a subject of bitter debate because it set the price for western participation in the nation. To the chagrin of many westerners, moreover, the very institutions of the nation – the Department of the Interior, the federal party system, the tariff and freight rate structure – seemed to favour central Canadian interests. Western protesters wanted a review of the terms of Confederation in order that Canadians should have equal opportunities and a fair return for their labour.

The very fact that such warm debates had developed by the turn of the century suggests how great was the change in the region during just one generation. In the 1870s, westerners worried about the buffalo; by 1900, they worried about the cost of transporting wheat, of importing farm implements, and of purchasing nearby quarter-sections. A new age had begun.

# 9

## Manitoba 1870–1900: First new province of the dominion

The new province of Manitoba was a metis settlement when it entered Confederation in 1870. By the time it elected its first and only metis premier, in 1878, however, it was rapidly completing the transition to a British-Ontarian community, a transition that was completed during the 1880s. And the Liberal administration of Premier Thomas Greenway, which governed the province from 1888 to 1899 and contained such zealous defenders of Ontario-style civilization as Joseph Martin and Clifford Sifton, made certain that the gristle of the new culture would harden into bone without serious challenge. By the close of the nineteenth century, a stable and comfortable civilization had been set in place, perhaps not as prosperous or populous as dreamers had predicted but none the less fixed in its ways and more or less satisfied with its accomplishment.

The fate of the metis in Manitoba, particularly those who were French-speaking, was sad. From the moment Wolseley's troops streamed into Upper Fort Garry, the metis were made to feel strangers in their own land. Catcalls and fistfights in front of Winnipeg's saloons were simply the most visible signs of a process that ended in exile for some, silence and shame for others. The first violent confrontations occurred before the troops were even fully settled in their new camp. Liquor flowed at Monchamp's and Dutch

George's 'rumshops,' men disputed, 'actually rolling and fighting in the miry mudholes of Winnipeg' and drunken orgies took place. Francois Guillemette was killed on the trail one night, Andre Nault was beaten nearly to death, and Elzear Goulet, fleeing from some cutthroats, was drowned in the Red River. The violence was not just a brief outburst but plagued the province for several years. As late as the autumn of 1872, the distinguished young French-Canadian lawyer Joseph Dubuc, by then a leader of the French community in the province and a member of the legislature, was accosted in the streets of Winnipeg, badly beaten, and left blinded in one eye for life. The new order must have seemed violent and even disgusting to many of the old settlers.[1]

The skirmishes with young hotheads from Ontario were upsetting but, had they been a unique phenomenon in an otherwise untroubled society, the metis would have lived on without undue difficulty because the hunters among them were accustomed to trials of strength and could handle themselves in plains wars and street fights with equal facility. But they faced an economic crisis in the 1870s that seemed insoluble. Part of the problem lay with the hunt; it had been the basis of the Red River food supply for over forty years but now was growing unreliable as a result of depredations on the buffalo population on both sides of the border. The buffalo herds no longer approached the Red River Valley and, indeed, no longer crossed the Riding Mountain–Turtle Mountain axis one hundred miles to the west. Because the metis hunters had to travel farther each season, they began to establish semi-permanent camps on the western rivers and even to trade there, at forts Edmonton and Carlton on the North Saskatchewan or Benton on the Missouri, rather than at Red River. At St Laurent on the South Saskatchewan, not far from Fort Carlton, Gabriel Dumont and his friends organized an informal provisional government in 1875, and petitions for assistance with land claims were forwarded to the Canadian government by metis at Prince Albert, Qu'Appelle, and Cypress Hills as well as St Laurent in 1878. These communities, as well as others on the upper Missouri in Montana Territory, were composed largely of Red River metis families who had moved west within the decade.[2]

The outward migration from Manitoba was partly caused by the fortunes of the hunt but was also the result of the poisonous atmosphere in Red River itself. A political solution to the central outstanding issue of 1870 – the amnesty – was long in coming, and settlement of a crucial promise of the Manitoba Act, the metis land grant, seemed even more elusive. Amnesty for those who had participated in the resistance of 1869–70 had been negotiated by the Red River delegates and had been implied in Cartier's promises to Bishop Taché, but the understanding was never put in writing. Instead, Macdonald procured $1,000 to be paid as a bribe to Riel and Ambroise Lepine in order to keep them out of the country.[3] It was a sordid bargain and yet, in the face of an Ontario government offer of a $5,000 reward to any person bringing about the arrest and conviction of Scott's 'murderers,' and the invasion of Riel's own house in St Vital by several armed men, flight was perhaps the safest alternative. Riel often returned to Manitoba from his exile in Minnesota during the next two years, sufficiently often that he could have taken the federal riding of Provencher in 1872 had he not withdrawn in favour of Sir George-Etienne Cartier, and he won the seat by acclamation after Cartier's death in 1873 and again in the general election of 1874. But when he walked quietly into the House of Commons to take the oath of office and just as quietly slipped out of the capital city that same evening, the uproar could be heard across the continent. Despite re-election by acclamation in the autumn of 1874, and Prime Minister Mackenzie's eventual decision that he and Lepine should be granted an amnesty after a further five years' banishment from Canada, Riel was a hunted man. He had been hounded into exile where, in fear and depression, he slowly lost his grip on reality. As with the violence in the streets of Winnipeg, the handling of the amnesty question was sad evidence of the Canadian administration's lack of concern for the metis.

But the story of the metis land problem was the most tragic evidence of Canadian misrule. Security of their land holdings had been one of the central concerns of the metis in the resistance of 1869–70 and had seemed to be answered by Manitoba assurances of security of tenure and of a grant of 1.4 million acres 'for the benefit of *families* of the half-breed residents,' acreage that was to be divided 'among the *children* of the *half-breed heads of families*.' But the implementation of these provisions was plagued by delays, speculation, and downright theft. At this distance, it is difficult to determine whether the politicians and administrators themselves were dishonest or whether they simply permitted speculators to wreak havoc, but it is certain that, one way or another, the metis acquired only a fraction of the land to which they were entitled. Four years of debate settled the 'hay privilege' – the customary right to cut hay on the two miles of land behind one's river lot – largely but not entirely in favour of the original settlers, but the issue of the 1.4-million-acre grant was much more difficult. If the grant was intended only for metis children, then their parents could not participate in it. Nor could Europeans, such as the Selkirk settlers, who had no Indian blood. Thus, in 1873, to remedy alleged inequities, the Selkirk settlers were offered 140 acres per head, and in 1874, the 'half-breed heads of families' were also recognized by passage of legislation offering them $160 of scrip that could be used to purchase dominion lands. The precise location of the 1.4 million acres, like that of the land represented by the scrip of the adult metis, remained unresolved as late as 1875. Was this right to be extinguished by the reservation of specific parcels of land – perhaps favoured parcels near present parishes – or did it imply that each metis, like other incoming settlers, could claim any available quarter-section in the usual manner at a dominion lands office? Were there reserves, in other words, wherein the metis communities could develop the old parish and kin network, and wherein metis children, as they reached the age of majority, could claim land of their own? Or was the land to be opened to all, in order that an individualistic system could be established?[4]

A compromise of sorts was reached. The scrip of the adult metis was to be redeemable in cash or vacant dominion lands; the children were allotted land in reserves. The adults' scrip became an article of speculation even before it appeared on the streets, and very little of it actually was used to establish new metis-owned farms in Manitoba. The children's lands were partially protected from speculation because, until the children reached the age of majority, they could not legally divest themselves of their property except after strict investigation of the circumstances. Despite these careful rules, thousands of 'infant' land transactions passed through the Manitoba courts. The grant to the children of Joseph Carrière, which was transferred to the lawyer and politician A.W. Ross, was one illustration of this shady business. The petition by Carrière to sell the children's grants was signed in the home of Napoléon Bonneau, a metis shill employed by Ross, and witnessed by another of Ross's staff, R.P. Wood, grandson of Manitoba's chief justice. Mr Justice Wood then passed the petition, and the land was purchased by Mr Ross. What is remarkable about this transaction is that none of the

Carrière family had seen the land, Bonneau set the price, and the children, far from being in dire need, were then attending school. The speculators, aided by the courts, were bending the law to the breaking point in thus bilking the metis children, and as a result the Manitoba government eventually found it necessary to pass an extraordinary series of statutes culminating in an 1885 bill that declared that all previous sales of infant metis lands were legal, notwithstanding any defect, irregularity, or omission. It has been estimated that about 75 per cent of the infant lands found their way to the courts and thereby into the hands of new owners. As lawyer Heber Archibald commented, 'It was the opinion of nine out of ten members of the profession that it was an improvident grant to the Half Breeds – in the first place – that it would bring them more harm than good – and that the sooner the whole of these lands was settled the better.'[5]

The loss of grant lands may seem unexceptionable because these gifts were intended principally as a boon for the metis, a means of extinguishing their Indian title, and did not affect their farms on the banks of the Assiniboine, Red, Seine, and Sale rivers. One might assume that here, on the family river lots, the metis would continue their lives as before. And yet, within a decade of the resistance, many of these Manitoba metis, too, had moved on. Was this a voluntary exodus? The answer has yet to be obtained but recent findings suggest not. The metis residents of river lot farms were required to apply to a dominion official to obtain clear title, a process that became more and more difficult as the decade passed. Those who stayed on their land for only a few weeks each year to gather hay and harvest a small crop of vegetables and grain but spent months away on the hunt (a common enough pattern as the buffalo herds became more distant from Red River) were apparently given short shrift by government officers. One example was the scattered settlement at Rat River: 93 metis claims to river lots were filed but 84 were rejected outright because the occupants had insufficient cultivated land and either no dwelling or an unacceptable one; 5 claimants who had adequate houses and at least 5 cultivated acres received 40-acre grants; 4 claimants who had houses and at least 10 cultivated acres received 80-acre grants. In sum, over 90 per cent of the claims were rejected and even those who earned grants did not secure large farms. As Senator M.A. Girard, a French-Canadian representative from Manitoba, complained, 'We hear of confiscation everywhere. The people are told they cannot remain any longer on the lands on which they have been settled for years.' If this isolated example is representative, the metis did not leave Manitoba happily but rather were driven out.[6]

In a democratic parliamentary system with fully representative government, the metis land crisis would inevitably have found its way into public debate. And yet few metis complaints about this stunning dispossession were aired in the legislature. Why was so little heard from the metis? The answer seems to lie in the political system of Manitoba as it evolved in the first decade after Confederation. The government of Manitoba in the early 1870s consisted of an elected legislative assembly (twelve French-speaking and twelve English-speaking ridings), an appointed legislative council, and an appointed lieutenant-governor who acted as premier, at least until 1874. The tenure (1870–2) of the first lieutenant-governor, Adams Archibald, was marked by careful management of electoral affairs and reliance upon the equally judicious Archbishop Taché. The administration was composed of moderates and therefore excluded both John Christian Schultz and his 'loyalists' and Louis Riel and his 'provisional government.' Archbishop Taché's 'young men,' able Québécois such as Joseph Royal, Joseph Dubuc, and Henry J. Clarke, who had been sent west at the urging of Cartier to represent the Catholic cause in Manitoba, dominated the French-speaking contingent in the legislature. On the other side, moderate Ontarians such as Alfred Boyd and Robert Davis allied with the old settlers such as the English metis John Norquay to ensure that vociferous Protestants had little influence on policy. The workmanlike sessions of the assembly were marked by relative moderation, no mean feat when one considers the tinder-box that was contemporary Manitoba society. Discussion of the painful experiences of the metis was phrased in the polite language of parliamentary questions about the amnesty and the long-delayed grants.

Beneath the surface calm lay anxiety and hardship. The French-speaking metis had to adjust to the arrival of hundreds of immigrants, French- and German-speaking as well as English, and to work with land regulations that were undoubtedly difficult. Their accustomed employment in cart brigades and boat brigades was disappearing with the fall of the local fur trade and the rise of the steamboat. If they had managed to retain or claim land, their farms were struck by devastating plagues of grasshoppers in 1873, 1874, and 1875, and the seed grain loans from the federal government, initially a godsend, soon came to be feared as a means of foreclosure for debt. Where could they turn except to their church leaders and their political representatives? Yet Taché had been discredited by his failure to secure Riel's amnesty and his insistence on patience; H.J. Clarke had abandoned Riel and, what was worse in the eyes of the church had left his wife to take up with another man's wife; Girard and Dubuc spoke well but they had accomplished little. Thus, the so-called French party in Manitoba experienced fatal divisions in the late 1870s. Eventually, the metis, led by Charles Nolin and the Lepine brothers, challenged the French Canadians.

The metis political unrest accomplished little beyond precipitating a ministerial crisis in June 1879. Joseph Royal, erstwhile leader of the French party in the assembly, was replaced by Marc Girard; the official status of the French language in the province was briefly threatened; and an electoral redistribution reduced the French to about 6 or 7 instead of 9 seats in the 24-seat house.[7] More important was the decline in influence of the French- and English-speaking metis. Their alliance, which united many of the old settlers, collapsed with the redistribution of 1879. Henceforth, the English metis controlled only one seat, John Norquay's riding of St Andrews. And with the disappearance of his old political base, the metis premier acquiesced in the assaults on his countrymen. The Norquay era in provincial politics saw the utter collapse of metis defences against manipulation of their land grants. Some metis moved west to follow the buffalo herds in the 1870s; many more followed in search of new lands for farming in the last years of the decade and in the early 1880s. Manitoba had by then ceased to be a metis community.

The census of 1870 established that the provincial population was about 12,000, of whom about half were French-speaking metis, one-third English-speaking metis, and less than one-sixth European or Canadian in origin. If we examine the population of the entire area that became southern Manitoba after the boundary extension of 1881, there were 19,000 citizens in the territory bounded by Lake of the Woods and Fort Ellice. Fully 7,000 people lived outside the Red River Valley and Assiniboine heartland of the old Red River settlement. This population increased slowly in the first half of the 1870s as Ontarians, French Canadians, and Mennonites moved in to take

up farms near the rivers and on former metis holdings. Still, it is
unlikely that the population was more than 30–35,000 in 1876–7 and
despite the dramatic upturn in immigration in the late 1870s caused
especially by hard times in eastern Canada and the agricultural depression in Great Britain the population of the enlarged province in
1881 was only 66,000. The boom that accompanied the railway inspired further immigration, much of it from Ontario and the British
Isles but also including emigrants from the United States. By 1886,
the population was 109,000, and the ethnic composition had altered
irrevocably. Only 7 per cent were metis, whether French- or English-speaking, and the Roman Catholic proportion had shrunk from
one-half in 1870 to about one-eighth. The province was now dominated by those of English origin (24 per cent), Scottish origin (24 per
cent) and Irish origin (20 per cent). Over 70 per cent had been born
in Canada, and another 18 per cent in the British Isles.[8]

The physical balance of the provincial population had also altered
in these fifteen years. Winnipeg had contained perhaps 200 residents in 1871; it was in 1886 a thriving city of 20,000. The old rural
river lot community on the Red and Assiniboine had contained over
two-thirds of the province's population in 1871; this area contained
40 per cent by 1886, including important new clusters in the two
Mennonite reserves and west around Portage la Prairie and Gladstone. Settlements in the outlying agricultural districts were the
most important new feature of the Manitoba landscape. Southwest
of Winnipeg, beyond the swampy lands around Lowe Farm, a
populous and lively farm community had grown up around Crystal
City, Manitou, and Glenboro; further west, another area was developing south of Brandon, itself rapidly becoming recognized as the
province's second city; in this southern area, around such towns as
Hartney, Killarney, Deloraine, and Souris, prosperous farms were
taking shape and a settled social and political life was being established. Similarly, north of Brandon, in an area that included Neepawa and Minnedosa but stretched as far west as Birtle and Russell,
yet another sub-region was taking form. Much remained to be done
in rural Manitoba, for according to the 1886 census only 18 per cent
of the 4 million occupied acres had been cultivated. But the establishment of a rural society was well under way.[9] Here were the
vitality and conviction to create a distinct provincial culture and to
contest with Winnipeg for the leadership of the province. That one
of these communities, near the Pembina Mountains, should rename

the Rivière aux Îlets de Bois the Boyne to commemorate a Protestant victory over Roman Catholics in Ireland was an illustration of the new cultural temper.

The foundation of every district was the agricultural settler. These 'pioneers' had chosen the Canadian west as the site to fulfil their dreams for a variety of reasons, but most often because someone they knew had done the same. And their predecessors, the first links in this 'chain migration,' would have been attracted by newspaper and government publicity, by organized colonization companies, or perhaps by word of mouth and the prospect of adventure. Whatever the source of this crucial first decision, the settlers would leave eastern Canada, for this was inevitably the point of embarkation for British and Canadian travellers alike, by one of two routes. A few hardy souls tried the steamers on the Great Lakes and endured the terrible overland trek to Winnipeg via the Dawson trail, but the three-week duration and the unspeakable discomfort of the trip forced the closure of the all-Canadian route in 1875. Thereafter, most immigrants wisely decided not to exchange the train for wagon and shank's mare until it was absolutely necessary. Until the CPR transcontinental service opened in 1886, they reached the western prairies by American trains: they could depart from Duluth, the Lake Superior port of the lake steamers, and travel by rail to the Minnesota landing on the Red River; or they could take the train direct from Toronto to Chicago and St Paul, a three-day trip. The steamboat journey, which required one week, or a stage-coach connection, which entailed fifty-eight consecutive hours of bone-wrenching agony, carried the immigrants from Minnesota to Manitoba until the end of 1878, when the opening of the St Paul, Minneapolis and Manitoba Railway provided a fast and convenient alternative. Thereafter Winnipeg was only four days from Quebec City.[10]

Once in the west, prospective settlers had still to find vacant lands. Before the railways, they often struck west from the Red River on the boundary commission trail along the forty-ninth parallel, or, if they left from Winnipeg, they would follow the Saskatchewan trail, the 'trunk line to the interior,' which despite its mud and ruts, carried long lines of metis cartmen and new settlers to their destinations. Steamboats were also very prominent for a brief period in the late 1870s, but with the spanning of the province by the CPR at the end of 1881, these well-appointed and gracious but invariably slow vessels were displaced to the districts further north and west. Because so few settlers had arrived in Manitoba during the 1870s, the location of the CPR main line and the four largest branch rail lines of the 1880s were pivotal in the determination of settlement patterns. The most important years in the alienation of Manitoba lands were 1881 and 1882, the years when the transcontinental crossed the province, and though some of these land transactions were later cancelled this was the period when western Manitoba took shape. The rest of the decade was a time of consolidation and slower growth.

This boom era was dominated by settlers of British or English-Canadian origin, but the sheer numbers of continental European arrivals should not be ignored. Parties of Hungarians and Scandinavians (near Minnedosa), Icelanders (rural municipality of Argyle), Danes (Montrose), Swedes (Manson), Belgians (La Grande Clairière), French Canadians (St Félix), and Germans (Alcester and Gilbert Plains) help to underline one significant feature of all the immigration activity: the importance of 'primary decision-makers,' the first links in a developing chain of migrants from the old home to the new. Whether they came to specific reserves, were organized by colonization companies, were part of groups, or travelled as individuals, the contact with earlier arrivals was often crucial in the settlers' choice of location. In a careful survey of one rural municipality, D.M. Loveridge concluded that as few as fifty or sixty individuals were primary in the location of almost all the 1,500 settlers in the rural municipality of Sifton; links to the Bruce Peninsula, Truro, a Belgian emigration scheme, and Sandhurst Military College in England explained the presence of many of the settlers in this district south of Brandon.[11]

They set up their homes, learned to farm in an unfamiliar environment, and met in the farms and villages, perhaps in a living-room or a rude church or a bare hall over a hardware store, to form local governments, school districts, and political parties. It was a time of new starts, a time when society was defined and forms of cultural expression were set in place. Literary or artistic definitions of rural Manitoba were left to the richer, more leisured circles of the empire's metropolises, but there were lively cultural statements in song and dance, sermon and editorial. They demonstrated conclusively that the new Manitoba was Protestant, conservative, and very British. It was also 'western Canadian,' though a clearer definition of that sentiment would have to await significant public issues and indigenous literary works.

Manitoba was a rural community, but it also possessed a rough-hewn metropolis. Winnipeg was 'never a merely provincial city' because, according to W.L. Morton, among its citizens there existed a 'sense of imperial past ... that habit of independence and command' that survived well beyond the turn of the twentieth century.

Winnipeg was confirmed in its position as western Canada's first metropolis after a struggle with several pretenders. Its site, the junction of the Red and Assiniboine rivers, had been a focus of the fur trade at least since the days of La Vérendrye in the eighteenth century; Lord Selkirk's colonization experiment made it the heart of the growing Red River settlement in the first half of the nineteenth century. Upper Fort Garry, situated at the Forks, was Riel's bastion in 1869–70, and this site became the administrative capital of the west with the arrival of Wolseley's troops and Lieutenant-Governor Archibald. The construction of a number of government and business offices on the road known as Main Street between the Upper Fort and Point Douglas in the 1870s ensured that the administrative and financial centre of the west remained in this vicinity. But the selection of a rail route across the prairies, and particularly of the Red River crossing, were the crucial determinants of the site of the prairie's metropolis. From 1874 to 1878, to the dismay of Winnipeg citizens, that crossing was fixed at Selkirk, a rival town situated twenty miles north of the Red-Assiniboine junction at a point where the banks of the river were higher and where the floods that regularly inundated Winnipeg had never caused serious problems. Recognizing that Selkirk was the first choice of the railway surveyors and that the so-called Pembina Branch railway to the American border was located east of the Red River in St Boniface, Winnipeg businessmen decided to force the hand of the CPR. They would build a bridge across the Red River with the city's resources. In case the lure of a bridge was not enough to win the transcontinental, the Winnipeggers also planned to secure two additional rail loops that linked the St Paul railway and a new provincial branch line, the Manitoba South-Western Railway, to the city centre as well as to the CPR.[12]

The bridge had been built and construction of the rail lines north-west and southwest of Winnipeg was under way when the CPR syndicate took over the transcontinental in early 1881. The syndicate was interested in the development of Winnipeg because Donald Smith's other large investment, the Hudson's Bay Company, owned 500 acres in the area of the Upper Fort, and because the bridge was already in place. But the CPR drove a hard bargain. In exchange for sending the main line through the city and establishing the CPR western yards and shops there, the CPR received free passage on the bridge (a city investment worth $2–300,000), a bonus of $200,000 that had been intended for the Manitoba South-Western Railway, free land for the station, and exemption in perpetuity from municipal taxation on railway property. But Winnipeg had secured its future: its businessmen, sure that they occupied the transportation intersection of the west and with visions of real estate fortunes to be won, set out to create a metropolis that would rival Chicago and St Louis, the models, it seems, for every aspiring town in western North America.

The sixteen months following the rail decision seem like sheer madness in retrospect. The population of Winnipeg tripled, from about 8,000 to well over 20,000, though there was no attempt to keep track of the so-called floating population. Transients from across the continent and around the world moved in, following the lure of quick money and big talk. Rumours of huge profits and sure investments passed through the bars and the tent cities, as did equally credible tales of $300 champagne baths for the winners and of canny hoteliers who bottled this unusual bath water for resale to thirsty celebrants. Levi Thomson, a young man working his way in this bizarre atmosphere, reported:

> In Winnipeg in April, 1882, almost every day you could hear eloquent auctioneers, trying to sell town lots in some place, real or imaginary, in some part of Manitoba or the North-west. One morning at the breakfast table there was some discussion as to an offer said to have been made for one of the best corner lots in the city, of $1000 per foot frontage. Some thought the price unreasonably high, others held a contrary opinion. I ventured to suggest that in my opinion it was too high and gave as my reason, that a short time before it became necessary in connection with a certain transaction in Toronto, to put a price on the unimproved land value of a corner lot at the intersection of King and Yonge streets, and it was placed at $1,000 per foot. 'Oh,' said someone, 'that is no criterion. That is only Toronto. This is Winnipeg.'[13]

The speculation had to end some time, and so the floods of April 1882 were merely the occasion for a return to reality. Attempts to start a new round of buying by means of an auction of Edmonton town lots did not produce the expected profits, and not even an imported auctioneer could whip up interest in now-flooded Red River town lots. The recession deepened in 1882 and became a serious depression in the following year. Bank loans became scarce and then unavailable as eastern investors fled in fright from the crash; property values plummeted as the possibility of resale ended; inventories in local stores became worthless as wages fell and the careless buyer of 1881 became the tight-fisted consumer of 1883. Business failures were an almost daily occurrence in 1883, and by 1885 a retrenching city council resolved that it must cut civic expenditures by at least 60 per cent to restore the city's credit. Winnipeg had acquired instant fame in the North Atlantic world, but with the collapse of the boom the glamour turned to notoriety in the investment community. Some observers have suggested, indeed, that the lull in immigration to the west was a result of the reputation acquired in 1882–3.

It is easy to exaggerate the consequences of such a spectacular crash. We might well conclude instead that Winnipeg had made its name and that, like Chicago, it could not fail to benefit from the attention. It had become the prairie metropolis in two short years. A city of 20,000 or more, it had acquired a stable economic base with the construction of the railway shops. It now possessed a number of small manufacturing enterprises, including an ironworks and several flour mills, brick factories, lumber mills, breweries, carriage and wagon works, garment-making shops, and printing shops. In addition, the city contained about 400 retail merchants and another 80 or more wholesale traders by 1886. This was sufficient economic activity to endure; it sustained a steady if unspectacular turnover until the end of the century.[14]

A reliable index to Winnipeg's future was the activity of the wholesale merchants. In this body of able individuals the business community found its strength and pride. Men such as A.G.B. Bannatyne and J.H. Ashdown were independent, perceptive, and, it would seem, tough. They had built their trade on the city's historic links with St Paul and London and as late as the end of the 1870s still divided their imports about equally among the United States, Great Britain, and eastern Canada. Despite an influx of commission agents and jobbers from eastern Canadian firms after the CPR syndicate was created, these local houses controlled much of the prairie wholesale trade through the 1880s. In addition to their success in business, they dominated the activity of city council, the board of trade, and even, in certain matters, the provincial government. These were the men who led the campaign to secure a bridge and to woo the CPR. Once successful, they moved to challenge Toronto's control of the Canadian grain export business, and with the help of Winnipeg millers, a group second in importance only to the wholesalers in the local economy, soon won the right to control wheat grading within Manitoba. When disputes arose over the relative qualities of eastern and western wheat, the board of trade demanded and won special recognition for the hard spring wheat of the prairies. Thus were born two new western institutions: Manitoba No. 1 Hard, a premium grade in world wheat markets, the standards of which were set by western boards of trade alone, and the Winnipeg Grain and Produce Exchange, an institution that asserted Winnipeg's primacy in the Canadian grain business.

While this struggle was being waged, the wholesalers turned their energies to the crucial matter of freight rates. The CPR had a monopoly on western freight because it had been given the Pembina Branch in the 1881 contract and, of course, had secured the so-called monopoly clause that guaranteed freedom from American rail competition. In its 1883 rate schedule, however, the company discriminated against Winnipeg distributors by raising the cost of freight. This preference for eastern shippers was unacceptable to the wholesalers on Winnipeg's board of trade, who sent protest after protest to Ottawa and Montreal. Eventually, the CPR agreed to establish a 'town tariff' for the Manitoba capital, that is, to levy a special lower rate on merchandise shipments from eastern Canada to Winnipeg only, thus ensuring a preference to Winnipeg wholesale firms over potential rivals in other western centres. A fleet of travelling salesmen was soon assembled in the Manitoba capital; the railway had brought Banff as close to them as the little towns in southeastern Manitoba, and these merchants were determined to take advantage of their position: 'The effects of the policies of the commercial elite on the urban geography of the region were striking. By defeating Selkirk in its bid for the railway, by winning freight rate and other concessions from the CPR, and by attaining control of the grain trade, merchant wholesalers and traders made possible the emergence of Winnipeg as the primate [sic] city of the eastern Prairies.'[15] With these victories, the wholesalers and their allies 'had made the Winnipeg Board of Trade a power to be reckoned with in western and national affairs.'[16]

The power of the board of trade and particularly of a handful of its most prominent members has led to much discussion about the contribution of such an élite to the community's development. The earliest interpretations were usually celebrations and took their cue from George Ham's glowing recollections written in 1921: 'They were big men, come together with big purpose. Their ideas were big, and they fought for the realization of them. They struggled for place and power and advantage, not with regard to the little isolated village which was the field of their activities and endeavours; but always with an eye to the city that now is and to the great plains as they now are.'[17] This celebration of mercantile ambitions was reflected in Ruben Bellan's pioneering study and in J.M.S. Careless's survey of the city's formative years. Both scholars were struck by the fact that the first generation of mercantile leaders, unlike later generations of businessmen who might stay in the city at one stage in a national or international career, were first and foremost Winnipeggers, loyal beyond question and devoted beyond the call of duty to the city's development. They owed their success to the city, just as it owed its position to them.[18]

Recent revisions of this view have examined the businessmen's record not with an eye to their victories alone but also with a concern for their shortcomings. This judgment, presented especially by Alan Artibise, suggests that the businessmen sought economic growth 'at the expense of any and all other considerations ... Accordingly, habits of community life, an attention to the sharing of resources, and a willingness to care for all men, were not much in evidence in Winnipeg's struggle to become a 'great' city. Rather, the most noteworthy aspect of Winnipeg's history in this period was the systematic, organized and expensive promotion of economic enterprise by public and private groups within the city.'[19] The substance of this criticism of business leadership lies in the businessmen's legacy of 'physical fragmentation.' Once the CPR had been won, 'city council did everything to encourage railway development and nothing to control it. This attitude had serious long-range consequences for Winnipeg's physical appearance and social fabric,' because it created 'an uncoordinated and socially disruptive series of self-con-

tained ghettos.'[20] Artibise's criticism is inappropriate, at least in relation to the years before 1900. Winnipeg is divided into three parts by
its rivers, the primary cause of community isolation, and responsibility for the other crucial barrier to communication lies with the
transcontinental railway. There is no doubt that the yards, shops,
and tracks of the CPR created a distinct community in the city's north
end. But the location of the yards at this early stage in the growth of
the city would almost inevitably have created problems. Each of the
four or five alternative proposals for the rail route presented similar
defects; that the result was determined by real estate speculators
and political manoeuvring among the aspiring developers should
not be allowed to affect our judgment of a process that destroyed
the heart of cities throughout the continent.

If Artibise exaggerated the sins of civic leaders in his comments on
the railway, he made a valuable contribution by emphasizing the
development of segregated neighbourhoods. Though the phenomenon would not surprise a contemporary observer, its lessons have
been lost to view in our history books, and as a result we too often
think of the frontier city, like the frontier farm, as a classless world
where careers and fortunes accrued to talent rather than to vested
interest. There is truth in the myth of the self-made man, as the
Winnipeg merchants' victory over Selkirk demonstrated, but the
period of economic democracy and social egalitarianism was very
brief. By the mid-1880s, the physical appearance of Winnipeg was
marked by a high degree of residential segregation by class. In the
village of the 1870s there were no residential districts as such, but
the booming land values of 1881-2 created a specialized commercial
district. Dwellings were pushed out of the new business area and
practically sprang up in three new areas. The best of the three was
the so-called Hudson's Bay Reserve which was near the Assiniboine
River on the south edge of the city. Large lots, wide shady streets,
and the presence of leaders of the board of trade demonstrated that
the Reserve was the address for the respectable and tone-setting
group. In contrast, the district on the north edge of the business
area and already expanding beyond the CPR tracks was known as
Shanty Town. Poor Jewish, Icelandic, and British immigrants with
few or no skills to sell on the labour market lived in these shabby
dwellings and endured such slights from the better elements as the
suggestion that they fostered a 'Shanty Nuisance' and that their area
was 'attaining an unenviable notoriety in police circles as the resort

of criminals and half-breed prostitutes.' West of the business streets, in a district just translated from prairie and still without trees and shrubs, were the narrower lots and more modest frame-houses of the respectable but not wealthy citizens. Though only one index of social class, residential segregation illustrated the thesis that the frontier was quickly replaced by a settled community. Within a decade, the unequal distribution of wealth was a fact of life.[21]

We might wonder how variation in neighbourhoods as measured by house size or even possession of wealth would affect the development of the city. The thesis suggested by Artibise is that the neighbourhoods and thus the social classes developed in isolation from each other. Moreover, the important decisions within the urban community, on public health measures and water-supply and immigration campaigns, were inevitably made by the business class through its dominance of city council. To this, we might add a cultural factor: by means of such institutions as the Historical Society, the Manitoba Club, the Masonic Lodge, and the St George's Society, the respectable classes established and refined their own perception of the proper social order. This perception included loyalty to Britain, Canadian patriotism, and a western booster mentality, but also a faith in the virtue of Parliament and courts as an expression of popular democracy. It encompassed their faith in themselves and in their ability to make their own way in the world. It explained failure by reference to personal shortcomings. And it made charity a private or religious act rather than a public responsibility. The role of government, as V.C. Fowke explained and Artibise lamented, was to provide the conditions for economic growth.

The goal of the provincial government in Manitoba, like Winnipeg's city council and board of trade, was to provide the proper conditions for economic development. The administration of Premier John Norquay was preoccupied with these economic issues during the years between 1879, when it was reconfirmed in office, and 1887, when it fell. Construction of rail lines, completion of public works, and establishment of municipal institutions, especially to permit local borrowing for further railway and construction activity, were its chief concerns at home. Negotiations with federal authorities for increased financial support and boundary extension constituted its principal external activity.

The boundary extension was sought as a measure of economic relief and administrative convenience as well as for provincial self-respect because the tiny 1870 province had little revenue and no control over the burgeoning settlements west of Portage la Prairie. An extension of its boundary might have been obtained in the early 1870s, once Sir John A. Macdonald had been convinced of the reliability of the new province, but Alexander Mackenzie did not act and only after Macdonald's return to office was the extension negotiated. The new 1881 boundary extended from the narrows of Lake Winnipeg on the north to the forty-ninth parallel and from the present western boundary to an undetermined Ontario border on the east. This eastern line was a vexed question because Premier Mowat of Ontario wanted to control the Lake of the Woods district whereas Manitobans believed their rightful territory extended almost as far as the shore of Lake Superior at Thunder Bay. The disagreement had its bizarre side, as in 1883, when both provinces tried to administer Rat Portage (Kenora) on the Lake of the Woods. The case ended in the highest court in the British Empire, the Judicial Committee of the Privy Council in London, where Ontario was victorious. The decision was no doubt good law, wrote W.L. Morton,[22] but it came at the expense of historic and geographic ties between Red River and Lake Superior. In Manitoba, it was greeted as yet another eastern slight.

The 1881 boundary settlement was accompanied by an increased federal subsidy to Manitoba and, it has been argued, was part of a package deal in which Premier Norquay agreed, in return for these concessions, to leave the federal government a free hand in railway policy. The truth of this allegation is not likely to be settled, but we can be certain that Prime Minister Macdonald believed that he had Norquay's acquiescence and that Norquay denied there was a bargain whenever the political pressure in Manitoba became too intense. The provincial government did have the power to charter commercial companies and under this title issued many charters to railway companies in the early 1880s. Those that infringed the famous 'monopoly clause' of the CPR contract by raising the possibility of a connection to an American railway were systematically disallowed by the federal government in order to ensure the survival of the Canadian transcontinental. But, once they had become accustomed to the luxury of rail service, Manitobans wanted much more than the CPR was offering. They wanted branch lines throughout the agricultural districts in order to ensure that the longest haul to the grain buyer was not more than fifteen miles; and they wanted competition on freight rates for the haul to ocean-going ships. Conflict with the CPR, and hence with the federal government, ensued.

Possible solutions to the Manitoban problems included a railway to Hudson Bay, a favourite in mid-decade, and a tougher stand on the disallowance issue against the federal government. But because John Norquay was a Conservative in federal politics, he was alleged to be a weak defender of Manitoba 'rights.' Thus, in the early 1880s, a new Provincial Rights party was formed under Thomas Greenway, a prosperous immigration leader from Crystal City. Greenway had been a member of Parliament for an Ontario riding before his migration westward, a late but enthusiastic convert to Reform principles, and so his advocacy of the Ontario Liberal stance on provincial rights and his opposition to Norquay were predictable. And then, in late 1883, independent of the establishment of Greenway's small opposition group in the legislature, a Farmers' Protective Union was founded in southwestern Manitoba where the absence of branch lines was particularly galling. Though the movement collapsed within a few years, it has been viewed by some historians as the Manitoba counterpart of the Saskatchewan uprising of 1885 and certainly was a measure of the dissatisfaction felt by those rural dwellers beyond the reach of rail lines and grain buyers. In these circumstances only the preponderance of Red River valley seats in the legislature and a generous new subsidy offer from the prime minister saved Norquay's government in the election of 1886. The premier had taken a risk during the campaign, however, by matching Greenway's promise of American rail competition for the CPR. He lost his gamble within a year.

Norquay's political position was shaky. As a friend of the federal Conservative party, he was branded a Conservative in provincial politics, though he was never close to Macdonald's agents in Manitoba and was never trusted by them. Thus, his apparent double-cross of Macdonald in 1887, when he vowed to build the Red River Valley Railway to the American boundary over the objections of Ottawa, was tantamount to jettisoning the support of the Conservative machine. The only possible explanation for this apparently foolhardy course was that he trusted his local backers, particularly the leaders of the Winnipeg business community and the farmers who had complained so loudly, to sustain him through the crisis. But when the going got rough and Macdonald used his connections to cut off the possibility of a Manitoba bond sale in London and New York, Norquay's erstwhile supporters backed down. The premier was left without a friend, it seemed, and without funds to run the government. He is said to have wept with remorse when reproached for his disloyalty to Macdonald. He may have gone on a drinking spree when visiting New York, but nothing could have saved him by that point.

In the autumn of 1887, Macdonald moved to get rid of Norquay. In a letter to the lieutenant-governor, he raised the issue of financial irregularities in the Manitoba government, and a month later, surely not by accident, similar rumours began to circulate in Winnipeg. The government had no money to meet its payroll, the banks had bowed to the prime minister and refused to provide loans, and an illegal transfer of $256,000 to the Hudson Bay Railway, which had occurred almost a year earlier, was suddenly revealed by a Conservative member of the legislature. In this deal, Manitoba was to have received 256,000 acres of land from the federal government as compensation for the money grant, but the land transfer was never made. When a Manitoba cabinet member claimed that Ottawa had approved the transfer, at a meeting attended by the prime minister, Macdonald responded: 'I had to tell LaRiviere that he must have dreamt this story.' Norquay could not survive the scandal, and his weak replacement, D.H. Harrison, could not sustain the government. Within two months, the Liberal Thomas Greenway had become premier of Manitoba.[23]

It has been customary to describe the fall of the Norquay government as the end of the old order in Red River, but the old way of life was long gone by 1888. Norquay himself had become a creature of the new age, however uncertain his position. His administration was dedicated to rapid economic development according to the principles of industrial capitalism. The replacement of a quasi-Conservative by a Liberal provincial government was an event in party politics only, not a stage in the evolution of Manitoba or prairie culture.

The most noteworthy issues of the Greenway administration concerned two perennials of Canadian history, railways and schools. There were other items of legislation in the decade of the Greenway government, but interest in these two topics has obscured its achievements in many fields. The railway issue was interesting because Greenway had used it to hound his predecessor into the ill-fated Red River Valley line. Having attained office, however, he was saddled with that same railway. Greenway won an immediate victory by getting Macdonald to abandon the CPR monopoly clause. The negotiations were extremely difficult, and the Manitoba premier actually left Ottawa without an agreement only to be called back by telegram, but the eventual conclusion seemed to satisfy all the parties. The CPR was delighted to be rid of an embarrassing public relations problem and even happier to have secured federal financial guarantees on further bond issues. Manitoba won the right to rail competition. And Macdonald, who had to sacrifice a principle that he had protected for almost a decade, must have been happy to see the end of this cry for Manitoba rights.[24]

The responsibility for the next move shifted to Greenway, who had returned home a conquering hero but now had to find a worthy competitor for the CPR. To the chagrin of a number of local promoters who had poured money into his campaign in expectation of an appropriate return, he settled on the Northern Pacific. The victory of this American company, though logical, smacked of back-stage manoeuvring and, it was said, even larger contributions to Greenway's cause. If the short-term results of the deal were acceptable, long-term advantage in rail rates was marginal. Through its network of spies, the CPR soon learned of the proposed new freight schedule on the Northern Pacific system and lowered its own in order to provide still cheaper service. By the contract between the Northern Pacific and the Manitoba government, the Northern Pacific rates would not be higher than those of the CPR, but this was difficult to monitor. Certainly, Van Horne maintained a private deal with one large elevator company by which he provided rebates in order to keep the grain prices paid to farmers on the CPR lines higher than those along the Northern Pacific route. By 1890, the two lines seemed to have ended their competition, and by 1891 Greenway had given up on the Northern Pacific as a vehicle for branch line construction and was working again with the CPR.[25]

The second principal issue of the Greenway administration, the schools question, has become a chestnut in Canadian historical circles. The reason for the continuing interest in the topic lies in its eternal relevance for Canadian Confederation; it has implications for such polarities as 'Conservative-Liberal, federal-provincial, east-west, French-English, Catholic-Protestant, church-state,'[26] as Paul Crunican explained. The traditional view of the origin of the schools issue was that it descended upon Manitoba out of a clear blue sky when D'Alton McCarthy, a Protestant MP, whipped up a popular frenzy against Roman Catholic 'special privileges' in a speech at Portage la Prairie on 5 August 1889. Manitoba's attorney-general, Joseph Martin, who followed McCarthy on the platform and may have been stimulated by a little extra liquor as well as the aroused audience, matched McCarthy's fervour by promising to abolish the official use of French in Manitoba's legislative publications and to terminate the dual educational system which permitted Roman Catholics to operate their own tax-supported schools separate from and independent of the Protestant section.[27] This interpretation of the origins of the schools legislation, which relied heavily upon external initiative and found little inspiration in local events, was slightly revised by W.L. Morton, among others, who emphasized that Greenway may have sought a smokescreen for his corrupt practices in the Northern Pacific railway deal. Nevertheless, Morton, like others before and since, placed the origins of the controversy in the anti-Catholic agitation in Ontario and thus suggested that eastern-Canadian bigotry, imported into British-Canadian Manitoba in the late 1880s, was the cause of the new school laws and of the great public passion aroused by the debate. Had Manitoba been left to debate the issue alone, he suggested, the result would not have been different but the heated atmosphere of religious crisis would probably have been avoided.[28]

Recent research has substantially revised these views. J.R. Miller has argued that the Equal Rights Association and D'Alton McCarthy did not precipitate the issue; if McCarthy's speech in Portage had an effect, it was to encourage the elimination of French language rights, not Roman Catholic schools, because opposition to French was the burden of his message.[29] This view has been reinforced by J.A. Hilts, who suggested that the Manitoba cabinet had decided to revise the dual school system well before McCarthy arrived in Manitoba and had announced its intention on 1 August, four days before the Portage speeches. Hilts's explanation of the new government policy relied upon the views of J.A. Smart, minister of public works in the Greenway cabinet: Smart believed that Catholics were paying fewer tax dollars than Protestants and receiving larger grants per school from the public treasury; and Smart, like Greenway and others, no longer had faith in the quality of the Catholic schools, especially in an era of challenges to Protestant cultural leadership around the world and of growing British imperialist sentiment in Canada. Thus, in Hilts's view, the schools issue had a local origin. The Portage events had their own importance because they added the matter of French language rights to the planned changes in the school laws, but that was their unique significance.[30]

To question the rights of Roman Catholics to a public-supported school system as well as questioning the official status of the French language in the province was tantamount to challenging the very basis of Confederation. Language and school rights had seemed to be entrenched in the Manitoba Act and had been accepted as the norm for twenty years. And yet British-Canadian residents of the province were adamant once the decision had been taken: 'They were determined that Manitoba should be a British and Canadian province, and were convinced that they were right and justified in that determination. The old drive of Ontario to possess the West was prevailing over the counter-claim of Quebec that the West should be the dual heritage of French and English.'[31] Indeed, Greenway's administration was sustained at the polls in the general elections of 1892 and 1896 when this issue was placed squarely before the people.

Franco-Manitobans did not attempt to recover official status for their language by reference to the courts at this time, but they did make common cause with their English-speaking co-religionists in defence of the dual school system. When this principle, a variation of the Quebec system, appeared lost, the Manitobans tried to establish their right to apply their taxes to support of Catholic schools as was permitted in Ontario. But not even that compromise was conceded. The new school system would be 'national' according to the American model, non-denominational but not secular (though the presence of 'religious exercises,' inevitably Protestant in tone, would further alienate the Roman Catholic population); the system would be administered by a department of education and thus be responsible to the legislature through a minister. Denied federal intervention by Sir John A. Macdonald, Manitoban opponents tested the legislation in the courts. There they were told by the Judicial Committee of the Privy Council that the School Act was within the competence of the legislature but that they had the right to appeal to the federal government for remedial legislation. The latter ruling hastened the collapse of the federal Conservative government in 1896 and thus was an important factor in the victory of the Liberals under Wilfrid Laurier in the general election of that year. The national Liberal victory, in turn, ensured co-operation from the Liberal cabinet in Manitoba. By amendments in 1897, Catholic teachers would be employed where a specified number of Catholic children attended a school (forty Catholic students in an urban school, ten in a rural school); if ten heads of families so requested, religious instruction would be held at the end of the school day by a minister of their faith; and, in a measure quite unrelated to the issue of tax support for religious schools that had started the crisis, where ten pupils in any school spoke a language other than English, instruction could be in English and that other language 'upon the bi-lingual system.' This settlement was far from satisfactory: 'Catholics were left with the conviction that they had suffered a moral wrong at the hands of the majority, and some of the majority were uneasy as to the effect of the bilingual clause on the future of a province of which the population was already diversified, and which was to become even more so as new currents of immigration flowed in.'[32]

The years that stretched from the end of the boom in 1882 to the surge in prosperity around 1897 were not easy for Manitobans. Below-average rainfall during the growing seasons from 1889 to 1897, fewer immigrants than expected, difficulties in adjusting to the new style of agriculture, and crushing municipal debts were just a few of the factors that made the first western province seem less than utopia to its new residents. But it was a period of growth, however slow, and of consolidation, however uncertain, and it resulted in the establishment of a stable community and reasonable prosperity. This was a grain-growing province, but its farmers had sufficient animals and gardens to sustain their families in difficult times and its businessmen had sufficient trade throughout the west to sustain the city of Winnipeg, a community of over 40,000 by the turn of the century. A new provincial consciousness was taking shape: 'The greatness of the break made by the newcomers had created a strong sense of identity with the old-new community of the Red River basin, and the strange new land became familiar quickly because of its distance from the old homes. The struggle for better terms and provincial rights, moreover, hardened the consciousness of identity. With a speed which was often amusing the new settler of yesterday became the Manitoban of the morrow. But under these more brilliant stars and amid these wider horizons the farmsteads continued the rural life of Ontario to which the British settlers were assimilated.'[33] The character of the new Manitoba was changing yet again as the 1890s closed. The arrival of European immigrants and a new wave of prosperity at the end of the decade coincided with and perhaps stimulated the development of a nostalgia for the 'good old days':

> O, for the times that some despise
> At least I liked them, me whatever,
> Before the Transfer made us wise
> Or politics had made us clever.

Thus, in the pages of western histories of the time, one could find a glorification of the Selkirk settlement and an emphasis on the autonomy of western historical development, and in the pages of western novels, a celebration of the very spirit of the land.

# 10

## The North-West Territories 1870–1905: War and politics

The North-West Territories were less populous and less stable than Manitoba in the generation after 1870. They were also much larger and more diverse. The communities of metis and Europeans and Indians adapted only slowly to the new order. In the case of one group, the whites and metis of the Saskatchewan valley, the transition precipitated one of the most serious armed conflicts in Canadian domestic history. The 1885 uprising made plain that though the era may have seen considerable economic and social change, it was also a time of disappointment. The level of tariffs and freight rates, the absence of branch lines, and the federal government's dilatory response to western demands for 'home rule' all irritated the newcomers. The adjustment to prairie agriculture was more difficult in the Territories than in Manitoba, the decision to change the transcontinental route frustrated the ambitions of northern settlers, and the decimation of the buffalo had tragic consequences for many metis and Indians. But, as in Manitoba, so in the Territories the stream of immigrants might slow but it never stopped. Adaptation of agricultural techniques and improvement in every aspect of the mixed farm economy provided the foundation for rapid growth after 1896. The grant of provincial status in 1905 to Saskatchewan and Alberta seemed only just, though belated, to citizens of the west. They had, by this time, established firm foundations for their new society. That this involved the virtual isolation of the Indians and metis may have been a matter of regret to a few, but, for most, life was too full to worry about those left behind.

Settlement in the North-West Territories was clustered principally in four areas by the middle of the 1880s. Two of these concentrations, around Edmonton and Prince Albert, were associated with the rich food resources and potentially fertile soil of the North Saskatchewan River valley and the adjacent parkland belt. A third was the dry rangeland of the southwest which extended from the Cypress Hills to the foothills of the Rocky Mountains. The fourth was the farm district of Assiniboia, centred on the CPR main line between Moosomin and Moose Jaw. This vast empire was administered by an Ottawa-appointed government for half of the period and later by local representatives who were still bound by Ottawa's financial control. Long-distance supervision was difficult, especially in the volatile circumstances of the 1880s, and led to unnecessary conflict between residents of the Northwest and leaders of the federal government in Ottawa.

The society of the North-West Territories took shape in the early and mid-1880s. By this time, 10,000 citizens lived in the two districts associated with Edmonton and Prince Albert. For contact with the outside world, they relied on steamboat connections to Winnipeg and a telegraph line to Qu'Appelle as a supplement to the cart trails.[1] The settlements had been founded as religious missions or as metis hunting communities or in anticipation of the railway, and they would survive the anger that accompanied the CPR decision to change its route from the parkland to the southern prairies. Despite the disillusionment of the mid-1880s, the eternal optimism of the pioneer was quickly restored. P.G. Laurie, editor of the *Saskatchewan Herald*, lost all his possessions in the 1885 uprising and yet within two years was again singing the hymn of progress. By the end of the decade, rail lines were extended northward from the CPR: the Manitoba and North Western reached Yorkton in 1890; the Regina-Saskatoon–Prince Albert line was completed in the same year; and the Calgary–Edmonton railway was finished in 1891. At this point, one could say that the parklands were opened for settlement.

The southwestern district of the Territories was cattle country. In that favoured land, where hot autumn weather cured the short grass and warm winter winds melted the snow from time to time, year-round grazing was possible. Until the early 1880s, this district was closely associated with the American territory to the south, particularly Fort Benton in Montana, but completion of the CPR and the construction of a narrow-gauge railway from Medicine Hat to the coal mines at Lethbridge integrated it into the Canadian prairie west. Despite the American origins of this district, therefore, the arrival of many English and Ontario ranchers in the early 1880s created a quite different culture that was to dominate the region for years to come.

The fastest-growing part of the Territories in the early 1880s was the region closest to Manitoba and along the main line of the railway. This district was sufficiently diverse to include English colonies at Yorkton and Cannington Manor; Jews, Germans, Hungarians, and Icelanders on nominally reserved tracts usually within thirty miles of the CPR, and many Canadians scattered across the region. The population of this area in 1886 was over 25,000. Its cultivated acreage constituted over one-quarter of all the cultivated land in western Canada.[2] Yet, like the northern parkbelt area, this too was a region of great unhappiness in the mid-1880s. Part of the problem lay with the settlers themselves. Late seeding, drought, early fall frost, and simple mistakes such as sowing seed broadcast on the surface of the soil, where it shrivelled in the hot sun, were a source of disillusionment to many. Thus, the mid-1880s were a nightmare to pioneers while crop experimentation proceeded. The experience of Alexander Kindred was probably not exceptional:

[In 1885] we had only 10 bushels [per acre] of very badly-frosted wheat. I took some to Indian Head and traded it for flour, shorts, and bran. I had no money to pay expenses ... In 1886 we had 80 acres under crop. Not a drop of rain fell from the time it went in until it was harvested. I sowed 124 bushels and threshed 54. In 1888 we began to think we could not grow wheat in this country. I had now 120 to 125 acres under cultivation. We put in 25 acres of wheat, 10 to 15 acres of oats, and let the rest go back into prairie. That year we got 35 bushels [of wheat] to the acre! So we went to work and ploughed up again. The next year wheat headed out two inches high. Not a drop of rain fell that whole season until fall. We summer-fallowed that year [1889] for the first time, and, to show the optimism, we put in in 1890 every acre we could. We had wheat standing to the chin but on the 8th July a hailstorm destroyed absolutely everything. My hair turned grey that night.[3]

Between 1886 and 1891 population growth in Assiniboia was mini-mal and caused largely by the influx of immigrants, especially non-English-speaking people, rather than by natural increase. Indeed, the out-migration of English-speaking citizens in this half-decade was a matter of grave concern: 'Manifestly the English-speaking speculators, who had come in to cultivate the land and sell at a profit, and many a homesteader, who had failed to make good under the adverse conditions, had left the region, and the New Canadians had done little more than fill their place. In the process the whole complexion of Assiniboia had changed. In 1885 it was an English-speaking country. In 1891 it was already polyglot.'[4]

The political arrangements in the North-West Territories reflected Prime Minister Macdonald's original determination to retain central authority over his western empire. A lieutenant-governor appointed by Ottawa was to direct the local administration according to prin-ciples determined in the national capital. He would work with the aid of a small council also appointed by the federal authorities. Until 1876, the seat of territorial government was Winnipeg, and the lieu-tenant-governor served Manitoba in that same capacity. The main territorial business concerned police and native matters. When Alexander Mackenzie became prime minister, he instituted a new system of government. By the North-West Territories Act of 1875, a lieutenant-governor would henceforth be resident in the Territories. The capital was located at Battleford until 1882 when, with the arrival of the railway, it was moved to Regina. The territorial council remained an appointed body, but when the population increased elected councillors would join its ranks. As soon as twenty-one elected representatives were entitled to sit in the council, the appointees would be removed and the council would be translated into a legislative assembly. No provision was made for the achieve-ment of responsible government, and thus the lieutenant-governor and his Ottawa advisers would retain control over much of the budget and other crucial matters. Moreover, no allowance was made for territorial representation in the federal House of Commons and Senate. A dual schools system, like that in Manitoba, was created, and by amendment in 1877, French and English were made the official languages of the courts and the council. The early consti-tutional framework of the North-West Territories resembled that of a crown colony within the British Empire: the local inhabitants would learn the ropes by observing government, rather than by governing themselves.[5]

Had the administrators been well posted in local affairs and effectively assisted by their political masters in Ottawa, the system would undoubtedly have been a success. Territorial residents might have chafed at the restrictions on their freedom, but they would have recognized the advantages of the tutorial system of political education. The administration was less than successful, however, and resulted in tragedy. David Laird, lieutenant-governor from 1876 to 1881, was a careful and methodical administrator. Editor of a Charlottetown newspaper before his election to the House of Commons as one of Prince Edward Island's first members of Parliament, he probably had sufficient business experience to handle the North-West Territories, but a chronic lack of federal financial support for his government and the inadequacy of the arrangements for local government made his five-year term a most frustrating experience. Laird met the inevitable problems concerning stray animals, prairie fires, gambling, and the administration of civil justice with commendable patience, but he was unable to resolve the problems of the natives and of the disgruntled settlers in the North Saskatchewan valley.

Laird's successor was Edgar Dewdney, who had been indian commissioner since 1879 and would now occupy both demanding offices.[6] Dewdney seemed to attract trouble. Not only did he implement a severe policy concerning Indian food rations, which created considerable unrest, but he also moved the territorial capital from Battleford to Regina with breathtaking dispatch, which angered the residents of the northern district. Though the choice of Regina was defensible because of the revised CPR route, Dewdney then alienated his new-found friends in the south by entering an unseemly dispute with Van Horne, vice-president of the railway, over the location of the Regina town site. Government House and the Mounted Police barracks ended up on Dewdney's land; the CPR station was placed two miles away. The trek from the one 'downtown' to the other, whether during the swamp and mosquito season of summer or the icy blasts of winter, convinced many territorial residents that Dewdney was as interested in lining his pockets as in looking out for their interests.[7]

The lieutenant-governor was a very powerful figure in the early 1880s. Because the territorial council could convene only rarely and at great expense, Dewdney assumed a large number of delegated powers, from the appointment of important civil servants to the licensing of professionals and the administration of regulations for education, health, and agriculture. He also controlled most of the government budget and was a central figure in the administration of justice. But, as late as 1884, only five elected representatives assisted the appointed councillors in the government of the Territories, and the economic and political crisis of mid-decade developed in part because there was no parliamentary outlet for grievances.[8]

The most important source of discontent was the metis and white community in the Fort Carlton–Prince Albert–Batoche district, where the general economic crisis combined with local fears about land tenure to produce a volatile situation. The metis were undoubtedly militant. They had moved into the district more than a decade earlier and had established stable, often prosperous, farms along the South Saskatchewan. As in previous generations, they also served as freighters, translators, horse breeders, and in the dozen other occupations associated with their status as intermediaries between European Canadians and natives.[9] Their dwellings began as rude flat-roofed log cabins with buffalo parchments stretched over doors and windows, but more enterprising settlers soon moved on to finer structures. One leader in the Batoche–St Laurent area, Francois Xavier Letendre, or Batoche, as he was called, lived in a two-storey clapboard mansion with fieldstone foundation and log walls that featured a columned veranda, decorative barge-board on the gables, carpeted rooms, and chandeliers – the whole valued at $5,500, which was the approximate value of Winnipeg's finer houses. Georges Fisher, Solomon Venne, and Charles Nolin were substantial members of the same community. Gabriel Dumont possessed a whitewashed log house with two compartments, a living-sleeping area of about twenty feet square and an attached kitchen about fourteen feet square; in addition, he had a stable and a root cellar and twenty acres of cultivated land on which he grew potatoes and barley. Dumont operated a ferry service and a small store complete with billiard table.[10] These fragments of information emphasize what is too often forgotten: that the metis settlements were permanent, stable communities, with merchants, mills, farms, and churches. Far from transitory camps, these extended villages contained a population of over 1,500 and represented the metis's adaptation to the new economic order.

The St Laurent community experienced numerous frustrations in its dealings with the territorial and federal governments. The chief concern, as it had been for many in Manitoba, was security of land tenure. The absence of French-speaking land agents and surveyors, uncertainty about conflicting claims, and the lack of representation in government made the universal problems of climate, freight rates, and farm technology all the more frustrating. Many of these people had left a Manitoba home in search of a more peaceful existence in the North-West Territories and had created it by the mid-1880s. In the face of challenges to their land tenure and in the absence of official assurances of redress, the leading metis began to meet, first secretly, later openly, to plan a strategy that would convince the federal government to listen to them.

If the metis had been alone in their dissatisfaction, they would probably have engaged in years of administrative battles against a distant and unsympathetic bureaucracy. But Big Bear's campaign to renegotiate the treaties happened to coincide with the growing metis unrest and encouraged the metis to think in terms of a broader native resistance. Even more important, however, was the anger in the white communities along the North Saskatchewan. Farmers and businessmen around Prince Albert, Battleford, and Edmonton were more vitriolic in their attacks on Ottawa than even the natives and metis. Frank Oliver, editor of the *Edmonton Bulletin*, in an angry screed of February 1884 which was reprinted in the *Prince Albert Times*, argued that rebellion alone would make the Ottawa government listen to the territorial assertion of 'rights.'[11] The mix of angry whites and natives in the Saskatchewan valley created a more unstable situation than elsewhere in the western interior.

The serious trouble dated from several protest meetings in the Prince Albert district in 1883–4 that had produced strong words against the federal government and one prominent agitator in the Canadian community, William Jackson. Only twenty-three years of age and just returned from several years at the University of Toronto, Jackson differed slightly from his neighbours because he advocated the political unity of whites and metis. To attain that end, he had secured a meeting with the St Laurent metis in the spring of 1884.[12] From a discussion of a list of rights to be sent to Ottawa, talk had drifted to the need for a leader of their cause and the name of Louis Riel had been raised. During the next several months, as the sense of grievance continued to grow and the problem of leadership became apparent, the prospect of Riel's assistance became attractive to English- and French-speaking metis alike. After a meeting of the two groups had endorsed the plan in early May, a delegation travelled south in buggies to St Peter's Mission in Montana. They were kept waiting at a modest dwelling until morning mass had ended and were then greeted by Louis Riel himself: 'God wants you to understand that you have taken the right way, for there are four of you, and you have arrived on the fourth of June.'[13] Within a week, Riel, his wife, and two children and a few possessions had been loaded into a Red River cart and the expedition was heading north for the Saskatchewan country. Before they even reached the metis settlements, they were greeted by a mass of wagons and people. After an enthusiastic round of introductions, they were installed in the Batoche home of Charles Nolin, Riel's cousin. The arrival of Riel was the crucial event in the development of unrest in the North-West Territories.

The uprising of 1885 was a tragedy. It absorbed over $5 million at a crucial moment for federal finances and, despite the boost provided the federal government and the CPR by military success, this money was sorely needed in peace-time allocations for the Northwest. The uprising destroyed the native campaign to renegotiate the treaties, as we have seen, and was a severe handicap for the metis people of the Saskatchewan district during the next generation. It entrenched a perception of white superiority over the metis that was to plague Northwest society ever after. And it ended in the execution of Louis Riel.

When he returned to Canada in 1884, Riel was forty years old and a very different person from the decisive young leader of 1869. He had been hounded out of Canada in the years between 1870 and 1875 only to return as a patient in Quebec mental hospitals in 1876–8. His instability had taken the form of visions and of an overpowering sense of personal mission, on the one hand, and deep silent withdrawals on the other. After his release from hospital in early 1878, he had been an impoverished wanderer, now plotting native alliances, now afraid of further fights over his role in 1870, now chastising himself for his weakness and sinfulness. He married in these years and had several children and to support his family had accepted a teaching job at St Peter's, the centre of Roman Catholic native missions in Montana. If his external circumstances had assumed an air of reality, his private imaginings remained troubled and uncertain. He still dreamed that he had a divinely inspired mission to save his metis people; he still was determined to reform the corrupt church by transferring the papacy to North America and anointing a new pope; he still believed the metis were the people chosen by God to purify the human race and that he was their 'David,' the name he used on both his marriage certificate and his American citizenship. Riel was a modern example of Machiavelli's 'prophet in arms': the metis movement he led into rebellion was 'as much a religious movement as a political uprising.'[14]

The Northwest rising began, however, as a peaceful citizens' protest against government inefficiency. Public discussions were conducted in an atmosphere of reason during the summer and fall of 1884. The meetings in English-speaking districts that Riel attended were, to the surprise of many, attentive and concerned. Riel's talks with Big Bear were uneventful and, apparently, without result. Among the metis of St Laurent, Riel was treated as a friend and ally but not as an absolute ruler: indeed, his views on metis aboriginal rights to the soil were not included in the list of rights forwarded from the Northwest on 16 December 1884. But this statement did contain references to most of the critical issues of the day, including representation in government, provincial status, metis and native rights, and construction of a railway to Hudson Bay.

The one uncertainty in this apparently tranquil scene was the relationship between Riel and the church. He remained a loyal Catholic and attended church services at Batoche, but his dreams of radical alterations in the papacy remained alive and the old metis distrust of French Canadians surfaced in his several disagreements with Father André and Bishop Grandin. However, he did win church approval for a metis patron, Joseph, just as the French Canadians had St Jean-Baptiste, and a metis national day. Thus, his holy plans for the metis nation were being implemented even while peaceful discussions of political grievances continued. Despite some bitter conflicts with the priests, Riel remained within the church throughout 1884, chiefly because the clergy sympathized with this poor soul – as they saw him – who had been hunted for so long. It was an error made out of charity but a political error none the less. Had the priests tried to counter his influence in the metis communities in 1884, Riel's ascendancy would never have been so complete.

The federal government must bear most of the responsibility for the tragedy of 1885.[15] The clergy, the white Canadian settlers, and the English-speaking metis of the district might have affected the course of events, but Madonald and his ministers were duty-bound to do so. Their defence has been that they were preoccupied with other matters, that the nation could not afford to pay for additional food rations and other ameliorative measures, and that, in any case, resort to rebellion was unthinkable. Such excuses were inadequate. Within days of the outbreak of violence, Macdonald dispatched quantities of flour, bacon, tea, and tobacco to appease the Indians and, after years of delay, established an investigatory commission into metis land claims. He was too late.

As winter broke in early March 1885, Riel's calm deserted him and he began to talk excitedly of resistance, of sweeping changes in the Northwest, and of a provisional government. With rumours flying, the North-West Mounted Police decided to reinforce its detachment at Fort Carlton. Riel and Dumont immediately seized a supply of arms and ammunition at a Batoche store, took several hostages as bargaining counters, and on the next day, 19 March (St Joseph's day), declared the formation of a metis provisional government with Riel, now above the affairs of men, as God's prophet. Dumont would be adjutant-general, and Dumont's nominees would become members of the Exovedate (literally, 'from the flock of sheep'). They then demanded the surrender of Fort Carlton, only twenty miles distant from Batoche. Superintendent L.F. Crozier of the Mounted Police chose to respond with dignity, sending a small party to investigate the situation. However, when this group was turned back by armed metis horsemen, Crozier foolishly decided not to wait for reinforcements but instead dispatched a column of 100 armed men, including 53 Mounted Police, to Duck Lake in order to secure the food and arms in the village store. Dumont and his metis soldiers gathered near the town and, when the Police neared, scattered for cover in the woods that bordered the trail; a brief attempt at parley ended in shooting. Because of their cover and superior numbers, the metis were able to rake the police position with bullets. Twelve of Crozier's men were killed and 11 were wounded in thirty minutes, and only Riel's intervention permitted the rest to escape to Prince Albert. The metis lost only 5 men. The police then abandoned Fort Carlton, accidentally burning it as they left, and sent appeals for aid to white settlements across the northern territories. The Mounties' reputation as an invincible force had sustained a serious blow. Riel, meanwhile, attempted to rouse the countryside, metis and Indian, in support of his provisional government. The uprising had begun in earnest.

Macdonald responded as best he could to the metis challenge by calling for the immediate raising and dispatch of a Canadian militia force. Within days, thanks to the CPR and the troops' own strenuous efforts to bridge the railway gaps in northern Ontario, soldiers were heading west. Within two weeks, on 6 April, the first column of 800 under Maj-Gen Frederick Dobson Middleton marched north from Qu'Appelle toward the Saskatchewan country. By 13 April a second column of 550 moved out of Swift Current on its hard trek toward Battleford under Lt-Col William Otter. A third was dispatched north from Calgary under the eccentric Maj-Gen T.B. Strange. Canada's 'first truly national army' was thus launched.[16] Citizens clamoured to enlist and within two months no fewer than 8,000 soldiers were mobilized for the battle against the natives of the North-West Territories.

The military campaign was brief. Middleton's North-West Field Force of 800 would be confronting about 350 metis and Indians, of whom about 200 were armed. The general planned to march slowly and steadily toward Prince Albert in order to give his green troops time to learn the business of war and to permit Otter's men to join him for the final battle. The metis general, Gabriel Dumont, who had experience in the battles against the Sioux along the Missouri, wanted to conduct a guerrilla campaign, using fierce brief attacks at night in order to prevent the invaders from sleeping: after three nights of stupefying raids, he said, the English would be killing each other. Riel did not approve because he feared the loss of Dumont and because the dispatch of a raiding force would weaken the defences of Batoche itself. At the small coulée known as Fish Creek, however, where the Canadian troops would descend into a ravine, Dumont was given one opportunity to attack – treating them, he snorted, as one would treat buffalo. The battle was indecisive because the metis fired too soon, betraying their planned ambush, but they did stall Middleton's advance for a full two weeks. In this interval, the Canadians were reinforced by two companies of troops, the steamer *Northcote*, and a representative of an American manufacturer with the latest in military technology, a multi-barrel rapid-fire Gatling gun. Still, the Canadian force advanced slowly and cautiously.

Middleton finally decided to attack Batoche itself. The metis had dug in along the steep east bank of the South Saskatchewan River, their deep rifle pits well secured against the fire of the enemy. When Middleton inspected the defences after the battle, he professed to be 'astonished at the strength of the position and at the ingenuity and care displayed in the construction of the rifle pits.' Nevertheless, numbers and firepower were all. The metis, fighting against overwhelming odds, were reduced to duck shot and melted nails for ammunition and yet held out for three days. On the fourth, 12 May 1885, the Canadians had found their bearings and the metis had exhausted their resources. An angry charge by the Midland companies, apparently more spontaneous than planned, carried them through the rifle pits and scattered the metis. Batoche had fallen. At least six metis died in this last battle, including ninety-three-year-old Jose Ouellette and Joseph Vandal, aged seventy-five, and many more were captured in the days that followed. Riel surrendered on 15 May. Dumont escaped easily to the United States.

The federal government had spent over $5 million to quell an uprising that had originated in Macdonald's concern for economy. And yet, in the eyes of many, the campaign asserted Canada's sovereignty and struck a blow for national pride. A Calgary newspaper editorial captured the sense of nationalism that accompanied the military mobilization:

When the train containing troops came in sight of the station at Calgary hundreds of the populace went to the Depot, and could scarcely believe their eyes when they saw the 65th's [Carabiniers', from Montreal] officers and men debarking ... Before the arrival of the troops the Canadian Government was freely sworn at. Many did not know there was a Government, and a number who were aware of it did not desire to cultivate its acquaintance; but the fact that it was sending troops there to protect the people and relieve Edmonton struck a responsive chord. The officers and men had come a long way ...

The arrival of Col. Osborne Smith's Winnipeg Light Infantry shortly after the arrival of the Carbineers was followed by a total disappearance of anti-Canadianism. Here were men who had come from one distant part of the North-West to protect another part ... Even Calgarians are human, and if anything touched their hearts more than this fact it was not easy to find it ...

> A great number of the inhabitants of Alberta are not Canadians, and until very recently they had a very faint conception of what the Canadian Government and Canadian people could do. The military has swept away hostiles and rebels alike.[17]

But such noble words excluded the so-called rebels from the definition of the nation. Patriotism had been fostered at the expense of the Indians and the metis.

The native uprising of 1885 has interested students of history as much as any other single event in Canada's past. Shortly after the uprising, English-Canadian representatives spoke of Riel as a rebel, while his defenders – often French Canadians – saw him as a patriot. Over the years, as scholarly analysis has replaced cultural partisanship, some observers have chosen to emphasize Riel's alleged madness and, whether from the perspective of psychiatric training or not, to suggest that he misled his supporters. Others have emphasized the grievances of the citizens of the North Saskatchewan valley and have placed the uprising within the context of western political and economic frustrations. Another perspective suggested that in both 1870 and 1885 the metis were acting to protect a distinctive way of life against the encroachments of 'civilization'; this approach, explained most successfully by G.F.G. Stanley in 1936, thus interpreted the Northwest uprising in a fashion reminiscent of F.J. Turner's American frontier thesis, though Stanley himself preferred to see the incident as a clash of cultures. Stanley later described the uprisings as an expression of metis nationalism – 'the inevitable reaction of a small group, conscious of its own identity, against the threat of absorption by a larger group, of a weak culture against a strong and aggressive one, of a simple economy against a highly competitive one.'[18]

Biographical analysis, which inevitably concentrates upon Riel's mental state, has never rested comfortably with the traditional political history of western grievances. Why did the metis accept the leadership and the doctrines of this apparently unbalanced man? Thomas Flanagan has suggested that Riel's career was strikingly similar to that of other prophets and religious founders who have arisen in like cultural circumstances, especially among native populations seeking 'millenarian deliverance from colonial domination.' In this interpretation, Riel's ideas, like those of the Mahdi in the Sudan and the Black Muslims of the United States, created a syncretic religion. Thus, by taking a comparative perspective, Flanagan has argued that the metis movement, like many others, arose from a combination of Riel's personal frustrations and the social crisis of his people. Flanagan demonstrated, too, that the violence of 1885, like other such outbreaks, was triggered by disastrous economic circumstances, in this case the hard times following the disappearance of the buffalo and the agricultural failures of the early 1880s. As prophet, Riel conformed to a common pattern because he belonged wholly to neither the metis nor to the white community. He was 'charismatic' in the strict sense: 'that is, his claim to lead was based on the visible manifestations of the anointing of the Holy Spirit – miracles, revelations, prophesies and sanctity.' His teachings, too, show some identity with those of other millenarian movements. We can conclude that Riel was not simply an accidental immigrant to the Northwest whose symptoms of mental disorder resulted in a violent uprising. As Flanagan has argued, Riel's insanity 'was a message of hope. Common conceptions of what is normal may suffice for normal times, but they do not encompass the range of human response to adversity. We need a broader view of sanity to comprehend the actions of men in dark times.'[19]

Riel was not regarded with such understanding in 1885. He was charged under a British statute of 1352 with having violated his 'allegiance, fidelity and obedience' to the queen; despite his American citizenship, and doubts about the jurisdiction of the court in such cases, this ancient and imprecise statute was made to serve. The issue of the trial was not Riel's behaviour, however, for the facts of the uprising were beyond question, but his sanity. According to the severe McNaghten Rule in English criminal law that then governed the plea of insanity (and was revised in the 1890s), a person was assumed to be sane until proven to the contrary; moreover, the person could not be declared insane in a general or abstract way but must be shown not to have understood the distinction between right and wrong in the very act with which he was charged; finally, the act must have been committed when the accused did not 'know the nature and quality' of what he was doing or, if he did know, 'did not know he was doing what was wrong.' This was a very strict rule. It asked – to quote Sir John A. Macdonald – not whether Riel was 'subject to illusions or delusions but whether he is so bereft of reason as not to know right from wrong and as not to be an accountable being.' Riel was mentally ill, as we understand the phrase, but he was probably sane as the law understood the term in 1885. And, to repeat the judgment of several scholars, though it is by no means a unanimous opinion, his trial was fair, given the legal standards of the time.[20]

Riel defeated his own lawyer's plea of insanity by his statements from the prisoner's box. His eloquent defence of the metis cause and his own career, delivered in a crowded hushed courtroom, was a historic statement in itself. He prayed for the court and for himself. He insisted on his sanity, on the grievous errors of the federal government, and on the sufferings of his people. He argued that he had a mission: 'No one can say that the North West was not suffering last year ... but what I have done, and risked, and to which I have exposed myself, rested certainly on the conviction I had to do, was called upon to do something for my country.' He spoke for an hour in English, not always fluently but with force and effect: 'Even if I was going to be sentenced by you, gentlemen of the jury, I have the satisfaction if I die – that if I die I will not be reputed by all men as insane, as a lunatic ... My reputation, my liberty, my life are at your discretion.' His oratory won a recommendation of mercy from the six jurymen but convinced them, too, that he was sane and guilty. The magistrate pronounced the customary and chilling formula: 'Louis Riel, you have been found by a jury ... guilty ... For what you have done the law requires you to answer ... It is now my painful duty to pass the sentence of the court upon you, and that is that you be taken now from here to the police guard-room at Regina ... that on the 18th of September next you will be taken to the place appointed for your execution, and there be hanged by the neck till you are dead, and God have mercy on your soul.'[21]

Petitions for clemency piled up in Ottawa, a political storm developed in Quebec, and reprieves were three times granted while appeals were heard and another investigation of Riel's mental state was undertaken. But Prime Minister Macdonald remained unmoved by the petitions for mercy. On the clear cold morning of 16 November, Riel walked to the scaffold, accompanied by two priests, a police escort, and government officials; he calmly asked forgiveness for others and himself, prayed on his knees, and then rose to receive the mask and the rope. As he was saying the Lord's Prayer with Father McWilliams, the trap was sprung. A simple funeral followed, and three weeks later, when it was judged safe, the body was sent secretly by rail to St Boniface. The casket lay in Riel's mother's house in St Vital on the evening of 11 December, and the next day, from all the villages along the Red and the Seine and the Sale, sleighs and carriages converged in solemn procession on the cathedral in St Boniface. The bells tolled the death knell as the great doors were thrown open and the casket was placed upon a catafalque surrounded by lighted candles. Archbishop Taché sat in state on his throne, presiding over the requiem mass for the person he had sent to school in Montreal twenty-seven years before. A teenager later recalled the mourners: 'I saw people cry, I saw men cry, when I was walking by in the afternoon I saw the crowd at the grave. Everybody was dressed in black.'[22] Riel lies before the cathedral in the cemetery of French and metis leaders of the west. The stone on his grave reads, 'Riel 16 novembre 1885.'

The period after the uprising was difficult. Batoche and the other metis settlements were shattered, at least temporarily, as the troops looted and burned their way down the river valley. But did Riel's capture end 'the hopes and aspirations of the New Nation,' as George Stanley once suggested?[23] If we look on the metis as just one minor variation on the general theme of immigrant adaptation to Canada's market economy, then Stanley exaggerated the impact of 1885. After all, the citizens of Batoche and district gathered up their possessions – the furniture, animals, tools, and implements that had escaped the looters and souvenir hunters – and, as would any group in like circumstances, re-established their community. Those who had remained aloof from the revolt and had political allies in high places were granted reparations by the Rebellion Losses Commission: Xavier Letendre (Batoche) received over $19,000, and other merchants, including Boyer, Fisher, and Venne were 'similarly compensated.'[24] It is true that the others, the vast majority, had to contend with serious economic dislocation. Freighting jobs had almost disappeared, there were no crops in 1886, and the land claims, though finally being investigated, still had not been settled. It is also true that the metis, given the choice of money or land as a settlement of their aboriginal rights, often chose the cash grant. This was not, as one scholar suggested, because they were ignorant of land values and were unwilling to farm but was rather because they were in straitened circumstances and required immediate assistance.[25] Petitions were sent to Ottawa regularly in the 1890s and as a result of a new issue of scrip to metis children in 1899–1900 descendants of the original settlers eventually located on farms adjacent to the Batoche–St Laurent site. In this view, then, life went on as before, and the metis completed the difficult transition to the new order despite the problems of the 1880s and, in the process, maintained their distinctive language, culture, and community.

However, Riel's dreams of a sovereign metis nation were ended. The idea of metis control over an empire in the Northwest, which must have had a parallel in the plans of Big Bear, ended with the battle at Batoche. Though many metis survived on district farms until the boom at the turn of the century, others had already blazed new trails to more remote homelands. Some joined the developing communities in Montana or the older settlement in Dakota, and many more travelled north and west, to gather in villages at Battle River, Green Lake, Lac Ste Anne, Lac La Biche, and beyond.

The uprising did achieve some belated but valuable reforms for citizens of the Northwest. In addition to the Rebellion Losses Commission and the review of metis land claims, the Territories finally won representation in the House of Commons (four seats) and the Senate (two seats); land transfer regulations were simplified; the local assembly was granted the power to incorporate companies with territorial objects and to levy direct taxes; and a territorial court of appeals was created. Moreover, the federal grant to the Territories was doubled to over $65,000, largely for school purposes. In 1888, the Northwest was also granted a fully representative twenty-two seat legislative assembly, though it did not acquire a responsible executive council and full control over local financial affairs until the revisions of the Laurier government in 1897.[26] The reforms, though valuable, were too late to respond to native concerns, however, and served instead to consolidate white ascendancy in the Territories.

One portion of the territorial population remained entirely aloof from the political crises of the era and continued to prosper despite the Northwest rebellion. Southern Alberta, the country centred around Fort Macleod and Calgary, achieved its success as a result of federal government policy decisions but also as a consequence of accidents of economic and social development. By the end of the 1880s, it was a distinctive sub-region within the western interior, a status it has never relinquished. At the base of this society was the beef economy, on which was established a politically powerful and often wealthy élite. Ranch owners and professional ranch managers visited each other at the Grande Ball, the fox hunt, and meetings of the polo league, served brilliant dinners catered by their Chinese cooks, and, when financially possible, sent their children to Victoria, Montreal, or England for schooling. Their development in the 1880s was contemporaneous with the rise of the American cattle frontier but was emphatically not Yankee in origin or style. It was far from egalitarian in social organization, as the American frontier was reputed to be, and in its respect for the law was clearly removed from the violence of the vigilante committees south of the border.

The federal government had established the institutional basis of this world in its ranch policy of 1880–1 which permitted entrepreneurs to set up huge cattle operations at remarkably little expense. Under this system, ranchers could lease 100,000 acres for up to twenty-one years at an annual rental of one cent per acre. Their only responsibility was to establish a herd at a ratio of one head per ten acres (later lowered to twenty acres) within three years. Despite conflict with settlers who wished to take up some of this land as farms, the ranchers maintained their favoured position for two decades, in the process demanding and receiving extraordinary police protection for their operations. According to the historian David Breen, 'On no other frontier was the cattleman afforded such protection as he established his herds.' Because of federal resistance to settlers' incursions, and especially through the establishment of vast water reserves that ensured that creeks would not be fenced off, the Ottawa authorities did treat the semi-arid southwestern lands of the Territories as a country apart. A unique 'cattle kingdom' with a 'British and equestrian tradition' had been established.[27]

The cattle business became a viable investment in the 1880s as a result of British market demand and the simultaneous introduction of the western railway and the refrigerated ship. It remained an attractive proposition until at least the turn of the century. Power in this economy was centralized. By 1885, four companies controlled almost one million acres of leased land, 42 per cent of the total leased acreage, and a number of other ranches were small only by comparison.[28] Much of the capital came from central Canada, especially Montreal, and most of the remainder came from England. One example of the range cattle industry as investment was the ranch owned by the Allan interests of Montreal, which ran a herd of about ten thousand head in the mid-1880s. The Allan herds represented a capital investment of about $250,000 and, according to one estimate, paid annual dividends of 20 to 35 per cent.[29]

The capital of this kingdom was Calgary. The city was created by the CPR but it was never so much a rail and farm town as it was a ranchers' town. Having defeated Fort Macleod in the contest for control of the beef economy, Calgary soon acquired a stockyard, slaughterhouse, tannery, pork packing plant, cold storage plant, and brewery, all owned by local stockmen. Ranchers' nominees sat on the city council and represented the district in the territorial assembly and the House of Commons; ranchers' money controlled the Calgary *Herald* and built the water, light, and street railway systems and even much of the business district in the city. At the heart of the city's social life lay the Ranchmen's Club, founded in 1891 on the model of Montreal's St James' Club as an exclusive, leather-upholstered and wood-panelled duplicate of a Victorian gentleman's retreat. Rather than a 'cowtown,' with whisky and revolvers, as American images would suggest, Calgary was built upon the tea, the gymkhana, and entrenched wealth: 'Its founders provided a legacy of gentility and social exclusiveness that has persisted to the present. The cattlemen and the town business and professional community blended easily to create a stratified and elitist society in imitation of the social structure they had formerly known in the eastern cities and in Great Britain.'[30]

The hegemony of the rancher came into question around the turn of the century. As the settlement frontier moved west from Manitoba and north from the United States, the demand for homesteads pushed land values up. Thus, the isolation of the southwest subregion was threatened by thousands of immigrants searching for family farms. The Western Stock Growers' Association, which represented over 200 of the larger ranchers, was able to hold off these newcomers while Clifford Sifton was minister of the interior, but the high precipitation levels between 1896 and 1903 and the appointment of the farmers' friend, Frank Oliver, to Sifton's post in 1905, were important developments in the farm-ranch struggle. In the next five years, the giant cattle empires were dismantled, to be replaced by smaller, though still substantial, enterprises and numerous immigrant farmers.[31] By this time however, the character of the cattle kingdom had been established on firm foundations.

The influx of newcomers into the Northwest around 1900 created irresistible pressures for provincehood. But what should be the new provincial boundaries? Who should form the government? Where would the capital city be located? How would the eternal issue of school legislation be resolved? The questions were finally answered in 1905 when Saskatchewan and Alberta became the eighth and ninth provinces within Confederation. With the establishment of three self-governing provincial units west of Ontario, the history of the prairie west had completed another cycle.

The pressure for provincial status came from all sides of the political spectrum in the Northwest. Its origin was no mystery: as the population began to increase rapidly in the late 1890s, the demand for more government services put intolerable burdens upon the territorial treasury. To build new schools, control prairie fires, build roads, and license businesses, the local administration required rapid adjustments in the federal subsidy. But such a change in the per capita grant from Ottawa, which lay at the heart of the federal-provincial financial system, inevitably roused expressions of righteous indignation from seven provincial premiers and threatened to drag on for years. Only provincial status would permit the citizens of the Northwest to make their case for improved federal grants; only provincial status would give them a ghost of a chance to revise the subsidy system. Moreover, the Territories had no power to borrow money or to charter railways. The call for provincial status, because it stemmed from such reasonable demands, was widely supported. As the Regina *Leader* explained, 'Our autonomy demand was never due to any grievous lack of home rule, it was due to a grievous lack of money.'[32]

Once the issue entered federal party politics, it was resolved quickly. Robert Borden, the Conservative leader, promised his support for provincial status in 1902, and Laurier's Liberal government followed suit before the 1904 federal election. The events of the 1904 campaign settled the matter. Because the acknowledged leader of the territorial government, F.W.G. Haultain, supported the Conservatives in 1904, Laurier did not want to give him the patronage powers associated with the premiership of a single, large western province. Far better, the prime minister reasoned, to create two provinces of equal size divided by the fourth meridian and to ensure that the Liberal party controlled at least one of the governments.

Regina and Edmonton were named provisional capitals, subject to confirmation by the provincial legislatures. Two Liberals, Walter Scott in Saskatchewan and Alexander Rutherford in Alberta, were invited to form the governments that would call the first provincial elections and, incidentally, would set up the civil service and command the patronage therein. An army of Liberal homestead inspectors and highway supervisors no doubt assisted the two Liberal governments to convincing victories in the 1905 elections and thus ensured not only that the federal two-party system would be entrenched in the new provinces but that the Liberals would remain in control.

Two other aspects of the 1905 decision were noteworthy. Once again, Ottawa declined an opportunity to return public lands and natural resources to the local government. The decision to retain the lands in 1870 may have been prompted by Macdonald's distrust of the metis; no such excuse was available in 1905. Presumably, the wishes of Sifton and his federal bureaucracy had prevailed over British constitutional practice.

The second policy decision, on the school law, created a much more severe political storm in eastern Canada though it left the west remarkably untouched. Under the Territories Act of 1875, a system of public schools had been created but provision was also made for members of the religious minority (Catholic or Protestant) in a given locality to establish a 'separate' school and to tax themselves for its support. By 1901, the territorial government exercised complete control over both 'public' and 'separate' schools, including inspection, licensing of teachers, and selection of textbooks, and thus the Catholic or Protestant 'separate' schools were as much under government direction as were the non-sectarian 'public' schools. The first draft of Laurier's 1905 legislation for provincial status seemed to restore an independent Catholic school system as had existed in the 1880s, but, after the minister of the interior, Clifford Sifton, resigned from the cabinet, a compromise was reached that guaranteed a continuation of school administration according to the territorial ordinance of 1901. Was the first draft a product of Laurier's determination to extend Catholic rights in the new province? Some historians argue that Laurier knew he was expanding Catholic rights. Others, including H. Blair Neatby, argue that the prime minister was merely trying to ensure that the existing satisfactory system would be protected by constitutional guarantees. The number of scholars on each side of the issue suggests that we should call it a tie. The role of Clifford Sifton in these debates has also prompted discussion. Some accuse him of anti-French, anti-Catholic bigotry. Others, including his most recent biographer, David Hall, argue that he was motivated by an indigenous 'western' perspective on Confederation. Hall concedes that Sifton was unsympathetic to Catholics and French Canadians, but he believes Sifton's beliefs were grounded in the western assumption that all newcomers should be inculcated with British democratic ideals and that the English language should be the language of public life and public communication. Both schools have merit; Sifton's views were based on ethnocentric and bigoted judgments about French Catholics but they reflected his hopes for a different cultural definition of the Canadian nation. The popularity of his outlook merely suggested that the debates over cultural adaptation in Canada were far from over.[33]

Two new prairie provinces had been created. They would now take their place in Confederation and on the maps of the world. Inevitably, each community assumed a life of its own and began to develop a distinct identity. Saskatchewan grew fastest and was soon the most populous and powerful prairie province. Though its people were diverse in background, the very range of their cultures and the uniformity of their farm life somehow inspired a strong sense of provincehood. Alberta grew more slowly, was built on a broader economic base – more ranching, more mining, more irrigation – and on larger geographically cohesive ethnic groups. It also had, like Manitoba, a wider range of wealth and poverty. Perhaps for these reasons, the sense of a common provincial outlook and the sense of commitment to the provincial community were less in evidence. The wheel had turned, at all events, and the prairie west moved into the political storms and technological changes of the twentieth century as three provinces, as a single region, and as a European Canadian rather than a native society.

# 11

# Immigrant communities 1870–1940: The struggle for cultural survival

The prairie west adopted recognizably 'modern' institutions in the half-century after 1840. By the end of the 1890s, its residents simply assumed that a capitalistic labour market, private property, and individualism were part of the environment, like the plains and the river valleys. But there were further surprises in store. In the next three decades, prairie society changed almost as drastically as it had in the preceding three generations. Its population increased sixfold from just over 400,000 in 1901 to 2.4 million in 1931, and its ethnic composition, as a result of an influx of hundreds of thousands of Britons, Americans, and Europeans, was altered forever. Its major cities grew rapidly and, like their counterparts in other developed nations, endured increasing tension among social classes. A vast rural community was built on a foundation of thousands of schools and railway sidings, villages and churches. New solutions to the eternal human issues of freedom, order, justice, and equality were made the subjects of economic and political debate. New political parties contested elections. Around the turn of the twentieth century, in brief, the prairie west entered a new phase in its evolution as a region.

Cultural diversity was one striking feature of prairie society in the opening decades of this century according to visitors from eastern Canada and Great Britain. To descend from the train at the CPR station in Winnipeg was to enter an international bazaar: the noise of thousands of voices and a dozen tongues circled the high marble pillars and drifted out into the street, there to mingle with the sounds of construction, delivery wagons, perambulatory vendors, and labour recruiters. The crowds were equally dense on Main Street, just a block away, where shops displayed their wares in a fashion more European than British North American: fruits and vegetables, books and newspapers, coats and jackets stood on sidewalk tables and racks, even on the outer walls of buildings when weather permitted. The smell of fresh earth at an excavation site, of concrete being poured and lumber being stacked, reminded the visitor of the newness and vitality of the place. But the smells were mixed with beer and whisky and sweat and horse manure to remind one, too that this was not a polite and ordered society but rather was customarily described as Little Europe, Babel, New Jerusalem, or the Chicago of the North.

Prairie society was much more than cosmopolitan Winnipeg. Visitors who travelled further west might have chanced on quite different scenes: at the southeastern edge of the plains, where the rough wooded terrain of the parkland stretched to the international border, they would have discovered an English parish church identical to those in Surrey or Sussex except that it was constructed of wood rather than stone. In this district, now known as Manor, Saskatchewan, there were indeed, manor houses; near the church there was, if not a high street, at least the makings of one. On special occasions, visitors might have seen mounted huntsmen assemble at the sound of a horn to assault the unsuspecting coyote or might have watched neighbours congregate in the library for a reading evening. The observer could then have taken the new train service north through Saskatoon and alighted at Hague, to be greeted by utter silence. A buggy might move slowly past the single row of stores behind the station, dark-skirted women might avert their eyes, and a murmur of phrases in low German would identify the distinctiveness of a Mennonite village. The examples could be multiplied many times: Mormons at Cardston, Alberta, where the great white temple dominated the district; Ukrainians near Wakaw, Saskatchewan, where the small onion dome of their frame church transported one to the steppes of Russia; Jews at Bender Hamlet, where the rows of houses suggested yet another settlement on the steppes; Hungarians at Esterhazy, Doukhobors at Verigin, Swedes at Erickson; the map of the southern half of the western interior was a giant checker-board of culturally and linguistically distinctive settlements.

The population of the western interior had been overwhelmingly Canadian by birth and British by national origin in the late nineteenth century, but within one generation the cultural composition changed dramatically. Almost half of all prairie residents at the start of the First World War had been born in another country, and the proportion was still one in three as late as 1931. Those who were British by 'origin' (a census term defined by the ancestral roots of a family's male line) had similarly declined to about 50 per cent of the prairie total (of this group, half were English, one-quarter Scots), while the various eastern European groups (Ukrainian, Austro-Hungarian, Polish, and Russian) numbered about 20 per cent, and western Europeans (German, Dutch, French, including French Canadians) also numbered about 20 per cent.[1]

As a community of immigrants was created in the opening decades of the twentieth century, phrases such as 'New Canadians,' 'strangers within our gates,' 'foreigners,' and 'ethnic groups' gradually became part of the Canadian vocabulary. Even today, westerners use the term 'ethnic' in everyday language and make broad generalizations about ethnic behaviour, tell crude stories known as ethnic jokes, and celebrate the changing seasons with ethnic festivals.

Definitions of the term 'ethnic' or of its many close relatives, from 'immigrant' to 'New Canadian' and 'displaced person,' are vague. According to popular convention, however, the term 'ethnic group' does not apply to Canada's aboriginal peoples and founding nationalities but does include all other minority groups whose identity is derived from racial origin, national origin, language, religion, and historical or contemporary consciousness.[2] To exclude the British and the French in a discussion of ethnic groups in the western interior would be a mistake. Their unique status in the west derives more from linguistic and historical precedence – for French and English are Canada's 'official' languages – than from officially sanctioned cultural privileges. In other ways, the English and French, like all other peoples, were immigrants to western Canada and behaved as members of ethnic groups.

The western interior has experienced five significant infusions of immigrants in its history. The first, a product of the fur trade, resulted in the establishment of a fur post society and in the birth of the most numerous new element in the area, English- and French-speaking metis. The second occurred in the decades after Confederation and, because it was composed largely of British Canadians, resulted in the establishment of a new, Ontario-like agricultural community; despite the apparent homogeneity of this society it is well to underline that it contained pockets of a quite different nature, including British ranchers and artisans, non-British agricultural settlements of Mennonites and Icelanders and Jews and, of course, continuing communities of Indians and metis. The third infusion of immigrants, and by far the largest, occurred between 1897 and 1913, and was comprised in equal parts of British, Canadian, American, and continental European arrivals, with a sprinkling of others from around the globe. The fourth, an extension of the third in terms of national origin, took place in the 1920s. And the fifth significant addition occurred in the decades after the Second World War. The subject of our immediate concern is the extraordinary burst of immigration in the 1897–1929 era. The implications of this multinational migration for the host society, whether local, provincial, or regional, were undoubtedly important, just as the new environment was an important factor in the life of the immigrants. We are only now coming to unravel the two threads of this story – the adjustments of the larger society and of the immigrants who composed it.

Canadian immigration policy was, according to the BNA Act of 1867, a subject of concurrent jurisdiction between the federal and provincial governments (section 95), but the central government retained paramountcy in case of conflict. In practice, however, the federal government took the lead in the establishment of policy with its act of 1869 which established immigration offices in Britain and Europe, quarantine stations at the three ports of importance (Halifax, Saint John, and Grosse Isle, Quebec), and domestic branches of the service in a number of Canadian cities. Restrictions were few: the entry of immigrants who were destitute, or physically or mentally unfit, and thus likely to become a public charge, was permitted only on payment of a bond; and criminals could be denied admission. This unusually open policy was limited once in the following three decades: as of 1885, most Chinese immigrants were required to pay a tax.[3] Policy was established by regulation as well as by statute, however, and with the appointment of Clifford Sifton as minister of the interior in 1897, clear but informal guide-lines worked to encourage some immigrant groups and to discourage others. Sifton was young, pragmatic, a westerner, convinced of 'the potential of the West, and its centrality to the future development and prosperity of Canada.' Thus the promotion of immigration and settlement was, he believed, a crucial 'national enterprise' akin to the construction of the transcontinental railway or the passage of the BNA Act itself. He worked to encourage the immigration of experienced farmers by spending considerable sums in the agricultural districts of the United States, Britain, and Europe, and he tried to discourage others, such as blacks, Italians, Jews, Orientals, and urban Englishmen, who would not, he believed, succeed on farms and would thus end up in the cities. These informal recruitment and entry qualifications were based more on occupational than race criteria, therefore, and worked to encourage such diverse groups as Ukrainians and Doukhobors while also discouraging English mechanics. Sifton was aware of and not immune to criticism of this policy; moreover, like his critics, he believed in assimilation of the immigrants to a British-Canadian norm. But he was in the business of building a bigger, better Canada, and, as a 'long-term investment,' farmers, British or non-British, constituted blue-chip stock.[4]

Immigration policy changed course slightly when Sifton was replaced by Frank Oliver in 1905. A vigorous defender of western Canada's interests, Oliver was also staunchly British in an era when national reaction to 'foreign' newcomers was increasing. He was more inclined to reduce the recruiting activity in central and eastern Europe and to increase it in Great Britain, including its cities, in order to preserve the 'national fabric' of Canada. The official effect of Oliver's tenure was a series of revisions to the Immigration Act between 1906 and 1910 which prohibited entry to those deemed medically or morally unfit, to those who were likely to become public charges, to criminals, to those not on a continuous journey from their country of origin (immigrants originally from India were thus virtually excluded), and to those who advocated the violent overthrow of constituted authority. But the unofficial consequence of Oliver's rule was to permit and even encourage the immigration of many more British subjects, including thousands of paupers who were assisted by charitable organizations, and virtually to deny entry to blacks and orientals. Despite his preference for agriculturalists, Oliver was less successful than Sifton in resisting the pressure of business leaders and cabinet colleagues to recruit 'alien navvies.'

As railway construction activity increased after 1907, the demand for unsophisticated labourers also multiplied because the railway builders wanted nothing to do with workers who expected 'high wages, a feather bed and a bath tub' in their construction camps.[5] The result was free entry for 'foreign' navvies in 1910–11. Because Robert Borden's new Conservative government was equally sensitive to the demands of contractors, mine owners, and lumber entrepreneurs, the policy was continued until the outbreak of war in 1914. Untold thousands of immigrants in this era belonged to this category of foreign navvy, to the dismay of observers such as Clifford Sifton.

The hiatus in immigration caused by the war was extended into the early 1920s by the prohibition of Doukhobors, Hutterites, Mennonites, and 'enemy aliens,' including Ukrainians and Germans, two especially favoured groups of Sifton's days. The government also reimposed monetary requirements on all newcomers except those destined for farm or domestic work. But, in 1923, in the face of mounting pressure from such European peoples as Mennonites, who faced very difficult times in the Soviet Union, the ban on enemy aliens was lifted. The failure of British population sources and mounting Canadian emigration to the United States may also have had a bearing on this decision. And, in 1925, in an even more important policy change, Mackenzie King's government decided to permit the two Canadian railway companies, the Canadian National Railway (CNR) and the CPR to embark on an expensive recruitment campaign in central and eastern Europe among those very farmers who for almost five years had been viewed as 'non-preferred' classes. Nearly 370,000 continental citizens left for Canada in the next six years, half of them under the terms of the railway agreement.[6]

The tide of immigrants was simply too great to be absorbed easily into the Canadian economy during the late 1920s. As hostility to foreigners and demands for restriction increased, the federal government moved to reduce the numbers of new arrivals in 1929. In accordance with an election promise, King's successor, R.B. Bennett, cancelled the railway agreement in 1930. The gates of Canada were essentially closed to immigration for the next decade. Immigrants of Asian origin found it virtually impossible to enter, and from 1931 only certain British subjects and American citizens, wives and children of legal Canadian residents, or agriculturists 'having

TABLE 1
Canada's population record (in thousands) 1861–1941

| | Natural increase | Immigration | Emigration | Net migration | Population at end of decade |
|---|---|---|---|---|---|
| 1861 | | | | | 3,230 |
| 1861–71 | 650 | 186 | 376 | − 191 | 3,689 |
| 1871–81 | 720 | 353 | 438 | − 85 | 4,325 |
| 1881–91 | 714 | 903 | 1,108 | − 205 | 4,833 |
| 1891–1901 | 719 | 326 | 507 | − 181 | 5,371 |
| 1901–11 | 1,120 | 1,782 | 1,066 | 715 | 7,207 |
| 1911–21 | 1,349 | 1,592 | 1,360 | 233 | 8,788 |
| 1921–31 | 1,486 | 1,198 | 1,095 | 103 | 10,377 |
| 1931–41 | 1,242 | 149 | 262 | − 112 | 11,507 |

Source: David C. Corbett *Canada's Immigration Policy: A Critique* (Toronto 1957) 121

sufficient means to farm in Canada' were permitted to enter the country. Where 1.8 million immigrants arrived in Canada between 1911 and 1921, and 1.2 million immigrants arrived in 1921–31, only 140,000 arrived between 1931 and 1941.[7]

In view of the wide variation in immigration during Canada's first sixty years as a nation (see Table 1), one might wonder why the government had not acted to implement a system that regulated the intake more effectively. The short answer is that the government seemed to have little control over immigration totals. Canadian recruitment of immigrants in the generations around Confederation had been something of a disaster. In every decade from the 1860s to the 1890s, Canada lost more citizens through emigration to the United States than it gained through immigration. In the face of significant western settlement difficulties, the weakness of the national economy in the 1880s and early 1890s, and the overwhelming presence of the American competitor, not to mention Australia, Argentina, and Brazil, western Canada failed to make an impact on the popular imagination in Britain and Europe. The well-tried tactics of immigration pamphlets, recruiting offices, assisted passages, and free tours for delegates of various communities were employed consistently throughout these decades, but the results were meagre. The best results came as a consequence of negotiations with particular groups, especially those facing straitened circumstances or political oppression. These talks led to colony migrations of Mennonites,

Icelanders, French Canadians from New England, Hungarians, Scandinavians, Jews, and others. But each of these many colonies was established as the result of special circumstances rather than popular response to an advertising campaign. Canada was just too small and too little-known in the late nineteenth century to win an international reputation as an immigrant destination.[8]

What happened to change the circumstances in the late 1890s? The question has sparked much scholarly debate and a wide range of answers. First, the Canadian government established a more serious and much more effective recruiting campaign. Second, circumstances in the United States, Britain, and Europe all had changed in ways that favoured Canada's recruiters. Third, the situation of the prairie agricultural frontier was more attractive as a result of important breakthroughs in farm technology and farm practice. And, fourth, the agricultural boom stimulated booms in coal, lumber, and railway construction that offered the prospect of abundant jobs to international migrants who might, in time, become immigrants; whether they stayed in Canada or returned home, however, they swelled the entry rolls.

Traditional Canadian interpretations of the immigration boom have paid great attention to the role of Clifford Sifton, minister of the interior 1897–1905, in stimulating Canada's recruitment efforts. There can be no question of Sifton's effectiveness as an administrator and as a leader of the nation's search for new citizens. He simplified the homestead procedures, promoted vast irrigation schemes in the arid areas of southern Alberta, eliminated the so-called land-lock by forcing the railways to select and patent their grants, and imparted new life to the immigration branch, where previously 'the pall of death seemed to have fallen over the officials.' New employees, a larger budget, millions more of advertising pamphlets, dozens of displays at regional exhibitions in the United States and Great Britain, numerous tours for visiting journalists, and provision for many more colony migrations were products of his tenure. He enlarged the immigration service in the United States from 6 agents to 300 and asked them to pursue recruits rather than wait for inquiries. He ensured that a similarly aggressive campaign was undertaken in the rural areas of England and Scotland. Finally, in Europe, where immigration propaganda was declared illegal by a number of governments, Sifton expanded a secret bonusing system through the North Atlantic Trading Company whereby recruiters would receive a money grant for every adult dispatched to Canada. Between 1899 and 1906, when the system was halted, nearly 71,000 immigrants arrived in Canada by this system and over $350,000 was paid to recruiters.[9] That Sifton and his department's activity brought Canada to the attention of the world is undeniable; whether it convinced reluctant people to emigrate is unlikely.

Canadian economic historians have recently taken a different tack in their analysis of western agricultural expansion. In the past, their response had been to cite a 'conjuncture of favourable circumstances' in the 1890s: a rise in wheat prices caused by European and American industrialization, falling wheat transport costs as railway and ocean shipping became more efficient, the end of available free land in the United States, the resumption of international circulation of labour and capital after a prolonged depression, and scientific and technological breakthroughs in the production of wheat and flour. Recent analysis has suggested, however, that some of these factors were more important than others. Sub-humid land in central North America was always preferable to semi-arid land, and thus the eastern American plains inevitably were developed first. The filling in of these preferred sites, the development of appropriate dry-land farming techniques, the movements in relative real wages in the North Atlantic community, which made Canadian wages seem vastly higher than those in Europe, and the rise of world wheat prices are thus seen to be important and interrelated factors. By contrast, the extension of the prairie rail network and the increase in government advertising played a small role in the determination of the rate of settlement, chiefly by hastening the process that was under way, but were not of pivotal importance.[10]

Another avenue of explanation of the Canadian immigration boom juxtaposes the 'pull' factors – the attractions in North America that might persuade immigrants to try their luck in a new land – with the 'push' factors – reasons that brought immigrants to the conclusion that life in the home country was no longer acceptable or that it could be made agreeable only by visiting the new land for a period. Here the stories of departures were as diverse as the communities that contributed to the stream of emigrants. Great Britain, Scandinavia, Italy, the Austro-Hungarian Empire, Russia, the small nations of southeastern Europe, and the United States were the chief contributors to the growth of western Canada's population. Each had specific circumstances that encouraged thoughts of escape.

The extraordinary migration from Europe must be seen as a product of vast changes in the continent's society and economy. Without the revolution in industry that began in England in the eighteenth century and spread across Europe in the nineteenth century, this world-shaking phenomenon would not have commenced. The growth of industry was associated, in ways that are still debated by scholars, with amazing changes in population: birth rates rose and death rates plummeted, first in western Europe and, after 1870, in southern and eastern Europe. The resultant natural increases in population were unprecedented; local opportunities were never sufficient to provide adequate employment for the numbers of young adults who were ready and eager to leave their homes. Cities burst at the seams as the rural exodus gathered speed, and when European investment stimulated overseas development people began to take ship for the 'new world' – South Africa, Argentina, Brazil, Australia, and North America. Two waves of emigrants can be distinguished. The first, between 1820 and 1890, was drawn almost exclusively from northwestern Europe – Great Britain and Ireland, Germany, and Scandinavia – and was directed principally to the United States. The second, between 1890 and 1930, was dominated by emigrants from southern and eastern Europe and had many destinations.

What pushed this second wave? In Britain, rural poverty and the unending reminders of deadening class restrictions went far to explain the exodus. Skilled workers, farmers, and unskilled servants and labourers were the components of the emigration, and, except in the years just before the First World War, the skilled labourers were in a decided minority. Pauper emigration schemes also pulled residents from city slums and sent them across the Atlantic. One poignant part of this story was the fact that 80,000 slum children were exported – alone – to Canada between 1869 and 1925, some of them to the west.[11] The situation in Austria-Hungary was slightly different. There, population growth had fragmented rural land holdings and, because of rapid economic development and the continuance of class rule, had created vast numbers of landless or nearly landless peasants. Farms of one, three, or eight acres were common; in the most notorious case, the province of Galicia, over 1 million farms were smaller than eight acres and only 1,500 farms were larger than fifty acres. Tiny holdings could not sustain a family. Moreover, ethnic or linguistic tensions complicated the lives of many citizens in the Hungarian part of the empire; the national revival of the Magyars brought with it discrimination against other ethnic groups and the repression of other languages: Croats, Slovaks, Ukrainians, Germans, and Jews bore the brunt of these measures. In Russia, a similar revival brought comparable problems. The Jews suffered great pain as a result; and Mennonites, Doukhobors, German Lutherans, and German Catholics, though not subject to such overt physical attacks, also feared for their survival as religious and ethnic communities. The American exodus to Canada, when placed beside the European emigration, is unusual: in a few cases, such as the Hutterites, religious liberty was an issue, but in most the wish for greater economic opportunity was the motivation that caused families to move north of the border.

The migration of navvies was a special case. They were males, usually young, many of whom planned to return to their European villages after a season or two in North American construction, mine, or lumber camps. A common feature of the Canadian working classes from the days of the mid-nineteenth century Irish canal-labourer, these workers appeared first in western Canada as the builders of the CPR. Ten thousand Chinese were said to have been employed in the mountain sections of the railway, and numbers followed them into mines and other enterprises, almost exclusively in British Columbia, until the influx was more or less halted by anti-oriental riots and political pressure in 1907–8. The need to find disciplined obedient workers who were willing to accept rough conditions and low wages led the railway entrepreneurs next to the *padrones* who trafficked in Italian labourers. Despite the objections of the ministers of labour and the interior, business leaders were able to win cabinet support for the importation of navvies from Italy and the Balkans between 1908 and 1914. In these years the proportion of unskilled immigrants in the total of male immigrants rose from 31 per cent to 43 per cent, and the proportion of central and southern Europeans rose from 29 per cent to 48 per cent. Many of these men did return to their European homes, if not within a season or two then certainly within a decade. But others, more often the victims of fraud than fecklessness, stayed on and became members of the Canadian community.[12]

The journey to the western interior of Canada included, for many immigrants, an ocean voyage. Not for them, however, the indescribable chaos of the timber ships of the early nineteenth century. Rather, the post-1896 emigrants, whether embarking from Hamburg or Bremen, Liverpool or Trieste, voyaged on steamships constructed for the purpose of Atlantic passenger traffic. The entire system of emigration was similarly more efficient by this time. As families of Ukrainians left their villages in Galicia or Bukowina, a dance or parade and a church blessing would mark their departure. A cart ride would take them to the city and the railway. As they passed through Germany in fourth-class train carriages, buttons or ribbons affixed to their coats to distinguish their shipping line, they found hawkers on the station platforms selling sandwiches and drinks. When they arrived at Hamburg, they learned that entire streets of lodging-houses were ready to provide shelter in exchange for their scarce cash. Bags roped shut, children clutched firmly by the hand, the families endured the line-ups for medical inspection, vaccination certificates, baggage fumigation, and steamship places, and then, finally, they were shepherded up the gangway to the ship.

The vessels of the Atlantic varied from 5,000-ton antiques to 30,000- or even 50,000-ton palaces such as Cunard's *Mauretania* and Hamburg-America's *Imperator*, but the typical ship was perhaps 15,000–20,000 tons, about 700 feet long, and 70 feet wide, carrying 400 first-class, 300 second-class, and 1,000 or 1,500 steerage passengers. The crossings were ten or twelve days and, unlike the era of sail, occasioned few deaths at sea.

Early passenger vessels (1870–90) housed the steerage passengers in bunks that lined the walls of the large lower-deck dormitories; long tables down the centre of these spaces served as eating and public areas. Later vessels had compartments for single men and women and family cabins and also provided separate dining and public rooms. Washing and toilet facilities were generally primitive and, because few, of an unsavoury character. Food was plain but, despite the lumpy slices of bread, gristly beef, and cold potatoes complained of by one passenger, usually adequate on the North Atlantic runs. Steerage class out of a northern European port may have been cramped, smelly, and crowded, but it was tolerable. The southern ports offered less attractive sailing prospects: food, cleanliness, sleeping accommodation, washing facilities, and the amount of space in which to move and to find some peace all were inferior to the better ships in the British and German ports. Naturally, those who travelled first or second class might have been living on a different planet: their restaurants offered linen and silver on the tables, as well as painted ceilings and mahogany panelling; they listened to string orchestras in the lounges; their staterooms, each equipped with a steward, featured carpet on the floor, double beds, easy chairs, and discreet lighting; but, of course, such accommodation was available only to a limited number of wealthy travellers, few of whom were likely to be emigrants.[13]

Arrival was exciting for everyone. Passengers pushed forward to the rails to catch the first sight of land, cheered as the port came into view, rushed to collect their belongings and children, to put on their best clothes, or to have a last wash or shave as the horns and whistles sounded to announce arrival at the dock. What followed was bedlam: the noise, the confusion, the strangeness of the place and the language or the accent, the difficulty of ascertaining where to go and what to do; hawkers' cries, children's talk, officials' orders, baggage handlers' oaths; medical inspection followed by immigration review followed by money changing, food purchases, a search for baggage, and, finally, release from the immigration sheds and into the streets. If one was fortunate, one purchased without undue strain a ticket on a 'colonist car' to western Canada, but there were stories of cheats and sharpies who would offer a ticket to Edmonton but provide instead a taxi fare to Quebec's city centre. If fortune smiled, the family's belongings would remain intact. Inevitably, however, some people lost items of value, as did the two little Danish girls whose prized dolls were left behind.[14]

The colonist cars became little communities in themselves. The wooden seats could be made up into berths: James Minifie, the journalist, remembers as a young traveller sharing an upper with his mother and brother, while a family of four slept beneath them. At the end of their car was a tiny kitchen for the preparation of simple meals. Armed with 'yard of tickets' and a few supplies, the immigrants embarked upon the rough and, even for romantics, seemingly endless train journey through the trees and lakes of the Shield. The ride was interrupted by quick sorties to railside stores in the northern Ontario bush and by long waits on sidings for priority trains to roar through. Inevitably, talk turned to the future and to inquiries about 'what it was like.' Everyone had a calculation about how to start anew, but chance as much as plan must have affected many of those early decisions. Minifie's father had a ticket to Calgary but, on the strength of conversations with a seat mate and the train conductor – who assured him there was no good land left in

Alberta (this was 1909) and that farm labour was needed in the parts they were traversing – grabbed his bags and jumped off the train at Sintaluta, on the endless plains of southern Saskatchewan.[15] Other new arrivals were met by husbands, brothers, and cousins; but how many times was this moment of family reunion associated with a sinking heart? Mrs Johanne Frederiksen arrived at Ellis Island in New York harbour on 13 May 1911, and a week later she and her six children alighted from the train at Nokomis, Saskatchewan, to be met by her husband who had preceded them by a year: 'You must excuse me [she wrote to her family in Denmark] ... I haven't managed to write but we were all so exhausted ... It has been difficult just to get food ready three times a day ... When we were set out in the middle of the night in the cold at the last station in a driving snowstorm, we all cried but then my husband was there ... Here it's still so desolate and frightening on the wild prairie. It is like the ocean. We are a tiny midpoint in a circle ... You will ... understand that it looks terrifying, more than you can imagine.'[16]

For others, the first home was a government-run immigration hall in one of the larger cities. In a noisy 'family room' or a large dormitory for single men or women, troubles and ambitions were the currency of exchange as the arrivals sought a place to live, a job, a niche in the new environment. The hall would soon be replaced by a more permanent home, a room in a lodging-house in a poorer part of the city or, in the case of single men, a boarding-house. Here, strands that knit together a community would quickly be extended and knotted: a church, a social club, or a language-based association would be a place of meeting; the street, the shops, and the job, too, would provide instruction in the ways of the economy; and, most of all, the family – nuclear, extended, adopted, perhaps only spiritually present by means of letters and messages from the Old Country – would exert its influence as a source of stability and standards. The members of a boarding-house might be drawn from the same village or region and thus might re-establish a familiar outlook and behaviour with scarcely a misstep. But, too, the newcomer might soon leave the circle of children and women and old folk to take job in a work camp or resource town. There, he would face the brutalizing possibilities that accompanied hard labour and coarse life in 'the bush.'[17]

Adjustment to new circumstances was never automatic, as anyone who has ever changed residences or cities will attest. But was immigration a traumatic crisis, an event burned into the mind that left a numbness for months and even years?[18] Surely the impact of the move varied with the individual; but it would be useful to remember the resilience of youth and the willingness implied in the original departure to make a new start. If adjustment was difficult, it was none the less a task that most were able to master. As the Frederiksens learned, it was a battle 'against nature's fury, the unyielding soil, the harsh climate.' But, in another letter home, one of the family extended the list of difficulties when she described their life as 'a struggle for existence, a struggle against the loss of culture's benefits: church, school, parish, community. How deep roots a man has in his fatherland he may never know himself, until he loses them.' And therein lay the heart of the matter: adjustment meant both economic survival and cultural accommodation. Material rewards came, in some degree, to almost everyone; western Canada was soon a viable community insofar as food and shelter and health services could make it comfortable. But what about the cultural arrangements? On what terms was one to re-establish faith, learning, traditional customs, and the family? These matters were just as important as food. Should the Frederiksens allow their older girls to hire out? Was the boy big enough to work in the neighbour's fields? Dare they risk a winter with father away in a lumber or construction camp? Could the family and its ideals survive even the shortest separations? 'It is Sunday. We have just arranged ourselves around the table to have afternoon coffee and read your letter; thank you so much for it, it brings us great joy. This is the way it goes here. On Sunday, when we assemble, we read the weekly letter, the gospel, or some other reading ... It makes the day a holy one for us and I hope, gives the children something to remember.' But on another day the eldest son, Henning, then sixteen, was delayed at the neighbours where he was working from 5 a.m. to after 9 p.m.: 'Yesterday was Ellen's birthday (her seventh) and Henning was supposed to come over in the afternoon for hot chocolate and cake. He didn't come until eight in the evening and I told him at once that that was wrong. Still, we set the table, brought out the Danish flag and tried to look happy. But it happened as it has with so many others who have tried to have a celebration far, far from everyone – we couldn't do it ... Henning put his arms on the table and burst into tears. Marie ... and Ellen ... cried too ... That day Henning had been loading hay since early morning, the same the previous day ... It's a hard school he is in.'[19]

English-speaking newcomers also had to adjust to the strange ways of the west. The appearance of a dictionary of the western Canadian 'language' in 1912 was one small indication of the distance between the prairies and other English-speaking communities. The definitions were both social commentaries and linguistic aids. The definition of 'All aboard' was 'the train conductor's call to passengers when the train is about to pull out. At such a moment in the Old Country, the railway officials smilingly invite the first-class passengers and deadheads to "take your seats, gentlemen, please," and bang the doors on the third-class passengers' fingers.'[20]

The important adjustments for English immigrants were not in the realm of linguistic novelties, of course, for it was a simple matter to pick up the slang, if one chose, and even to moderate one's accent to meet the flat intonation and lazy rhythms of local speech. The greater challenge was to make one's way and to maintain 'standards.' Within weeks of his arrival in Saskatchewan, Philip Minifie learned to harness horses western-style, to plough a straight furrow, to exchange his tweeds for denim, and to purchase horsehide gloves and rawhide boots. Within a year, he had joined a group of Ontario men who were planning to homestead a new district in southwestern Saskatchewan. In two years, he was joined by his family. And within three – a measure of his acceptance in the wider community – he had added to his responsibilities as pioneer farmer those of secretary-treasurer of the local school board (District 717, Malvern Link, named after the Malvern Hills near his Shropshire home) and of the local branch of the Grain Growers' Association. Mrs Minifie was the organist at the Anglican church, a much more sedate institution than the hot gospel fellowship church that met at nearby Turkey Track school. And by 1916, seven years after Philip's arrival in Canada, his eldest son, sixteen-year-old James, was off to fight in the First World War. In 1919, James, who had returned from English army camps without ever seeing shots fired in anger, went to Regina College, and in 1920 he went to the University of Saskatchewan at Saskatoon. Two years later he travelled to Oxford as the province's Rhodes Scholar.[21]

The Minifies were not a typical English family, and yet their fortune was representative of a theme that recurs in prairie history.

The Minifie children found it easier than their European-born contemporaries to be loyal to the empire and to make their way in the world through education. Like members of other ethnic groups, the English tended to marry their own, to locate in boarding-houses run by their countrymen, to congregate in certain areas of the cities, and to support their own football teams, music halls, and fish and chip shops. One bastion of their community was the Church of England, the prairie wing of which was dominated by English immigrants after 1900. The familiar liturgy and accents were significant aspects of the transition to the new land. As a labourer said: 'When we are at church it seems much like home, and one feels the new life enter in him, after the toils of the week.' The strength of the Sons of England, a cultural society that presented social evenings on the model of the music hall, including rousing patriotic hymns and familiar anecdotes and even English refreshments, was another index to the solidarity of the group. The function of such rituals as the church service and social evening was economic as well as psychological. The newcomers wanted jobs and a secure income; they disdained their competitors, especially the strangers from southern Europe, and attempted to control jobs through their ethnic networks. To assert their ethnic superiority, they contrasted their language and manner with that of other newcomers: as one English maid explained, 'To tell the truth, I didn't bother with any foreign people. I was too English for that.' They sponsored their own when openings came up in mine or plant, and they dominated the hiring system in such companies as the T. Eaton Company department stores and the CPR shops.[22] The English were indeed different from western Canadians when they arrived and were often disliked for their superior airs and alleged 'softness.' But they spoke English, the public language of the prairies, they knew the rules of politics and social intercourse, and they were a repository of wisdom when the institutions of the new society – trade unions, school districts, political parties – were created.

French-speaking immigrants had a more difficult transition. They spoke Canada's other 'official' language, insofar as the British North America Act permitted the use of French in federal courts and Parliament, but their numbers in the west were never sufficient to entrench the bilingual promise of the Manitoba Act and the North-West Territories Act into daily usage in public life. Immigration was the central difficulty. From the earliest days of the west's existence in Confederation, French-speaking citizens of Quebec had not responded as had Ontarians to the call of the west. The reasons for this apparent lack of interest in a promising investment frontier are numerous. Québécois had their own 'frontier,' the Shield, which was promoted by church colonization societies and seemed much closer to home. Other restless Québécois would be attracted by the prospect of industrial jobs just a few miles to the south of the St Lawrence, in the mills and factories of New England. Fainter hearts would be deterred from western migration by Quebec newspaper attacks on 'Ontario fanaticism' which allegedly resulted in assaults on French rights during the 1869–70 troubles, the 1874–5 debates concerning Riel's amnesty, the 1879 Norquay ministerial crisis, the 1885 Territorial uprising, and the Manitoba school and language legislation of 1890. And, finally, if one scholar is correct, French-Canadian culture itself was inimical to adventure: according to Arthur Silver, Québécois were less likely to try their luck in an unknown land, preferring instead the familiar ambiance of their province or the niche already created for them by their compatriots in the eastern United States. The prairies were just too far away and too strange for Québécois.[23]

The failure to establish significant French-Canadian immigration in the first generation of settlement was fatal to the French cause in the west during the post-1900 boom. With only 23,000 French-speaking settlers in the region in 1901, there was little hope that chain migration – the links that encouraged residents of a community to join friends in a new land – would offset the tide of non-French arrivals. Moreover, the citizens of the prairie region, recognizing that the French and Roman Catholic element – the two loyalties were not synonymous but were closely linked – was small and weak, proceeded to cancel the institutional guarantees of a continued French-Canadian presence. The use of the French language in the Manitoba courts and legislature was ended by an enactment of the Manitoba government in 1890. The territorial assembly followed suit in 1892. The use of French as a language of instruction in the schools rather than merely a subject of study was cancelled by the Manitoba government in 1890, restored in 1897 as part of a 'bilingual' program in which English had primacy, and abolished again in 1916. The Territories eliminated French as a language of instruction except in the primary grades in 1892 but restored it in the upper grades for one hour per day at the end of the school day in

1901. In 1918, Saskatchewan reduced the use of French to the first year of school only, though the optional hour at the end of the school day was retained. In 1931, after continuing debates about papal influence and foreign subversion, the government of Premier J.T.M. Anderson virtually eliminated French as a language of instruction in Saskatchewan schools. Alberta permitted only limited use of languages other than English after a crackdown on abuses of the school regulations in 1913. The loss of official status for the French language in government and schools was another blow to the French-speaking peoples of the western provinces.[24] The result was that Canada's newest regional community did not provide the bilingual compromises of Canada's federal government, and did not appear to be a congenial destination to French-speaking immigrants in the years of prairie growth after 1900.

The pattern of French settlement in the west illustrated the meagre input of French immigration agencies. In the 1870s and 1880s, when recruitment fell largely to the Roman Catholic church and its Manitoba leader, Mgr Alexandre Taché, archbishop of St Boniface, the French were encouraged to settle in the Red River valley on lands vacated by the metis. However, the plan to concentrate the French in a homogeneous bloc was undercut by the rapid dispossession of the metis, by the relative failure of church efforts to win migrants in Quebec and New England, and by the weakness of the attempts to secure colonists in the French-speaking lands of Europe. Insofar as French, Belgian, and Swiss recruits did arrive in the following decades, they destroyed plans for a single bloc by setting up homes wherever larger groups could be accommodated. Thus, at St Albert under Bishop Grandin and Abbé Morin, at Grande Clairière under Abbé Gaire, at Montmartre, St Brieux, and Gravelbourg, French communities were created. In the end, the French had established something more important than a homogeneous bloc. Their communities constituted a chain of parishes across the west from the Red River to the Rockies, the spine as well as the creation of the Roman Catholic church in the region. French influence in culture and politics was to be important in the politics of cultural development for the next three decades.[25]

The English and the French were not ethnic groups like the others. They represented the two officially recognized languages of the country and the two largest national groups in Confederation; moreover they were the tacitly acknowledged leaders of the two dominant religious groups in Canada, the Roman Catholics and the Protestants.[26] Thus, the two collectivities derived their influence from much more than simply their roots in a single nation of origin, their religious identity, or their common tongue. Each represented an alternate vision of Canada. One, Protestant, English-speaking, and pan-Anglo Saxon in cultural tone, was in the ascendant. The other, Roman Catholic and French-speaking, was on the defensive, having lost important institutional guarantees in the preceding decades. Neither was prepared for the influx of strangers that changed the very nature of prairie society in the three decades after 1900.

Some of the newcomers accepted voluntarily and with few apparent reservations the principle that they should accommodate themselves to the standards and customs of the dominant English-Canadian culture. The Icelanders can be taken as representative of this outlook. This is not to suggest that they willingly abandoned their language and culture, for they did not, but rather that they wished to be seen as good citizens and to conform to the conventions of their new home. A few Icelanders had left their island in the North Atlantic in the mid-nineteenth century because of economic depression, but their numbers grew in the 1870s. About 2,000 Icelanders emigrated to Canada, first to the Muskoka district of Ontario and later, in 1875, to the western shore of Lake Winnipeg. There, in the district of Gimli ('Paradise'), just north of the province of Manitoba, they secured exclusive rights to a bloc of land and created a large self-governing settlement, the Republic of New Iceland. They immediately founded a school, churches, and an Icelandic-language newspaper. Despite some very dark days, the community survived. The hardest chapter of its early days occurred in 1876–7, just after the colony was founded, when a devastating smallpox epidemic struck. During this disastrous winter, the province of Manitoba provided no relief beyond the dispatch of three doctors and the imposition of an armed quarantine upon the entire settlement that lasted for seven months. Over 100 citizens, mainly the very young, died. A second crisis occurred in 1877–9 when settlers debated whether the broad-minded Church of Iceland or the conservative German Lutherans of the American Missouri Synod should lead them. This conflict exacerbated tensions created by floods in 1879 and 1880 and drove many settlers out of the settlement, some to the Dakotas and others to southern Manitoba. Nevertheless, the settlement grew and even prospered. It was integrated within the municipal system of Manitoba government, and with the rest of the province acquired community halls, farmers' institutes, debating clubs, and sports events. The Icelanders retained a newspaper in their own language and founded a national festival (*Islendingadagurinn*), but they used English as the language of instruction in their schools, even after the 1897 Laurier-Greenway compromise would have permitted the addition of Icelandic on a bilingual basis. In 1897, they acquiesced, too, in the federal government's decision to open the Icelandic reserve to 'any class of settlers.' In the next decade, as Icelanders became a part of Winnipeg and Manitoba society, and members of other cultures, particularly Ukrainians, moved into the former New Iceland, an identifiable Icelandic community ceased to exist. Aside from its clubs and magazines and the August festival, the 5,000 Icelanders had few means of public expression. But pride in nationality remained. The Icelandic ideal was a combination of public conformity to English-Canadian cultural norms and private, family-centred efforts to retain their language and culture and to instil in their children an awareness of and pride in their national heritage.[27]

The situation of the German community in western Canada was different, yet in many respects it led to a conclusion akin to the Icelandic example. The Germans who arrived in western Canada during the immigration boom came principally from the Austro-Hungarian and Russian empires rather than from Germany. Roman Catholic and Protestant, urban and rural, Low and High German–speaking, they were numerous in total but divided into so many parts and so affected by the events of world politics that they never achieved a pan-German identity in Canada. Eventually, they too accommodated to the British-Canadian norm.[28]

Jews began to arrive in numbers in western Canada as a direct result of the pogroms in tsarist Russia in the early 1880s. Similar pressures drove other Jews out of Poland, Austria-Hungary, and Germany in the following decades. Differences of national origin and form of worship, though important, were transcended by the things they shared, including their faith, their language, and, most of all, their history as a people apart. They gathered in Winnipeg, where employment could be obtained, friends of one's faith found, and a religious congregation established, but they were also to be found in the rural west, both in agricultural colonies such as those near Wapella, Hirsch, Cupar, Lipton, and Sonnenfeld in Saskatchewan; Rumsey, Alberta; and Bender Hamlet, Manitoba; and in the little towns of the agricultural region where the Jewish general store – at one time there were over 100 in Manitoba – was as common as the Chinese café.[29]

The Jewish agricultural settlements knew mixed fortunes. The first, New Jerusalem, near Moosomin, North-West Territories, met a succession of disasters from the time of its foundation in 1884, including early frost and a fire. Others, such as the Wapella colony, which was established in 1888 over the protests of some district residents, flourished for many years. But, whether success or failure, the settlements were homes for several thousand new Canadians. In Bender Hamlet, in the Interlake district of Manitoba, a European-style village was set out. Its half-mile of main street was lined on one side by houses with spruce logs chinked with a mixture of mud, straw and manure; fields were laid out, cropping routines established, animals purchased, gardens planted. Income was earned by hauling timber, cutting pulpwood, gathering seneca root, selling eggs, and, of course, attempting to raise grain on land that was better suited to raising rocks. Each spring the frost pushed a new crop of limestone boulders to the surface. The colony endured for twenty-five years and then collapsed, a victim of the children's need to find a wider world and, when they embarked on that search, of their refusal to return to poverty. The last individual to leave the Hamlet, Jack Lavitt's father, sold out, after a quarter-century of steady labour, for $700 in 1926. Like most of his contemporaries, young Jack had obtained only eight years of schooling, and yet, for all its poverty, he still recalls the riches of the community; he and his friends knew everyone, played pranks, attended *shul* on Saturday and Hebrew lessons after school, went to all the parties, picnics, bar mitzvahs, and weddings, and, eventually, moved to Winnipeg and started again: 'But we could work. We could get by. When everyone was out here at Bender, it was a happy place. A healthy place. It was a different world. You worked, you ate, you lived. And, you came out of there with ... something.'[30]

The life of a small-town Jewish merchant was uncertain for different reasons. He was a businessman in a society that distrusted 'middlemen,' and he was a Jew in a world where Protestant and Catholic alike might object to his presence. He never would be accepted unreservedly. His children, though part of the town concert and team and club, might feel the same distance during Christmas celebrations or high holidays. One never knew whether a debtor would renounce his obligation and start a new account across the street, all the while condemning 'the Jew store' in a loud voice; one never knew, either, whether one's contribution to the grade 3 bake sale would be accepted without a fuss. Novelist Adele Wiseman described it best:

> So there was I, overly sensitive, terribly high strung, a regular little bleeder. What could I do to protect myself, delicate little artist in the bud, against, for instance, my teachers?
>
>   We had a celebration in school and all the kids were supposed to bring stuff to eat. We didn't happen to have any weekday ordinary bread in the house, so Mom made my contribution, fancy little sandwiches, out of the Holy Sabbath egg bread. They were the only ones left on the plate one teacher was holding, and both teachers looked down at the plate and then at each other as though the plate had worms on it.
>
> Honest to God Historic Dialogue:
>   Mama: You're still crying? Why are you still crying? You've been
>             crying for hours.
>   Me:      I'll cry until I stop.[31]

There were quotas to restrict Jewish entrants to Manitoba's medical and law schools. A tacit covenant excluded them from a summer resort. But they made their way and found their salvation despite the slights.

In Winnipeg, Jews began as unskilled labourers and small businessmen. At the turn of the twentieth century, they congregated in the city's north end, in the slum area known to them as Mitzrayim (Egypt) and to the press as New Jerusalem. They were itinerant pedlars, draymen, scrap and rag collectors, garment workers, tailors, and storekeepers. And, with the exception of a few who quickly perceived the lay of the land, they were socialists: Zionist, Marxist, or democratic, almost all of them espoused some kind of socialist reform for Canadian and international society. As the years passed and prosperity favoured their community, politics and religion and even dwelling place changed. By the mid-1920s, Jews were leaving the city centre for the more spacious lots on the northern edge of the city and even for the British Canadian bastions south of the Assiniboine River. They were more likely to become Liberal or Conservative in politics, too, and to have exchanged the traditional for the reform branch of their faith.[32] But their group exclusiveness remained. They were still Jews in the census report, they were probably still described as members of a synagogue, and, to a degree unmatched by almost any other group, they still married within the faith. History and religion ensured their active rejection of Anglo-conformity but, as their place in school and business and politics demonstrated, in most other respects they conformed to the standards and the institutions of British Canada.

The migration to Canada of thousands of peasants from the Hapsburg provinces of Galicia (Halychyna) and Bukovina – Ruthenians to their contemporaries, Ukrainians in modern-day terms – created an ethnic group whose internal politics were complex and whose impact on the larger society is still being felt. The Ukrainians were not, in general, content to join Icelanders and Germans in passive accommodation to the British-Canadian norm, but they were not sufficiently united to join Hutterites and Doukhobors in active rejection of or isolation from the culture of the charter group. As much as any other single ethnic group, the Ukrainians were responsible for the official adoption of today's bilingual-multicultural definition of Canadian society. And the origins of this important departure lay in the internal battles of prairie Ukrainian-Canadian people in the four decades after 1900. Their tenacity and cultural loyalty overcame myriad divisions and eventually led to their establishment of a Canada-wide, pan-Ukrainian voice and thence to national ethnic assertiveness.

The Ukrainians were the most visible of all the southeastern European peasant cultures that came to the prairie west. They numbered at least 200,000 by 1931, and their striking characteristics – language, clothing, and housing – were obvious and distinctive features of the prairie environment.[33] Their sheepskin jackets, embroidered shirts, and baggy trousers were a common sight in rural districts for a generation; their two- or three-room log houses, whitewashed, thatched, and dominated inside by a large clay stove, dotted the countryside.[34] And their numerical strength imparted considerable importance to their internecine conflicts, and to their eventual unity.

Like other European peasant migrants, the Ukrainians left behind a world of poverty and carried with them little material wealth and few acquired skills. They were experienced farmers, however, and were prepared to work and to endure privation. They left regions where most citizens were illiterate, where most farms were too small for subsistence operations, where agricultural technology was primitive, and where drunkenness and indices of ill-health were proof of social crisis. Their two dominant religious institutions, the Greek Catholic church (the Uniates, product of a union between the Roman Catholic and Greek Orthodox churches in Poland in 1596) in Galicia and the Romanian-based Greek Orthodox church in Bukovina, were little inclined to press for social change. As a result, socialist and Protestant ideas had already taken root among their 'intelligentsia' – groups of literate reformers – in the late nineteenth century. These ideas came to Canada with the migrants. By the second decade of the twentieth century, the Ukrainian community was divided into four prominent factions and a number of smaller ones: the Protestants migrated into a Presbyterian-sponsored Greek independent church; the Marxists had joined the Ukrainian-language locals of the Social Democratic party or even the locals of the ideologically strict Socialist Party of Canada and eventually found their way into the Communist party and the Ukrainian Labor– Farmer Temple Association; the nationalists adhered to the reinvigorated Ukrainian (Greek) Orthodox church, which acquired a following after 1918; and the religious loyalists were members of the French-led Roman Catholic or Austrian-run Greek Catholic community.[35]

The impact on Canadian Ukrainians of the Russian revolution and the subsequent Ukrainian uprising in the steppes of southern Europe was considerable. Not only did it result in the emergence of a communist party but it also spawned monarchist and republican parties in Canada dedicated to the eventual creation of an independent Ukraine. One common thread can be discerned in this bewildering multiplicity of leagues and churches: the peasant culture was adapting to industrial capitalism. The oppressive conformity of the village, the brutal brawls of the drunken spree, the magic and superstition, and the proverbs that declared, for example, that 'an unbeaten wife is like an unsharpened scythe' were not mere figments of Protestant social workers' imaginations. They constituted centuries-old habits of a peasant society and were sources of tension when this society was re-established. What was especially significant in the Canadian setting was that, after the initial decades of hardship on pioneer farms, new ideas were debated and new courses of action were decided on. The world of the peasant was being transformed into the world of the ethnic politician. By 1940, under the pressure of war, the factions merged into the Ukrainian Canadian Committee, a loose coalition dedicated to democratic principles and British institutions, to promotion of Ukrainian cultural objects in Canada, and naturally, to support of the aspirations of Ukrainians in Europe.[36] Four decades on the prairies had created Ukrainian Canadians; their accommodation to North American technology was accompanied by religious and, to a greater degree than with the Jews, cultural continuity. They had been acculturated but not fully assimilated.

The Mennonites were even slower to adapt to British-Canadian ways, but in their case adjustment was delayed by their determination to remain separate from the materialism and godlessness that they associated with the larger prairie community. Mennonites first came to western North America in the years after 1874. They had sought large blocs of land where they might have freedom of religion, German-language schools, and exemption from military service and in 1874 were granted two exclusive tracts of land in southern Manitoba. The migration of about 7,000 souls from southern Russia was composed of Dutch–North German Anabaptists, descendants of the sixteenth-century left wing of the Reformation who had moved eastward in Europe in order to retain their group identity and religious freedoms. The increasing pan-Slav nationalism of the tsars had caused the most conservative among them, after a century of prosperity and expansion, to fear for their separate identity and thus to move once again.[37]

The Manitoba Mennonite colonies of the 1870s and their Saskatchewan descendants of the 1890s adapted their Russian agricultural pattern to the North American square survey. The basic unit of Mennonite settlement was the village rather than the homestead, and the units of cultivation were small strips of land rather than quarter-sections owned by individual farmers. To satisfy the homestead regulations individual Mennonites entered patents for 160 acres, but these formal requirements bore little relationship to their village-based farm system. The community itself determined the allocation of plots and the rotation of crops. The village, too, hired a herdsman who every morning walked the length of the single elm-shaded street to collect the cows at every gate and to lead them to the community pasture. The village had its own government, its own insurance or social security fund, and its own religious community. About 100 such villages functioned in Manitoba in the late nineteenth century, and others were established in Saskatchewan offshoots. With their own schools, churches, and agricultural systems, the villages seemed remote from the Canadian society that surrounded them.

The Mennonites themselves were also distant from other settlers on the prairies. They dressed austerely, they stayed largely among their own kind and married within their community, and they conversed almost entirely in Low German. Their domestic architecture, unvarying in pattern and yet quite different from house to house, was a distinctive variation on the peasant home: the neat front room was used only on formal occasions, and two or three bedrooms and kitchen completed the square. The focus of all such houses was the large stove and oven that heated the entire dwelling. What startled Canadians (though it was common in central Europe) was a passageway that linked house to barn, thus creating a single unit where the proper Anglo-Saxon assumed there should be no association. Despite their exclusiveness and the unusual aspects of their culture, the Mennonites were prosperous farmers who were interested in trade and accustomed to business dealings, and so their relations with neighbouring service towns were good.

If it seemed to some that the Mennonite commonwealth might flourish for generations, others recognized that the prairie environment was imposing new and different pressures on the group. Significant changes in theology and worship were affecting Christians around the world in the late nineteenth century, and several aspects of this change, including the rise of evangelical 'brethren' and the inevitable conflicts between conservatives and progressives over styles of worship, affected prairie Mennonites. So too did disagreements between ambitious expansion-minded farmers and the lazy, of whom every community has one or two: the nucleated village system held back the hard worker and bred resentment. Thus, by the late 1880s farmers were beginning to risk excommunication because they preferred to live and farm their own quarter-sections.

The construction of a railway through the West Reserve, the largest bloc of arable land in the Mennonite community, and its inevitable accompaniment of service centres complete with elevators and stores, altered the Mennonite situation again. The towns served as 'the bridgeheads for the assimilation of Mennonites into prairie society' because they enabled the individual farmer to survive outside the village system.[38] And the pressures of the provincial educational system began to affect the villages too. Schools have always been the crucial battleground for cultural ideals in western Canada and were the scene of a concerted Mennonite defence against the uniform English-language public education system. The most determined of the Mennonite idealists could not accept the unilingual and compulsory features of Manitoba's 1916 school law and within a decade had moved on to new promised lands in Mexico and Paraguay. In one of history's ironies, their lands in Manitoba were taken up by a second wave of Mennonite migrants fleeing the civil war in the Soviet Ukraine. Whether a 'Canadian' of the 1870s migration or a 'Russian' of the 1920s exodus, however, all the prairie Mennonites were learning to adapt to a wider Canadian environment in the inter-war decades. Radios and young people's groups, co-operatives and trunk highways were symbols of their rapid integration into the communications web of the 'modern' world. The village agricultural system and the separate school were things of the past; the language and the faith remained.[39]

Mennonites were often confused with two other groups of pacifists who settled in Canada, Doukhobors and Hutterites, but they were quite distinct from either. Doukhobors, the most famous of the three, were Russian rather than German-speaking; their faith developed out of eighteenth-century dissent within the Russian Orthodox church and was based on the rejection of formal church organization and of a mediatory priesthood. Their doctrine and history were preserved in hymns – 'The Living Book' – and were associated at some points in their history with a degree of Christian 'communism.' They fled Russian persecution in the 1890s and through the intervention of Tolstoy and Kropotkin, among others, eventually established three colonies in what became Saskatchewan. These 7,400 souls were mainly followers of the visionary Peter Verigin who accepted his insistence upon village-centred agriculture, communal labour, and collective ownership of property. But some did not, and soon conflicts arose over whether to acquiesce to the demands of 'the state' – in this case, Canadian government regulations that homesteads be patented and that births and deaths be recorded – and whether to maintain the communes. The most vehement Verigin loyalists, the fervent Sons of Freedom, in order to demonstrate their opposition to worldly wealth, began in 1902–3 to destroy their belongings and to embark on nude demonstrations as visible expressions of their faith. The colony survived these disruptions and even prospered in the next several years, but in 1906–7 Canada's new minister of the interior, Frank Oliver, began to revise his predecessor's rulings on Doukhobor lands, thus forcing them to conform to a strict reading of the law or lose their reserved blocs. In the ensuing conflict, over one-third of the community opted for individualism and the customary homestead. Under the leadership of Peter Makaroff of Blaine Lake, they ceased to practice communalism but retained their religious beliefs and pacifist principles as the Society of Independent Doukhobors. The larger fraction of the community joined Verigin in the creation of a new communal utopia in the interior of British Columbia where the familiar cycle of prosperity, collapse, and eventual migration occurred. The prairie Doukhobors were still a distinct community in the inter-war years. They spoke Russian, they lived in close proximity to each other in the districts of the three original blocs of land, and they continued to practise their religion. Not for them the excesses of the Sons of Freedom, or even the commune of the Veriginites, but rather the combination of faith, language, and community by which they were distinguished, like the Ukrainians and Mennonites, from the larger prairie society.[40]

Hutterites alone maintained the utopian communal ideal over several generations. They came late to the prairie west, having left Russia for the United States in the 1870s and then, in reaction to the overheated patriotism of South Dakota in 1917–19, negotiated entry into Canada, chiefly Manitoba and Alberta, between 1918 and 1922. Like the Mennonites, they were pacifists and descendants of the Anabaptist wing of the Reformation. They originated in the south Tyrol and Moravia and followed Jacob Hutter and a succession of others across central Europe in the sixteenth and seventeenth centuries. At each colony, they re-established their communal specialization of labour, with children's nursery, women's spinning hall, and a common dining-room, as well as dormitories with individual apartments for couples and their unmarried children. This was the pattern they re-created on the prairies. They retained the dress – black and white were predominant colours – and customs and simple manner of living of their ancestors and, though they spoke English and German, continued to communicate in an almost-extinct Tyrolean dialect. Their colonies would attain a population of 100 to 200 before a new branch community was established and, as exemplary social and economic democracies, were remarkably successful at meeting the material and spiritual needs of their members. Children were trained in the colonies' own schools to prepare for adult responsibilities within the faith; adults were taught to accept their roles, to suppress carnal desires, and to prepare for death. The communities prospered and the families multiplied. Aside from minor skirmishes with governments in their purchases of land for new colonies, they were left to live in peace. By the end of the 1920s, just as three centuries earlier, the Hutterian brethren remained self-sufficient, autonomous, and remote from the society in which they dwelt. Could they resist the assimilative pressures that had altered Mennonite and Ukrainian life? Could the state avoid intervention in colony affairs, especially during the creation of new communities? The answers remained to be given.[41]

One group of prairie Canadians remained almost as distant from its fellow citizens as did the Hutterites, though it lived in daily contact with the larger society. About 3,500 Chinese lived in Canada in 1880, and, in the five years of CPR construction, 1880–5, the Chinese population rose sharply to about 15,000 because of the recruitment of railway labourers. In the boom after 1900 it reached nearly 30,000, again because of the Canadian quest for hardy workers. Thus, several thousand Chinese resided in each prairie province in the first half of the twentieth century. Theirs was an unusual community not only because of its cultural roots but also because it was overwhelmingly male and apparently restricted in occupation. The ratio of Chinese women to men was 1:25 in prairie cities in 1921, for example, and about 80 per cent of the prairie Chinese work-force in 1931 was employed in two types of business – restaurants and laundries. The social life was narrow; they established their own political and benevolent associations but had only limited contact with Canadian institutions. From the 1890s, the Chinese were subject to hostility from the larger prairie community. There was a riot in Calgary in 1892 when a Chinese laundry worker was discovered to be a smallpox carrier, Saskatchewan disenfranchised the Chinese in 1908, and later both Saskatchewan and Manitoba enacted laws forbidding the employment of white women in Chinese restaurants. When the federal Chinese Immigration Act of 1923 ended further immigration to Canada, the growth of the community was effectively halted. Aging single men clustered in Chinatowns in the larger cities, victims of racist taunts and otherwise cut off from white society. In the prairie villages, however, the restaurant owner sometimes found a niche: 'When the hotel closed down, he started his own restaurant and a store as well ... He always put in a bag of candy for the children with an order ... He acted as a banker on Saturday nights ... He kept many people from starving during the Depression.'[42] It was a lonely life, none the less, and must have offered little to those who spent their declining years in such isolation.

What metaphor will crystallize the social and cultural composition of prairie society in the first four decades of this century? Perhaps one should think in terms not of melting pots or mosaics but of stews. Simmered long enough, the ingredients might indeed assume a uniform consistency as in a melting pot, but, in the period that concerns us, between 1900 and the 1930s, that process had not occurred. Ethnic identity remained, in this period, unmistakeable.

To extend the metaphor, many of the stew's ingredients were imported. Prairie population growth, from 400,000 in 1901 to 2 million in 1921 to 2.4 million in 1941 (a ratio of 1:5:6), was fuelled by immigration. This prairie 'stew' relied not only on imported ingredients but also on constant replenishment as it was drained off by other, chiefly American and European, consumers. The prairie population was always changing. We must beware the convenient assumption that individuals descended from an immigrant car, selected a home in city or country, and there remained to raise a family and grow old. This is certainly wrong. Prairie people were on the move, from farm to city, construction camp to coal mine to homestead, southern prairie to northern parkland, and, most of all, out of the region entirely. They migrated to the Pacific, to the United States, or back to Europe. If one estimate of this migration is accurate, as few as 800,000 of the original 2 million immigrants (two of five) remained in the prairies by 1931.[43]

One significant characteristic of these unassimilated elements was their 'foreign' character. By 1940, five prairie residents in ten acknowledged paternal origins other than British, two of these in eastern Europe and another two in western Europe. One more would be from England rather than British Canadian. And, to a degree that is difficult to imagine today, these ethnic peoples lived in discrete blocs. Whether the result of organized group settlement (Icelandic, Mennonite, Hutterite, Doukhobor), of chain settlements (links in the place of origin that were re-established in the new home as in the Hungarian case), or of gravitation group settlement (migrants who arrived independently but were drawn together by mutual attractions, as with Ukrainians and Germans), ethnic groups peopled vast areas of the prairies. Some of the nearly exclusive enclaves included up to thirty towns and villages within a single district. The enclaves were isolated from each other and, to a remarkable degree, from the larger prairie community. They retained such localisms as the dialect, customs, and traditions peculiar to their home districts in Europe, and they possessed an amazing institutional completeness. In matters as small as cuisine and as large as choice of marriage partner, the blocs remained relatively distinct in the 1920s and 1930s. A rough calculation based on the federal census suggests that at least 6 in 10 Scandinavians, 7 in 10 French and Germans, 8 in 10 Slavs, including 9.4 of 10 Ukrainians, in north-central Saskatchewan still spoke their mother tongue at home in 1941; other statistics suggest that this underestimated the persistence of languages other than English.[44] Ethnic identity remained a real and important factor in the life of many paririe Canadians in the 1930s.

When Stephen Leacock undertook his famous speaking tour through western Canada in the 1930s he learned quickly enough that the talk of 'balkanization' and 'bohemianization' and 'ruthenization' of the prairies that had filtered into eastern Canadian circles did not convey an accurate picture of the region. He concluded that one of his fondest assumptions about racial character seemed to be borne out in the west as in every other advanced society: give Scotsmen the smallest opening, he loved to say, and they would soon rule the roost. His conclusion was pure Leacock, but it was perceptive: after three decades of European immigration, the cultural standards of prairie society remained British; social and economic leadership rested firmly in the hands of the British Canadian; and, even in politics, where notions such as socialism and social credit were bandied about, British institutions and principles were as yet unshaken. But we must not assume that the mix of ingredients in this community was so diverse that each sample drawn from the whole was different in composition from every other: there was, I am certain, a consistency in prairie society, as in the stock of a stew, that was obvious in its dominant flavour if subtle in its variations.

# 12

# Capital and labour 1900–40: Cities, resource towns, and frontier camps

[If the arrival of hundreds of thousands of newcomers imposed great strains on prairie economic and social institutions, the tensions were made worse by the growth of large urban centres and the widening gap between rich and poor. Too often the prairie west is perceived as a monolithic agricultural community. But it also contained cities, mine towns, timber camps, and railway construction sites] These communities were just as important as farms in creating the character of the region. And the obvious divisions between prosperity and poverty, or power and powerlessness, helped to shape another fundamental aspect of the prairie social outlook: in the decades after 1900, social class became a fact of life for western Canadians. By the end of the 1930s, one could speak without fear of contradiction about 'workers' and 'the working class part of town,' and about the 'prosperous elements' and their 'better residential areas.'

The region boasted two important urban centres in 1891, Winnipeg (26,000) and Calgary (4,000). By 1941, with the addition to this category of Regina, Saskatoon, and Edmonton, it could claim five. Besides these important cities, another ten centres might be described as cities (their population exceeded 5,000 in 1941) and can be included at least to some degree in the discussion that follows. In 1941, the five major urban centres contained 24 per cent of the total regional population and 70 per cent of the prairie urban population.

The ten sub-metropolitan centres contained an additional 4 per cent of the regional population and 12 per cent of the urban total.[1] Within their boundaries, as in the grimy coal towns and isolated camps, those who sought a new start came face to face with the realities of economic hardship and political frustration.

The pre-eminence of Winnipeg as regional metropolis had been established during the 1880s and 1890s but was confirmed, in most emphatic terms, by the boom years between 1900 and 1913. Once the agricultural economy had been set in place, as it was by 1913, Winnipeg's growth slowed markedly, but as late as 1941 no other cities seemed to be serious challengers for the role of dominant urban centre of the prairies. In that year, Winnipeg's population, when the suburbs and the satellites were included, was as large as the combined totals of Regina, Saskatoon, Calgary, and Edmonton. Its proportion of wholesale employment was at least one-third of the regional total, its proportion of employees in the financial and insurance industries was about one-half, and it provided a like proportion of jobs in the transportation and communications industries. Yet one could argue that Winnipeg had already lost its role as regional metropolis by 1914; from that date, slowly but surely, its functions and powers as the dominant urban centre of the prairies were eroded. Rather than a single metropolis, the prairies had five sub-metropolitan centres and ten smaller cities by 1941.

Winnipeg's rise to prominence was based on the railway, the grain trade, the wholesale trade, and a limited range of manufacturing and financial activities. Rail service was crucial in its ascendancy. And, once the CPR and Northern Pacific lines were secured, the development of an expanded rail network based on the Manitoba capital followed quickly. The Laurier government's decision to support the construction of the Canadian Northern and the Grand Trunk–National Transcontinental systems enhanced Winnipeg's position because both lines were to be built through the 'western gateway.' The Canadian Northern located its administrative offices and repair shops in the city, and the new Grand Trunk Pacific–National Transcontinental line established its workshop in the suburb of Transcona. The CPR also expanded its old shops and yards and later built new yards in Transcona. With the growth of freight traffic, the major railways also enlarged their freight sheds. 'By 1911, twenty-four railway lines radiated out from Winnipeg, conferring upon the city a commanding position in Prairie trade, in terms both of receiving the products of the West for shipment east, and of distributing throughout the West merchandise originating in Eastern Canada or Europe.'[2]

The products of the west that flowed through the city were primarily agricultural goods, especially grain and cattle. As a result, both found their focus in Winnipeg and contributed much to the boom era. As grain inspection headquarters (Winnipeg inspection was made compulsory by the federal Grain Act of 1899), shipping base, and marketing centre, the city gained an international reputation in a few short years. By 1902, it was receiving more wheat than Chicago; its grain futures market, together with those in Buenos Aires, Chicago, and Liverpool, became the arbiter of world prices. Long-established and new grain companies, buyers and exporters alike, flocked to the city, and soon names such as Richardson (formerly of Kingston), Searle and Peavey (of Minneapolis), and the Grain Growers' Grain Company (a farmer-owned company, renamed the United Grain Growers in 1917) became identified with the huge new Winnipeg Grain Exchange building (1908) on Lombard Street, one block from Portage and Main. Similarly, the burgeoning livestock industry, though centred in southern Alberta, also contributed to Winnipeg's prosperity. A local firm, Gordon, Ironsides and Fares, became the world's largest cattle-exporter in 1906, and as a result of the joint sponsorship of the provincial government and the three largest railway companies, St Boniface became the site of the Empire's largest stockyards in 1907–12. Having built a trade centre for the agricultural boom, Winnipeg boosters reveled in its growing wealth.

Aside from the activity generated by grain and cattle, Winnipeg's economy continued to rely heavily on the wholesale trade. The board of trade's successful campaign for freight rate reduction in the 1880s was repeated in the next decade and resulted in further concessions from the railway between 1897 and 1901. For the next few years, Winnipeg wholesalers enjoyed substantial preferences – as much as 15 to 30 per cent reductions in freight rates – over competitors in eastern Canada and in other prairie cities, as well as the advantages of large inventories and relatively rapid response time when orders arrived. Between 1909 and 1913, the annual value of the trade was estimated to be over $100 million and to require the employment of 3,000 travelling salesmen in addition to manufacturer's agents and local office and warehouse staff. The centre of the city, where the rail lines converged, was rebuilt in this era, and the new streets of huge wholesale buildings constituted an impressive 'warehouse area,' still today a striking feature of the urban landscape. The wholesale function was further enhanced with the rise of mail order houses; the removal of Eaton's catalogue warehouse from Toronto to a nine-storey building in Winnipeg in 1920 gave the city yet another important source of wealth and jobs. Winnipeg was to remain a wholesale centre despite the rise of competitors. As H.J. Symington, president of the board of trade, argued in 1927:

A large proportion of the goods throughout the West will be distributed from Winnipeg. It is so today ... although Winnipeg cannot compete in the Regina area, although it cannot compete in the Saskatoon area, it does in fact sell goods in these areas and in fact sells them right through to British Columbia. Why? – The merchant in the country makes a purchasing trip: where does he go? He goes where he has a large range of selection, his specialties, everything required for his general business, ... and he buys in carload lots, mixed carload lots, and he sends it in the fall and in the spring to his store for distribution ... Matters of credit are most important. Credit arrangements are with the big firms in Winnipeg or Vancouver.[3]

With its rapid growth in population and agricultural production, the prairie economy – particularly Winnipeg – acquired some elements of a manufacturing sector (see Table 2). The first and most obvious enterprises in this category were the plants that processed farm products – abattoirs, flour mills, malting facilities, breweries, and dairies – or produced construction materials – paint, lumber, bricks, finished steel, and cement. But a wide range of products, including clothing and printed materials, were soon added to this list.

Winnipeg was also important as a labour market. Because it was the largest prairie city and sat at the gateway to the prairies and to the north, those seeking work and those seeking workers gravitated to the streets stretching from the CPR rail station into the heart of the business district. Small employment agencies, often little more than ramshackle store fronts, posted sheets of jobs on their walls, doors, and windows and thus acted as clearing-houses in this great labour bazaar. And the workers came, to finger the sheets, to discuss the

TABLE 2
Manufacturing in Winnipeg 1891, 1901, 1911

|  | Number of employees | Wages and salaries ($000) | Cost of materials ($000) | Value of production ($000) |
| --- | --- | --- | --- | --- |
| 1891 | 1,410 | 984 | 4,764 | 6,701 |
| 1901 | 3,155 | 1,811 | 5,046 | 8,616 |
| 1911 | 11,705 | 7,615 | 18,429 | 32,699 |
| 1914 (estimates) | 18,000 |  |  | 50,000 |

Source: Ruben Bellan *Winnipeg First Century: An Economic History* (Winnipeg 1978) 115n, 124

alternatives, and to sign on for a winter in a timber camp in Peace River, a harvest on a farm near Old Wives Lake, a stint on a rail crew heading toward Prince Rupert.

Because of its pre-eminence at the start of the boom, Manitoba's capital was also one of Canada's financial centres during the west's first era of prosperity. The foundation of local fire, life, and property insurance companies, trust companies, a stock exchange – as well as an extraordinary increase in bank clearings – demonstrated that Winnipeg was generating its own financial base. W.F. Alloway and H.T. Champion of the city expanded their private bank to the point where it became the largest such operation in Canadian history. A number of head offices of financial enterprises moved to Winnipeg, and by 1910 two chartered banks, the Union and the Home, each with assets of over $100 million, had established their headquarters there.

In addition to housing these enterprises, the city was also a base for construction activity, for a flourishing retail trade, and for important educational and administrative services. Its future must have seemed boundless in the golden years between 1900 and 1913: 'Its grain traders completely controlled the marketing of the great staple product of prairie agriculture, its wholesalers dominated merchandise trade from the Great Lakes to the Rockies, its financial community exercised authority throughout the region, its industry furnished a major proportion of building materials required by Western construction activity, and its railway shops and yards were crucial to the operation and maintenance of the Western railway network.'[4]

The dreams of infinite expansion for the Winnipeg economy were not realized. One by one, the city's prairie-wide functions were whittled away; by 1940, though still the first city of the prairies, it had been reduced to a status not far removed from that of Edmonton or Regina. It had become merely the capital of a province, the economic and transportation centre of a limited trading area, rather than the metropolis of the entire western interior. Its setbacks were numerous, its opponents relentless. Other prairie cities wanted their share of the economic activity and, by the 1920s, had removed almost all of Winnipeg's freight rate preferences and thus undercut its wholesalers. They wanted industry and competed for the new plums: Calgary won a large CPR shop in 1912 and Regina was promised a General Motors assembly plant in 1928. They wanted to be transportation centres, and, as a result of the opening of the Panama Canal in 1914 and the freight rate revisions, one of these challengers, Vancouver, suddenly acquired extraordinary prominence in the western interior. By the mid-1920s, the Pacific port was handling all of Alberta's crop and some of the Saskatchewan harvest as well, and Vancouver wholesalers were now sending agents into the western prairies.[5] In addition, changes in manufacturing and advertising techniques affected the merchandising system in this era; where brand names and huge enterprises could influence an entire market, direct contacts between producer and retailer were more common, to the exclusion of the wholesaler. Finally, the sharp increase in industrial activity in central Canada began to take its toll in the 1920s: plans for western manufacturing plants were moth-balled, western regional offices were reduced in size, and western head offices, as in the case of both the Home and the Union banks, were absorbed into larger operations and transferred to Canada's heartland.

This is not meant to imply that Winnipeg ceased to develop after 1914. With the emergence of the airplane as an important mode of transportation in the inter-war years, Winnipeg became the headquarters for James A. Richardson's Western Canada Airways (1926) and later for Trans-Canada Airlines (1937). The rise of tourism and conventions, another aspect of the growing service sector, also focused attention on the city. In 1927, for example, 10,000 Masons and several thousand Conservatives added considerable money to the local economy. The development of northern Manitoba's mineral resources and the further exploitation of its hydro-electric potential also contributed to the wealth of the province's capital city. But the pace of economic development had slowed dramatically. Perhaps the city's poor reputation in labour-management relations had had an effect, but the most likely explanation was that the creation of the wheat economy had been completed by the 1920s. Winnipeg had boomed because it had maintained a monopoly control over 'the commercial, financial and transportation services necessary to the marketing of agricultural products and distribution of goods and services to the hinterland.' It entered a relative decline as its monopoly was slowly eroded.[6]

The economic functions that continued to support Winnipeg's sub-metropolitan status in the inter-war period also distinguished the other four prairie cities from the smaller centres of the region. The administrative activities of a capital city, the educational services of a university town, the health facilities and retail and wholesale outlets that served a hinterland with a radius of 100 miles or more provided part of the explanation for the size of Regina, Saskatoon, Edmonton, and Calgary. They all owed something to the railway, as well, and to special advantages that were shared by no other prospective metropolis.

In the case of Calgary, the cattle industry, including stockyards, abattoirs, and tanneries, accounted for 25 per cent of Alberta's manufacturing activity by 1911 and was thus one pillar of the local economy. A second was oil, which was discovered at Turner Valley, twenty miles southwest of the city, in May 1914. Though the discovery did not produce a sustained boom, it did result in the establishment of Turner Valley as Canada's most important oilfield. With the construction of a refinery, the growth of local management and technical services, and, in 1938, the creation of the Alberta Oil and Gas Conservation Board, Calgary became the centre of the Western Canadian petroleum industry.[7]

The rise of Edmondon was slower and more uncertain. The old fur trade post on the north bank of the North Saskatchewan River became a trade and administrative centre in the northern part of the Territories, but its pre-eminence was challenged by the establishment in 1891 of a rival town on the south bank of the river, at the terminus of the Calgary and Edmonton Railway. In the continuing absence of a bridge, this settlement, known first as South Edmonton and from 1899 as Strathcona, was able to compete for leadership of the district. Home of freight yards, several flour mills, and a small cattle trade and timber mill, Strathcona was a town of over 1,500 in 1901; though well below Edmonton's population of 2,600, it seemed to possess potential for growth. But Edmonton easily and quickly defeated the challenge of its south bank rival. Within five years, Edmonton's aggressive board of trade had built the necessary bridge across the North Saskatchewan and had secured the services of the two new transcontinental railways. Moreover, with the aid of its combative MP, Frank Oliver, Edmonton had also been named the capital of the new province of Alberta. Calgary, in contrast, had the misfortune to be represented in Ottawa during these crucial months in 1905 by a member of the Conservative opposition. Though Strathcona did become the site of the new provincial university, even this plum could be seen as an Edmonton victory because it retained that important service within Edmonton's hinterland rather than permitting it to go to the south. By 1912, the leaders of Strathcona were quite willing to merge with their aggressive colleagues in the enlarged city of Edmonton.

The success of Edmonton was an object lesson in the role of lobbyists. Not only had the northern city become the capital and the metropolis of a vast hinterland, but it had also become the dominant force in provincial politics. Because its own MP had drawn the new provincial electoral map, Edmonton and its satellite, Strathcona, each acquired one representative in the provincial legislature; in addition, four other ridings radiated from the city like wedges of a pie, and two more were clearly in the city's immediate hinterland. Eight of 25 seats were within the city's orbit, and 5 more, at least, belonged in the general category of 'northern Alberta.' In contrast, Calgary could claim only 3 or 4 seats within its orbit, and the entire 'southern' portion of the province, including Red Deer, which straddled the divide, encompassed only 12 ridings. Thus was Edmonton's hold on the province consolidated. Its administrative functions, its university, its railways and health services provided a safe and secure economic base for a generation.

Edmonton had always relied on the rich farm lands of central Alberta to provide it with wholesale and retail functions, and in the years of rapid western growth the construction boom supported local lumber mills and brick yards. The basic energy source of that era, coal, was available in abundance in local mines, and the discovery of natural gas at Viking supplemented this advantage when a pipeline to the capital was completed in 1923. Moreover, because Edmonton was the only large centre in the area, its cattle trade was eventually large enough to sustain an important meat-packing sector. But little was added to these economic activities. Only the interest of mining and petroleum companies in northern Canada's resource potential provided hope for the future: the development of a local group of bush pilots and local air transport services was one of the few bright spots in the unchanging economic scene of the interwar years.[8]

Saskatchewan's urban pattern was even more the product of the requirements of an agricultural economy. Two large cities and six smaller ones anchored a network of villages and towns that covered an expanse of agricultural land larger than France. Decentralization of the urban centres was appropriate to the low density of the population. Regina had been the capital of the Territories and retained that position in the new province despite a slanging match with the Saskatoon newspapers, but the second plum of the new provincial community, the university, went to Saskatoon by decision of the university's board of governors, after heated skirmishes with Prince Albert, Regina, and Moose Jaw. Though founded by a Methodist temperance colonization society, Saskatoon grew to prominence because of the energy and ambition of its leading entrepreneurs. Using a tactic common in this era, the 'boomers' incorporated the community as a town (1903) and later a city (1906) in order to increase its borrowing power and thus were able to build the public works – streets, sidewalks, sewers, and fire services – that would attract further investment. The gamble paid off. Between 1905 and 1907, the city, which had had only one rail line (the Regina–Prince Albert service) acquired connections to all three transcontinentals and an extensive branch line system. The transportation services and public works, in turn, were an important factor in the wooing of the university. And they were also crucial to the attraction of about 100 wholesale firms that set up shop between 1906 and 1912. Saskatoon had acquired its present shape and role by 1912: a decade of furious activity was enough to make all the difference between a hamlet and a prominent city. During the following generation, with the agricultural economy in place, Saskatoon and its sister cities on the prairies changed very little. In physical structure and economic function, the cities of 1912 were the cities of 1940.[9]

Historians have been attracted to the role of 'boosters' in the development of the prairies because the selection of a handful of city sites out of a thousand competitors is best explained by reference to these committed entrepreneurs. Their gambles to secure pre-eminent status by early incorporation, heavy civic borrowing, and rapid expenditure on public works and city services were dramatic and, in the case of the winners, allegedly far-sighted. And their philosophy, 'that cities are made by the initiative and enterprise of their citizens,' as the *Regina Leader* proclaimed, thus became entrenched in urban political life in the west.

It is important to look beneath the boosters' rhetoric to the political and social implications of their message. The roots of the outlook can be seen in the recollections of one Saskatoon merchant: 'All were imbued with an optimism that Saskatoon was destined to become an important centre. Newcomers in business were welcomed and encouraged; everyone pulled together to develop and boom the town; there were no petty jealousies of one another.'[10] Competitors lay not within the town but in the next towns down the line. That is why inter-city rivalry in the west could reach such vituperative heights. And, even more important, it is part of the explanation as to why internal social divisions in western cities were so little discussed by contemporaries and later by scholars. A 'knocker,' as he was described in those days of boosterism, was one who questioned the optimism of the economic developers, saw flaws in the plans of the real estate promoters, and commented publicly on such social problems as inadequate housing, substandard water and sewage services, and serious problems associated with vice and violence. The 'knocker' was the most reviled of all creatures in the circles of the boosters. According to one student of the subject, 'the attitude of boosters toward organized labour and the poor and disadvantaged was one of scorn, and the cities the boosters dominated spent only a small fraction of their budgets on such community services as sanitation, health departments, or welfare – far less than was spent on promoting growth.'[11] In a booster atmosphere, class-based debates – that is, serious differences of interest on the spending of public funds and serious differences in perceptions of community needs – were not welcomed. The greatest victory of the boosters was not the creation of their metropolis but the creation of an ethos of community solidarity that transcended class, income, and occupation.

Social gradation existed in prairie cities, however, and should be seen as a powerful distinguishing characteristic of prairie society in the post-1900 decades. A novel by Douglas Durkin, who won a minor literary reputation in the 1920s and 1930s, is a guide to popular perceptions of social composition. In *The Magpie* (1923), a returned war hero was confronted with the uncomfortable truth that the Great War had not improved social conditions in his own country. He discovered, shortly after his return from the Front, that his closest comrade from the trenches lived in a shack-like house on the edge of a western metropolis, clearly Winnipeg. Durkin describes the setting in detail, including the tomato plants growing along one edge of the front yard and cucumber vines along the front porch. This labourer expressed political views which, in their support for other workers, would have sounded dangerously close to subversion in middle-class parlours. The labourer exuded sympathy for the strikers of 1919 and distaste for the 'big fellows who called out the Mounties and had the streets cleared with bullets.' The chap's wife presided serenely over linoleum floors, cheap wicker chairs, and dime-store reproductions of Victorian message paintings such as *The Angelus* and *The Age of Innocence*; on her face was an expression of 'old sadness ... the same expression he had seen in the faces of the English and French women of the lower classes even during the height of the rejoicing that followed the close of the war. It had a certain ineradicable beauty – like shadow caught in a tree that is full of sunlight.' In contrast, when the war hero visited the home of a business leader, he found a landscaped mansion with vast ranks of windows and formal reception rooms looking out upon a riverbank vista. In this home, dinners were formal events, preceded by cocktails – illegal in this prohibition era – and followed by cigars in the library for men and coffee in the drawing-room for the ladies. Servants helped lighten the burden of entertaining, particularly during 'the season,' when social events were more formal and numerous. The political views expressed in this setting were similarly distant from those of the working-class representative. According to Durkin, at least, the 'leading business men of the city' saw themselves as a group under siege in 1919, ready and eager to do battle with the

labour radicals. Though described as 'a novel of post-war disillusionment,' *The Magpie* can better be seen as a graphic revelation of
class consciousness in western Canada.[12]

Fiction in this case corresponds with fact. The first four decades
marked the discovery of class consciousness in Winnipeg and, to a
lesser degree, in the other cities of the west. At one extreme, it was
revealed in the 'conspicuous consumption' of the wealthy; at the
other, by the wretched poverty of some city slums. A macabre pas-
time united the two worlds: working-class families would tour the
summer resorts of the rich in order to admire the 'conspicuous
leisure' habits of their superiors; and the upper classes, especially
their youth, occasionally embarked on automobile adventures into
the 'howling chaos' of the slums.[13] But class consciousness was also
revealed in other ways, particularly in labour-management conflicts
and in important civic political issues. During the four decades after
1900, Winnipeg and the smaller prairie cities discovered 'modern'
class relations.

The case of Edmonton was instructive. A town of 2,600 in 1901,
the city had grown to 11,000 by 1906 and had already taken on the
social characteristics it was to display for a generation. The west end
of the city, especially the area close to the banks of the North Saskatchewan, was increasingly the residential quarter of 'prosperous
businessmen, professionals and civil servants.' East of First Street
and north of Jasper Avenue lived a high proportion of 'the labourers, tradesmen, marginal businessmen and alien ethnic newcomers.' The pattern evident in this residential segregation was repeated in other expressions of community outlook in 1906. In the
newly established *Saturday News*, a showy women's section described At Homes, luncheons, parties, and dances in which aspiring
leaders of society entertained each other in carefully staged rituals.
Membership in the exclusive Edmonton Club was already becoming
a measure of prominence in local business and public life. For the
most part, these community leaders were from Ontario or Great
Britain, were Anglican or Presbyterian, and about half of them had
obtained advanced education in universities or colleges or apprenticeship programs. It is no surprise to learn that labourers had correspondingly less education, smaller houses on smaller lots, and were
more diverse in ethnicity and religion. Those who lived further from
the centre of town lacked electricity and sewer and water service for
a number of years and thus lived with coal oil lamps and sad irons,

outdoor privies and indoor pails, and the necessity of buying water from the horse-drawn tank wagons that circulated through the neighbourhood. And, if it was too early to describe the distinctions between the business-professional group and the labourers as a class division, growing class assumptions were none the less present in civic politics in this era. The location of rail lines, an isolation hospital, and a garbage incinerator all worked to divide east end residents from the wealthier west end in one city election campaign. As a workers' spokesman commented about the incinerator: 'They tell us that this garbage doesn't smell; that the plant will be a nice place – in fact an ornament. All right. Then we will locate the plant somewhere along McKay or Victoria. I think about a block from the new parliament buildings would suit.' Electoral results bear out the thesis of an east-west conflict within the city.[14]

The existence of a group of wealthy powerful families in pre-1914 western cities is not likely to be disputed by modern historians. James Ashdown of Winnipeg and Pat Burns and A.E. Cross of Calgary, three of the best-known of this group, merely represented the several hundred entrepreneurs, financiers, merchants, and government and church leaders who 'set the tone' or established the rules in the new society. They took up where the preceding generation had left off, asserting the rule of law, the power of the church, the influence of the school lesson, and the inevitable correctness of British traditions. In addition to creating the conditions for social stability, they were determined to promote rapid economic growth within their empire and were not generally exercised by the evidence of growing social inequality. Social Darwinists when on the public platform, they would explain that life was a struggle in which the fittest prospered; in the dining room of the Ranchmen's Club or the Manitoba Club, they would amend this pious assertion by noting that, having struggled and survived, they were now exempt from competition to some degree and thus could strike an appropriate co-operative note – call it a cartel or a price-fixing deal or simply business statesmanship – for the good of the local business community. These men and women were undeniably sincere in their determination to build a better world in western Canada; that they had prospered in the process, and therefore led important public institutions, was an appropriate – if heavy – responsibility, in their view.[15]

The environment created by this group matched their aspirations. Their houses, often designed by architects, were the wonders of their respective cities: in 1912 alone, twenty-six houses that cost more than $20,000 each were constructed in Winnipeg. The finest summer 'cottages' at Lake of the Woods – rambling log structures with boat houses and sleeping cabins – were valued at $5,000 to $10,000. (The appropriate comparison would be a frame-house in a working-class district of Winnipeg which sold in 1900 for $1,500 to $3,000). In Winnipeg, their leisure activities included an automobile touring club based at Lower Fort Garry, the famous headquarters of Sir George Simpson. In the ranch district near Calgary, recreation often centred around the horse, including gymkhanas, polo, and 'the hunt.' This group of social leaders was establishing a private social circle: it now had its own clubs for golfing and dining, its own circle of receptions for the debutantes who were 'coming out,' its own organizations for the wives who were charged with reinforcement of their husbands' status, its own residential districts, and even its own schools: thus was the social distance between classes extended.[16]

Political behaviour is the ultimate test of class. Though we will consider it later in more detail, a few preliminary observations on the political activities of this group can be made. If they were far too busy to run for office regularly, the tone-setters nevertheless did participate when the occasion offered and especially when trouble arose. Their promotion of civic expenditure on immigration propaganda rather than health and welfare measures has been noted. They had considerable influence in elections, especially in Winnipeg where the wards were gerrymandered and where multiple voting (one aldermanic vote in each ward where the citizen owned property) was permitted. And they were consistently active in such private-public interest groups as the board of trade, the policies of which were often crucial to the direction of urban public life. In promoting their perception of the civic good, they promoted the interests of their class.[17]

The condition, outlook, and consciousness of the working class on the prairies have been the subject of many generalizations and little investigation. A 1909 federal government survey in Winnipeg found 120 families (837 individuals) living in forty-one homes. The average house, which had about seven rooms, thus contained three families and an additional nine or ten unmarried boarders. The family of James Gray, the prairie historian, moved a dozen times in his childhood, and, as a result, Gray attended twelve different Winnipeg public schools in nine years. But what is representative of prairie working-class life is unknown.[18] Studies of workers' incomes and the cost of living in Toronto and Montreal around the turn of the century have demonstrated that the wages of one adult, even if the individual were employed throughout the year, would not be sufficient to raise a family of five above the 'poverty line.' Winnipeg, Edmonton, and Calgary may have offered slightly better circumstances because of temporary shortages of labour, but there is little reason to believe that one adult wage-earner could provide more than the bare minimum in food, clothing, and housing for a family. Most workers' households would have required supplementary income; whether a wife took on a part-time job, a daughter spent a few years as a domestic, or a son brought home his wages from the time he entered his teens, the working-class household was a viable economic unit only with these supplements. The loss of the main breadwinner's job because of illness, mistakes, or an economic slump could cause serious problems. But these crises, like layoffs and drunkenness, were only a few of many common evils to be dreaded. Even marriage and children were mixed blessings in the labourer's household, because they often meant the end of income supplements for aging parents and a start of a decade of great difficulty for young adults.[19]

How can a picture of this life be drawn in the absence of adequate studies? We know that a serious outbreak of typhoid in Winnipeg in 1904–6 was confined largely to a working-class area where an investigator compared the situation created by open ditches and outdoor toilets to that in medieval European cities. Winnipeg's typhoid death rate in this period was higher than that of any other major city in Europe and North America. We know, too, that disproportionately high numbers of infant deaths, owing primarily to gastrointestinal diseases (the causes – improper feeding and contaminated milk – are commonly associated with poverty), occurred in Winnipeg's north end, especially among families from central and southern Europe. (The rate of deaths per 1,000 live births was over three times higher than for families of British or Canadian origin). We know that overcrowding and unsanitary living conditions were regular features of Winnipeg building and health inspectors' reports: 'A ten-roomed house was found to have nine separate tenants (only one of whom had two rooms) each living independently and doing their own cooking on gas stoves and eating and sleeping in one room. To make matters worse, not one of the gas stoves had a hood or pipe to carry off noxious gases. Imagine these rooms ... in winter with double sashes on. There was only one water closet and one sink in the house.'[20] But to translate the dispassionate words of official reports into the cries that echo in a crowded dirty house is very difficult; and to determine the outlines of the 'typical' life of labourers and their families is similarly far beyond our reach at the moment.

The political outlook of the workers also defies easy generalization. For every activist who joined a revolutionary movement, there were dozens who avoided politics entirely and dozens more who were recruited into the old-line parties. But there was sufficient interest in labour, socialist, and syndicalist movements in western Canada throughout the four decades after 1900 to suggest that working-class consciousness was becoming a reflex action. Though stronger in British Columbia than on the prairies, these radical and reformist movements found real support in Winnipeg and, to a lesser degree, Edmonton and Calgary. In moments of agitation, such as the spring of 1919, they also affected smaller cities such as Brandon, Moose Jaw, and Prince Albert. One irony of this growing class awareness, however, was that it was more likely to be expressed in civic election campaigns – where radical political alternatives would be least effective – than in national contests and thus has been neglected by national historians.

We do know that urban workers increased dramatically in numbers during the post-1900 western boom and that, as was the pattern elsewhere, their workplaces became larger and more impersonal in the same era. In 1911, about 35,000 were employed in manufacturing on the prairies and another 146,000 in construction, transportation, and domestic trades. By 1929, these sectors employed 61,000 and 190,000, respectively. A quarter of a million people, many of them living in urban centres, constituted a sizeable constituency for the appeals of labour organizers and socialist politicians.[21]

The existence of a third social grouping somewhere between the business and cultural leaders and the labourers is more difficult to substantiate. Still, one can argue reasonably not only that such a group existed but also that it provided the glue that held the community together. Teachers, preachers, health care workers, government employees – the 'professional and service' sector – comprised

7 per cent of Winnipeg's population in 1881, almost 13 per cent in 1911. By 1929, the proportion of workers in the 'personal and professional service and government' category in the three prairie provinces was nearing one in five (18 per cent), or about 160,000 in a work-force of 900,000. These professionals accepted the challenge of smoothing the rough edges of the new society, thus making it more spiritual, more open to the talents of ambitious and mobile newcomers, and less harsh in its treatment of some of its citizens.

The heart of the professionals' activity was the school, an instrument through which a democratic and prosperous society would be achieved. It was no mere coincidence, therefore, that schools continued to be the subject of intense political debate in the early twentieth century and that the state of local classrooms and the behaviour of teachers were always topics of intense interest in prairie communities. At one level, the school was an agent of assimilation that would transform unskilled, dangerous foreigners into loyal, respectable subjects of the crown. At another, the school would ensure that all children, newcomer and Canadian-born alike, attained the work discipline and basic skills necessary in a changing world. With such heavy responsibilities, the education system grew rapidly in size and importance.[22]

The churches, especially the Protestant churches, had an equally important role in the eyes of the professionals. They provided charity, sought to alleviate blatant social injustice, and, of course, reminded all citizens, rich and poor alike, that salvation was the object of life. But their role as agents of social assistance and social change distinguished them from the religious institutions of the preceding generation. The new church was not simply a building dedicated to Sunday service, mid-week Bible study, and parish visits; it had become the focus for settlement houses, educational forums, distribution of food and clothing, and even mediation in labour disputes. The minister's staff had thus expanded to include trained parish workers and dozens of volunteers who assisted him in his work among the poor, the sick, the foreign, the young, the old, and the disturbed.[23]

No church could continue to meet the demands made on it by means simply of the informal voluntary programs that it provided. As the community's educational skills increased, as the awareness of contemporary social problems developed and the idea of public responsibility took hold, a corps of 'social professionals' was created. Public health nurses taught hygiene, supervised pre- and post-natal classes, and examined countless school children for health problems. Child care workers investigated allegations of child neglect, supervised dozens of foster homes, and arranged adoption procedures. Other welfare or social aid workers controlled food and housing relief programs and attempted to provide some counselling, however meagre, for people who sought help. The so-called welfare state was being launched in every industrial nation, and prairie Canada simply followed British, American, and Ontario examples in the first half of the twentieth century.[24]

Members of the new social group – personal, professional, and government services – were not as wealthy as the business leaders or as prominent as individual cultural leaders, but they were not as poor or as lacking in control over their environment as labouring people. They were, indeed in the middle. They were not Karl Marx's bourgeoisie, and they should not, one suspects, be lumped in with the business leaders on political and social matters. They did not constitute a conscious social class at all and thus ruined the calculations of all the political party theorists, left and right, by their adherence to a wide variety of loyalties and ideals. Their style of life was often closer to the business leaders. They joined the Canadian Club to hear luncheon addresses on public issues; they joined the historical society or the naturalists' society to continue their program of public and self-improvement; they attended church and ethnic associations and provided lay leadership in each; they lived in middle-level housing in middle-level areas and, generally speaking, were middle-income earners, too. But the very demands of their professions made them conscious of the condition of the working people and the poor. Thus, in politics and in public debate, they sometimes sided with the leaders of social reform and, at other times, backed the business leaders' calls for economic progress and social austerity.[25]

The cities of the west and, to a lesser degree, the towns and villages, too, were becoming identical to the urban centres of the industrial capitalist world. One aspect of this remarkable homogenizing process was the creation of a comparable urban social structure: it comprised a large working class, a professional service class, and the business leaders. The many elements ignored by this simplistic design, such as the thousands of small merchants, salesmen, and clerks, found their place by choosing the social identity to which they were most closely allied.

Frontier camps represented yet another social environment. Simple, rough, and unforgiving, they provided newcomers with the harshest introduction to western Canada. Their rate of population turnover was exceptionally high, and their political atmosphere, including direct labour action, was unstable. Nowhere should consciousness of social class have been more in evidence, and yet the camps were rarely the scene of significant expressions of class solidarity. About 7,000 worked in the forests and mines of the western interior in 1911, and about 20,000 in 1929.[26] But the number who worked at any one time in the construction camps is impossible to know. The extraordinary railway boom in the early twentieth century added thousands of miles to Canada's transportation system, and the smaller boom in prairie branch lines in the 1920s added another 2,000 miles; every mile required the labour of hundreds of navvies. One scholar has estimated that there were between 50,000 and 70,000 'blanketstiffs' – they carried their blanket-beds on their back from job to job – employed annually in railway construction in the peak years 1907–13. And one of the rail companies estimated that, to maintain a work-force of 2,800 men on one section, it had to engage 'as many as 5,000 men in the period of one month.' Thus, to the question 'how many?,' one can reply only that camp and resource town population varied with the season and the condition of the economy. A range of 25,000–125,000 in any given year would be a reasonable guess.[27]

One outstanding characteristic of unskilled workers was their mobility. If they were young, single, and in quest of a grubstake, they might travel the breadth of the country and hold a half-dozen jobs in as many industries in the space of a year. If they were married or had a homestead, they might take to the camps for six months of each year, returning to family or farm in the intervals. A significant proportion of this population was 'foreign' (that is, their mother tongue was neither English nor French), and some of them were more attached to the 'old country' than to the new. How many of these workers returned to Europe for brief periods or permanently is not certain, but the phenomenon of the 'guest worker' was as well-known in western Canada in the early twentieth century as it is in western Europe today.

The influence of ethnicity on work and leisure in these communities was apparent to many observers. The term 'white men' was reserved for English and French-speaking Canadians, Americans, British, and Scandinavians; the term 'foreigner' was applied to eastern and southern Europeans. The work of the railway construction crews actually seemed to be divided along such rough lines: the 'whites' predominated in supervisory positions and in the softer jobs such as on the track layers, the steam shovels, the locomotive repair teams, and the bridge crews; the 'foreigners' worked beyond the end of steel and in the unskilled tasks requiring brute strength. Edmund Bradwin, who travelled through hundreds of these camps during his years with Frontier College, an educational mission to the workers, estimated that about one-third of the labour force in the 1920s was British, Canadian, and American (one in three of these was French-speaking), one-third was Slavic, and a slightly smaller fraction (25 per cent) was Scandinavian and Finnish, with a sizeable number of Italians and a few other nationalities besides.[28] The crews would undoubtedly segregate by nationality in working and sleeping arrangements, but the largest camps must have seemed like Towers of Babel to newcomers.

The employment system was a striking illustration of the capitalist labour market in action. The employer took no responsibility for the worker beyond the bounds of the job; when the contract ended, or when the worker was found wanting, employment ceased. When it rained, there was no pay. Not for these contractors the paternalism that accompanied long-term employment and loyal retainers: even the cost of transportation to and from remote camps was customarily deducted from the employee's wages. Until 1916, when federal government employment offices took control of placement, private employment agencies or 'shipping offices' recruited workers in return for a commission from the construction and logging companies. Cheating, misrepresentation, locked trains, and even guarded convoys were said to have been a part of the system. The step from steerage in an Atlantic vessel to the rocks and pines of the Canadian Shield must have seemed instantaneous to the European labourer who signed a contract at dockside and was shipped without ceremony or delay to a remote construction camp.

The work itself varied. The semi-skilled jobs required constant labour but often were reasonable in their physical demands. The work assignments for the unskilled were sheer hell because the physical demands never ended. Mucking clay, loading rock, and clearing bush were heavy tasks at the best of times, but in dreary rainy autumns, bitterly cold winters, and even the baking summer sun, among the remarkable species of biting insects that inhabit the mid-Canadian forest, work was often misery itself. It was also dangerous. The number of deaths and injuries on the construction sites has never been established, but scattered reports suggest that it was high. Wages were competitive when listed in the advertisements on the walls of a job agency but rarely converted into cash at the promised rate. The problem was 'deductions.' Transportation costs, blankets and clothing from the company store, board at camp, medical expenses, and time lost through machine breakdowns or blizzards all counted against the day labourer: it sometimes seemed that the 'stiff' was lucky to get away without owing the company!

Living conditions ranged from crude to indescribable. Temporary camps might consist of tents, bunk cars, or log bunk-houses, but, whatever the housing material, they were invariably dirty, smelly, and lousy. Double bunks on two levels lined the walls of the bunk-house; a large stove sat in the centre of the floor; the large room – perhaps thirty by sixty feet – was dark because windows let in the cold in winter and insects in summer. Tales and gossip alone enlivened leisure hours, but even these bright moments were rare in work-weary lives. Recreation at the camp was consequently limited and was found instead during the classic escape – the spree. A 'good drunk' would be a weekend or a week evening spent drinking, fighting, gambling, and visiting prostitutes. This type of outlet provided excitement, a memorable break in the monotonous rhythm of camp life.

The blanketstiffs and bunk-house men were labourers and yet, perhaps because of their mobility and isolation, were rarely integrated into the larger working class. Their condition was temporary, they would have explained, and they planned to climb the ladder of status from lumber camp to railway construction camp and then 'head out' to a homestead or a skilled trade as soon as possible. In moments of crisis, therefore, these men might support a class movement, but the more typical situation was silence; they usually saw themselves, during their camp career at least, as being beyond the reach of the Canadian labour community, out of touch and perhaps even out of sympathy with their colleagues in the cities and the mine towns.

The western interior had its share of resource towns in the opening decades of the twentieth century because it possessed then, as it does to this day, vast coal reserves as well as a variety of minerals and significant timber stands. In an era when coal was a crucial source of energy not only for home heating but also for thermal electricity, railway locomotives, and steel production, coal mines were an important part of prairie economic activity. In the lignite mines around Estevan, Saskatchewan, in 1931, over 400 miners and labourers were employed, not to mention several hundred others who wished to be employed. In Alberta, where coal-bearing forma-tions underlie most of the southern half of the province, over 7,000 miners and mine labourers, exclusive of supervisors and other trades, were employed in the same year. Mineral discoveries in Manitoba, particularly the great Flin Flon ore body which contained copper, gold, lead, and zinc, also contributed to economic activity in the inter-war years. Despite ups and downs, the Flin Flon develop-ment and the gold mines in central Manitoba each employed several hundred workers. Forestry activities in the western interior were tiny in comparison to those in British Columbia but none the less resulted in revenues of about $400,000 in 1931 (British Columbia – $2 million) and the employment of about 1,000 lumbermen. (The output increased to $1.6 million in 1941 [British Columbia – $4.7 mil-lion], and employment rose commensurately.) Finally, the hydro-electric potential of Manitoba's rivers was an important factor both in the development of a smelter at Flin Flon and a paper mill on the Winnipeg River. The power plants, like the industrial plants that they supplied, became sites of small towns. Thus, the mines, the mills, and the dams sustained in the western interior as in the rest of the 'mid-Canada corridor' another important economic and social phenomenon – the resource town, or, as it was often called, the company town.[29]

Life in such a community was more stable than in the frontier camps, but it was still difficult. The towns were distant from larger centres of population, they often lacked social organizations or re-creational facilities, and they were plagued by extraordinary rates of population turnover. Moreover, they possessed a narrow segment of the larger population, chiefly young adult males, and thus lacked the very old, the very young, and, of course, women. Like the camps, then, such towns were often viewed as stopping places on a trip to another destination and suffered the problems generated by short-term community social arrangements.

The coal towns were the most numerous of the resource-based industries in the interior. They had a remarkable and depressing sameness to them, whether situated in the stark landscape of southern Saskatchewan, the badlands of central Alberta, or the majestic valleys of the Rockies. They were dominated by the fortune and the routine of the mine. The hours of the shift change, the prices at the store, the conditions of bunk-house or shack, and the quality of the school all were determined by 'the company.'

One important determinant of the worker's life was his actual task. Most western coal mining was done by the room-and-pillar method, in which small teams of two or three men built 'rooms' in the coal seam and hauled out the coal. The team members were dependent on each other both for output and safety but were otherwise extremely independent because they determined their own pace of work and method of operation. Their job was dangerous, as the average of thirty-odd fatalities per year in the inter-war era suggests, and their wages were low.[30] The skilled experienced men who were paid on the contract system (set fee per unit mined) could earn good wages when the going was smooth, but seasonal layoffs and disruptions in underground operations make reference to a daily wage misleading. Western markets required coal chiefly in fall and winter, and few miners managed to work regularly. In the Saskatchewan fields during the Second World War, over half the miners worked fewer than 100 shifts in a year though they would have been prepared to work 250 shifts (based on a five-day, fifty-week year). In Alberta 'domestic' coal fields, the same proportion was evident throughout the 1930s. Even in the busy 'steam' coal-fields (high-quality bituminous coal) of Alberta, only three miners in ten worked 200–300 shifts per year during the 1930s. Annual earnings were low as a result. In the 1930s, most western miners were earning less than $1,000 per year, though those in the steam coal-fields secured up to $1,500 in good years.[31]

Complaints about housing, water-supply, sewage service, schools, and company stores were a common feature of western mine life. A 1919 commission of inquiry in Alberta produced numer-

ous tales of domestic squalor: twenty to twenty-four children stud-
ied in 'an awfully small shack' that served as school for one town;
five or six men slept in each 'chicken coop' (as they called the four-
teen-foot-square shacks) at Wayne, Alberta; about forty of these
men used one toilet, which had no drainage system, and one had
recently acquired 'a doze of crabs' from the toilet; these same men
recalled bedbugs in their pancakes. At Lovett, after much grumbling
by the men and sixteen deaths caused by 'flu,' a general clean-up of
the rows of company houses produced '64 wagonloads of tins
alone.' Near Cadomin, sanitation arrangements were hopeless: 'Refuse is thrown out of doors on the street, a collection of empty cans,
potato peelings, ashes and slime, and greasy and dirty water being
the result. Toilets are earth closets and are let go too long without
new holes being dug.' The cesspool that served the hotel at Brulé,
Alberta, was too close to some of the company houses and sometimes overflowed. The water-supply at Canmore was so dangerous
that a typhoid epidemic was said to be an annual event.[32]

Even the more prosperous stable mining communities had difficulties with schools and sanitation facilities, but, if one scholar's
picture of the Slocan valley of British Columbia is representative,
their most significant feature was social division. According to Cole
Harris, the miners (one of the two important social groups) were
diverse in ethnic background, itinerant, young, and hard-working.
Whether they lived in bunk-houses near the rivers or in cheap
hotels in the towns, they rarely attended middle-class functions
such as church services or church socials and found it hard to meet
women other than prostitutes. They had their own celebrations – 24
May, 1 July, Labour Day – when horse and foot races, rock-drilling
contests, and a dance would brighten their existence. Their union
served as social centre and welfare agency and, in a way, their
church: as with the middle-class denominations, the labourers'
ideals included brotherhood and the Co-operative Commonwealth.
But a job, a little extra money, and a chance to marry and settle down
in a more attractive occupation were foremost in their thoughts.

The other social group Harris labelled 'the citizens.' These businessmen and their families thought of the valley as their home.
Their lives rarely overlapped with the miners except when they met
in stores and at sporting events. They built tennis courts, planted
small orchards, attended meetings of the Masons, sailed yachts,
and, it seemed, lived quite independently of the miners. They were

predominantly British or British Canadian, and their status came not from inheritance, family name, or institutional association but, as much as anything, from personal attributes and from permanence.

Was this an example of a class-based society, an illustration of Marx's proletariat and bourgeoisie? The miners did develop 'a sense of common identity' and an 'instrument of class defence,' the union. But, especially in the early years of a mine, their place of work was separated from their place of residence, past or future, by hundreds and perhaps thousands of miles. Their life in this western camp or town was temporary and therefore did not require or deserve permanent economic or political remedies. However, the 'citizens' enjoyed a 'family-centred ethic of freedom and self-reliance.' They would support the miners' wage demands, for example, but reject their union-based collective vision because it infringed on the rights of others, including both the rights of the property-owner and of other workers. Access to resources in this new land was neither Turnerian (that is, available to all) nor Marxian (that is, determined by past and present property arrangements). The workers may have been members of the proletariat, but, because they had not settled permanently in this place or for this fate, they retained expectations of a better future; they assumed that they would all be 'citizens' one day. Members of the 'middle class' had achieved their status by their head start and by their permanence; they would welcome new residents to their ranks who possessed the prerequisites – enough money to start a business and a commitment to settle down.[33] We can conclude that during the early years in the Slocan valley the foundations of two social classes were laid.

This social distance between societies developed simultaneously with the development of the mines in the 1890s and the early years of the twentieth century. What happened during the next several decades? Clear answers have yet to be given, but the preliminary outline suggests that social distinctions became ever more deeply entrenched in the inter-war years. Mr Krkosky, a Slovak, spent a year in the collieries in Fernie, British Columbia, around the turn of the century before returning to his home in Europe. His son, perhaps entranced by family stories of wealth and adventure, followed suit in 1902. But this second visitor to Canada, Joe Krkosky Sr, married a member of the Fernie Slovakian community and eventually settled down with his new family in Blairmore, hub of the

Alberta coal economy. His son, Joe Jr, having won prizes at the local elementary school, followed him into the mines, put down roots in the community, married, and, at the age of about thirty, in the early 1940s, became the father of a boy who was thus a 'third-generation' Canadian. As a union leader and civic councillor, 'merciful Joe' (Joe Jr,) won widespread affection and respect during his years in the town. He worked for the West Canadian Collieries as a skilled miner and shared a 'room' in the pits with his brother, Martin. Another brother and an uncle also worked for the company. Joe Jr died instantly in this room when struck by 'a fall of top coal' on 11 October 1944. He was thirty-five years old.

Joe Krkosky Jr can be taken as a representative of a social class. In 1941, half the mine workers in Alberta were European-born and another 10 per cent were children of Europeans. Six in ten, therefore, belonged to a language group other than English. One of the six would be Italian, one would be 'northern European' – that is, Scandinavian or Finnish or French (from Belgium or France rather than Quebec), and the other four would be 'Slavic' (Ukrainians, Slovaks, Czechs, Poles, Serbs, Croats, and others). Despite the significant differences among their number, these ethnic workers can be viewed as an increasingly united bloc within the mine towns. Led by the radical leadership of the Ukrainian Farmer–Labour Temple Association and affiliated in a dozen similar cultural associations, they were brought together by sporting teams, cultural events, reading groups, benevolent funds, and especially by political action and strikes. In Blairmore, for example, a bitter seven-month strike in 1932 was succeeded by the election of a workers' slate to the town council in 1933, including Joe Krkosky Jr, and, despite several attempts by 'average rate payers' to turn them out in succeeding years, working-class solidarity was sufficient to permit the union to control city hall for the next decade. The political outlook of the group can be inferred from council's action in renaming the main street Tim Buck Boulevard after the leader of the Canadian Communist party who was imprisoned for his political views in 1932. In the 1945 federal election, 54 per cent of Blairmore's votes were cast for the Labour Progressive (Communist) party candidate.

Not only the eastern Europeans but also many other miners had memories of class lines and a consciousness of class identity. And they did work together. A multiracial concert in Hillcrest in 1924, sponsored by the English, Italian, and Ukrainian branches of the

Workers' Party, was a great success. A newspaper reported: 'Songs in many languages ... of industrial and political solidarity, whilst Comrade Bartholomew drove home the message in a short but powerful speech. Then away went the chairs ... The floor was crowded until four in the morning, and even then, the Italian comrades continued to serenade, singing revolutionary and operatic music with great gusto.'

A working class existed in the mines and resource communities of western Canada. As Allen Seager concluded: 'The Bohemian and the Belgian, the Finn and the Friulan, the peasant and the artisan, thrown together into the crucible of Canadian industrial capitalism, had been forged into a class. The process was not one which stripped these people bare, erasing their memories and their heritage, but rather one which adapted them to new conditions, some familiar, some not so familiar. There was thus a definite relationship between class, ethnicity, and culture in the coalfields, but not one which is easily reducible to a simple formula.'[34]

The rapid growth of prairie cities, the existence of resource towns and frontier camps, and the development of a booster ethos and class awareness were important aspects of prairie society during the first three decades of the twentieth century. The cities and towns provided the environment in which North America's version of modern industrial capitalist society was established. The camps provided a sizeable proportion of the prairie male population with some experience of a rough working-class existence and, even more important, an opportunity to participate in the North American dream of social advancement. The booster ethos, so fervently expounded by boards of trade, civic leaders, and even school boards, asserted the primacy of community over class and ethnic loyalties.

Though not always as clearly expressed as in Winnipeg, awareness of class differences permeated political discussion and social relations across the prairie west. In the cities, resource towns, and camps of the region, class distinctions were evident. Whether they were perceived to be permanent features of society is harder to determine. Given the pervasiveness of boosterism, the power of the North American dream, and the promise of free homesteads, we must conclude that upward mobility – 'progress' – was an integral part of the prairie creed and that class identity was correspondingly weak.

# 13

---

# The rural west 1900–30:
# The farm, the village,
# and King Wheat

The prairie west was intended to be Canada's settlement frontier. The cities, the railways, the coal towns, and the lumber mills had as their common purpose the development of one of the world's great agricultural regions. The precise nature of this farm society was not fully determined during the first generation after Confederation but, in the years between 1900 and 1914, the extent of prairie potential became clear and the rural economy assumed its modern form. The farmers' choices were reinforced by the unusual circumstances of the First World War. By 1920, prairie agriculture specialized in the production of wheat for export. By 1928, Canadian wheat sales constituted nearly half the world export market. An entire society was organized to facilitate this activity. It was built upon rural village and transportation networks, a grain marketing system, and a family economy attuned to the rhythms of the seasons and the demands of the work itself. In this period, at least six of every ten prairie citizens lived in rural areas, either on farms or in villages that existed to serve farms. Thus, in the course of two generations, 1880–1930, the farm had become the paramount institution in the prairie west.

Pioneers were the heroes of the prairie agricultural epic. Male or female, young or old, British or European or American, these newcomers faced the problems of adaptation to a difficult environment with relatively little help from outside sources. They could begin life anew, an opportunity of incalculable value, but the likelihood that they would succeed on the homestead was not nearly as great as they were led to believe. Still, the myth of the frontier flourished in the prairie west as it had among successive generations of Americans and, indeed, as it had flourished in Australia, South Africa, Argentina, and wherever else free land offered a new start.

The expectations of the homesteaders were shaped by the publicists who preceded them, particularly by the Canadian expansionists of the mid-nineteenth century. Typical of the propagandists' enthusiasm was H.Y. Hind's declaration after touring the region for the Canadian government: 'It is a physical reality of the highest importance to the interest of British North America that this continuous belt can be settled and cultivated from a few miles west of the Lake of the Woods to the passes of the Rocky Mountains, and any line of communication, whether by waggon road or railroad, passing through it, will eventually enjoy the great advantage of being fed by an agricultural population from one extremity to another.'[1] The qualifications made by the British and Canadian expeditions of the late 1850s, especially Palliser's concern about the aridity of the southern plains, were forgotten in the desire to settle the west in the following decades. The single most important advocate of western fertility was the botanist John Macoun, who worked for the CPR and later for the Department of the Interior, and who attacked Palliser's generalizations about the Great American Desert with a fervour that bordered upon recklessness.[2] But Macoun was just one among many who celebrated western potential in the generation after Confederation. Together, the expansionists wove a thread of utopianism into the western fabric. They described the landscape as 'the largest flower garden on the continent' and the climate as 'very much the same as it was in England 30 years ago.'[3] The countryside was invariably pastoral, dotted with 'protected glades' and carpeted by flowers. Even the noxious dandelion could be seen as a cloth of gold.[4] The climate was described as bracing and healthy rather than extreme. Prospects for successful farming were excellent if one were prepared to work; by implication, only the feckless would fail. In E.R. Peacock's *Canada, A Descriptive Textbook* commissioned by the Department of the Interior, British immigrants were told that on the prairies 'every settler is given, practically free, a large farm in a country which produces the best wheat in the world.' The society was egalitarian, Peacock explained, and the neighbours friendly: 'The feeling of equality with one's neighbours, and particularly the knowledge that the land is one's own is worth a great deal.' Children have their own horses, he implied, and soon become 'capital shots and get many a bag of prairie chickens.' The immigration literature created an image of wonderland: the prairie west offered a new start, success, equal social status, and a comfortable environment. It was a site for utopia.[5]

The images conjured up by immigration leaflets might have been dismissed as exaggerations had they not been embedded in the western mystique by travel literature and popular fiction. Because western Canada was an investment frontier at a time when European empires were again contemplating overseas enterprises, the region was discussed often by emigration promoters and investment analysts alike. About 100 travel volumes dealing with Canada were published in the settlement era, and countless more articles appeared in newspapers and journals, and most emphasized the optimism and confidence of the west. This was the 'New Canada,' materialistic, work-obsessed, impatient, rude, and bound for greatness.[6]

Ralph Connor gave immortality to the image of a cultivated utopia in the prairie west. Connor was actually Reverend Charles W. Gordon, a Presbyterian minister in Winnipeg who wrote fiction to publicize the mission needs of the western church. His books, which appeared first as serials in a church magazine, sold 5 million copies and caught the imagination of a generation. They told the stories of western missionaries, doctors, and Mounted Policemen – good-hearted and manly men – who confronted the rough life of bush camps and mine towns. Naturally, the good guys won victories for the temperance movement and the church. To modern readers his characters seem stereotyped and his plots contrived but, at the time, the prairie settings were revelations. The novels discussed the development of individuals and the development of society – a Christian and western Canadian society – in a manner that was believable and exciting.[7] Most important for our purposes, they suggested that the prairie west was a place where any individual could begin again and, with a little honest effort, could succeed. Connor built this image of the west upon a series of comparisons between the new land and other societies: it was a society close to nature, not urban; it was young, not old; it was free, not bound by convention. The prairie west, indeed, could re-create the individual just as it improved upon the social order. In one of his novels, Connor described some well-bred young men from England who, 'freed from the restraints of custom and surrounding, soon shed all that was superficial in their make-up and stood forth in the naked simplicity of their native manhood.'[8] In another, a Scottish girl fell in love with a Russian immigrant youth – the descendant of a noble family, to be sure – and exclaimed in delight, 'How wonderful the power of this country of yours to transform men!' The object of her affection, Kalman Kalmar, she described as 'my Canadian foreigner.'[9] Given the superlatives of the promoters, the homesteaders' expectations were understandable.

The era of rapid prairie development before 1914 happened to be the last time in recent history, with the exception perhaps of the conservation boom of the late 1960s, when the organs of public opinion glorified rural life. In the decades after 1920, when urban standards and urban technology dominated cultural works, 'rural' became a synonym for backwardness. But, at the turn of the century, country life was associated with images of purity and productiveness. Reverend Mr Gordon was uttering the conventional wisdom when he told a luncheon meeting that 'the foundation ... of national development and national progress is the soil. The country that grows wheat can, as the [Presbyterian] Superintendent of the West used to say, grow men.'[10] Not only was rural life purer because it was closer to nature but it was also, according to the physiocratic notion of wealth, the source of national prosperity. Another prairie novelist repeated the common belief that 'up from the soil comes all life, all progress, all development.'[11] So it happened that the pioneers opened the continent's 'last, best west' in an age when agriculture was celebrated and the farm was believed to be the foundation of the economy. Such ideas could only sustain their faith in themselves and in their task.

The celebration of rural life has survived in western Canadian culture as reverence for the original settlers of the region. The myth of the prairie pioneer is too well entrenched and too attractive ever to be dislodged from its place at the centre of western history. As Stephen Leacock once explained, 'Going West, to a Canadian, is like going after the Holy Grail to a knight of King Arthur. All Canadian families had, like mine, their Western Odyssey.'[12] References to the difficult early years on a pioneer farm are invariably couched, as with Leacock, in sprritual and mystical phrases. The simple dwelling, often of logs in Manitoba and of sod on the plains further west, sanctified its builder; the simple diet, based on flour, potatoes, and oatmeal supplemented by such store-bought luxuries, where possible, as coffee, tea, and sugar, purified those who received it; the first furrows in virgin soil, cut with the new chilled-steel plough and the recently purchased team of oxen, represented a holy act and a contribution to the extension of God's empire; the endless bone-shattering hours on the trail were a testing as severe as the natural calamities of hail, blizzard, frost, and drought; and the social gatherings, whether dances, church services, or picnics, were somehow happier and more unified in spirit than any of those that followed. The pioneer days acquired a lustre over the years that only success and comfort could have polished so brightly. Failure was forgotten; the world was young again; a society was being created.

To say that the pioneer became a folk myth is not to deny that their lives were difficult or their achievements hard-won. It is impossible to read pioneer recollections without being moved by the determination, the ingenuity, the sadness, and the joy of their lives. One member of the Tyhurst family who was raised in a sod house on the open plains west of Fielding, Saskatchewan, recalled in a memoir the cool water from a well that her father had dug by hand. She spoke fondly of the fresh milk, eggs, and home-churned butter, the coal-oil lamps for evening homework, and her delight in a single Mandarin orange and 'bought biscuits' on Christmas day. Sunday church service, though three miles distant, was an important part of her week, and the school Christmas concert, with its skits, songs, lunch, and Santa Claus, was a highlight of her year. She recalled, too, that her English-born mother never once spoke of the first year on the farm. At the age of twenty-three, in 1906, Mrs Tyhurst had arrived on a scene made black and desolate by prairie fire, and within six months she saw all her own belongings but one trunk burn with her first sod house. The soddy was replaced with a frame-house after six years, and two years later, in 1914, the Tyhursts bought their first 'real furniture,' an oak sideboard, chairs and table, and an organ. Four of the six Tyhurst children lived to maturity and saw their parents established in a 'nice new house' in the 1930s. But the farm work, especially the field operations with a team of big horses, became more difficult for Mr Tyhurst as he grew older; in

1944, at the age of sixty-six, he sold the farm for $8,000.[13] The story of the Tyhurst family is repeated many times in the hundreds of volumes of community histories now being compiled by descendants of the pioneers. Drifts of snow that came through the walls and covered the bedclothes during a fierce blizzard, hail storms that killed poultry and destroyed crops, dances that sparked romance, schools that encouraged dreams of scholarship, and doctors whose devotion to the district was legendary are the stuff of pioneer life and, now, of the pioneer myth.

The tasks of the pioneers did call for initiative, independence, and ingenuity. Even more, they demanded perseverance. By choosing a quarter-section and filing a claim with the government's land office, Philip Minifie was promising to break thirty acres of prairie, to construct a house worth $300, and to reside on the land for half of each year for three years. If he fulfilled these conditions, 160 acres of prairie land, valued at perhaps ten or fifteen dollars an acre on the open market, would be his at the end of the three-year period. Minifie then purchased a wagon and oxen, plough, groceries, kitchen utensils, building materials, and a few luxuries such as tobacco and set out on his new career. He found the deep wide hole with the stake that marked his land, briefly surveyed his empire, collected some dung for a fire over which he cooked some oatmeal, and then, on that first morning, began to plough. As he walked the first furrows,

> He began to be aware of the ruthless pressure of time that bears down on the shoulders of every farmer and particularly of every new farmer. There is never enough time on the prairie. Ploughing cannot start until the frost is out of the ground, for the prairies freeze a foot or more deep during the long winter. Once the land is ploughed, seed must be thrown in as fast as possible at what the farmer guesses or senses is the optimum soil condition. Planted too early the seedlings can be damaged by late frost, frequent in May. Planted too late they risk frost damage before the grain has matured in August. Then the crop must be cut and stooked, again in a wild rush to secure optimum conditions, and threshed as soon as possible to get a good price before the new crop deluges the market and sends the price sliding downwards. In between seeding and binding, hay must be cut, cured, and stored against winter; summer-fallow must be worked, granaries and bins built, harness and machinery repaired, seed cleaned for next

year, fences built and repaired, and all the thousand and six daily chores performed – cows milked, stables cleaned out, eggs collected, chickens feathered, peas picked and shelled, gardens weeded, leaks in the roof mended, wells cleaned out, potatoes dug and stored, hogs butchered, sausage ground, bacon cured, horses shod, shares sharpened, cream skimmed and churned, outhouse moved to a new pit and last season's Eaton's mail-order catalogue hung on the wall.[14]

Despite the pressures of time, the relative dryness of his district, and the problems that accompanied inexperience, Minifie made ends meet on his farm. His wife and two sons joined him a year later in the house he had constructed – 'Built her myself, every nail and board,' as he proudly related – and soon converted the bare drab single room into a colourful, relatively comfortable home. The family established its daily and seasonal routines: father rose at 4:30 a.m. to lay the fire, round up and harness the horses, milk the cow, and feed the animals: he then ate breakfast and started ploughing by 7 a.m. He ate a big lunch at noon and then worked in the fields until 6 or 7. Then, he fed and bedded down the animals, ate supper, and fell into bed himself, assured that daylight would come soon enough. The details differed with the season, the district, and the family, but the pattern was everywhere the same.

The work week of farm women varied so much that normal or typical routines did not exist for them. Kathleen Strange, a member of a successful farm family in a settled district of Alberta, recalled her week and year as ones of unending labour. Saturday was preparation day for Sunday visitors, which included cooking a large roast (as much as twenty or thirty pounds), peeling a pailful of potatoes, baking a 'big batch of bread, two large cakes, numerous cookies and at least six pies.' The household would be cleaned and the kitchen scrubbed, so that Sunday would be a day of rest. Monday was again a baking day, and in the evening all the soiled clothing was placed to soak in tubs. Tuesday was wash day: water was hauled from the well and heated in two galvanized wash-boilers on the stove. Then, by 9 a.m., after the breakfast dishes were done, the cream separator scoured, the beds made, the floors swept, and the table set for dinner (the unvarying pattern of the day between 6 and 9 a.m.), she was ready to do the washing. She carried pailfuls of hot water from the stove to the tubs – burning herself more than once – and scrubbed by hand, on the washboard, the mountain of laundry created by a household of eight to fifteen, depending on the season. Clothes were hung on the line in summer but were draped all over the house in winter, much to her disgust, because underwear and flannel shirts took several days to dry. Wednesday was for ironing, mending, and more baking, this time ten loaves and batches of cinnamon buns. The ironing was heavy work, because it was done with a sad iron heated on the stove. Thursday and Friday were lighter days; aside from the three meals and the usual housework, they were reserved for special chores such as sewing. Another of her tasks was 'canning.' In a world without refrigeration, the larder had to be stocked with home-made preserves, so pork and poultry, vegetables and fruit, wild berries and pickles all were 'put up' in crocks or glass sealers. Aside from the daily round of the house, Mrs Strange also managed the vegetable and flowers in the house garden, the chickens and eggs, and oversaw the milking and cream separating – though she did not, as did many of her contemporaries, do all the milking herself. It remains to be noted that this child of an English family, raised in London itself, loved her life on a prairie farm.[15]

Was the prairie homestead just another version of the American frontier? The frontier of settlement in the United States has long been seen as the great equalizer in human affairs, the birthplace of democratic politics and egalitarian social relations where careers were open to the talented and wealth accrued to the diligent. The classic statement of this belief, which underlies the free enterprise philosophy so common in western North America, was Frederick Jackson Turner's address to an academic audience in 1894 on the theme of 'The Significance of the Frontier in American History.' Since that time, the idea of the frontier and studies of its impact on society have been associated with Turner.[16] The frontier, according to his view, was an area of sparse population customarily many miles west of settled or civilized communities, to which migrated the ambitious, the innovative, the self-sufficient, and those who simply desired a new start. The frontier was therefore a place, constantly moving west and renewing itself with the expansion of settlement into new territories. But it was also a process that moulded new character traits in the individual – inventiveness, materialism, wastefulness, and love of mobility – and created a new type of society marked by anti-intellectualism, a taste for abundance, opposition to conservation, an assumption that political and social equality were available to all, and a strong belief that class distinctions were irrelevant. These characteristics, many of which remain vital in the American way of life, have affected our view of the settlement era in the Canadian west. We assume, for example, that the Canadian frontier was marked by social equality. We believe, too, that the free homestead ensured a more or less equal start for everyone in the economic sweepstakes of the new society. And we accept that the rewards were earned by the diligent.

What is the truth of such generalizations? The establishment of prairie rural society and the operation of settlement policy have not yet been examined in detail by modern scholarship. We do not know, for example, whether the settler's choice of land determined whether he would succeed as a homesteader. We cannot yet generalize about settlers' fortunes on the basis of such factors as ethnic group or initial capital investment. However, some recent research suggests several lines of investigation. Proximity to friends, easy access to a railway shipping point, and quality of land, including soil quality and type of vegetation cover, were crucial factors in the initial selection of land. But whether they affected the rate of success is doubtful. The rate of attrition – the failure of the homesteader to 'prove up' and thus obtain a patent for his quarter-section – was extraordinary. Chester Martin long ago calculated that four in ten prairie homestead applications were never fulfilled. Though admittedly rough, his statistics indicated a rate of failure of 20 per cent in Manitoba (1870–1905), 57 per cent in Saskatchewan (1911–31), and 45 per cent in Alberta (1905–30). This led him to note in his ironic fashion that 'in some respects "free" homesteads have been costly beyond computation.'[17] V.C. Fowke, who was closer to the homestead in temperament as well as personal experience, suggested that the discrepancy between entries for homesteads and the achievement of patent 'is so pronounced as to indicate a wastefulness little less than shocking.'[18] D.M. Loveridge's careful analysis of the rural municipality of Sifton in Manitoba, which included an examination of sales contracts as well as homestead entries, demonstrated that 18.2 per cent of all disposals of Dominion Lands – homesteads and sales – ended in cancellation and thus was very close to Martin's tally for the entire province of Manitoba.[19]

Explanation of these high failure rates has been slow to accumulate. Martin's pioneering study suggested that European immigrants were more successful in the homesteading process than were

Anglo-Saxons, a result he attributed to their group solidarity. A recent study of two districts near the Qu'Appelle valley suggests that he was partly correct. On the rocky inferior soils and wooded marshy terrain of the Neudorf area, the settler's attrition rate was 28 per cent, (25 cancelled homestead applications of 89), whereas on the first-class soil and easily cultivated plains of the Abernethy area, it was 59 per cent. The explanation of the differences lies not in the land quality, but in the nature of the settler and the time of settlement. Abernethy was first settled in the tough years of the early and mid-1880s, Neudorf in the early 1890s. The predominantly German community around Neudorf comprised older men who could not afford to fail and who could rely on their families and neighbours to pull them through a difficult time; the largely British or British-Canadian community of Abernethy had a much higher proportion of young bachelors who did not have to prove up in order to ensure family survival and who, because they spoke the language of the continent and were not constrained by home ties, were free to try again elsewhere.[20] But failure is not an easy matter. That four of every ten prospective landowners did not secure their homestead quarter-section would seem to be an indictment of policy and a measure of environmental unsuitability rather than an index to individual character weaknesses.

The capital costs of establishing a farm ranged from almost nil, for the very poor, to many thousands of dollars for the well-heeled immigrant. John Burton arrived from Bruce County in Ontario with $65 in his purse and established a prosperous farm near Abernethy. Samuel Copithorn was similarly successful, though he was fortunate enough to start with $200. A Ukrainian colony near Batoche contained fifty families, whose original capital investment ranged from $40 to $1,000 each. But the minimum initial investment could not be reduced by very much. Whether by dint of hard work in northern logging operations, western mines, railway construction sites, or itinerant harvesting crews, whether by virtue of neighbourly assistance or family contributions, each homestead unit would require a capital outlay of several thousand dollars in the period of proving up (three to eight years, generally speaking).

Was this a frontier of opportunity? For the first-generation pioneers who were able to survive and prove up the answer was yes. The work was hard, the neighbours distant, and the returns few, but their hopes were high and their willingness to endure present hardship in the expectation of future reward was undeniable. For those who lived on the edge of poverty for a few years, perhaps even several decades, and then failed, however, the experience was cruel. They had had dreams, too, but had not found the key to open the riches of this last frontier. For the prairie west was 'next-year country' not just in the dreams of better crops and better prices but also in the pioneers' determination that their children should not be caught in the cycle of poverty that had held back countless generations of their forbears. This is why education was so critically important in prairie society and why reform politics and co-operative economics were as much a part of prairie life as the post office box and the mail order catalogue: utopian it may have been, as the dean of prairie historians, W.L. Morton, once suggested, but those millions of advertisements for Canada's free lands had inspired in western settlers, as in immigrants to America before them, dreams of independence and of success – perhaps even greatness – for their children.

One interesting aspect of the pioneer myth was the suggestion that there were no significant social distinctions or gradations on the prairie frontier. 'We were all just folks together,' the refrain goes, and to make any suggestion to the contrary was to behave like a 'knocker' in a society of boosters. The issue has not yet received much attention in historical research, but the few pieces of available evidence suggest a picture different from that painted by the nostalgia of pioneers.

No one would deny that the early days of settlement in any district were marked by co-operation among all types of citizens and by a considerable degree of social cohesion. But this era was short-lived, perhaps five or ten years at the very most, and was followed by twenty to forty years of relative stability. Was this later period similarly noteworthy for co-operation, social equality, and community cohesion? Was it a seamless generation, unchanging in social characteristics? I believe that the answer to both questions is no.

A social history of prairie agriculture between 1880 and 1930 might be divided into three eras. The first, as we have seen, was the day of the pioneer and of Ralph Connor's novels, when simple log shacks and soddies, like equality of social status, were the rule. The second era, beginning around the turn of the century, was the period when social relationships were being confirmed but still offered a degree of flexibility. This era, which we could associate with the reform spirit and optimism of Nellie McClung, was a time when the patterns of land and wealth distribution became clear and when a version of English or Australian class relations seemed to be developing. The First World War can be seen as the next watershed. The demand for food production put great pressure on prairie farmers, hastened an increase in farm size, encouraged the adoption of new farm technology, and broke down the developing patterns of rural class relations, establishing instead a system much closer to the American Midwestern model. This was a time of testing for agriculture when, as the novels of Robert Stead suggested, the agrarian myth could no longer be accepted as a prevailing truth. In addition to the delineation of three distinct eras in rural social history before 1930, we should emphasize that, from the turn of the century, there were social and economic distinctions within rural communities. Though these were not Marx's social classes, the very existence of a social hierarchy suggested that the prairie west did not offer the same opportunities to everyone.

An introduction to the history of rural life is provided by prairie fiction. There was a distinct change in perceptions of agriculture in pre- and post-war novels, and this transition, as seen for example in the writing of Nellie McClung and Robert Stead, reflected a change in the role and even the self-esteem of farmers. McClung, a leader of temperance and suffragist campaigns, was a popular writer in the years before the First World War. In one of her stories, the heroine, wife of a pioneer farmer, was invited to address a high-toned literary club in Ottawa. The sweet, unaffected, and unfashionably dressed farm woman conquered her listeners: 'Whatever the attitude of the audience was at first, they soon followed her with eager intent as she told them, in her easy way, simple stories of the people she knew so well, and so lovingly understood. There was no art in the telling, only a sweet naturalness and apparent honesty – the honesty of purpose that comes to people in lonely places ... Men and women country-born, who had forgotten the voices of their youth, heard them calling across the years.' The woman writer's farm husband was likened to 'good brown bread'; an eastern smoothie who attempted to lead her astray was a diet of 'popcorn and chocolate.'[21] These stereotypes for farm and city, west and east, were repeated many times in magazine articles and after-dinner speeches before 1914. But then, with the Great War and its aftermath, popular perceptions changed. In Canada, the new realities included a community that was more industrialized than ever before, more than ever plagued by French-English tensions, and as preoccupied by regional problems in the Maritimes as in the west. The era of farm supremacy was over. The agrarian myth was forgotten, and the new phenomenon was, as a Canadian critic observed in the early 1920s, 'The Cityward Bias of Literature.'[22]

In their critique of farm and small-town society, Canadians were part of an international trend in popular culture. In the United States, Sinclair Lewis mocked small-town Main Street society, and a contingent that included F. Scott Fitzgerald and Ernest Hemingway fled North America for the cultural sophistication of Paris and Madrid. In Britain, the Bloomsbury of the 1920s included Lytton Strachey, whose devastating portrait, *Eminent Victorians*, was published in 1918, and Virginia Woolf, who wished to remake the literary expressions and reconstruct the taste of a generation. The work of Canadian writers, with the exception of Morley Callaghan, one of the expatriates in Paris, was not at the forefront of international literature in the 1920s, but it often acknowledged the issues that the international giants raised. Prairie writers, in particular, were attracted to the themes of lost innocence and damnable materialism that had assumed a new prominence. The disillusioned pacifist Frances Marion Beynon, the struggling lecturer Douglas Durkin, and Durkin's protégé and eventual consort, Martha Ostenso, all wrote novels of importance that provided local expressions of these issues – and all eventually left Winnipeg for New York. But the best-known prairie novelist of the era was Robert Stead. In his work, one sees most clearly the crisis of farm society in the post-war decade.

Robert J.C. Stead grew up in Manitoba and edited small-town newspapers before becoming a publicist in Calgary in 1911. He wrote several volumes of poetry of the Robert Service type and between 1912 and 1926 wrote seven novels that were well received in the west; the best sold as many as 70,000 copies, and none sold fewer than 5,000, respectable totals by any measure. They presented a prairie version of the quest theme, in which the pioneer's dream of independence was ruined by his monomaniacal concentration on the future at the expense of the present, and a prairie version of 'innocence vs sophistication' wherein the simple farm life was contrasted with the arts and skills of urban society. If McClung's pre-war work, like that of Ralph Connor, was distinguished by an uncritical faith in the frontier, Stead's novels were remarkable for their emphasis on the problems of the farm. In five of his seven prairie novels, Stead employed eastern-Canadian, British, or simply 'urban' ideals and standards to suggest that the rural west required a 'spiritual leaven' – a generous infusion of 'the arts' – if it were to become a vital community. He noted the 'peculiarity of the agriculturist that, among all professions, he holds his own in the worst repute.'[23] His visionary hero in *Dennison Grant* wished 'to break up the rectangular survey of the West for something with humanizing possibilities ... which will permit of settlement in groups – villages if you like – where I shall install all the modern conveniences of the city – including movie shows.'[24] In Stead, the perceptions of city and farm had undergone a crucial change. The city was now exciting, a source of art and creativity. The countryside was less attractive because its deadening, work-dominated routine led to boredom and stultification. The contrast was central to prairie rural history in the settlement era.

The change in public perception was not the only significant transition in prairie agriculture after 1900. Even more important, in the long run, were the changes in the social and economic structure of the farm community. The pioneer days had been the era of bachelors and young families; the early farms had been closer to subsistence operations that to export-oriented grain producers; the early technology had been almost biblical in nature: farmers relied on oxen for power and seeded by hand (broadcasting), and, despite the presence of nineteenth-century inventions such as the binder and threshing machine, their harvest still was dependent on large crews and considerable manual labour; finally, social institutions were informal and likely to consist of house parties, overnight dances, and Friday night gatherings at the post office or café. Within a brief period, certainly by the early years of the twentieth century, the frontier had given way to a settled society. Children were older and required advanced education or, more perplexing, entry into farming; the early problems of farm production had been addressed and now the farmers were concerned about transportation and grain handling and the world market; modern farm machinery was available to the more prosperous settler and soon steam engines and gasoline tractors were being tested in prairie fields; farm labour requirements increased, too, and many farms relied not only on huge crews at threshing time but on one or two hired hands in the growing season; regular meetings of clubs and associations replaced the informal social calendar and, predictably, contributed to the development of district hierarchies as people became executive material or membership material or not worthy of an invitation; the new codes were still flexible, and prairie citizens were still sufficiently close to the frontier to look on others as potential equals, but the rules of society were now hardening into convention.

The life of W.R. Motherwell, farm leader and politician, illustrates this transition. Motherwell arrived in the Abernethy area just north of the Qu'Appelle valley in 1882 as a twenty-two-year-old graduate of the Ontario Agricultural College. He built a modest three-room log house and, a year later, brought his new bride to his homestead. Despite the tragic death of their first two children in infancy, the pioneers worked steadily over the next two decades and by the early years of the new century were leaders of the district. Their large farm and handsome horses and vehicles – both a two-seater buggy and a four-seater surrey – were well-known. But even better-known was their new house, constructed in 1897 of field stone selected during annual searches by Motherwell himself. Its size and design made it closer to a country home on an English estate than to a prairie farmhouse. Its interior was based on the concept of two communities, the family and the servants, as was common in the Victorian middle class and, by the skilful use of hallways, doorways, and decorative treatment, ensured that the servants, their utilitarian functions such as cooking, and their living quarters would be segregated from the family quarters and the public or 'ceremonial' areas of the building. The death of Mrs Motherwell in 1905 disrupted W.R.'s family life, but his elevation to the Saskatchewan cabinet in the same year required him to resume his public career. He remarried in 1908 and continued to be a community leader. His family pew was occupied every Sunday that he was at home, his daughter was sent to Germany for a year of study, and his son, Talmage, who had attended a university agriculture course, was given two quarter-sections and written out of his will when he married – apparently beneath the family's station – in 1913. Motherwell was a bastion of the new society and, with other community leaders, a defender of its 'respectable' values.[25]

The settled society of the post-1900 prairie west was, as the Motherwell example suggests, imbued with the atmosphere of Victorian England and Ontario. The co-operative ethos of the frontier had been succeeded by an individualism that would have done business leaders proud. And the egalitarianism of the early years had been replaced by an increasingly firm stratification. The prairie west did not start out as an essentially 'classless' community, as S.M. Lipset, the sociologist, once suggested, but rather was clearly divided into strata that might in time become rigid social classes.[26] In the top level of this hierarchy were families like the Motherwells, whose English-Canadian background, material wealth, and personal capacities ensured that they would set the tone of local society. These families possessed large farms and considerable material wealth; they were sustained by the labour of a number of male and female 'hired hands.' The next level of the hierarchy was occupied by the respectable families whose farms approximated the district average in size and who might employ one or two labourers during the growing season. A variety of factors might distinguish the third level. The poorer families on farms of marginal size could rarely afford to hire help and, indeed, would themselves enter the labour market to make ends meet. But income was only one definition of membership in this category. Ethnicity was also an important criterion because citizens of south-eastern European origin and of certain other groups could rarely aspire, in these pre-war years, to higher social standing. And if a member of a family was a slovenly farmer, a drunkard, or in some other way had seriously offended against the rules of respectability, that would affect the standing of all the family members. Finally, those citizens who possessed no property – the maids and hired hands – also belonged in this category. They worked very long hours for very low pay and, especially in the case of the hired women, were often excluded from the life of 'the family.' Such generalizations about rural social structure are rough approximations, of course, but they do suggest that in the farm community, as in prairie cities, there was a hierarchy that influenced the development of community standards and the locus of political power.

It should be possible to be more precise about the distribution of wealth in farm districts, but prairie scholarship has not yet addressed this issue in detail. A survey conducted in southeastern Saskatchewan in the early 1930s revealed that the upper 15 per cent of farmers possessed 676 acres, on average, and a net worth of $37,580, for a total of about 30 per cent of farm wealth in the district. The bottom

33 per cent of farmers possessed an average of less than 300 acres, and a net worth of $7,579, for a total of about 18 per cent of district farm wealth. Perhaps the most significant finding of the survey was its discovery that net worth in the 1930s seemed to depend on net worth at the start of the farmers' careers: those who commenced farming with about $7,000 possessed almost exactly that amount thirty years later; those who commenced farming with $17–18,000 had doubled their net worth during the first generation.[27] This extraordinary conclusion was supported by an analysis of landholding in Manitoba's Rural Municipality of Sifton. There, D.A. Loveridge concluded, the 632 farmers' initial land acquisitions could determine their fate: 'Of those [521] who took only one or two quarters in 1881–1920, 25.7% still held land in 1930; of those [81] taking either three or four quarters, 44.4%; and of those [30] taking from five to nine, 62.5% survived. Of the people who acquired ten or more quarter-sections, fully 83.3% still held land … [in 1930].' And, to reinforce this perception that some of the rich were indeed getting richer, 60 per cent of the 190 surviving 'family groups' (original settlers and their heirs) had increased their original holdings.[28] Loveridge's study, like that of southeastern Saskatchewan, indicated significant gradations in the distribution of wealth in the rural west.

Another measure of success on the farm was the decision of the individual or family to stay on the homestead after the patent had been earned. The study of Sifton municipality demonstrated that the original settlers and their descendants still owned 60 per cent of the land in the area in 1930, but it also concluded that these individuals constituted only 30 per cent (190 of 632) of the people who had acquired land in the first generation of settlement. Thus, 18 per cent of the early arrivals in Sifton failed to complete land acquisitions and another 61 per cent did not remain on the land in this area; only one in four of the original families survived to form the bulwark of this one rural community. Lyle Dick's analysis was even more enlightening because it demonstrated that in the densely settled yet difficult land of the community around Neudorf the Germans left very soon after they had proved up. Within five years, 30 per cent of the successful homesteaders moved on and another 20 per cent left in the next five years: thus, one in every two settlers was gone within the decade. Around the British-Canadian community of Abernethy, however, persistence was twice as likely: only 30 per cent had left the patented homestead after ten years, and even after twenty years 40 per cent of the residents – twice as many as in the Neudorf district – remained in the original district. The Germans, in other words, stayed only long enough to establish some equity before they sold out and moved to more attractive lands or occupations. If these studies are representative, rural mobility in the prairie west was much greater than scholars have ever imagined.[29]

An old prairie joke tells the story of three winners of a million-dollar lottery: the conservatively dressed banker explained that he would invest his windfall in bonds and earn a secure return; the flamboyant salesperson announced that she would invest in mining stocks and multiply her fortune; and the slow-speaking farm couple explained carefully that they would just keep on farming until the money was all gone. Allowing for the usual hyperbole, was this a reasonable depiction of the homesteader's finances? Surveys conducted at the start of the 1930s, before the Great Depression had done its worst, suggest that is was not entirely accurate. Pioneer farmers reinvested a large portion of their total income in their farm businesses. As late as 1930, very few had substantial savings or investment outside the farm. They earned, on the average, about $600 per year, though the actual income ranged from a loss of $100 per year to gains of over $1,500 per year. Inevitably, those whose initial investment was low earned the least. The 1931 federal census reported that over one-third of all prairie farms were mortgaged, and a more detailed survey in the same year concluded that many farmers also were indebted to implement companies, banks, and stores. These debts mounted as the Depression deepened. Though averages are misleading, we might venture that the 'average' prairie farm family possessed total capital of $14,000 and debts of about $3,000 in 1930–1. Most of their wealth lay in their land, which in 1931 represented about two-thirds of the farm's net worth. The prairie farm family was land-rich and wage-poor. Its estate would be much larger than that of the urban labourer, but its daily fare, especially in the long hard months of winter, would be no more lavish than that of its city cousins.[30] We must remember that averages conceal the peaks and valleys: in the rural west, there were wealthy families with large holdings, struggling families that managed to get by on the 'typical' 300–400 acre farm, and poor or landless individuals who belonged on the lowest rung of society's ladder.

The crucial factor that prevented these strata from seeming like rigid determinants of an individual's fate was the rapid change in the structure of the farm economy after 1914. Many thousands of prairie farmers in the pre-war years had been, of necessity, part-time labourers. They sustained their homestead gamble – as the economists would say, their 'undercapitalized' business – by working on larger neighbouring farms as hired hands, by joining itinerant threshing crews, and by heading out for a road or rail construction site, logging camp, or mine town. As late as 1936, 75 per cent of the agricultural labour force in Alberta (100,000 people) relied on wage labour to supplement their farm incomes, but only 7 per cent (9,000 people) were year-round farm hands.[31] These marginal farmer-labourers often lost their homestead gamble. Even for the first generations of winners, the economic uncertainties associated with the boom times of farm production during the war, the agricultural depression of the early 1920s, and the renewed cycle of boom and bust in the following decade were sufficient to turn success into defeat. The introduction of such important technological innovations as the tractor, combine, and truck, all of which gained acceptance in the 1920s, also required significant alterations in the farm economy. By increasing the farmers' need for capital and multiplying the acreage that could be handled by the household labour unit, this new wave of mechanization undercut the demand for wage labourers in the rural economy. The completion of rail and road networks and sharp cuts in government works budgets in the 1930s similarly reduced off-farm employment opportunities for marginal farmers and their children. The prairie labour force in the 1920s and 1930s, far from being fixed or rigid in structure, was inherently unstable. If thousands did not leave their farms in this period, it was because they had no place to go, not because their lot was satisfactory. And if marginal farm couples and their children did not become members of a rural proletariat, it was because the size of the prairie farm grew larger, the demand for hired labour dropped, and the employment unit in the region became the household. A class of hired hands, or of labourers and servants, did not exist for any length of time in the rural prairie west, and consciousness of fixed class relations was not a crucial factor in rural political life before 1930.

Social distinctions were a part of rural communities in the Canadian west as they were in many other agricultural communities around the world. Had these distinctions endured for several generations, they would have influenced individual perceptions and political behavior. But because they changed so rapidly they were not perceived to be permanent barriers to self-improvement or significant indicators of family fortunes. The Victorian class lines evident in the architecture of W.R. Motherwell's house had been modified by 1920, and even that famous building reflected the new outlook; the system of halls and doorways was revised, several walls were removed to open the 'parlour' to the view of guests at the front door, the formal dining room became a family living area, and meals were henceforth served in a large 'winter kitchen.' Such alterations symbolized the replacement of a stern separation between the classes by the flexibility of North America's superficial egalitarianism. They also reflected a change in the labour market; large numbers of hired hands under the supervision of an estate manager might have been economic in some countries, but on the Canadian prairies a household could now handle a fairly large farm with the aid of the new technology.

All farmers, rich or poor, confronted a different circumstance after the First World War. They had once been in the van of economic progress, the admired pioneers of empire and nation; now they were perceived to be slow-witted, eternally bitching 'sons of the soil.' They had once possessed political influence; now they had to fight for every adjustment in national economic policy. Farmers, whatever their social status, were beginning to see themselves as a distinct 'class' in the 1920s.

Rural society included towns and villages as well as farms. Were the residents of these centres to be included with farm families as part of the rural west? Or were they part of the urban society? It was a moot point and one upon which there was no consensus. Perhaps we might follow a recent student of the rural west, Paul Voisey, and agree that 'villages' with less than 1,000 people identified closely with the surrounding farm areas and that larger towns assumed airs of self-importance and independence. For purposes of discussion, the towns and villages of the prairie west can be considered part of a developing rural society in which comparable themes such as site selection and class distinction may be discerned.

A hierarchy of towns developed between 1870 and 1930. At the top were the five largest cities of the prairies, where universities and the largest health care institutions and government services were located. On the second tier, ten cities such as Medicine Hat, Moose Jaw, and Brandon, all between 5,000 and 20,000 in population, served as supply centres for subregions that might stretch for fifty miles in each direction. On the third level were the sixty towns with populations between 1,000 and 5,000. Larger than the local village, smaller than the true cities, these centres – Dauphin, Estevan, Melville, Hanna, Red Deer – offered forty to seventy businesses, a wider selection of clothing and furniture, professional services such as lawyers and doctors, and an opportunity to see a motion picture and were perhaps the nearest convenient centre in which an ambitious student could complete the senior grades in high school. The fourth level included about 1,000 villages with populations between 50 and 500. Offering as few as eight or as many as thirty-odd businesses, these towns were the mainstay of prairie farm society because they provided the grocery, mail, automobile, farm implement, hardware, and lumber services – not to mention hotel, café, community hall, and rink – that might be used on a weekly basis by the residents of the surrounding rural districts. And the fifth level included a large number of hamlets, perhaps 1,300–1,400 in the late 1920s, with fewer than 50 residents and fewer than six businesses. Many of these centres were little more than a signpost and a general store or garage at a crossroads, and many more consisted of a single elevator at the railway track. They offered only the services that could not be obtained easily without an extra six or ten-mile journey in a slow buggy or an uncertain farm truck. About 2,500 trade centres existed to serve the grain economy by the 1920s; the far-flung and complex network was intended to offer the essential retail services and to meet the social requirements of a new community but was basically designed to facilitate the production and transportation of grains.[32]

The choice of the precise site for each town was a matter of much speculation because fortunes could be won and lost in the blink of a negotiator's eye. Brandon was an example of how the game was played. Anyone in Manitoba who cared about land sales would have known that the transcontinental railway required a divisional point in the western part of the province and could have measured the hundred-odd miles to the potential sites along the wide sloping valley of the Assiniboine River. From there, it was a simple enough matter to squat on a likely quarter-section, put up a shack, plough a few token acres, and hope that the CPR would come knocking on one's door with an offer of cash. But at the ideal location, on the east bank of the river, the speculators found Dugald McVicar, his wife and his brother John from Perth, Ontario, who had been living in a sod house for two years while they tried their hand at farming. In anticipation of the railway decision, ambitious tradesmen began to erect a general store, a sawmill, and a canvas hotel at the river side, on the McVicar quarter, meanwhile filling the McVicars with stories of instant wealth. And thus, when the CPR arrived, McVicar asked for more money – reports on his price range from $40,000 to $80,000 – than the company was prepared to offer. With the alleged retort 'I'll be dammed if a town of any kind is ever built here,' the CPR official moved two miles west, across the river, and purchased the land of another, more amiable speculator, for one-tenth or even one-twentieth of McVicar's request. As a measure of the value of this type of adventure, another group of speculators who subdivided the quarter-section adjoining the CPR station and town site reportedly earned $200,000 on the subsequent land sales. Within three months of the CPR decision on location, the Brandon site was a sea of billowing canvas tents; the noise of hammers and steamer whistles combined with the jangling of horse harness and the rumbling of wagons to suggest prosperity for all who shared in this adventure. The McVicars eventually sold their small farm for $1,500.[33]

This same kind of jockeying accompanied the selection of many town sites. In the case of Minnedosa, three and perhaps four potential rail crossing points on the Little Saskatchewan River were promoted by competing groups of speculators. The group that was able to incorporate a town and offer a large bonus – a grant of $30,000, land for the right of way, tax exemption for twenty years, and a free gift of 1,000 town lots – won the railway station and a promise that no station would be constructed for six miles in either direction. In the case of the town of De Winton, the CPR head office apparently discovered that its own agent, General Rosser, owned the entire town site and planned to make a tidy sum from sales to the growing number of merchants and residents who were congregating around the station. Rather than permit this unofficial profiteering to continue, the CPR moved the station under cover of darkness to a temporary location, and only after a month of very difficult negotiations did it buy the present site of Carberry from a settler for $32,000. (That settler, who had bought the land for $500 in scrip, was entirely satisfied; Rosser lost his job. Forever true to the colours of confidence men, Rosser then sold the De Winton site to another speculator.) Another common experience was that of the town of Millford

on the Souris River, which contained a dozen commercial establishments and many houses when its residents gave up hope of obtain-
ing rail service and moved their entire settlement – houses, stores,
hotels, and all – to the railhead at Glenboro. As these citizens had
demonstrated, the railway could make or break a town site on the
prairies.[34]

The boom era for a small town was brief and turbulent. Carmangay, Alberta, was rushed into existence in 1909 on the site where a
branch rail line in the Calgary-Lethbridge area crossed the Little
Bow River. Forty buildings rose within two weeks of the town site
sale, a railway gang of 200 men demanded food and drink, dozens
of other labourers worked on the construction sites in town, and
soon building lots were trading, sight unseen, in New England,
Britain, and across Canada. By 1914, 60 per cent of the 1,400-odd
town lots were held by Ontario investors and only 8 per cent by
residents of Carmangay itself. Population turnover was very high in
the early years. Of 125 businessmen resident in the six villages along
this branch line in 1914, 74 per cent were replaced by newcomers by
1920. The village, like so many others, never lived up to the dreams
of the speculators. Taxes went unpaid on town lots for years, and by
the 1920s Carmangay's fate as a village of 300 souls was sealed. By
the 1970s, it had shrunk still further, but it had not disappeared. As
a centre for sports and social gatherings and a place of residence for
district farmers, it had become 'more like the villages that characterized rural society throughout much of the world.'[35]

One critic of prairie architecture has suggested that the railway was
the determining feature of a town's character. Main Street ran either
at right angles to or parallel with the track and the elevators. The
street pattern, usually a grid, was in keeping with this spirit of
utility and efficiency. Neither natural nor architectural advantages,
whether streams, churches, memorials, or the elevators themselves,
were singled out to provide a focus for local architecture. The
abnormally wide main street, often sixty to eighty feet from boardwalk to boardwalk, was created to serve horse and wagon in muddy
weather rather than human beings who had to endure the storms of
winter. The chief architectural feature of Main Street was the 'false
front,' square slabs of frame, masonry, or even imported pre-cast
metal, that concealed the steeply pitched roofs behind and were
intended to give an air of solidity and permanence. E.A. McCourt,

the prairie novelist, described the small towns as 'alien eruptions on the face of nature'; a harsher critic said that this kind of town was a 'mechanical achievement,' the product of 'agricultural fundamental-ism,' and suggested that its purely functional origins resulted in the establishment of a 'bleak and depressing environment.' But hind-sight is no guide to what filled the eyes of the town's founders. As they regarded the muddy streets, unpainted lumber store fronts, and raw plank sidewalks, they saw a future of prosperity and stability.[36]

Towns existed to serve the farmer but in most cases acquired their own identity as the years passed. They would begin with an eleva-tor, a post office, and a number of stores; then a lumber yard would be added, a hotel or boarding-house, a blacksmith's shop, a grain buyer, and perhaps a grist or even a roller mill. As the population grew, the local citizens were quick to establish schools, churches, and, in many cases, a weekly newspaper. These institutions were outgrowths of the needs of the rural hinterland, but were also and even primarily products of the town itself. Within a few years, a decade at most, the substantial towns – those with a population of 1,000 or more – had an existence that seemed only partly dependent on the farmer. Struggles with competing centres over the trading district did continue, and each merchant was presumably careful to treat his customers well, but the town as institution – its council, its teams, its clubs, and its schools – was increasingly divorced from all but the closest of the surrounding farmers. The result was a new layer of rural society, the town society, with its own secrets, classes, and determinants of status.

Despite regular disclaimers by prairie residents and the absence of scholarly work on the topic, social divisions were definitely a part of town life. The 'lower orders' were the hired servants, the casual labourers, the unskilled railway maintenance men, and the like. They were transitory figures on the local scene – the more suspect for their impermanence – and they lived in rented rooms or the hotel. The best of the lower orders were those who held similarly undistinguished jobs but had permanent residences, often a two- or three-room house, and were clearly rooted in the community as section foreman, bookkeeper, or desk clerk. These people worked ten to twelve hours a day, six days a week, and earned between $200 and $400 a year. They rarely figured as executives of local societies, and they travelled through life without leaving a mark on the historical record except as an address in the trade directory.

The people with status were merchants and professionals, many of whom would be only slightly above the lower orders in wealth but all of whom could claim independent status. The poorest among them might own a barber shop or a small smithy and have a net worth of between $500 and $3,000. The dozen wealthiest men might have businesses worth $5–10,000 in the 1880s, double that sum by 1910, and triple by 1930. These were the individuals who dominated the town council, served on the executives of the clubs and associations, and thus set the tone of the 'better class.' Any one of their number might build a great brick mansion on the edge of town, purchase a grand piano, take a holiday in 'the East,' or send his children to school in Winnipeg, Regina, or Calgary. Between the lower orders and the wealthiest business and professional people were the rest of the 'better class' – teachers, clergymen, policemen, and other civil servants – who upheld the values of the status quo. Women shared the status of their husbands or, if they were unmarried, took their status from their family, job, or place of residence. They were not active in public life except in the exclusively female associations within the churches.

The typical town existed as an outpost of British-Canadian civilization. It was patriotic, as the celebrations of Queen Victoria's birthday attested; it upheld the virtues of order and respectability, as the lessons in the church and school made plain; and it accepted the dictates of the national and international economy. In Minnedosa, in the late 1880s, then a town of 600, all of the agricultural implement dealers (6), mortgage and loan companies (5), insurance companies (8), and real estate companies (3) were local franchises of provincial, national, or international operations. It was a bastion of empire, in economic and cultural terms.[37]

Relations between farm and country town were never quite as easy as cheerful recollection would have it. Villagers often assumed the role of propagandists, politicians, and social convenors in prairie society. But with the passage of time and the development of rural social networks, which were usually based on the school as site for Christmas concert, church service, and summer picnic, farm-dwellers developed an alternate social and political system that included only those of like minds and occupations. Then, too, as the town developed, its leaders were preoccupied with 'larger' matters than merely serving the old clientele: they might be campaigning for roads to new hinterlands, for improved rail service to the 'city,' and for telephone or electricity networks or cement sidewalks within the town itself. That the town's most pressing need, in the view of farm families, was a comfortable room where rural visitors might rest, wash, use a toilet, and change diapers could thus be overlooked by the civic leaders.

Beneath the superficial irritants in town-country relations lay a more serious issue: the eternal mistrust between merchant and consumer. Prairie folk tales and literature, like those of other rural societies, were once replete with stories about fast-talking city salesmen and slow-witted country men and women. The jokes simply reflected a particular version of reality. After the first era of community-building, in which town and farm worked together, the two worlds achieved a kind of stability and came to recognize their differences. And as the balance of international cultural approval shifted from wilderness and nature to civilization and city, the prairie townsfolk, no matter how small their 'urban' centre, gained an opportunity to put on airs in front of their country cousins. Whether because they talked faster, knew a more recent slang, or saw more movies, the townsfolk could, if they wished, assume a superior stance. And, of course, they set the prices for consumer goods. In many communities where goodwill dissolved the irritants, the resultant social tensions were so slight as to be irrelevant. But they sometimes got out of hand. Credit policy and prices in the local stores, problems with the elevator agent, disputes about mail order houses such as Eaton's, and eternal debates about 'producers' (the farmer) and 'parasites' (the 'middleman' or merchant) could divide farm folk from townsfolk. In the area around Hanna, Alberta, these sentiments erupted in complaints in the years after the First World War. Political organizations were split by the move of the United Farmers of Alberta into politics. Community relations were likewise made difficult by the UFA candidate's outburst, 'We don't want the support of the Town of Hanna.'[38] The development of farmer-run producers' and consumers' co-operatives in the next decade also may have alienated the two groups. But town-country relations, like relations between any two communities or individuals, were not fixed for all time by such conflicts. In Hanna, the common problems of the Depression and the widespread interest in co-operatives brought the farmers and townspeople together again. In southwest Manitoba, where the era of mistrust was more likely to have occurred earlier, the 1920s saw the re-establishment of a common cause in the face of the growing spectre of metropolitan hegemony over rural culture. Modern views in magazines, schools, and even in the school curriculum seemed to conspire against rural life and to depict farm and village folk alike as unfashionable or out of touch. But the automobile, the radio, and the telephone worked to counteract the isolation and the loneliness of rural life, to bring farm and town closer together, and to re-establish bonds of friendship between them.[39]

The business of the prairies during the half-century after 1880 was, first and foremost, agriculture. Crop prospects, the weather, and wheat prices were part of daily conversation because they affected the fate of the region. In these years, a complex system for raising, handling, transporting, and marketing grain was built on the foundations provided by village and farm residents. And when farmers believed the system to be unfair or inefficient, they united in protest. As a result, discussion of economic issues became, willy-nilly, partisan political debate. King Wheat, as he was known, inspired intense disagreements among his subjects.

Wheat became an important international commodity in the nineteenth century because bread became a food staple in the industrial nations of the North Atlantic world. As the decades passed, Europe's increasing preference in bread was baked from a snow white dough, high in gluten (protein), which was especially characteristic of hard spring wheat raised on the western plains of North America. The world's largest market for wheat was England, which had a food deficit that increased sharply during the century while its rapidly growing population moved into urban centres and concentrated on industrial and commercial activities. By 1900, British farmers could supply domestic requirements for only two months of every twelve, and the docks at Liverpool, Hull, and London were busy in every season unloading the tons of grain – 5 million tons in 1914 alone – purchased in Argentina, Australia, India, Russia, the United States, and, as the prairie west was developed, Canada. The 'second industrial revolution' spread across Europe in the nineteenth century, and the new industrial giants such as Belgium and Germany, with their new enterprises associated with steel, chemicals, and electricity, also increased their imports of food products. Henceforth, it was plain, the New World would feed the Old.[40]

Called into being by these changing European circumstances, the Canadian agricultural frontier experienced eras of rapid expansion and sudden contraction just as did the European economies. During the 1880s and 1890s, the largest proportion of settlers established farms in the Manitoba park belt where brown soils and a growing-season precipitation of over fifteen inches promised crop conditions closer to those of Ontario or the midwestern United States. However, the development of two significant movements of protest, in 1883–5 and again in 1892–6, suggested that these pioneer farmers faced considerable difficulty in making ends meet. The next era of prairie agricultural settlement might be defined as extending from the point when immigration increased, around 1897, to the occupation of much of the best semi-arid territory, around 1907–8. The area that was filled in during this decade was the arc of semi-arid land lying between the parkbelt and the driest portion of Palliser's Triangle. Too often this subregion is regarded as part of the driest area of the western interior, but, as V.C. Fowke has emphasized, its dark brown soils and higher precipitation offered greater hope to prospective homesteaders. This decade of settlement can be associated, too, with the rapid expansion of the prairie rail system, especially in southern and central Saskatchewan, and the completion of a relatively efficient grain-handling system.

The next phase in prairie agricultural history, the decade after 1908, was marked by a great error in Canadian domestic policy. In throwing open to settlement the relatively dry regions of southwest Saskatchewan and southeast Alberta – the drainage basin of the South Saskatchewan River – where the light brown soils indicated a historic absence of vegetation, the Canadian government was taking a great risk. Settlers in this district suffered the painful consequences of the government's excessive optimism when several thousand of these farms were abandoned during the lengthy drought after 1917. Aside from the development of Palliser's Triangle, the decade 1908–18 was noteworthy for rural prosperity. During the First World War, when British demand for Canadian wheat was high and world wheat prices rose sharply, prairie farmers pressed all available land into cultivation and went into debt to expand their farms even more. Wheat production increased tremendously, and, some would argue, the fatal prairie habit of dependence on a single export commodity was established. Another misfortune was the inability of the two new transcontinental rail systems to weather the economic fluctuations. Both collapsed during the war and were amalgamated into a government-owned Canadian National Railways system.

With the passing of the boom associated with high wartime wheat prices and increases in cultivated acreage, prairie farmers experienced very hard times. From 1919 to 1924, near-drought conditions existed in the southern prairies, and the consequent drop in production, when combined with a price collapse in world grain markets, ended the brave experiment of many homesteaders. But the last half of the 1920s brought renewed prosperity and optimism. Immigration resumed, and, especially along the northern fringe of the prairies and in the Peace River district of northern Alberta, boom times returned. Railway construction again provided off-farm employment, and world markets offered high returns for wheat exports. By 1929, when the rains failed and world markets again were glutted, prairie farmers could look on their problems with a degree of patience because they had grown accustomed to the instability of their occupation. They had reached a kind of plateau in the economic history of their region. In the preceding half-century, but chiefly within the last thirty years, they had increased the area of improved land from 6 million acres in 1901 and 34 million in 1916 to about 60 million acres. Wheat production in the same period had also attained a plateau and now ranged from an annual total of nearly 300 to above 500 million bushels. Canada's wheat exports occupied 40 per cent of the world export market in the late 1920s and provided breads, pastas, crêpes, and pancakes for tables in the United Kingdom and continental Europe in about equal proportions. The 'wheat economy,' as it was known, including numerous grading and marketing institutions, was firmly established by 1929.[41]

At the base of this economic pyramid were the farmers. Their yearly cycle of labour began in the early spring, when they cleaned grain in fanning mills to ensure that the seed would be free of weeds and other impurities and 'pickled' it in copper sulphate or formaldehyde to make it smut-resistant. When the fields were dry enough, farmers prepared for seeding by harrowing the soil – that is, by having the horses pull an iron-toothed, rake-like implement across the surface. As soon as possible, the farmers were walking behind or riding on drill-seeders pulled by teams of horses. These implements poured a fine stream of grain into furrows of soil that collapsed to cover the kernels. Later, the fields were harrowed again to ensure that the seed was well covered. Seeding activities lasted about two months, from mid-April to mid-June, and required long hours behind the horses, but speed was essential if the grain was to mature before the first fall frosts.

The next month, from mid-June to mid-July, farmers devoted to cultivation of summer fallow and additional soil-breaking or tree-clearing as well as odd jobs such as the repair of grain bins and work around the home buildings and garden. Summerfallow, the cultivation of idle fields, was used to preserve moisture, to kill weeds, and to prepare the soil for the next year's crop. The practice might seem unusual because it entailed the loss of productive capacity and the expenditure of labour equivalent to that of seeding, but it was perceived to be essential in the semi-arid parts of the prairies, where the hazards of variable precipitation might be offset by 'storing' one year's moisture for next year's crop. Recent research suggests that in most of the prairie west summerfallow was rarely 'economic' – that is, the yield of two seasons on previously cropped land would usually have been greater than the enhanced yield of the crop sown on summer fallow. But it was widely employed because, despite the forgone income implied by reduced crop acreage, the wide variations in annual return were reduced and the risk of total crop failure was much lower. Summerfallow, in short, was a reasonable response to the uncertainty of prairie crop conditions.[42]

The last weeks of July were occupied by haying, a hot and miserable job, and by preparing the farm for the big event of the year, harvest. Women put in hundreds of hours preserving pickles, sauerkraut, and berries, filling stone crocks with onions, corn, and cabbage, baking extra butter tarts, carrot loaves, and date squares, while the men readied the machinery, the spare parts, and the animals for the burst of activity on which their way of life depended. In early August, the binder was pulled into the fields to cut the grain and tie it into bundles. Two or three men followed on foot, thrusting eight or ten sheaves firmly into the soil, heads up, in a circular formation that produced a pyramid or 'stook,' where the grain could dry and ripen and be a little safer from the perils of the weather until the threshing commenced. When the threshing crew arrived, sometimes early, sometimes late in the fall, the activity was intense. From twelve to over twenty men descended on the farm, set up the threshing machine – which separated the grain from straw and chaff – and prepared living quarters that ranged from portable bunk-houses to spare granaries. An engineer ran the machine, a tank man hauled water for the steam engine (these were replaced by gasoline engines around the First World War), two pitchers threw sheaves into the separator, a half-dozen teamsters hauled the bundles from the stooked fields, and another two or three teamsters hauled the threshed grain to granaries. Other men with pitchforks loaded bundles in the fields, and someone – imagine the pride of a younger boy or the mixed emotions of a teenage daughter – carried mid-morning and mid-afternoon snacks to the crews to ensure that a minimum of time was sacrificed in a day that regularly began at 6 a.m. and ended at 8 or 9 p.m., with an hour's break in between for lunch. Harvest was a time of great excitement, a time to meet some easterners (or even, in some years, Britons) who travelled west in 'harvest excursions,' a time to rekindle the camaraderie of the pioneer years while labouring at a common task, a time to sample the cuisine of a dozen households, to run the risk – as James Minifie noted – of drinking from many different wells and consequently enduring diarrhoea in a region bereft of toilet facilities: 'Squatting at night in a field of stubble qualifies for Dante's Purgatorio', Minifie claimed. Once the grain was in, it had to be shovelled onto the wagon or sleigh and hauled to market – a task that could occupy the entire winter if the rail line was some distance from the farm.[43]

The next phase of the farmers' business, grain marketing, was as critical to survival as the harvest itself. And it was subject to as many variables. The economic fluctuations of the farm business began in the field. Climatic changes such as drought, hail, or early frost and the problems caused by insect pests such as grasshoppers and by plant diseases such as stem rust could destroy an entire crop. The grade of the grain was another important variable. The plump hard red kernels of No. 1 Northern wheat commanded a premium in the marketplace, of course, but an invasion of weed seeds (adulteration), an early frost (discolouring), too much moisture (shrinkage), or crude harvesting equipment (chipping kernels) would result in a discount to No. 2 or 3 or lower. The price of wheat on the international market also varied, depending on crops around the world, the availability of shipping, and the demands and incomes of European consumers. Wheat prices ranged downward in the late nineteenth century, rose sharply to the end of the First World War, collapsed in the early 1920s, rose again later in the decade, and then plummeted in 1930–2. Farmers' costs, too, varied with changes in the price of such capital goods as seed, machinery, binder twine, and imported food products such as coffee and sugar. All of these factors – yield, grade, market price, and input costs – resulted in large and unpredictable fluctuations in the farmer's net income. These fluctuations were often made worse by the farmers' investment and debt management practices. Purchases of land and machinery naturally increased the vulnerability of farmers by tying them to fixed interest rates. One poor crop might jeopardize the entire enterprise, and several crop failures in succession would almost inevitably lead to liens and foreclosures. In the end, prairie farmers found themselves in a struggle for survival. Very quickly, they focused their reform efforts on the issues associated with the price they received for their grain.[44]

When they reached the railway shipping point, farmers had to choose between selling their wheat immediately to the elevator agent for the 'street' price, loading a rail car and then selling the carload for the 'track' price, or shipping the carload to an export terminal where it could be sold on the world market for the 'spot' price. The differential between these three prices, which could be considerable, was the cause of much discontent. Farmers who sold their wheat at the street price were taking a substantial discount, perhaps three or four cents a bushel below the track price, and yet over half of all western grain handled by country elevators in 1923 was purchased on this basis, and the proportion was undoubtedly higher in earlier years.[45] Farmers were forced to accept street prices because they could not fill a boxcar with a particular variety and grade of grain within the limited time permitted by the rail companies. They were, as a result, subject to the local elevator agent's terms regarding price, weight, grade, and dockage (reduction for impurities). When they saw the spread in price between street and track grain, farmers were angry. They knew that the large elevator companies were owned by a few Winnipeg-based firms that were said to belong to a cartel whose members fixed prices and eschewed competitive practices. As early as the 1890s, farmers blamed the absence of competition on the concentration of ownership of elevators, the collusion on price among these companies, and the actions of the CPR, which were intended to encourage the construction of more efficient standard elevators but which, farmers believed, also favoured the big elevator syndicates. Their agitation led to the first significant reforms of the grain handling system which were enshrined in the Manitoba Grain Act of 1900.[46]

The results of government intervention in the grain trade can be established by following a typical farmer's wagon. Normally, grain was delivered to a country elevator where it was weighed, graded, and then dumped into a hopper beneath the scales. Then it was elevated by conveyor cups and, depending upon type and grade, funnelled into one of many vertical storage bins, where it joined the product of other farms to await loading into a rail car. If farmers wished to avoid the elevator, they could use loading platforms next to the track – another product of their protest campaigns – but this inefficient method was useful chiefly as a competitive spur to the elevator companies.[47] At the elevator, farmer and elevator agent agreed on grade, weight, dockage, and shrinkage according to regulations established by the federal Board of Grain Commissioners. The railway companies allocated boxcars to elevators according to principles regulated by this same federal agency – yet another victory of the protestors – and by the late 1920s were hauling grain from 5,000-odd elevators to Pacific, Atlantic, and Great Lakes terminals. En route, the grain was officially inspected and weighed to ensure that it met the standards for each grade established by federal statutes and by milling and baking experts in federal laboratories. The inspectors in Winnipeg, for example, carefully probed the contents of selected rail cars to choose representative samples for an examination in which weight, colour, moisture content, and impurities were considered. The rail cars proceeded to the export terminals where inspection again occurred before the grain was transferred into ships or, in rarer instances, rail cars, for shipment to market. Terminal operations were subject to particularly close scrutiny because millions of bushels were mixed in these facilities to meet the average standards for each of the six grades of wheat and comparable grades of oats and barley. Most prairie grain before 1930 travelled by lake freighter from the Thunder Bay ports to terminals on the lower Great Lakes – on Georgian Bay and at Buffalo and Port Colborne – where, once again, trans-shipment to rail cars for the final voyage to the ocean took place.

The establishment of a government regulatory agency and of specific rules for the handling of grain was just the first fruit of farmers' political protest. Equally important, in the long run, was the development of a farmers' co-operative movement. The movement began in a number of local initiatives to set up farmer-owned elevators, of which sixty existed in 1910. The financial experience of these enterprises was generally unsatisfactory, but the education they provided benefited the entire farming community. A second experiment in farmers' co-operation, the Grain Growers' Grain Company, also operated in the terminal market. It was the brainchild of E.A. Partridge, 'the sage of Sintaluta,' who in 1904–5 had been delegated by his local of the Grain Growers' Association to study the Winnipeg grain market and had concluded that it was 'a combine' with 'a gambling hell thrown in.' After several years of struggle, the farmer-owned marketing operation that Partridge devised was able to compete effectively with the private traders – described by Partridge as 'three milling companies and five exporting firms' – and to establish an integrated system of terminals and country elevators.[48] The farmer-controlled co-operative elevator system expanded rapidly after 1910 with the assistance of the provincial governments. After the union of the Alberta line with the Grain Growers' Grain Company to form the United Grain Growers in 1917, that enterprise and its counterpart, the Saskatchewan Co-Operative Elevator Company, operated 650 local elevators at about half the shipping points on the prairies and controlled about one-third of the terminal capacity at Thunder Bay. 'By the early inter-war years,' V.C. Fowke concluded, 'the farmers' commercial grain companies had revolutionized the competitive position of the western grain grower in the markets in which he disposed of his cereal products ... The farmers' companies had it within their power ... to set the pattern of elevator services and of price relationships which would be most acceptable to their grower owners.'[49]

It remains to be noted that these farmers' co-operative companies operated within the open market system and on ' free enterprise' principles. All the pre-1920 reforms in the grain handling system were designed to improve the market system and to ensure that it was 'fair' – that is, properly competitive – rather than to bypass it. Farmers' demands for nationalization of country elevators, for example, had been answered by government assistance to farmer-controlled co-operatives. Farmers' proposals for government-owned terminal elevators had prompted the establishment of a few terminals under the Board of Grain Commissioners, but these were never major factors in the grain trade. Within the system that had evolved, government regulation rather than ownership was the rule. The First World War interrupted this practice but did not constitute a rejection of the principle. In 1916, Britain and its allies had created a centralized cereal purchasing agency in order to deal with the uncertainties of wartime food procurement. Canada responded in early 1917 by instituting a Board of Grain Supervisors to control the distribution of Canadian wheat, and in 1919 this was translated into a Canadian Wheat Board. For three years, 1917–20, a government agency controlled the marketing of Canadian wheat. However, as soon as possible, at the opening of the crop year in 1920, the federal government ended the Wheat Board and returned the wheat trade to private merchants. The open market system was restored.

The dramatic collapse in wheat prices in 1920, just as Canada returned to the private grain trade, was at the root of farm protest for the next decade. Prices had been high during the era of government marketing; they had been low before the war and were low again in the early 1920s. The farmers' conclusion was inescapable: no longer would they be satisfied with mere regulation of the open market system; henceforth, they would be committed to abolition of the private grain trade. The Winnipeg Grain Exchange had become the enemy. The importance of this institution derived from the fact that Winnipeg, which was situated at the point where Canadian railways from east and west converged, became the centre of western grain inspection and later of trading in grain futures. And the trade in futures was the issue.

A futures contract is simply an agreement to deliver or to take delivery of a specified quantity and quality of a good at a specified date and price. Such a contract is so explicit and so liquid that, unlike a deal to build a house or buy a car, it can easily be bought and sold on the open market. And this is what occurred on the Winnipeg exchange and in the other great grain commodities markets of Chicago, Buenos Aires, and Liverpool. Millers who required 1,000 bushels of wheat in March could, if they chose, act in September to 'lock in' a favourable price by purchasing a futures contract for delivery at that date. No one objected to such admirable examples of foresight and planning. But not all or even many transactions in the futures market were made with the intention of taking or making delivery. Rather, the more common event – over 99 per cent of the time according to an American study of the mid-1920s – was to speculate that the price of the commodity would change in the dealer's favour before the delivery date arrived. At that point, the speculators would offset the first contract – if they had agreed to take delivery, they would agree to deliver – with a second and, thus, the Exchange clearing-house would cancel their obligations and the speculators would pocket the difference. Futures prices moved with changes in world-wide harvest prospects and global weather patterns, shifts in interest rates and transportation costs, and numerous other factors, but, according to defenders of the system, they provided an extremely sensitive means of determining commodity price levels.

Critics argued that the speculators drove prices down in the fall and up in the spring – on each occasion to the detriment of the producer. Three federal royal commissions considered the farmers' criticisms during the inter-war years and found them to be unsubstantiated. A clear difference of political opinion had developed within Confederation, according to V.C. Fowke:

> There was no longer any possibility of harmony between the views underlying agrarian protest and those of any substantial section of federal leadership. The conviction of the western wheat grower that the Winnipeg Grain Exchange ought to be abolished ... rested upon a belief – diametrically opposed to the free enterprise tenets underlying the national policy – that the open market or competitive system, the system of freely moving prices, ought not to govern the marketing of western grain ... [The private speculative trade would have to be] replaced by a governmental agency with power to control prices. The western wheat farmer reasoned that there was serious inadequacy in national policies which assured the subsidization of transportation interests by land and money grants and security guarantees, provided for the protection of industry by tariff walls, permitted to economic interests generally the greatest possible freedom in their efforts to avoid the hazards of competition by combination and agreement and, at the same time, left the agricultural producer exposed to the full rigours of competition both nationally and internationally.[50]

Farmers campaigned from 1920 to 1923 to restore government marketing of wheat and to eliminate the futures market, at least for that one crop. When this option seemed more distant than ever, they turned to their second-best alternative, the pool. The pooling concept had won favour in several parts of the United States and

was founded on co-operative principles. No other recommendations were necessary in many segments of the farm movement. As
the term implies, the pool would create a single large common fund
or stock – in this case, wheat – and distribute the net returns after
the entire crop had been marketed. It was yet another producer-
controlled alternative to the open market system, but, unlike the
co-operative elevator, it dealt with the sale of the farmer's products
rather than with the farmer's purchase of services. Put another way,
the pool addressed the problem of the export or spot price rather
than the spreads between the street, track, and spot prices. The
prairie pool system followed American precedents: farmers voluntarily signed an agreement to deliver all their wheat to the pool for
five years and would receive, in return, an initial payment per
bushel and the remainder in interim and final payments based on
the actual return for that grade. The pool's promise was that it
would avoid the annual autumn glut on the market and, as a result
of its 'direct and orderly marketing,' would eliminate middlemen
and speculators, thereby increasing the average return to the farmer. Some pool advocates were even more aggressive; they believed that a giant centralized agency such as theirs could actually
drive up the world price. This difference of opinion, though the
source of heated debate in the inner councils of the pool, did not
result in significant changes in policy in the early years. Nevertheless, it was a fundamental disagreement in political philosophy: the
radicals wished to set a fair price based on their costs of production
and, through Canada's role in world food production, to maintain
this price in the export market. They were unable to do so in the late
1920s, no doubt because world price control was beyond their grasp
but also because they only marketed half of all Canadian wheat
deliveries. This failure led to calls for a compulsory pool, especially
in Saskatchewan, where over 75 per cent of wheat acreage was
already under contract to the pool. The campaign preoccupied farm
leaders for four years but, despite Saskatchewan legislation that
would have tested farm support for the idea, opponents forced the
issue into the courts, where it died in 1931. By then, however, the
pools had greater problems with which to contend.

The pool as a marketing innovation collapsed in 1929–31 with the
crisis of the world economy. Its directors cannot be blamed for the
debacle. They simply had more wheat than they could sell, had
offered too high initial prices, and could no longer convince the

banks to extend their credit. The federal government then intervened to liquidate the pool's wheat and to wind up its operations. Henceforth, the three provincial pools would exist as elevator companies but their international marketing system would cease. And the farmers would recommence their campaign to replace the private grain trade with a government-controlled wheat marketing board.

A cycle in prairie agricultural history had been completed by 1930. The grain economy rested on sure foundations. The family farm and the rural village were functioning as their architects would have wished. The complex structure of the grain production, handling, and grading systems was similarly accepted on all sides. But the onset of a world depression made evident the one crucial unresolved issue in farm politics; as V.C. Fowke, the pre-eminent scholar of the wheat economy, has written: 'One of the most significant features of the national policy has been a persistent disregard of the competitive inferiority of agriculture within the price system. The major era of the national policy which ended in 1930 witnessed no serious attempt on the part of the government to ameliorate or even to assess that inferiority.'[51] The crisis of the 1930s was so great, however, that the federal government and the Canadian people were forced to reconsider their reliance on the competitive market for agricultural exports.

Group portrait after the 1885 troubles
(Horse Child and Big Bear, front left, Poundmaker, front right)

Winnipeg, ca 1880: Main Street south from Portage

Carlton House, 1871

Ukrainian mother and child, ca 1903

Jean Stewart's third birthday: a British-Canadian family in 1915

W.R. Motherwell at his farmstead, ca 1909

Houseboys at Chateau Lake Louise, 1905

A Mennonite family in Saskatchewan, ca 1914

Anglican mission school, Blackfoot Reserve, Alberta, ca 1900

Old Sun Blackfoot school, Alberta, 1901

Harvey school, Alberta, 1915

Queen Elizabeth visiting Biggar, Sask, 1939

Storm over Lake Winnipegosis

Greek Catholic church near Winnipegosis

Ranch pond near Coleman, BC

Abandoned store, Saskatchewan

Dust storm in southern Alberta, 1942

Oil wells, Woodbend field, Alberta, 1946

# 14

# Politics and culture
## 1900-29

The composition of the prairie population changed substantially in the opening decades of the twentieth century. And the structure of the economy – the function and location of cities, the size and influence of towns and villages, the nature of the grain export business – changed in comparable degree. Given the speed of such developments and the range of ethnic and occupational diversity, political tensions were an inevitable part of prairie life. Liberals and Conservatives there were aplenty, of course, but Wobblies and United Farmers and Independent Labourers also contested for popular support and challenged the conventional wisdom about the proper course of this new society. The prairie west was, most emphatically, a land of new beginnings. And, in the opinion of a diverse band of political activists, it had a mission to fulfil.

The political groups differed in their diagnosis of Canadian ills. The western wings of the old-line parties were often restive within the national Liberal and Conservative organizations, but, for all the acrimony of the west-east disputes, they were still engaged in domestic quarrels. Even when federal and provincial wings of the national parties separated, they retained a common outlook because they expressed the will of the established groups in the prairies and the nation. Among the groups that did not share the political philosophy of the Liberals and Conservatives, the various socialist and syndicalist movements offered truly radical alternatives. Less revolutionary in ideological hue but more powerful in electoral politics were the numerous farm protest and 'Progressive' movements that emerged at the close of the First World War and swept the prairies with dramatic intensity in the following three years. Most lasting of these political alternatives, however, was the union of labour moderates, farm protesters, and liberal professional reformers that became the Co-operative Commonwealth Federation in 1933. Each of the four political perspectives – the perspectives embodied in the western wings of the old-line parties, the radical labour groups, the Progressives, and the labour-farm-CCF coalitions – was offered as a solution to national problems by its western proponents. And each figured prominently in prairie debates about the social and economic principles on which the ideal community should be founded.

Many nations and cultures assume missions at some time in their history as the holy wars of Islam and the international leadership of the Soviet Union and the United States bear witness. Though more modest in expression, Canadians too have at times believed that they had a distinctive destiny as a nation. In the nineteenth century, the purpose of the French Canadian was to keep alive in the New World the pre-revolutionary faith and civilizing ethos of Roman Catholic and French Europe. In the same period, English-speaking central Canadians believed that they combined the best of European tradition and North American innovation.[1] Later, in the boom of the early twentieth century, the confidence inspired by the western frontier and the social impulse of a new outlook in the Protestant churches was assimilated to the British-Canadian inheritance to create a powerful new regional image that transcended earlier definitions of the national mission: the promise of the west became the promise of Canada.

The old-line political parties of the prairie west, the Liberals and Conservatives, won their spurs as protest parties – and as representatives of this western mission – in the last decades of the nineteenth century. Under John Norquay, Manitoba Conservatives had fought the disallowance policy of Sir John A. Macdonald's Conservative government, and Premier Thomas Greenway, a Liberal, had resisted federal Conservative attempts to change Manitoba school legislation. This pattern of provincial opposition to federal policy prevailed for the next decade. The federal Liberal government of Sir

Wilfrid Laurier used Clifford Sifton, minister of the interior, as prairie lieutenant, controller of patronage, and supervisor of electoral machinery between 1897 and 1905; Sifton's power, magnified by the role of his ministry in the west, made him the natural target of the Conservatives. The Manitoba Conservative government of Rodmond P. Roblin, which ruled the province from 1900 to 1915, consistently directed its election campaigns against the federal Liberal government and Sifton himself.

Federal party lines had not been a part of Territorial politics, but as soon as provincial status was offered Saskatchewan and Alberta wings of the federal parties came into existence. In each province, the Conservatives assumed the role of defenders of 'provincial rights' and depicted the local Liberals as the dupes of a distant Ottawa Leviathan. The provincial Liberal parties were not shaken. In both provinces, competent administrations and efficient electoral machines were established with the help of federal patronage; each survived minor scandals and changes of first minister to outlive its Manitoba counterpart. The Liberal government in Saskatchewan began under Premier Walter Scott in 1905, was passed to W.M. Martin in 1916 and to Charles A. Dunning in 1922; it was still thriving under James Gardiner when Dunning left for Ottawa in 1926. The first Alberta premier, A.C. Rutherford, ran into serious problems over a railway scandal in 1909–10 and was replaced by Arthur Sifton, Clifford's older brother. When Arthur entered the federal cabinet in 1917, Charles Stewart carried on and the Liberal machine seemed as powerful as ever. Only in Manitoba were the Conservatives more effective than the Liberals. Nevertheless, the machine established by Roblin and his colleague Robert Rogers collapsed in 1915. Part of the reason for its failure was a dramatic financial scandal, but an equally important factor was the ability of Liberal leader T.C. Norris to unite suffragists, prohibitionists, and farm and labour protesters within his party. Though the Conservative party was less successful in Saskatchewan and Alberta, the old-line parties were sufficiently active in the prairie provinces in the first two decades of the twentieth century to sustain the generalization that a viable two-party system existed in the region.[2]

Despite the apparent life-and-death tone of their rhetoric and their electoral contests, the two parties did not differ significantly. Both were dependent on British Canadians for leadership, both were laissez-faire in economic policy, and both were loyal to the

British Empire in moments of crisis. The Conservatives may have been slightly more British, the Liberals more American, in cultural ideals, but this was a matter of degree. Both parties were proponents of a western Canadian mission in the early twentieth century, and both were controlled by an urban-rural coalition that united the major spokesmen of the business class and the leaders of the farm community. Both were aggressive in their advocacy of the assimilation of European immigrants, and though their support in the ethnic communities varied from province to province, both were willing to create foreign-language electoral machines. In brief, the Liberals and Conservatives were parties with eastern Canadian roots and British intellectual forbears; they may have expressed significant differences in those communities, but in their translation to the prairie west they came to represent two versions of the same class and cultural loyalties.[3]

At the base of their western Canadian perspective was a peculiar version of their British inheritance. Late Victorian and Edwardian England was an aggressive imperial power, and western Grits and Tories saw the Boer War and the naval armaments race with Germany, like the celebrations of Queen Victoria's Diamond Jubilee in 1897, as simply expressions of the greatness of an empire on which the sun never set. This militant view of British civilization was a crucial aspect of the western Canadian image. But, if western Canadian leaders were proud of their British heritage, they were not complacent about British social achievements. They insisted that they lived on a frontier and had the freedom to improve upon the parent culture. What better way to create a perfect society than to build it on virgin land, to employ the finest raw material of a dozen lands, and to work to plans inherited from the world's greatest civilization? The frontier, in western Canada as in the United States, was the land of new beginnings. Where all citizens started as social equals, merit and virtue rather than class would be rewarded. Where farms and rural life, rather than factories and cities, were the foundations of the economy, true wealth would be created. Where life was lived close to nature, individuals learned the lessons of God at first hand. Calculations of prairie greatness and celebrations of imperial power inevitably ran together; the west would have a population of 100 million; it would be the bread-basket of the world; it would become the centre of gravity of all Canada; and, if it ruled Canada, and Canada led the empire (as it soon would), then, as anyone could see, the west would lead the world.

The institutions that had taken shape in the region in the three decades after Confederation were, by and large, appropriate to the ambitions of the Liberal and Conservative leaders. The Mounted Police were effective, colourful, and, best of all, committed to the tone that these leaders wished to establish. The Protestant churches were finally committing missionaries and money to the vast but crucial task of Christianizing the prairies. The issue of publicly supported Roman Catholic schools had been faced in both Manitoba and the North-West Territories and had been won: non-denominational systems that expressed the outlook of the Protestant God had been set up in the two jurisdictions in the 1890s. And, in the same decade, the Manitoba and Territorial assemblies had overruled earlier guarantees of French-English bilingualism by declaring English the only official language of debate and record. Thus, at the turn of the twentieth century, the goal of prairie social leaders – a Protestant, law-respecting, English-speaking community in which democracy and social equality were fundamental assumptions – seemed within reach. The extraordinary boom of the following decade did not cause the social leaders to doubt their mission or to question that they would ultimately prevail. Rather, the leaders of the prairie west became even more conscious of the region's identity and increasingly aware of its mission to the nation.

The development of a prairie bias in the ranks of the old-line parties was, in part, the product of political circumstances. Time after time, residents of the west were made to feel that they resided in a colony controlled by an imperial power. The federal government, which exerted extraordinary authority over economic development in the region, was regularly accused of insensitivity. The western provinces, according to many local political leaders, were dominated by authorities in Ottawa who served their own conception of the national interest and ignored the legitimate aspirations of western Canadians. The prairie litany seemed endless. Ottawa disallowed Manitoba railway legislation in the 1880s; Ottawa tried to overrule Manitoba's school legislation in 1895-6; Ottawa delayed the grant of responsible government and provincial status to the North-West Territories until long after the citizens were ready for these responsibilities; and Ottawa retained control of the crucial natural resource of the west, the public lands, thus depriving the provinces of their most important source of revenue and, potentially, their most important administrative task. Though any federal system is ready-made for regional confrontation with the central government, the peculiar circumstance of the Canadian case, including thirty-five years of territorial rule, the federal government's heavy reliance on the CPR, and federal retention of public lands, was especially productive of tensions between the prairie provinces and Ottawa. Was it any wonder that a regional consciousness developed?

The growing regional tensions within Canada were contained within the two-party system for a number of years. This was a fact of some significance in the first decade of the century because east-west disputes and charges of eastern imperialism were becoming urgent. Westerners complained of regional imbalance in the composition of important decision-making bodies such as the Supreme Court, of 'eastern domination' in national delegate-controlled assemblies such as the Trades and Labor Congress, and of 'eastern ignorance' in the governing councils of national voluntary associations such as the Methodist church. In each case, the westerners were cast in the role of aggressive newcomers and others – invariably described as 'the East' – were made to appear conservative defenders of vested interests. When western delegates to the Trades and Labor Congress descended from their trains at Fort William in 1910, they feared they would be described as 'rampant revolutionaries.'[3] When they tried to turn the congress toward a more radical industrial and political stance in 1907, they were cautioned that 'it might suit them in the West, but ... it was unfair to ... introduce this resolution in advance of the opinions of those whom eastern delegates represented.'[4] The leaders of the Methodist church were sufficiently concerned about the differences between east and west that they created a western general superintendent and a western advisory committee to serve the special needs of the region.[5] Speeches at the luncheons of the various Canadian Clubs of the nation, always a barometer of public interests, were often directed at this new question of 'east-west' relations. The stereotypes were clear, if shop-worn: 'The west seems to have lost all sense of perspective. Living in an air of continual self-advertisement, it is in danger of absorbing the idea that all that is of value is west of the great lakes. The West is grand, but it can still be reminded of some facts about the older East.'[6]

It was a measure of the strength of the old-line parties and of their embodiment of the western mission that their leaders handled the most pressing social question of the boom era – the influx of hundreds of thousands of 'foreigners' – with forbearance. The wave of newcomers did elicit expressions of concern, but it did not, except in a few isolated incidents, result in ugly nativist conflicts and did not, in the years before 1914, produce a concerted campaign against European immigration. The explanation of this social calm lies in the prairie leaders' confident assumption that they could 'Canadianize' the newcomers. The attributes of the new society – education, religion, the law, economic opportunity, and social equality – were sufficient, they believed, to mould recalcitrant peasants into good citizens.

The parties relied on their allies, the church leaders, to assist them in the process of Canadianization. In a nation where no established church existed, those denominations with large memberships and an institutional presence from coast to coast could quite justifiably claim a central role in the body politic. And three denominations, the Methodists, Presbyterians, and Baptists, relishing their newly acquired status as national institutions, accepted the responsibility of Christianizing Canada's newest region and assimilating its newest citizens. They were motivated in part by the needs of the immigrants, but they were also motivated by a concern for the fate of the nation. Many of the new arrivals were Greek Catholic or Greek Orthodox, faiths that to Canadian Protestant eyes fostered idolatry, servility, and superstition. The reformers concluded that these immigrants would require considerable guidance if they were to become responsible citizens in a democracy. Many more immigrants were under the sway of the Roman Catholic church, an institution that was said to be long on ceremony and hierarchy, short on free thought and inter-faith co-operation. The three Protestant denominations established several dozen institutions – medical missions, schools, student residences, and settlement houses – in rural districts and in city neighbourhoods where Ukrainians and other citizens of eastern European origin predominated. Evangelization of the individual and amelioration of the material conditions of the community went hand in hand in their campaign to convert 'foreigners ... into English-speaking Christian citizens who are clean, educated, and loyal to the Dominion and to Greater Britain.'[7]

Another central institution dedicated to the assimilation of newcomers was actually guided by the political party hierarchies. This was the public school. Observers of prairie public affairs believed that the most certain method of building the new utopia was by moulding the outlook and character of children. In schoolrooms across the region, the two essentials of assimilation – community of language and common ideals of citizenship – were gravely inculcated as if the very future of the west depended on comprehension of 'would' and 'should' or upon instant recognition of the pink-coloured nations on the Mercator projection of the world. As J.W. Dafoe explained: 'In a country like ours where so many nationalities are settling in our midst, it is imperative that the children of these different nationalities should be taught the same language, the same aspirations, the same ideals of citizenship as our natural-born Canadians.'[8] The lessons of the education system in each province were consciously directed at the creation of a new British-based western Canadian race. Students memorized the classic verses and songs of British imperialism such as *We'll Never Let the Old Flag Fall*, *Children of the Empire*, *Union Jack*, *Rule Britannia*, and *England, My England*. Their history classes were built around an appreciation of British history and parliamentary government. One textbook explained, for example, that India had attained maturity only by reason of the guidance and protection of British rule. The anonymous author celebrated the generosity of British colonial leaders who respected even native 'prejudices,' except, of course, where intervention was necessary to prevent crime or to abolish 'brutal customs.'[9] If they were to become good Canadians, Canada's newcomers would have to learn the lessons of Britain's thousand-year march to liberty.

The story of school legislation and languages of instruction – a story usually associated with the wartime west – was not just another chapter in war-inspired anti-foreign sentiment but rather had been troubling prairie party leaders from the early years of the new century. As early as 1907, Manitoba's Conservative government had required that all schools fly the Union Jack, and two years later the Liberal *Manitoba Free Press* had commenced an extraordinary editorial campaign demanding that the provincial government institute unilingual English-language instruction for all Manitoba children. This concentration on the schools as the crucial agent of assimilation became the rule among prairie social reformers. In the pre-1914 era, the school systems of the three prairie provinces permitted a good deal of latitude in the use of languages other than English for regular instruction. From the time of the Laurier-Greenway compromise in 1897, Manitoba had no compulsory attendance law and permitted instruction in English and 'another language on a bi-lingual basis'; the consequence was the development of entire school systems – including institutions for teacher instruction – in French, German, Polish, and Ukrainian.

In Saskatchewan's publicly supported schools, instruction in another language than English was permitted in the primary grades and for one hour at the close of the school day, and it was also permitted in private schools; almost 300 of the province's schools employed a language other than English for significant parts of the school day. This was especially noticeable in an era when children were likely to receive much if not all of their education in those very primary grades where languages other than English were employed. One-half of all Saskatchewan pupils in 1916–17, for example, were in Grade 1. As early as 1913, Alberta Education authorities, who faced similar problems, had begun to enforce existing regulations in order to increase school attendance and to ensure that English-language instruction became general. Such measures were implemented in Manitoba and Saskatchewan in the following five years. But, despite the coincidence, the war should be seen as the occasion for the new educational regulations rather than the cause of their imposition.[10] The enforcement of compulsory unilingual English-language instruction was just one more expression of the mission espoused by the prairie wings of the old-line parties. To a remarkable degree, the Canadianization campaign was a subject of bipartisan agreement in the pre-war years.

The first phase of the immigration boom slowed during the economic recession of 1913 and halted at the outbreak of war in August 1914. With these events, too, the tolerant optimistic attitude of the prairie Grits and Tories was replaced by increasing suspicion of newcomers from European homelands. The prairie leaders' enthusiasm for the creation of a great new society ran headlong into the realities of a bitter and taxing war. The flower of prairie youth – too often British-Canadian youth, in their view – was crushed in that tragic distant conflict, and the patience of prairie leaders at home wore thin when they overheard the languages of enemies in the markets and meeting halls of Winnipeg, Edmonton, and the rural west. The expansive confidence of the prairie Grits and Tories – the generosity of spirit and the aggressive competitiveness that marked their distinctive mission to Canada and their perspective on the world – was one of the most striking features of the pre-1914 boom. Its disappearance was equally significant.

The First World War had an extraordinary impact on the course of politics and on the relations among cultural groups in the prairie west. Not that the experience of war was itself responsible for the decisive changes – such a claim would be an exaggeration. Rather, the pressures imposed on prairie society in wartime reinforced tendencies that had been present before 1914, encouraged popular movements that might otherwise have remained in obscurity or matured more slowly, and, perhaps most serious of all, poisoned social relations, both among classes and among linguistic or national groups, to a degree that would have been unimaginable to a pre-war observer. The consequence was the breakdown of the region-wide bipartisan consensus on political priorities and the regional ideal.

The outbreak of war was even more of a surprise in the prairie west than it was in Surrey or Lancashire. Western Canadian newspapers had almost ignored the assassination of the Austrian archduke in Sarajevo and had not perceived the implications of the diplomatic manoeuvrings that ensued. But Britain's declaration of war brought spontaneous demonstrations of loyalty. Flags flew and bands played in Saskatoon as in London. Surprise gave way quickly to newspaper stories, mostly false, about battles and to enthusiastic offers of gifts to the war effort. Recruiting for what was assumed would be a short war, probably three and certainly less than twelve months, began immediately and produced remarkable results on the prairies. Partly because of the patriotism of the many recently arrived British but even more because of the unemployment and uncertain prospects of a flat economy, thousands of men were pleased to accept a uniform and a rifle in exchange for a trip home and a brief exercise in educating the Germans in their proper place.[11]

Canadians went to war gladly because it was their duty, but as the months of struggle lengthened into years they discovered new strengths within their nation and a new perspective on the world. The conflict became not just Britain's war, in which loyal Canadians supported a parent in time of need, but a battle in which Canada, like the other fighting nations, was a principal. The war was a continuation of the struggle to create a humane civilization, part of the mission that western Canadians had espoused for several decades, and thus, for many prairie citizens, was the first chapter in the extension of their mission to a wider world. Their ideal was 'democracy.' Their empire was dedicated to the peaceful evolution of self-governing peoples, as was attested by their own experience in territories that had moved from 'wilderness' to provincial status. In standing against the 'autocracy' and the 'militarism' of the kaiser and his 'Prussian' staff, they represented the fraternity, equality, and liberty of a nobler civilization. The prairie Protestant churches, particularly, condemned the German evil and, far from proclaiming brotherhood with the enemy, lauded the war as a Christian mission.[12] Though these expressions of the purpose of the war were common in the English-speaking world, western Canadians believed that they, above all, embodied the ideals of the Allied cause.

The impact of the war on the Canadian economy accentuated the distinctiveness of the prairie region. The recession of 1913–14 continued in western urban centres for the next five years, though it was masked by the return of rural prosperity. Private construction projects and public works had fuelled the economy of the cities in the first decade of the century, but by the end of 1912 the construction of the urban west, or as much as was needed for a generation, was complete. And the only significant wartime boon for manufacturing cities, munitions production, bypassed the prairies. Some blamed the National Policy for its structuring of the Canadian economy, some blamed the location of metals and the cost of freight, some blamed the regional biases of the decision-makers, but no one disputed that the prairies received less than 1 per cent of the $1 billion of Canadian munition production. Another regional grievance was born. What is more, the prolongation of the urban recession did not bode well for the post-war society in which thousands of returned soldiers would be looking for work.[13]

The same theme, lack of economic diversification, was prominent in prairie agriculture during the war. Improved farm acreage doubled in these years, a direct response to the tripling of the price of wheat, as farmers put all their efforts into grain, especially wheat production. The gamble was probably inevitable, given the potential rewards, but it struck at the roots of provincial government campaigns favouring diversification into livestock production which would spread the risk of cash crop specialization. The heavy reliance on a single crop also increased the debt burden of the many farmers who bought land, implements, horses, and, the newest wonder, automobiles, in the expectation that price inflation would be sustained. The debts and the absence of diversification increased farmers' economic vulnerability, of course, and thus contributed to the crises of post-war readjustment in the west.

The events of wartime introduced significant new divisions into the ranks of the old-line parties. Where, in earlier years, they had been united in support of pragmatic and progressive goals, they now experienced fallings-out as pro- and anti-suffragists, pro- and anti-temperance advocates, and supporters and opponents of school language uniformity and military conscription emerged within each party. One important measure of these differences was the reaction of political leaders to the new religious perspectives within the Protestant churches. Nineteenth-century Ontario had been dominated by an evangelical Protestantism with a message of salvation directed to the individual. But in the last decades of the century new currents altered the religious beliefs and the social perspective of the Protestant churches.

In a remarkable conjuncture of circumstances, this new outlook, the 'Social Gospel,' became an important influence in western Canadian life and the driving force in the development of a distinct western Canadian mission. The Social Gospel was the product of many intellectual currents. In an age when powerful evangelists crossed the continent with the message that God could provoke changes in the life of an individual, hope for such change became widespread. Centralized national churches, the product of unions within both the Presbyterian and Methodist denominations between 1874 and 1884, created newly influential and strikingly large institutions. Moreover, the establishment of new agencies within these churches, agencies that were active in young people's, women's, and children's work, brought thousands of Canadians into contact with social questions and public issues.

Important departures in Christian social thought turned the attention of Protestant leaders away from individual sin and salvation to the environment in which the individual was required to make his way. One of these departures was led by the American Henry George, whose Christian roots and training in economics led him to condemn the effects of private landholding – a revolutionary stance in that day – and to argue that land should be taxed in order to give the entire community the rents that now accrued to wealthy individuals. But George was just the most influential among many thinkers whose Christian concern for the community led to defences of the poor and attacks upon the wealthy in the late nineteenth century. Their political nostrums, eccentric or practical, were made more biting by the popular currents of reform Darwinism that preoccupied many thinkers in the 1890s. Recognizing that 'survival of the fittest' applied to species rather than to individuals, one of these philosophers, the Russian Kropotkin, concluded that successful behaviour was based on co-operation rather than competition. Jesus was the expression of the final evolutionary stage in human society because his teachings supported a co-operative social order.

In an era when theologians were becoming more critical of social wrongs, and philosophers such as T.H. Green were advocating a positive interventionist state, prairie ministers increasingly denounced social injustice and called for government action. The Social Gospel was progressive, optimistic, and driven by a crusading zeal; it was strongest within the Protestant churches that were strongest on the prairies; it provided the support of the churches and the gospel – crucial elements in that age – for campaigns of social reform and regeneration; it was at the very heart of western Canada's developing sense of mission to the wider world because it came of age with and expressed the ideals of the new west. But it separated Liberal from Liberal, Conservative from Conservative, because it demanded further reforms when some citizens desired only retrenchment, more brotherly love when some citizens feared loss of status or loss of their distinctive British Canada to the alien forces they described as 'Huns.'[14]

War fever brought to western Canada, as to many parts of the world, intensified campaigns on behalf of female suffrage and prohibition of alcoholic beverages. On the prairies, as in these other jurisdictions, both were victorious. The arguments that convinced prairie audiences were similar to those presented by reformers in England and the United States: abolition of drink would protect young soldiers from 'the low life' and increase the efficiency of the domestic war effort; female votes would purify politics and ensure that the nation did not revert to materialistic and sinful ways after the war. And yet there were special lessons in the prairie reform campaign. Victory in the suffrage and prohibition movements was neither a surprise nor an end in itself to the local leaders but rather was proof of the malleability of their society. The struggle to win referenda and to persuade legislators offered laboratories in which to test political tactics. The strategy sessions and public meetings introduced people of similar views – especially women – and thus were an instrument in the establishment of reform solidarity. The leaders of these reform causes were not worried, it seemed, by the accusation that removal of someone's source of pleasure – alcohol in this case – was presumptuous and even authoritarian. Their goal was a united society, they responded, where sacrifice was sometimes necessary and where the will of the majority prevailed.[15] Once again, such an attitude cut across party lines; once again, reformer was at loggerheads with conservative, radical social gospeller with traditional evangelical; and, once again, the affiliations of Conservative and Liberal neither expressed not accommodated the fundamental divisions in the community.

The majoritarian outlook of some militant Protestant reformers weighed heavily on certain groups of prairie residents during the war years, particularly those who came from the Austro-Hungarian and German empires and those others, largely from Russia, who spoke German. Included in these categories were most prairie Ukrainians and Germans, about 37,000 adult males. Nearly 8,000 of these 'enemy aliens,' the term that designated citizens of the enemy nations, became inmates of internment camps, though most were eventually paroled in order to alleviate labour shortages.

Other events were to touch prairie ethnic relations more directly. Before the outbreak of the war, Canadians had treated Germans as another Nordic people, as civilized as the British. The early months of hostilities did not change this perception. Canadians blamed the kaiser and his military advisers, not the German people, for the conflict. But the sinking of the *Lusitania* and the release of a report on alleged German atrocities in Belgium commenced the re-education of British subjects on the nature of German civilization and character. Combined with this growing hatred of all things German was the British Canadian's low estimate of southeastern Europeans, including especially the Ukrainian immigrants from the Hapsburg empire, and of the European pacifists, including Doukhobors and Mennonites. These concerns were supplemented by contemporary Protestant distrust of the Roman Catholic that was fuelled by charges that French Canadians were not doing their part in the war effort. Thus, the inevitable Canadian suspicion of 'enemy aliens' evident in the establishemnt of internment camps in 1914 grew with the horror of the Great War to encompass more aliens and, eventually, many loyal Canadian citizens whose national origin was not British. This attitude can be termed 'nativism.'

British-Canadian hostility toward 'foreigners' was expressed in a number of political movements. The female suffrage movement, which was led by English-speaking Protestants, at times employed the argument that British-Canadian women deserved the vote because the franchise had already been entrusted to naturalized immigrant males from central Europe, many of whom were presumed to be targets for corrupt electoral practices. The prairie prohibition movement, which was also led by Protestant British Canadians, encountered its stiffest opposition among Roman Catholic and European settlers, which was seen in some quarters to be further proof that these newcomers were unsuitable for the western Canadian utopia. And the rhetoric of soldier recruitment and of patriotic ceremonies, perhaps inevitably, turned to condemnations of laggards, pacifists, and, at times, the 'foreign' people of the prairies.[16]

The wartime election of 1917 demonstrated how serious was this British-Canadian hostility toward foreigners. Prime Minister Robert Borden, in his determination to prosecute the war effectively and to support 'the boys' overseas, had introduced conscription and negotiated a union with his lifelong opponents, the Liberals. He had also sanctioned a new election act that enfranchised female relatives – wives, widows, mothers, sisters, and daughters – of soldiers who had served or were serving overseas. But the act disfranchised Canadian citizens who were pacifists or conscientious objectors, who habitually spoke an 'enemy' language, or who had come from enemy countries and been naturalized after 1902. It was an extraordinary step: to make the basic right of citizenship dependent on any such qualification was to tamper with the very foundation of a democratic state. But this was not the only federal measure marked by ethnic intolerance. The creation of the Union government in 1917 had united most English-speaking Canadians behind Borden and conscription, but it had alienated the French, who remained with Sir Wilfrid Laurier and the Liberal party. In the bitter, racist election campaign that followed, some western Canadians, as irresponsible as they were angry, accused French Canadians of cowardice and implied that Laurier, their hero only a few years earlier, was a secret ally of the Hun. Thus, in the heated days of 1917–18, the definition of enemy was extended by some fanatics to include the French Canadian.

In the closing months of the war, political events threatened the established order of the Atlantic world more seriously than at any time in the previous half-century. The Bolshevik revolution in Russia had inspired responses in various reform and revolutionary movements in western Europe and North America, and profound social conflict seemed imminent. Who was behind such dangerous talk? Surely it was the enemy – the Hun, the Bolshevik, the alien – said some English Canadians. By early 1919, the British-Canadian exclusivist sentiment had become widespread. The foreign war was over, though the need to resist the Bolsheviks in Russia was now attracting sympathy, but the domestic war had begun in earnest. Talk of deportation of aliens was commonplace in some prairie cities, especially Winnipeg, and was receiving serious support. An editorial in the Winnipeg *Telegram* argued that 'The deportation proceedings should not be confined to the enemy aliens that were interned. They should be extended to every alien enemy whose sympathy with the Allied cause has not been capable of the clearest proof from the beginning of the war. Canada wants none of these.'[17] Late in January 1919, a full-scale race riot broke out in Winnipeg. The rioters, most of whom were returned soldiers, attacked 'aliens' and 'Bolsheviks' alike: their initial goal was to disrupt a memorial meeting in remembrance of the German socialists, Rosa Luxemburg and Karl Liebknecht, who had been assassinated in Berlin, but when that meeting was not held, they roamed the streets of the north end for two days, smashing windows, breaking into houses and shops, demanding naturalization papers, and forcing people to kneel on the pavement to kiss the Union Jack. No arrests seem to have resulted from this exceptional occurrence, and little official disapproval was apparent. The *Telegram* noted that 'there are worse things than violence' and went on to enumerate the greater evils, including 'toleration of treason among us' and, significantly, 'toleration of destructive propaganda by citizens of hostile alien race.'[18] The enemy had been translated from 'Hun' to 'alien' to 'Bolshevik'; it was a short step from there to 'socialist.' In the eyes of a large segment of the old-line parties, Canada's enemies could be defined not just by nationality or ethnic group loyalty but by political ideology: socialism, in this perspective, was another facet of the 'Hun conspiracy.'

A few months earlier, in the autumn of 1918, as a result of its concern about a Bolshevik plot against the Canadian state, the federal government had suppressed publications in 'enemy alien' languages – German, Russian, Ukrainian, Hungarian, Finnish, and others – and outlawed a number of organizations, chief among which were the Ukrainian Social Democratic party and its Russian and Finnish equivalents. In the next nine months, the official identification of aliens with revolutionary socialist doctrine became complete.

Between 1914 and 1919, the western Canadian ideals of social reform and majoritarian democracy had moved ever closer to repression and nativism. The angry atmosphere of public life in the closing months of this period can be seen as an outgrowth of war-inspired anxieties and, thus, as different in kind and source from the attitude toward immigrants that prevailed before 1914.[19] Revenge, fear, and hostility had replaced confidence and concern for improvement as the primary sentiments of many reformers; deportation and repressive legislation rather than schools and missions were becoming the focus of so-called reform campaigns. The time of crisis had arrived, and the western Canadian mission of the old-line parties had lost its confident idealism. Increasingly, it was assuming the tenor of a narrowly British-Canadian and business-class movement. Rather than celebrating the social and ethnic democracy of the west, as it had done in the pre-war years, the prairie élite now stressed its British-Canadian roots and its superior social character. The challenge from below, it argued with increasing concern, must be contained.

The most important challenge to this British-Canadian middle-class definition of the prairie mission came from the labour movement. Though they were divided by political allegiance and union loyalty, separated by their places of employment, the workers of western Canada produced a substantial critique of the established economic and social system during the first two decades of the twentieth century. And then, in the troubled winter of 1918–19, when a group of revolutionaries assumed control of their program, they came as close as ever North American workers have come to seizing the instruments of power in their communities. Their revolt collapsed, utterly and completely, in the summer of 1919. Its failure marked the demise of a political movement and of a political philosophy. Thereafter, a more moderate and less Marxist critique of Canadian society became the dominant strain of left-wing politics. Reform rather than revolution, British labourism rather than Soviet or German socialism, were henceforth the most significant perspectives within the western Canadian left.

Unions in western Canada represented about one worker in ten in the years before 1914. They were strongest in Winnipeg, Vancouver, and the coal mining towns of Alberta and British Columbia, and as early as the turn of the century they were reputed to be more radical than their eastern Canadian counterparts. In their support for socialism and for unions that organized by industry rather than by craft (and which thus defended the unskilled and the apprentice as well as the skilled labourer) and their interest in an independent political party for labour, western workers probably deserved their reputation. They were less comfortable than were the skilled crafts-men of central Canada with the leadership of Samuel Gompers's American Federation of Labor. They were less trusting, too, of Gompers's acceptance of the rules of modern capitalism. And they were repelled by his use of business unionism and political support for labour's friends to protect the skilled worker's niche within the status quo. The westerners were innovators, ready to test their strength against their employers.[20]

There were at least four important strains in western Canadian labour politics. The syndicalists were revolutionaries who sought to overthrow the established order by building large industrial unions that would eventually constitute a state within a state; then, on the appointed day of revolution, they believed, a great general strike would replace capitalism with a workers' commonwealth. The Industrial Workers of the World, an American-bred movement that organized coal, construction, and lumber workers in Alberta and British Columbia in the years from 1909 to 1914 was the chief advo-cate of this philosophy in western Canada.

The Socialist Party of Canada (SPC) represented a second revolu-tionary perspective. Marxist in outlook, disciplined in organization, this small cadre believed that a socialist revolution was inevitable. Its task was to educate the masses and to preserve the ideals of socialism until the day of upheaval; *der Tag*, the SPC assumed, would probably be peaceful and perhaps be achieved through the ballot box. Members of the SPC in western Canada were called 'Impossi-blists' because they resolutely refused to co-operate with others on the left for 'short-term' economic or political advantage.

Akin to the SPC in its espousal of a Marxist ideology but more sympathetic to a strategy of short-term advantage, whether in saw-offs at election time or at the bargaining table, was a third political alternative, the Social Democratic Party. The SDP was especially strong among the European ethnic communities where 'language locals' – Finnish, Ukrainian, Russian – were the rule. They main-tained close contact with socialist politics in Europe and thought of themselves as a part of the international workers' movement against an international capitalist class.

The largest political parties in the working class were the various independent 'Labour parties' that developed in the main western Canadian cities. The perspective of this fourth political alternative varied but was generally reformist rather than revolutionary in intent and eager to win short-term gains rather than to debate about some distant revolution. The four strains of labour politics demonstrated the range of political thought on the western Canadian left and the importance of the workers' disaffection from capitalism. These were not irrelevant cells of a few dozen malcontents but well-established, intellectually creative organizations with perhaps ten or twenty thousand members – and thousands more supporters – by the close of the war.

The 'political' movements had ambiguous relationships with the trade union movement in western Canada. Because three of the four political options, the SPC, the SDP, and the Industrial Workers of the World, supported a workers' revolution, they were anathema to the leadership of the skilled trades unions. Not all western unionists were in the American-dominated 'international' craft unions, of course, but the most numerous crafts, including most of the machinists and metal workers, the railway running trades, the construction trades, and the printing shops, or about 70 per cent of western unionists, did belong to the American unions. Coal-miners, who constituted a district of the United Mine Workers of America, were a special case. Because of their particular circumstances, they enjoyed considerable latitude in decisions concerning both the workplace and political activity. Whatever their job or craft, however, western Canadian union members, like their eastern brethren, accepted a dual leadership. Negotiations on issues of the workplace such as hours, wages, and conditions were affected by decisions at the international headquarters, especially if strike action was contemplated; other benefits, including insurance and funeral payments, were also organized by the American office. The Canadian political environment, including legislation on immigration, accident compensation, minimum wage, and other social insurance measures, was discussed in labour's version of a national parliament, the Trades and Labor Congress (TLC). This body was composed of delegates from most Canadian union locals and met once a year to determine a national stance on matters of concern to labour.

Because the TLC was dominated by the more numerous craft unions of central Canada and because the 'eastern' union leaders took their direction from American craft union headquarters, the TLC abided by the 'business union' philosophy of Samuel Gompers. As a result, it regarded even an independent labour party as dangerous. Its leaders preferred to back the Liberal party or, perhaps, to elect 'independent worker's candidates' to Parliament, legislature, and city council. Thus, western Canadian workers found they were confined by the conservatism of the American Federation of Labor (AFL) when they sought changes in national or provincial politics.[21]

Such constraints did not hold them back. British Columbia's workers elected representatives to the provincial legislature as early as the 1890s, and labour candidates became commonplace in civic and provincial campaigns in both British Columbia and Manitoba after 1900. However, aside from a few 'moral victories,' the western worker had little to cheer about until the closing years of the war. Then, suddenly, radical political and union organizations won adherents as never before. What had changed? Why was this radicalism so much more pervasive in the west than in the rest of Canada or North America?

Explanations of western labour radicalism are numerous. Some historians emphasize the structure of the western Canadian economy, with its dependence on the boom and bust cycle of primary production; they argue that employers in the west were interested in the short rather than the long term and thus treated their workers more harshly than did their counterparts in eastern Canada or elsewhere.[22] Other historians have emphasized the frontier environment of western Canada. In this view, workers in the west were immigrants who were seeking 'a new start and better opportunities'; when they ran up against the poverty and class divisions of urban slums and isolated mining towns, they resorted first to unions and, when that instrument proved futile, attacked the very structure of society by joining radical organizations.[23] These explanations have merit but are rather general. Examination of the events leading to the crisis of 1919 suggests more obvious explanations of western radicalism.

The militant socialist movements were based in the coal towns, where class lines were sharply drawn and worker misery was evident, and in a few skilled urban trades, such as machinists and construction workers, where union members had faced boom and bust cycles with frustrating regularity between 1906 and 1914. Their goals were 'production for use, not for profit' and 'a fair day's wage for a fair day's work.' Such ideals assumed a stable society and some modification of the capitalistic labour market. But the First World War altered their fortunes. Inflation upset household calculations and encouraged recurrent battles at the bargaining table; registration of manpower and conscription, especially when juxtaposed with alleged profiteering by wealthy capitalists, convinced many workers that their class alone bore the brunt of the war effort; and the prospect of war's end, with an overcrowded labour market, further price instability, and a final opportunity to secure the ideals of liberty and justice, suggested that they must act immediately if they were to defend their interests and secure reforms. Thus they turned to new tactics, such as the general strike and the industrial union, to strengthen their hand. This was not peculiar to the west but rather was manifested in groups as diverse as Britain's 'triple alliance' (miners, dockers, and railwaymen) and America's machinists. But what was unique to the Canadian situation was the readiness of westerners to blame 'the East' when such reform proposals did not receive support in the national labour movement. Perhaps the smaller constituency of the west was more easily pushed in a new direction, especially in this moment of crisis, than was the larger, more diverse constituency of all Canada or North America. Certainly, when western delegates lost crucial votes on industrial unionism and the general strike tactic at the TLC convention in Quebec City in September 1918, they returned to the west with the conviction that they alone had the insight and the freedom to adopt the new tactics required by new circumstances. This was untrue as a depiction of the vote at Quebec City – many easterners supported their stand – but it served as an explanation and as an excuse for the next step. They then joined the radical socialists in a very militant program, hoping all the while that the nation and the continent would follow suit.[24]

During the extraordinary turmoil of the winter of 1918–19, which saw the deadly influenza epidemic, the return of hundreds of thousands of soldiers, and federal government repression of foreign-language publications and some socialist organizations, calls for social reconstruction emanated from such diverse groups as the

British Columbia Federation of Labour and the Methodist church. But the most important move toward social change was led by the revolutionaries in the SPC, a predominantly western group with headquarters in Vancouver, which took the lead in the western Canadian labour movement. They arranged an unprecedented Western Labour Conference for Calgary in March 1919 and convinced the unions of all four western provinces to send delegates. Their ostensible goal was nothing more dramatic than a united western front on such matters as industrial unionism and the use of the general strike as a bargaining weapon – a united front that might exert greater influence at the TLC convention in the autumn of 1919. But matters got out of hand. SPC leaders found themselves leading a work-force whose militancy was as great as their own. The Calgary conference of March 1919 became an enthusiastic revolutionary love-in. The delegates cheered radical speeches and roared their disapproval when voices of moderation were tentatively raised. They endorsed the principle of 'proletarian dictatorship' as a means of translating capitalist private property into communal wealth, and they sent fraternal greetings to such groups as the Russian Bolsheviks and German Spartacists. And when the SPC leaders offered a specific program of action, the delegates overwhelmingly endorsed it: one region-wide referendum would determine whether western workers should secede from international (AFL) craft unions and create their own industry-based organization, the One Big Union; and another referendum would ask whether workers wished to call a general strike to enforce a number of demands, including a thirty-hour work week, to alleviate the expected unemployment crisis.

The radicals believed that a great proletarian victory was within their grasp in the early spring of 1919. To their dismay, their movement disintegrated within four months. Perhaps what they needed was a Lenin, who would move decisively to seize the instruments of power. But all they had was the SPC and the Impossibilist crew – Bill Pritchard, Jack Kavanagh, and Victor Midgley of Vancouver; Bob Russell and Dick Johns of Winnipeg; Joe Knight and his wife in Edmonton – who adhered to a different political philosophy, who indeed believed that capitalism would collapse of its own weight. Thus, when the opportunity for revolution was presented to them, they treated it as an educational event and an exercise in collective bargaining.

The crisis occurred in Winnipeg, then the most volatile of Canadian communities. 'Injunction City,' as union leaders called it, was notorious for the aggressive self-confidence of its capitalists and for the gulf that separated the north end, Elmwood, Transcona, and St Boniface, the working-class districts, from the more prosperous neighbourhoods south of the Assiniboine River. The misunderstandings had been growing since the early years of the century. In April 1919, when the increased militancy of the workers faced the determination of the employers, two relatively minor bargaining stalemates in the construction and metal trades were quickly transformed into a city-wide confrontation. The workers bore part of the responsibility for the crisis because they decided to test the newly fashionable weapon of the 'general strike,' the mere threat of which, they thought, had won a similar contest in Winnipeg in the summer of 1918. And the employers bore part of the responsibility because, having bowed to the general strike threat a year earlier, and having heard the revolutionary talk of the labour leaders, they were not prepared to budge. They viewed this test as a pivotal moment in labour-capital relations, not just for Winnipeg but for the nation and the continent. Huns, Bolsheviks, aliens – in short, revolutionaries – were threatening to destroy their dreams.

In the view of these businessmen, Calvinist in perspective if not in faith, God rewarded those who had earned material rewards and so the prevailing distribution of wealth and its natural concomitant, power, was more or less just. If someone found it inappropriate, as their version of the western Canadian dream made plain, hard work in this land of opportunity would set matters right. A.J. Andrews, a corporation lawyer, later explained that the Labour church, a workers' institution prominent in 1918–19, taught doctrines that 'were intended to make you forget all you were ever taught at your mother's knee. Their aim is to remove the word "duty" from the dictionary ... The whole vile doctrine preaches duty to class, self before country.'[25] The employers and their allies were not afraid. Rather, with determination and even glee, they would put the workers in their proper place. Newspaper advertisements were sent across the nation to explain that the issue in Winnipeg was 'the Union Jack or the Red Flag'; calls to the federal cabinet warned that a Bolshevik conspiracy was exploding in western Canada; and, in the city itself, a well-organized Citizens' Committee of One Thousand ensured that the ranks of the employers, and the support of the elected officials of city and province, remained firm.[26]

When the building and metal trades union asked for help from the city's Trades and Labour Council, they received almost unanimous support in a general strike ballot. On 15 May 25,000 workers across the city put down tools, picked up jackets and dinner pails, and headed for home. But this time, use of the big weapon did not force the employers' capitulation. Instead, the unions found themselves in a different and very difficult situation; their goals, as they repeated over and over, were a living wage and the right of collective bargaining in the building and metal trades. Their major contention was that they would be stronger if they won recognition of larger, multi-shop bargaining units, a version of the then-popular industrial union strategy. But, as they soon realized, they were responsible for shutting down an entire city. And perhaps for running it! A strikers' council soon negotiated the continuance of milk and bread deliveries with company owners and city council, but this very assumption of power, accompanied by placards on the horse-drawn wagons – 'Permitted by authority of the Strike Committee' – demonstrated their dilemma. The strikers sought limited goals, but in pursuit of these short-term ends they had taken control of the very necessities of life in prairie Canada's largest city. Thus did an economic confrontation become a political one. Winnipeg workers had not planned a revolution, but they were now, as the employers rightly appreciated, in a position to make one.

The response of employers, governments, and craft union leaders was identical: if they defeated the general strike, they would defeat the One Big Union and 'The Revolution.' Their actions during the next six weeks were increasingly arranged in concert. The federal government told postal workers to return or be fired; the provincial government issued the same ultimatum to telephone employees; rather than trust its police, who had voted to support the strike but remained on the job at the request of the Strike Committee, the municipal government fired almost 200 and replaced them with nearly 2,000 'special police' hired at $6 a day, twice the temporary discharge allowance given returned soldiers. And then, after four weeks of strike, when the mediation efforts of the federal minister of labour had produced some minor concessions on the employers' part – and thus defused the serious threat of a national rail tie-up – the federal government struck the fatal blow. Before dawn on 17

June, eight strike leaders, all British-born but for one Ontario native, and four European Canadians were arrested. (The latter were definitely not leaders of the strike but were leaders in their communities; their arrests lent credence to tales of alien conspiracy). It was the penultimate blow in the campaign to defeat the strike.

The final chapter in the Winnipeg story was also the saddest. To demonstrate that the strike was ending, and at the urging of the city council and the Citizen's Committee, civic officials agreed to restore streetcar service. This action, when a face-saving compromise was almost within reach, provoked another confrontation on the streets. This time, unlike several earlier demonstrations, the circumstances were ready-made for violence. The strikers and the returned soldiers who supported them were frustrated; members of the citizens' committee scented victory. And the Royal Northwest Mounted Police and the special police were ready for action. The police were assembled, drawn up in order, and, in the case of the specials, issued revolvers and wagon spokes, as the demonstrators gathered. When the crowds failed to disperse, the mayor read the Riot Act from city hall steps. At the moment when the Mounties rode out to clear Portage Avenue and Main Street, the strikers halted a streetcar in front of city hall and set it on fire. The Mounties charged through the masses of demonstrators, wheeled, and raced again down the street. Meeting a hail of stones and sticks, they fired into the crowd. Within minutes, the main streets were clear, the specials were cruising the side streets, and militia in machine-gun trucks were patrolling the downtown area. Two men had died of gunshot wounds, and many others, including four police, were injured. Within a week of 'Bloody Saturday,' the strike had collapsed.

The Winnipeg strike, though a result of local labour-management troubles, dealt a fatal blow to the western labour movement's hopes for radical social change. The two crucial planks in the radical platform had been denied: employers would not accept industry-wide collective bargaining, as events in Winnipeg had made plain, and the state would not countenance general strikes, as was demonstrated by the federal government's willingness to fire workers, to order out the militia, and, eventually, to charge the leaders with seditious conspiracy. Moreover, as if the opposition of business and government were not enough, the workers were themselves divided and exhausted. After the Winnipeg strike had started, sympathy walkouts occurred in a number of western cities, thus draining the workers' energy and money in what proved to be a lost cause. The counter-offensive of the AFL-affiliated craft unions severely handicapped the One Big Union in its attempts to secure a foothold in the west. And the Winnipeg strike trials preoccupied some of the most important talents in the movement for over a year. Factionalism and recrimination within the left undercut what remained of the workers' will to effect significant social change. Many urban westerners had been made aware, intensely aware, of class interests and class lines in their communities – none more so than Winnipeg – but that was the extent of the change evoked by the remarkable outburst of the working people in 1918–19.

The flowering of revolutionary socialism was a significant event in the history of western Canadian politics, but, having withered so quickly, it was quickly forgotten in the wider community. Other more moderate solutions to social injustice soon competed for public attention and, within months, seemed to be the only viable alternatives to the established order. Revolution was then left behind, and reform became the dominant concern of the dissatisfied. Throughout the 1920s, reformist amelioration of the Canadian capitalist system was discussed in church, union, and farm meetings. The central topics in most debates were the 'progressive movement' and its kin, the 'farmers' political parties,' but many allied themes, including co-operatives, the United Church, and labourism, were also touched on.

One reason for the preoccupation with reform lay in the changed social structure of western Canada in the decades after 1900. Whereas the radical industrial and mine workers organized in a constituency of perhaps 250,000, the moderates of the prairies could expect support from 2 million citizens – at least four of five in the regional population. Farmers and professionals were fundamental to the new reform movement. The 'professionals' – teachers, ministers, newspaper men and women, health and social workers, government employees – had become much more numerous and, because of their education and skills, more important as commentators on and participants in public affairs, and their rise to prominence was one reason for significant new departures in the reform camp. The background of these individuals was often rural, one suspects, because most Canadians lived in rural communities before 1900, but they became city or town dwellers when they pursued advanced education and they remained in the city or maintained their contact with 'urban' life when they took up full-time jobs. They were mostly Protestant, English-speaking, and Canadian or British-born, though there were significant exceptions, and they were attuned to the language of urban social reform that was so prominent in the early twentieth century. They were the heart of the 'middle' group, between business leaders and labourers, in city and town. Some of them would have claimed to be Social Gospellers, others evangelical Christians, but almost all would have acknowledged the power of religion in their lives. Moreover, they were infected by the contagion of the 'western myth': they believed that they lived in a democratic malleable community and thus could effect significant social change. These reformers of the 'middle' class allied with the farm men and women of the prairies to create powerful social reform movements in the 1920s.

If the urban professional group seemed a new factor in the prairie political community, the farmers' world had changed to such a degree that it, too, could be described as substantially different in character from its pre-1900 equivalent. The place of farm dwellers in the prairie social order has not been established satisfactorily by students of prairie history. Some farmers were only a short step from the illiteracy and poverty of the most primitive Old Country peasant or slum conditions, but many others were just as literate as their counterparts in the offices and professions of the Atlantic world's urban centres. They had been raised in the era of the educational reforms of Victorian England and Canada; their generation shared an unusually rich, unusually democratic introduction to the entire history of English culture. These farmers, men and women, should be viewed in the context suggested by Paul Fussell's survey of English literature in the First World War:

> By 1914, it was possible for soldiers to be not merely literate but vigorously literary, for the Great War occurred at a special historical moment when two 'liberal' forces were powerfully coinciding in England. On the one hand, the belief in the educative powers of classical and English literature was still extremely strong. On the other, the appeal of popular education and 'self-improvement' was at its peak, and such education was still conceived largely in humanistic terms. It was imagined that the study of literature at Workmen's Institutes and through such schemes as the National Home Reading

Union would actively assist those of modest origins to rise in the class system ... The intersection of these two forces, the one 'aristocratic,' the other 'democratic,' established an atmosphere of public respect for literature unique in modern times ... In 1914 there was virtually no cinema; there was no radio at all; and there was certainly no television. Except for sex and drinking, amusement was largely found in language formally arranged, either in books and periodicals or at the theater and music hall, or in one's friends' anecdotes, rumors, or clever structuring of words.[27]

Studies of Canadian society may eventually demonstrate that this same literary and scientific sophistication was present in a significant proportion of prairie farm families.[28] Many farmers, like many of their city cousins, were literate and forceful. They were able to think their way through tracts of agrarian reformism and selections of Victorian poetry and to reach conclusions concerning political change.

If one thing was soon apparent to western Canadian activists, urban and rural, in the anxious years of 1918 and 1919, it was the uselessness of the Union government. For a group that had been elected with such widespread support on the prairies in the late autumn of 1917, the Borden Unionists had frittered away their advantage with remarkable dispatch. The budget of 1918 brought little relief to the west and, if anything, only made more evident how different were the economic interests of central and prairie Canada. The Unionist transportation policy included nationalization of the Canadian Northern Railway, which was welcomed, but the Crow's Nest rates were still suspended. Moreover, as a result of wartime inflation, freight rates were increased as soon as the new administration thought it feasible – that is, a week after the 1917 election. The rising cost of living was a matter of concern to every citizen, and, in the prairie west in particular, the rulings of both the food controller and the fuel controller were subject to harsh criticism because they did not take into account the special circumstances of life on the prairies, especially on the prairie farm. Perhaps the failure of the Union government was due to errors not of policy but of communication; certainly, prairie dwellers took strong exception to its secrecy, its rule by order-in-council, and its refusal to explain its course. But, whether the problem had several explanations or very few, the Unionists were a disappointment.[29]

Where to turn? The customary answer in Canadian politics was the Liberal party, but the events of the war had made that an unlikely alternative for most westerners. Laurier's defence of French-Canadian language rights had displeased many prominent prairie Liberals in 1916, and such influential party members as John Dafoe, editor of the *Manitoba Free Press*, now advocated the creation of a separate western Liberal party: 'These developments at the capital must tend to strengthen the feeling which has been growing steadily for years that Western Liberals need not look to the East, at present, for effective and progressive leadership. The time is ripe for Western Liberals to decide that they will rely upon themselves – and thus do their own thinking, formulate their own policies and provide their own leaders. Canadian public life will thus be given what it sorely needs – a group of convinced radicals who will be far more interested in the furthering of their programme than in office-holding ... "To your tents, O Israel."'[30] In this statement, one sees both the regional sentiment and the desire for reform that characterized so much western political rhetoric in this era.

Many Canadians who wished to reform their nation turned to another political force, the Progressive movement, as the vehicle to implement their ideals. The Progressive uprising was a complex phenomenon. It has been described as a farm movement, a sectional protest, a vehicle for the social gospel, and a quest for cheaper government; it was all of these things and more. In its name, 'third party' provincial governments were elected in Ontario (1919), Alberta (1921), and Manitoba (1922), and significant movements under similar titles influenced the course of politics in all the other provinces; 65 members of the federal Parliament were elected under its banner in 1921, and 12 remained under variants of that name after the 1930 federal election. It was the most important departure from the two-party system since the consolidation of the Liberals and Conservatives in the 1870s and can be seen as the forerunner of the 'protest' parties of the 1930s. The Progressive movement was, for most of the 1920s, the focus of prairie reform activity and ideological debate.[31]

Western farmers provided one bulwark of the Progressive campaign. They had borne the costs of the settlement experiment and had had to struggle for every dollar. They had campaigned for branch lines, for regulation of grain grading and weighing practices, and for competitive elevator and grain buying systems. They had risked heavy investments, including years of their own labour, in the dangerous gamble on weather and price that was the eternal lot of the farmer. Thus they knew the benefits of organization and lobbying campaigns and had sufficient reasons – tariff reform, restoration of the Crow's Nest freight rates, completion of the Hudson Bay railway, and a revised grain marketing system – to want to continue their political activities. The war slowed their campaign, but during 1919 the farmers made important strides.

Two components of this 'agrarian revolt' made it much larger than merely a prairie phenomenon. The first, which prairie farmers shared to some extent with farmers across the nation and across the continent, was rooted in the consciousness of their distinctiveness as an occupational group. To be a farmer was to be a unique and valuable contributor to the social and economic fabric of the nation, in this perspective, and to have special interests in common that were not acknowledged by governments in power. This agrarian mystique drew strength from ideas as old as western civilization and from relatively recent insights. On the one hand, agriculture was a way of life: Virgil's honest yeoman celebrated life on the soil and the physiocrats of the French Enlightenment claimed that agriculture was the foundation of all wealth; the Romantics and the modern apostles who advocated a 'return to the land' seemed to provide proof that rural life created purer character. But, beside these nostalgic and essentially undemonstrable – however popular – notions, there was a sense that modern farmers were also 'professionals.' They were scientists, insofar as they had to understand and implement the findings of entomolgists and plant breeders and soil surveyors; they were engineers when they repaired equipment; they were accountants when they balanced revenues against expenditures; they were 'modern' – for which one should read 'educated and respectable' – in the increasingly urban-determined definition of society and culture. And like businessmen and manufacturers, they recognized that modern times required the organization of an economic interest group if their viewpoint was to be presented forcefully to public and government alike. In the identity created by occupational and romantic definitions of their life, all Canadian farmers could find common ground. Such views lay behind the foundation of the Canadian Council of Agriculture in 1909, a national institution in which farmers could lament the continued evil of the tariff and warn of the dangers of rural depopulation. Such campaigns sustained farmers' self-esteem in the face of fashionable literary denunciations of rural life and demonstrated that they were an occupational group distinct from all others. Indeed, in the rhetoric of some, they were a 'class.'

Canadian farmers, like other occupational groups, did not have a complete identity of interests. Though they were united by their anger against the growing urban derision directed at rural life, for example, they found that BC fruit growers, Quebec dairy farmers, and Saskatchewan grain exporters did not have a common perspective on government policies that affected agriculture. Where a Nova Scotia farmer was moved by his concern for the Intercolonial, his Manitoban counterpart was anxious about the Crow's Nest rate and the Hudson Bay or Peace River rail outlets. In this sense, farm protests were marked by a second significant defining characteristic – they were provoked by a regional as well as an occupational consciousness. Thus, where traditional prairie grievances about central Canadian politicians, manufacturers, and bankers fed the prairie farm revolt, other grievances fuelled similar farm revolts in other regions.

Another element in the post-war movement can best be described as a product of the 'middle group' – neither radical labourer nor business leader – that had become a force in prairie society. These people have not often figured in accounts of the Progressive movement, and yet they must have been central to it. Protestant ministers, for example, helped to develop reform ideas because they were often present at farm meetings, delivering the prayers and brief biblical illustrations that provided a convincing religious interpretation of the otherwise unconventional talk about a new party. It is reasonable to assume, too, that where regional and occupational interests coincided with Progressive platform planks, as was the case for prairie elevator agents or maritime fishermen, there would Progressive supporters be found. But, as we learn more about this unusual protest movement, we learn that its support was even more widespread and diverse. In Nova Scotia and New Brunswick, the Progressives were briefly the vehicle of the broadly based Maritime Rights activists in 1919–20. In Ontario, the United Farmers joined with the labour movement to form a provincial government in 1919; surely, the 'Progressive' reform platform had a wide economic and occupational appeal in that province. And, on the prairies, town dwellers as well as farmers voted for Progressive candidates in the

1921 federal election; they also voted for UFA candidates in Alberta in 1921 when farmers formed the provincial government, for UFM candidates in 1922 when they formed the Manitoba government, and for the Progressives who ran in Saskatchewan provincial contests, with less success, in 1921 and 1925. As was the case for farmers, so with non-farmers, the appeal of the Progressives varied with the region and the riding. Thus, on the prairies, traditional regional stereotypes and economic interests may have created the impression that the Progressives were the party of regional and farmers' occupational protest, but they were more.

As many observers recognized, and as the support of teachers, elevator agents, and shopkeepers made evident, the Progressives were seeking significant social and economic change. In part, theirs was a campaign for regional justice because it called for the redistribution of wealth from the urban heartland to the periphery. In addition, though the analysis was rudimentary and the term was not used in today's sense, it was a campaign for 'class' justice. The Progressives recognized the growing danger of the concentration of capital in fewer and fewer hands; they feared the emergence in Canada of an aristocracy of wealth that would be every bit as oppressive as the entrenched oligarchies in European societies; and they were determined to ensure that democracy in politics and just rewards in income would be the lot of every Canadian. Their stand on the tariff was not just an expression of the farmers' interest in cheaper imported implements but was a defence of 'the people of Canada' against the 'protected interests'; the 'privileged class' must not be permitted to become richer at the expense of the 'poor' or 'the masses'; and these privileged citizens should not continue to subvert the old-line parties by contributing 'lavishly' to campaign funds, thus lowering 'the standard of public morality.' These quotations, taken from the Progressive platforms prepared by the Canadian Council of Agriculture in 1916 and 1918, demonstrated the movement's awareness of the divergence of class interests in Canada. And the Progressive solution for the revenue shortfalls entailed by tariff reform – to tax the value of unimproved land and to employ graduated taxes on personal income, large estates, and corporation profits – also constituted an attack on concentrations of wealth and power.[32]

Progressivism appealed to a wide range of voters. It represented an inchoate movement for 'betterment' that could be depicted as

cheaper government in Manitoba, cleaner government in Saskatchewan, regionally and occupationally fairer government in Nova Scotia or Ottawa, and, in every venue, democratic and godly government. William Irvine, the Alberta minister and farm-labour MP,
wrote at this time: 'The line between the sacred and the secular is
being rubbed out' because 'everything is becoming sacred.' The
ideals of the social gospel became, for many, the ideals of the political movement. Salvation was thus transformed into a matter of concern to legislatures.[33]

Despite their apparent consensus on the nation's ills, Progressives never did agree on a diagnosis or a remedy. Two schools of
Progressive thought can be distinguished for purposes of discussion. The dominant perspective in the early 1920s, led by T.A. Crerar, president of the United Grain Growers and cabinet minister in
the Union government, was strongest in Manitoba and Saskatchewan and most complacent about the achievements of prairie society.
As represented by Crerar and his two allies, George Chipman of the
*Grain Growers' Guide* and John Dafoe of the *Manitoba Free Press*, these
'Manitoba' Progressives believed that a few changes in federal policy would effect vast improvements in the nation. Most important,
they believed that these changes could be achieved within the existing political system. If the Liberal party would adopt a low-tariff
plank and shed its big business ties in eastern Canada, the transformation of the party system would be complete. Crerar and Dafoe
were the foremost exponents of the western mission to the nation.
The democracy and opportunity of the region had permitted them
and, in their observation, hundreds of thousands of others to get a
new start and to establish a secure existence. If only these principles
could be communicated to the rest of Canada, they believed, it
would become one of the world's finest societies.[34]

The second perspective was expressed by H.W. Wood, president
of the United Farmers of Alberta, and was strongest in that province and among some Ontario farmers.[35] These 'Albertans' shared
neither Crerar's satisfaction with the contemporary west nor Dafoe's
confidence in the two-party parliamentary system. They argued that
Canada's political institutions must be scrapped because big business, by means of its control of secret well-disciplined party caucuses, subverted the will of the people. The Albertans asserted that
a new world order was just around the corner: individual and social
perfectibility could be achieved when, as appeared likely, the grow-

ing hostility of industries, classes, and nations finally drove the competitors to acknowledge that 'co-operation' alone would save them from extinction. The victory of this superior principle – that is, recognition that co-operation arose from and superseded 'competition' as the fundamental organizing principle in society – would be achieved in the domestic political arena when the futile wars of the obsolete party system were replaced by the harmony of 'group government.'[36]

Though never entirely explained, group government depended on an assumption that economic interests provided individuals with their primary identity. Thus the inevitable emergence of economic organizations based on the division of labour, in the Albertan perspective, would intensify the conflict among labourers, capitalists, and farmers until they agreed to co-operate for the good of all. Achievement of group government and of 'co-operation,' an extraordinary departure for any society, was the Albertan equivalent of the syndicalists' general strike or the revolutionary socialists' day of proletarian revolution. According to Calgary's philosopher-politician William Irvine, group government would be the farmers' great contribution to social harmony – because farmers, of all the occupational groups, realized the virtues of co-operation: 'Although fathered by oppression, the farmers' movement has escaped that bitterness of feeling against capital, and that extreme rashness both of expression and action, so characteristic of labor. The farmer, in reality, combines in his own profession, the two antagonists. He is both capitalist and laborer. He knows that production is not furthered when war is going on between the two. He sees, also the hopeless deadlock between organized capital and organized labor in the world of industry and commerce, and is thus led to the discovery of co-operation as the synthesis without which progress cannot be made.'[37] Here was an alternate vision of the world and an alternate version of the reform mission. Rooted in the western Canadian preference for non-partisan politics and also in the national demand for reform, it was also a rejection – at least in part – of the Marxists' insistence on the primacy of property relations. Instead, the Albertans added a form of British guild socialism – an evolutionary rather than a revolutionary outlook – to reform Darwinism and co-operativism.[38] And they insisted that the very process of farming created a 'class' or occupational identity.

Manitoban and Albertan Progressives shared aspects of an out-look. Both were reformist in comparison to the revolutionary social-ists of the labour movement because they accepted then-current relations of property. Both believed the old-line political parties were corrupt tools of the Big Vested Interests (so-called, according to farmer-philosopher E.A. Partridge, because of the size of the owners' vests). But the Albertans were more radical than the Mani-tobans and, in their way, as radical as any member of the One Big Union, because they believed that a change in the political system could transform power and status relations in an entire society. Marxists would condemn as naive the Albertans' refusal to tinker with the ownership of property; conservatives would smile at their ideal of individual and social perfectibility; but the Albertans did make an important contribution to the shaping of Canadian political institutions.

At first glance, Progressivism must seem an utter failure. It col-lapsed quickly in the Maritimes, was merely a one-term administra-tion in Ontario, and never did achieve power in Saskatchewan. The farm governments in Manitoba and even in Alberta, despite the professed ideology of the 'Albertan' camp, accepted the conven-tions and customs of the parliamentary system, including the lead-ing role of the cabinet, caucus discipline, and advisory but not authoritative party meetings. Both prairie farmer governments were noted for responsible, cautious, even conservative legislation and administration in the 1920s. There was nothing in the provincial record, it might appear, that suggested long-term significance for this reform outburst.

The federal Progressives seemed to be even less effective. Though they briefly controlled the balance of power in the House of Com-mons, and were sufficiently numerous to be offered the leadership of His Majesty's Opposition, they were caught between the Manito-bans' desire for rapid reform of the party system and the Albertans' determination to create a new governmental structure.[39] In the end, dread of caucus discipline led them to reject both coalition with the Liberals and the leadership of the opposition. Instead, they sat as a third force in the House of Commons, voted as individuals rather than a party, and gradually lost their force and their purpose. Crerar resigned as their leader in 1922, to be replaced by the mild Robert Forke, and, by the time of the budget debate in 1924, when they suffered a serious split, their effectiveness had ended. They elected only 24 MPs in the 1925 general election and 20 in 1926, by which time they were obviously a spent force on the national scene. The fall of the Progressive party was as abrupt as its rise.

The collapse of the Progressive movement in national electoral politics and its apparent conservatism in prairie provincial politics should not be construed as proof of its futility. Rather, as the experienced journalist, John Dafoe commented, progressivism remained a vital force in public life: 'The Progressives represented a western outlook, which has not vanished by any means. If it does not present itself through the media of Progressives it will appear in some other form. That point should not be lost sight of.'[40] Its ideals underlay the organization of the wheat pools and the consumer co-operatives. Its successes included partial restoration of the Crow rate. Its sense of mission was an important influence in the creation in 1925 of a new national Protestant church, the United Church of Canada, from the Methodist, Presbyterian, and Congregational churches. And its determination to counteract the rise of powerful industrial and merchant capitalists found an outlet in other better-organized, better-based political movements. Of these, the most important in the long run, though only a splinter in the 1920s, was the labour group. Thus progressivism should be seen as a step in the development of a Canadian critique of monopoly capitalism. It collapsed because its tactics and leadership were insufficient to meet the challenges of the time.

As much as any other single factor, the development of a third party in Canadian politics depended on farm and labour co-operation in the prairie provinces. And the political possibilities in these jurisdictions were shaped by the events of 1918–30. Had there been no revolutionary socialist crisis and no Progressivism, the Co-operative Commonwealth Federation could never have developed into a significant ideological alternative in prairie public life. If the electorates in the prairie metropolis and the wheat provinces had not been cultivated to accept just such a message as the CCF espoused, a single nation-wide third force could never have developed. This might seem an exaggeration in the light of British experience, but we must remember the American example and, indeed, the weakness of the left in eastern Canada. Among the false starts and failed dreams of the 1920s, therefore, the establishment of the Independent Labour parties and farmers' socialist movements in Winnipeg and the prairies was an important, if obscure, point of departure for the modern party system in Canada.

The nature of Canada's socialism can be illustrated by two Winnipeg events. In October 1909, Big Bill Haywood, the famous American syndicalist, spoke to a quiet attentive audience of respectable size in the Winnipeg Trades Hall. In the same week, Will Crooks, a Labour member of the British Parliament, received an overwhelming response when he rose to address a much larger crowd in that very hall; after the moving ovation, he began, 'I thought I was a stranger in a strange land.'[41] In the contrast lies an important fact: prairie socialism was led by Britons and British Canadians who deferred to the British example, not on specific planks but on matters of fundamental principle; most prairie socialists believed they were as loyal to the crown and respectful of the law as any other British subject. Like their counterparts in the 'Mother Country,' they insisted on a pragmatic evolutionary party that aimed to work within the parliamentary system. They were the inheritors, they would have said, of the British tradition of liberty and democracy, but they believed, too, in the worth of working people and in just rewards for their labour.

One of the ironies of politics – and an illustration of the British legacy – was that the prairie socialist alternative was founded on the contribution of an opponent of socialism, F.J. Dixon. He, more than J.S. Woodsworth or R.B. Russell, first made the movement viable. Son of a coachman on an English estate, Dixon left school at thirteen, came to Canada at nineteen, and, by twenty-nine, was making a living as a full-time political organizer in Winnipeg. Strikingly handsome, an able platform speaker, and a courageous, independent politician, Dixon made his name on two issues, the single tax and direct legislation. The former was indicative of his debt to Henry George, the American reformer, who would redistribute wealth by taxing land and returning the revenue to the people through government works and services. The latter was rooted in a determination, especially evident on the prairies, to prevent the development of the 'special interests' by the implementation of such conventions as the referendum, the initiative, and the recall, which were expected to permit the public to exert greater control over government. As the leader of a Direct Legislation League and a League for the Taxation of Land Values, Dixon won a large following both in Winnipeg and in the rural west among reformers of all political stripes. His column in the *Grain Growers' Guide*, his position in the Manitoba legislature (he was elected in 1914 as an Independent), and his ties with the working-class community in Winnipeg ensured that he would be widely known and appreciated. And, though it won him only pain during the war, his insistence on the inalienability of human rights, including the right to life, and thus to be a pacifist and to resist conscription, further demonstrated both his integrity and his profound faith in what he saw as the British tradition of individual liberty. His pacifism drove him away from an informal alliance with the Liberal government of Manitoba and resulted in his return to the provincial legislature as a candidate for the Dominion Labour Party in 1920. But he soon renounced his affiliation with the DLP because of its continuing quarrels with other labour and socialist movements over who should be blamed for the 1919 crisis. Later in 1920, Dixon led his followers into an Independent Labour Party. As its provincial House leader, Dixon was the embodiment of the ILP. He dropped his pre-war praise of competition and attacks on socialism, replacing them with support of co-operativism and even of group government: 'There must be some progressive form [of government] which would give the workers a greater voice in the management of industry, a greater share of the wealth they produced and the establishment of the principle of co-operation in industry ... co-operation in distribution and co-operation in production.'[42] But he continued to believe in the competitive market economy. Given the opportunity, he might nationalize public utilities and national resources; he might levy a severe land tax; but he would not abolish the capitalist's quest for private profit. Privilege would be abolished by such measures as free trade, but liberty must remain. Thus Dixon led a party that was, in its own way, as inclusive and pragmatic – and as liberal – as its old-line opponents. The ILP included radical socialists but also progressives and free enterprisers; its deepest commitment was not to socialism, as defined by Marxist or Fabian theory, but to peaceful, gradual, practical reform.

The Saskatchewan left had similarly diverse origins. One of its crucial figures, M.J. Coldwell, was, like Dixon, a moderate. Coldwell was born in 1888 in Devon, England, son of a businessman whose indifferent success pushed the family to take in boarders. But his parents scrimped in order to educate the children, and, before

Coldwell sailed for Canada at the age of twenty-two to try his luck as a teacher in the new west, he had earned a university certificate in teacher training and had spent several golden years – rugger, pipe-smoking, tea with a young lady whom he later returned to marry – at University College, Exeter. An able teacher in an occupation that was just assuming professional status in Saskatchewan, Coldwell rose rapidly to a principalship in Regina, a coveted post, and helped to organize a teachers' professional association. He also became active in reform politics, first as a concerned and unconventional city alderman, then as a leader in a long-running lecture series on public issues, and finally as a Progressive party candidate in the 1925 federal election. He was not a socialist or even a labour party representative in the mid-1920s, but he was keenly aware of the economic circumstances of urban workers and of farmers because he had taught in both city and village schools. Coldwell espoused the usual western Canadian critique of eastern-dominated party caucuses; his was a 'people's party,' aiming to 'hasten the day when the forces of special privileges will be decisively defeated.' By the late 1920s, when Progressivism faltered, he moved easily into an alliance with the Saskatchewan labour movement – the province's Independent Labour Party was formed in 1929 – and thence into a coalition with representatives of the farm movement. For Coldwell as for Dixon, sympathy with working people and a commitment to 'loyalty, fair play and honesty' rather than to socialist ideology were the underpinnings of a public career.[43]

Saskatchewan farmers, not urban radicals, injected a strain of socialism into prairie provincial politics in the 1920s. But to distinguish one perspective or leader is impossible. George Williams was probably the most influential spokesman in the long run. He was born in Binscarth, Manitoba, in 1894, fought overseas, and then became a farmer near Semans, in the Touchwood Hills district of south-central Saskatchewan that for some reason seemed to raise radical farmers along with wheat. Williams belonged to a left-wing caucus in the farmers' movement, spoke of the 'exploitation of the mass of the people, agricultural and industrial alike by the capitalistic class,' and wished to create a co-operative commonwealth distinguished by 'producer control of industry and the powers of government.' On his left were Marxists such as Frank Eliason, former member of the SPC, and W.E. Wiggins, an admirer of the Soviet Union; and on his right were the thousands of farmers who supported the pools and wished to reform farm credit arrangements but had no thought of changing the economic system. The crisis of 1929–31 pushed all of them to the left, however, and at the same time into an alliance with Coldwell and the ILP.[44]

Though the story has yet to be told, there is little reason to think that the Alberta farm and labour movements did not evolve in a fashion similar to those of Saskatchewan. Urban labour councils and political parties were well established by the early 1920s and, despite the One Big Union upheaval, were able to elect representatives to city councils and to the provincial assembly in that decade. The farm movement, of course, was much more successful in Alberta politics, having elected a government in 1921 and returned it to power in 1926 and 1930. But even this success did not appease the radical farmers, and, as the economic crisis deepened in 1929–30, they, like their Saskatchewan and Manitoba counterparts, turned to thoughts of a farm-labour alliance to renew their movement and, particularly through action at the national level, to reform the economy.[45]

The development of farm-labour connections in each of the three prairie provinces was accompanied by the emergence of a national spokesman for the cause. James Shaver Woodsworth was the ILP representative for Centre Winnipeg and, as the decade passed, the leading parliamentary critic of the old-line parties. Around him gathered the more radical farmers, the disgruntled independents, and the rare Labour MPs. Around him, eventually, a party was formed. By such accidents of personality as well as the impersonal forces of class and region were the institutions of the nation directed into new channels.[46]

Woodsworth was an austere and even rigid person to be the leader of a party, but his many strengths were made even greater by his apparent asceticism. Son of one of the most important Methodist missionary administrators in late-nineteenth-century western Canada, Woodsworth grew up in the narrow confident world of British Canada's Manitoba, attended the Methodist Wesley College in Winnipeg, and, in his early twenties, became a circuit-rider among the farm communities in the southwest of the province. But he then went to Toronto and to England for further study before settling down to the inevitable mark of success – a city church. His encounter with other cities, cultures, and approaches to the church were revelations. He was shocked by the discovery that thousands, even millions, of his fellows lived in poverty and misery in the slums of eastern Canada and Britain. And, when he returned to Winnipeg, he was shocked to find that the same tragedy had arrived in western Canada. The religious doubts of a Methodist who possessed neither the fiery conviction of the circuit-rider nor the intellectual patience of the theologian were combined in Woodsworth with a will for improvement and a horror at things as they were. Several times he tried to resign from the church because he could not accept Methodist doctrines and because his own faith seemed uncertain, but his problems were pushed aside by more flexible supervisors. Then, having concluded that his own work should be devoted to the needy rather than to the comfortable, Woodsworth moved from the pulpit to a variety of social reform occupations – superintendent of All Peoples' Mission in Winnipeg's north end (1907–13), secretary of the national office of the Canadian Welfare League (1913–16), and director of a prairie-wide government-sponsored Bureau of Social Research (1916–17). The war provoked a final crisis, however, and in 1918, having concluded that his pacifism was the last of many causes that separated him from his fellow Methodists, he left the church for good. Within months, he had become a longshoreman in Vancouver. Once immersed in the extraordinary debates about socialist revolution and social reform of 1918–19, he opted decisively for the evolutionary and parliamentary path to the end which, he believed, all radicals aspired: 'collective ownership and democratic control of the means of wealth production.' He saw his path as the middle way, the compromise between the conservatism of Gompers's supporters and the radicalism of the One Big Union. His closest friend in Winnipeg, F.J. Dixon, reinforced this view, and when the ILP sought a nominee in Central Winnipeg for the 1921 federal election Dixon and others of like mind pushed him forward. Woodsworth carried the riding and, at forty-six, began his career as a politician.[47]

When he attended the opening of Parliament in 1922, in the middle of the post-war depression, Woodsworth was taken aback by the pageantry of the glittering occasion and by the easy familiarity of those in the inner circles of government, business, and 'high society': 'Only now am I beginning to sense the fact that we have a governing class ... as I saw Clifford Sifton and his wife who, during my boyhood days in Brandon I had known as neighbours, I wondered whether, after all, the majority of this grand assembly were not very ordinary folk. The whole affair appeared to me very false and superficial – an attempt to impress upon our young democracy the vestigial remains of the feudalism of Europe.' But his strategy for dealing with the tragic circumstances of Canada was only beginning to take shape. He concluded that human welfare must replace private profit as the organizing principle of society. He believed that, just to start the process, the power of banks must be broken, the problem of unemployment faced, and the national economy placed on a properly planned foundation. But as his Labour colleague William Irvine explained to the House, their party of two ('the honourable Member for Centre Winnipeg is the leader of the labour group – and I am the group') also assumed that the parliamentary system should itself be reformed by the adoption of the 'group government' idea.[48]

It was a hopeless cause, as the Labour and Progressive members learned to their cost. By 1924, the absence of discipline in Progressive ranks had left that group in disarray. Woodsworth then forced them to confront their ambivalence. In the debate on the budget, a measure that disappointed the Progressives in particular, Woodsworth moved an amendment calling for a lowered tariff, the revenue shortfall to be made up by taxes on unearned income, unimproved land values, and a graduated inheritance tax. The motion was a direct steal from the Progressive platform and thus forced the Progressives to choose between the King government and their principles. Fourteen Progressives supported the amendment, and ten of them later left the Progressive fold to sit as a 'ginger group.' These ten were the strongest 'group movement' advocates in the Commons, but, because of their distaste for the compromises of the King government, they were also the closest in sympathy with the Labour MPs. In the Parliament of 1925–6, the Progressives defeated two governments without securing a single concession, while the two-member Labour group, which also held part of the balance of power in the narrowly divided chamber, secured King's agreement to introduce old age pensions. The lesson was obvious. A party could exert leverage in the parliamentary system where a loosely organized movement, handicapped by the absence of group discipline and even of common principles, could not.

Party organization came to seem essential to the reformers who wished to work within the parliamentary system. Thus, in federal politics as in the provinces, the ideology of group government gave way to the formation of a party – and to practical discussions about permanent offices, paid memberships, and centrally directed educational campaigns. The reform movement was already, by the late 1920s, being translated into a reform party. Progressivism did not die, in other words, but rather underwent a time of testing, in which the less committed dropped away. It emerged as a smaller, more disciplined group with agreement on ideology and tactics that made possible the eventual formation of a third party. Significantly, this was a national and a provincial rather than regional party. The idea of a western mission to rebuild Canada, which had informed the pre-war prairie reformers and had remained a powerful force in the outlook of 'Manitoban' Progressives, was not an important factor in the labour-farm coalition of the late 1920s. Instead, a new national reform outlook was beginning to emerge: British in cultural memory, Canadian in loyalty, this outlook praised the 'worker,' reviled the 'parasite,' and promised economic justice through democratic government.

While the west was the focus of Canadian attention and the recipient of international publicity between 1900 and 1914, it was the fulfilment of hopes kindled a half-century earlier in the days of John A. Macdonald and George Brown. In the years following the First World War, westerners attempted to seize the initiative in Canadian public life. Various versions of the new Confederation were promoted by western political movements, but none was adopted. By the end of the 1920s, the prairie west was merely one – and not the first – among Canada's regions. The abrupt end of western dreams marked the end, too, of a national purpose that had inspired Canadians since the birth of their nation. But something permanent had been added to the national fabric: the dominant group in prairie public life had asserted itself against radical and 'ethnic' newcomers and, to the relief of British Canadians from coast to coast, had consolidated its economic and social control; the moderate reformers had secured notable victories on such issues as temperance and the formation of the United Church and, in the process, had reinforced the tradition of western protest in national public life; and, finally, after a number of failed attempts to overthrow or purify the national political parties, prairie reformers had laid the foundation for a new, uniquely Canadian party system.

# 15

# The Depression 1930–40

The Dirty Thirties. The drought. The Great Depression. Hard Times. Ragged drifters moving through a world made desolate by dust and grasshoppers. Cold winds slicing through the city's heart, tossing drifts of snow, toying with scraps of paper. And outbursts of high spirits. The images have become clichés and yet they are accurate. The 1930s stand out in prairie history because they provided a collective experience that was as important in the development of a regional society as the era of the pioneer. Not that others in North America or around the world didn't experience hard times: rather, that the people of the prairie west faced the crisis together.

The decade was distinguished, first and foremost, by the agricultural crisis. But it was also an era of urban poverty, as the bread lines and relief payments will suggest. Political behaviour, too, was distinctive; students of politics think of the decade as one of experiment, especially because of the influence of two new parties, Social Credit and the Co-operative Commonwealth Federation, but also because federal-provincial relations were re-examined for the first time since Confederation, partly because of pleas emanating from prairie governments. The 1930s were the years of trial. Residents of the prairies entered the era of the Second World War more aware of their regional identity and, paradoxically, of their dependence on the nation than ever before. Despite the expressions of class and ethnic division during the decade, they were also more united than at any time in the past.

The Great Depression assumed different aspects in various parts of the world. In western Europe, it was associated with the problems of war debts and reparation payments arising from the 1919 Paris peace settlement. In the offices and homes of the northeastern United States, it was often ascribed to the collapse in October 1929 of the notorious financial house of cards on Wall Street. In Australia and Argentina, the Depression was discussed in terms of the extraordinary drop in agricultural prices and the virtual disappearance of farm export markets. And in many parts of the globe, it was related to the unexpected failure of precipitation – a drought that struck at the very foundation of crop and animal production and thus at the base of human existence.

These problems all had their impact on the prairie west. Drought, agricultural price declines, and the failure of foreign markets hit prairie farmers like hammer blows. The rigidities of the financial system locked them into fixed interest payments on debts contracted in a more optimistic era. And the lack of income among prairie consumers meant that the light industry of the prairie cities, as well as the wholesale and service sectors, could not continue at pre-1929 levels. Had it lasted two or three years, as in the previous recessions of 1907–8, 1913–15, and 1920–3, it would have been forgotten with the others. But a peculiar combination of factors ensured that it would hang on in western Canada, year after year, even when the rest of the world was recovering, until only the return of war provided an ironic release.

The agricultural depression was devastating. Prairie farmers had known uncertain times in the preceding fifteen years but the trend, seen from the perspective of the late 1920s, was to higher yields and better cash returns. Acreage in field crops had increased dramatically during the First World War and had then levelled off at about 22 million acres in the mid-1920s. It was slightly above that level, at 25 million acres, in 1928–9. Yields in the 1920s had been satisfactory, too, culminating in a record harvest in 1928. Prices had also been satisfactory, despite a drop in 1928–9.[1] In the late 1920s, the optimism generated by yield, acreage, and price was reinforced by growing faith in the marketing system, due in large measure to the farmers' establishment of their own marketing agents – the wheat

pools. With this mechanism in place, they hoped, individual farmers would be shielded from the worst vagaries of the competitive
market. All in all, prairie farmers had good reason for optimism in
the late 1920s.

Agricultural prospects were not without blemish. Most important
among the potential problems was the reliance on a single economic
activity and a single export crop. The prairie farmer, contrary to the
advice of some experts, had continued to specialize in wheat production: 60 per cent of field crop cash income came from wheat sales
(1926–9). Moreover, 70 per cent of that wheat was exported. And
the world wheat market was not stable: by the late 1920s, over-pro-
duction in exporting countries was being combined with reduced
purchases by importing nations. Quotas and embargos introduced
by France, Germany, and Italy, combined with high domestic support prices in those countries, seriously affected Canadian cereal
grain sales. The expansion of prairie field crop acreage also implied
that farmers were taking greater risks in their annual bets against
soils and climate: cultivation of the arid lands of Palliser's Triangle
and neglect of summerfallow and other moisture conservation practices could only be seen as poor risks in the long run. Moreover, it
was estimated that nearly 30 per cent of prairie farm capital was
borrowed at fixed charges. The assumption of such heavy fixed debt
obligations during the optimistic 1920s – debts for more land, new
field equipment, mechanization, and such consumer items as better
houses and clothing – ensured that the day of reckoning, if it came,
would be very dark indeed.[1]

The agricultural crisis, like the Canadian industrial recession, began before the Wall Street crash. World wheat prices were dropping
in the summer of 1929, and to make matters worse the prairie crop
was disappointingly small. For some parts of the west, indeed, the
drought began in the summer of 1929. Despite the low income that
this combination of lower prices and smaller harvests would create,
the farmers' representatives on the boards of the pools attempted to
flex their muscles in world markets. If the pooling theory was valid,
they argued, united action among the sellers of a major exporting
nation such as Canada to hold a large fraction of world production
off the markets should drive the price up. So the pools held back on
sales, hoping for a price rise. The commencement of a new crop year
in August 1930 saw the pool directors steadfast in their optimism.
Thus, despite a continuing decline in wheat prices, they promised

farmers an initial payment of one dollar per bushel. The stunning drop in world commodity prices in late 1930 made a hash of these calculations. The pools headed for receivership and the farmers for poverty. The combination of American business troubles and the collapse of commodity prices led in turn, by 1931, to an international financial crisis and the utter failure of world trade and capital flows. By 1933, the total value of world trade had fallen 65 per cent as compared with 1929. The Winnipeg price of wheat fell below forty cents per bushel for No. 1 Northern in late December 1932, 'a price which had no parallel in its world counterpart throughout the preceding four hundred years.'[2] Recovery of the international economy began in 1933, but by then domestic circumstances had ensured that the prairie farmer would see little of the world trade expansion.

The farmer was triply cursed: even when the international market began to recover, Canadian economic policy and prairie growing conditions combined to keep him in bondage. One of these difficult circumstances was at least within the control of human action. Tariffs had long been the bane of prairie farmers and the touchstone of Canadian manufacturing interests. As the Depression deepened, manufacturers called for increased protection against the 'dumping' of foreign products in Canada. This appeal was reinforced by government economic advisers who argued that higher tariffs would force Canada's trading partners to reconsider their protectionist trade policies and, consequently, to negotiate reciprocal reductions in tariffs. In the memorable phrase of Prime Minister R.B. Bennett, Canada would 'blast her way into the markets of the world.' It was a bold policy, but prairie farmers were Bennett's cannon fodder. While the share of national income earned by those in the service industries and other better-insulated occupations rose from 29 per cent to 35 per cent (1929–32), and the share earned by workers in manufacturing remained almost stable (14 per cent and 15 per cent), the portion earned by primary producers (including farmers) was cut in half (23 per cent to 12 per cent). What is worse, the primary products of the central provinces – newsprint, wood pulp, non-ferrous metals, hydro-electric power – were to some degree protected by the continuing market in the United States; the western farmer remained tied to traditional markets in the United Kingdom and Europe. Thus, in the 1930s, this tariff policy was a further source of east-west antagonism. Federal tariff policies protected Canadian industry at the expense of primary producers. No major Canadian industry suffered as much as agriculture in the economic down-swing, and none recovered so slowly. As the economist A.E. Safarian commented, 'Western agriculture bore the whole brunt of both fluctuating export income and the rigid costs of the Canadian economy.'[3]

Stories of the Dirty Thirties – the name expresses the image – began with the weather. Every prairie child has heard how, in that dark time, parents determined whether kids could go to school: they threw a gopher into the air and if he didn't come down they knew he had dug a burrow – and it was much too dusty to risk the trip. The dust storms began in 1931. Hot dry winds blew steadily day after day in the month of June when, normally, soft rains are expected to assist crop germination. On 1 July, the customary Dominion Day baseball tournaments in towns across the prairies were disrupted by blowing dust; fans who braved the stinging blasts in the open bleachers of a hundred ball diamonds were as preoccupied with the utter failure of their crops as with the prospect of a community supper and dance. The next two years were not as severe, but the summer of 1934 was even worse. Soil began to blow in mid-June, to destroy gardens and crops, to drift across window and door sills, and by mid-summer, for the first time in living memory, to cause the cancellation of many fairs in villages across the southern plains: the ball games and dances might still proceed, but the garden competitions could hardly continue without entrants. The weather of 1935 was not quite as forbidding, but 1936 was a disaster. The coldest winter in history, with chilling records compounded by blizzard after blizzard, offered one slight ray of hope in that the snow promised moisture for the spring. But the summer brought new records – the longest hottest summer yet – with temperatures regularly above 100 degrees Fahrenheit, deaths from heat prostration, and, most serious, intimations that the drought and high winds were causing desert-like conditions to spread over the southern plain. It was becoming apparent that, like the Sahara, the prairie desert was moving and growing. The customary autumn rains never did arrive to relieve the gloom in many districts in 1936, the winter was again unusually cold, and the summer of 1937 crushed the little hope that remained. May and June of that year were even hotter, drier, windier, and dirtier than the year before. Dust storms reduced visibility to a few feet, lakes went dry, and farmers actually raced to cut Russian thistle in order to feed starving cattle. Needless to say, there was no crop – not even enough for seed – on the southern plain. Then, in mid-July, the baleful blue and brown of the drought-burned skies gave way to the low clouds of the fabled three-day rain. Relief had come. Even the subsequent disasters of stem rust and grasshoppers in 1938 could not take away the belief that the climate had finally righted itself.[4]

Heat, wind, and the absence of moisture were only part of the prairie tragedy. With the drought's ideal conditions, grasshoppers proliferated into a plague of biblical proportions. In 1930, they infested several thousand square miles; by the end of the decade, as abandoned farms offered growing numbers of incubation beds, they were a serious problem in several hundred thousand square miles – almost the entire western interior with the exception of parts of Manitoba. The appetites of the so-called Rocky Mountain locusts seemed insatiable, their tastes diverse. It is hard to separate tall tale from fact, but they were said to have consumed not only gardens and crops but also shrubs, the sweaty part of pitchfork handles, clothes on the line, and even shirts on their owners' backs. They died in drifts, they carpeted sidewalks, they flew in clouds that darkened the sky and hummed like squadrons of alien invaders. And, as if grasshoppers were not enough, sawfly, army worm, and cutworm infestations also destroyed crops and gardens in record numbers. Gophers, too, flourished in this climate, burrowing beneath the fields, eating and destroying grain by the bushel. They became a dietary supplement for impoverished families and, for thousands of school children, a profitable source of sport; both Saskatchewan and Alberta offered a penny a piece for gopher tails and, in peak years, paid over a million claims. Yet another enemy of the farmer was plant disease. In the years when rain did fall, as in 1935, wheat stem rust cut into the plant and toppled the grain or prevented it from heading out; farmers walked through apparently bountiful crops to discover that there was nothing to harvest, and the red dust on their overalls announced that Marquis wheat, the famous wheat strain developed in the pre-war years, had been made obsolete by these new conditions.

Proof that the disaster was complete was provided by the annual compilations of yield and income. An average prairie wheat crop in the 1920s produced 350 million bushels (17 bushels per seeded acre), whereas in the five terrible years 1933–7 it produced an average of 230 million bushels (9.5 bushels per seeded acre). Averages concealed the peaks and valleys: Saskatchewan in 1937 produced an average of 2.6 bushels per acre. The price experience followed the same pattern. One government estimate of wheat prices (all grades considered) was one dollar per bushel in the last half of the 1920s, forty-six cents per bushel in the first half of the 1930s, and sixty-six cents per bushel in the second half. Naturally, farm income was drastically reduced. In the late 1920s, income from the sale of farm products averaged well over $500 million per year, but in the early 1930s it reached barely $180 million (just over one-third as much) and for the 1930s it averaged only $250 million per year, or one-half of the standard attained in the 1926–9 era. In the austere language of the economist: 'Producers throughout the wheat economy were destitute and relief was required on an unprecedented scale to avert disaster. In the drought area the repeated crop failures wiped out not only the livelihood but also the entire working capital of resident farmers, and rural relief requirements included not only food, fuel, clothing, and shelter, as for unemployed wage earners in urban centres, but seed, feed, tractor fuel, and supplies as well.' The crisis was worst in the wheat belt of Saskatchewan where, by the end of the terrible crop failure of 1937, it was estimated that two in three members of the farm population were destitute.[5]

One response to the crisis was to leave. About 250,000 people moved out of the prairies between 1931 and 1941, reversing the flow of population for the first time since 1870. Saskatchewan was actually declining in total population in the late 1930s, and neither Manitoba nor Alberta was growing at a rate equivalent to its natural increase. In addition to the out-migration, however, prairie society was also affected by dramatic movements of population within the region, especially by an exodus from the short-grass plains of the south to the wooded parkbelt farther north. The number of families who abandoned the dust bowl is uncertain, but the 1936 census reported almost 14,000 abandoned farms on the prairies, of which 8,200 were in Saskatchewan and 5,000 in Alberta, encompassing 3 million acres. Saskatchewan's worst year was yet to come. About 15,000 families moved from the plains to the parkland. The new was probably better than the old, but the transition was not made easily. What could be expected when the uprooted had neither capital equipment nor experience with the different conditions of agriculture in wooded terrain?[6]

Families left the dry belt quietly, for the most part, beaten by the wind, the dust, and the hunger, hauling a lifetime's earnings in a couple of wagons or hay-racks behind a team of emaciated horses or in old and even dangerous cars and trucks. They carried a few clothes and utensils, some furniture and lumber, and perhaps a cow; they said good-bye to neighbours, to friendships built in the shared circumstances of pioneering, and set off for the north. They headed for the heavily wooded, even swampy lands north of the Carrot River, near Meadow Lake, or past Peace River. Palliser's Triangle or government policy errors had defeated them, and now they would confront new problems in the very different agriculture of the northern prairie fringe. But, with the assistance of government agencies, forests were cleared, muskegs drained, and log cabins built. The cycle of prairie pioneering took one more – and final – turn.[7]

Aside from these understandable departures, what is surprising and even inspiring in retrospect is the determination of the farm community in the southern prairies to confront the Depression head on and defeat it. Scientists, administrators, and farmers contributed a great deal to the ultimate recovery of the agricultural economy. One victim of the rehabilitation program was the cultivation practice of the preceding two generations. It had become the custom in the semi-arid prairies to leave a field fallow in a three- or even a two-year rotation to conserve moisture. In order to combat weed growth on the idle fields, the maintenance of 'black' summerfallow – deep cultivation followed by careful and repeated surface tilling – had become common. (The proud farmer would point to his neat black fields and claim that they were proof of his attention to duty.) The extra cultivation killed weeds, to be sure, but in a succession of dry years, the pulverized, fibreless topsoil was ready to fly with the first high wind, thus eroding the surface and sand-blasting the plants in adjacent fields. On bad days in the mid-1930s it was impossible to drive alongside open fields, so heavy was the dust and so limited the visibility.[8]

The problem of soil erosion was tackled by a new phenomenon of prairie life – the agricultural scientist. Staff scientists at the Dominion Experimental Farm in Swift Current, Saskatchewan, and their colleagues at similar stations in Scott and Indian Head and at Medicine Hat, Alberta, as well as in the agricultural schools of the three prairie universities were now available to make such matters their business. Agriculture was becoming a profession; and, as in other fields, the practitioners were to be aided by science: professionals would ensure that farmers, like doctors and teachers, would have the best available information and practice when they undertook their assignments.

Scientists' answers to the problem of soil drifting, which had been available for several decades, were applied in the last half of the 1930s. They had proved that weeds, not capillary action, consumed moisture in summerfallow. They had demonstrated, too, that a lumpy weed-free fallow would provide the essential drift-resistant and moisture-retaining properties in soil. How to achieve this type of limited cultivation? Farmers must abandon the regular use of the mould board plough and harrows, which raked the soil into a dry 'dust mulch,' and adopt instead a shallower cutting edge: no more ploughing of dry soil and no fall ploughing in the high wind of Palliser's Triangle. The new implement did not emerge overnight. Instead, the tried and tested techniques of listing shovels (which ploughed high furrows that caught drifting soil) and strip farming, which had been used for years in the United States and in southern Alberta, were used in the interim. In the longer term, one crucial innovation was 'stubble-mulch,' often known by the term 'trash farming,' in which weeds were uprooted early but left on the surface of the fallow to prevent wind erosion. Another was the development of drought-resistant grass that could outgrow weeds and could root in even the most drift-prone soil.

But what was essential was a new method of soil cultivation that would cut the weeds, permit summerfallow to retain moisture, but not encourage wind erosion. Here the farmers were as important as the agricultural engineers. Charles S. Noble was the most persistent of a dozen farmer experimenters in Alberta, and his invention, the Noble Blade for cultivators, refined with the aid of scientists and other farmers in the late 1930s, became popular in his province. Saskatchewan farmers concentrated on a different type of soil-cutting tool, the disc, and produced dozens of variations in backyard smithies during the 1930s. So intense was popular participation in the project that, when the University of Saskatchewan co-operated with local inventors to test promising new models at Kindersley in May and June 1945, hundreds of farmers converged on the town to watch the trials. Within a year, dozens of home-made discers were emerging from the machine and blacksmith shops of the Saskatchewan plains, their quantity limited only by the availability of steel pipe and wheels in local junk yards. That farmers were deadly serious should not be forgotten: at one such meeting on dry-land farming technique, the lecturer, straight from his laboratory at the Swift Current experimental farm, was greeted abruptly by a farmer: 'We aren't here today for social talk and we didn't come here just to visit with you. We're here to learn how to control soil drifting. We've got a problem and we want you to tell us how to fix it. If you can't do that, tell us right now and we'll go home. But if you've got any answers for us ... we will stay with you till the cows come home.'[9]

These scientists produced results by co-operating with and learning from their pupils. In some cases, the student became the teacher, and in others the local boy or girl returned to tackle local problems. Norman Criddle had become the federal government's entomologist for Manitoba in the 1920s. Some years before, as a young man on his father's ranch near Brandon, he had observed that grasshoppers swarmed on the fresh manure that he cleaned out of the barn each morning. His later experiments led him to conclude that, in the early morning hours, the grasshoppers were attracted by moisture. He was soon testing various mixtures of bait – wet bran and sawdust in particular – with poisons. Without his breakthrough, and the co-operation of tens of thousands of farmers who travelled to government-sponsored 'mixing stations' to pick up poison bait, the grasshoppers would never have been defeated in the 1930s.

Farm-scientist co-operation improved as the decade proceeded. By 1938, Saskatchewan was able to organize a vast 'short-course' scheme in which the government billeted the farmers while universities and experimental farms supplied the speakers for ten-day schools that were conducted in a dozen centres around the province. Agricultural Improvement Associations were similarly influential. Organized by the Dominion Experimental Farms, 109 local instructional groups with 14,000 members were formed within two years of the movement's initiation in 1935. At the centre of the activity was an ungainly creature known to prairie citizens as the PFRA, the Prairie Farm Rehabilitation Administration. The PFRA, an agency of the federal government, was created in 1935 to salvage the worst-hit areas of the agricultural economy. Only the infusion of federal money, indeed, was adequate to the task. These grants permitted the establishment of forty-eight experimental substations where farmers could be taught how to deal with the problem of severe soil drifting. A second significant PFRA program dealt with water conservation and land reclamation. Grants and engineering advice created not only a number of community irrigation schemes but also encouraged thousands of farmers to undertake small projects such as dug-outs and dams that collected and stored spring run-off for watering small herds of farm animals.[10] Associated with this work was an attempt to correct the tragic mistakes of 1908 when the driest areas of Palliser's Triangle were taken from ranchers and opened for homesteads, often with far too many farms on too little land. This reclamation had begun in the Tilley East area of Alberta in 1927 and was now extended to other areas where soil drifting was a problem, especially on abandoned land such as that around Melita, Manitoba, and Cadillac, Saskatchewan. In both provinces, control of the worst lands was transferred to the crown – thorny problem though such assembly was – and the areas were then fenced, seeded with grass, and turned over to local 'community pasture' associations that determined grazing rights. Not only did projects stop soil erosion and save livestock, but they also provided work, relief money, and even adequate machinery for communities that lacked all three.[11]

The soil reclamation projects were an undoubted success, and the water conservation and land use schemes did much to correct the errors of an earlier generation of policy-makers. Nevertheless, discussion of the victories should not be allowed to conceal the facts of defeat. The migration of 250,000 people out of the region and of another 50,000 or more from their accustomed homes to new and very difficult circumstances on the northern prairie fringe was a failure of serious dimensions. The loss of annual income equivalent to about half the farmers' annual returns – and the even heavier burdens imposed on this limited revenue by fixed charges for interest and taxes – were similarly serious. The decimation of accumulated capital, whether in the form of deteriorating houses, worn-out implements, or starving livestock, was proof that farm families had been reduced to the barest minimum.

A reform as fundamental in its implications as the scientific breakthroughs and the PFRA was the federal government's decision to intervene in the grain marketing process. This intervention had been sought by some farmers as early as the First World War but, to their disappointment, Prime Minister Meighen had approved a return to the futures market and the private grain trade in 1920. The wheat pool system, to which reform-minded farmers had turned after that setback, was, in their view, a 'second best' alternative. The failure of the pools in 1930 and the collapse of international commodity markets again brought the question of government grain marketing to the fore. R.B. Bennett's cabinet was under enormous pressure to relieve the burdens on farmers and, to judge by the leaders of prairie farm movements, the prairie preference was for a national wheat marketing board. In early 1935, Bennett yielded on this, as he did on so many proposals for government intervention in the economy. Faced with continuing economic crisis and an imminent election, he finally decided to use the power of government to correct abuses that private enterprise had failed to remedy. His original proposal for the Canadian Wheat Board was stunning: the draft legislation would have nationalized the entire western elevator system, would have created a monopoly agency for the sale of the major field crops – wheat, oats, barley, rye, and flax seed – and would have established this board as the exclusive dealer in these commodities both at home and abroad. But when the private traders had completed their lobby, the board was a shadow of its former self: it became a wheat, not a grain marketing agency; its elevator system was never created; and its compulsory features were eliminated, leaving it to establish an annual minimum price for wheat that farmers were free to accept or to reject in favour of the offers of private companies. The Canadian Wheat Board, as created in 1935, was simply 'an optional marketing channel which freed producers from dependence on the open market system without in any way interfering with that system.'[12] But the act did mark an important turning point. The federal government was now marketing grain and, more important, was guaranteeing a minimum price for Canada's most important crop. Henceforth, the government could be seen as 'a buffer between chaotic conditions in the international wheat market and the farmers on the land in western Canada.'[13]

The significance of this safety net for western farmers became evident in 1939. In that year, Mackenzie King's government planned to eliminate the Wheat Board until prairie farmers rose in wrath. King quickly backed down and, in order to mollify western critics before the next election was called, extended the farmers' safety net by introducing the Prairie Farm Assistance Act (1939). Taken together, the amendments to the Wheat Board Act and the new PFAA provided maximum protection to the small producer and instituted an insurance plan against crop failures. Ottawa had capitulated to the prairie campaign. The federal government would now be the guarantor of a 'fair price' for prairie wheat. As D.A. MacGibbon concluded: 'The really significant fact was that the Government had tried to get out of the business of selling wheat and had failed.'[14]

No community could have sustained such a prolonged and devastating calamity as the Great Depression without direct assistance payments to its citizens. And thus, for prairie residents, rural and urban alike, 'relief' was a disagreeable necessity. The payments commenced as early as 1929 in some districts of rural Saskatchewan and continued without break for a decade. Saskatchewan's municipal and provincial authorities started on a modest scale with road work and seed loans, but by 1931 the problem was so general that a newly created Relief Commission divided much of the province into three categories of disaster for the distribution of food, fodder, clothing, fuel, farm supplies, and even school relief. Supplementary government payments to doctors, too, enabled many districts to maintain a degree of medical care. Churches and welfare organizations in the rest of Canada dispatched thousands of rail car loads of fruit, vegetables, clothing, fuel, and blankets during the decade. For prairie folk, the sweetest luxury was a box of apples; the most perplexing donation was rumoured to be Maritime dried cod, which, to several dry-landers unaccustomed to its preparation, seemed better suited to shingling outhouses than to alleviating hunger.

To people raised on the virtues of hard work and independence, relief was a humiliation. They lined up at a relief office where clerks – in rural areas often acquaintances – would fill out the forms listing their dependants, their assets, and their needs in order to determine eligibility for food chits. The relief was called a loan in Saskatchewan, partly to discourage abuses, but also to preserve the family's self-respect. Did the relief recipient really need to operate a car? Was it true that he somtimes drank a beer on Saturday night? Had he skipped the compulsory stint on the work detail? To the person on relief, the issue was phrased in a slightly different fashion – to wit, how to find the essential $1.50 that maintained self-respect. According to James Gray, who had firsthand experience, this extra cash was the margin on which one's character was maintained: the relief voucher system often covered food and fuel but not tobacco, toothpaste, lipstick, movies, haircuts, newspapers, or, indeed, that tantalizing glass of beer. Any one of these 'luxuries' might express just a little of one's independence and thus relieve the gloom.[15]

Relief administration varied with the locality, but almost everywhere the chief concern of the municipal government – whose responsibility for the relief of permanent residents could not be denied – was to keep expenses to a minimum. Vigilant officers in the relief agency took pains to ensure that unqualified candidates were cut from the list. The nativist attitude of one such public servant – 'I somewhat resent from an Austrian the inference that I have not a right to express my opinion' – illustrated the slights that accompanied the bureaucratic forms.[16]

The urban relief system was more rigid than its rural counterpart. Urban administrations made elaborate attempts to establish commodity lists that would provide an inexpensive balanced diet, to weigh the lobbies of retail merchants against the cost advantages of a central food depot, to avoid the stigma – especially for children – of drab, poor-quality 'relief clothing,' to distinguish 'legitimate' residents from migrants who were 'exploiting' the resources of the city, and thereby attested to the uncomfortable and unpleasant aspects of the new order. That almost one in five Saskatoon residents was on relief in the mid-1930s was an index to the scope of the problem.

The Winnipeg relief program can be seen as a special case because of its size, but it was probably typical in its origin and philosophy. It had been set in motion by the dual motivation of concern for one's impoverished fellows and fear of social conflict. A march of unemployed men, most of them European, had shocked the civic establishment on 1 May 1908 and prompted the creation of an Associated Charities organization that was supposed to dispense relief efficiently. Delegations to the provincial government, first of British tradesmen and then of central European unskilled workers, in the spring of 1915 forced the institution of a public works program. Later in the year, continuing civic concern about relief payments led to city council control over the program which had formerly been operated by the churches. And the long post-war recession produced a series of relief schemes in which the federal, provincial, and municipal governments participated. This last period of economic weakness set the pattern for the relief efforts of the 1930s as, for five winters in succession, from 1920–1 to 1924–5, from $200,000 to almost $500,000 was spent annually on direct relief for about 7,000 to 12,000 people or 5 per cent of the city's population.

The principles of the system, as established by the political leaders and their allies, the businessmen and socially concerned professions, were refined but not significantly altered during these two decades. Because the concept of unemployment – especially endemic unemployment – was unthinkable in the land of economic promise, relief was seen as a charitable handout in the depths of winter rather than an insurance program or a job-creation scheme. The worst evil in such relief systems was thought to be the creation of 'pauperism,' where individuals lost their initiative and became dependent on charity. Therefore, city officials offered only the barest minimum and, even then, only if the able-bodied male recipients were prepared to prove their worthiness by taking a 'work test' – that is, showing that they actually wanted to work by labouring cheerfully in the civic wood yard. Prevention of social upheaval, strict economy in operation, and the provision of emergency supplies rather than of jobs or insurance were the guiding principles of the system.

The size of the system should put the lie to careless generalizations, as much the product of home-grown myth-makers as of Hollywood, that the years before the 1930s constituted a boomtime. In fact, far from a roaring flamboyant decade, the 1920s were an era of recession and economic uncertainty, especially in the urban centres of western Canada. That 5 per cent of the residents of the regions's largest city required direct assistance during the winter months of five years is an index to the needs of the poor. The relief rolls contained over 2,200 male family heads in 1924–5, most of them unskilled labourers, though one in five worked in the building trades. Three in ten were European born, a similar proportion were born in Canada, and four in ten were British by birth. Most of the family heads were young adults, between 20 and 40 years of age. They had three children, on average, and lived in rented accommodation, for which many paid less than $15 per month. Four families in ten occupied four to six rooms; another four families in ten occupied two or three rooms; and 15 per cent of the families (about 350 in total) occupied only one room. Relief expenditures averaged over $250,000 in the first half of the 1920s, but tough rules and improvement in the economy reduced this sum to an average of $50,000 per year in the four years after 1925. Then, in the winter of 1929–30, another slump forced expenditures up. When the summer came, the problem did not disappear but instead became worse. Now single men as well as fathers of families were lining up at the civic offices looking for work and relief money. Their numbers were simply incredible. The city expenditure on relief averaged $3 million a year from 1930–1 to 1939–40 and began to drop only in 1941 and 1942. The number of people on relief and in relief work was about 17,000 in 1930–1 and remained between 30,000 and 40,000 for most of the decade. At least one in seven Winnipeggers was on relief for part of each year in the 1930s. It was an extraordinary crisis.[17]

Even if the relief vouchers enabled one to survive, the struggle was endless. The pleading letters in the files of Prime Minister R.B. Bennett constitute painful documentation of the sense of hopelessness and futility of the time:

Benton, Alberta
February 19,1935

... I suppose I am silly to write this letter but I haven't anyone else to write to ...

We are just one of many on relief and trying to keep our place without being starved out. Have a good 1/2 section not bad buildings and trying to get a start without any money and 5 children all small. Have been trying to send 3 to school and live on $10.00 a month relief for everything, medicine meat flour butter scribblers. Haven't had any milk for 3 months but will have 2 cows fresh in March some time. Am nursing a 10 months old baby and doing all the work cooking washing mending on bread and potatoes some days. This is our worst winter as my husband has had to be home to look after the outside chores. Other winters he always made some money as we lived in town and I could manage alone.

Am so worried on account of the children as we never have any vegetables except potatoes and almost no fruit and baby hasn't any shoes have kept him in old socks instead but now he is getting so he creeps and pulls them off so often. I would like to get a couple of little pigs this spring I am sure we can make a go of this place as its good land and doesn't blow if we would just manage until fall. Just had 70 acreas in last year and the dry spell just caught it right along with the grasshopper although we poisoned most of them there were hardly any left by fall. I can't hardly sleep for worrying about it ...

Please help me by lending me some money and I will send you my engagement ring and wedding ring as security ... My two rings cost over $100.00 15 yrs ago but what good are they when the flour is nearly all done and there isn't much to eat in the house in the city I could pawn them but away out here I haven't been off the farm this winter.[18]

Bennett sent five dollars as a gift.

One category of relief recipient was not handled with the rest. Chits and boondoggles could not mollify the single unemployed young men of the prairies – indeed, of the nation – who were becoming a serious concern to public authorities by the second and third years of the crisis. Homeless, penniless, and desperate, they 'rode the rods' beneath the boxcars from one city to the next, begged for food and clothing, camped in shantytowns outside major cities, and beseiged relief hostels when food and shelter could be scrounged nowhere else. Theirs was a sad and angry state, as a letter from one of them illustrated: 'Would you like to have us lie down like a bunch of spineless whelps and be contented as slaves? Is that all our grandfathers toiled for? Canada ... young nation ... letting her youth go to hell! Are you not proud of her? How can you sleep at nights while thousands of us are idle in brain and body, in want and privation? You who would cheer us on to the battlefield today send us to hell! What fools our mothers were to bear us! 'Tis to be hoped that there will be a stop made to bringing kids into this hopeless world if all they are to [be] offered is a relief camp! We who should be the pride of the nation are the derelicts! The curse!'[19] These young men, perhaps 50–70,000 of them in any given summer of the Depression, had to be treated carefully.[20] They were dangerous, for one thing, in an age when political violence and social upheaval were far from unknown; and they were delicate, for no leader wished to be responsible for destroying the health or the self-respect of the nation's youth. The answer was labour camps. For four years from their establishment in 1932, an average of 20,000 single homeless 'volunteers' were employed and housed under the supervision of the Department of National Defence. Their wage of twenty cents a day made them the regiment of the Royal Twenty Centers. They received lodging in camp bunk-houses, three square meals of army grub, and worked forty-four hours per week on road and airport construction or land reclamation projects. If they didn't like the regime, the young men could leave. But where could they go?

Because of the limitations of camp life, the young men were not always placid. Their chief complaints, aside from predictable mutterings about the food, were that they were wasting their lives and that the twenty-cent wage was an insult. Their dissatisfaction was fed by the politically conscious among them, often labelled 'agitators,' who organized and taught them and goaded them to rebel. The unrest bred violence. In the Saskatoon camp, an attempt to move fifty of these political 'leaders' to Regina in 1933 caused a clash between police and relief camp men in which one RCMP officer was killed and many police and campers were injured. Twenty-six young men were brought to trial on charges of rioting and unlawful assembly. Premier Anderson, having won federal approval for the establishment of a new camp at Dundurn, near Saskatoon, denounced the 'Communists' who were alleged to be infiltrating the district: 'As long as I live in public life I shall do all in my power to drive those disciples of the "Red Flag" out of Saskatoon and out of the province.'[21]

The single most dramatic incident in the history of these relief projects also occurred in Saskatchewan, though it was more a product of frustrations built up in Alberta and British Columbia than of those in the eastern prairies. With the aid of organizers from the Workers Unity League (an affiliate of the Red International of Labour Unions), relief camp workers in British Columbia had gone on strike to demand a national work-and-wages program. Two months of hand-to-mouth existence in Vancouver convinced them that they must apply pressure where it would be felt, and in June they set out for Ottawa, 1,000 strong, riding boxcars and scavenging food and shelter in hospitable towns along the way. Prime Minister Bennett stopped them in Regina. No rail cars or trucks carrying strikers were to proceed further. The presence of a large detachment of Mounted Police in the Saskatchewan capital must have played a part in the prime minister's calculations, but the embarrassment visited upon Liberal Premier Jimmy Gardiner, a long-time enemy of the Tories, cannot have been accidental. The trekkers bedded down on straw in Regina's Exhibition Grounds (to night-time calls of 'Mooo!'), living on tag days and donated food while negotiations between strike leaders and Ottawa officials determined what would become of their protest. Bennett rejected their demands and, after permitting them to remain in the city for two weeks, ordered the arrest of the leaders. His timing was poor. On the evening of Canada's birthday, 1 July, at a meeting in the market square organized to consider the strikers' next move, the RCMP arrested seven strike leaders. The Canadian Press wire report made headlines across the nation: 'One Dead, One Dying in Regina Battle  Regina, July 1 (CP)  Gun-fire blazed out in riot-torn Regina tonight leaving one policeman dead and a striker dying as steel-helmeted Royal Canadian Mounted Police clashed with 3,000 relief-camp deserters and sympathizers. City Detective Miller [sic] was seized by the strikers and beaten to death, eyewitnesses said.'[22] Over eighty were injured in the Regina riot, a like number were arrested, and thousands of dollars in damage was done to buildings in the city centre. But little was achieved. The strikers were dispersed, as the prime minister wished; a royal commission concluded that 'communists' had instigated the violence; and the people of Canada were strengthened in their determination to defeat Bennett in the federal election of 1935. But the problems could not be solved so easily. The very foundations of the Canadian and the prairie communities were being called into question. The experience of relief had not been a happy one.

The unprecedented economic failures and related political issues naturally affected the course of parties and the party system in the prairies. Each province followed a different tack in its attempt to ameliorate local conditions. Manitoba moved toward a coalition government, as befitted a moderate administration in time of crisis. It has been argued that the Bracken government almost transcended political partisanship while retaining party lines. Saskatchewan began the decade with a Conservative-Progressive coalition, shifted to the Liberals in 1934, and moved leftward to the Co-operative Commonwealth Federation in 1944, just after the crisis ended. Despite these remarkable changes, a two-party system remained entrenched in the province at the end of the period. Alberta had had a left-of-centre administration in the United Farmers under Premier Brownlee and turned to the right when it sought an alternative government in 1935. The Social Credit sweep was remarkable for its suddenness but also for its completeness: almost nothing remained of the opposition parties by 1944. But were these apparently different party systems simply manifestations of a single region-wide phenomenon? Were they outgrowths of a prairie drive to create utopia – or of a prairie susceptibility to populist leaders and movements? Did they demonstrate that the prairies were not affected by class allegiances? Such generalizations have been made and should be noted in an analysis of Depression politics in the west.

Manitoba, according to many observers, has always been the most conservative of the three prairie provinces.[23] As if to prove the point, Manitoba alone did not experience a change of government during the Depression. Indeed, despite two changes of premier, in 1943 and 1948, the 'Progressive' group first elected in 1922 retained power for well over three decades until its defeat in 1958.

One factor in the success of John Bracken's United Farmer and Progessive administration was steady support in two areas of the province, the southwest countryside and the southern portion of Winnipeg. Throughout the 1920s and 1930s, Bracken could count on at least 20 rural seats in the 55-seat house, chiefly drawn from the prosperous farming areas and small towns of southern Manitoba where citizens of British-Canadian stock predominated. He could also rely on Winnipeg for a few seats because his economy-minded administration appealed to the more prosperous British-Canadian middle class of the capital's south side.

A second factor in Bracken's success was his ability to divide and to absorb the opposition. When the United Farmers of Manitoba resolved to leave politics in the late 1920s, Bracken was forced to canvass more widely for electoral support. His first stop, after a careful courtship, was in the Liberal camp, where he achieved a meeting of minds just before the 1932 provincial election. The Progressive-Liberal coalition thereby secured another majority. But in the following election, in 1936, popular dissatisfaction with Bracken's financial policies and the Depression itself caused the Progressive-Liberal coalition government to be defeated by 31 seats to 22. However, by extending his alliance to the newly organized Social Credit group of 5, Bracken was able to secure a one-seat majority in the legislature. In 1941, he moved even farther afield by bringing the Conservatives and the CCF into his fold in order, he argued, that Manitoba might face the wartime crisis united. As in 1932, so in 1936 and 1941, Bracken had been able to convince the crucial members that times of crisis required a united front. His success seemed to bear out his contention that, in small communities such as Manitoba, coalition governments could represent all interest groups. The province had no need, in his view, for a competitive party system.[24]

Bracken's success in transcending Manitoba's obvious class and ethnic divisions was astonishing. Winnipeg politics demonstrated sharp divisions along class, ethnic, and neighbourhood lines, and, despite an unusually complex ten-member city riding that undercut worker solidarity, these differences of outlook were evident in the election results. In 1920, according to one calculation, Liberals and Conservatives won six city seats with 44 per cent of the popular vote while the Labour candidates won four seats with 56 per cent of the vote. Rural elections were also affected by class loyalties. The support for opposition parties was considerable in the poorer areas of the province – the southwest, Interlake, and northwest – where non-British immigrants had settled on poorer brush land and established near-subsistence operations. However, these groups were only slowly establishing themselves and articulating a common consciousness because they remained preoccupied by the battles of earlier times and earlier homes. Only in 1936 did the French unite behind Social Credit candidates. The Ukrainians were divided by European-based loyalties; the Germans were divided by religion and, to a lesser degree, by European loyalties; Indians could not vote. Thus, for lack of a united opposition, the myth of a 'non-partisan' government and a homogeneous community was perpetuated. Voter turnout was around 70 per cent in elections from 1922 to 1932 but dropped to 66 per cent in 1936 and ranged between only 50 and 55 per cent in the 1940s. In retrospect, one has the impression that, whether through boredom or disgust, Manitobans had permitted their government to abolish politics entirely. But this is only partly true. The opposition received over half the votes cast in most of these elections, but this support was divided into a number of camps – CCF, Social Credit, Independent, and Communist – and, in the first-past-the-post system, earned few representatives.[25]

John Bracken was the architect of this remarkable dynasty in Manitoba politics. His strong personality, non-partisan approach to the problem of government, and unshakeable faith in the essential unity of Manitobans sustained his administration for two decades and imparted the style that was to carry the Garson and Campbell governments for another sixteen years after his departure. Bracken was a no-nonsense farm boy from eastern Ontario who had become an agricultural extension officer and eventually a professor of agriculture. He had absorbed the strict teachings of a Methodist household and combined them with an unusual flair for organization and exposition, on the one hand, and for instilling loyalty and a sense of common purpose, on the other. Bracken was a rugby star in his youth and a team captain all his life. His leadership was founded on an athletic metaphor: cabinet members were the natural leaders of the 'team,' the members of the legislation were 'supporting players,' and their favourite compliment was to say someone was a 'team man.' Opposition lay not within the community – thus the clear preference for abolishing partisan politics – but outside, in Ottawa, the international markets, or, more often, in adversity itself. And, as the professor of agriculture would explain, proper method and disciplined application would handle the problems as they arose. More could not be asked or expected.[26]

The Manitobe Progressive government was cautious, reasonable, and pragmatic. It secured some important economic activity in the late 1920s, including mining, pulp and paper, and hydro-electric enterprises, and it maintained Manitoba's solvency in the crisis of the Depression. But by accepting the necessity of balancing the budget – at the urging of the prime minister and the province's bankers – Bracken became the very epitome of the conservative financier. Only British Columbia among Canada's nine provinces could join Manitoba in reporting balanced accounts (always exclusive of relief payments) in the late 1930s. The costs of such rigid fiscal rectitude were borne by Manitobans in the form of reduced public works programs, school services, and civil service salaries and a notorious wage tax. Bracken's defenders argued that his was the responsible course; his detractors would probably have accepted the risk of provincial default in order to provide greater assistance to the people. There is no absolute right and wrong in such a debate. Bracken pursued the course with utter devotion; by a remarkable feat of political legerdemain, he maintained the support of a majority in the legislature. Just as remarkable, the province never wavered from its acceptance of the legislature's authority.

Provincial politics in Saskatchewan had been relatively undisturbed by the farmers' revolt of the post-war period. The ruling Liberal party had divorced itself from its federal wing as early as 1920, and had replaced Premier W.M. Martin, a Regina lawyer, with Charles A. Dunning, a farm leader, in 1922, thereby consolidating its position as the farmers' best ally. But when Dunning left for the federal cabinet in 1926, the new premier, James G. Gardiner, returned to the narrow partisanship that had distinguished the pre-war Liberals. Jimmy was a scrapper, his followers fondly said, one of that special type of partisan who fought tenaciously for party 'principles' and believed that the other side was always wrong. He was also a crucial figure in the operation of the Liberal 'machine.' As one Liberal organizer put it, Gardiner was 'somewhat of a Puritan and outside of elections has kept all the Commandments from his youth up.'[27] But, in the late 1920s, Gardiner ran into troubles that could not be settled easily by reference either to his machine or to customary Liberal principle. The issues were not the usual Saskatchewan political fare of freight rates and grain marketing but rather centred on European immigration, education, and – extraordinary as it may sound – the Ku Klux Klan.

Critics of the Liberal party had never been happy with its activity in Saskatchewan's Roman Catholic and European settlements. The federal Liberal government's decision in 1925, at the urging of the railways, to encourage the recruitment of more immigrants from central and eastern Europe was another indication, in their critics' view, that the Liberals were blind to the problems created by 'alien' communities. Gardiner's failure to remove nuns ('sectarian staff') from Saskatchewan schools and crucifixes ('sectarian emblems') from classroom walls was taken by these critics as a measure of the premier's own lack of concern. And beneath these issues lay the critics' long-standing suspicions of Liberal electoral organization: built on highways inspectors and the judicious use of patronage, this exceptional organization had been in the background of political debate until Gardiner assumed the premiership. But Gardiner continued to control the machine from the premier's office and thus became the target for those who believed that political corruption and European immigration were jointly responsible for the ills of the province. Dr J.T.M. Anderson, a former school inspector and author of *The Education of the New Canadian: A Treatise on Canada's Greatest Problem* (1918), who became Conservative leader in 1924, did much to revive his party by attacking the Liberals on just this point. He was careful to insist that he stood for assimilation of the European, not for anti-alien prejudice, but his very choice of position on the issue ensured that he would win widespread support from nativists. The largely British-Canadian Saskatchewan Grain Growers' Association also injected a strain of anti-European, anti-Catholic prejudice into provincial life, and its successor, the United Farmers of Canada, Saskatchewan Section, was similarly exercised by Ottawa's failure to restrict immigration. The movement that converted the muted complaints into an ugly explosion was the Klan.

In search of profitable fields for expansion, the Ku Klux Klan entered Ontario from the United States in the mid-1920s and spread to Saskatchewan in December 1926. Its first venture ended in ignominy within nine months when its two organizers absconded with the membership funds, but local supporters regrouped and, by 1929, had established over 100 locals with perhaps 10,000 or 20,000 members and were conducting enthusiastic revival meetings across the province. Hooded figures, burning crosses, Imperial Wizards, Exalted Cyclops, Kleagles and Kligrapps might have seemed out of place in the rural west. But Saskatchewan was experiencing the nativist backlash against immigration that had earlier poisoned Manitoba. The distrust of Roman Catholics and central Europeans that had marked public debates over languages of instruction and public aid to Roman Catholic schools now was translated into demands for 'selective immigration' and the removal of French-language materials and Catholic clerical personnel from the schools. The nativists' abusive rhetoric was shocking. *The Orange Sentinel*, journal of the Orange Order, asked: 'Would you like to have a black-skirted "she-cat"' of a Nun teach your children in a public school that you are a heretic?' The Anglican bishop of Saskatchewan, Dr G.E. Lloyd, described the European newcomers as 'these dirty, ignorant, garlic-smelling, non-preferred continentals' and promised to get rid of the Gardiner government because of its 'miserable conduct in connection with the objectionable French textbook.' In short, there had developed in Saskatchewan a widespread concern about the effect of non-British immigration that had been linked to the ever-present suspicion of the Roman Catholic church and, now, to the Liberal party. The Klan did not create this nativist uprising. Rather, it provided a new focus for the anger and, by building on a fundamentalist religious base, associated it with elements of traditional Protestant teachings. With hymns such as *When I Survey the Wondrous Cross* and fluent speakers whose message was built on references to the gospel, the Klan could be mistaken for a fundamentalist crusade.[28]

The Liberals misread the depth of the nativist movement and, in so doing, laid the basis for the transformation of the Saskatchewan political system. Instead of resorting to the usual tactics of investigating commissions and revised departmental regulations, Gardiner tackled nativist opinion head on. Rather than delegate control of the party organization and permit opposition examination of civil servants, he insisted that his record was clean. The muttering continued. Gossip had it that the Roman Catholic archbishop occupied a small room behind the Speaker's chair in the legislative assembly, whither the premier repaired for advice during debates. The currency of such rumours demonstrated that Gardiner was losing the allegiance of Protestant English-speaking Liberals. The election of 1929, in which Gardiner won 30 seats to the 35 of his opponents, proved that his errors were important. His defeat was the opening phase of a decade-long shift in the provincial political system.

The new 'Cooperative' government, a mixed bag of Conservatives, Progressives, and Independents under the leadership of J.T.M. Anderson, was betrayed by weather and markets shortly after it took office. Elected on religious and racial issues – one might charitably describe the victory as a mandate for a new cultural policy – Anderson and his inexperienced cabinet were forced to deal with the most severe economic crisis in prairie history. Immigration and schools were replaced by relief and rehabilitation as the chief concerns of the people. The government's emergency policies were not ineffectual, but they alienated some Conservative supporters, especially businessmen, and provided ample opportunity for the experienced Liberal opposition to make them appear fools. The result was an unmitigated disaster for the Anderson government. As one former Liberal cabinet minister wrote privately to Mackenzie King: 'Everytime we have a Tory gov't there follows as the night, the day, depression, drought, etc. These days show the difference between a Liberal and a Conservative. One battling for existence and the other living in luxury as the result of special privilege.'[29] That such smug nonsense could pass for political thought was a measure of the depth of partisanship in Saskatchewan public life. But it was also an index to the public's dissaffection from its government. In the general election of 1934, the Liberals won 50 of the 55 seats behind the slogan 'Liberal Ways Bring Brighter Days.' The Conservatives won not a single riding. These changes were consolidated four years later. W.J. Patterson had replaced Gardiner as premier in 1935 when Jimmy was called to the federal cabinet by Mackenzie King, but the new Liberal government was otherwise remarkably similar to Gardiner's earlier administration. It was preoccupied by the depression crisis, devoting its time to seed grain advances, tax sales, and relief distribution, and it appeared to be a competent – though admittedly patronage-based – government. In the general election of 1938, the Liberals' administrative success was attested by victory in 38 of 52 ridings. With their eighth victory in the nine Saskatchewan general elections since provincehood, the Liberals had been confirmed as the 'government party.'

The crucial political change of the decade concerned the other side of the political spectrum. The Conservative party had ceased to be a significant force by 1938. The Social Credit challenge – this new movement was now the dominant force in Alberta – had failed. And only one party remained to dominate the opposition benches: a Farmer-Labour coalition, renamed the Co-operative Commonwealth Federation, had become the second party in Saskatchewan's return to the two-party system. The new order, in which the Liberals and the CCF were the sole significant competitors for political power in the province, was to endure for over three decades. In retrospect, we can see that a significant shift in voter allegiance began in 1929. In that nativist campaign, accustomed loyalties had been challenged by the ethnic and religious bigotry of the Klan, and the consequence, it seems, was a small but important erosion of Liberal strength in some British-Canadian Protestant communities. In 1934, some Conservatives who had given up on the Anderson government but who refused to vote for the hated Liberals, transferred their support to the Farmer-Labour group. And in the same campaign eastern European voters, both Orthodox and Ukrainian Catholic, ignored the Roman Catholic attacks on socialism as they shifted their support from the Liberals to the Farmer-Labour candidates who spoke the language of economic justice and who organized as intensively as ever the Liberals had done. Generally, too, voters who lived in the parkbelt axis stretching from Yorkton to Lloydminster, and in the drought-stricken agricultural region north of Rosetown, were more likely to support the Farmer-Labour party; both of these areas had a Progressive tradition and, in the case of many British immigrants, a Labour party heritage in the Mother Country. To the surprise of the politicians, it was not the very poor who supported the protest party; rather, the poorest citizens voted Liberal in order to defeat Anderson, but the more prosperous voted Farmer-Labour, perhaps to effect more significant changes in the economic system. The election of 1938 consolidated the trends of 1934: parkland protest, eastern European protest, and British Labour protest sustained the CCF and, though its share of the popular vote declined slightly, helped to double its legislative representation from five to ten.[30]

Much has been written about the ideological perspective of the Farmer-Labour or CCF movement and its slow evolution from radical socialism to moderate social democracy. The first full-scale treatment of the Saskatchewan CCF, by the sociologist S.M. Lipset, argued that the party was not socialist at all. Rather, Lipset said, the

CCF, when placed in the context of economic protest in the wheat-growing regions of North America, was of a piece with earlier agrarian protest crusades such as the Populists and the Non-Partisan League. It was, like them, a product of the relatively malleable institutions of a recently settled 'frontier.' Its popularity was due to the absence of serious economic cleavages in the rural districts, to the typical wheat growers' protests against the international market economy, and to the Depression itself, which reinforced agrarian unrest. In Lipset's view, the Farmer-Labour party was the offspring of socialists, among others, but it had dropped this aspect of its outlook by 1936 and adopted in its place the philosophy and vocabulary of traditional agrarian and social reform movements. The CCF, he wrote, like Social Credit in Alberta or the Non-Partisan League in North Dakota, blamed the Depression on 'eastern' capitalists: the Saskatchewan party 'gave farmers a different interpretation of the nucleus of external economic power, though essentially it played the same role of providing an external scapegoat for the personal misfortunes of farmers.'[31]

Lipset's interpretation has aroused much discussion in the intervening generation. One group of scholars, mainly but not exclusively Marxist in perspective, has followed Lipset in emphasizing the similarities among North American populist protests and the essentially conservative cast of their ideologies. Another group, more sympathetic to the party, had insisted that it was as socialist as any other democratic socialist movement in the countries that share North Atlantic cultural perspectives. The most uncompromising assertion of the latter view was written by Lewis H. Thomas, a historian who was Saskatchewan's archivist during the early CCF administrations. Thomas emphasized the social gospel and co-operative heritage of the Saskatchewan party and the varied social backgrounds – farmers, professionals, and labourers – of its members. The CCF government of 1944 differed from its Liberal predecessor, he argued, by reason of its commitment to civil service reform – merit rather than patronage – and its introduction of such measures as a government-owned insurance company and 'true crown corporation' status for the telephone and power companies, a status that ensured that public accountability and entrepreneurial independence would be a part of their character. If the 'strong minded, vigorous, and colorful personalities' of the Saskatchewan CCF 'were not socialists within the great tradition of English-speaking socialism,' Thomas concluded, 'a more precise and accurate designation has not yet been supplied by Canada's historians.'[32]

The debate involves more than semantics. The CCF was neither revolutionary socialist, as was the 1919 Socialist Party of Canada, nor capitalist in the manner of the Liberal and Conservative parties. Whether it was another agrarian or petit bourgeois response to industrial capitalism and, thus, essentially comparable to Social Credit, we shall consider later. For the moment, we can conclude that the voters of Saskatchewan chose a new path when they elected a CCF government in 1944. The CCF was prairie Canada's version of socialism; it was an alliance of farmers, labourers, and professionals who shared a deep faith in British parliamentary institutions and an abiding distrust of the competitive market economy; it was quite willing to mix private enterprise with state ownership, but it would not, given the opportunity, permit the market to dictate the availability of health and education services, to bankrupt thousands of family farms, or to develop provincial resources in such a manner that the people did not benefit. It was an indigenous response to long-term urban and class issues as well as to the immediate crisis of the agricultural depression. The CCF was a movement, at times radical, at times moderate in outlook, seeking economic security and the amelioration of social injustice. And it was, most assuredly, a party. The CCF was exceptionally well organized, even in such former Liberal strongholds as the eastern European settlements. Moreover, it had seized the advantage in Saskatchewan politics by claiming the reform position – another former prerogative of the Liberals – in provincial politics. As one party in the classic reform-conservative pattern of two-party systems, the CCF also acquired the legitimacy and the sense of responsibility associated with its new status as a potential government.

Alberta's experience was superficially very different from that of Manitoba and Saskatchewan. The so-called farmers' revolt of the post-war years had put the United Farmers of Alberta into office in 1921, and the continuing activity of the farm movement as well as the relative success of the government ensured its re-election in 1926 and 1930. But the crisis of the Depression drove the UFA from power and chased every UFA member from the legislature in 1935. Its successor, Social Credit, remained in office for thirty-six years, first under its founder, William Aberhart, and later, after his death in 1943, under Ernest Manning, who was premier from 1943 to 1968, and Harry Strom, who led the government from 1968 to 1971. The sudden sweeping changes in the elections of 1921, 1935, and 1971, coupled with the weakness of the oppositions throughout the century, have prompted observers to suggest that Albertans developed an unusual type of political representation – a 'quasi-party system' – and that their political outlook was more conservative, despite a utopian strain, than the prairie or Canadian norm. Alberta's anomalies took root, observers suggest, during the UFA and Social Credit years.

The United Farmers of Alberta – the farmers' movement, not the government – was dominated by its president from 1916 to 1930, Henry Wise Wood. And Wood, a native of Missouri, brought a distinctive combination of Christianity and social reform to his work. Having seen the collapse of American farm organizations after they failed to secure political office, he resisted the entry of the UFA into provincial politics. And when he saw that this could no longer be prevented, he argued that the UFA should seek to replace the old party system and its competitive approach with a co-operative spirit and 'group government' principles. The implementation of such ideas was no easy matter in a parliamentary system, however, and both the UFA premier from 1921 to 1925, Herbert Greenfield, and his successor, J.E. Brownlee, were soon using cabinet and caucus discipline just as their predecessors had done. Particularly under the administration of former UFA solicitor Brownlee, the farmer government provided sensible, effective guidance in public affairs. It negotiated an end to the costly railway problems of northern Alberta and, despite some quarrels over schools policy, secured the transfer of natural resources from federal to provincial control. Moreover, it dealt forthrightly with the problems of rural drought, seed grain relief, and credit.

If there was an intimation of UFA weakness in the late 1920s and early 1930s, it lay in two related problems: first, Alberta farm unrest focused to an unusual degree on issues of monetary reform such as debt moratoria, the creation of provincial banks, and such inflationary measures as increases in the money supply; second, the UFA government and its ally, the farm movement, were founders of the wheat pool and suffered correspondingly when it collapsed in 1930–1. The drought and the international depression accentuated the weaknesses of the UFA government. Brownlee, an Edmonton lawyer, offered orthodox responses to the demands for debt moratoria and created only a Debt Adjustment Board that would review creditors' applications for foreclosures. The apparent failure of the international market system, the near-bankruptcy of the provincial government, and the compelling stories of individual suffering at the hands of 'big' banks and financial institutions evoked UFA expressions of concern but not new policies. Still, if the UFA government seemed feeble in 1934, it was not yet dead. The spirit of co-operativism championed by the late H.W. Wood remained a force in provincial politics. Then the coincidence of a number of forces – accidents, if you will – carried Alberta away from the political consensus established by the UFA and into paths far distant from those chosen by Saskatchewan and Manitoba.[33]

The UFA government fell in the 1935 election in part because of internal weaknesses but chiefly because its opponent was irresistible. Among the government's own failures, the scandalous divorce of a cabinet minister and the even more shocking revelations that accompanied legal charges that Premier Brownlee had seduced a young secretary were probably most important. The conflict within its own ranks over monetary policy was also a factor in its collapse. Though Brownlee, like Bracken, was orthodox in his economic views, some of his allies, including the influential Labour MP for Calgary East, William Irvine, advocated drastic reform of the currency and banking systems. If such disagreements contributed to the rise of an alternate party, however, they played only a small part in the larger story. The depth of the Depression and the irresistible force that was William Aberhart explain the extraordinary rise to power of Social Credit.

Aberhart's story would be best told in a gothic novel or a modern melodrama because his life was a matter of blacks and whites rather than shadings and nuances. The atmosphere of his 1935 election crusade is captured in the bawdy serendipity of Robert Kroetsch's *The Words of My Roaring*, though the modern novelist attributes more sexual enjoyment and less repression, more humour and less earnest study to that era than the historian would dare. Aberhart was born in 1878 in rural Ontario and in the boom years before the First World War moved to Calgary, where he won prominence as a teacher and administrator. A disciplined worker with boundless energy, he became a fundamental Baptist and then founded the Calgary Prophetic Bible Institute and an exceptionally popular Sunday afternoon radio broadcast which, at its height, reached 350,000 listeners in the three prairie provinces and nearby states. All this was in addition to his regular duties as teacher and principal – he was outstanding in both capacities – at a local high school. In his lectures to students, he emphasized enthusiasm, ambition, and hard work. In his church and radio lessons, he insisted upon the literal truth of the Bible and the importance of the prophetic texts. And, when the Depression struck, he seized upon the economic doctrine propounded by the Englishman C.H. Douglas as the secular equivalent of biblical truth. This unusual combination of economic ideas and biblical readings was soon part of the Sunday afternoon radio fare. Aberhart was an exceptional orator with a remarkable speaking voice, but he was also a respected, sincere educator and religious leader. If he saw a way out of the economic morass and could associate this plan with biblical prophecy, then he offered hope to thousands who had little else left.[34]

Social Credit originated with an English engineer, Major C.H. Douglas. It was another of the twentieth-century ideologies that explained the course of world history, placed the blame for contemporary ills on a scapegoat, and demonstrated how a few simple political and economic measures would bring about a just society. 'The gist of the social credit theory,' wrote political theorist C.B. Macpherson, 'was that modern technology had made possible an era of great plenty and leisure both of which could and should be distributed throughout the community as unearned income, and that this could be done by some comparatively simple monetary devices, which would not interfere with the structure of ownership and private enterprise.'[35] The wealth was made possible by the technological advances of the Industrial Revolution and the use of new energy sources – these Douglas described as the 'cultural' or 'technological heritage.' His scapegoat was the international financial community, whose pursuit of private advantage was a public crime. The A + B theorem was one explanation of Douglas's solution: if A stands for all payments made to individuals and B stands for all payments made to other organizations (for example, the cost of raw materials and bank charges), and the price of a good is A plus B, then individuals, with salaries equivalent to A, could not purchase all they produced. But if the control of credit were taken from financiers and placed in the hands of the people, if a national 'dividend' based on the unearned increment from the technological heritage were issued to consumers, and if producers received subsidies in return for lower prices, then the deficiency of consumer purchasing power would be remedied and a humane society would be ensured. The theory not only explained contemporary shortages but also defended 'the right to private ownership of capital' and the virtue of 'private management of industry and agriculture, on grounds of administrative efficiency.'[36] It was simple in explanation, sweeping in implication; its credit reforms were radical, yet its treatment of property relations – excepting the property of a few 'financiers' – was conservative. Its impulse was moral and, in the hands of Aberhart, apparently as sound as Christianity itself.

Readings in Social Credit and the Bible went together in William Aberhart's radio study groups until early 1935, when it became apparent that the UFA government would not implement the new economic doctrine. Aberhart then sanctioned the creation of a Social Credit political organization. In five months, between the first party convention on 4 April and the provincial election of 22 August 1935, Aberhart and Social Credit simply overwhelmed the old political parties. His highly centralized system of study groups became the core of a political machine. His radio broadcasts made effective public relations. 'Monster picnics' and other summer-time gatherings, usually opened by a hymn such as *O God Our Help in Ages Past* – the Social Credit party anthem – and capped by Aberhart's 'stem-winder' oratory, were infectious. Aberhart himself chose his party's candidates and determined its platform. The result, 56 seats of 63, and 54 per cent of the popular vote, was a personal victory. The UFA returned not a single member and disappeared forever as a political party.

When, shortly thereafter, Stephen Leacock toured the west to expound his vision of Confederation, he concluded that the doctrine of Social Credit was like a religion of 'the South Sea islands' and included 'a god so exalted they must not even pronounce his real name. He is just called Oom. Social Credit is going to be the Oom of the Canadian West.' It was, he wrote, 'a sacred ideal, too holy for current use.'[37] This was a fair conclusion despite its crude articulation. Aberhart would not accept and perhaps did not understand the policy recommendations of C.H. Douglas, on the one hand, and did assume the customary responsibilities and structure of cabinet government and the parliamentary system, on the other. His tenure was noteworthy for administrative reforms, especially in the organization of rural municipal government and the provincial education system, and for its commitment to the principles of a social welfare state. None the less, after a back-benchers' revolt in 1937, the government passed a number of bills concerning the banking system, reduction of interest on the public debt, and reductions of principal and interest on ceratin private or farm debts, among other topics. In the period between 1937 and 1941, eleven of these Alberta statutes were disallowed and ten were declared *ultra vires* by the Supreme Court of Canada.[38] But 'it is difficult,' as L.H. Thomas suggested, 'to know how Aberhart viewed the fate of this legislation, most of which was inspired by his critics.'[39] In the end, we can say with confidence only that Aberhart was a social reformer of a unique sort. He had explained in 1935 that Social Credit's aim was 'to feed, clothe and shelter the people' and, in 1938, that Social Credit was 'merely Christianity applied to everyday economics.'[40] When confronted with the realities of Canada's economic system and political institutions, he was less a disciple of C.H. Douglas than a master of his own school. His dictum was that 'Prudence will get us what nothing else can. Prudence combines two important qualities, piety and practical sagacity.' Here was the proper definition of Aberhart's political philosophy.

Two scholarly interpretations of the Social Credit era in Alberta might supplement this judgment. The first, enunciated by the political philosopher, C.B. Macpherson, explained Alberta's propensity for single-party domination of the legislature by reference to the province's relatively homogeneous social composition and to its 'quasi-colonial' status within the Canadian economy and the federal system:

> The absence of any serious opposition of class interests within the province meant that alternate parties were not needed either to express or to moderate a perennial conflict of interests. There was apparently, therefore, no positive basis for an alternate-party system. The quasi-colonial position of the western provinces made it a primary requirement of their provincial political systems that they should be able to stand up to the national government, that is, able to make effective demands on it and to resist national legislation which they regarded as exploitive.

The result was a 'quasi-party system' as opposed to the alternate-party system that was the norm in the British and Canadian tradition; the voters of Alberta had undertaken 'a series of experiments in control of representative government by popular movements, without a party system; experiments not in direct democracy ... but in delegate democracy.'[41] Despite the criticisms of several scholars, Macpherson's judgment was a sensitive estimate of the Alberta situation in the first half of the twentieth century.

The second scholarly interpretation suggests that the Alberta Social Credit movement was, in its essence, quite like the Saskatchewan ccf: both were 'populist' revolts, 'the characteristic political response of the agrarian *petit-bourgeoisie* ... to the consequences of capitalist modernization for them as a class.'[42] In each province, according to this view, farmers were being forced either to enlarge their farms or to join the ranks of wage labour. Though they remained loyal to the concepts of private property and small commodity production, farmers were critical of the unremitting competitiveness of the modern capitalist system. Their protest was 'populist.' Richards and Pratt, in their study *Prairie Capitalism*, distinguish three crucial characteristics of populism: the nature of its electoral alliance, the extent of its critique of capitalism, and the scope of its reform policies. In each case, they suggest, the ccf chose the 'left' variant of the populist outlook and Social Credit chose the 'right.'

Left populist strategy attempted to build a farm-labour alliance, right populists minimized conflict among groups within the prairies and attempted a regional alliance of all classes indigenous to the plains against eastern interests. Second, left populism erected a relatively general critique of all sectors of corporate capitalism ... right populists concentrated their critiques, to the point of obsession, upon the power of the banks to limit the money supply and control the cost of credit. Finally, all populists consistently supported the institutions of the individual family-owned farms, and to that extent all were 'capitalists' defending private property. However left populist organizations typically emerged from the extensive rural cooperatives of the plains and tended to a chiliastic belief in cooperatives as the morally just way to organize economic activity ... Left populism demanded of government not only a regulatory role to promote competition, but also the generation of countervailing power on farmers' behalf by a variety of entrepreneurial means – public ownership of utilities and railroads, and government-run marketing agencies. Conversely right populism had few links to the cooperative movement and, beyond the use of the state to break the stranglehold of banks over the money supply, it viewed the achievement of well-functioning competitive markets as a sufficient goal.[43]

If, as these scholars contend, the CCF and Social Credit were variants of the same phenomenon, they were still very different one from the other. In the language of twentieth-century political thought, the CCF was a social democratic and social gospel movement; the Aberhart party was reform capitalist and Christian fundamentalist.

Could Alberta have voted CCF or Saskatchewan have gone Social Credit? Was there something in the society of each province that predisposed it to the left- or right-wing alternative? Perhaps, but the case has yet to be made. We can agree that accidents of electoral history and the power of individual personalities were part of the difference. Because the CCF had been discredited by the UFA failures, and because of Aberhart himself, Alberta turned to the right. Conservative and Liberal weakness and the insistent CCF organization turned Saskatchewan to the left. Once chosen, there was no turning back. At any given moment, according to one theory of political behaviour, communities are divided into several 'political generations,' each of which 'may have undergone socialization to political matters under quite different conditions.'[44] Having been innoculated in the 1930s and 1940s, Saskatchewan and Alberta voters acquired immunity to the appeals of the opposing philosophy. Henceforth, they lived in dramatically different political systems. As it happened, the accidents of personality and party fortune left Saskatchewan with the classic two-party model and Alberta with a quasi-party system.

The 1930s were a decade of trial for residents of the prairie west. Like the boomtime at the turn of the century, the Depression was an identifiable period that affected the psychology of individual citizens, the fate of entire communities, and the image of the region. In some respects, it was a turning point: never again would the prairie farm appear to offer certain prosperity; never again could governments avoid a measure of responsibility for agricultural income or, indeed, for the social security of individuals and the direction of the economy; never again would Canadian politics be based on a two-party system. But, in the other respects, the decade was a period of stasis: urban citizens on relief and farm families faced with crop failure worried about survival, not political change; economic disaster made people conservative in their protests, as the prairie preference for the Liberals, the CCF, and Social Credit made plain; and, despite the availability of technology that would have revolutionized the farm economy, rural incomes were so limited that the era of horsepower was extended for another decade. The period has been described as 'ten lost years,' but perhaps the more apt title is James Gray's *The Winter Years*; that the prairie west was spared the political extremes and the violence of other nations was a measure of its poverty but also of the stability of its institutions.

# 16

# The new west since 1940: Political and economic change

After ten years of crisis, the prairie west slowly adjusted to wartime activity and then to the economic boom of the post-war era. For the next three decades, steady and even spectacular economic growth was the rule. As the years passed, prairie society became increasingly like that in other parts of the 'developed' world. It was much more urban than rural; it was less dependent on agricultural income; its labour force included more representatives of the liberal professions and more managers and clerical workers; it was still heavily engaged in natural resource production and preoccupied by the activity of world markets but it had a reasonably diversified base of resources and the incomes of its residents were close to the national average; it was swept by the new trends in family formation, as was the rest of the developed world, and it succumbed to the trappings of material culture that guided, amused, adorned, or eased daily living in Lyons, Belgrade, Wichita, and Leeds. It became a part of the North Atlantic welfare state. By the 1980s, the region seemed to be just another neighbourhood of a single homogenized global metropolis.

There were distinctive aspects to this apparent homogeneity, however, as prairie residents were quick to assert. Despite the continuing importance of agriculture, the provincial economies grew increasingly apart. The political variations that had begun in earlier decades were consolidated by the post-war generation into unique approaches to politics and parties in the three provinces. And the mix of the constituent elements of each provincial society – business and labour, ethnic groups and natives, urban and rural residents – created three quite distinctive communities.]

In 1941 Manitoba's population was 730,000, having changed very little in the preceding decade. By 1961, it had increased to 920,000, and in 1981 it was about 1,026,000. The province was not really growing; indeed it was unable to maintain its natural increase. The change was particularly evident in rural areas where the trend resulted in the disappearance of some hamlets and the depopulation of many farm areas. Only the largest cities – Winnipeg and Brandon – and a few favoured small towns – Winkler, Altona, Morden, Neepawa, and others – grew at a reasonable pace. Winnipeg, as one of Canada's metropolises, benefited most from the dramatic drift from farm to city, especially in the 1950s, and almost doubled in size from 300,000 to 600,000 in these forty years. The only other feature of note in the geographic distribution of population was the increase 'north of 53,' where mining and hydro-electric developments resulted in significant settlements at such places as Thompson and Lynn Lake.[1] Manitoba was a stable community in this era, adapting slowly to changing world circumstances but existing on the periphery rather than at the centre of new developments.

The provincial economy was stronger than the tale of population growth would suggest. From the 1940s, Manitoba attained an enviable degree of economic diversification, and if personal income per capita was slightly below the Canadian average it was none the less stable.[2] Thus, in an age of boom and bust for grain and mining production, such fluctuations in income were offset to some degree by a large manufacturing sector, construction activity, and other resource industries. Within the manufacturing sector, the brightest spots were the aerospace industry, garment making, agricultural implements, and other light industries. but even agricultural production in the post-1940 era was more consistent than in the first decades of the century. Manitoba had never been as dependent as its sister provinces on wheat, and as early as 1921 more than half the seeded acreage was devoted to other crops. Potatoes, vegetables, sugar beets, sunflowers, corn, and, increasingly, rape seed were the principal field crop alternatives. Cattle were also an important component of provincial agricultural income.[3]

The growth of the mining and resource industries was another notable change in Manitoba's economy. The paper mill at Pine Falls was supplemented by a forestry complex, including a paper plant, at The Pas; hydro developments on the Churchill and Nelson rivers spurred business activity, especially in the 1970s; and steady production of nickel and other minerals at Thompson and at Lynn Lake underlined the role of mining in the provincial economic outlook.

Manitoba politics reflected the stability of the economy and the glacial slowness of population change. The province had been governed by a Liberal-Progressive coalition in the 1930s, and, despite the departure of Premier Bracken to the federal Conservative leadership in 1942 and of Premier Garson to the federal Liberal cabinet in 1948, the 'non-partisan' coalition government carried on without a misstep in the general elections of 1949 and 1953. The new premier, Douglas Campbell, articulate, reasonable, and a shrewd judge of people, remained satisfied with the non-partisan stance of the old Bracken-Garson 'team' which, he said, 'has eliminated politics from the business of government and ... made up for what it lacks in color by gaining in efficiency.' But the times were changing. The city was being wooed by a revitalized Conservative party; poorer rural areas, where Ukrainians and other European ethnic minorities predominated, were swinging to the CCF. When, in 1958, Winnipeg finally achieved seats proportionate to its population, it helped to elect a new Conservative government led by Duff Roblin, grandson of R.P. Roblin.

The new administration was progressive, business-oriented, and affiliated with the old British-Canadian élite of the province. Roblin increased government spending on health, education, and public works. He set in motion plans for a Winnipeg floodway, consolidated schools, and new sports and cultural facilities associated with the Pan-American Games and the national and provincial centennials. After Roblin left Manitoba in quest of the federal Conservative leadership in 1967, his successor, Walter Weir, took the party on a tack to the right: opposition to the federal medical care and bilingualism programs and a determination to reduce government spending produced an image of negativism at a time when Canadians, in the wake of Expo'67, Trudeaumania, and the 'youth revolution,' were confident and upbeat. The provincial Liberals, far from offering a distinctive alternative, were as conservative in policy and as dependent on the British- and French-Canadian élites as the government. The new force in Manitoba politics was the New Democratic Party, whose young leader, Ed Schreyer, embodied the party's links with the 'little people' – Roman Catholics, non-British ethnic groups, and the working class.

The election of 1969 marked a significant shift in Manitoba political and social history. Having failed to establish itself as a clear alternative, the Liberal party commenced its slide into oblivion. In 1966 it got 34 per cent of the popular vote; in 1969, 25 per cent; in 1973, 19 per cent; in 1977, 12 per cent; and in 1981, 6 per cent. After a period of division and confusion, the Conservatives continued their turn to the right; they were the party of business, the advocates of reduced government intervention in society, and the inheritors of Bracken's south Winnipeg–southwest Manitoba electoral alliance. They carried the province in the anti-government swing in 1977, but lost in 1969, 1973, and 1981. The new 'governing party' in Manitoba was the New Democratic Party. It was led by Schreyer until his elevation to the post of governor-general of Canada in 1979 and then by Howard Pawley, a lawyer from the town of Selkirk. The NDP administrators combined defence of human rights and extension of social welfare programs with experiments in economic development. This emphasis on positive government, as opposed to Conservative Premier Sterling Lyon's (1977–81) advocacy of reductions in government size and services, fitted well with their support among the lower classes, non-British Canadians, and the so-called new forces in provincial politics – natives, recent immigrants, and working women.

To describe the Conservative-NDP contests as 'class-based' required careful definition of the term. Neither party was committed to drastic redistributions of property, and if the NDP wished to provide the disadvantaged with greater access to the instruments of power it was not offering significant changes in the process or goals of government. As T.E. Peterson has concluded: 'Compared with the past, the classes were closer in many respects than ever before. The local upper classes were neither as wealthy nor as remote as their predecessors; and the lower classes, assisted by the two decades of postwar prosperity, were neither as poor nor as submerged. Class competition evidently became more acute as rival classes were

less sharply distinguished.'[4] Thus, if Manitobans had seemed prepared to tear the province apart in the opening decades of the twentieth century because of social and cultural divisions, they were, in
the years after 1940, living in a more open and harmonious community where disagreements could be discussed vehemently and yet
without profound consequences for the social fabric. Isolated and
impoverished citizens remained, social inequality had not been
abolished, but a single community now existed where in the preceding century such unity was never achieved.

Saskatchewan, too, underwent rapid change in the four decades
after 1940 but, despite obvious similarities with Manitoba's experience, its differing heritage produced important variations in outlook
and institutions. The most obvious parallel between the two provinces was in population change. Saskatchewan also ceased to grow
in the 1930s; its population shrank steadily from 1936 to 1951 and
stabilized between 900,000 and 1,000,000 in the 1960s and 1970s –
just where it had been in the 1930s. Similarly, the big-city share of
the population – distributed between Regina and Saskatoon rather
than concentrated as in Winnipeg – increased rapidly from 11 per
cent in 1941 to 28.5 per cent in 1971. Small cities and larger towns
(1,000–35,000) also grew apace, increasing their share of the provincial total from 10 per cent to 25 per cent. The corresponding decline
in the rural population, was, as in Manitoba, an extraordinary development: in this most agricultural province of the nation, where
700,000 citizens, 8 in 10, had lived on farms and in small villages in
1941, only 400,000, or just under 4 in 10, were classified as rural in
1981.[5] It was a rapid and difficult transition, the more so for being
only dimly perceived as a social revolution by those who participated in it.

Saskatchewan's economy, despite these apparent signs of weakness, grew increasingly prosperous in the post-war decades and
was, by the 1970s, one of the richest and most diversified in the
country. Like the urbanization process, so the trend to wealth required difficult adjustments in a community grown accustomed to
calamities during the 1930s. Just after the Second World War, 60 per
cent of Saskatchewan's wealth was produced by agriculture, under
20 per cent by manufacturing, and less than 10 per cent by mining
and other resource industries. By the late 1970s, the proportions had
shifted dramatically: annual mining and natural resource revenue,
led by potash, petroleum, and uranium, sky-rocketed to about $1.5

billion, and its share of Saskatchewan wealth increased to about 27 per cent of the entire economy. Agriculture's share declined to under 40 per cent. Still unstable to some degree because it relied on world markets and prices, Saskatchewan's economy was nevertheless infinitely healthier than it had been in the first half of the century because it had finally achieved a diversified base.[6]

Management of resources, as of social arrangements, fell to successive provincial governments. But politics was not only a matter of government, it was also the first-ranked sport in Saskatchewan, outpacing even curling in participants and observers for more than a generation. A sociological study in the 1940s concluded that 125,000 Saskatchewan farmers, in their wheat pools, credit unions, and farm organizations, elected representatives to 40,000–60,000 offices – one elected position for every two or three farmers.[7] Provincial contests in Saskatchewan drew above 80 per cent of eligible voters in every general election but one after 1934. The average turnout (mean and median) in the 11 elections 1934–75 was 83 per cent; the 11 elections in Alberta 1935–75 drew a mean average of 67 per cent and a median of 64 per cent; and the 13 in Manitoba 1932–77 drew 64 per cent (mean and median). One of every nine voters in Saskatchewan was a card-carrying party member at the time of the 1975 election.[8] This was a community that took self-government seriously; the electorate followed political debate with close attention, chose sides with dramatic effect, and insisted on partisanship on every issue, whether the rights of trade unions, the nature of health care, the marketing of grain, or the closure of unprofitable rail lines. In a large province with a scattered and diverse population, political debate was one of the few things that all citizens had in common. At the heart of Saskatchewan's popular culture was consciousness of and participation in politics.

The party system was very competitive throughout these four decades. Just as in the province's first forty years the Liberals were the governing party, so in the next forty there was a single dominant group, the CCF/NDP. And just as the chief opposition party changed in the first period, so in recent decades the Conservatives replaced the Liberals as the single alternative in the continuing two-party system. The CCF/NDP held office for 31 of 38 years (1944–64 and 1971–82), the Liberals for 7 (1964–71), and the Conservatives took office in 1982 for the first time since the Depression in a landslide as devastating as it was unexpected.

But were the parties different? As in Manitoba in recent years, the answer was a qualified yes. In a study based on electoral results in the 1960s and early 1970s, when the Liberals and CCF/NDP were the chief parties, two political scientists concluded:

The following have tended to give more support to the Liberals than to the CCF/NDP: those with above-average incomes; the more prosperous farmers; voters under 45 years of age; sales, managerial and professional occupational groups; Roman Catholics, Anglicans, Jews, and Mennonites; and those with at least three years' secondary school education. Alternatively, the following have given more support to the CCF/NDP than to the Liberal party: individuals with below-average incomes; the less prosperous farmers; voters 55 years of age and over; laborers, craftsmen, and transportation and service workers; United Church members, Presbyterians, and Lutherans; and those with less than three years' secondary school education.[9]

The nature of their support – the prairie west version of left and right or liberal and conservative on a political spectrum – was a measure of the outlook of the CCF/NDP and of its opponents, whether Liberal or Conservative.

The CCF/NDP came into office as a reform movement with a social gospel–socialist-labour heritage. In its first years, as it attempted to diversify the economy, it established a large number of crown-owned enterprises, including a shoe factory, a brick manufacturing plant, and a woollen mill, in addition to more obvious businesses such as bus and air transportation companies. Perhaps not surprisingly, the factories did not prosper, but the transportation, insurance, and utilities companies performed smoothly. However, the most significant contributions of the first CCF governments to innovative policy in Canada lay in the fields of health, social services, and education. The schools system was centralized, teachers' salaries and qualifications were upgraded, and the universities were expanded. Mental health care became a priority of government for the first time, and, in fulfilment of a long-time plank in the party platform, universal hospital insurance at nominal cost was inaugurated in 1947.

The greatest single step toward the social welfare state, and the issue that ensured the continuing politicization of the Saskatchewan community, was the introduction of a universal compulsory prepaid medical care plan in 1961–2. The plan was introduced just as Tommy Douglas left Saskatchewan to become leader of the newly formed New Democratic Party in November 1961. His successor as Premier, Woodrow Lloyd, lacked Douglas's witty platform style and obvious enjoyment of a scrap and was unable to swing the entire community behind the plan – though one might doubt whether even Tommy Douglas could have averted the crisis. The medicare battle began in early 1962. Recognizing that there was no half-way measure between resistance and acquiescence, the doctors of the province simply refused to accept medicare. With the backing of the Canadian and American medical associations, they saw themselves as defending individual freedom and the doctor-patient relationship against the red tide of socialism. The threat of a large migration of doctors to the United States, accusations of Bolshevism, the formation of Keep Our Doctors committees, and mass meetings and motorcades were used by the opponents of medicare to whip up public concern about the issue. Government supporters responded with Keep our Democracy committes, an advertising campaign, and plans to set up community health clinics. Eventually, in July 1962, the doctors of the province went on strike for over three weeks. It is no exaggeration to say that friendships and even families were disrupted by the dispute. One of the handful of doctors on the government team, Dr Orville Hjertaas of Prince Albert, saw his business associations destroyed, his family pilloried, and his qualifications questioned. But the plan went into effect, was accepted almost universally within a short period, and was translated into a national program before the decade was out. The CCF/NDP had borne the brunt of the opposition, however, and Saskatchewan had redefined political party loyalties in the process. More clearly than ever before, CCF now meant 'social reform' and government action whereas Liberal meant 'freedom' and fewer government social initiatives.[10]

The 'medicare crisis,' as it was known, sapped the strength of the government and provided ideal ground for a Liberal resurgence. Led by former CCF MP Ross Thatcher, owner of a small chain of hardware stores, the Liberals staked out the right side of the political spectrum. As Thatcher explained, 'I am opposed to socialism and all that it stands for, because I think, given time, socialism erodes and destroys man's initiative and independence. I believe that a greater investment of capital in Saskatchewan is the one vital step towards the achievement of virtually every economic and social goal which we hold dear. I believe that you cannot make a nation ... strong ... by fermenting [sic] class hatred.'[11] The Liberals won the 1964 and 1967 elections but, in the harder times of 1971, lost to the resurgent NDP under Allan Blakeney. Thatcher died suddenly a month after the election, and the Liberal slide began. The 1975 general election saw the Liberals drop a large fraction of their popular vote – from 43 per cent (1971) to 32 per cent (1975) – and they fell to 14 per cent in 1978 and less than 5 per cent in 1982. At the same time, Conservative fortunes revived.

The explanation of this extraordinary shift in the allegiance of the 'other half' of the political spectrum, the non–New Democrat population, must be the decline in popularity of the federal Liberal government in the west. When the federal Liberals rebuilt their party after the Diefenbaker Conservative landslide of 1958 and, again, in the wake of Pierre Elliot Trudeau's success in 1968, they chose systems – the 'mass party' of the early 1960s and the 'participatory democracy' of the late 1960s – that appealed to central Canada's urban middle class and undercut the long-time agricultural base of the Liberal party in the prairie west. When the Ottawa Liberals produced new policies, they were often accused of being too 'socialist' – meaning they were taking too much control of the economy and were meddling in areas where they had no business, such as language and metric measures; but they were also criticized for being too 'right wing' – meaning that government was applying principles of economic efficiency to the detriment of the most sacred facet of prairie life, the family farm. And the one prairie Liberal who might have assumed the mantle of Jimmy Gardiner, Otto Lang, was too coolly rational, too desirous of modernizing farm society, to be seen as the crucial defender of prairie interests in Ottawa. When Lang lost his Saskatoon-Humbolt seat in 1978, the last hope of an early Liberal revival in Saskatchewan was extinguished.[12]

The fall of the Liberals was directly related to the rise of the Conservatives. The Conservative share of the provincial popular vote was 2 per cent in 1971, but under the brash articulate Dick Collver it rose rapidly to 28 per cent in 1975 and 38 per cent in 1978. After Collver's departure from the party, Grant Devine, an agricultural economist, led the Conservatives to a stunning victory in 1982 in which the party won 55 seats and 54 per cent of the popular vote. It would be wrong to think that this transition from Liberal to Conservative as the alternative to the NDP in Saskatchewan's two-party system marked a great shift in popular perspective. Instead, both Liberals and Tories represented the right side of the Saskatchewan political spectrum because both were closer to business and farther from labour than their NDP opponents. Both Liberals and Tories were closer to youth and farther from the elderly than were the NDP. Both Liberals and Tories were perceived to be less sympathetic to government intervention in the economy and to social experiments. As in Manitoba, so in Saskatchewan a new two-party system had evolved. That the system excluded the Liberals, the governing party in the national capital, was a serious regional and national problem, but it was caused by the Liberals themselves and by the fortunes of electoral contests.

Alberta was Canada's Cinderella in the post-1940 decades. Not for Albertans the deadly debates over economic growth as in Manitoba or even about government ownership as in Saskatchewan. Alberta was in a category by itself. Nowhere was growth so rapid, the increase in wealth so obvious, the atmosphere of confidence so palpable. The discovery of oil at Leduc in 1947 was as significant an event in regional history as the original influx of homesteaders before the First World War, and the implications of the windfall were still being worked out in the 1970s and 1980s.

The most obvious consequence of the petroleum boom was the emergence of Alberta as the largest prairie province. Where its population was about 800,000 in 1941, 33 per cent of the regional total, it was 1.3 million in 1961 (40 per cent of the prairie population) and 2.2 million in 1981, or over half (53 per cent) the total population of the prairie west. Just as striking was the growing influence of Edmonton and Calgary. The prairies had had a single metropolis, Winnipeg, in 1941, with a population half as large again as that of Edmonton and Calgary combined, but the two Alberta cities grew so rapidly that, by 1981, they were both slightly larger than the Manitoba capital. Like its sister provinces, Alberta also experienced a rapid population decline in its rural community from over three-fifths (66.6 per cent) in 1941 to about one-fifth (22.8 per cent) of the total provincial population in 1981. And, too, it saw significant growth in its northern reaches as tar sands and agricultural expansion spurred growth in the Peace River and Fort McMurray areas.

This extraordinary population increase was the result of a booming economy. And prosperity was due to petroleum. In 1935, just over 50 per cent of Alberta's wealth was a consequence of agricultural production, and just over 10 per cent was the result of mining, including petroleum. A generation later, in 1971, agriculture's share was less than 15 per cent, and the proportion due to mining was about 40 per cent. After the oil crisis of 1973–4, the value of mining production rose even higher, to more than half of Alberta's wealth in the late 1970s. Agriculture in Alberta, as in Manitoba, was diversified. Ranching remained a significant activity in the Calgary region, sheep and a variety of field crops – potatoes, vegetables, and sugar beets – were raised in the south, and rape seed and grass seed were important on the northern margins of agriculture near Edmonton and in the Peace River country. The dominant fact in Alberta history after 1940 was diversified wealth. Prairie communities had never before, not even in the pre-1914 boom, had to cope with such prosperity.[13]

The political history of Alberta also diverged from the pattern in the two neighbouring prairie provinces in the modern era.[14] As competitive two-party systems evolved in Manitoba and Saskatchewan, the quasi-party system described by C.B. Macpherson became more firmly entrenched in Alberta. And, what is more remarkable, when the province finally rejected the Social Credit party in the 1971 election, it supported the Conservatives in such decisive fashion that a new era of single-party dominance was inaugurated under Premier Peter Lougheed. The Conservative position was consolidated in the general elections of 1975, 1979, and 1982. Social Credit simply collapsed during the decade, and the New Democratic Party, which did retain one seat throughout this period, won fewer than 20 per cent of the popular vote in each of the three elections. The Liberals, despite strong showings in the election campaigns, were unable to convert this support into seats and thus were relegated to the status of bystander in political debates. The biggest noise in Alberta politics was made by a 'separatist' movement in the late 1970s and early 1980s. Eventually coalescing around the Western Canada Concept, this group criticized the federal Liberal government and advocated either the creation of a new nation or a drastically revised Confederation. It lamented the drain of western wealth to eastern Canada, the entrenchment of French as one of Canada's official languages, the transition from imperial to metric measures, and the allegedly socialistic nature of eastern Canada's political leadership. And it raised the long story of prairie dissatisfaction with national tariff and transportation policies that had allegedly exploited the region for eastern purposes. But the separatist anger was not sufficiently widespread to produce electoral victories in the 1982 provincial contest and seemed to wane quickly during the recession of 1982–3. No one would deny that there were continuing tensions within Confederation, or that resource-rich Alberta was a centre of dissatisfaction with federal policies, but separation from Canada seemed an unlikely alternative for provincial residents as Lougheed's Conservatives commenced their fourth government.

Casual observers of the prairie west might be forgiven for assuming that, like the oil barons, farmers were prosperous and successful in the decades after 1940. Despite annual worries about the weather and periodic protests about federal policy, farm families seemed better housed, better equipped, richer than ever before. For a proportion of the rural population this was certainly true. But the success story had its darker side. Rural society in the prairie west was drastically changed in this period. During the first four decades of the twentieth century, the institutions of the rural west were set in place, tested, and revised to meet the crisis of the Depression; during the next four decades, the structure was changed so much as to be almost unrecognizable to the pioneer. Thus, there were as many individual failures and departures as victories, as many dying villages as growing towns, as many painful readjustments – in place of residence, method of cultivation, circle of friends – as smooth transitions.[15]

The degree of change was remarkable. The number of farms was cut in half in the forty years after 1940. The farm population was reduced by over half. Whereas over 60 per cent of the prairie population was rural in 1941, under 30 per cent was 'rural' in 1981, and only 11 per cent lived on farms. The rural west was home to 750,000 fewer inhabitants in 1981 than in 1941. In contrast to the golden days of rural life, the countryside was empty. And without people to participate and observe, the schools, churches, ball teams, and sports days ceased to exist.

Fewer people were farming the prairies, and yet they were cultivating a larger area than when the rural population was at its height. Obviously, the size of individual farms increased dramatically.[16] Such growth raised concerns about farm ownership and particularly the possibility of large-scale leasing. Legislation was introduced in each of the three provinces to halt the rapid trend to foreign and non-resident Canadian ownership of land. (It stood at about 5 per cent of prairie farm lands in 1980.) But the development of a new phenomenon, the partly owned, partly rented farm, probably indicated that a new feudalism – absentee landlords and wage-labour farmers – would not soon become entrenched in the west. (Over one-third of prairie farm units were in this category in 1976, whereas only 6–8 per cent were run solely by a tenant and 55–65 per cent were owned completely by the operator.) Thus, the most sacred of prairie rural institutions, the family farm, seemed safe, though the farm unit was now much larger than it had been in the early decades of this century.[17]

Rural areas were depopulated and farm units grew larger because city life seemed more attractive and because individual farmers were physically capable of handling larger acreages than ever before. Some scholars have contended that the development of more efficient farm machinery was the fundamental explanation of the rural exodus. Their argument focuses on the horse, the growing season, and the tractor. In the era when the draughthorse ruled the farm, one man could handle up to an eight-horse team and could work the horses for about eight hours each day. In this manner, he could seed 300 acres in about 21–35 days. A reasonable estimate of the growing season, 110–125 days, and of the wheat maturing season, about 90–100 days, suggests that 300 acres was the optimum crop size for a one-person farm. Until the 1920s, the gasoline tractor was a poor economic bet compared to the horse because these new machines were unreliable, difficult to repair, and unsuited to the horse-drawn implements of the prairie farm. Moreover, as any fool could see, the tractor, with its metal wheels and winter-time obstinacy, could not replace the horse for the Sunday trip to town or the weekday grain hauling chores, and, worse than that, cost more to feed than old King and Queen in the barn. Technology worked wonders, however, and a lighter, stronger, more reliable tractor, equipped with rubber wheels and power take-off (a device that extended the spinning drive shaft behind the rear axle and thus permitted the engine power to operate towed implements), was soon available. What is more, combines, trucks, and cars eliminated the need for horses in other phases of the farm operation. But the Depression and the war intervened, putting mechanization out of reach of many farmers until the 1940s.[18] In 1941, there was one tractor for every two and a half prairie farms; by 1976, two tractors for every farm. The 'tractor

TABLE 3
Change in prairie agriculture

|                         | 1941    | 1976    |
|-------------------------|---------|---------|
| Number of farms         | 296,469 | 164,192 |
| Cars on prairie farms   | 128,257 | 148,095 |
| Trucks                  | 43,363  | 304,434 |
| Tractors                | 112,624 | 326,599 |
| Combines                | 18,081  | 127,755 |

explosion' of the late 1940s was followed by the 'horsepower explosion' of the 1960s and 1970s. Now farmers could work twenty-four-hour days, if they wished, and till their fields with large implements at speeds four or five times greater than horses could manage. Inevitably, the horse disappeared from prairie farms and the capacity of the individual farm labourer was multiplied many times.[19]

In 1941, there was one car for two farms, one tractor for two and a half farms, one truck for every seven farms, one combine for eleven farms; and in 1976, there was one car per farm, two trucks, two tractors, and nearly one combine (see Table 3).[20]

The demands of farm ownership changed just as rapidly as the shape of the farm community. Farmers who sold out in 1940 would not have had the skills to operate these same farms – now three times as large – in the 1980s. If they did try to resume their old occupation they would soon learn to manage the giant tractors, combines, and field implements, of course, but the cultivation strategy would be unfamiliar, the choice of herbicides, pesticides, and fertilizers would be bewildering, and the financial decisions would be frightening. Debates over soil fertility – especially concerning nitrogen loss and the increase in soil salinity – would force them to decide whether summerfallow acreage should be sharply reduced. Correspondingly, the use of nitrogen and phosphorus fertilizers (sales of which took off in the 1960s and 1970s) would preoccupy them with the scientific measurement of the soil's health. Despite debates over the implications of the use of herbicides and insecticides, such chemicals were increasingly common on prairie farms and, especially if the farmer opted for reduced tillage and continuous cropping, would have to be considered.[21] Surely the crops must be the same, our returning farmers might protest. And again, the answer would not reassure. Wheat – new breeds to be sure – was still the king on prairie farms, but its relative importance had declined. Of the new crops, rape (canola) and flax – used for their oil content – were very important, and so too were vegetables and a wide range of other specialty crops.[22]

Behind the trend to larger farms, larger machines, and chemical analysis lay the basic issue of any business – the matter of profit and loss. Here, the 1940 farmer who returned in 1980 would find the decisions nothing less than shocking. Farm operating expenses rose by a factor of five in the two decades from 1956 to 1976 while farm net income rose by a factor of three. Farm lands that were valued at $20–$40 per acre in 1940 might be sold for $500 per acre and even, on the best soils, $1,000 per acre. Because the modern farm was likely to have been expanded recently, the interest payments on the price of the additional quarter-section would have to be met. Fuel costs, fertilizer costs, and machinery costs were rising rapidly. Thus, the farmer of the 1980s worked with financial calculations on a daily basis where his predecessor would rarely have bothered, except in spring and fall, to estimate seasonal budgets. Where the farmers of the 1940s were accustomed to calculations based on units of $1,000 and $10,000, the farmers of the 1980s would speak in units of $100,000 and even $1 million. The negotiation of credit and the payment of interest were now part of the farmer's monthly calendar, too, and occurred in a new world of federal, provincial, credit union, and chartered bank agencies for agricultural loans. As interest rates rose and fell, the prospects of the farm dimmed or brightened. And, if it had seemed unclear before, the crucial reason for the exodus from the rural west would now be apparent: the farm was no longer the foundation of a rural way of life where, as in a self-sufficient garrison, the family could surmount the vagaries of world price changes and even of the weather. The farm was instead a large, capital-intensive business that operated on a line of credit and relied on Mother Nature to produce satisfactory earnings.

The analogy of a $1 million business, wherein the farm was little different in kind from an urban enterprise of similar size, could be extended to include the work process and the consumption patterns of the farm family. Many farmers worked in the fields in air-conditioned, dust- and sound-filtered tractor and combine cabs that could be likened to the work environment of a factory or office. Many of their other tasks were similarly reliant on labour-saving equipment such as augers and truck hoists, two-way radios and mechanical milkers. The farm home, equipped with car, refrigerator, running water, inside toilet, and television, differed little from its town equivalent. Groceries and clothing were purchased in the shopping centres frequented by urban dwellers. Consolidated schools provided educational facilities that differed only in after-school programs (as had been the case forty years before, the farm children must not miss the bus). None the less, the proportion of farm children attending and staying in school now approximated the levels of their town and city counterparts.[23] Urbanization, in other words, was a two-way phenomenon in the decades after 1940. Thousands of farm families moved to the city, of course, but the city – or its material culture – also invaded the farm. As a business, a residence, and a type of labour, farming on the prairies was almost as 'urban' as plumbing in Edmonton or clerking in Weyburn. Only the neighbourhood was different. Farmers had ceased to be self-sufficient; like urban dwellers, they had become consumers.

The structure of the grain business had also changed. Canadian institutions for handling, transporting, and marketing grain had evolved in the era of steam locomotives, wooden boxcars, and the Winnipeg Grain Exchange, but after the Depression the system slowly entered the world of diesel engines and computers. The most visible change was the abandonment of the elevators and branch railway lines, the maintenance costs of which were no longer justified in the eyes of company accountants.[24] There were 5,758 elevators in 1933 and only 3,506 in 1978 (a 40 per cent drop). Naturally, this trend pushed the burdens of grain storage, longer hauls, and better highway maintenance back on the farmer. Like elevator consolidation, abandonment of branch lines was the product of cost accounting in which social factors were not to be considered. In the early decades of prairie settlement, 20,000 miles of branch lines had been built to accommodate the stately pace of the horse-drawn grain wagon. In recent decades, because railways were seen to be public utilities, the maintenance or reduction of this network was a burning public issue in every prairie community. After a quarter-century of debate, several protracted investigations, and much uncertainty, about 3,000 miles of track had been abandoned and the issue was far from settled. Empty town sites such as Floral, Saskatchewan, home of Gordie Howe of hockey fame, thus became symbols in continuing discussions, and pictures of weather-beaten false fronts, abandoned main streets, and rusted rails overgrown with weeds were proof alternately of the wisdom or the folly of abandoning branch lines.

The cost of grain transportation was an even hotter item in prairie politics. No one needed an explanation when talk of Crow was in the air. But no one had a ready solution to the impasse on the Crow's Nest freight rates. The railway companies, required by federal legislation to maintain low rates on grain and flour, did not want to invest in the grain transport system when it was already losing millions of dollars. The farmers did not want to forgo a valuable subsidy which, many argued, was their equivalent of the manufacturers' tariffs, their share of the National Policy bargain. But change was coming, even to this most untouchable principle of the prairie farm economy. The railways were alleged to be losing several hundred million dollars annually if grain transport was calculated as a separate item. And the profits on the other parts of the rail corporations, such as the CPR's smelters, airlines, and forest and real estate holdings, all of which were the outgrowth of the Canadian people's original investment in the rail line, were rarely discussed in the freight rate equation. As in the operation of the individual farm, so in transportation, the 'grain industry' had become the field of analysis and the industry's balance sheet had a separate entry for grain shipment costs. In addition to the obvious opposition from the railway companies, the Crow rate was criticized by other western interests. Representatives of the livestock industry argued that the Crow undercut their operations: it was cheaper to ship feed grain out of the region than to produce finished meat products for shipment to central Canada. The same argument was raised by those who wished to establish oilseed-crushing plants on the prairies. Then, in the late 1970s, an increasing number of grain farmers, swayed perhaps by the federal civil servants' agitation, by the railway companies' lobby, or by arguments concerning the need for modernization of the rail network, began to lean toward change in the Crow rate system. Thus, after more than a half-century of debate, a new rate structure and large federal government subsidies to the railways were finally implemented in 1983.[25]

A significant new element in farm thought and, perhaps, a pivotal factor in the Crow debate was the unexpected intervention of the Canadian Wheat Board into the politics of grain in the late 1970s. The board had become the exclusive international sales agent for Canadian wheat in 1943 and, later, for oats and barley. Through a quota system it regulated the flow of these grains from the farm into the elevators. Its system of block shipping co-ordinated the movement of grain by rail from country elevators to export position at Great Lakes or ocean terminals. Aside from its role as marketing and transportation agent, however, the board had evolved into the farmers' adviser on production strategy – which crops to grow, how much acreage to seed, what prices might be expected. Thus its intervention in grain politics in the late 1970s was, in the eyes of many observers, a natural extension of its role; its act, a deceptively simple one, was to establish 'export goals' for 1985, 1990, and 2000. These goals were very high: grain exports of 30 million tonnes in 1985 would be 50 per cent above the totals actually attained in the late 1970s, when farmers and shippers were said to be working at or near full capacity, and levels of 36 million tonnes in 1990 and 46 million tonnes in 2000 were undeniably beyond the reach of the present system and current production techniques. Moreover, they flew in the face of critics of increased grain exports, including the Science Council of Canada and the National Farmers' Union, both of which preferred less reliance on exports and greater emphasis on Canadian agricultural self-sufficiency. (These dissenters noted that Canadian grain exports earned $3 billion in foreign exchange but that food imports, especially nutritionally important commodities such as fruit and vegetables, cost over $2 billion.) But the attention paid to rapid increases in production, shipment, and sales of grain soon dominated prairie grain debates and significantly affected decisions on cultivation, transportation, and, it seems, even freight rates.[26]

The family farm was, by 1980, a business rather than a way of life. Its production techniques were those of a highly mechanized, highly efficient, capital-intensive industry. Its domestic economy was almost indistinguishable from its urban counterparts. The larger economic system in which it operated – the handling, transportation, and marketing of farm products – was undergoing its own restructuring as the demands upon it became more insistent. Though agriculture remained a defining element of the prairie west in the 1980s as it had been in 1940 and 1900, its relative influence had declined sharply with the drop in farm population, and, even more important, its practitioners – the farm families – had become almost as 'urban' as city-dwellers.

The most significant indication of the urban character of prairie farming was its growing degree of 'class' division. Farmers had done to themselves what they prevented external institutions from doing: they forced many of their number off the land and created distinct divisions within their own society.

The farmer's replacement as the focus of prairie social mythology was the business leader. Not since the heady days at the opening of the century had prairie entrepreneurs seemed fit subjects for hero worship, but in the 1980s the names of Pocklington, Gallagher, and Blair challenged even the politicians for front-page coverage and certainly crowded the names of farm leaders into specialist journals. Even more unusual, perhaps, was the obvious rise and apparent eclipse of multinational mining corporations during these four decades. Two new patterns of resource development – an Alberta model based on local capitalists and a Saskatchewan model based on state control – became prominent, largely at the expense of the foreign-owned multinational enterprises. These developments in the non-farm sectors of the prairie economy signalled the opening of a new era and the emergence of three provincial empires where a single region had once existed; whether they were proof of continuing local control of the political and economic environment had yet to be determined.

The centres of the new west where Regina and Saskatoon as well as Calgary and Edmonton. The growth of the Saskatchewan cities was, however, quieter and apparently less noteworthy than that of their larger Alberta counterparts. The model of state control upon which it was built had far-reaching implications. Not even a change of government from 'social democrat' to 'free enterprise' in 1982 was likely to affect the growth of provincial crown corporations or the provincial Heritage Fund.[27] Saskatchewan was the model of contemporary state capitalism in Canada.

Crown corporations and co-operative institutions in Saskatchewan dominated some of the most important sectors of the economy. The Crown Investments Corporation, the holdings of which included the provincial telephone and power utilities, the bus company, the potash enterprise, oil and mining companies, and part of a steel company, possessed assets of $5 billion at the close of 1981 and was one of Canada's largest business corporations. The premier grain-handling company in the province was Saskatchewan Wheat Pool, a farm-owned co-operative, and another co-operative, United Grain Growers, was also prominent in the field. One of the largest enterprises in grocer and retail wholesaling was Federated Cooperatives; its Saskatoon head offices supervised extensive operations and $1.3 billion in sales in 1981. One of the largest farm machinery suppliers was Canadian Co-operative Industries Ltd, with Winnipeg offices controlling an empire with $100 million in sales in 1981. Even in finance, where the Toronto and Montreal headquarters of Canada's chartered banks exercised immense influence, local institutions, including Co-operative Trust Company of Saskatoon, and numerous credit unions, led by Sherwood Credit Union of Regina, were prominent. Most important, perhaps, the province had established a powerful source of investment capital in its Heritage Fund. About one-third of the province's annual non-renewable resource revenue had been placed in the fund, and as of 1981 its $1.3 billion in assets had been used to 'patriate, strengthen and diversify' resource production through the provincially owned crown corporations.[28] It was an impressive accomplishment for a community of fewer than 1 million people and even more remarkable for the fact that most of these locally controlled institutions had not existed in 1940.

To understand the dramatic change in Saskatchewan one must begin with the oil, potash, and uranium discoveries of these four decades. One must also appreciate the significance of two crucial influences in the modern province, the experience of the Depression and the impact of the CCF/NDP. The provincial attitude to the resource bonanza was shaped by the fear of another economic crisis as devastating as the one of the 1930s and by a perspective on political economy that might be termed 'prairie socialist.' When the first CCF government embarked on its program of 'planned economic development' and 'social ownership of natural resources' in the 1940s, it experienced more setbacks than victories. Nevertheless its ideal – diversification – emerged unscathed. If ever the province was to escape the boom and bust syndrome of a one-crop economy, the CCF leaders argued, new resources and new enterprises would have to be developed. Private enterprise was allowed to undertake the new ventures in the 1950s and 1960s because the CCF, stung by the failure of its five competitive companies, hesitated to embark on a second campaign for social ownership.[29]

Despite this bitter experience, its modest ventures in resource control – fur, fish, and timber corporations and a sodium sulphate mine – were moderately successful. Thus, during the seven years of Liberal government 1964–71, when the New Democrats had time to reflect on their record, and to react to the prodding of an adventurous party leader, Woodrow Lloyd, some party members began to insist on greater public control of natural resource development. Noting that the province had lost substantial revenue from the exploitation of oil and potash deposits, these new reformers, many briefly associated with the so-called Waffle socialist-nationalist movement within the NDP, won greater support when the price of potash, like that of petroleum, quadrupled between 1969 and 1975. The Blakeney government, elected in 1971, acted quickly to tax some of the ensuing profits. After re-election in 1975, when the provincial taxation law was challenged by the federal government and the multinationals, Blakeney took advantage of the public ownership sentiment in the party and the province to nationalize a portion of the industry. Within three years, despite a hail of criticism from the opposition and the multinationals, 40 per cent of provincial capacity had been purchased. Thereafter, the steady flow of resource revenue into provincial coffers and the atmosphere of success within the civil service sustained new crown ventures and a virtual celebration of the advantages of state-controlled economic development.

Whether this reliance on government entrepreneurs, rather than on private enterprise, satisfied provincial voters was difficult to estimate. Some scholars have argued that the NDP program of state ownership in the 1970s was conducted 'with little attention to the cultivation of popular participation and support' and, thus, that there were real tensions between the bureaucrats and the voters.[30] The 1982 election, in which the New Democrats were soundly defeated, seemed to indicate that the party had failed to understand public opinion but not, it should be underlined, that crown enterprises were disliked. Rather, the people seemed to be asking that some of the new wealth be distributed immediately. State capitalism, it appeared, was presumed to make everyone a little richer. Just as important for the fate of the local economy, state capitalism placed enormous wealth and power in the hands of local entrepreneurs – albeit civil servants – whose criteria for investment and for decisions on the social costs of economic change were alleged to be more responsive to community priorities than their national and multinational counterparts. Therein lay the crucial principle of and the uncertainty within the Saskatchewan experiment. Whether the NDP contention was valid, and local government entrepreneurship worked, only time would tell. For the moment, one could say that

Saskatchewan pinned its economic hopes on civil service entrepreneurs.

The Alberta government also faced public criticism for its policy on natural resource income in the 1980s. As in Saskatchewan, the administration had responded to rapid rises in mineral prices by creating a Heritage Fund into which was placed 30 per cent of the annual revenue from non-renewable resources. As in Saskatchewan, much of the revenue from the Trust Fund was invested in provincial crown enterprises (50–60 per cent of the Trust Fund until the economic recession of 1982), including a housing corporation, a home mortgage corporation, a municipal financing corporation, a farm loan corporation, a small business loan corporation, and the provincial telephone company. And, as in Saskatchewan, some voters perceived the fund as 'a tightly controlled, private preserve of big, insensitive government.'[31] But the similarities between Saskatchewan and Alberta were far outweighed by the differences. Most important, Alberta's fund was far larger; if it had been a corporation, like its Saskatchewan counterpart, its $11 billion assets in 1981 (vs $1.3 billion in Saskatchewan's Crown Investment Corporation) would have made it Canada's fourth largest company, as measured by assets, after Hydro-Québec, Ontario Hydro, and Canadian Pacific. Moreover, the Alberta Heritage Fund supported crown enterprises that serviced the provincial economy but were not near its productive heart, such as communications and small loans, rather than resource ownership. The Alberta government had followed a different path with its Heritage Fund from that pioneered by the NDP in Saskatchewan.

An outsider might have assumed that Albertans were very like their neighbours in their perspective on political economy. Aside from the Heritage Fund, Alberta too had a huge Wheat Pool and a Dairy Pool, an extensive credit union system, and an important provincial financial enterprise; it operated a crown-owned airline (Pacific Western Airlines) and a telephone company (Alberta Government Telephones) as well as an energy company (Alberta Energy Company).[32] But the structure of the Alberta economy was entirely different from that of Saskatchewan and so was the provincial outlook on the proper mix of government and private enterprise. If Saskatchewan was Canada's model of democratic socialism, Alberta was its guide to state support of private entrepreneurs.

Alberta's extraordinary economic transition from near-bank-ruptcy to super-wealth began before 1940, when, to a large degree, Canada was heated, illuminated, and driven by coal, wood, and horse power. To a greater degree, it was fuelled by oil and natural gas in the 1970s and 1980s. During the four decades of change, from the 1930s to the 1970s, most of Canada's production of these two crucial resources was located in Alberta. This crucial conjuncture – Alberta discoveries and the modernization of Canada's patterns of energy consumption – guaranteed the accumulation of wealth in the westernmost prairie province. The policies of successive Social Credit administrations (1935–71) directed the economic windfall into the hands of private enterprise. The policies of the Lougheed Con-servative government (from 1971) ensured that not only the pri-vately owned multinational energy companies but also, to an even greater degree, a new class of local entrepreneurs would secure an important share of petroleum wealth. Thus, there were two differ-ent phases in the establishment of Alberta's policy of state reliance on private entrepreneurs.

Natural gas was discovered early in Alberta's history. It had heated and illuminated Medicine Hat from 1904 and Calgary from 1912, but, despite the discovery of a huge reservoir at Turner Valley in 1913, gas was perceived as a nuisance rather than a boon. Crude oil and naphtha could be marketed, natural gas could not. Thus the gas was burned off as a waste, millions of cubic feet, night and day, especially after further discoveries in 1924 far outpaced the needs of the region. Alberta was powerless to intervene until 1930, when control over natural resources was transferred from Ottawa to the prairie governments. But the province remained uncertain about its course of action until further gas and oil strikes in 1936 produced serious quarrels among the oil companies. At this point, the obvious waste and the threat of a damaging race to exploit the new basin that involved Imperial Oil, Canada's largest purchaser of crude and distributor of petroleum products, forced the hand of Alberta's new Social Credit government.[33] Its response was to follow American precedent.

To understand the resulting Alberta policy, one must understand the physical and legal systems of oil ownership. Oil and gas lie in great underground 'reservoirs' that can be tapped from as many surface sites as the dimensions of the reservoir permit; the legal principle known as the rule of capture confers title to the resource on the person who brings it to the surface; where ownership of surface parcels is divided among a number of competitors, the potential for a destructive race to drain the reservoir – and to flood the marketplace – is obvious. This dilemma was resolved in the United States by two expedients: first, the major international oil production and marketing corporations, the so-called Seven Sisters – Exxon, Shell, British Petroleum, Mobil, Texaco, Socal, and Gulf – agreed in secret on their shares of the world market. These shares would henceforth dictate their level of production. They then arranged a price system for oil based on the cost of production and delivery of expensive East Texas oil. Second, the American majors forced 'supply management' on oilfields in the United States; state-controlled 'conservation agencies' would henceforth estimate market demand, allocate this demand to the various petroleum reservoirs, and distribute the reservoir allocation among individual wells.[34] From the 1930s, the oil industry restricted production, shared markets, and set prices with the aid of American government regulatory agencies. The alternatives, which included nationalization and outright competition, were ignored in favour of creating a large American branch of the international petroleum cartel.

The Alberta government accepted the American example when it created its Oil and Gas Conservation Board in 1938. Henceforth, petroleum and natural gas markets would be assessed and each producer allocated a share. But, after the discovery of huge new reserves of natural gas in the late 1940s and early 1950s, producers demanded permits to export this remarkable commodity beyond provincial borders, both to eastern Canada and to the United States. Gas was a touchy subject in Alberta politics, however, because it had long been seen as both a crucial domestic endowment and the ticket to eventual industrial development. Under pressure from business interests and from the federal minister of trade and commerce, C.D. Howe, to permit gas exports, the Social Credit government of Ernest Manning moved to assert Alberta's ownership rights. Fearing that Ottawa might want a share of the windfall, Manning consolidated Alberta control over the gas by establishing a single pipeline 'collection' system within the province. This pipeline corporation would collect the gas at well-head and deliver it to local consumers as well as to export companies on the provincial borders. In this way, federal intervention to regulate the Alberta gas industry was made politically difficult. Though he had been encouraged to consider multinational and crown corporation ownership of this new vehicle, Premier Manning chose to create an ingenious new enterprise, the Alberta Gas Trunk Line Company, now known as Nova An Alberta Corporation. Non-voting shares were sold to the public, but sales were restricted initially to Alberta residents. Voting shares totalling 2,002 were divided among gas producers, gas exporters, Alberta's gas utilities, and the Alberta government in such a way that no single group could control company policy or, worse, sell the enterprise to an outside group. With this remarkable stroke, Manning avoided what he saw as the evils of government ownership and of untrammelled capitalism, secured Alberta's control over natural gas development, and created a new financial giant.[35]

The implications of the Manning policy became clear in the 1970s. Whatever the expectations of its founders, Alberta Gas Trunk became one of Canada's largest corporate empires. As gas prices rose, its profits permitted expansion into petrochemicals, the purchase of a large oil company (Husky Oil), and the successful giant-killing bid to build the proposed Arctic gas pipeline, which may eventually carry Alaskan and Canadian polar gas to southern markets. The president of the company, Robert Blair, an Albertan for most of his working life, became a giant in Canadian business. His nationalist and socially conscious opinions received much attention in the corporate world but also among a wider public. The political economists John Richards and Larry Pratt believe that Nova would not have been a leading force in the rise of Alberta business if it had been a crown corporation 'because the motivation – private accumulation – would have been missing. In creating Alberta Gas Trunk Line, Manning himself helped set the process of regional accumulation in motion – an interesting example of the unintended consequences of government intervention'[36]

Manning had a different experience with the oil industry. Oil became big business in Alberta in February 1947 when Leduc No. 1, a few miles south of Edmonton, blew in. For the next decade, as field after field came into production, millions of investment dollars flowed into the province. By the mid 1950s, Canadian subsidiaries of six integrated multinationals controlled or leased 75 per cent of the proven resources, all the major oil pipelines and most of the major refineries in the region. As in the United States, the oil was pumped from the ground under a market prorationing system supervised by a government agency, in this case Alberta's Oil and Gas Conservation Board. Moreover, the Alberta government, eager to see the exploitation of provincial petroleum reserves, granted generous royalty and lease provisions to the multinationals. Manning believed, apparently, that the multinational energy giants alone could mobilize the necessary investment capital and would do so only if Alberta resource policy seemed stable. Thus, despite its ownership of 80 per cent of the minerals in the ground, including oil and gas, Manning's administration chose to rely on private enterprise to gather risk capital, drill the holes, and market the product. The policy was safe, relatively lucrative, and resulted in rapid development; but it meant the sale of the province's assets at a lower price and a faster rate than might have been achieved with government participation in the industry. It also meant that development remained in the hands of the multinationals and that the growth of a local entrepreneurial class, which might have contributed to the diversification of the Albertan economy, was truncated.

Social Credit's failure was Peter Lougheed's opportunity. His fundamental argument from 1965, when he took the Conservative leadership, to 1971, when his party took over the government, was that Alberta had squandered its petroleum revenue by failing to invest in local industries. His allies were the urban professionals – the businessmen, lawyers, and resource industry experts in Alberta's new bourgeoisie – who agreed with him that the province must prepare for the day when the multinationals left – and the morning after, when the oil itself was gone. Lougheed's timing was perfect. The 'Alberta first' ethos in his administration and the aggressive spirit of Alberta's new entrepreneurs happened to coincide with a revolution in the international energy industry in the 1970s. Rapid increases in world consumption, the absence of new discoveries, and the consolidation of the major producing nations into the Organization of Petroleum Exporting Countries drove energy prices to astonishing levels in the next few years, from an international reference price of $3 per barrel in mid-1973 to $28–30 per barrel in the early 1980s. Albertans – citizens, government and entrepreneurs alike – reaped the benefits.

Lougheed pursued an updated version of Manning's policy of state support for private entrepreneurs. Not that he was an apostle of out-and-out free enterprise. His revision of the petroleum royalties system without consulting the oil companies was a crucial step away from Social Credit practice. So, too, was his support for such crown enterprises as Pacific Western Airlines and the Alberta Energy Company. Rather than bowing to the demands of the multi-national energy giants, Lougheed skimmed off a larger proportion of the oil revenue and created the infrastructure for an industrial-ized, diversified local economy. The heart of the policy was his plan for a local petrochemical industry, including an ethane-ethylene enterprise owned jointly by the multinational Dow Chemicals and two Alberta companies, Dome Petroleum and Nova. And if such projects required further government support, he would give sym-pathetic consideration to such proposals. As Lougheed understood, political influence often worked together with economic factors to determine the location of industries and willy-nilly of investment capital and voting power.

What drove Lougheed? Much was made in the popular press of the Alberta premier's family history as a determining influence in his policy choices. It was true that his grandfather, Conservative Senator James Lougheed, was one of the most powerful – and rich-est – figures in the turn-of-the-century west and that his father and mother experienced serious financial and personal difficulties in the 1930s, when he was growing up. Whether the family crisis, which undoubtedly was an important factor in shaping his character, also established Lougheed's outlook on policy is dubious. Allan Blake-ney, who grew up in Nova Scotia, was just as determined to diver-sify Saskatchewan's economic base as was Lougheed Alberta's. The Lougheed family was again wealthy by the time Peter Lougheed went to the University of Alberta for law studies and to the Harvard Business School for graduate work in the early 1950s. Aside from the family heritage, Lougheed learned about business in the legal community of Calgary and the boardrooms of one of the west's most powerful and most conservative entrepreneurs, Frederick C. Mannix, of the construction and engineering firm Loram. There, surrounded by western regionalists and fierce free-enterprisers, he learned to be concerned about the eventual exhaustion of the oil reserves and the necessity for diversification into industrial and petrochemical operations. Like his colleagues, he attributed his frustration to a central Canadian 'establishment,' which was said to be sustained by an 'Eastern-dominated' federal government. The Ottawa-Edmonton confrontation over energy policy that began in 1973–4 and continued for eight years was, in the eyes of Lougheed and his Alberta supporters, just another chapter in prairie resistance to central Canadian exploitation of a hinterland region. Lougheed's goal was to establish real economic power – local direction of the local environment – in Alberta. Thus did he explain the three objectives of his government:

> The first one is to strengthen the control by Albertans over our future and to reduce the dependency for our continued quality of life on governments, institutions or corporations directed from outside the province. Secondly, to do this as much as possible through the private sector and only to move through the public sector if the private sector is not in a position to move in essential new directions and then only in exceptional and very specific circumstances. And thirdly, to strengthen competitive free enterprise by Albertans which to us means giving priority to our locally-owned businesses. Our basic guidepost [is] to maximize the number of our citizens controlling their own destiny.[37]

Distrust of the 'East' and fear of economic collapse went hand in hand in Lougheed's philosophy. His family history was probably much less influential in shaping the Alberta government's outlook than the provincial experience of a century of the National Policy and a decade of Depression.

If Lougheed was the political star of the 1970s in western Canada, the Alberta entrepreneurs were the heroes of the media. One might imagine them in the stereotype roles of a frontier movie or a Ralph Connor novel. Robert Blair of Nova was the teacher-missionary, because he was cool and able and could be seen as the conscience of the corporate world. Jack Gallagher of Dome was the gambler, smiling through good times and bad as he built a multi-billion-dollar petroleum empire that was often referred to as the 'flagship' of Ottawa's frontier exploration policy. Peter Pocklington, whose interests in sports enterprises, retail sales, and property development were said to total $1 billion, was the gunslinger; his flashy style of life and aggressive free-enterprise speeches made him the epitome of the self-made, self-conscious individualist. And they were supported by a cast of thousands, most of them closer to Pocklington than to Blair, wearing cowboy boots and stetsons with their three-piece western-style suits. A recent study of 349 Calgary oilmen, including managers and research professionals as well as entrepreneurs, discovered that eight of ten were Canadian and that seven of ten were raised in western Canada. They were strongly 'free enterprise' in politics and voted overwhelmingly for the Conservative party, federally and provincially, because it was closest to their outlook, though even Tories were suspected of being too 'socialistic.'[38] These were Lougheed's backers in the crucial revolution in Alberta's party system, and one suspects they were admirers of Gallagher and Pocklington because those two stood up for the west and did so with flair.

Western capital came of age in the 1970s. Journals of business contrasted western growth and eastern stagnation, the rise of Calgary and the decline of Montreal, the power of western resource industries and the weakness of the eastern manufacturing sector. As with most such generalizations, some truth was buried in the hyperbole. Both Saskatchewan's model of socialism – or state capitalism – and Alberta's emphasis on 'people's capitalism,' or state support for selected private entrepreneurs, had been in place long enough to have proven their worth. Significant portions of the two provincial economies were now under the control of local people. It was a far cry from the weak, dependent, and nearly bankrupt economies of the late 1930s.

'Western alienation' became a prominent theme in popular descriptions of federal-provincial relations during the 1970s and early 1980s. Because it seemed to arise more or less simultaneously with the crisis concerning Quebec's place in Confederation, this western unrest might be interpreted as similar to the French-Canadian challenge to national unity. But such a conclusion would be misleading. Despite acrimonious discussions between westerners and other Canadians concerning revenue-sharing, resource policies, freight rates, and official languages, the prairie west remained firmly Canadian. Indeed, 'alienation' was an inaccurate label for the western perspective. The prairie dissent was not led by estranged secessionists; rather, the important spokesmen of the western cause – Lougheed, Blakeney, Schreyer, and Lyon – posed a serious threat to the central Canadian political and economic establishment. It was the prairie determination to revise national policy, not to shrug it off, that made sparks fly.[39]

The origin of prairie protest lay in the previous century of regional history and in the physical structure of the northern half of North

America. From the time of Confederation, this island of settlement was separated from other communities on the continent by an international frontier and by physical barriers that could be transcended only at considerable expense. The protest was rooted, too, in an economic structure established by international markets and federal government decree: wheat exports became the heart of the prairie economy, and the so-called National Policy – tariff, railway, freight rate, settlement, immigration, police, and Indian policies – shaped the local economy and society. Was it any wonder that prairie 'subordination' to the 'East' – to the federal government and to the leaders of central Canada's business community – should have been a preoccupation of early prairie politicians? Prairie protest was also built on regional consciousness itself. The sense of a unique landscape and site, the struggle of the pioneer, federal-provincial bickering, the turn-of-the-century boom and the Depression catastrophe of the 1930s, and the intense experience of nativism and ethnic acculturation all contributed to the development of a common identity rooted in place and past. The expressions of prairie culture – photographs, paintings, novels, and histories in particular – were both another cause of regional sentiment and an illustration of regional maturity. By the 1970s, the people of the prairie west had undergone their time of testing and wished to have a hand in shaping their region and the nation. Their relative weakness in national political debates seemed to be a continuation of the inferior status that their ancestors had railed against in the preceding century.

The adoption of a federal system of government in 1867 and the establishment of three prairie provinces were pivotal factors in shaping the political expression of prairie residents. By the first decade of the twentieth century, prairie electors were integrated into the two-party system of central and Maritime Canada. However, as the development of Progressive, CCF, and Social Credit movements made plain, the old-line Liberal and Conservative parties could not always represent the multiplicity of ethnic, class, and regional perspectives within the nation. In the elections of the 1920s and 1930s, the two old-line parties shared the hustings – and the benches of the legislatures – with new 'third' parties. Never again were they able to dominate the political spectrum as they had done before the First World War.

The development of viable third parties in the 1930s coincided with a crisis in federal-provincial finances and in the economic structure of Confederation. The governments of Alberta and Saskatchewan were nearly bankrupt in this decade and the Manitoba government was little better off. Relief payments were putting intolerable burdens on prairie taxpayers, but when the federal government tried to provide assistance in 1935 its legislation was declared unconstitutional by the courts.[40] A Royal Commission on Dominion-Provincial Relations (the Rowell-Sirois commission) was appointed in 1937 to examine these problems. Despite its remarkable scholarly output, it was much less influential than the outbreak of war in revising Canadian federalism. During the wartime emergency, a new federal-provincial taxation system was implemented. From 1941, the federal government and the provinces shared tax revenues and, in accord with one of the crucial recommendations of the Rowell-Sirois report, tried to ensure that a minimum standard of services was maintained across the nation by means of federal redistribution of revenue from the richer 'have' provinces to the poorer 'have nots.' This was an important forward step, in the view of prairie Canadians, because they were henceforth to be protected as much as possible from a disaster like that of the 1930s.[41]

Prairie voters remained firmly attached to the federal government and the old-line federal parties in the 1950s and early 1960s. Their political protest movements had grown older and more traditional – were 'provincialized,' as one political scientist explained – and no longer seemed to present a challenge to Confederation. A favourite son, John Diefenbaker, led the national Progressive Conservative party for eleven years (1956–67) and provided vocal proof of prairie integration into the Canadian family. But Diefenbaker was replaced as Conservative leader in 1967 in what seemed to some of his supporters to be an 'eastern' coup. And Canada elected a new Liberal prime minister in 1968, Pierre Trudeau, who had had little contact with the region. Trudeau was both an eastern Canadian and an unswerving advocate of two official languages for Canada. To make matters worse, in the view of some prairie people, his attempts at party renewal undercut traditional Liberal strength in the west. Suddenly, the litany of prairie impatience with Ottawa assumed a new relevance: federal policies on tariffs, freight rates, grain sales, French-language services, and provincial control of natural resources were as contentious in the 1970s as they had been in the 1920s or 1890s.

Prairie criticism of the federal Liberal government was made more urgent by the unusual circumstances of the federal-provincial relationship in this era. Whereas, before 1930, the prairies had been Ottawa's colony, administered by the Department of the Interior and shaped by Canada's 'National Policies,' after 1945 they became part of the extraordinary bargaining process that increasingly distinguished relations between the two levels of government. Having presented ample proof that Ottawa's policies perpetuated the economic dominance of central Canada at the expense of the west, and having made little headway at special prairie consultations with the federal government such as the Western Economic Opportunities Conference of 1973, prairie governments and voters were increasingly restive. And an economic downturn in 1969–71, which was especially hard on prairie farmers, contributed to growing pressure on politicians to provide solutions. Each of the three incumbent provincial governments was defeated in this period, and criticism of the federal administration increased in intensity.

A few issues stood out in federal-prairie relations in the 1970s and 1980s. The most dramatic was the Alberta-Ottawa confrontation over energy, a decade-long battle that constituted an extraordinary chapter in the history of Canadian federal-provincial relations. It was a battle over money (should Albertans reap the advantage from rising international oil and gas prices or should they subsidize energy consumers in the rest of Canada?), but it was also a contest over the provincial right to resource ownership and, therefore, over which jurisdiction would establish policy in this crucial field. Another important issue arose from the Saskatchewan government's attempts to regulate the potash industry and to tax the 'windfall' gains of oil producers. The Saskatchewan legislation was opposed by the federal government and eventually declared unconstitutional by the Supreme Court. In Manitoba, the Pawley government's attempt to establish limited government services in the French language and to entrench French as an official language was interpreted by the Conservative opposition, and by crowds of protesters, as the extension of Ottawa's language policy to the province. That the legislation was allowed to die on the order paper was evidence of prairie unease in the face of the federal Liberal government's bilingualism policy. In each case, Ottawa was alleged to be the 'bad guy' because federal policy challenged positions established by successive generations of prairie provincial leaders.

On the question of resource policy, there was unanimity in the west. The resources belonged to the provinces, the prairie premiers

'Clout': Premiers Bennett, Lougheed, Blakeney, and Lyon
(Roy Peterson, *Vancouver Sun*, 25 April 1980)

insisted, and must pay for the establishment of diversified economies that would possess potential for long-term growth; this was
the root of the pre-1930 prairie campaign for the control of natural
resources, they said, and the message hidden in the disaster of the
1930s. Premier Allan Blakeney of Saskatchewan declared in 1979:

> As a provincial government we intend vigorously to protect what is
> constitutionally ours – in particular the revenue from our natural
> resources – but we understand that in order to reap the benefits of
> Confederation, we must be willing to give a little ... And, in recent
> years, that is just what Saskatchewan has done. For the good of all
> Canadians, we – and Alberta – have accepted substantially less than
> the world price for our oil ... You will find few separatists in Sas-
> katchewan. You *will* find people who believe that for too long Sas-
> katchewan has not had its fair share of the benefits, those who are
> tired of the West being considered a hinterland for the industrial tri-
> angle of the St. Lawrence valley.[42]

Ottawa's National Energy Policy (1980) and the rapid growth of Ottawa's crown-owned energy company, Petro-Canada, also prompted
outbursts of rage in provincial capitals, particularly Edmonton.
Only significant compromises enabled the federal government to
avert serious confrontation.[43]

The language rights of French- and English-speaking citizens
have bedevilled Canadian policy-makers for over two centuries and
have been a recurrent issue in prairie history since the creation of
Manitoba in 1870. Legislation to end the official status of French in
the region was passed in the 1890s, and bilingual educational privileges were reduced or eliminated during the First World War. But
the issue cropped up again, most notably in the late 1920s in association with the Ku Klux Klan in Saskatchewan and in the 1960s when
the Royal Commission on Bilingualism and Biculturalism ran into
opposition in the west. Memories of these episodes were revived
during the Manitoba language debate of 1983–4. The evident hostility to French, though widespread, was probably not critical to the
course of Canadian history. It did demonstrate that the interpretation of Canada as a French-English or dual nationality was simply
not accepted in the prairie west. Many prairie-dwellers would have
endorsed Donald Creighton's attack on the Royal Commission on
Bilingualism and Biculturalism: 'It grotesquely exaggerated the im-

portance of language and culture; it absurdly minimized the importance of everything else.'[44] However, the spread of French-language
education and the growing acceptance of bilingualism in the professions was an important contrasting trend and, perhaps, an indicator
of changes in prairie public opinion in the longer term.

Federal agricultural policy also angered the prairie governments.
After a period of indecisiveness in the 1960s, the Liberal administration in Ottawa tackled western farm problems with vigour in the
Trudeau years. Its goal was the creation of a new economic climate
'in which agriculture can fight for its progress,' but, rhetoric aside, it
was streamlining an 'industry,' encouraging the disappearance of
small farm units, and offering an insurance plan (grain income sta-
bilization) to protect against drastic drops in farm income. The abandonment of branch rail lines and of the subsidized 'Crow' freight
rates on grain was merely an aspect of a wholesale revision in federal agricultural policy, and, quite predictably, such policies caused
trouble because they undermined vested interests.[45]

What was not immediately apparent in the federal-provincial
storms of the 1970s and early 1980s was the considerable influence
of prairie spokesmen in national affairs. An interesting illustration
of their new power was the role of prairie premiers in the creation of
the Constitution Act of 1982. In the negotiations that preceded that
legislation, prairie administrations achieved significant concessions.
The clarification of provincial ownership of natural resources and
the extension of provincial taxation powers addressed two of the
crucial issues in prairie-Ottawa relations. The entrenchment of
equalization payments and programs to reduce regional disparities
established that a national minimum level of services was the right
of every Canadian; this had been a concern of prairie leaders since
the Depression. The entrenched Charter of Rights raised serious
philosophical debates about the relative powers of courts and legislatures in the law-making process: the provision of a mechanism by
which legislatures could ensure that their statutes might override
the general rights outlined in certain sections of the Charter was
another concession sought by the prairie premiers. The formula for
amending the constitution requires the agreement of the Senate and
House of Commons and the legislatures of seven of the ten provinces having, in aggregate, at least 50 per cent of Canada's population. This avoids the problem of earlier proposals – as westerners
saw it – of giving a specific veto over constitutional change to

Ontario and/or Quebec, and it ensures that, given current population expectations, the four western provinces can unite to defeat a constitutional amendment. Because these were four matters of substance on the constitutional agenda (from the original list of twelve items set out by Prime Minister Trudeau in 1980), the conclusion was a noteworthy victory for the prairie premiers and a significant prairie contribution to Canada's constitution.[46]

Despite continued tension in federal-provincial relations, the relationship between the prairie west and Ottawa was not as close to disintegration as some observers believed. The tension arose from two circumstances: economic forces that were international as well as local in origin created a boom in the resource-rich west and a recession (even 'deindustrialization') in central Canada; and the electoral fortunes of the federal Liberal government, due to accidents of personality and history that beset any party but also to deliberate policy choices, reached their nadir in the west during this period of economic crisis. However, what an economic crisis had failed to rend asunder in the 1930s would probably be left intact in the 1980s. Accidents of personality and choices of policy-makers could revive a party's electoral fortunes in a region very quickly. Surely the prairie loyalty to Confederation was more enduring than these temporary reverses in federal-provincial relations in the Trudeau years might imply.

In the decades after 1945, the prairie west moved increasingly toward a homogeneous international culture and was increasingly subject to the dictates of the transnational corporate economy. The Hollywood entertainment industry and the mass production–mass consumption style of work and leisure activities were as influential in the prairie west as in the United States or western Europe. And yet a spate of fictions, histories, and museum exhibits was proof that prairie cultural expressions were not only growing in volume but also in their concern to articulate local experience. International homogeneity and multinational power; local distinctiveness and local autonomy: which was the more telling trend in economic and cultural history? The delicate balance between global and local forces was a subject of concern for many peoples in the years after 1945 and, not least, for the citizens of the prairie west.

The assumption of global uniformity figured prominently in Canadian scholarship. The philosopher George Grant argued that since the Second World War Canada's ruling class, the people who controlled its great corporations, have become a northern extension of a continental ruling class, just as the nation's economy became a branch plant and the nation's military an errand boy. In the modern age, he wrote, it was impossible for many citizens to live outside the dominant assumptions of their world: democracy could not save Canadians from absorption into a 'homogenized continental culture.' His argument was based on the assumption that Canada was 'a local culture' and on the assertion that 'modern civilization,' especially 'modern science,' made all local cultures obsolete. Grant's essay reached a stinging conclusion: because conservatism was impossible, and because Canadian existence had hitherto been predicated upon the conservatism of Canadian society and its leaders, then the existence of Canada – a local conservative culture – was impossible.[47]

These generalizations have found considerable support among students of Canadian and prairie society. A distinguished Canadian economist, Harry Johnson, argued that Canada was increasingly a part of the larger North American economy: 'Both politically and economically, the general trend of world evolution is toward ... political and economic organization on a continental ... rather than national scale.' The best-known Canadian student of communications in the 1960s, Marshall McLuhan, was making comparable statements about the effects of the electronic media. The economist Paul Phillips suggested that regionalism had always been a central characteristic of the Canadian economy but that, in recent decades, the multinational corporation and continental capital integration, not the Canadian government, were the crucial forces in decision-making. The historian J.E. Rea, in his discussion of 'the most persistent social theme' in prairie history, 'the struggle for cultural dominance,' said that ethnic minorities were assimilated in the post-1945 period: 'What has evolved is a Prairie culture which is more diverse, but not essentially different from that established at the end of the nineteenth century. The premises of the Ontario migrants, and the social institutions which they planted, have generally remained intact.' The political scientist Roger Gibbins perceived a 'decline of political regionalism' in the prairie west. Among the reasons for the decline, he argued, were the urbanization of the population, the erosion of ethnicity, the transformation of agriculture, and, finally, 'the loss of a distinctive prairie culture, or the lost opportunity to

create a distinctive prairie culture,' which he associated with pressures from urban multinational mass media. What these scholars
had in common was the assumption that the forces of modern economic organization, modern transportation and communications
technology, and even of modern politics were eliminating the possibility of local autonomy, region-wide political identity, and a distinctive local culture.[48]

There is merit in this view, but it is only half the story. The
argument for a decline of local control over the economy, for example, should be tempered by recognition of the areas of considerable regional power. As long as prairie-based co-operatives owned
three-quarters of the country elevators and were relatively responsive to their membership, there was a measure of local control in the
wheat economy. As long as the Wheat Board acted as the central
agency for the sale of Canadian grain, and was reasonably responsive to the needs and desires of its constituents, its important functions were subject to a measure of local control. And as long as
decisions on freight rates remained within the political system, even
there a measure of local control was possible. It is true that determinants of prices and yields were still beyond the farmers' grasp, but
security of return had become greater than ever before, owing in
good measure to the efforts of the local pools and the local agricultural scientists and extension educators. These trends did not suggest homogenization or loss of local autonomy.

Within the rest of the prairie economy, the strength of the thesis
regarding international capital flows and transnational enterprises
was evident. But at the same time, given the inevitable context of an
increasingly integrated global economy, the degree of local control
over the non-agricultural portions of the prairie economy merited a
closer look. Three developments contradicted the conventional wisdom. First, co-operative enterprises and credit unions were extremely important in the prairie economy. In the early 1980s, five of
Canada's ten largest co-operatives were based in the prairie west,
and the prairie credit unions possessed assets of nearly $7 billion.
Second, the number and importance of prairie-based industrial enterprises grew substantially in the four decades. Though in several
cases these corporations were themselves transnational enterprises,
their owners – the prairie super-rich – demanded recognition as
local entrepreneurs who reflected a regional bias in their approach
to the economy. The power associated with such families as Rich-

ardson, Poole, Mannix, and Southern could not be discounted and, to the degree that this power was exercised with the future of the community or the region in mind, must be recognized as another kind of local control. The third theme in prairie economic self-determination concerned the role of the state. Prairie governments had always been prepared to intervene in the economy on behalf of local citizens. By the early 1980s, it was a rule of thumb that Canadian governments – that is, all levels of government – spent, on direct purchases and transfers of income, roughly 40 per cent of the total value of goods and services produced in Canada. Large state-owned institutions such as the three prairie telephone corporations, the two power corporations, the Alberta airline company, the Alberta energy company and treasury branches, the Alberta Heritage Fund, the Saskatchewan Crown Investments Corporation, and even that unusual hybrid Nova An Alberta Corporation were subject to direction from the people's representatives. In sum, the degree of local control over the local economy was much greater in 1980 than in 1940.[49]

If the argument for increasing international homogeneity and multinational power could be contrasted with a trend to local control in the case of the prairie economy, a similar duality was evident in the case of social organization and social structure. Ethnicity, native-white relations, and social class were the chief subjects at issue. The conventional wisdom in North American sociology, a product of Robert Park's work many years ago, has been that ethnic minorities inevitably were assimilated during the passage of several generations. This perspective seemed reasonable because it corresponded to daily observations on the replacement of folk architecture by tract home, the decline in the use of traditional languages, the exogamy of young people, and the secularism of daily life, to cite a few obvious illustrations. But the fieldwork of prairie sociologists found evidence that did not entirely confirm Park's thesis. Despite a significant province-wide decline in the use of traditional languages, ethnic languages and other characteristics of group identity were still important in the rural bloc settlements of north-central Saskatchewan. Continuing minority group loyalties and institutional completeness were also evident in Winnipeg's ethnic communities. There were relatively meltable and unmeltable individuals and groups, in other words, and the latter – the 'unmeltables' – created institutions parallel to those of the mainstream and climbed parallel ladders to success. This distinction between cultural assimilation (adaptation to mainstream values and material culture) and structural assimilation (entry into the important institutions of mainstream society) itself raised problems, but it did emphasize the continuing importance of ethnic identity in the prairie west.[50]

Native identity, like ethnic identity, did not disappear during this generation. There were 68,000 native people in the prairie west in 1941, most of whom lived in rural surroundings, and about 200,000 in 1981. By the latter date, natives constituted about 7 per cent of Manitoba's and Saskatchewan's populations and about 4 per cent of Alberta's. About one-quarter of the registered Indians lived off their reserves by 1976, and it was estimated that this proportion would reach one-third by the mid-1980s. Generalizations about the economic and social status of the urban and rural native population appeared frequently in the press and almost without exception emphasized that native birth rates were higher than white, that native unemployment rates were higher and native household incomes lower than white, that transfer payments were a primary source of native income, and that violence was endemic in native communities. The catalogue of negatives was so well-known that it must have had some accuracy, but it also rang chords that were familiar to students of prairie immigration history. The questions asked and the values implicit in the analysis sounded very much like the social surveys of central European immigrant communities in the prairie west before 1930. Like those surveys, contemporary reports reflected a sincere concern for the members of the native community, but they also imposed goals that were not necessarily those of the natives. A different perspective would have emphasized that prairie Indian bands differed from their counterparts in the rest of Canada. As one sociologist concluded: 'The typical prairie band is larger and grows rapidly due to the unusually high fertility rates. It is remarkably cohesive, well-developed at the community level, and relatively likely to retain the use of native languages. The typical non-prairie band is the obverse in many respects, being more fully integrated into the mainstream through education, employment, and off-reserve residence.'[51]

Native identity in the prairie west was consolidated in the postwar decades. Campaigns for native rights and celebrations of native culture produced a clearer and more insistent articulation of native identity than had occurred in the preceding half-century. Despite the assimilationist drive of the federal government, indeed, the natives forced the larger society to acknowledge a new political status – or new statuses – for them. And within the larger Canadian community, the distinctive characteristics of the prairie Indian associations and of the metis and non-status Indian communities were evident.

Prairie literature has also been seen as distinctive. Dick Harrison, the literary critic, suggested that a central theme in the history of prairie literature was the 'struggle for an indigenous prairie fiction'; the first task of the critic, he wrote, was to reconcile 'the incongruities between the culture and the land.' W.L. Morton's literary confession emphasized similar themes. Even Wallace Stegner contended with this kind of problem: 'Contradictory voices tell you who you are. You grow up speaking one dialect and reading and writing another ... all forces of culture and snobbery are against your *writing* by ear and making contact with your natural audience. Your natural audience, for one thing, doesn't read – it *isn't* an audience. You grow out of touch with your dialect because learning and literature lead you another way unless you consciously resist.'[52] This is the gap between nature and culture, America and Europe, west and east, country and city, body and mind that has been expressed many times from many perspectives. But in the post-1945 prairie west, one was struck not by an exceptionally wide gap between literature and life or by the absence of an audience, but by the very eagerness for locally created, locally inspired art and by the quest to bridge the gap between 'memory' and 'history.' Was this not the inspiration for the fiftieth and seventy-fifth provincial birthdays in Alberta and Saskatchewan, the many centennial celebrations, and the boom in local history publications, heritage movements, and family reunions? A regional voice and a regional audience – two very different things – have developed in the prairie west since the Second World War. As John Hirsch said of the Manitoba Theatre Centre, which was founded in 1957–8 but had its formative years in the preceding decade, there came together in Winnipeg the physical and financial support, the artistic talent, and the audiences to support an institution devoted to drama. The prairie west was now prepared to see its life translated into and its perceptions shaped by literature.

The expression of this interest in one's past and one's environment often began at an artistic level inferior to that of the metropolises of the English-speaking world. Despite a continuing self-consciousness, however, there was a growing maturity, especially in literature, where the growing influence of the university was evident. The finest prairie writers had learned to speak of local concerns in an international idiom. And for that reason the language of their imagination created a vision that became a focus for the community. It also attracted international attention. Northrop Frye has suggested that the best literature depends on local identification. And he went on to defend its quality in Canada, to argue that the gap between colonialism and maturity had narrowed: 'There is no reason for cultural lag or for a difference between sophisticated writers in large centres and naive writers in smaller ones. A world like ours produces a single international style of which all existing literatures are regional developments. This international style is not a bag of rhetorical tricks but a way of seeing and thinking in a world controlled by uniform patterns of technology, and the regional development is a way of escaping from that uniformity.'[53]

Every type of cultural expression has its own technology and its own historical rhythms of patronage, circulation, production, content, and form. What may have been true for prairie literature had no necessary relationship to developments in architecture, film, television, newspapers, painting, or other kinds of cultural production. In each of these areas, there were contradictory pressures toward a distinctive indigenous expression, on the one hand, and toward international uniformity, on the other. But communications technology was changing so rapidly in these decades that generalizations about international cultural homogeneity – as in the common fear of Hollywood and American network television – were premature.

Evidence about local distinctiveness was most striking in prairie politics. As the twentieth century passed, provinces became increasingly important units in Confederation and provincial identities became important in culture and politics. One aspect – even creator of – these identities was the provincial party system. A distinctive local blend of personalities and popular preferences moulded distinctive provincial governments and political institutions. In the period after 1945, the various communities in each province – native, ethnic, class, occupational, rural, and urban – became more closely integrated into a single community. The political parties reinforced provincial distinctiveness by pursuing significantly different brands of political education. The result was the development of ideological divisions within each prairie province and, thus, of indigenous party systems. These were not simply brokerage parties, in other words, but rather were parties based on ideological differences. None the less, the prairie west continued to be Canadian. Its local politics possessed distinctive elements, but its distinctiveness did not imply disloyalty.[54]

In these forty years, the prairie west was affected profoundly by international forces, but it also retained elements of individuality. Sweeping generalizations concerning cultural homogeneity and the concentration of global decision-making presented only one perspective on a complex story. As W.L. Morton once commented, 'There are sections as well as nations, nations as well as civilizations. The sub-society which is a section ... possesses some degree of integrity and character.'[55] The people of the Canadian prairies discovered new patterns in their heritage, contours in their environment, and depths in their common experience as they adapted to life in the closing decades of the twentieth century.

# 17

## Conclusion

'Here was the least common denominator of nature, the skeleton requirements simply, of land and sky – Saskatchewan prairie. It lay wide around the town, stretching tan to the far line of the sky, shimmering under the June sun and waiting for the unfailing visitation of wind, gentle at first, barely stroking the long grasses and giving them life; later, a long hot gusting that would lift the black topsoil and pile it in barrow pits along the roads, or in deep banks against the fences.'[1] W.O. Mitchell's *Who Has Seen the Wind*, like many of the finest statements of prairie art, begins with the land. And that is where the history of a region must begin.

Soon enough, human communities possessed the territory. But they never tied it down or controlled it in the way that seemed possible in some other parts of the world. And because the west was an 'empty' land, it offered vistas of natural splendour and intimations of longer perspectives that moved even detached observers to song. The surveyor Simon J. Dawson recorded in his journal for 7 June 1858: 'As we passed through Swan Lake, the sun was setting behind a range of hills which rose over a low wooded country to the west. To the south the blue outline of the Duck Mountain was just discernible on the verge of the horizon; while we, in our tiny craft, were gliding on through woody islands, rich in the first green drapery of a summer.'[2] Such passages were commonplace in nineteenth-century travel literature, and they remain a staple of prairie prose.

Into this idyllic setting came human beings who were prepared to contest for control of its resources. Thereafter the history of the Canadian prairies, like that of all communities, is one of accommodation and negotiation, of victory and defeat. When the telegraph line reached the district of Fort Carlton in 1875, the head chiefs, Mistawasis and Ahtahkakoop, sent a scout to warn the construction party: 'We have been expecting a commissioner to come and make a treaty with us. When I saw the [telegraph] wire and heard nothing of the commissioner I felt as if something was sticking in my throat ... If you insist on going ahead we will soon get enough Crees to make you stop. All our people are of the same opinion. When a treaty is made our rights to the land and the country will be the government's. Until then the rights are ours, and we tell you to stop.'[3] And so the story has continued for the past three centuries: co-operation and conflict, tragedy and triumph.

The first inhabitants of the region, the native people, relied on plants and animals for food and moved regularly between resource zones according to the produce of the season, the fortunes of the hunt, and their diplomatic relationships with neighbouring groups. Their material existence was probably comfortable, given the limitations imposed by their travel and the varying cycles of the ecosystem. In the first two centuries after the advent of Europeans, they hunted, fished, and traded as they had done in preceding centuries. They used European trade goods such as axes and knives and were affected by some European innovations, particularly the gun and the horse, but they remained in control of their domestic economies and their diplomatic alliances. Native autonomy was lost in the nineteenth century because of population pressure from eastern North America and the destruction of the single crucial element in the plains economy, the buffalo. From the 1870s, treaties were negotiated by representatives of the Canadian government and the natives of the western interior in which native sovereignty over the land was extinguished in exchange for government promises of economic assistance, educational facilities, and the creation of reserves for native people. In a few short decades, the natives of the western interior ceased to be autonomous peoples and became wards of the state.

From the European perspective, the history of the western interior between the 1640s and the 1860s was the story of competing fur trade enterprises. The Hudson's Bay Company of England, founded in 1670 on the initiative of Radisson and Groseilliers, traded from posts on Hudson Bay such as York Factory until, under the pressure of competition, it began to establish inland houses in the 1770s. The French and later the North West Company, with Montreal as headquarters, relied on an extensive network of posts that was pushed into the prairie west by La Vérendrye in the 1730s and greatly extended by Peter Pond and Alexander Mackenzie. Competition between the Hudson's Bay Company and the Nor'Westers, which involved the deaths of at least twenty of Lord Selkirk's colonists in 1816 and of sixteen Hudson's Bay traders in the Athabasca War, finally forced the coalition of the two companies in 1821. Under a new leader, Governor George Simpson, the Hudson's Bay Company ruled the fur trade and the region for another five decades.

Some of the western fur traders established liaisons with native women and had children. Their offspring, whether French- or English-speaking metis, were sufficiently numerous by the early nineteenth century to constitute the largest group in the Red River colony and an important component of the lower ranks of fur company operations. And, when international concern for the region quickened between the 1840s and the 1860s, the metis led the defence of local interests against incoming speculators. Canada eventually secured sovereignty over the northwest but only after an armed metis resistance led by Louis Riel in 1869–70 that resulted in significant revisions to the terms of the region's entry into Confederation.

Because of the great powers of the federal government but also because of Prime Minister Macdonald's decision to retain central control of western lands, the policy framework for prairie development was created in Ottawa. Decisions on the dispatch of the North-West Mounted Police, the square survey, the homestead policy, and immigration recruitment activities were taken between 1870 and 1874 and remained cornerstones of prairie history for two generations. Two other crucial decisions, on tariff policy and the Canadian Pacific Railway, followed in 1879–80. The prairie west was to become an agricultural hinterland, built on international immigration, the family farm, and grain exports. It was also to be integrated with a growing manufacturing sector in central and Maritime Canada. As the failure of the Northwest uprising of 1885 and the passage of Manitoba legislation on schools and language in 1890 made plain, the defining elements of prairie society were henceforth to be

Protestant, English-speaking, and British. The creation of two new provinces, Saskatchewan and Alberta, in 1905 seemed to demonstrate to the established classes that the British tradition of peaceful evolution from colony to self-governing state had been fulfilled.

New forces at work in the prairie west around the turn of the twentieth century made such complacency inappropriate. One source of concern for the social leaders was the arrival of hundreds of thousands of non-British immigrants who placed great strains on prairie institutions during the next few decades. Seen from the immigrants' perspective, however, the struggle to make a secure home in a new environment while retaining meaningful elements of their heritage was very trying. In the end, they gave up much of their traditional cultures as they helped to build the new prairie west. Swedes and Germans assimilated quickly; Mennonites, Jews, and Ukrainians sought to retain more of their cultural heritage and, eventually, helped to create a 'multicultural' definition of Canada; Hutterites remained isolated from the larger community; and some other religious groups – notably a few Doukhobors and Mennonites – preferred to leave the region rather than accommodate to its norms. By the 1940s, the prairies were less British than they had been in 1900 but were far closer to a British-Canadian cultural model than to any other.

Political institutions, too, underwent severe testing in the early twentieth century. The existence of a wide gap between the wealthy and the poor produced real tension in parts of the prairie west. In the larger cities, such as Winnipeg and Calgary, luxurious homes in segregated residential areas, exclusive clubs, colleges, and social events, and the concentration of political and economic power in the hands of a few were signs that a ruling class was taking shape in the region. By contrast, the squalour of some slum areas such as Winnipeg's north end, of frontier construction camps, and of resource towns such as Lovett and Cadomin, Alberta, suggested that a class struggle of the nineteenth-century British type was in the making. The intensity of labour-management struggles, especially in Winnipeg and in the Alberta coal towns, should be seen in this context.

That a full-scale class struggle did not develop in the first half of the twentieth century was due to at least three factors. First, the ready availability of a 160-acre homestead, which cost ten dollars and three years' residence, undercut the militancy of many camp and mine workers because it offered a ready alternative, a modest living, and hope for the future. At this early stage in the development of the agricultural frontier, the constant flux prevented the maintenance of firm class identities among farmers. Second, there was the development of a liberal professional group. As in the larger Atlantic world, these teachers, doctors, social workers, and journalists belonged neither to the business élite nor to the working class. They were in the middle in social status, political perspective, and income, simultaneously tempering the harshness of economic circumstances while offering aid and hope to the workers. Third, the Depression of 1929–39 was so devastating in its combination of drought, international trade crisis, commodity price declines, and the disappearance of local investment that prairie society went into prolonged stasis. Nativist hostility, which was serious in the late 1920s as the emergence of the Ku Klux Klan in Saskatchewan demonstrated, declined in importance – though it did not disappear – in the face of this more serious crisis. And political expressions of anger were channelled into either the moderate Co-operative Commonwealth Federation, the new left-wing party led by J.S. Woodsworth, or into Alberta's Christian variant of the Social Credit movement led by William Aberhart. The prairie west entered the Second World War poorer than at any time since the turn of the century. None the less prairie residents still accepted the rule of law and the legitimacy of the parliamentary system.

The period after 1940 saw a remarkable shift in prairie fortunes. Wealth flowed into the region as oil, potash, hydro-electricity, uranium, and other minerals diversified an economy that once relied on King Wheat. Improvements in agriculture, which ranged from larger equipment to fertilizers, herbicides, and new plant strains, increased productivity and hastened the departure of farm children to urban centres. Accompanying the economic gains was a significant change in material culture. Television, cars, airplanes, and universities brought the prairie west closer to a growing global cultural consensus. As the differences between the region and the developed world dissolved, social issues within the region increasingly resembled those in other nations: the native peoples' renaissance – part of an international political and cultural phenomenon – was unmistakable in the prairie west; the growing gulf between fundamentalists and modernists in the churches was part of an international trend; and political debates about the fate of the region, as in other nations, were grounded upon local perceptions of multinational corporations and the global balance of power. Similarly, social change assumed an international cast: the remarkable changes in the family that accompanied widespread birth control, higher employment rates for women, more single-parent families, and increases in life span were evident in the prairie west and around the North Atlantic world. Prairie art was also international: though rooted firmly, even self-consciously, in local images, prairie artists, novelists, and performers in theatre and dance found their context, their standards, and their audience in an international rather than a local or regional community.

But the prairie provinces were distinctive neighbourhoods in the North Atlantic cultural metropolis. Local control over the economy was greater than at any point in the twentieth century. Local ethnic loyalists contributed a vital and important element in social organization and cultural expression. The same was true of native identity, which was stronger and more aggressive than ever before. Prairie literature, especially drama, fiction, and poetry, was never as healthy as in the decades after 1960. And, though prairie political movements were notoriously difficult to anticipate, it seemed that the provincial party systems offered ample expression to the preferences of the people.

The Canadian prairies have strengths and weaknesses, as do the thousands of other homeland regions around the world. Among its problems is a strain of majoritarian complacency that denies the necessity of critical comment and minority rights. At times, the arrogant materialism of some prairie residents suggests an unattractive impatience with the needs of others at home and abroad. The curious inferiority complex that produces angry reactions to slights from outsiders – especially easterners – is also indicative of prairie uncertainties. But, cold winters aside, the prairie west is also a pleasant home. It offers a vast and pleasing landscape to the traveller, from the sweep of the wide prairie to the Rocky Mountains, and from the sheltered parklands to the endless miles of forest, rock, and lake. It offers relative abundance to most of its residents, though, like other communities, it does not distribute the wealth equally or even generously to every household. It offers freedom of worship, freedom of expression, and a considerable degree of social harmony, especially when compared to the constraints and conflicts in some parts of the globe, but there are limits to this flexibility, too. It is very fortunate in its inheritance of adaptable political institutions. It has transcended staggering economic reverses. It introduced the nation to the provision of universal health care. It has tolerated the works of local artists and supported the research of several generations of scientists. It has provided a harbour and hope to hundreds of thousands of immigrants. The struggles, sacrifices, and successes of its residents during the past three centuries constitute a rich heritage.

# Notes

CHAPTER ONE: INTRODUCTION

1 Eric Ross *Beyond the River and the Bay* (Toronto 1973) 130
2 W.A. Mackintosh *Prairie Settlement: The Geographical Setting* (Toronto 1934) 4–10
3 Peter B. Clibbon and Louis-Edmond Hamelin 'Landforms' in John Warkentin ed *Canada: A Geographical Interpretation* (Toronto 1968) 72
4 Ross *Beyond the River* 8
5 Cited in J.G. Nelson 'Animals, Fire and Landscape in the Northwestern Plains of North America in Pre and Early European Days' in A.W. Rasporich and H.C. Klassen eds *Prairie Perspectives* II (Toronto 1973) 67

CHAPTER TWO: NATIVE HISTORY: AN INTRODUCTION

1 Olive Patricia Dickason 'A Historical Reconstruction for the Northwestern Plains' *Prairie Forum* 5 no 1 (spring 1980)
2 John Bartlett Brebner *The Explorers of North America 1492–1806* first pub 1933 (London 1955) 47
3 E. Leigh Syms 'Cultural Ecology and Ecological Dynamics of the Ceramic Period in Southwestern Manitoba' *Plains Anthropologist* Memoir 12 vol 22 no 76 part 2 (May 1977)
4 A variety of perspectives upon these questions are presented in Leo Pettipas ed *Directions in Manitoba Prehistory: Papers in Honour of Chris Vickers* (Winnipeg 1980).

5 Karl W. Butzer 'This Is Indian Country' *Geographical Magazine* 52 no 2 (November 1979) 140–8; at Alberta's World Heritage Site, Estipah-Sikikini-Kots (Head-Smashed-In) Buffalo Jump, the bone pile is at least 30 feet deep.

6 David Mandelbaum 'Anthropology and People: The World of the Plains Cree' University of Saskatchewan, University Lectures no 12 (Saskatoon 1967) 8

7 Hugh Dempsey *Crowfoot: Chief of the Blackfeet* (Edmonton 1972) 25

8 Wilcomb E. Washburn *The Indian in America* (New York 1975) 51–62

9 Mandelbaum 'Anthropology' 8–9

10 Washburn *Indian* 51

11 Wilcomb B. Washburn *Red Man's Land, White Man's Law: A Study of the Past and Present Status of the American Indian* (New York 1971)

12 Leonard Mason 'The Swampy Cree: A Study in Acculturation' National Museum of Canada *Anthropology Papers* no 13 (January 1967)

13 Marshall Sahlins *Stone Age Economics* (New York 1974) 1–39; Marvin Harris *Cannibals and Kings: The Origins of Cultures* (New York 1978)

14 Eileen Power *Medieval People* first pub 1924 (London 1963) 18–38; Emmanuel LeRoy Ladurie *Montaillou: Cathars and Catholics in a French Village 1294–1324* (London 1978)

CHAPTER THREE: THE NATIVES' FUR TRADE 1640–1840

1 Wilcomb E. Washburn *The Indian in America* (New York 1975) xvi

2 A helpful survey of Ojibwa history is presented in Charles A. Bishop *The Northern Ojibwa and the Fur Trade: An Historical and Ecological Study* (Toronto 1974).

3 Introductions to this era include Arthur J. Ray *Indians in the Fur Trade: Their Role as Hunters, Trappers and Middlemen in the Lands Southwest of Hudson Bay* (Toronto 1974); Charles Bishop 'Ojibwa, Cree and the Hudson's Bay Company in Northern Ontario: Culture and Conflict in the Eighteenth Century' in Anthony W. Rasporich ed *Western Canada Past and Present* (Calgary 1975) 150–67; and David G. Mandelbaum *The Plains Cree: An Ethnographic, Historical, Comparative Study* first pub 1940 (Regina 1979).

4 Ray *Indians* and John S. Milloy 'The Plains Cree: A Preliminary Trade and Military Chronology 1670–1870' MA thesis, Carleton University, 1972

5 Oscar Lewis *The Effects of White Contact upon Blackfoot Culture, with Special Reference to the Role of the Fur Trade* (New York 1942)

6 James W. Vanstone *Athapaskan Adaptations: Hunters and Fishermen of the Sub-arctic Forests* (Chicago 1974). Around 1900, Vanstone reports, there were about 2,400 Chipewyan, 850 Slave, and 830 Beaver and Sarsi in Canada.

7 Ray *Indians* 40–3

8 Ibid 35–40 and 46–8 and Milloy 'Plains Cree' 107–66

9 Arthur J. Ray and Donald B. Freeman *'Give Us Good Measure': An Economic*

*Analysis of Relations between the Indians and the Hudson's Bay Company before 1763* (Toronto 1978) 224; also Ray *Indians* 13

10 Milloy 'Plains Cree' 64–76

11 Ray *Indians* 70

12 Ray and Freeman *Measure* 53–62

13 The best description is Edward Umfreville *The Present State of Hudson's Bay* (London 1790) reprint ed W. Stewart Wallace (Toronto 1954) 28–32.

14 This issue was addressed in an interesting manner by E.E. Rich 'Trade Habits and Economic Motivation among the Indians of North America' *Canadian Journal of Economics and Political Science* 26 (1960) 35–53.

15 Ray and Freeman *Measure* 231–60

16 Ray *Indians* 68 and 85–7 MB, or Made Beaver, was an accounting device – a kind of currency – which established an equivalence between European goods and native purchasing power in terms of a prime, whole beaver pelt.

17 E.E. Rich *The Fur Trade and the NorthWest to 1857* (Toronto 1967) 102

18 Toby Morantz 'The Fur Trade and the Cree of James Bay' in Carol M. Judd and Arthur J. Ray eds *Old Trails and New Directions: Papers of the Third North American Fur Trade Conference* (Toronto 1980) 39–58

19 Abraham Rotstein 'Fur Trade and Empire: An Institutional Analysis' PhD dissertation, University of Toronto, 1967

20 A. Rotstein 'Trade and Politics: An Institutional Approach' *Western Canadian Journal of Anthropology* 3 no 1 (1973)

21 Ray and Freeman *Measure*

22 I am indebted to Dr Jean Friesen for this material on reciprocity. See her paper 'My Birthright and My Land' unpublished paper presented to Brandon University Native Studies Conference 1981

23 Frank Raymond Secoy *Changing Military Patterns on the Great Plains (17th Century through Early 19th Century)* (New York 1953); Preston Holder *The Hoe and Horse on the Plains: A Study of Cultural Development among North American Indians* (Lincoln 1974)

24 Richard Glover ed *David Thompson's Narrative 1784–1812* (Toronto 1962) 241–3

25 Holder *Hoe and Horse*

26 Ray *Indians* 131

27 Milloy 'Plains Cree' 168 and 200–1

28 Quoted in Ray *Indians* 207

29 Lewis *Blackfoot Culture*; Irene Spry 'The Great Transformation: The Disappearance of the Commons in Western Canada' in Richard Allen ed *Man and Nature on the Prairies* (Regina 1976) 21–45

30 Lewis *Blackfoot Culture*

31 Bishop *Northern Ojibwa* 11–12, 202–22, 262–304; also Charles A. Bishop 'The Emergence of Hunting Territories among the Northern Ojibwa' *Ethnology* 9 (1970) 1–15

32 John F. Taylor 'Sociocultural Effects of Epidemics on the Northern Plains: 1734–1850' *Western Canadian Journal of Anthropology* 7 (1977) 55–81

CHAPTER FOUR: THE EUROPEANS' FUR TRADE 1640–1805

1 The classic account of the fur trade is Harold Adams Innis's *The Fur Trade in Canada: An Introduction to Canadian Economic History* (New Haven 1930). A revised edition, which is cited hereafter, was published in Toronto in 1956. The most extensive discussion of the western fur trade is Arthur S. Morton *A History of the Canadian West to 1870–71* first pub 1939, L.G. Thomas ed (Toronto 1973).
2 Innis *Fur Trade* 6
3 Innis *Fur Trade* 118
4 This interpretation is presented by W.J. Eccles *The Canadian Frontier 1534–1760* (Hinsdale, Illinois, 1969) 128–31.
5 Glyndwr Williams 'Highlights of the First 200 Years of the Hudson's Bay Company' *The Beaver* Outfit 301 (autumn 1970) 5; also useful are Grace Lee Nute 'Médard Chouart des Groseilliers' *Dictionary of Canadian Biography* I *1000–1700* (Toronto 1966) 223–8 and 'Pierre-Esprit Radisson' *Dictionary of Canadian Biography* II *1701–40* (Toronto 1969) 535–540.
6 Williams 'Highlights' 8; the most thorough history of the company is E.E. Rich *Hudson's Bay Company 1670–1870* 3 vols first pub 1958, 1960 (Toronto 1960).
7 Williams 'Highlights' 10–13
8 Eccles *The Canadian Frontier* 132–46
9 Williams 'Highlights' 16
10 Rich *Hudson's Bay Company* I 556–86
11 E.E. Rich *The Fur Trade and the Northwest to 1857* (Toronto 1967) 82–95; Yves F. Zoltvany 'Pierre Gaultier de Varennes et de La Vérendrye' *Dictionary of Canadian Biography* III *1740–1770* (Toronto 1974) 246–54; L.J. Burpee ed *Journals and Letters of Pierre Gaultier de Varennes et de La Vérendrye and His Sons* (Toronto 1927)
12 K.G. Davies 'Henry Kelsey' *Dictionary of Canadian Biography* II *1701–40* 307–15; A.G. Doughty and Chester Martin ed *The Kelsey Papers* (Ottawa 1929)
13 Morton *A History of the Canadian West* 239–50; Ray *Indians in the Fur Trade* (Toronto 1974) 90–1; Clifford Wilson 'Anthony Henday' *Dictionary of Canadian Biography* III *1740–1770* (Toronto 1974) 285–7
14 Williams 'Highlights' 29; Glyndwr Williams ed *Andrew Graham's Observations on Hudson's Bay, 1767–91* (London 1969)
15 Paul Clifford Thistle 'Indian-Trader Relations: An Ethnohistory of Western Woods Cree–Hudson's Bay Company Trader Contact in the Cumberland House–The Pas Region to 1840' MA thesis, University of Manitoba, 1983, 113
16 Williams 'Highlights' 33; Joseph Burr Tyrrell ed *Journals of Samuel Hearne and Philip Turnor* (Toronto 1934)
17 Rich *The Fur Trade and the Northwest* 163–85; W. Stewart Wallace ed *Documents Relating to the North West Company* (Toronto 1934)

18 Williams 'Highlights' 29; Rich *Hudson's Bay Company* II 1–43
19 Morton *A History of the Canadian West* 421–530; Rich *The Fur Trade and the Northwest* 186–208; Richard Glover ed *David Thompson's Narrative 1784–1812* (Toronto 1962)
20 Rich *The Fur Trade and the Northwest* 194; W. Kaye Lamb ed *The Journals and Letters of Sir Alexander Mackenzie* (Toronto 1970); W. Kaye Lamb ed *The Letters and Journals of Simon Fraser 1806–1808* (Toronto 1960)

CHAPTER FIVE: MAINTAINING THE OLD ORDER 1805–44

1 Sylvia Van Kirk *'Many Tender Ties': Women in Fur-Trade Society in Western Canada, 1670–1870* (Winnipeg 1980) 23
2 Ibid 28–52
3 Jacqueline Peterson 'The People in between: Indian-White Marriage and the Genesis of a Metis Society and Culture in the Great Lakes Region, 1680–1830' PhD dissertation, University of Illinois at Chicago Circle, 1981
4 Jennifer S.H. Brown *Strangers in Blood: Fur Trade Families in Indian Country* (Vancouver 1980) 68–70
5 Ibid 96–7
6 J.E. Foster 'The Origins of the Mixed Bloods in the Canadian West' in L.H. Thomas ed *Essays on Western History* (Edmonton 1976): Margaret MacLeod and W.L. Morton *Cuthbert Grant of Grantown: Warden of the Plains of Red River* first pub 1963 (Toronto 1974)
7 John Morgan Gray *Lord Selkirk of Red River* (Toronto 1964)
8 E.E. Rich *The Fur Trade and the Northwest to 1857* (Toronto 1967) 203–8 and Arthur S. Morton *A History of the Canadian West to 1870–71* first pub 1939, L.G. Thomas ed (Toronto 1973) 518–37
9 Barry Kaye 'Selkirk's Colony in the Wilderness: An Analysis of the Geographical Circumstances Surrounding the Establishment of the Red River Settlement' (forthcoming article). I would like to thank Professor Kaye for his advice on aspects of Red River history.
10 E.E. Rich *Hudson's Bay Company* II *1763–1820* (Toronto 1960) 296–301 and Morton *Canadian West* 532–7
11 Rich *Fur Trade* 210
12 Ibid 219
13 Morton *Canadian West* 497–518
14 MacLeod and Morton *Grant* 24–5
15 Ibid 36–7
16 The song is translated in ibid 50–1; metis rights are discussed in ibid 28–30 and in Jennifer S.H. Brown 'Metis Matriorganization: Questions and Problems' paper presented to the Metis Symposium, Winnipeg, 1982
17 Rich *Fur Trade* 229
18 MacLeod and Morton *Grant* 64–5

19 Rich *Fur Trade* 228
20 Glyndwr Williams 'Highlights of the First 200 Years of the Hudson's Bay Company' *The Beaver Outfit* 301 (autumn 1970) 45
21 Rich *Fur Trade* 242–3 and E.E. Rich *Hudson's Bay Company* III (Toronto 1960) 412
22 Rich *Fur Trade* 233–5; Williams 'Highlights' 47–9; John S. Galbraith *The Little Emperor: Governor Simpson of the Hudson's Bay Company* (Toronto 1976); Arthur S. Morton *Sir George Simpson* (Toronto 1944)
23 Rich *HBC* III 415 and Williams 'Highlights' 47
24 Williams 'Highlights' 48; Morton *A History of the Canadian West* 623–42
25 Williams 'Highlights' 49–50; Rich *HBC* III 469–530
26 John S. Galbraith *The Hudson's Bay Company as an Imperial Factor 1821–1869* (Toronto 1957) 233–50
27 Rich *Fur Trade* 283

CHAPTER SIX: THE METIS AND THE RED RIVER SETTLEMENT 1844–70

1 H.C. Pentland 'The Development of a Capitalistic Labour Market in Canada' *Canadian Journal of Economics and Political Science* 25 no 4 (November 1959) 450–61
2 Irene Spry 'The Great Transformation: The Disappearance of the Commons in Western Canada' in Richard Allan ed *Man and Nature on the Prairies* (Regina 1976) 21–45
3 Public Archives of Canada, Hargrave Papers, Letitia Hargrave to Mrs MacTavish, 1 April 1848; Letitia Hargrave to Flora, 7 July 1853
4 E.J. Hobsbawm *The Age of Capital 1848–1875* (London 1977); Jean Usher [Friesen] *William Duncan of Metlakatla: A Victorian Missionary in British Columbia* (Ottawa 1974); Christine Bolt *Victorian Attitudes to Race* (London 1971); George W. Stocking Jr *Race, Culture and Evolution: Essays in the History of Anthropology* 2nd ed (Chicago 1982); Sylvia van Kirk *'Many Tender Ties': Women in Fur-Trade Society in Western Canada, 1670–1870* (Winnipeg 1980) and '"What if Mama is an Indian?": The Cultural Ambivalence of the Alexander Ross Family' in John E. Foster ed *The Developing West: Essays in Canadian History in Honour of Lewis H. Thomas* (Edmonton 1983) 123–36
5 Walter E. Houghton *The Victorian Frame of Mind 1830–1870* (New Haven 1957) 120
6 Van Kirk *Many Tender Ties* 145–230; Frits Pannekoek 'The Social Origins of the Riel Protest of 1869–1870' unpublished ms. I would like to thank Dr Pannekoek for permission to use this work.
7 Carol Judd 'Native Labour and Social Stratification in the Hudson's Bay Company's Northern Department, 1770–1870' *Canadian Review of Sociology and Anthropology* 17 no 4 (1980) 305–14 and '"Mixt Bands of Many Nations":

1821–70' in Carol Judd and Arthur J. Ray eds *Old Trails and New Directions: Papers of the Third North American Fur Trade Conference* (Toronto 1980) 127–46

8 Cited in Judd 'Native Labour' unpublished ms; see also Carol Livermore [Judd] 'Lower Fort Garry, The Fur Trade and the Settlement at Red River' Parks Canada Ms Report no 202 (1976). I would like to thank Ms Judd for copies of these manuscripts.

9 Philip Goldring 'Papers on the Labour System of the Hudson's Bay Company, 1821–1900' I (1979) and II (1980), Parks Canada Mss. I would like to thank the author, who permitted me to see preliminary drafts of these reports.

10 John S. Galbraith *The Hudson's Bay Company as an Imperial Factor, 1821–1869* (Toronto 1957)

11 Irene M. Spry 'The "Private Adventurers" of Rupert's Land' in Foster ed *The Developing West* 49–70

12 E.E. Rich *Hudson's Bay Company* III (Toronto 1960) 412

13 This account follows W.L. Morton's valuable 'Introduction' to E.E. Rich ed *London Correspondence inward from Eden Colvile 1849–1852* (London 1956) lxxix–lxxxvi.

14 Spry 'Private Adventurers'; Alvin C. Gluek Jr *Minnesota and the Manifest Destiny of the Canadian Northwest: A Study in Canadian-American Relations* (Toronto 1965); Morton *Colvile* xxxvii

15 Irene M. Spry ed *The Papers of the Palliser Expedition 1857–1860* (Toronto 1968) 190–1

16 D.W. Moodie 'Early British Images of Rupert's Land' in Richard Allen ed *Man and Nature on the Prairies* (Regina 1976) 1

17 Ibid 3–8

18 Ibid 7

19 Doug Owram *Promise of Eden: The Canadian Expansionist Movement and the Idea of the West* (Toronto 1980) 32

20 R.M. Ballantyne *The Young Fur Traders* (London n.d.) 200–1

21 William F. Butler *The Great Lone Land* (London 1872). For a survey of these writings, see Irene Spry 'Early Visitors to the Canadian Prairies' in Brian W. Blouet and Merlin P. Lawson eds *Images of the Plains: The Role of Human Nature in Settlement* (Lincoln 1975) 165–80.

22 Owram *Eden* 71, quoting H.Y. Hind

23 Ibid 23–30

24 Ibid 27

25 John Warkentin *The Western Interior of Canada: A Record of Geographical Discovery 1612–1917* (Toronto 1964) 144–230 and John Warkentin 'Steppe, Desert and Empire' in A.W. Rasporich and H.C. Klassen eds *Prairie Perspectives* II (Toronto 1973)

26 Warkentin *Western Interior* 147

27 Warkentin 'Steppe, Desert' 121
28 Gary S. Dunbar 'Isotherms and Politics: Perception of the Northwest in the 1850s' in Rasporich and Klassen eds *Prairie Perspectives* II 94
29 Cited in Owram *Eden* 72
30 W.L. Morton *The Critical Years: The Union of British North America 1857–1873* (Toronto 1964) 21–40 and David McNab 'The Colonial Office and the Prairies in the Mid-Nineteenth Century' *Prairie Forum* 3 no 1 (spring 1978) 21–38
31 Gluek *Minnesota and the Manifest Destiny* 78, 117, 158–91 and Gluek *Manitoba and the Hudson's Bay Company* (Winnipeg 1973)
32 Owram *Eden* 59–78
33 Toronto *Globe* 26 December 1856, cited in Morton *Critical Years* 32
34 Alexander Morris *The Hudson's Bay and Pacific Territories* (Montreal 1859), as discussed in Owram *Eden* 72–8
35 George F.G. Stanley *The Birth of Western Canada: A History of the Riel Rebellions* first pub 1936 (Toronto 1960) 48–9
36 Pannekoek's views were expressed in several published articles, including 'The Anglican Church and the Disintegration of Red River Society, 1818–1870' in Carl Berger and Ramsay Cook eds *The West and the Nation: Essays in Honor of W.L. Morton* (Toronto 1976) 72–90; 'Some Comments on the Social Origin of the Riel Protest of 1869' *Historical and Scientific Society of Manitoba* series III no 34 (1977–8) 39–48; 'The Rev. Griffiths Owen Corbett and the Red River Civil War of 1869–70' *Canadian Historical Review* 57 no 2 (June 1976) 133–49
37 Frits Pannekoek 'The Social Origin of the Riel Protest of 1869–70'
38 Robert M. Gosman 'The Riel and Lagimodière Families in Metis Society 1840–1860' Parks Canada Manuscript Report no 171 (Ottawa 1975 and 1977)
39 Morton *Critical Years* 60–71
40 Spry 'The Great Transformation'
41 W.L. Morton *Manitoba: A History* first pub 1957 (Toronto 1967) 117. A more detailed analysis of this era by Morton is his 'Introduction' to *Alexander Begg's Red River Journal and Other Papers Relative to the Red River Resistance of 1869–70* (Toronto 1956).
42 The most complete biography is George F.G. Stanley *Louis Riel* (Toronto 1963). Another useful source is Lewis H. Thomas 'Louis Riel' *Dictionary of Canadian Biography* XI *1881–90* (Toronto 1982) 736–52; a different perspective on his mental state is Thomas Flanagan *Louis 'David' Riel: 'Prophet of the New World'* (Toronto 1979).
43 Morton *Begg's Journal* 76
44 Morton *Manitoba* 141; the purposes of the federal government are discussed in D.J. Hall '"The Spirit of Confederation": Ralph Heintzman, Professor Creighton, and the Bicultural Compact Theory' *Journal of Canadian Studies* 9 no 4 (1974) 24–43.
45 Morton *Begg's Journal* 144

46 W.L. Morton 'The Bias of Prairie Politics' *Transactions of the Royal Society of Canada* series III 49 (1955) 57–66

## CHAPTER SEVEN: PRAIRIE INDIANS 1840–1900

1 Arthur J. Ray *Indians in the Fur Trade: Their Role as Hunters, Trappers and Middlemen in the Lands Southwest of Hudson Bay* (Toronto 1974) 225

2 John S. Milloy 'The Plains Cree: A Preliminary Trade and Military Chronology 1670–1870' MA thesis, Carleton University, 1972

3 Isaac Cowie *The Company of Adventurers: A Narrative of Seven Years in the Service of the Hudson's Bay Company during 1867–1874 on the Great Buffalo Plains* (Toronto 1913) 302–3

4 John McDougall *In the Days of the Red River Rebellion: Life and Adventure in the Far West of Canada (1868–1872)* (Toronto 1903) 50–1

5 Paul F. Sharp *Whoop-Up Country: The Canadian-American West, 1865–1885* first pub 1955 (Helena 1960) 33–55

6 Milloy 'Plains Cree' 258–60

7 Philip Goldring 'Whisky, Horses and Death: The Cypress Hills Massacre and Its Sequel' Canadian Historic Sites no 21, 41–70

8 Jean Friesen 'My Birthright and Land' unpublished paper presented to Brandon University Native Studies Conference 1981. The prairie treaties are discussed in detail in John Leonard Taylor 'The Development of an Indian Policy for the Canadian North-West, 1869–79' PHD dissertation, Queen's University, 1975

9 Peter A. Cumming and Neil H. Mickenberg eds *Native Rights in Canada* second edition (Toronto 1972) 121–2

10 Taylor 'Indian Policy' 55–80

11 Alexander Morris *The Treaties of Canada with the Indians of Manitoba and the North-West Territories* first pub Toronto 1880 (reprinted Toronto 1971) 48–9

12 Friesen 'My Birthright and Land' and Taylor 'Indian Policy' 115–37

13 Raoul J. McKay 'A History of Indian Treaty Number Four and Government Policies in Its Implementation 1874–1905' MA thesis, University of Manitoba, 1973, 22

14 Morris *Treaties* 77–125 and Taylor 'Indian Policy' 144–56

15 Morris *Treaties* 143–67 and Taylor 'Indian Policy' 185–92

16 Morris *Treaties* 182–4, 201–2

17 Cited in Taylor 'Indian Policy' 203, 206

18 Hugh Dempsey *Crowfoot Chief of the Blackfeet* (Norman, Oklahoma, 1972) 98

19 Treaty 8 was not just a repetition of the earlier numbered treaties. Among the significant differences was the provision for 'reserves' of land either for an entire band or for families and individuals on the basis of 640 acres per family of five or 160 acres per individual. This treaty also noted Indian con-

cerns about government schools and promised 'non-interference with the religion of the Indians'; Richard Daniel 'The Spirit and Terms of Treaty Eight'
in Richard Price ed *The Spirit of the Alberta Indian Treaties* (Montreal 1980)
47–100.

20 Spry 'The Great Transformation: The Disappearance of the Commons in
Western Canada' in Richard Allen ed *Man and Nature on the Prairies* (Regina
1976) 21–45

21 J.E. Foster 'The Saulteaux and the Numbered Treaties: An Aboriginal Rights
Position' in Richard Price ed *The Spirit of the Alberta Indian Treaties* (Montreal
1980) 162–3

22 Friesen 'My Birthright and Land'

23 Jean Friesen 'Notes for Treaty 5 Historical Research' unpublished paper prepared for Treaty 5 Chiefs Native Constitutional Conference, Ottawa, March
1983

24 Morris *Treaties* 29

25 Frank Gilbert Roe *The North American Buffalo: A Critical Study of the Species in
Its Wild State* first pub 1951 (Toronto 1970)

26 Noel E. Dyck 'The Administration of Federal Indian Aid in the North-West
Territories 1879–1885' MA thesis, University of Saskatchewan, 1970, 28

27 For this and the following material, I am indebted to Dr John L. Tobias who
permitted me to see 'Canada's Subjugation of the Plains Cree 1879–1885'
before its publication in the *Canadian Historical Review* 64 (1983) 519–48.

28 William Bleasdell Cameron *The War Trail of Big Bear* (Boston 1927) 243; W.B.
Fraser 'Big Bear, Indian Patriot' in Donald Swainson ed *Historical Essays on the
Prairie Provinces* (Toronto 1970) 71–88; and R.S. Allen 'Big Bear' *Saskatchewan
History* 25 no 1 (winter 1972) 1–17

29 Stuart Hughes ed *The Frog Lake 'Massacre': Personal Perspectives on Ethnic
Conflict* (Toronto 1976)

30 Tobias 'Subjugation'

31 Dempsey *Crowfoot* 164–70, 189–93

32 Desmond Morton *The Last War Drum: The Northwest Campaign of 1885* (Toronto
1972) 128–30

33 George T. Denison, cited in Peter B. Waite *Canada 1874–1896: Arduous Destiny*
(Toronto 1971) 162; also Sandra Estlin Bingaman 'The Trials of Poundmaker
and Big Bear, 1885' *Saskatchewan History* 28 no 3 (autumn 1975) 81–94

34 The classic studies of this type are Ralph Linton *Acculturation in Seven American Indian Tribes* (New York 1940) and Melville Herskovits *Acculturation: The
Study of Culture Contact* (Gloucester, Mass, 1938).

35 John S. Milloy 'The Era of Civilization: British Policy for the Indians of
Canada 1830–1860' DPhil thesis, Oxford University, 1978, and John S. Milloy
'The Early Indian Acts: Developmental Strategy and Constitutional Change'
paper presented to Brandon Native Studies Conference 1981

36 Robert J. Surtees *The Original People* (Toronto 1971); J.D. Leighton 'The Development of Federal Indian Policy in Canada 1840–1890' PhD dissertation, University of Western Ontario, 1975; Sally M. Weaver *Making Canadian Indian Policy: The Hidden Agenda 1968–70* (Toronto 1981); Canada Department of Indian and Northern Affairs (Policy Planning and Research Branch) *The Historical Development of the Indian Act* (Ottawa 1975)

37 Sarah Carter 'Agriculture and Agitation on the Oak River Reserve, 1875–1895' *Manitoba History* 6 (fall 1983) 2–9

38 Hugh Dempsey 'One Hundred Years of Treaty Seven' in Ian A.L. Getty and Donald B. Smith eds *One Century Later: Western Canadian Reserve Indians since Treaty 7* (Vancouver 1978); A.J. Looy 'The Indian Agent and His Role in the Administration of the North-West Superintendency 1876–1893' PhD dissertation, Queen's University, 1977; Esther S. Goldfrank *Changing Configurations in the Social Organization of a Blackfoot Tribe during the Reserve Period* (New York 1945); Lucien M. Hanks Jr and Jane Richardson Hanks *Tribe under Trust: A Study of the Blackfoot Reserve of Alberta* (Toronto 1950); D.J. Hall 'Clifford Sifton and Canadian Indian Administration 1896–1905' *Prairie Forum* 2 no 2 (1977) 127–51; Stuart Raby 'Indian Land Surrenders in Southern Saskatchewan' *Canadian Geographer* 17 (1973) 36–52

39 Jacqueline J. Kennedy [Gresko] 'Qu'Appelle Industrial School: White "Rites" for the Indians of the Old North West' MA thesis, Carleton University, 1970; and Jacqueline Gresko 'White "Rites" and Indian "Rites": Indian Education and Native Responses in the West, 1870–1910' in Anthony W. Rasporich ed *Western Canada Past and Present* (Calgary 1975) 163–82

40 As note 39

CHAPTER EIGHT: CANADA'S EMPIRE 1870–1900

1 Vernon C. Fowke *The National Policy and the Wheat Economy* (Toronto 1957) 5

2 Dick Harrison *Unnamed Country: The Struggle for a Canadian Prairie Fiction* (Edmonton 1977) 154–64 and Dick Harrison ed *Best Mounted Police Stories* (Edmonton 1978)

3 Gilbert Parker *Pierre and His People: Tales of the Far North* (Toronto 1897) 90, 92; Ralph Connor [C.W. Gordon] *Corporal Cameron of the North West Mounted Police: A Tale of the Macleod Trail* (Toronto 1912) 383

4 Harrison *Unnamed Country* 77–8

5 H.A. Cody *The Long Patrol: A Tale of the Mounted Police* (Toronto n.d.) 55

6 R.C. Macleod *The NWMP and Law Enforcement 1873–1905* (Toronto 1976)

7 Ibid 4

8 Ibid 8

9 S.W. Horrall 'Sir John A. Macdonald and the Mounted Police Force for the Northwest Territories' *Canadian Historical Review* 53 no 2 (June 1972) 179–200

10  Macleod *NWMP* 7–72

11  Ibid 81

12  This quotation is from ibid 130 and the one above from 36–7.

13  Donald Creighton *John A. Macdonald* II *The Old Chieftain* (Toronto 1955) 301–2
    and Donald Creighton *Dominion of the North* (Toronto 1944) 348

14  Creighton *Macdonald* II 309

15  The best recent study of the CPR is W. Kaye Lamb *History of the Canadian
    Pacific Railway* (New York 1977). See also Pierre Berton *The National Dream:
    The Great Railway 1871–1881* (Toronto 1970) and *The Last Spike: The Great Rail-
    way 1881–1885* (Toronto 1971). An examination of its original coup is Dolores
    Greenberg 'A Study of Capital Alliances: The St Paul & Pacific' *Canadian His-
    torical Review* 57 no 1 (March 1976) 25–39; an older, useful study is Harold A.
    Innis *A History of the Canadian Pacific Railway* first pub 1923, (Toronto 1971)

16  University of London, School of Oriental and African Studies, Mackinnon
    Papers, S.P. Huntington to William Mackinnon 5 November 1888, 19 June
    1889, 18 March 1890, and Huntington to H.M. Stanley 28 January 1891

17  Lamb *CPR* 79–80. The issue is raised by Owram *Eden* 159–67 and placed in an
    interesting new context by E.A. Mitchener 'William Pearce and Federal Gov-
    ernment Activity in Western Canada 1882–1904' PhD dissertation, University
    of Alberta, 1971

18  T.D. Regehr 'Contracting for the Canadian Pacific Railway' in Lewis H.
    Thomas ed *Essays on Western History* (Edmonton 1976) 111–26

19  Lamb *CPR* 135

20  Chester Martin *'Dominion Lands' Policy* first pub 1938, republished Lewis H.
    Thomas ed (Toronto 1973) 14

21  Ibid 15

22  Ibid 12

23  Dominion Lands Act 1872 cited in ibid 104

24  Fowke *National Policy* 59

25  Vernon C. Fowke *Canadian Agricultural Policy: The Historical Pattern* (Toronto
    1946) 165–77

26  Arthur S. Morton *History of Prairie Settlement* (Toronto 1938) 65–118; Fowke
    *Agricultural Policy* 176–80; A.N. Lalonde 'Colonization Companies in the
    1880's' *Saskatchewan History* 24 (1971) 101–14

27  Innis *CPR* 294

28  Fowke *National Policy* 62–6

29  Ibid 64

30  A survey of the debate is presented in Kenneth H. Norrie 'The National Pol-
    icy and the Rate of Prairie Settlement: A Review' *Journal of Canadian Studies* 14
    no 3 (fall 1979) 63–76

31  Kenneth H. Norrie 'The National Policy and Prairie Economic Discrimination,
    1870–1930' in Donald H. Akenson ed *Canadian Papers in Rural History* I (Gana-
    noque 1978) 24. The western case is presented in Western Premiers 'Eco-

nomic and Industrial Development Opportunities' Western Economic Opportunities Conference, 24–6 July 1973.

32 T.D. Regehr 'Western Canada and the Burden of National Transportation Policies' in David Jay Bercuson ed *Canada and the Burden of Unity* (Toronto 1977) 115–41

33 Paul Phillips 'The National Policy Revisited' *Journal of Canadian Studies* 14 no 3 (fall 1979) 3–13

34 Relevant comparisons are not easy to establish, but the 1888 CPR rate for wheat was about 28 cents per hundredweight; in the mid-1890s it was about 17–24 cents; after the Crow agreement it was about 14 cents; T.D. Regehr 'The Canadian Northern Railway: The West's Own Product' *Canadian Historical Review* 51 no 2 (1970) 177–87.

35 W.L. Morton 'Canada: The One and the Many' in A.B. McKillop ed *Contexts of Canada's Past: Selected Essays of W.L. Morton* (Toronto 1980) 288

36 A survey of the issue is Howard Darling *The Politics of Freight Rates: The Railway Freight Rate Issue in Canada* (Toronto 1980).

CHAPTER NINE: MANITOBA 1870–1900

1 George F.G. Stanley *Louis Riel* (Toronto 1963) 159–61; A.H. de Tremaudan *Hold High Your Heads* trans Elizabeth Maguet (Winnipeg 1982) first pub 1936 as *Histoire de la nation métisse dans l'ouest canadien* 2nd ed (St Boniface 1979) 103–6; George Young *Manitoba Memories: Leaves from My Life in the Prairie Province 1868–1884* (Toronto 1897) 187–91; 'L'Honorable Joseph Dubuc, K.S.M.G.' (Winnipeg 1981)

2 George F.G. Stanley *The Birth of Western Canada: A History of the Riel Rebellions* first pub 1936 (Toronto 1960) 177–82; Stanley *Louis Riel* 252–60; Marcel Giraud *Le Métis canadien : son rôle dans l'histoire des provinces de l'ouest* (Paris 1945)

3 At Bishop Taché's urging, Donald A. Smith added £600 to this fund, which was first used in February 1872; Stanley *Riel* 178–81.

4 D.N. Sprague 'The Manitoba Land Question, 1870–1882' *Journal of Canadian Studies* 15 no 3 (fall 1980) 74–84

5 Gerhard Ens 'Metis Lands in Manitoba' *Manitoba History* 5 (spring 1983) 2–11

6 The issue was before the Manitoba courts in 1982–3; see Douglas N. Sprague, 'Government Lawlessness in the Administration of Manitoba Land Claims, 1870–1887' *Manitoba Law Journal* 10 (1980) 415–42.

7 Gerald Friesen 'Homeland to Hinterland: Political Transition in Manitoba, 1870 to 1879' Canadian Historical Association *Historical Papers* (1979) 33–47. The lieutenant-governor reserved the Manitoba act which would have eliminated publication in French of the Orders of the Day and the Sessional Papers.

8 The birthplaces of Manitoba residents according to the 1885–6 census broke down in the following manner: 31 per cent born in Manitoba, 31 per cent in

Ontario, 8 per cent in other provinces – a total of 71 per cent in Canada; 9 per cent were born in England, 5 per cent in Scotland, and 3 per cent in Ireland – a total of 18 per cent in the United Kingdom (the totals are rounded).

9 John H. Warkentin 'Western Canada in 1886' Historical and Scientific Society of Manitoba *Transactions* series III no 20 (1963–4) 85–116; W.L. Morton *Manitoba: A History* first pub 1957 (Toronto 1967) 176–233

10 John Langton Tyman *By Section, Township, and Range: Studies in Prairie Settlement* (Brandon 1972) 31–2

11 Donald Merwin Loveridge 'The Settlement of the Rural Municipality of Sifton 1881–1920' MA thesis, University of Manitoba, 1977, 190–205

12 Randolph Richard Rostecki 'The Growth of Winnipeg, 1870–1886' MA thesis, University of Manitoba, 1980, 29–49

13 Arthur S. Morton *History of Prairie Settlement* (Toronto 1938) 60

14 Ruben Bellan *Winnipeg First Century: An Economic History* (Winnipeg 1978) 25–58

15 Donald Kerr 'Wholesale Trade on the Canadian Plains in the Late Nineteenth Century: Winnipeg and Its Competition' in Howard Palmer ed *The Settlement of the West* (Calgary 1977) 151–2

16 Ruben Bellen, cited in J.M.S. Careless 'The Development of the Winnipeg Business Community, 1870–1890' *Transactions of the Royal Society of Canada* 8 series IV (1970) 254

17 George H. Ham *Reminiscences of a Raconteur* (1921), cited in Alan F.J. Artibise *Winnipeg: A Social History of Urban Growth 1874–1914* (Montreal 1975) 22

18 Careless 'Winnipeg Business Community'

19 Artibise *Winnipeg: A Social History* 23

20 Alan Artibise *Winnipeg: An Illustrated History* (Toronto 1977) 26 and Artibise *Winnipeg: A Social History* 76

21 Rostecki 'Growth of Winnipeg' 94–111

22 Morton *Manitoba* 219

23 Gerald Friesen 'John Norquay' *Dictionary of Canadian Biography* XI 1881–1890 (Toronto 1982) 642–7

24 Joseph A. Hilts 'The Political Career of Thomas Greenway' PHD dissertation, University of Manitoba, 1974, 104–75 and W. Kaye Lamb *History of the Canadian Pacific Railway* (New York 1977) 155–64

25 D.J. Hall *Clifford Sifton* I *The Young Napoleon 1861–1900* (Vancouver 1981) 58–9

26 Paul Crunican *Priests and Politicians: Manitoba Schools and the Election of 1896* (Toronto 1974) 4

27 John W. Dafoe *Clifford Sifton in Relation to His Times* (Toronto 1931) 36–43 and Lovell Clark *The Manitoba School Question: Majority Rule or Minority Rights?* (Toronto 1968) 2–5

28 W.L. Morton 'Manitoba Schools and Canadian Nationality, 1890–1923' Canadian Historical Association *Report* 1951 51–4 and Morton *Manitoba* 240–50

29 J.R. Miller 'D'Alton McCarthy, Equal Rights, and the Origins of the Manitoba School Question' *Canadian Historical Review* 54 no 4 (December 1973) 369–92
30 Hilts 'Greenway' 196–221
31 Morton *Manitoba* 245
32 Ibid 272
33 Ibid 224–5

CHAPTER TEN: THE NORTH-WEST TERRITORIES 1870–1905

1 The steamboat trip from Winnipeg included a two-day voyage down Lake Winnipeg to Grand Rapids and fifteen days on the Saskatchewan River to Edmonton. The Swift Current to Battleford stage-coach journey required ninety-six hours.
2 Warkentin 'Western Canada in 1886' Historical and Scientific Society of Manitoba *Transactions* series III no 20 (1963–4) 85–116
3 Arthur S. Morton *History of Prairie Settlement* (Toronto 1938) 86
4 Ibid 88
5 Lewis H. Thomas *The North-West Territories 1870–1905* Canadian Historical Association Booklet no 26 (Ottawa 1970)
6 Lewis Herbert Thomas *The Struggle for Responsible Government in the North-West Territories 1870–97* first pub 1956 (Toronto 1978) 99–145. Dewdney was lieutenant-governor from 1881 to 1888.
7 Pierre Berton *The Last Spike: The Great Railway 1881–1885* (Toronto 1971) 113–25
8 Thomas *Struggle* 107–11
9 Diane Payment 'Monsieur Batoche' *Saskatchewan History* 32 no 3 (autumn 1979) 89; Diane Payment *Batoche (1870–1910)* (St Boniface 1983)
10 George Woodcock *Gabriel Dumont: The Metis Chief and His Lost World* (Edmonton 1975) 86–90
11 Thomas *Struggle* 123–4
12 Donald B. Smith 'William Henry Jackson: Riel's Disciple' in A.S. Lussier ed *Pelletier-Lathlin Memorial Lecture Series, Brandon University 1979–80* (Brandon 1980) 47–71
13 Woodcock *Dumont* 140
14 Thomas Flanagan *Louis 'David' Riel: 'Prophet of the New World'* (Toronto 1979) 121 and George F.G. Stanley *Louis Riel* (Toronto 1963)
15 Thomas *Struggle* 129–30; another view is presented in Donald Creighton *John A. MacDonald* II *The Old Chieftain* (Toronto 1955) 411–18.
16 Stanley *Riel* 324. The story is told in Desmond Morton *The Last War Drum: The North West Campaign of 1885* (Toronto 1972).
17 Peter B. Waite *Canada 1874–1896: Arduous Destiny* (Toronto 1971) 160
18 E.R. Markson 'The Life and Death of Louis Riel: A Study in Forensic Psychia-

try' *Canadian Psychiatric Association Journal* 10 no 4 (August 1965) 244–64. See also Thomas *Struggle* and Stanley *The Birth of Western Canada: A History of the Riel Rebellions* first pub 1936 (Toronto 1960). The quotation is from G.F.G. Stanley 'Louis Riel' in Robert L. McDougall ed *Our Living Tradition* fifth series (Toronto 1965) 29. A review of the discussion is Douglas Owram 'The Myth of Louis Riel' *Canadian Historical Review* 53 no 3 (1982) 315–36

19 Flanagan *Prophet* 179, 184, 186

20 Creighton *Macdonald* II 430–9; Thomas Flanagan and Neil Watson 'The Riel Trial Revisited: Criminal Procedure and the Law in 1885' *Saskatchewan History* 34 no 2 (spring 1981) 57–73; Desmond Morton *The Queen v Louis Riel* (Toronto 1974); Lewis H. Thomas 'A Judicial Murder – The Trial of Louis Riel' in Howard Palmer ed *The Settlement of the West* (Calgary 1977) 37–59

21 Hartwell Bowsfield *Louis Riel: The Rebel and the Hero* (Toronto 1971) 140–5

22 Winnipeg *Tribune* 12 December 1970. On the evening of 12 December 1885 Riel was burned in effigy on a Winnipeg street corner, just across the river from the cemetery; A.H. de Tremaudan *Hold High Your Heads* trans Elizabeth Maguet (Winnipeg 1982) first pub 1936 as *Histoire de la nation métisse dans l'ouest Canadien* 2nd ed (St Boniface 1979) 155.

23 Stanley *Riel* 339

24 Payment 'Batoche' 96

25 Marcel Giraud 'Metis Settlement in the North-west Territories' *Saskatchewan History* 7 no 1 (winter 1954) 1–16 and 'The Western Metis after the Insurrection' *Saskatchewan History* 9 no 1 (winter 1956) 1–15; Payment 'Batoche' 98–9

26 Thomas *Struggle* 130–9

27 David H. Breen *The Canadian Prairie West and the Ranching Frontier 1874–1924* (Toronto 1983). All quotations are from his PhD dissertation, 'The Canadian West and the Ranching Frontier, 1875–1922' University of Alberta, 1972; see 170–80.

28 Simon Evans 'Spatial Aspects of the Cattle Kingdom: The First Decade, 1882–1892' in Anthony W. Rasporich and Henry C. Klassen eds *Frontier Calgary: Town, City, and Region 1875–1914* (Calgary 1975) 47

29 Breen 'Ranching' 135–41

30 Ibid 204; Lewis G. Thomas 'The Rancher and the City: Calgary and the Cattlemen, 1883–1914' *Transactions of the Royal Society of Canada* 6 series IV (1968); Shelagh S. Jameson 'The Social Elite of the Ranch Community and Calgary' in Anthony W. Rasporich and Henry C. Klassen eds *Frontier Calgary: Town, City, and Region 1875–1914* (Calgary 1975) 57–70

31 Breen 'Ranching' 285ff

32 Regina *Leader* 28 December 1904, cited in Evelyn Eager *Saskatchewan Government: Politics and Pragmatism* (Saskatoon 1980) 23

33 A review of literature on the 1905 issue is presented in J. William Brennan 'The "Autonomy Question" and the Creation of Alberta and Saskatchewan,

1905' in Howard Palmer and Donald Smith eds *The New Provinces: Alberta and Saskatchewan 1905–1980* (Vancouver 1980) 43–63.

## CHAPTER ELEVEN: IMMIGRANT COMMUNITIES 1870–1940

1 Canada *Census* 1901, 1911, 1921, 1931; A.S. Whiteley 'The Peopling of the Prairie Provinces of Canada' *American Journal of Sociology* 38 (1932–3) 240–52
2 Joseph R. Manyoni 'Ethnics and Non-Ethnics: Facts and Fads in the Study of Intergroup Relations' in Martin L. Kovacs ed *Ethnic Canadians: Culture and Education* (Regina 1978) 27–42
3 Warren E. Kalbach *The Impact of Immigration on Canada's Population* (Ottawa 1970) 12–13. The 1885 Chinese 'head tax' was $50; in 1903 it was raised to $500.
4 D.J. Hall 'Clifford Sifton: Immigration and Settlement Policy, 1896–1905' in Howard Palmer ed *The Settlement of the West* (Calgary 1977) 62, 68
5 The statement was made by President Thomas Shaughnessy of the CPR. The navvy issue is discussed in Donald Avery *'Dangerous Foreigners': European Immigrant Workers and Labour Radicalism in Canada 1896–1932* (Toronto 1979) 25–37.
6 Ibid 90–112
7 Canada, Royal Commission on Bilingualism and Biculturalism, cited in Howard Palmer ed *Immigration and the Rise of Multiculturalism* (Toronto 1975) 12
8 Vernon C. Fowke *Canadian Agricultural Policy: The Historical Pattern* (Toronto 1946) 161–77; the quotation on homestead policy is from 179–80.
9 Hall 'Sifton' 68, 71–2
10 Kenneth H. Norrie 'The National Policy and the Rate of Prairie Settlement: A Review' *Journal of Canadian Studies* 14 no 3 (fall 1979) 65–72
11 Joy Parr *Labouring Children: British Immigrant Apprentices to Canada, 1869–1924* (London 1980)
12 Donald Avery 'Canadian Immigration Policy and the "Foreign" Navvy 1896–1914' Canadian Historical Association *Historical Papers* (1972) 143–5
13 Philip Taylor *The Distant Magnet: European Emigration to the U.S.A.* (New York 1971)
14 Jorgen Dahlie 'Scandinavian Experiences on the Prairies, 1890–1920: The Frederiksens of Nokomis' in Howard Palmer ed *The Settlement of the West* (Calgary 1977) 257 n
15 James M. Minifie *Homesteader: A Prairie Boyhood Recalled* (Toronto 1972) 30–1
16 Dahlie 'Scandinavian' 106–7
17 Robert Harney 'Men without Women: Italian Migrants in Canada, 1885–1930' *Canadian Ethnic Studies* 11 no 1 (1979) 29–47
18 Oscar Handlin *The Uprooted: The Epic Story of the Great Migrations That Made the American People* (New York 1951) provides one American perspective on dislocation. Another view is presented in Timothy L. Smith 'New Approaches

to the History of Immigration in Twentieth-Century America' *American Historical Review* 71 no 4 (July 1966) 1265–79.

19 Dahlie 'Scandinavian' 109, 111

20 John Sandilands ed *Western Canadian Dictionary and Phrase-Book: Things a Newcomer Wants to Know* first pub Winnipeg 1913 (facsimile edition Edmonton 1977) 3

21 Minifie *Homesteader*

22 Ross McCormack 'Cloth Caps and Jobs: The Ethnicity of English Immigrants in Canada, 1900–1914' in Jorgen Dahlie and Tissa Fernando eds *Ethnicity, Power and Politics in Canada* (Toronto 1981) 38–55

23 A.I. Silver 'French Canada and the Prairie Frontier, 1870–90' *Canadian Historical Review* 50 no 1 (March 1969) 11–36; Robert Painchaud 'French Canadian Historiography and Franco-Canadian Settlement in Western Canada, 1870–1915' *Canadian Historical Review* 54 no 4 (1978) 447–66

24 Keith A. McLeod 'Politics, Schools and the French Language, 1881–1931' in Norman Ward and Duff Spafford eds *Politics in Saskatchewan* (Don Mills 1968) 124–50; John Herd Thompson *The Harvests of War: The Prairie West, 1914–1918* (Toronto 1978) 87–94; Raymond Huel 'French Language Education in Saskatchewan' in Susan Mann Trofimenkoff ed *The Twenties in Western Canada* (Ottawa 1972) 230–42; the 'French' population of the prairies was 136,000 in 1931.

25 Robert Painchaud 'Les exigences linguistiques dans le recrutement d'un clergé pour l'ouest canadien, 1818–1920' and Gilbert-Louis Comeault 'Les rapports de Mgr L.-P.-A. Langevin avec les groupes ethniques minoritaires et leurs répercussions sur le statut de la langue francaise au Manitoba, 1895–1916' both in La Societé canadienne d'histoire de l'église catholique *Sessions d'étude* (1975) 43–64, 65–85

26 Canada *Census* 1901, 1911, 1921, 1931. The Anglicans, Presbyterians, and Methodists together included 45 per cent of Canada's population between 1900 and 1925.

27 W. Kristjanson *The Icelandic People in Manitoba: A Manitoba Saga* (Winnipeg 1965); Laura Goodman Salverson *The Viking Heart* first pub 1947 (Toronto 1975) and *Confessions of an Immigrant's Daughter* first pub 1939 (Toronto 1981)

28 Arthur Grenke 'The Formation and Early Development of an Urban Ethnic Community: A Case Study of the Germans in Winnipeg, 1872–1919' PhD dissertation, University of Manitoba, 1975

29 Arthur A. Chiel *The Jews in Manitoba: A Social History* (Toronto 1961)

30 Ted Allan 'New Jerusalem Just a Memory' *Winnipeg Free Press* 10 December 1980, 57

31 Adele Wiseman 'A Brief Anatomy of an Honest Attempt at a Pithy Statement about the Impact of the Manitoba Environment on My Development as an Artist' *Mosaic* 3 no 3 (spring 1970) 101. Another fascinating perspective is Fredelle Bruser Maynard *Raisins and Almonds* (Don Mills 1964).

32 R. Usiskin 'Toward a Theoretical Reformulation of the Relationship between Political Ideology, Class and Ethnicity: A Case Study of the Winnipeg Jewish Radical Community 1905–1920' MA thesis, University of Manitoba, 1978

33 Canada *Census* 1931

34 John C. Lehr 'The Government and the Immigrant: Perspectives on Ukrainian Block Settlement in the Canadian West' *Canadian Ethnic Studies* 11 no 2 (1977) 42–52 and John C. Lehr *Ukrainian Vernacular Architecture in Alberta* Alberta Historic Sites Service Occasional Paper no 1 (1976)

35 Orest T. Martynowycz 'Village Radicals and Peasant Immigrants: The Social Roots of Factionalism among Ukrainian Immigrants in Canada 1896–1918' MA thesis, University of Manitoba, 1978; John Marlyn *Under the Ribs of Death* first pub 1957 (Toronto 1964)

36 Oleh W. Gerus 'The Ukrainian Canadian Committee' in Manoly R. Lupul ed *A Heritage in Transition: Essays in the History of Ukrainians in Canada* (Toronto 1982) 195–214

37 Frank H. Epp *Mennonites in Canada, 1786–1920: The History of a Separate People* (Toronto 1974). The Mennonite immigrants to western Canada were distinct from the various Swiss-German Mennonites who joined William Penn's colony and then migrated north to Upper Canada with the Loyalists in the late eighteenth and early nineteenth centuries.

38 John H. Warkentin 'The Mennonite Settlements of Southern Manitoba' PhD dissertation, University of Toronto, 1960, 147

39 E.K. Francis *In Search of Utopia: The Mennonites in Manitoba* (Altona, Manitoba, 1955) and Frank H. Epp *Mennonites in Canada, 1920–1940: A People's Struggle for Survival* (Toronto 1982)

40 George Woodcock and Ivan Avakumovic *The Doukhobors* (Toronto 1968)

41 Victor Peters *All Things Common: The Hutterian Way of Life* first pub 1965 (New York 1971), and John Ryan *The Agricultural Economy of Manitoba Hutterite Colonies* (Toronto 1977)

42 J. Brian Dawson 'The Chinese Experience in Frontier Calgary: 1885–1910' in Rasporich and Klassen eds *Frontier Calgary*; Harry Con et al *From China to Canada: A History of the Chinese Communities in Canada* (Toronto 1982)

43 J.H. Richards 'Retrospect and Prospect' in P.J. Smith ed *The Prairie Provinces* (Toronto 1972) 131

44 Alan B. Anderson 'Linguistic Trends among Saskatchewan Ethnic Groups' in Martin L. Kovacs ed *Ethnic Canadians: Culture and Education* (Regina 1978) 63–86

CHAPTER TWELVE: CAPITAL AND LABOUR 1900–40

1 Canada *Census* 1941

2 Ruben Bellan *Winnipeg First Century: An Economic History* (Winnipeg 1978) 100; also Paul Phillips 'The Prairie Urban System, 1911–1961: Specialization

and Change' in Alan F.J. Artibise ed *Town and City: Aspects of Western Canadian Urban Development* (Regina 1981) 7–30

3 Bellan *Winnipeg* 175–6

4 Ibid 113

5 Carl A. Dawson and Eva R. Younge *Pioneering in the Prairie Provinces: The Social Side of the Settlement Process* (Toronto 1940) 41. In 1931–2 and 1932–3, Vancouver wheat shipments were 74 million and 93 million bushels respectively; Montreal shipments were 46 million and 58 million respectively.

6 Phillips 'Prairie Urban system' 28

7 David Breen 'Calgary: The City and the Petroleum Industry since World War Two' *Urban History Review* 6 no 2 (1977) 55–71; Max Foran *Calgary: An Illustrated History* (Toronto 1978)

8 John Gilpin 'Failed Metropolis: The City of Strathcona, 1891–1912' in Artibise ed *Town and City* 259–88; John C. Weaver 'Edmonton's Perilous Course, 1904–29' *Urban History Review* 6 no 2 (1977) 20–32; Alexander Bruce Kilpatrick 'A Lesson in Boosterism: The Contest for the Alberta Provincial Capital 1904–06' *Urban History Review* 8 no 3 (February 1980) 47–110; J.G. MacGregor *Edmonton: A History* (Edmonton 1967)

9 Earl G. Drake *Regina: The Queen City* (Toronto 1955); Stan Hanson and Don Kerr *Saskatoon: The First Half-Century* (Edmonton 1982); Lewis H. Thomas 'Saskatoon, 1883–1920: The Formative Years' in Artibise ed *Town and City* 237–58

10 Thomas 'Saskatoon' 251

11 Alan Artibise 'Boosterism and the Development of Prairie Cities, 1871–1913' in Artibise ed *Town and City* 216

12 Douglas Durkin *The Magpie* (Toronto 1923). A good survey of Durkin's career is provided by Peter Rider in 'Introduction' to the reprint of *The Magpie* (Toronto 1974).

13 Conspicuous consumption was described by Thorstein Veblen in *The Theory of the Leisure Class: An Economic Study of Institutions* first pub 1899 (New York 1953). The 'chaos' was described by John Marlyn in his north end Winnipeg novel, *Under the Ribs of Death* (Toronto 1957) and by Ralph Connor (C.W. Gordon) in *The Foreigner: A Tale of Saskatchewan* (Toronto 1909).

14 Carl Betke 'The Original City of Edmonton: A Derivative Prairie Urban Community' in Artibise ed *Town and City* 309–46; and MacGregor *Edmonton* 143

15 Studies of the social thought of business leaders are not common. One recent work is A.A. den Otter *Civilizing the West: The Galts and the Development of Western Canada* (Edmonton 1982). See also Michael Bliss *A Living Profit: Studies in the Social History of Canadian Business, 1883–1911* (Toronto 1974) and *A Canadian Millionaire: The Life and Business Times of Sir Joseph Flavelle, Bart. 1858–1939* (Toronto 1978).

16 Sheilagh S. Jameson 'The Social Elite of the Ranch Community and Calgary' in A.W. Rasporich and H.C. Klassen eds *Frontier Calgary: Town, City and*

*Region* (Calgary 1975) 57–70; and Alan F.J. Artibise *Winnipeg: A Social History of Urban Growth 1874–1914* (Montreal 1975).

17  This argument is presented in Artibise *Winnipeg: A Social History*.

18  Bellan *Winnipeg* 115–6 n; James H. Gray *The Boy from Winnipeg* (Toronto 1970) 19

19  An outline of Winnipeg workers' budgets is provided in Artibise *Winnipeg: A Social History* 308–19. Careful studies of the subject are presented in Terry Copp *The Anatomy of Poverty: The Condition of the Working Class in Montreal 1897–1929* (Toronto 1974) and Michael Piva *The Condition of the Working Class in Toronto, 1900–1921* (Ottawa 1979)

20  Artibise *Winnipeg: A Social History* 241, also 225–40

21  Alan G. Green *Regional Aspects of Canada's Economic Growth* (Toronto 1971)

22  David C. Jones, Nancy M. Sheehan, and Robert M. Stamp eds *Shaping the Schools of the Canadian West* (Calgary 1979)

23  Richard Allen *The Social Passion: Religion and Social Reform in Canada 1914–28* (Toronto 1971)

24  Lorna Fay Hurl 'An Analysis of Social Welfare Policy: A Case Study of the Development of Child Welfare Policies and Programmes in Manitoba 1870–1924' MSW thesis, University of Manitoba, 1981; H.C. Klassen 'In Search of Neglected and Delinquent Children: The Calgary Children's Aid Society, 1909–20' in Artibise ed *Town and City* 375–91

25  Discussions of class lines in the modern community are readily available but often difficult to work with. One introduction is T.B. Bottomore *Classes in Modern Society* (New York 1966). A more advanced study is Anthony Giddens *The Class Structure of the Advanced Societies* 2nd ed (London 1980).

26  Green *Regional Aspects* calculated from Appendix C

27  Donald Avery *'Dangerous Foreigners': European Immigrant Workers and Labour Radicalism in Canada 1896–1932* (Toronto 1979) 27; A. Ross McCormack 'The Blanketstiffs' *Canada's Visual History* 13 (Ottawa 1974) 1

28  Edmund W. Bradwin *The Bunkhouse Man: A Study of Work and Pay in the Camps of Canada 1903–14* first pub 1928 (Toronto 1972) 92–112, 249

29  Data on output is from Canada *Census* 1931 and 1941; *Report* of the Royal Commission on Coal 1946; and Rex A. Lucas *Minetown, Milltown, Railtown: Life in Canadian Communities of Single Industry* (Toronto 1971).

30  Allen Seager kindly permitted me to see material from his forthcoming work on the Alberta coal communities.

31  *Report* of the Royal Commission on Coal 1946, 296, 304–6. Such statistics require a context: according to Terry Copp, a family of five supported by a semi-skilled worker in Montreal in 1929 would be below the 'poverty line' if the breadwinner earned less than $1,500 per year – a sum well above the average annual income for such a worker (*Anatomy of Poverty*).

32  David Jay Bercuson ed *Alberta's Coal Industry 1919* (Calgary 1978) 117, 183–6, 194–5, 200, 221

33 The views of F.J. Turner are discussed below, 308–20; Cole Harris presented his perspective on Sandon in an unpublished paper at the British Columbia Studies Conference, University of Victoria, 1979. A different view is presented in A.A. den Otter 'Social Life of a Mining Community: The Coal Branch' *Alberta Historical Review* 17 (1969) 1–11.

34 Allen Seager '"A Forecast of the Parliament of Man": Aspects of the Alberta Miners' Movement 1905–1945' unpublished paper presented to McGill University Conference on Class and Culture 1979

CHAPTER THIRTEEN: THE RURAL WEST 1900–30

1 H.Y. Hind, cited in Doug Owram *Promise of Eden: The Canadian Expansionist Movement and the Idea of the West* (Toronto 1980) 69

2 Ibid 149–67

3 Ibid 165

4 Klaus Peter Stich '"Canada's Century": The Rhetoric of Propaganda' *Prairie Forum* 1 no 1 (April 1976) 19–30

5 Another perspective is presented in Patrick A. Dunae '"Making Good": The Canadian West in British Boys' Literature, 1890–1914' *Prairie Forum* 4 no 2 (fall 1979) 165–82.

6 L.H. Thomas 'British Visitors' Perceptions of the West, 1885–1914' in A.W. Rasporich and H.C. Klassen eds *Prairie Perspectives* II (Toronto 1973)

7 One example is Ralph Connor (C.W. Gordon) *Corporal Cameron of the North West Mounted Police: A Tale of the Macleod Trail* (Toronto 1912) 308. Critical studies include J. Lee Thompson and John H. Thompson 'Ralph Connor and the Canadian Identity' *Queen's Quarterly* 79 no 2 (summer 1972) 159–70; F.W. Watt 'Western Myth – The World of Ralph Connor' *Canadian Literature* 1 (summer 1959) 26–36.

8 Ralph Connor (C.W. Gordon) *The Sky Pilot: A Tale of the Foothills* (Toronto 1899) 27

9 Ralph Connor (C.W. Gordon) *The Foreigner: A Tale of Saskatchewan* (Toronto 1909) 378, 384

10 Ralph Connor (C.W. Gordon) 'The Future of Canada' Canadian Club of Toronto *Addresses and Proceedings* (1904–5) 148

11 Robert J.C. Stead *Dennison Grant: A Novel of To-Day* (Toronto 1920) 291

12 Stephen Leacock *My Discovery of the West: A Discussion of East and West in Canada* (Toronto 1937) Preface

13 Maymont Library Board *From Sod to Solar: Fielding, Lilac, Maymont, Ruddell* (Altona, Manitoba, 1980) 474–8

14 James M. Minifie *Homesteader: A Prairie Boyhood Recalled* (Toronto 1972) 52–3

15 Kathleen Strange *With the West in Her Eyes: The Story of a Modern Pioneer* (Toronto 1937) 218–31

16 Ray Allen Billington ed *Frontier and Section: Selected Essays of Frederick Jackson Turner* 37–62

17 Chester Martin *'Dominion Lands' Policy* first pub 1938, Lewis H. Thomas ed (Toronto 1973) 169–72, 240–1

18 Vernon C. Fowke *The National Policy and the Wheat Economy* (Toronto 1957) 285. Fowke argues that the crucial failure of land policy was the absence of land or climatic surveys that would have excluded areas 'totally unfit' for farming.

19 Donald Merwin Loveridge 'The Settlement of the Rural Municipality of Sifton 1881–1920' MA thesis, University of Manitoba, 1977, 217

20 Lyle Dick 'A Social and Economic History of the Abernethy District, Saskatchewan, 1880–1920' Parks Canada ms (Winnipeg 1983). I would like to thank Mr Dick for permitting me to see an advance copy of this valuable report.

21 Nellie L. McClung *The Black Creek Stopping House and Other Stories* (Toronto 1912) 166, 175–6

22 B.K. Sandwell 'The Cityward Bias of Literature' *Queen's Quarterly* 31 (1923–4) 148; also H.F. Gadsby 'The Sons of the Soil' *Toronto Saturday Night* (1 June 1918)

23 Robert J.C. Stead *The Homesteaders: A Novel of the Canadian West* (London 1916) 123–4

24 Robert J.C. Stead *Dennison Grant* 271

25 Sarah Carter 'Material Culture and the W.R. Motherwell Home' *Prairie Forum* 8 no 1 (1983) 99–111; Dick 'Abernethy'; Allan R. Turner 'W.R. Motherwell: The Emergence of a Farm Leader' *Saskatchewan History* 11 no 3 (autumn 1958) 94–103

26 Seymour Martin Lipset *Agrarian Socialism: The Cooperative Commonwealth Federation in Saskatchewan: A Study in Political Sociology* first pub 1950, revised ed (New York 1968) 247

27 William Allen, W.C. Hope, and F.C. Hitchcock Studies of Farm Indebtedness and Financial Progress of Saskatchewan Farmers Report no 3 *Surveys Made at Indian Head and Balcarres; Grenfell and Wolseley; and Neudorf and Lemberg* University of Saskatchewan College of Agriculture Extension Bulletin 68 (Saskatoon 1935)

28 Loveridge 'Sifton' 237–8

29 Ibid 227–32; Dick 'Abernethy' 40–4

30 Calculated from the Canadian Pioneer Problems Committee survey, 1930–1, in R.W. Murchie et al *Agricultural Progress on the Prairie Frontier* (Toronto 1936) 72–9. Of 2,078 farms, 1,646 (80 per cent) reported debts ranging from $1,900 to $5,900. These 1,646 indebted farms also reported assets of $8,000–$25,000 and a debt/asset relationship of 15 per cent to 30 per cent. A useful survey is Lyle Dick 'Estimates of Farm-Making Costs in Saskatchewan, 1882–1914' *Prairie Forum* 6 no 2 (1981) 183–201.

31 D. McGinnis 'Farm Labour in Transition: Occupational Structure and Economic Dependency in Alberta, 1921–1951' in Howard Palmer ed *The Settlement of the West* (Calgary 1977) 182

32 Nathan Laselle Whetten 'The Social and Economic Structure of the Trade
   Centres in the Canadian Prairie Provinces with Special Reference to Its
   Changes 1910–1930' PhD thesis, Harvard University, 1932; C.A. Dawson and
   Eva R. Younge *Pioneering in the Prairie Provinces: The Social Side of the Settlement
   Process* (Toronto 1940) 39–59
33 Pierre Berton *The Last Spike: The Great Railway 1881–1885* (Toronto 1971) 23–32
34 Barry Potyondi 'In Quest of Limited Urban Status: The Town Building Process in Minnedosa 1879–1904' in Alan F.J. Artibise ed *Town and City: Aspects
   of Western Canadian Urban Development* (Regina 1981) 121–7; John Langton
   Tyman *By Section, Township, and Range: Studies in Prairie Settlement* (Brandon
   1972) 42–3, 55
35 Paul Voisey 'Boosting the Small Prairie Town 1904–31: An Example from
   Southern Alberta' in Artibise ed *Town and City* 147–76
36 Ronald Rees 'The Small Towns of Saskatchewan' *Landscape* 18 no 3 (fall 1969)
   29–33
37 Barry Stephen Potyondi 'Country Town: The History of Minnedosa, Manitoba 1879–1922' MA thesis, University of Manitoba, 1978, 37–56
38 Jean Burnet *Next-Year Country: A Study of Rural Social Organization in Alberta*
   (Toronto 1951) 82
39 J.F. Newman 'The Impact of Technology upon Rural Southwestern Manitoba
   1920–30' MA thesis, Queen's University, 1971; and Potyondi 'Country Town'
   119
40 Dan Morgan *Merchants of Grain* (New York 1979)
41 The ups and downs of the grain economy are discussed in Fowke *National
   Policy*. Also useful are Arthur S. Morton *History of Prairie Settlement* (Toronto
   1938) and R.W. Murchie et al *Agricultural Progress on the Prairie Frontier*
   (Toronto 1936).
42 Kenneth Norrie 'Dry Farming and the Economics of Risk Bearing: The Canadian Prairies 1870–1930' *Agricultural History* 51 no 1 (January 1977) 134–48
43 The calendar is discussed in Dick 'Abernethy' and Minifie *Homesteader*.
44 Murchie et al *Agricultural Progress* 67–131 and W.A. Mackintosh *Economic
   Problems of the Prairie Provinces* (Toronto 1935) 20–32
45 Duncan Alexander MacGibbon *The Canadian Grain Trade* (Toronto 1932) 102–3
46 Fowke *National Policy* 153–65 and D.J. Hall 'The Manitoba Grain Act: An
   "Agarian Magna Carta?"' *Prairie Forum* 4 no 1 (spring 1979) 105–20
47 In 1928–9, 94 per cent of all grain shipped was loaded by country elevators;
   MacGibbon *The Canadian Grain Trade* 90.
48 These quotations appear in W.A. Mackintosh *Agricultural Co-operation in
   Western Canada* (Kingston and Toronto 1924) 19; on the issue, see Ian Mac-
   Pherson *Each for All: A History of the Co-operative Movement in English Canada
   1900–1945* (Toronto 1979).
49 Fowke *National Policy* 149
50 Ibid 191–2

51 Ibid 290

CHAPTER FOURTEEN: POLITICS AND CULTURE 1900–29

1 Allan Smith 'American Culture and the Concept of Mission in Nineteenth Century English Canada,' Canadian Historical Association *Historical Papers* (1971) 169–82
2 W.L. Morton *Manitoba: A History* first pub 1957 (Toronto 1967); David E. Smith *Prairie Liberalism: The Liberal Party in Saskatchewan 1905–71* (Toronto 1975); L.G. Thomas *The Liberal Party in Alberta: A History of Politics in the Province of Alberta 1905–1921* (Toronto 1959)
3 *The Voice* 16 September 1910
4 Ibid 23 September 1907
5 George Neil Emery 'Methodism on the Canadian Prairies, 1896 to 1914: The Dynamics of an Institution in a New Environment' PhD dissertation, University of British Columbia, 1970
6 T.A. Russell 'The Grain Growers and the Manufacturers' in Canadian Club of Toronto *Addresses and Proceedings* (1910–11) 121
7 Cited in Marilyn Barber 'Nationalism, Nativism and the Social Gospel' in Richard Allen ed *The Social Gospel in Canada* (Ottawa 1972) 223; the Anglican church did not participate in this missionary activity directed at Ukrainians because it acknowledged the authority of the Greek communion and the primacy of the Ukrainians' own clergy.
8 Cited in J.E. Rea 'My Main Line Is the Kiddies ...' in W. Isajiw ed *Identities: The Impact of Ethnicity on Canadian Society* (Toronto 1977) 5–6
9 *England's Story*, cited in Morris K. Mott 'The "Foreign Peril": Nativism in Winnipeg, 1916–1923' MA thesis, University of Manitoba, 1970, 85
10 John Herd Thompson *The Harvests of War: The Prairie West, 1914–1918* (Toronto 1978) 92
11 Ibid 12–26
12 Richard Allen *The Social Passion: Religion and Social Reform in Canada 1914–28* (Toronto 1971) 35–62 and Michael Bliss 'The Methodist Church and World War I' *Canadian Historical Review* 49 no 3 (September 1968) 213–33
13 Thompson *Harvests* 144–72
14 Richard Allen 'The Background of the Social Gospel in Canada' in Richard Allen ed *The Social Gospel in Canada* (Ottawa 1972) 2–34
15 Thompson *Harvests* 95–114
16 Ibid 73–94
17 Mott 'Nativism' 22; the *Telegram* editorial was entitled 'Deport the Whole Brood.'
18 Ibid 23–5
19 J.H. Thompson does not agree; *Harvests* 73–4.
20 Martin Robin *Radical Politics and Canadian Labour 1880–1930* (Kingston 1968);

Paul Phillips *No Power Greater: A Century of Labour in British Columbia* (Vancouver 1967); A. Ross McCormack *Reformers, Rebels, and Revolutionaries: The Western Canadian Radical Movement 1899–1919* (Toronto 1977); David J. Bercuson *Fools and Wise Men: The Rise and Fall of the One Big Union* (Toronto 1978)

21 Robert H. Babcock *Gompers in Canada: A Study in American Continentalism before the First World War* (Toronto 1974) 145–6; Gerald Friesen 'Studies in the Development of Western Canadian Regional Consciousness 1870–1925' PhD dissertation, University of Toronto, 1973, 186–233

22 Paul Phillips 'The National Policy and the Development of the Western Canadian Labour Movement' in A.W. Rasporich and H.C. Klassen eds *Prairie Perspectives* II (Toronto 1973) 55–6; H. Clare Pentland 'The Western Canadian Labour Movement, 1897–1919' *Canadian Journal of Political and Social Theory* 3 no 2 (1979) 53–78

23 David Jay Bercuson 'Labour Radicalism and the Western Industrial Frontier: 1897–1919' *Canadian Historical Review* 58 no 2 (June 1977) 154–75

24 Gerald Friesen 'Yours in Revolt': The Socialist Party of Canada and the Western Labour Movement' *Labour/Le Travailleur* I (1976) 139–57

25 Kenneth McNaught and David J. Bercuson *The Winnipeg Strike: 1919* (Don Mills 1974) 63

26 The two most complete discussions of the strike are David Jay Bercuson *Confrontation at Winnipeg: Labour, Industrial Relations, and the General Strike* (Montreal 1974) and D.C. Masters *The Winnipeg General Strike* first pub 1950 (Toronto 1973).

27 Paul Fussell *The Great War and Modern Memory* (New York 1977) 157–8

28 Sarah Carter 'Material Culture and the W.R. Motherwell Home' *Prairie Forum* 8 no 1 (1983) 99–111; Ian Clarke, Lyle Dick, Sarah Carter *Motherwell Historic Park* History and Archaeology no 66 (Ottawa 1983)

29 Thompson *Harvests* 153–61; Robert Craig Brown *Robert Laird Borden: A Biography* II 1914–1937 (Toronto 1980)

30 *Manitoba Free Press* 13 May 1916

31 W.L. Morton *The Progressive Party in Canada* (Toronto 1950)

32 The platforms are reprinted in ibid 300–5. As T.A. Crerar, soon to be the leader of the movement, explained to Alberta farm leader H.W. Wood, the Progressives 'must proceed on broad, sane lines of policy, and not from a sectional or class point of view'; Crerar to Wood, 15 March 1918, in George Chipman Papers, Queen's University.

33 Richard Allen 'The Social Gospel as the Religion of the Agrarian Revolt' in Carl Berger and Ramsay Cook eds *The West and the Nation: Essays in Honour of W.L. Morton* (Toronto 1976) 181–4, 185

34 Morton *The Progressive Party* 106–19, 160–4; Ramsay Cook *The Politics of John W. Dafoe and the Free Press* (Toronto 1963); Ian MacPherson 'George Chipman and the Institutionalization of a Reform Movement' Historical and Scientific Society of Manitoba *Transactions* series III no 32 (1975–6) 53–65

35 C.B. Macpherson *Democracy in Alberta: Social Credit and the Party System* (Toronto 1953); W.L. Morton 'The Social Philosophy of Henry Wise Wood' in A.B. McKillop ed *Contexts of Canada's Past: Selected Essays of W.L. Morton* (Toronto 1980)

36 Reginald Whittaker, Introduction to the Carleton Library Edition, in William Irvine *The Farmers in Politics* first pub 1920 (Toronto 1976) xv–xxv

37 Irvine *Farmers* 101–2

38 Ian MacPherson 'Selected Borrowings: The American Impact upon the Prairie Co-operative Movement, 1920–39' *Canadian Review of American Studies* 10 no 2 (fall 1979)

39 The party standings after the 1921 elections were Liberals 116, Progressives 65, Conservatives 50, Labour 2, other 2.

40 *Manitoba Free Press* 30 October 1925

41 Quoted in D. James Naylor 'Labourism, *The Voice* and the British Connection' unpublished manuscript

42 Allen Mills, 'Single Tax, Socialism and the Independent Labour Party of Manitoba: The Political Ideas of F.J. Dixon and S.J. Farmer' *Labour/Le Travailleur* 5 (spring 1980) 52. Also helpful is Duncan Norman Irvine 'Reform, War and Industrial Crisis in Manitoba: F.J. Dixon and the Framework of Consensus, 1903–1920' MA thesis, University of Manitoba, 1981

43 Walter D. Young 'M.J. Coldwell, the Making of a Social Democrat' *Journal of Canadian Studies* 9 no 3 (1974) 50–60

44 Duff Spafford 'The "Left Wing" 1921–1931' in Norman Ward and Duff Spafford eds *Politics in Saskatchewan* (Don Mills 1968) 44–58

45 Anthony Mardiros *William Irvine: The Life of a Prairie Radical* (Toronto 1979)

46 There were two Labour MPs, Woodsworth and William Irvine (Calgary), in 1921–5; two again, Woodsworth and A.A. Heaps (Winnipeg), in 1925–6; and three, Woodsworth, Irvine, and Heaps, in 1926–30.

47 The best biography is Kenneth McNaught *A Prophet in Politics: A Biography of J.S. Woodsworth* (Toronto 1959).

48 Ibid 163–4, 167

CHAPTER FIFTEEN: THE DEPRESSION 1930–40

1 A.E. Safarian *The Canadian Economy in the Great Depression* (Toronto 1970); W.A. Mackintosh *The Economic Background of Dominion-Provincial Relations* ed J.H. Dales (Toronto 1964)

2 Vernon C. Fowke *The National Policy and the Wheat Economy* (Toronto 1957) 259

3 Safarian *Depression* 120, 56

4 The story of the weather is told in James Gray *Men against the Desert* (Saskatoon 1967) and *The Winter Years: The Depression on the Prairies* (Toronto 1966) 104–16.

5 G.E. Britnell and V.C. Fowke *Canadian Agriculture in War and Peace 1935–50*

(Stanford 1962) 71–4, 444–7; also G.E. Britnell *The Wheat Economy* (Toronto 1939)

6 Britnell and Fowke *Agriculture* 74–7, 189–91; Britnell *Wheat* 37–8, 202–3, 225

7 A.W. Bailey 'The Year We Moved' *Saskatchewan History* 20 (1967) 19–31

8 Descriptions of the dust storms are often chilling. One is provided by James Gray in *The Winter Years* 161–81.

9 Gray *Desert* 112

10 Dugouts were nothing more than excavations, perhaps 20 × 50 yards in extent and 4 yards deep. Eventually, 80,000 dugouts as well as 10,000 dams and 5,000 irrigation projects dotted the prairie landscape; Gray *Desert* 183.

11 Seventy community pastures were completed or under way in Saskatchewan by 1939. Manitoba joined the programe later, but Alberta, jealous of its newly won control over provincial lands, never did participate. In the end, 2.3 million acres, nearly 2 per cent of prairie farm lands, were in community pastures; Gray *Desert* 184–5, 136; Britnell *Wheat* 232: Britnell and Fowke *Agriculture* 76.

12 Fowke *National Policy* 265

13 T.W. Grindley et al *The Canadian Wheat Board 1935–46* (Ottawa 1947), cited in Fowke *National Policy* 266

14 D.A. MacGibbon *The Canadian Grain Trade 1931–1951* (Toronto 1952) 47. The board was designed to aid the small producer, in particular, because it was permitted to buy only 5,000 bushels from any one farmer at the minimum or 'support' price. Farmers in a district where failure was adjudged to have occurred would receive a compensation payment based on the size of their farm but with a ceiling of $200 to $500. A 1 per cent levy on all grain sales from western Canada sustained the fund.

15 Gray *The Winter Years* 27–36

16 Alma Newman 'Relief Administration in Saskatoon during the Depression' in D.H. Bocking ed *Pages from the Past: Essays on Saskatchewan History* (Saskatoon 1979) 246. In Winnipeg, the reaction was sharper: 'The Dominion Government is admitting Central Europeans, late alien enemies ... before we have finished burying our gas-poisoned soldiers, and who, if our present policy of employing the foreigner on municipal work is continued, will quite likely tend the graves of the men they killed'; Michael R. Goeres 'Disorder, Dependency and Fiscal Responsibility: Unemployment Relief in Winnipeg, 1907–42' MA thesis, University of Manitoba, 1981, 111.

17 This story is surveyed in Goeres 'Relief in Winnipeg.'

18 Michiel Horn ed *The Dirty Thirties: Canadians in the Great Depression* (Toronto 1972) 236–7

19 Letter to the *Vancouver Sun* May 1935, cited in Horn ed *The Dirty Thirties* 340

20 Lorne A. Brown 'Unemployment Relief Camps in Saskatchewan, 1933–36' *Saskatchewan History* 23 (1970) 82; H. Blair Neatby *The Politics of Chaos: Canada in the Thirties* (Toronto 1972) 33–5

21 Brown 'Relief Camps' 90
22 Toronto *Globe*, 2 July 1935, cited in Horn ed *The Dirty Thirties* 385. The story of the trek is told in Victor Hoar ed *Recollections of the On to Ottawa Trek* (Toronto 1973)
23 Murray S. Donnelly *The Government of Manitoba* (Toronto 1963) 58
24 The 1932 result was 38 Bracken Liberal-Progressives, 10 Conservatives, 5 Independent-Labour, and 2 Independents. The Bracken outlook is explained in John Kendle *John Bracken: A Political Biography* (Toronto 1979). Another view is contained in T.E. Peterson's 'Manitoba: Ethnic and Class Politics' in Martin Robin ed *Canadian Provincial Politics: The Party Systems of the Ten Provinces* 2nd ed (Scarborough 1978) 61–119; also useful are W.L. Morton *Manitoba: A History* first pub 1957 (Toronto 1967) and Donnelly *Government of Manitoba*.
25 Peterson 'Manitoba'
26 Douglas L. Campbell, in an interview with the author, 1980; also Kendle *Bracken*
27 H. Blair Neatby *William Lyon Mackenzie King 1924–1932: The Lonely Heights* (Toronto 1963) 94
28 William Calderwood 'Pulpit, Press and Political Reactions to the Ku Klux Klan in Saskatchewan' in S.M. Trofimenkoff ed *The Twenties in Western Canada* (Ottawa 1972) 191–229; Patrick Kyba 'Ballots and Burning Crosses' in Norman Ward and Duff Spafford eds *Politics in Saskatchewan* (Don Mills 1968) 105–23; David E. Smith *Prairie Liberalism: The Liberal Party in Saskatchewan 1905–71* (Toronto 1975) 108–97
29 T.C. Davis to W.L.M. King, 28 May 1931, cited in Smith *Prairie Liberalism* 206. P.A. Russell 'The Co-operative Government's Response to the Depression, 1930–1934' *Saskatchewan History* 24 (1971) 81–100
30 Smith *Prairie Liberalism* 198–243; Andrew Milnor 'The New Politics and Ethnic Revolt, 1929–1938' in Ward and Spafford eds *Politics in Saskatchewan* 151–77
31 Seymour Martin Lipset *Agrarian Socialism: The Cooperative Commonwealth Federation in Saskatchewan: A Study in Political Sociology* first pub 1950 (New York 1968) 157. This debate can be followed in Lewis H. Thomas 'The CCF Victory in Saskatchewan, 1944' *Saskatchewan History* 34 no 1 (winter 1981) 1–16; George Hoffman 'The Saskatchewan Farmer-Labor Party, 1932–1934: How Radical Was It as Its Origin?' *Saskatchewan History* 28 no 2 (spring 1975) 52–64; Peter R. Sinclair 'The Saskatchewan CCF: Ascent to Power and the Decline of Socialism' *Canadian Historical Review* 54 no 4 (December 1973) 419–33 Evelyn Eager 'The Conservatism of the Saskatchewan Electorate' in Ward and Spafford eds *Politics in Saskatchewan*; Walter D. Young *The Anatomy of a Party: The National CCF 1932–61* (Toronto 1969).
32 Thomas 'CCF' 15
33 Carl F. Betke 'The United Farmers of Alberta, 1921–1935' in Carlo Caldarola ed *Society and Politics in Alberta: Research Papers* (Toronto 1979) 14–32

34 C.B. Macpherson *Democracy in Alberta: Social Credit and the Party System* (Toronto 1953); Harold J. Schultz 'Portrait of a Premier: William Aberhart' *Canadian Historical Review* 45 no 3 (1964) 185–211; John A. Irving *The Social Credit Movement in Alberta* (Toronto 1959); Lewis H. Thomas ed *William Aberhart and Social Credit in Alberta* (Toronto 1977)

35 Macpherson *Democracy in Alberta* 94; John L. Finlay *Social Credit: The English Origins* (Montreal 1972)

36 Macpherson *Democracy in Alberta* 114

37 Leacock *My Discovery of the West* (Toronto 1937) 136

38 J.R. Mallory *Social Credit and the Federal Power in Canada* (Toronto 1954)

39 Thomas ed *Social Credit* 89

40 Schultz 'Aberhart' 199–200

41 Macpherson *Democracy in Alberta* 21, 5

42 J.F. Conway 'The Prairie Populist Resistance to the National Policy: Some Reconsiderations' *Journal of Canadian Studies* 14 no 3 (fall 1979) 77–91; Peter R. Sinclair 'Class Structure and Populist Protest: The Case of Western Canada' in Caldarola ed *Alberta* 73–86

43 John Richards and Larry Pratt *Prairie Capitalism: Power and Influence in the New West* (Toronto 1979) 22–3

44 The idea is presented in David Butler and Donald Stokes *Political Change in Britain* (New York 1976) and reviewed in J. Paul Johnston 'Demographic Change in the Alberta Electorate, 1955–1975' in Caldarola ed *Alberta* 287–303. Another useful view is Myron Johnson 'The Failure of the CCF in Alberta: An Accident of History' in Caldarola ed *Alberta* 87–107.

CHAPTER SIXTEEN: THE NEW WEST SINCE 1940

1 Canada *Census* 1941, 1951, 1961, 1971, 1981; see Gerald Friesen 'The Prairie West since 1945: A Historical Survey' in A.W. Rasporich ed *Making of the Modern West: Western Canada Since 1945* forthcoming University of Calgary Press.

2 Brenton M. Barr 'Reorganization of the Economy since 1945' in P.J. Smith ed *The Prairie Provinces* (Toronto 1972) 65–82

3 Bruce Proudfoot 'Agriculture' in P.J. Smith ed *The Prairie Provinces* (Toronto 1972) 51–64

4 T.E. Peterson 'Manitoba: Ethnic and Class Politics' in Martin Robin ed *Canadian Provincial Politics: The Party Systems of the Ten Provinces* 2nd ed (Scarborough 1978) 61–119; Frances Russell 'The NDP Creates a New Political Majority' Winnipeg *Free Press* 18 November 1981

5 Canada *Census* 1941, 1981; Friesen 'The Prairie West since 1945'

6 Barr 'Reorganization of the Economy' and John H. Archer *Saskatchewan: A History* (Saskatoon 1980) 344, 364–5

7 Lipset *Agrarian Socialism* 244–5; 'census value added': a measure of total net production of an industry, including the value of goods and/or services produced plus costs of purchased services and overhead charges.

8 John C. Courtney and David E. Smith 'Saskatchewan: Parties in a Politically Competitive Province' in Martin Robin ed *Canadian Provincial Politics: The Party Systems of the Ten Provinces* 2nd ed (Scarborough, 1978) 312, 302

9 Ibid 304

10 E.A. Tollefson *Bitter Medicine: The Saskatchewan Medicare Feud* (Saskatoon 1963)

11 John Richards and Larry Pratt *Prairie Capitalism: Power and Influence in the New West* (Toronto 1979) 199–200; also David E. Smith *Prairie Liberalism: The Liberal Party in Saskatchewan 1905–71* (Toronto 1975) 280–320

12 The best survey of this development is David E. Smith *The Regional Decline of a National Party: Liberals on the Prairies* (Toronto 1981).

13 Richards and Pratt *Prairie Capitalism* 138–62; Barr 'Reorganization of the Economy'; Proudfoot 'Agriculture'

14 Carlo Caldarola ed *Society and Politics in Alberta: Research Papers* (Toronto 1979) contains a number of valuable articles.

15 A useful American survey is Gilbert C. Fite *American Farmers: The New Minority* (Bloomington, Indiana 1981); the Canadian story is told in John W. Bennett *Of Time and the Enterprise: North American Family Farm Management in a Context of Resource Marginality* (Minneapolis 1982).

16 Several surveys are contained in Marc-Adélard Tremblay and Walton J. Anderson eds *Rural Canada in Transition* (Ottawa 1966).

17 Barry Wilson *Beyond the Harvest: Canadian Grain at the Crossroads* (Saskatoon 1981) 92–101; Earl J. Tyler 'The Farmer as Social Class in the Prairie Region' in Marc-Adélard Tremblay and Walton J. Anderson eds *Rural Canada in Transition* (Ottawa 1966) 317–21

18 Robert E. Ankli, H. Dan Helsberg, and John Herd Thompson 'Adoption of the Gasoline Tractor in Western Canada,' in Donald H. Akenson ed *Canadian Papers in Rural History* II (Gananoque, Ontario, 1980) 9–39

19 The average prairie tractor of the early 1920s was rated at about 20 horsepower; the average size rose to about 30–40 horsepower in the 1950s and, in 1967, to over 80 horsepower. By the late 1970s, many new tractors were rated over 150 horsepower.

20 Agriculture Canada *Selected Agricultural Statistics for Canada and the Provinces, 1982*

21 Wilson *Harvest* 19–34

22 Wheat was sown on 45 per cent of the cultivated acreage in the late 1930s but on only 32–34 per cent in the late 1970s. Oilseeds were sown on 7–10 per cent of cultivated acreage and produced nearly 10 per cent of farm cash receipts – over $500 million per year – between 1976 and 1981.

23 Tyler 'Farmer as Social Class' 39–41, 285, 290, 322; Donald R. Whyte 'Rural Canada in Transition' in Marc-Adélard Tremblay and Walton J. Anderson eds *Rural Canada in Transition* (Ottawa 1966) 64–71

24 Wilson *Harvest* 126–7

25 A survey of the issue is presented in Howard Darling *The Politics of Freight Rates: The Railway Freight Rate Issue in Canada* (Toronto 1980).

26 Wilson *Harvest* 147–52
27 'Rule by Devine Right' *Saskatchewan Business* July–August 1982
28 On the *Financial Post 500*, Saskatchewan Crown Investments Corporation was ranked fourteenth by assets and forty-eighth by sales in 1981. The Pool, with nearly $2 billion in sales, was fortieth by sales. Co-op Trust had assets of over $600 million in 1981. Sherwood Credit Union had assets of over $300 million. On the Heritage Fund, one useful discussion is Giles Gherson 'Time to Get Cracking' *The Financial Post 500* (1982).
29 Comparative advantage did not favour import substitution manufacturing in Saskatchewan. Within a few years, the woollen mill, brick manufacturing plant, shoe factory, tannery, and box factory failed.
30 Richards and Pratt *Prairie Capitalism* 274; Jeanne Kirk Laux and Maureen Appel Mollot 'The Potash Corporation of Saskatchewan' in Allan A. Tupper and G. Bruce Doern eds *Public Corporations and Public Policy in Canada* (Montreal 1981) 189–219
31 Gherson 'Time to Get Cracking' 26
32 Alberta Pool: $1.4 billion in sales (1981); Dairy Pool: $124 million in sales (1981); Province of Alberta Treasury Branches: $2.4 billion in assets (1981); Pacific Western Airlines: over $300 million in sales (1981); Alberta Government Telephones: over $2 billion in assets (1981); Alberta Energy Company: $1 billion in assets (1981); source: *Financial Post 500* (1981)
33 The value of the waste gas in today's market might be $5 billion, according to Peter Foster *The Blue-Eyed Sheiks: The Canadian Oil Establishment* (Toronto 1979) 197. In the early 1940s, mining contributed 10 per cent of Alberta's total value of production. In the 1950s, it produced 20 per cent. In the 1960s, it rose to over 30 per cent and in the 1970s to over 50 per cent. The dollar figures (given in millions) were more remarkable:

| | 1945 | 1950 | 1955 | 1960 | 1965 | 1970 | 1975 | 1979 |
|---|---|---|---|---|---|---|---|---|
| Net value of production in mining sector | 42 | 123 | 304 | 349 | 690 | 1,260 | 5,363 | 11,930 (est) |

| | 1946 | 1951 | 1956 | 1961 | 1966 | 1971 | 1976 | 1979 |
|---|---|---|---|---|---|---|---|---|
| Value of production | | | | | | | | |
| Crude oil | 14 | 114 | 353 | 371 | 523 | 1,032 | 3,262 | 5,680 |
| Natural gas | 7 | 3 | – | 51 | 136 | 266 | 2,101 | 4,128 |
| Coal | 33 | 41 | 39 | 10 | 32 | 42 | 234 | 253 (est) |

These figures are from Alberta Treasury, Bureau of Statistics *Alberta Statistical Review* 75 Anniversary Edition (1980).

34 An entertaining insight into these deals is provided by Anthony Sampson *The Seven Sisters: The Great Oil Companies and the World They Shaped* (New York 1975). Crucial in this secret arrangement was the international pricing system which was based on the cost of production and transportation of relatively expensive Texas oil. Thus, for example, Iranian oil delivered in Rome was priced not on the basis of its low cost of production and shipment but rather as if it had been produced in and shipped from Texas. The difference between the cost to the producer and the cost to the buyer was described as 'phantom freight.' A useful survey of the oil business, Alberta- and Seven Sisters–style, is presented in Richards and Pratt *Prairie Capitalism* 46–61.

35 Nova had sales of $2.7 billion and assets of $5 billion in 1981; *Financial Post 500*. Its development is discussed in Richards and Pratt *Prairie Capitalism* 61–91.

36 Richards and Pratt *Prairie Capitalism* 68

37 Cited in ibid 233. The statement was made in September 1974. The most complete discussion of Lougheed's life and outlook is Allan Hustak *Peter Lougheed: A Biography* (Toronto 1979).

38 J.D. House *The Last of the Free Enterprisers: The Oilmen of Calgary* (Toronto 1980)

39 A valuable introduction to this story is Donald V. Smiley *Canada in Question: Federalism in the Eighties* 3rd ed (Toronto 1980).

40 J.R. Mallory *Social Credit and the Federal Power in Canada* (Toronto 1954)

41 D.V. Smiley 'The Rowell-Sirois Report, Provincial Autonomy, and Post-War Canadian Federalism' *Canadian Journal of Economics and Political Science* 28 no 1 (February 1962) 54–69

42 Quoted in J.F. Conway *The West: The History of a Region in Confederation* (Toronto 1983) 201–2

43 Larry Pratt 'Energy: The Roots of National Policy' *Studies in Political Economy: A Socialist Review* 7 (winter 1982) 27–59; Larry Pratt 'Petro-Canada' in Allan Tupper and G. Bruce Doern eds *Public Corporations and Public Policy in Canada* (Montreal 1981) 95–148. On the two Saskatchewan cases, *Central Canada Potash Co. Ltd. et al.* v *Government of Saskatchewan et al.* and *Canadian Industrial Gas and Oil Ltd.* [CIGOL] v *Government of Saskatchewan et al.*, see Wendy Macdonald *Constitutional Change and the Mining Industry in Canada* (Kingston 1980).

44 Smiley *Canada in Question* 262

45 Smith *Regional Decline* 90–103

46 The story is surveyed from several angles in Keith Banting and Richard Simeon eds *And No One Cheered: Federalism, Democracy and the Constitution Act* (Toronto 1983). The relevant sections of the act are: (a) natural resources (section 92A); (b) equalization (section 36); (c) override (section 33); and (d) amending formula (section 38).

47 George Grant *Lament for a Nation: The Defeat of Canadian Nationalism* (Toronto 1965)

48 Harry G. Johnson *The Canadian Quandary: Economic Problems and Policies* first
pub 1963 (Toronto 1977) 103; Marshall McLuhan *Understanding Media: The Extension of Man* (Toronto 1964); Paul Phillips 'National Policy, Continental Economics, and National Disintegration' in David Jay Bercuson ed *Canada and the
Burden of Unity* (Toronto 1977) 19–43; J.E. Rea 'The Roots of Prairie Society' in
David Gagan ed *Prairie Perspectives* (Toronto 1970) 46–55; Roger Gibbins *Prairie
Politics and Society: Regionalism in Decline* (Toronto 1980)

49 Canadian Co-operative Credit Society Ltd *Annual Report* 1982, 20; *Financial
Post 500* June 1982; Marsha Gordon *Government in Business* (Montreal 1981)

50 Alan Anderson 'Linguistic Trends among Saskatchewan Ethnic Groups' in
Martin L. Kovacs ed *Ethnic Canadians: Culture and Education* (Regina 1978)
63–86, Alan Anderson 'Ethnic Identity in Saskatchewan Bloc Settlements: A
Sociological Appraisal' in Howard Palmer ed *The Settlement of the West* (Calgary 1977) 187–225; Leo Driedger 'In Search of Cultural Identity Factors: A
Comparison of Ethnic Students' *Canadian Review of Sociology and Anthropology*
12 (1975) 150–62; Leo Driedger 'Multicultural Regionalism: Toward Understanding the Canadian West' paper presented to Western Canadian Studies
Conference, Banff, 1983; I would like to thank Professor Driedger for permitting me to see an early draft of this paper.

51 Linda Gerber 'The Development of Canadian Indian Communities: A Two-
dimensional Typology Reflecting Strategies of Adaptation to the Modern
World' *Canadian Review of Sociology and Anthropology* 16 (1979) 404–24; Stewart
J. Clatworthy and Jonathan P. Gunn 'Economic Circumstances of Native
People in Selected Metropolitan Centres in Western Canada' Institute of
Urban Studies, University of Winnipeg, December 1981

52 Wallace Stegner *Wolf Willow: A History, A Story and a Memory of the Last Plains
Frontier* (New York 1955, 1966) 25–6; Dick Harrison *Unnamed Country: The
Struggle for a Canadian Prairie Fiction* (Edmonton 1977) xii; W.L. Morton 'See-
ing an Unliterary Landscape' *Mosaic* 3 no 3 (spring 1970) 1–10; also Eli Man-
del 'Writing West: On the Road to Wood Mountain' in Eli Mandel *Another
Time* (Erin 1977) 68–78

53 Northrop Frye 'Across the River and Out of the Trees' in James Polk ed
*Northrop Frye: Divisions on a Ground: Essays on Canadian Culture* (Toronto 1982)
31

54 A useful perspective on the trend toward provincial empire is Alan C. Cairns
'The Governments and Societies of Canadian Federalism; *Canadian Journal of
Political Science* 10 no 4 (December 1977) 695–725. Also useful is David Elton
'Regional Politics and Western Alienation' presented to the 1983 Western
Canadian Studies Conference. A different view is contained in Larry Pratt
and Garth Stevenson eds *Western Separatism: The Myths, Realities and Dangers*
(Edmonton 1981). Finally, a strong survey of recent politics is Smith *Regional
Decline*.

55 W.L. Morton 'The Bias of Prairie Politics' in A.B. McKillop ed *Contexts of Canada's Past: Selected Essays of W.L. Morton* (Toronto 1980) 159 and W.L. Morton 'A Century of Plain and Parkland' in Richard Allen ed *A Region of the Mind* (Regina 1973) 179

CHAPTER SEVENTEEN: CONCLUSION

1 W.O. Mitchell *Who Has Seen the Wind* (Toronto 1947) 3
2 John Warkentin ed *The Western Interior of Canada: A Record of Geographical Discovery 1612–1917* (Toronto 1964) 198
3 Allen Ronaghan 'Three Scouts and the Cart Train' *Alberta History* 25 no 1 (winter 1977) 12–14

# Bibliographical essay

Many articles and books have been written about the prairie west in the last two decades and many more in the preceding half-century. Because a large number of these works have been cited in the notes, this brief essay is merely an introduction to the literature of the region.

Each province supports a historical journal – *Alberta History*, *Saskatchewan History*, and *Manitoba History* (formerly *Transactions* of the Manitoba Historical Society) – and these are complemented by *Prairie Forum*, an interdisciplinary scholarly journal, and *The Beaver*, chiefly devoted to northern Canada and the fur trade. The twelve volumes of papers presented to the Western Canadian Studies Conferences, an event organized by the Department of History of the University of Calgary, have also had a great impact on prairie scholarship.

The basic prairie bibliography is Bruce Braden Peel *A Bibliography of the Prairie Provinces to 1953 with Biographical Index* first pub 1956 (Toronto 1973), and this has been updated by Gloria M. Strathern comp *Alberta, 1954–1979: A Provincial Bibliography* (Edmonton 1982) and Ved Arora ed *The Saskatchewan Bibliography* (Regina 1980). The best general guide to recent historical works on the post-1870 era is Alan F.J. Artibise ed *Western Canada since 1870: A Select Bibliography and Guide* (Vancouver 1978).

The Indian's fur trade is reviewed in Arthur J. Ray *Indians in the Fur Trade: Their Role as Hunters, Trappers and Middlemen in the Lands Southwest of Hudson Bay* (Toronto 1974). Newer work is surveyed in Jacqueline Peterson and John Anfison 'The Indian and the Fur Trade: A Review of Recent Literature' *Manitoba History* forthcoming (1984–5). Two valuable works on the social history of the era are Sylvia Van Kirk *'Many Tender Ties': Women in Fur-Trade Society in Western Canada 1670–1870* (Winnipeg 1980) and Jennifer S.H. Brown *Strangers in Blood: Fur Trade Families in Indian Country* (Vancouver 1980).

The best short survey of the Europeans' fur trade is Glyndwr Williams 'The Hudson's Bay Company and the Fur Trade: 1670–1870' *The Beaver* Outfit 314: 2 (autumn 1983) 4–86. A longer, popular version is James K. Smith *Wilderness of Fortune: The Story of Western Canada* (Vancouver 1983). The scholarly literature is discussed in Sylvia Van Kirk 'Fur Trade Social History: Some Recent Trends' in Carol M. Judd and Arthur J. Ray eds *Old Trails and New Directions: Papers of the Third North American Fur Trade Conference* (Toronto 1980). One scholarly survey, now a little dated, is E.E. Rich *The Fur Trade and the Northwest to 1857* (Toronto 1967), and a much longer version is Arthur S. Morton *A History of the Canadian West to 1870–71* first pub 1939, L.G. Thomas ed (Toronto 1973). Less advanced students will prefer Conrad E. Heidenreich and Arthur J. Ray *The Early Fur Trades: A Study in Cultural Interaction* (Toronto 1976). One invaluable source for the fur trade, as for much else in Canadian history, is the multivolume *Dictionary of Canadian Biography*.

Alexander Ross's discussion of his own experiences in *The Red River Settlement: Its Rise, Progress, and Present State* first pub 1856 (Edmonton 1972) is a classic account of that topic, and W.L. Morton's introductory essays to E.E. Rich ed *London Correspondence inward from Eden Colvile 1849–1852* (London 1956) and to *Alexander Begg's Red River Journal and Other Papers Relative to the Red River Resistance of 1869–70* (Torotno 1956) are his most extensive statements on the northwest before 1870. The dated but exhaustive study by Marcel Giraud, *Le Métis canadien: son role dans l'histoire des provinces de l'ouest* (Paris 1945), and George F.G. Stanley's *Louis Riel* (Toronto 1963) are important introductions to the history of the metis.

Two fine studies of the post-1870 west are Vernon C. Fowke *The National Policy and the Wheat Economy* (Toronto 1957) and Lewis Herbert Thomas *The Struggle for Responsible Government in the North-West Territories 1870–97* first pub 1956 (Toronto 1978). A useful perspective on land policy is presented in John Langton Tyman *By Section, Township and Range: Studies in Prairie Settlement* (Brandon 1972). Still important is Arthur S. Morton *History of Prairie Settlement* (Toronto 1938) and, also from the Frontiers of Settlement series, Chester Martin *'Dominion Lands' Policy* first pub 1938, Lewis H. Thomas ed (Toronto 1973). A different aspect of the settlement era is addressed in David H. Breen *The Canadian Prairie West and the Ranching Frontier 1874–1924* (Toronto 1983). My favourite narrative of homestead life is James M. Minifie *Homesteader: A Prairie Boyhood Recalled* (Toronto 1972), and an interesting contrast is presented in James H. Gray *The Boy from Winnipeg* (Toronto 1970). Doug Owram *Promise of Eden: The Canadian Expansionist Movement and the Idea of the West* (Toronto 1980) and R.C. Macleod *The NWMP and Law Enforcement 1873–1905* (Toronto 1976) are valuable new books that address significant subjects.

Among the studies of agriculture three works of note are Ian MacPherson *Each for All: A History of the Co-operative Movement in English Canada, 1900–1945* (Toronto 1979), C.F. Wilson *A Century of Canadian Grain: Government Policy to 1951* (Saskatoon 1978), and Barry Wilson *Beyond the Harvest: Canadian Grain at the Crossroads* (Saskatoon 1981). One of the few business histories is A.A. den Otter *Civilizing the West: The Galts and the Development of Western Canada* (Edmonton 1982), and, on education, one might consult David C. Jones, Nancy M. Sheehan, and Robert M. Stamp eds *Shaping the Schools of the Canadian West* (Calgary 1979).

Social history is not a new invention, as the valuable work Carl A. Dawson and Eva R. Younge *Pioneering in the Prairie Provinces: The Social Side of the Settlement Process* (Toronto 1940) demonstrates. Equally valuable are Jean Burnet *Next-Year Country: A Study of Rural Social Organization in Alberta* first pub 1951 (Toronto 1978) and, also from the Social Credit in Alberta series, W.E. Mann *Sect, Cult and Church in Alberta* first pub 1955 (Toronto 1972). Urban history can best be sampled in Alan F.J. Artibise ed *Town and City: Aspects of Western Canadian Urban Development* (Regina 1981) and his *Winnipeg: A Social History of Urban Growth 1874–1914* (Montreal 1975). Among the many recent works in western labour history the following are important: David Bercuson *Confrontation at Winnipeg: Labour, Industrial Relations and the General Strike* (Montreal 1974), A. Ross

McCormack *Reformers, Rebels, and Revolutionaries: The Western Canadian Radical Movement 1899–1919* (Toronto 1977), and Donald Avery *'Dangerous Foreigners': European Immigrant Workers and Labor Radicalism in Canada 1896–1932* (Toronto 1979). A fine memoir of the Depression is James H. Gray *The Winter Years: The Depression on the Prairies* (Toronto 1966). Among the few studies of prairie culture, Dick Harrison's *Unnamed Country: The Struggle for a Canadian Prairie Fiction* (Edmonton 1977) stands out. A survey of the many recent works in another field is Howard Palmer 'Canadian Immigration and Ethnic History in the 1970s and 1980s' *Journal of Canadian Studies* 17 no 1 (spring 1982) 35–50, and a related monograph is his *Patterns of Prejudice: A History of Nativism in Alberta* (Toronto 1982).

The list of books on prairie politics might seem endless. Three reliable surveys from the national perspective are the volumes in the Centenary series: W.L. Morton *The Critical Years: the Union of British North America 1857–1873* (Toronto 1964), Peter B. Waite *Canada 1874–1896: Arduous Destiny* (Toronto 1971), and Robert Craig Brown and Ramsay Cook *Canada 1896–1921: A Nation Transformed* (Toronto 1971). Another useful viewpoint is presented by D.J. Hall in *Clifford Sifton* I *The Young Napoleon 1861–1900* (Vancouver 1981) and II (forthcoming). Yet another is Ramsay Cook *The Politics of John W. Dafoe and the Free Press* (Toronto 1963). Two valuable biographies are John Kendle *John Bracken: A Political Biography* (Toronto 1979) and Kenneth McNaught *A Prophet in Politics: A Biography of J.S. Woodsworth* (Toronto 1959). A narrower span is addressed in John Herd Thompson's *The Harvests of War: The Prairie West 1914–1918* (Toronto 1978). Provincial politics are surveyed in M.S. Donnelly *The Government of Manitoba* (Toronto 1963), David E. Smith *Prairie Liberalism: The Liberal Party in Saskatchewan 1905–71* (Toronto 1975), Evelyn Eager *Saskatchewan Government: Politics and Pragmatism* (Saskatoon 1980), Lewis G. Thomas *The Liberal Party in Alberta: A History of Politics in the Province of Alberta 1905–1921* (Toronto 1959), and Carlo Caldarola ed *Society and Politics in Alberta: Research Papers* (Toronto 1979). I would single out from the railway histories T.D. Regehr *The Canadian Northern Railway: Pioneer Road of the Northern Prairies, 1895–1918* (Toronto 1976) and W. Kaye Lamb *History of the Canadian Pacific Railway* (New York 1977). An important study of recent political economy is John Richards and Larry Pratt *Prairie Capitalism: Power and Influence in the New West* (Toronto 1979). Another is David E. Smith *The Regional Decline of a National Party: Liberals on the Prairies* (Toronto 1981). Also useful is Roger Gibbins *Prairie Politics and Society: Regionalism in Decline* (Toronto 1980).

An introduction to historiography is provided by Carl Berger *The Writing of Canadian History: Aspects of English-Canadian Historical Writing: 1900–1970* (Toronto 1976) and A.B. McKillop ed *Contexts of Canada's Past: Selected Essays of W.L. Morton* (Toronto 1980). Longer bibliographical essays are included in Richard Allen ed *A Region of the Mind: Interpreting the Western Canadian Plains* (Regina 1973), especially L.G. Thomas 'Historiography of the Fur Trade Era' (73–86) and T.D. Regehr 'Historiography of the Canadian Plains after 1870' (87–102).

Manitoba boasts two provincial histories, W.L. Morton *Manitoba: A History* first pub 1957 (Toronto 1967) and James A. Jackson *The Centennial History of Manitoba* (Toronto 1970). John H. Archer has written *Saskatchewan: A History* (Saskatoon 1980).

One of the finest narratives of prairie life is Wallace Stegner *Wolf Willow: A History, A Story and a Memory of the Last Plains Frontier* first pub 1955 (New York 1966). Among novelists, Ralph Connor (C.W. Gordon), F.P. Grove, and Robert Stead should be sampled for a taste of pre-1930 styles, but the main works appear after that date: Sinclair Ross *As for Me and My House* first pub 1941 (Toronto 1957), W.O. Mitchell *Who Has Seen the Wind* first pub 1947 (Toronto 1960), Margaret Laurence *The Stone Angel* first pub 1964 (Toronto 1968) and *The Diviners* first pub 1974 (Toronto 1975), Robert Kroetsch *The Studhorse Man* (Toronto 1969), Henry Kreisel *The Betrayal* (Toronto 1964), David Williams *The River Horseman* (Toronto 1981), Rudy Wiebe *The Blue Mountains of China* (Toronto 1970) and *The Temptations of Big Bear* (Toronto 1973), and Guy Vanderhaeghe *Man Descending: Selected Stories* (Toronto 1982).

# Index